A Guide to Reviewing
English Composition and Grammar, Benchmark Edition
Second Course

English Composition and Grammar (grades 6–12) focuses on effective composition and mastery of the writing process. The program teaches students to think through the writing process and to apply it to all forms of composition—expository, persuasive, narrative, and descriptive.

Use the list below as a convenient guide to reviewing ***English Composition and Grammar***. Page references provide examples of key features.

- A complete chapter, **Writing and Thinking: The Writing Process,** teaches students to think clearly, logically, and creatively for better organized, more effective composition (page 3).
- Each course presents writing as a recursive process focusing on prewriting (page 5), writing (page 29), evaluating (page 31), revising (page 34), proofreading (page 38), and making the final copy (page 40).
- Special features—**Before You Write** (page 5), **When You Write** (page 30), **When You Evaluate** (page 31), **When You Revise** (page 34), and **When You Proofread** (page 38)—provide cues that remind students of key points at each stage of the writing process.
- Helpful features—**Guidelines for Evaluating Your Writing** (page 32), **Revising a Draft** (page 35), and **Guidelines for Proofreading** (page 39)—summarize key points of the evaluating, revising, and proofreading stages of the writing process.
- **Critical Thinking** sections, followed by practical exercises, help students strengthen thinking skills and apply them to writing (pages 18 and 19).
- A variety of photographs, many full-color, helps students generate ideas for writing (page IW1).
- **Tools for Writing and Revising**, a complete section, presents important principles of grammar, usage, and mechanics that can be applied to writing and revising, as well as to speaking (page 263).
- Functional **Writing Applications** enable students to see the connection between composition and the principles of grammar, usage, and mechanics (page 301).
- Each course offers practical instruction in a variety of important special topics—studying and test taking (page 647), speaking and listening (page 669), completing forms (page 220), preparing reports based on sources (page 178), and writing in other courses (page 658).
- A wealth of supplements, including the *Annotated Teacher's Edition* and the *Teacher's ResourceBank™*, provides a rich variety of teaching resources for ***English Composition and Grammar***.

Harcourt Brace Jovanovich, Inc.
School Department

ENGLISH COMPOSITION AND GRAMMAR

BENCHMARK EDITION

Grades 6-12

COMPOSITION FROM THE START!

The thinking writing connection!

- ☐ Complete coverage of the vital thinking-writing connection
- ☐ Comprehensive development of composition through the writing process
- ☐ Practical instruction in grammar, usage, and mechanics
- ☐ An unprecedented variety of teaching resources

The thinking writing connection!

English Composition and Grammar, Benchmark Edition, helps students connect thinking and writing. In every level, a full chapter—**Writing and Thinking: The Writing Process**—provides the foundation for the entire course of study. It teaches students to think clearly, logically, and creatively for better organized, more effective composition. The **Writing and Thinking** chapter enables students to relate critical-thinking skills—observation, application, classification, analysis, synthesis, and evaluation—to stages of the writing process. Throughout the program, composition chapters emphasize thinking skills.

Critical Thinking sections strengthen the reasoning abilities essential to clear, logical writing.

From *Fourth Course*

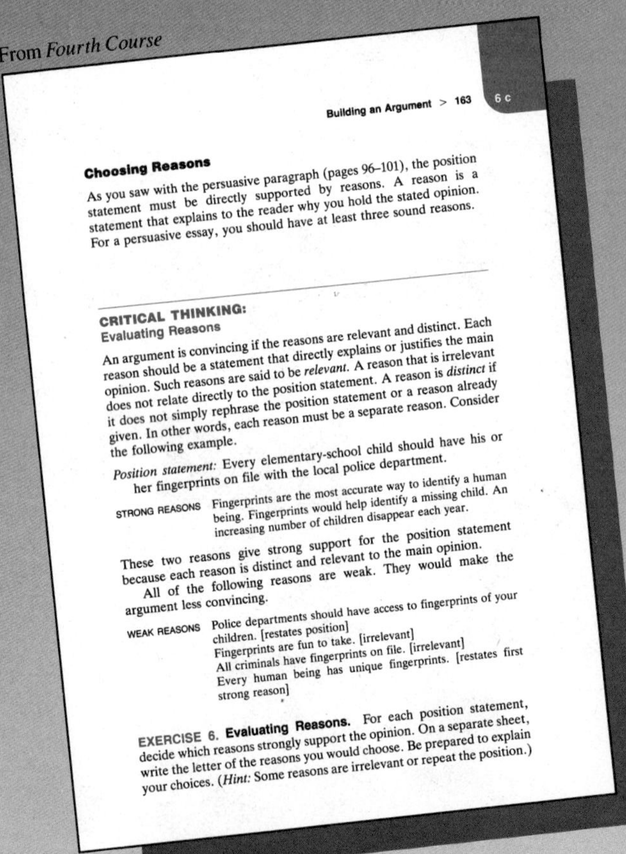

Building an Argument > 163 6 c

Choosing Reasons

As you saw with the persuasive paragraph (pages 96–101), the position statement must be directly supported by reasons. A reason is a statement that explains to the reader why you hold the stated opinion. For a persuasive essay, you should have at least three sound reasons.

CRITICAL THINKING:
Evaluating Reasons

An argument is convincing if the reasons are relevant and distinct. Each reason should be a statement that directly explains or justifies the main opinion. Such reasons are said to be *relevant.* A reason that is irrelevant does not relate directly to the position statement. A reason is *distinct* if it does not simply rephrase the position statement or a reason already given. In other words, each reason must be a separate reason. Consider the following example.

Position statement: Every elementary-school child should have his or her fingerprints on file with the local police department.

STRONG REASONS Fingerprints are the most accurate way to identify a human being. Fingerprints would help identify a missing child. An increasing number of children disappear each year.

These two reasons give strong support for the position statement because each reason is distinct and relevant to the main opinion.

All of the following reasons are weak. They would make the argument less convincing.

WEAK REASONS Police departments should have access to fingerprints of your children. [restates position]
Fingerprints are fun to take. [irrelevant]
All criminals have fingerprints on file. [irrelevant]
Every human being has unique fingerprints. [restates first strong reason]

EXERCISE 6. **Evaluating Reasons.** For each position statement, decide which reasons strongly support the opinion. On a separate sheet, write the letter of the reasons you would choose. Be prepared to explain your choices. (*Hint:* Some reasons are irrelevant or repeat the position.)

Students apply critical-thinking skills to carefully chosen writing activities.

Clear, logical instruction

The textbook develops critical-thinking skills through orderly, consistent instruction. It defines and illustrates skills that students then apply in practical exercises.

Sample pages are reduced. Actual sizes are $5\frac{15}{16}'' \times 8\frac{3}{8}''$.

Focus on composition—from the start!

Logically organized for the contemporary classroom, ***English Composition and Grammar*** focuses on effective composition and mastery of the writing process. Composition chapters open each level, emphasizing the writing process in expository, persuasive, narrative, and descriptive writing through both paragraph and essay forms. Activities help students apply the writing process while developing and practicing specific writing skills.

A composition-based program, ***English Composition and Grammar*** begins with the writing process.

From *Fourth Course*

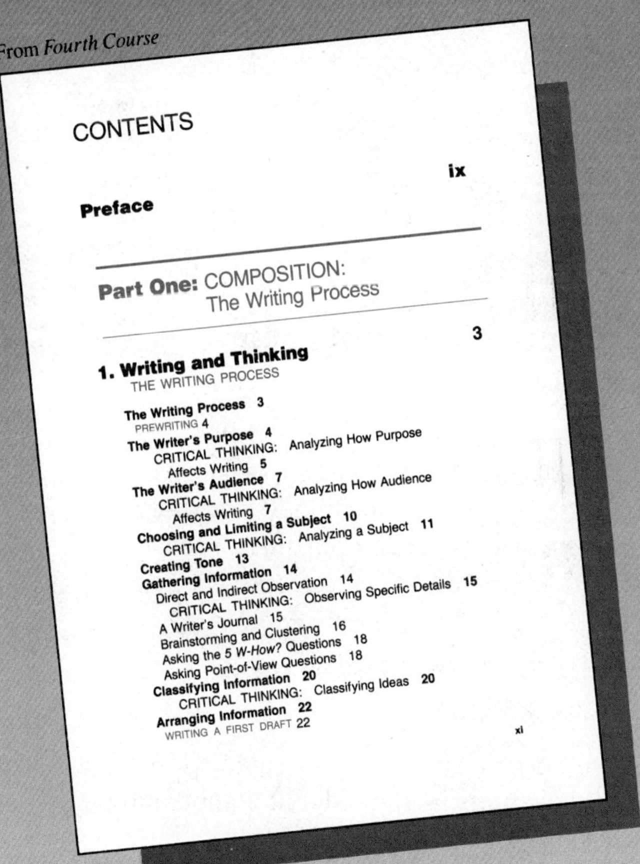

CONTENTS

xi

Composition instruction helps students carefully think through each stage of the writing process and ask key questions when preparing to write.

From *Introductory Course*

A variety of photographs, many full-color, helps students generate ideas for writing.

Six logical steps to mastery of the writing process

A manageable six-stage writing process

The program incorporates a recursive writing process that students can easily manage—(1) prewriting, (2) writing the first draft, (3) evaluating, (4) revising, (5) proofreading, and (6) writing the final version. This unique six-stage process clearly distinguishes between determining strengths and weaknesses in a draft (evaluation) and making changes to improve it (revision).

Instruction students can comprehend

Straightforward explanations and clear examples enable students to apply the six-stage writing process to all types of writing—from short paragraphs to longer compositions, such as reports, letters, essays, and research papers.

Flexible organization for a variety of uses

Because each chapter is self-contained, teachers can use chapters in any order or combination to meet special learning needs or teaching preferences.

From *Fifth Course*

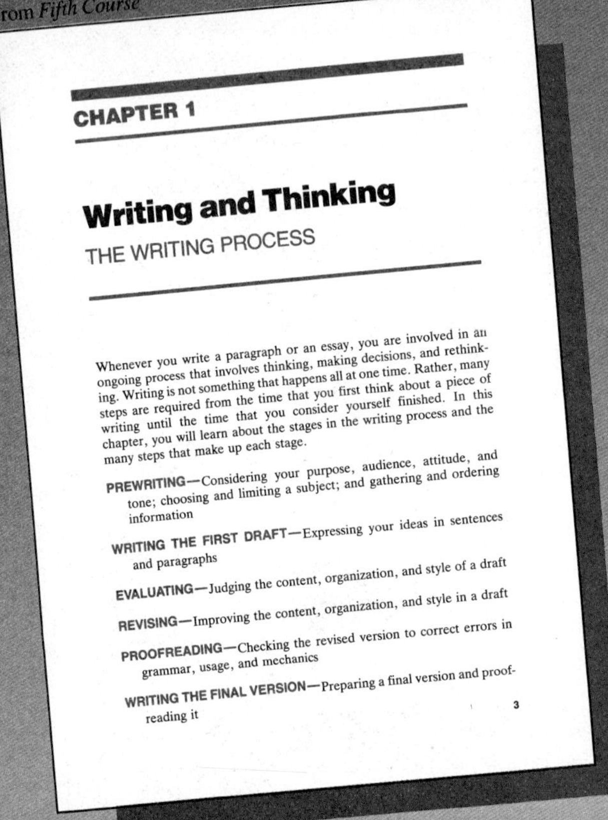

CHAPTER 1

Writing and Thinking

THE WRITING PROCESS

Whenever you write a paragraph or an essay, you are involved in an ongoing process that involves thinking, making decisions, and rethinking. Writing is not something that happens all at one time. Rather, many steps are required from the time that you first think about a piece of writing until the time that you consider yourself finished. In this chapter, you will learn about the stages in the writing process and the many steps that make up each stage.

PREWRITING—Considering your purpose, audience, attitude, and tone; choosing and limiting a subject; and gathering and ordering information

WRITING THE FIRST DRAFT—Expressing your ideas in sentences and paragraphs

EVALUATING—Judging the content, organization, and style of a draft

REVISING—Improving the content, organization, and style in a draft

PROOFREADING—Checking the revised version to correct errors in grammar, usage, and mechanics

WRITING THE FINAL VERSION—Preparing a final version and proofreading it

3

In each level, the **Writing and Thinking** chapter develops all six stages of the writing process through clear examples and practical exercises.

The **prewriting** stage includes considering the audience and identifying the purpose, as well as selecting subjects and gathering information.

In the **evaluating** stage, students critically review their writing and decide what to change.

The fourth stage separates the complex, thoughtful process of **revising** from the fifth stage, the more mechanical act of **proofreading.**

Sample pages are reduced. Actual sizes are 5¹⁵⁄₁₆″ × 8⅜″.

Guidelines for Evaluating in the composition section help students think critically as they review their writing in the evaluating stage.

From *Third Course*

28 < **Writing and Thinking**

The following Guidelines for Evaluating can be used with almost any form of writing. Use them as a checklist when you reread your draft in order to identify any problems that you should address. Then use the symbols on page 41 to mark the problems you discover, so you can locate them easily when you are ready to make improvements.

GUIDELINES FOR EVALUATING

Content		
Purpose	1.	Do the ideas and information included in the paper help to explain, to describe, to persuade, or to tell the story?
Audience	2.	Will the audience find the paper interesting? Are unfamiliar terms explained and necessary background information supplied to help the audience understand?
Topic Development	3.	Are enough information and details provided to help the audience understand the topic? Does all of the information "belong" in this paper?
Organization		
Order	4.	Are the ideas arranged in a way that will be clear to the reader? Is the pattern of organization appropriate for the paper?
Transitions	5.	Are the ideas smoothly joined by connecting words and phrases? Are the relationships between sentences obvious, rather than confusing and unclear?
Style		
Tone	6.	Does the paper sound serious or light enough for the audience to accept what is said? Does the tone seem suitable for the purpose of the paper?
Sentence Structure	7.	Do the sentences vary in length to avoid monotony? Do the sentences begin in different ways and follow different patterns?
Word Choice	8.	Does the writing contain precise, specific words? Do the words make the meaning clear rather than general and fuzzy?

will be a best seller, although it is aimed at "a very general audience."

"I suppose I know about roughly the state of knowledge on it now," he says of Mayan hieroglyphics, but he observes that "no one is really able yet" to interpret the glyphs fully. There is no Rosetta Stone to unravel the Mayan puzzle, he says, adding, "I'm working slowly to break little pieces here and there."

RICHARD HAITCH

If you rewrote this same information for an audience of ten-year-olds, you would give background information (what hieroglyphics are, what an archaeologist does, where and when the Mayan culture existed), explain references (the Rosetta Stone), and simplify sentence length and vocabulary (*cognoscenti, comprehend*).

As you analyze audience, you will also consider purpose, for the two are closely related. In persuasive writing, for example, readers' beliefs and feelings are particularly important.

Techniques for Prewriting. To determine how your audience will affect your writing, ask yourself the following questions:

- Who is the audience? Friends? Acquaintances? Strangers? A combination of these groups?
- What does the audience already know about the topic?
- What background or technical information must I supply?
- What language and style are most appropriate for the audience: simple or complex words and sentences, casual or formal presentation?
- Does the audience have any strong feelings about the topic that could affect my writing?

From *Fourth Course*

Practical guidelines for writing

Clear guidelines and charts summarize key ideas and provide concise suggestions for effective writing.

Throughout the composition chapters, **Revising** charts identify specific problems in writing and provide techniques, with examples, for revising.

From *Fifth Course*

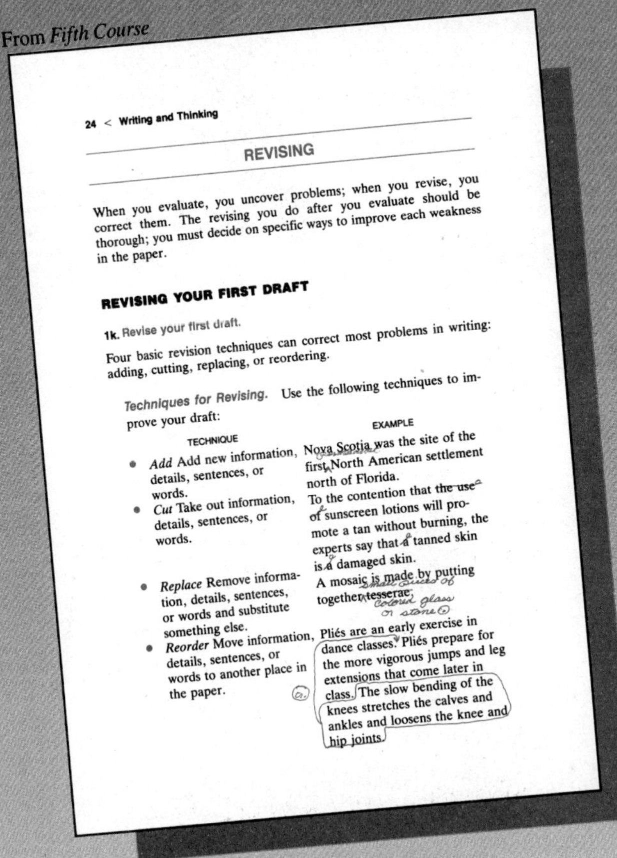

24 < **Writing and Thinking**

REVISING

When you evaluate, you uncover problems; when you revise, you correct them. The revising you do after you evaluate should be thorough; you must decide on specific ways to improve each weakness in the paper.

REVISING YOUR FIRST DRAFT

1k. Revise your first draft.

Four basic revision techniques can correct most problems in writing: adding, cutting, replacing, or reordering.

Techniques for Revising. Use the following techniques to improve your draft:

TECHNIQUE	EXAMPLE
• *Add* Add new information, details, sentences, or words.	Nova Scotia was the site of the first North American settlement north of Florida.
• *Cut* Take out information, details, sentences, or words.	To the contention that the use of sunscreen lotions will promote a tan without burning, the experts say that a tanned skin is a damaged skin.
• *Replace* Remove information, details, sentences, or words and substitute something else.	A mosaic is made by putting together tesserae. small pieces of colored glass or stone
• *Reorder* Move information, details, sentences, or words to another place in the paper.	Pliés are an early exercise in dance classes. Pliés prepare for the more vigorous jumps and leg extensions that come later in class. The slow bending of the knees stretches the calves and ankles and loosens the knee and hip joints.

Special features throughout the program provide cues that remind students of key points at each stage of the writing process.

Tools for clear, effective writing and revising

Instruction in effective English to complement the writing process

A complete section, **Tools for Writing and Revising,** presents important principles of grammar, usage, and mechanics that can be applied to writing and revising, as well as to speaking. Tabbed pages allow quick and easy reference during writing.

From *Third Course*

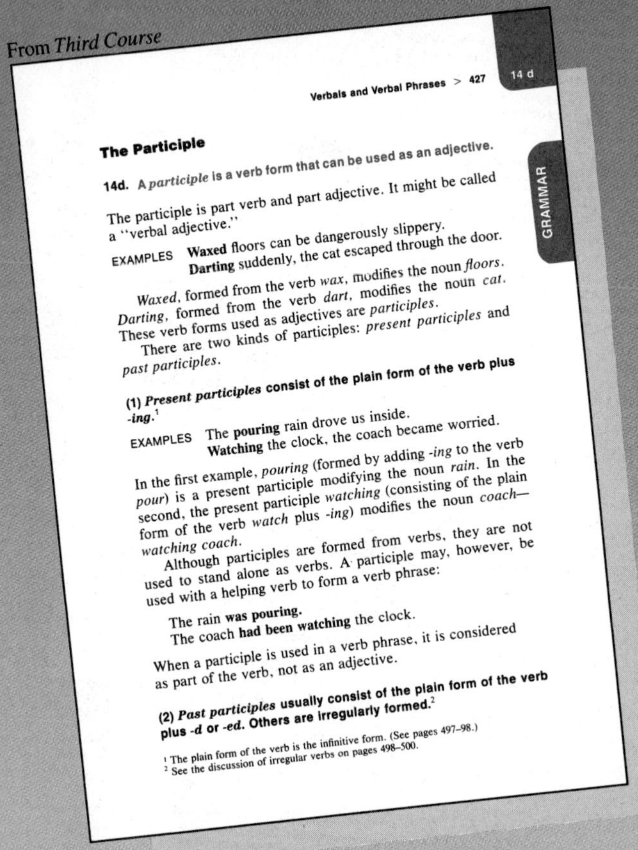

Verbals and Verbal Phrases > 427

14 d

GRAMMAR

The Participle

14d. A *participle* is a verb form that can be used as an adjective.

The participle is part verb and part adjective. It might be called a "verbal adjective."

EXAMPLES **Waxed** floors can be dangerously slippery.
Darting suddenly, the cat escaped through the door.

Waxed, formed from the verb *wax*, modifies the noun *floors*. *Darting*, formed from the verb *dart*, modifies the noun *cat*. These verb forms used as adjectives are *participles*.

There are two kinds of participles: *present participles* and *past participles*.

(1) *Present participles* consist of the plain form of the verb plus *-ing*.[1]

EXAMPLES The **pouring** rain drove us inside.
Watching the clock, the coach became worried.

In the first example, *pouring* (formed by adding *-ing* to the verb *pour*) is a present participle modifying the noun *rain*. In the second, the present participle *watching* (consisting of the plain form of the verb *watch* plus *-ing*) modifies the noun *coach—watching coach*.

Although participles are formed from verbs, they are not used to stand alone as verbs. A participle may, however, be used with a helping verb to form a verb phrase:

The rain **was pouring**.
The coach **had been watching** the clock.

When a participle is used in a verb phrase, it is considered as part of the verb, not as an adjective.

(2) *Past participles* usually consist of the plain form of the verb plus *-d* or *-ed*. Others are irregularly formed.[2]

[1] The plain form of the verb is the infinitive form. (See pages 497–98.)
[2] See the discussion of irregular verbs on pages 498–500.

Each principle is simply stated, illustrated by clear examples, and followed by a variety of exercises.

From *Second Course*

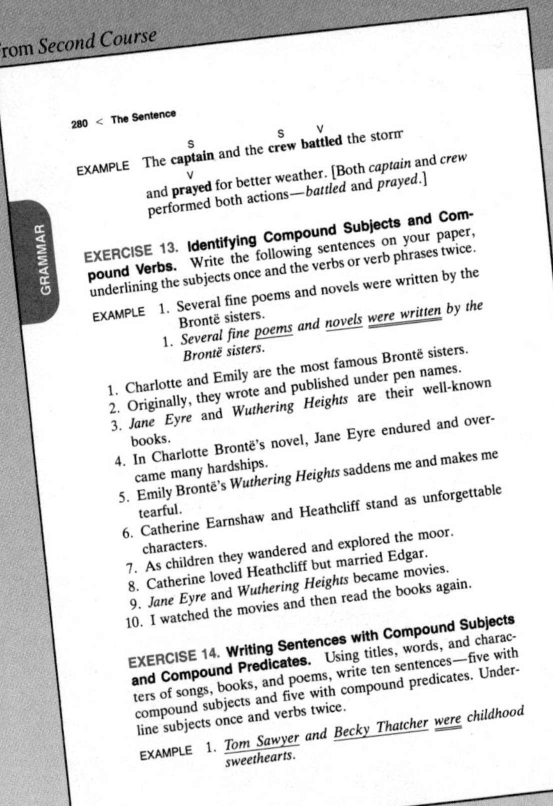

280 < The Sentence

GRAMMAR

EXAMPLE The **captain** (S) and the **crew** (S) **battled** (V) the storm and **prayed** (V) for better weather. [Both *captain* and *crew* performed both actions—*battled* and *prayed*.]

EXERCISE 13. Identifying Compound Subjects and Compound Verbs. Write the following sentences on your paper, underlining the subjects once and the verbs or verb phrases twice.

EXAMPLE 1. Several fine poems and novels were written by the Brontë sisters.
1. *Several fine poems and novels were written by the Brontë sisters.*

1. Charlotte and Emily are the most famous Brontë sisters.
2. Originally, they wrote and published under pen names.
3. *Jane Eyre* and *Wuthering Heights* are their well-known books.
4. In Charlotte Brontë's novel, Jane Eyre endured and overcame many hardships.
5. Emily Brontë's *Wuthering Heights* saddens me and makes me tearful.
6. Catherine Earnshaw and Heathcliff stand as unforgettable characters.
7. As children they wandered and explored the moor.
8. Catherine loved Heathcliff but married Edgar.
9. *Jane Eyre* and *Wuthering Heights* became movies.
10. I watched the movies and then read the books again.

EXERCISE 14. Writing Sentences with Compound Subjects and Compound Predicates. Using titles, words, and characters of songs, books, and poems, write ten sentences—five with compound subjects and five with compound predicates. Underline subjects once and verbs twice.

EXAMPLE 1. *Tom Sawyer and Becky Thatcher were childhood sweethearts.*

Clearly labeled exercises identify objectives and help students relate them to the writing process.

Writing Applications that increase understanding

Functional **Writing Applications** enable students to see the connection between composition and the principles of grammar, usage, and mechanics. Each explains an element or technique, illustrates it, and provides an exercise for practical application to writing.

From *Introductory Course*

Adverb Phrases > 255

5. Tall candles tower over the centerpiece.
6. A small cardboard pilgrim stands beside each plate.
7. The roast turkey sits on a huge platter.
8. Vegetables are arranged around it.
9. Beside the turkey is Grandmother's cranberry salad.
10. I will remember these wonderful Thanksgivings at my grandparents' house for a long time.

GRAMMAR

WRITING APPLICATION B:
Using Variety in Placing Adverb Phrases

If you eat cereal for breakfast, you probably don't eat the same kind every day: most people like variety. One way to put variety into your writing is to be aware of, and make use of, the several possible positions for the adverb phrase. Notice where the adverb phrases are placed in these examples.

EXAMPLES **In the morning** we take a crafts class. [The adverb phrase comes first in the sentence.]
Then **at noon,** we eat lunch. [The adverb phrase comes in the middle of the sentence.]
We go to swimming class **in the afternoon.** [The adverb phrase comes last.]

Writing Assignment

Step into a time machine and begin your journey into the past or the future. Describe an adventure you have. Use at least five adverb phrases and try to vary their position in the sentence. Underline these phrases. A portion of a sample description is shown.

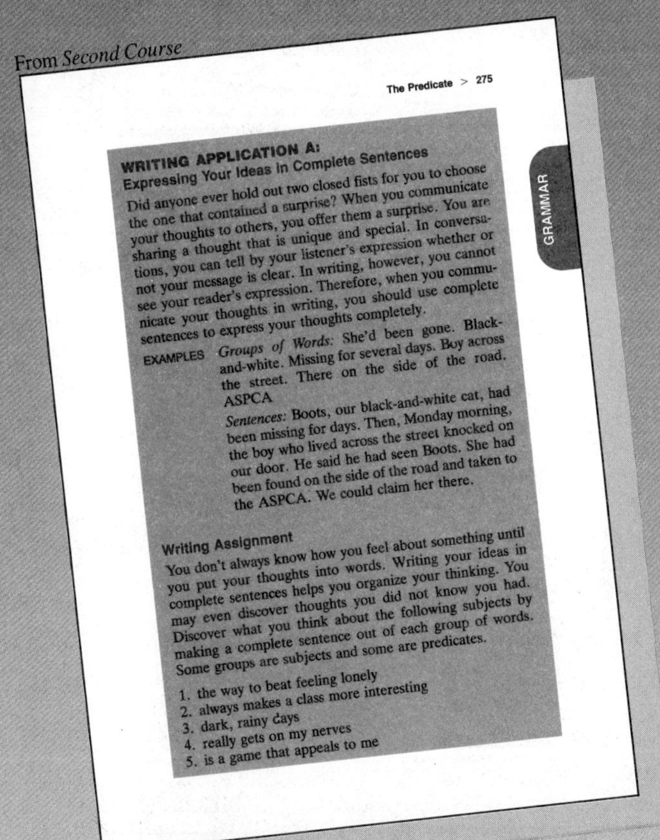

From *Second Course*

The Predicate > 275

WRITING APPLICATION A:
Expressing Your Ideas in Complete Sentences

Did anyone ever hold out two closed fists for you to choose the one that contained a surprise? When you communicate your thoughts to others, you offer them a surprise. You are sharing a thought that is unique and special. In conversations, you can tell by your listener's expression whether or not your message is clear. In writing, however, you cannot see your reader's expression. Therefore, when you communicate your thoughts in writing, you should use complete sentences to express your thoughts completely.

EXAMPLES *Groups of Words:* She'd been gone. Black-and-white. Missing for several days. Boy across the street. There on the side of the road. ASPCA

Sentences: Boots, our black-and-white cat, had been missing for days. Then, Monday morning, the boy who lived across the street knocked on our door. He said he had seen Boots. She had been found on the side of the road and taken to the ASPCA. We could claim her there.

Writing Assignment

You don't always know how you feel about something until you put your thoughts into words. Writing your ideas in complete sentences helps you organize your thinking. You may even discover thoughts you did not know you had. Discover what you think about the following subjects by making a complete sentence out of each group of words. Some groups are subjects and some are predicates.

1. the way to beat feeling lonely
2. always makes a class more interesting
3. dark, rainy days
4. really gets on my nerves
5. is a game that appeals to me

GRAMMAR

Standard Uses of Capital Letters > 623

29 a-c

WRITING APPLICATION A:
Using Capitalization Correctly to Make Your Writing Clear

By now, you have probably begun to analyze and evaluate statements you encounter in the news media. Whether you agree or disagree with a statement, if you respond to it in writing you should be sure to use capitalization correctly to make your meaning clear. Notice in the following excerpt from a letter to the editor that the writer correctly capitalized the first word in her sentence as well as the first word of the statement she was responding to. These capital letters make clear which words are hers and which are those of the other letter writer.

EXAMPLE A recent letter to the editor contained the following statement: The newspaper does not have the right to print subversive material under somebody's byline.

The writer of this letter went on to explain why she disagreed with the statement, arguing her case by citing facts as evidence.

Writing Assignment

Find a statement with which you strongly agree or disagree in an editorial or a letter to the editor. Write a letter to the editor responding to the statement, using capitalization correctly and arguing your case by citing facts.

29b. Capitalize the pronoun *I* and the interjection *O*.

You will probably have little use for the interjection *O*, which is used only in such rare expressions as "O happy day, come soon!" The common interjection *oh* ("Oh, what a beautiful morning!") is capitalized only when it appears at the beginning of a sentence. *Oh* is usually followed by a mark of punctuation, but *O* is rarely followed by punctuation.

EXAMPLES Rejoice in the Lord, **O** ye righteous!
He was doing, **oh**, about 35 miles an hour.

29c. Capitalize proper nouns and proper adjectives.

A proper noun is the name of a particular person, place, or thing. A common noun names a kind or type. Words that name a kind or a type

MECHANICS

From *Complete Course*

Sample pages are reduced. Actual sizes are 5 15/16" × 8 3/8".

Special emphasis on useful skills

English Composition and Grammar offers practical instruction in a variety of important special topics—studying and test taking, speaking and listening, understanding mass media, completing forms, preparing detailed reports, and writing in other subject areas.

From *Third Course*

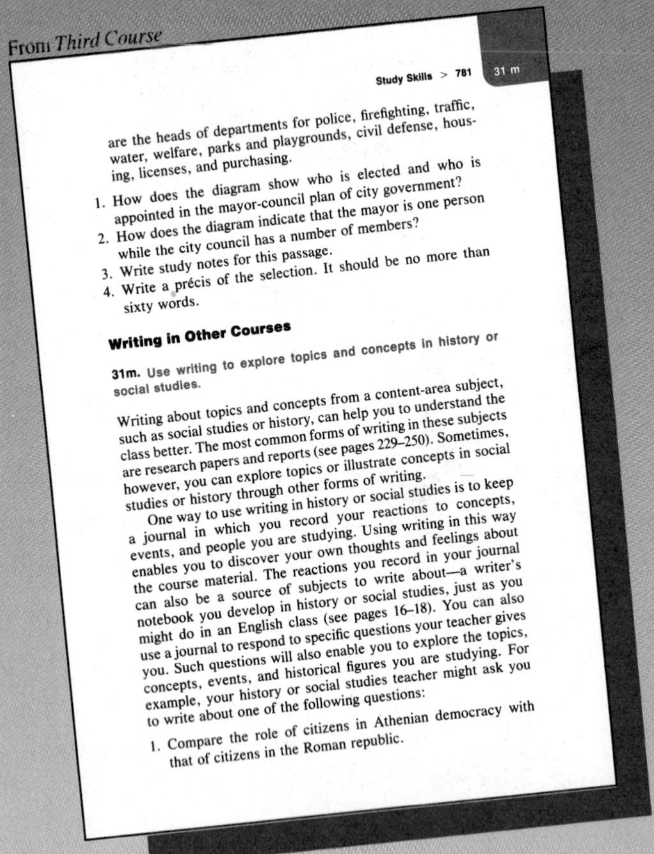

Study Skills > 781 31 m

are the heads of departments for police, firefighting, traffic, water, welfare, parks and playgrounds, civil defense, housing, licenses, and purchasing.

1. How does the diagram show who is elected and who is appointed in the mayor-council plan of city government?
2. How does the diagram indicate that the mayor is one person while the city council has a number of members?
3. Write study notes for this passage.
4. Write a précis of the selection. It should be no more than sixty words.

Writing in Other Courses

31m. Use writing to explore topics and concepts in history or social studies.

Writing about topics and concepts from a content-area subject, such as social studies or history, can help you to understand the class better. The most common forms of writing in these subjects are research papers and reports (see pages 229–250). Sometimes, however, you can explore topics or illustrate concepts in social studies or history through other forms of writing.

One way to use writing in history or social studies is to keep a journal in which you record your reactions to concepts, events, and people you are studying. Using writing in this way enables you to discover your own thoughts and feelings about the course material. The reactions you record in your journal can also be a source of subjects to write about—a writer's notebook you develop in history or social studies, just as you might do in an English class (see pages 16–18). You can also use a journal to respond to specific questions your teacher gives you. Such questions will also enable you to explore the topics, concepts, events, and historical figures you are studying. For example, your history or social studies teacher might ask you to write about one of the following questions:

1. Compare the role of citizens in Athenian democracy with that of citizens in the Roman republic.

Special features present useful techniques for writing in other subject areas, including science, history, and literature.

From *Third Course*

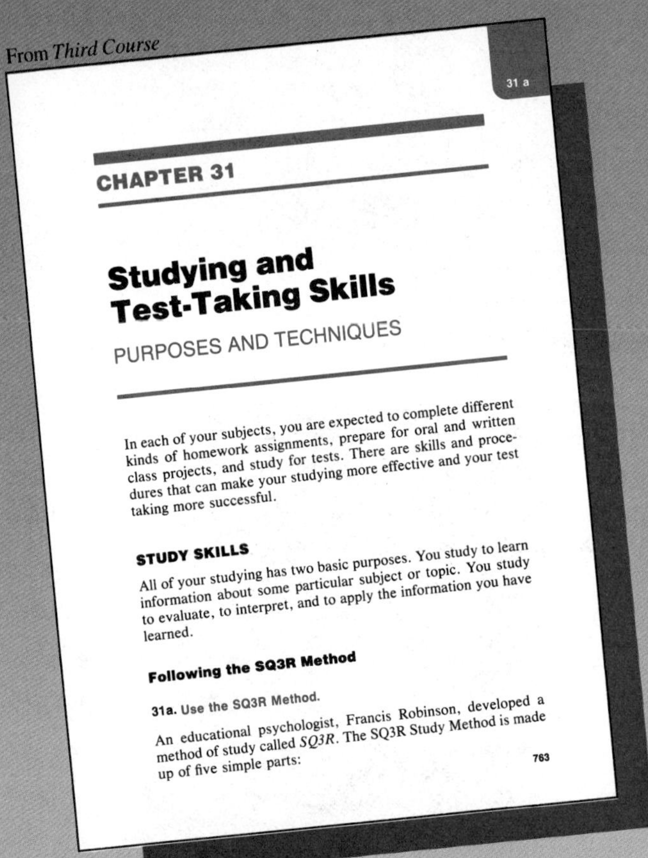

31 a

CHAPTER 31

Studying and Test-Taking Skills

PURPOSES AND TECHNIQUES

In each of your subjects, you are expected to complete different kinds of homework assignments, prepare for oral and written class projects, and study for tests. There are skills and procedures that can make your studying more effective and your test taking more successful.

STUDY SKILLS

All of your studying has two basic purposes. You study to learn information about some particular subject or topic. You study to evaluate, to interpret, and to apply the information you have learned.

Following the SQ3R Method

31a. Use the SQ3R Method.

An educational psychologist, Francis Robinson, developed a method of study called *SQ3R*. The SQ3R Study Method is made up of five simple parts:

763

Chapters at every level offer practical instruction in studying and test taking. Both the *Fifth Course* and *Complete Course* also include sections on preparing for college entrance examinations.

Chapters on effective speaking and listening in each book (not shown) develop practical skills—interviewing, discussing, and public speaking—that students can use for a lifetime.

Sample pages are reduced. Actual sizes are 5 15/16″ × 8 3/8″.

Annotated Teacher's Edition... for a range of instructional needs!

The *Annotated Teacher's Edition* contains full-sized student pages surrounded by expanded margins with teaching notes and suggested answers. The *Annotated Teacher's Edition* also includes invaluable teacher material that provides:

- A thorough discussion of effective techniques for teaching composition—from adapting the writing process for different ability levels to evaluating papers;
- Numerous helpful teaching suggestions, including ways to check understanding and teach students of varying abilities;
- Instructional objectives for every chapter;
- A suggested course of study;
- Model lesson plans;
- A suggested sequence of composition assignments and, for easy reference, a composition summary chart.

From *Fourth Course*

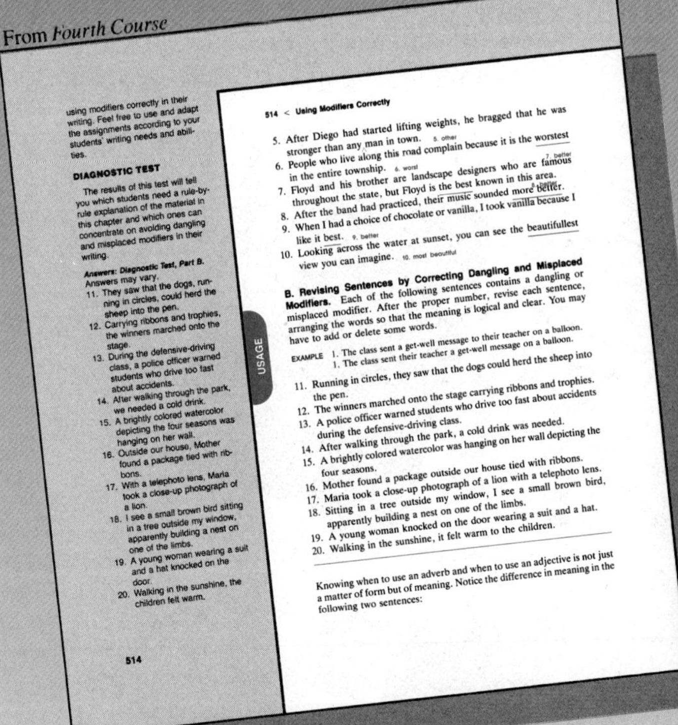

using modifiers correctly in their writing. Feel free to use and adapt the assignments according to your students' writing needs and abilities.

DIAGNOSTIC TEST

The results of this test will tell you which students need a rule-by-rule explanation of the material in this chapter and which ones can concentrate on avoiding dangling and misplaced modifiers in their writing.

Answers: Diagnostic Test, Part B.
Answers may vary.
11. They saw that the dogs, running in circles, could herd the sheep into the pen.
12. Carrying ribbons and trophies, the winners marched onto the stage.
13. During the defensive-driving class, a police officer warned students who drive too fast about accidents.
14. After walking through the park, we needed a cold drink.
15. A brightly colored watercolor depicting the four seasons was hanging on her wall.
16. Outside our house, Mother found a package tied with ribbons.
17. With a telephoto lens, Maria took a close-up photograph of a lion.
18. I see a small brown bird sitting in a tree outside my window, apparently building a nest on one of the limbs.
19. A young woman wearing a suit and a hat knocked on the door.
20. Walking in the sunshine, the children felt warm.

514

514 < **Using Modifiers Correctly**

5. After Diego had started lifting weights, he bragged that he was stronger than any man in town. *5. other*
6. People who live along this road complain because it is the worstest in the entire township. *6. worst*
7. Floyd and his brother are landscape designers who are famous throughout the state, but Floyd is the best known in this area. *7. better*
8. After the band had practiced, their music sounded more better. *8. better*
9. When I had a choice of chocolate or vanilla, I took vanilla because I like it best. *9. better*
10. Looking across the water at sunset, you can see the beautifullest view you can imagine. *10. most beautiful*

B. Revising Sentences by Correcting Dangling and Misplaced Modifiers. Each of the following sentences contains a dangling or misplaced modifier. After the proper number, revise each sentence, arranging the words so that the meaning is logical and clear. You may have to add or delete some words.

EXAMPLE 1. The class sent a get-well message to their teacher on a balloon.
1. The class sent their teacher a get-well message on a balloon.

11. Running in circles, they saw that the dogs could herd the sheep into the pen.
12. The winners marched onto the stage carrying ribbons and trophies.
13. A police officer warned students who drive too fast about accidents during the defensive-driving class.
14. After walking through the park, a cold drink was needed.
15. A brightly colored watercolor was hanging on her wall depicting the four seasons.
16. Mother found a package outside our house tied with ribbons.
17. Maria took a close-up photograph of a lion with a telephoto lens.
18. Sitting in a tree outside my window, I see a small brown bird, apparently building a nest on one of the limbs.
19. A young woman knocked on the door wearing a suit and a hat.
20. Walking in the sunshine, it felt warm to the children.

Knowing when to use an adverb and when to use an adjective is not just a matter of form but of meaning. Notice the difference in meaning in the following two sentences:

USAGE

Clear annotations provide answers, and extended margins offer helpful teaching notes.

From *First Course*

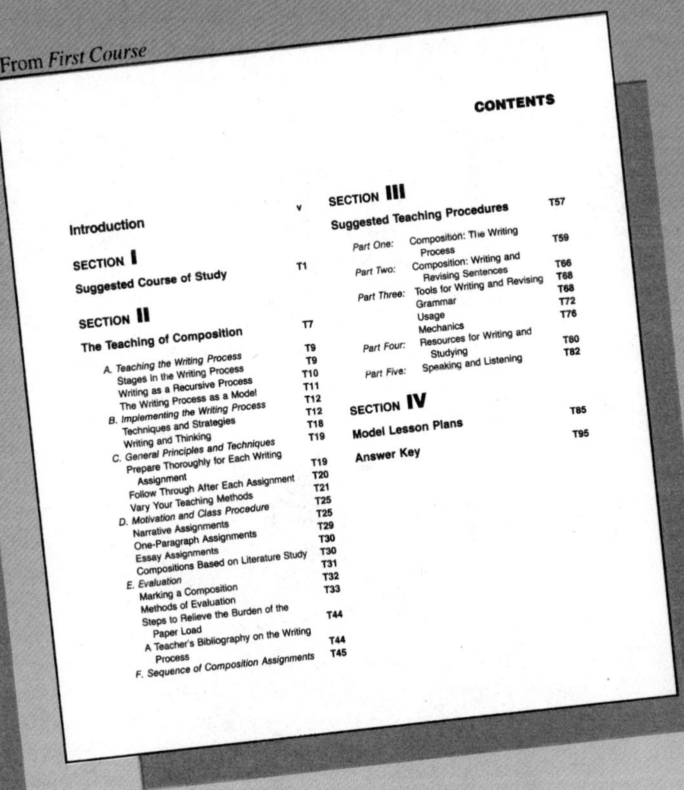

CONTENTS

The **Teaching of Composition** section, based on current research, helps teachers provide comprehensive, systematic instruction that promotes success in writing.

Sample pages are reduced. Actual sizes are 8½″ × 9⅛″.

Teacher's ResourceBank™... packed with practical supplements!

A comprehensive *Teacher's ResourceBank™* makes classroom instruction easy. This useful component includes the *Teacher's Resource Book,* as well as overhead transparencies, classroom posters, a booklet of tips for teaching the writing process, correlations, and a tab key index. A three-ring binder with convenient tabbed dividers provides organized storage for teaching resources.

Teacher's Resource Book

The *Teacher's Resource Book* includes tests and a wealth of copying masters for reinforcing writing, grammar, usage, and mechanics skills. A generous collection of worksheets for less-advanced students provides practice in composition, grammar, mechanics, and usage—all correlated to student textbooks. The *Teacher's Resource Book* also contains composition and speech evaluation forms that allow both teachers and students to assess and critique student writing and speaking.

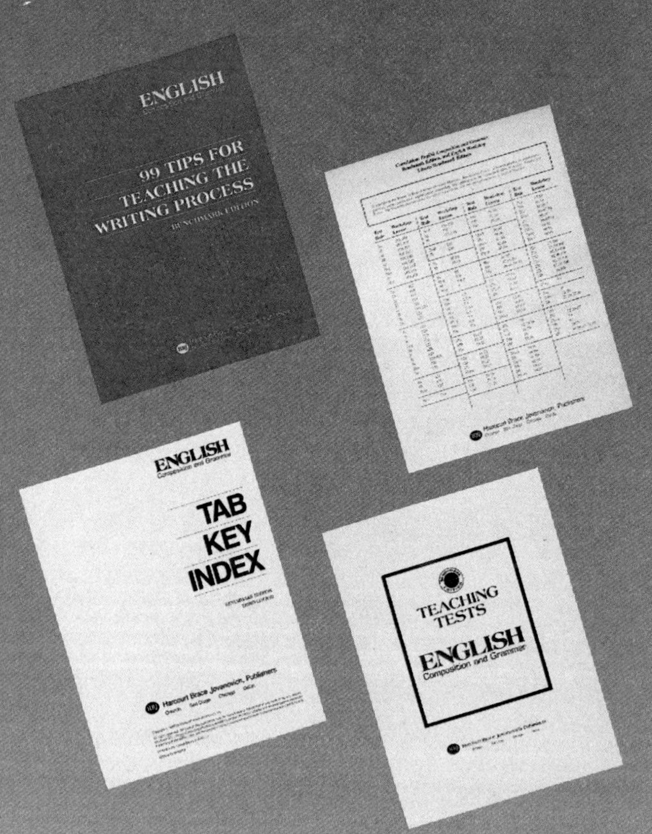

Transparencies for Writing Instruction

Transparencies for Writing Instruction include visuals that illustrate stages of the writing process, as well as color photo-transparencies that help students generate ideas for writing. Copying-master writing exercises enhance the color photo-transparencies.

Thinking and Writing Posters

Two kinds of posters supplement instruction. Wall charts detail the stages of the writing process, while full-color classroom posters stimulate ideas for writing.

99 Tips for Teaching the Writing Process

This resource booklet provides 99 helpful suggestions for teaching the stages of the writing process—from prewriting to writing the final draft.

Correlations

Charts, lesson plans, and reproducible writing assignments correlate specific lessons in ***English Composition and Grammar*** to ***Adventures in Literature.*** Charts also correlate lessons in ***English Composition and Grammar*** to ***English Workshop*** (see page P12).

Tab Key Index

The Tab Key Index allows quick and easy location of specific information in the textbook. Teachers may use it for individualizing instruction, improving student writing skills, and simplifying evaluation.

Additional components

Teaching Tests

Teaching Tests for each level include tests for appropriate textbook chapters. Pre-tests for grammar, usage, mechanics, sentence structure, and composition help determine learning needs before instruction begins. Following instruction, Mastery Tests evaluate skills in grammar, usage, mechanics, sentence structure, and composition.

Photo-Transparencies

Picture the Possibilities: Photo-Transparencies to Motivate Writing include four-color photo-transparencies that help students generate ideas for writing.

Writing Process Transparencies

Writing Process Transparencies illustrate the stages of the writing process and provide additional writing practice.

Microcomputer software

English Grammar, Usage, and Mechanics Exercise Bank and Word Processing Software packages for each level contain review bank disks and a word processing disk. Review bank disks enable students to sharpen grammar, usage, and mechanics skills. Teachers can add their own exercises for classroom use or can print exercise sheets for home use. Word processing disks help students write and revise compositions. A complete Teacher's Manual provides instructions and helpful suggestions.

Related programs

Vocabulary Workshop, Benchmark Edition

Vocabulary Workshop (grades 6–12) develops vocabulary power for improved expression. Based on word lists in corresponding levels of ***English Composition and Grammar, Vocabulary Workshop*** may be used as an independent vocabulary program. The new ***Benchmark Edition:***

- Systematically builds vocabulary with six different types of activities;
- Provides valuable practice in dictionary reference;
- Introduces words gradually—in groups of ten—and treats each word in at least four contexts per lesson;
- Includes worksheets on analogies that challenge students' critical-thinking skills;
- Tests students' grasp of new words and reviews and reinforces words from previous lessons;
- Uses a standardized-test format for cumulative quizzes at five-lesson intervals;
- Features a separate Teacher's Answer Key and Mastery Tests.

English Workshop, Liberty/Benchmark Edition

English Workshop (grades 6–12) is a consumable work-text for practicing and reinforcing language skills. Its solid combination of step-by-step instruction and exercises leads to mastery of essentials in grammar, usage, mechanics, vocabulary, and spelling for effective composition. The program includes:

- Exercises built on high-interest themes, in a format students can follow on their own;
- Chapters on sentence combining to help students add variety, clarity, and rhythm to their writing;
- Composition lessons focusing on writing topic sentences and on developing the four types of paragraphs;
- A separate Teacher's Answer Key and Mastery Tests for each level.

Composition: Models and Exercises, Liberty/Benchmark Edition

Composition: Models and Exercises and ***Advanced Composition: A Book of Models for Writing*** (grades 7-12) present writing techniques used by hundreds of highly respected authors. The series emphasizes success in composition through models that illustrate specific skills and exercises that put those skills to work. The program includes Teacher's Manuals with Answer Keys—one for *First* through *Fifth Courses* and one for ***Advanced Composition.***

A thoroughly flexible program, the series serves as a self-contained composition program or as a complement to ***English Composition and Grammar.***

About the author

John E. Warriner taught English for many years in junior and senior high schools and in colleges. He was the primary author of ***English Composition and Grammar, Benchmark Edition,*** an author of ***English Workshop,*** general editor of ***Composition: Models and Exercises,*** and editor of ***Short Stories: Characters in Conflict.***

BENCHMARK EDITION

ANNOTATED
TEACHER'S EDITION

ENGLISH
Composition and Grammar

John E. Warriner

SECOND COURSE

HBJ **Harcourt Brace Jovanovich, Publishers**
Orlando San Diego Chicago Dallas

The Annotated Teacher's Edition, and the Teacher's Resource Book, when used with the pupil's textbook, provide a complete composition and grammar program.

An Annotated Teacher's Edition and a Teacher's Resource Book are not automatically included with each shipment of a classroom set of textbooks. However, each will be forwarded when requested by a teacher, an administrator, or a representative of Harcourt Brace Jovanovich, Inc.

The Teacher's Resource Book is available for every level of *English Composition and Grammar.* For information, please contact your sales representative.

John E. Warriner taught English for thirty-two years in junior and senior high schools and in college. He is chief author of the *English Composition and Grammar* series, coauthor of the *English Workshop* series, general editor of the *Composition: Models and Exercises* series, and editor of *Short Stories: Characters in Conflict.* His coauthors are all active in English education.

Printed in the United States of America
ISBN 0–15–311739–7

CONTENTS

CRITICAL READERS

We wish to thank the following people, who helped to evaluate the materials in the pupil's edition:

John H. Bushman	Professor of Curriculum and Instruction at University of Kansas, Lawrence, Kansas
Myles Eley	English Department Chairman at Warren Central High School, Indianapolis, Indiana
Norbert Elliot	Coordinator of Composition at East Texas State University, Commerce, Texas, and Director of the Northeast Texas Writing Project
David England	Associate Professor of English Education and Director of the LSU Writing Project at Louisiana State University, Baton Rouge, Louisiana
Kent Gill	Head of the English Department at Holmes Junior High School, Davis, California
Cheri L. Hannon	Language Arts Instructional Specialist for Shawnee Mission Community Schools and Consultant for the Shawnee Mission Writing Project, Shawnee Mission, Kansas
Sandra I. Jackson	English Teacher at Palm Beach Gardens Community High School, Palm Beach Gardens, Florida
Eloise Livingston	Former Elementary Teacher, Director of Library and Media Services for Morgan County Schools, Decatur, Alabama
Patricia J. Marston	English Teacher at Semmes Middle School, Semmes, Alabama
Donna Miller	Program Consultant for Language Arts for Orange County Schools, Orlando, Florida
Cheryl Olsen	District Coordinator of Language Arts for Natrona County School District # 1, Casper, Wyoming
Sydell Rabin	Department Head of English at Columbia High School, Maplewood, New Jersey
William D. Renn	English Department Chair at Valley High School and Adjunct Professor of English at Jefferson Community College, Southwest, Louisville, Kentucky
Connie Sears	English Department Chair at Minco High School, Minco, Oklahoma
Kathy Steckloff	English Teacher at Englewood High School, Jacksonville, Florida
Jocelyne Tord	Assistant Principal at Wagner Junior High School 167, New York City, New York
Annette Van Dusen	Curriculum Supervisor for Oklahoma City Public Schools, Oklahoma City, Oklahoma
Paul Wheeler	English Teacher at Berkshire Middle School, Birmingham, Michigan

INTRODUCTION

A Basic Text

The *English Composition and Grammar* series consists of seven books for use as basic texts in grades 6 to 12. The rich store of supplementary teaching materials in English, including media other than the textbook, serves to emphasize the need for a single, coordinated basic language text as the center of the instructional program in most English classes.

Content

In content and organization the *English Composition and Grammar* series reflects the author's belief that the primary function of an English textbook is to provide the subject matter of English in a clear and flexible arrangement. Each book contains separate sections of the following study areas: composition, sentence structure, grammar, usage, mechanics, library and reference tools, speaking, and listening. Also, a vocabulary program and a spelling program run throughout the series. Each section, as well as each chapter within a section, is an independent unit, a fact which enables the teacher to use the books with any course of study and in any sequence.

Books in the series have been carefully graded to meet the language needs of students at each level. For example, the number of chapters devoted to the construction of clear and smooth sentences increases from two in *Introductory Course* and *First Course* to ten in *Complete Course. Introductory Course* introduces adjective and adverb phrases, while *First Course* introduces adjective and adverb clauses and two of the verbals—the participle and the infinitive. *Second Course* adds the noun clause and the gerund.

Refinements in usage are added each year as the student becomes able to understand them and employ them in speaking and writing. Work in expository writing moves from simple explanations and reports in the early books to the formal research paper and the logical presentation of argument in the later ones. In all areas, each book reviews what students have studied in the preceding years and carries on the teaching in greater depth.

Presentation

Subject matter is the province of the textbook; method, however, is the province of teachers. The texts are intended to aid teachers; they do not usurp their proper role in motivation and method. A textbook which can be taught by only one method and in only one sequence may easily get in the way of teachers who prefer their own approaches or who wish to follow a local course of study.

Although the presentation of material in the texts is straightforward and deductive, the material can, and in many instances should, be taught inductively, the teacher leading the class through specific examples to the formulation of the principle underlying them. Then, in the text, the class will find the principle fully explained and followed by practice exercises. The "Model Lesson Plans" near the end of this teacher material, as well as the page-by-page discussion in the "Suggested Teaching Procedures" section, show specifically how to employ the inductive method. (Note, however, that for review, which is a basic process in each year of English, the deductive method is usually more efficient than the inductive, and for advanced classes it is often as effective and far less time-consuming even for the presentation of new skills.)

Everything taught in the *English Composition and Grammar* series has a practical application to speaking and writing. Although addressed informally to the student, the instruction is concise and businesslike. It does not strain to be entertaining, nor does it rely on decorative art and discursive one-way chats with the student to make English study palatable. The subject matter of English is English. The author is convinced that it cannot be taught successfully by means of digressions and excursions into other fields. The wide acceptance of the previous editions reinforced the author's belief that both students and teachers appreciate this serious, straightforward presentation.

A Reference Handbook

For most students, especially those in the upper grades, a basic English textbook serves another useful function—that of a reference book. In order to increase their effectiveness a reference tools, the *English Composition and Grammar* books follow the handbook format. The organization by subject-matter areas, the use of color for important definitions and rules, the tab key system, and the omission of extraneous materials help students to find with ease answers to their questions about English. This easy reference feature of the books is especially appropriate in today's classrooms, where students are encouraged to work independently, to do more studying on their own. In such matter-of-fact areas as usage, punctuation, capitalization, manuscript form, letter writing, and sentence structure, and student can find the answer to a specific problem by referring to the text, where all rules are clearly stated and typographically highlighted.

Composition

English teachers are keenly aware of the importance to their students of achieving competence in writing. Inability to express ideas adequately in writing handicaps the student in all kinds of work. For this reason the major emphasis in all books in the *English Composition and Grammar* series is on the writing process, with expository writing receiving the most attention.

In one sense, the ability to write well is acquired through the mastery of a great many individual skills, and textbook exercises provide practice in employing them. Through the teacher's guidance and insistence, students learn to carry over into all their writing the skills they have learned from their textbook.

In another sense, the ability to write well requires, among other things, accurate observation, a stimulated imagination, strong interest in words, and an awareness of logical thinking and clear organization. These are the intangibles of the writing art. To a degree they are teachable. Each book in the series deals with them. For the most part, however, they are acquired through broad personal experience and through the analysis and emulation of models of good writing.

Grammar

The *English Composition and Grammar* series teaches grammar for two main reasons—to provide a basis for instruction in usage and to facilitate the teaching of writing. While it cannot be demonstrated that ignorance of grammar ever prevented students from writing well, it is possible that such ignorance can prevent them from profiting from the teacher's instruction and corrections. The experienced teacher knows that teaching compostion is never easy; without a vocabulary for discussing sentence structure, it is often more. Similarly, the teaching of grammar will not in itself necessarily change usage habits, but it does make possible the efficient teaching of such broad concepts as agreement, pronoun reference, and proper placement of modifiers.

For both of these purposes—the teaching of writing and the teaching of usage—the author believes traditional grammar to be particularly well suited. Its vocabulary is already partly familiar to most students, even in the earlier grades; its essential concepts can be taught in a fairly short time; and its common-sense statements, though sometimes unscientific, have a direct and obvious bearing on matters of usage and composition. By advocating the use of traditional grammar in teaching usage and composition, however, the author is not suggesting that other linguistic approaches be ignored.

The Benchmark Edition also contains many Writing Applications that show connections between principles of grammar, usage, and mechanics and concrete writing techniques.

The *Composition: Models and Exercises* Series

Since space for models is necessarily limited in a general English textbook, a companion series of texts, *Composition: Models and Exercises,* has been prepared to reinforce the teaching in *English Composition and Grammar. Composition: Models and Exercises* consists of five books paralleling *First Course* through *Fifth Course. Advanced Composition: A Book of Models for Writing* is recommended for use with *Complete Course.*

The *English Workshop* Series

Since the need for additional practice and drill in the essentials of grammar, usage, punctuation, capitalization, composition, vocabulary, and spelling will vary from class to class, a companion series of workbooks, *English Workshop,* has been prepared to supplement the exercises found in *English Composition and Grammar. English Workshop* consists of seven books. *Introductory Course* through *Fifth Course* is recommended for use along with *Introductory Course* through *Fifth Course* of *English Composition and Grammar. Review Course* is recommended for use with *Complete Course.*

The *Vocabulary Workshop* Series

To supplement your course work in the study of vocabulary, a companion series of vocabulary workbooks, *Vocabulary Workshop,* has been prepared to accompany *English Composition and Grammar. Vocabulary Workshop* consists of seven books. *Introductory Course* through *Complete Course* is recommended for use along with *Introductory Course* through *Complete Course of English Composition and Grammar.*

Teaching Tests

A complete testing program accompanies the *English Composition and Grammar* series. Each test booklet contains Pretests, Chapter Tests, and Mastery Tests, which may be used to measure achievement in grammar, usage, mechanics, sentence structure, and composition. The test booklets, *Teaching Tests,* are available from the publisher at a small cost. Printed tests are often more highly respected than mimeographed tests prepared by the teacher, and they relieve the teacher of a vast amount of work in preparing and duplicating tests for class use.

Annotated Teacher's Edition

Each pupil's textbook in the *English Composition and Grammar* series is complemented by an *Annotated Teacher's Edition*. The *Annotated Teacher's Edition* includes all pages from the pupil's edition, an answer key, annotated textbook exercises, and professional information to aid the teacher in presenting textbook content: chapter overviews, instructional objectives, suggestions for adapting content to students' needs and abilities, and suggested teaching procedures. This professional information is printed in the margins of the extended pages in the *Annotated Teacher's Edition*. In addition, each *Annotated Teacher's Edition* includes a course of study for the year's work in English. In an extensive discussion of the teaching of composition, it also presents methods and materials for teaching compositon, forms for evaluating student papers, and a sequence of composition assignments. The *Annotated Teacher's Edition* is designed for the teacher's convenience, reference, and ease of use.

Teacher's Resource Book

A *Teacher's Resource Book* is available for each level of the *English Composition and Grammar* series. Each book contains copying masters of the following items: reteaching/enrichment worksheets in composition, grammar, usage, mechanics; teaching tests; evaluation forms (peer editing and analytic scales); and charts.

SECTION I

Suggested Course of Study

Chapters in *English Composition and Grammar, Second Course* are grouped according to content—the composition chapters in Parts One and Two, the grammar, usage, and mechanics chapters in Part Three, etc. The book is arranged this way so that students can use it as a handbook to look up a question of spelling or grammar or punctuation easily and quickly. This arrangement means, however, that the book is not designed for teaching straight through. While students must begin writing compositions at the beginning of the year if they are to have maximum opportunity to improve their writing, they must concurrently study grammar, usage, and mechanics. If the book were taught straight through, a class would not reach the mechanics chapters until well into the second semester.

In most school systems where a course of study is established, teachers will simply teach chapters in the text in the order called for by the local course. Since each chapter is an independent unit, any chapter, with a few necessary exceptions, may be taught at any point in the year. Teachers who are expected to determine their own order may wish to adopt the sequence suggested in the course of study that follows. The chapters in the suggested course of study are grouped into quarters of the school year; the exact sequence of chapters within any quarter, however, is left up to the teacher. (In the suggested course of study, the chapters in each quarter are merely listed numerically.) It is assumed that a quarter will consist of approximately nine weeks. It is also assumed that roughly one half of the English course will be devoted to language and language skills, the province of this text, and the other half will be devoted to reading and literature.

Certain chapters, although scheduled for intensive study at a later time, contain materials that should be introduced early in the first quarter and taught on a regular basis throughout the year; for example, the list of spelling words at the end of Chapter 25 and the list of vocabulary words at the end of Chapter 28 can be assigned in weekly groups of ten to fifteen words. The chapters on capitalization and punctuation should be pointed out to the class at the beginning of the year so that students can refer to them at any time they need help in these subjects.

A SUGGESTED PLACEMENT OF CHAPTERS BY QUARTERS OF THE SCHOOL YEAR

FIRST QUARTER

Compositon: The Writing Process

Chapter **1** Writing and Thinking

Tools for Writing and Revising

Grammar

Chapter **10** The Sentence
Chapter **11** The Parts of Speech: Noun, Pronoun, Adjective
Chapter **12** The Parts of Speech: Verb, Adverb, Preposition, Conjunction, Interjection

Usage

Chapter **17** Agreement

Mechanics

Chapter **22** Capital Letters

Resources for Writing and Studying

Chapter **29** Studing and Test Taking

SECOND QUARTER

Composition: The Writing Process

Chapter **2** Writing Paragraphs: Structure and Development
Chapter **4** Writing Stories

Composition: Writing and Revising Sentences

Chapter **8** Writing Complete Sentences

Tools For Writing and Revising

Grammar

Chapter	**13**	Complements
Chapter	**14**	The Phrase
Chapter	**15**	The Clause

Usage

Chapter	**18**	Using Verbs Correctly

Mechanics

Chapter	**23**	Punctuation: End Marks, Commas, Semicolons, Colons

Resources for Writing and Studying

Chapter	**26**	Using the Dictionary

THIRD QUARTER

Composition: The Writing Process

Chapter	**3**	Writing Paragraphs: Four Types of Paragraphs
Chapter	**5**	Writing Exposition: The Whole Composition

Composition: Writing and Revising Sentences

Chapter	**9**	Writing Effective Sentences

Tools for Writing and Revising

Grammar

Chapter	**16**	The Kinds of Sentence Structure

Usage

Chapter	**19**	Using Pronouns Correctly
Chapter	**20**	Using Modifiers Correctly

Mechanics

Chapter	**24**	Punctuation: Italics, Quotation Marks, Apostrophes, Hyphens

Resources for Writing and Studying

Chapter	**27**	Using the Library

FOURTH QUARTER

Composition: The Writing Process

Chapter	**6**	Writing Exposition: Summaries and Reports
Chapter	**7**	Writing Letters and Completing Forms

Tools for Writing and Revising

Usage

Chapter	**21**	Glossary of Usage

Mechanics

Chapter	**25**	Spelling

Resources for Writing and Studying

Chapter	**28**	Vocabulary

Speaking and Listening

Chapter	**30**	Speaking
Chapter	**31**	Listening

EXPLANATORY NOTES ON THE COURSE OF STUDY

FIRST QUARTER

Since "Writing and Thinking," will give your students a basic foundation in the writing and thinking processes, you may want to begin the year with Chapter 1. Before you make your first writing assignment, you will probably want to go over with your students the section on manuscript form on text pages 40–42.

Chapters 10, 11, and 12, dealing with the sentence and the parts of speech, provide an early review of the grammar taught in the seventh grade. Some classes or students may require you to reteach this material rather than review it.

Chapter 29, "Studying and Test Taking," is placed in the first quarter so that students will be able to practice effective studying and test-taking techniques throughout the school year.

Chapter 22, "Capital Letters," serves as a reminder of some of the conventions of writing. If you teach the chapter during the first quarter, your students will be able to use it for reference throughout the year.

Chapter 17, "Agreement," puts to practical use some of the information the students have studied in the chapters on grammar.

SECOND QUARTER

After students have reviewed the writing and thinking process in the first quarter, Chapter 4, "Writing Stories," is a natural way to continue with the year's work in composition. Personal-experience narratives are the easiest and most enjoyable kind of writing for most eighth-graders. After the pleasant experience of writing stories, the students will be more interested in a serious study of the structure and development of paragraphs, Chapter 2.

Chapters 13, 14, and 15, will give students a basic understanding of the grammar of a sentence and will prepare them for Chapter 8, "Writing Complete Sentences." Chapter 18, "Using Verbs Correctly," presents some additional grammatical information about verbs (tense and conjugation) and provides practice in overcoming common usage problems.

In this quarter students can continue their study of mechanics with the first punctuation chapter, Chapter 23. You may teach the entire chapter at this point, but many teachers prefer to take up the points in the chapter throughout the course of the year.

Chapter 26, "Using the Dictionary," should be taught early in the school year so that students will be able to apply what they have learned to their study of vocabulary and spelling. In addition, students can be encouraged to refer to their dictionaries during the proofreading stage of the writing process.

THIRD QUARTER

In this quarter, students will continue their study of the paragraph, concentrating on the four types of paragraphs (Chapter 3). After a study of narrative, descriptive, expository, and persuasive paragraphs, students will be ready to approach the expository composition, Chapter 5.

The final grammar chapter, "The Kinds of Sentence Structure," and the usage chapters, "Using Pronouns Correctly" and "Using Modifiers Correctly," should be taught early in the quarter. Chapter 9, "Writing Effective Sentences," provides an opportunity for follow-up and application of the student's work in grammar and usage.

Chapter 24, "Punctuation," covers italics, quotation marks, apostrophes, and hyphens. As with Chapter 23, you may want to teach the chapter all at once or cover the various types of punctuation marks as needed during the course of the school year.

Chapter 27, "Using the Library," logically follows the study of the dictionary in the second quarter and precedes the chapter on writing reports in the fourth quarter.

FOURTH QUARTER

Fewer chapters are assigned to the fourth quarter. If your classes have fallen behind during the first three quarters, you will be able to use the extra time to catch up.

If you have used Chapter 21, "Glossary of Usage," for reference throughout the year, you may wish to omit it entirely or confine the study to those usage problems most prevalent in your classes.

Students will continue their study of exposition with Chapter 6, subtitled "Summaries and Reports." Letter writing is one kind of writing eighth-graders may be doing during their summer vacation. Teaching Chapter 7 in the fourth quarter provides a timely reminder, not only of the conventions of letter form, but also of the kind of content that makes a friendly letter interesting and the kind that makes a business letter effective.

Chapter 28, "Vocabulary," and Chapter 25, "Spelling," are a natural pair. Work on the vocabulary and spelling lists should have started early in the first quarter, but you can use this time for systematic study of word spellings and meanings.

The chapter on speaking, Chapter 30, is a logical follow-up to the study of summaries and reports (Chapter 6). The work that has already been done in planning a composition will contribute to the work on planning a talk. You may also wish to coordinate the teaching of Chapter 31, "Listening," with Chapter 30, teaching audience listening along with speaking.

SECTION II

The Teaching of Composition

Composition work should be a regular part of the class routine. If you think you can manage the paper work, you may wish to begin the year by telling your classes that they will write weekly or biweekly. Naturally, the time you allot for each paper will vary with the difficulty of the assignment. For example, while one week is sufficient time to write a short personal-experience narrative, more than one week may be needed to write a report based on reference sources. (On pages T44–T55 you will find a series of fifteen suggested composition assignments that can provide the basis for a year's program.) Tell the class that you will always let them know in advance when each paper will be due. Although you may wish at times to omit an assignment or to add an extra assignment, ordinarily you should avoid such breaks in the routine.

When you make writing assignments, indicate when you expect to receive papers from students. Uphold your requirements, but also try to return papers promptly. In this way, students will receive your feedback about their writing while their interest in a particular assignment still runs high. With higher interest, students might also be more motivated to devote serious effort to evaluating and revising their papers. Even when you are teaching a concentrated unit in literature, you may want to keep up the composition assignments, perhaps basing them on the literature being studied. It is not necessary to be so rigid as to designate the same day every week or every two weeks as composition-due day, but it is advisable to keep the writing on a clearly regular basis.

A. TEACHING THE WRITING PROCESS

The Benchmark Edition provides a more comprehensive and systematic treatment of the writing process than previous editions. It draws upon current research which reveals that mature writers follow a recursive sequence of thinking and planning, drafting, evaluating, revising, and proofreading. Immature writers often understand that they need to create a particular written product which exhibits certain characteristics, but they have little understanding of how to achieve that product. Current practices in the teaching of writing seek to fill this gap by balancing the traditional emphasis on product with a new emphasis on process. This new emphasis on a mastery of composing skills and an understanding of how and when writers apply these skills holds greater promise of ensuring students' success.

STAGES IN THE WRITING PROCESS

The terminology used to describe and delineate aspects of the writing process varies widely. Some educators speak of invention or discovery rather than of prewriting; others refer to editing rather than proofreading as a stage in the process.

The following chart outlines the writing process as it appears in *English Composition and Grammar.* At each grade level, the writing process is presented as a sequence of six stages. The first, **prewriting,** encompasses all the thinking and planning activities that occur before the writer begins a first draft. To clarify the various kinds of thinking and planning that go on at this stage and to help students master specific skills, the prewriting stage is further divided in the text and presented as a series of steps moving from consideration of purpose and audience to the arrangement of ideas in a logical order. **Writing,** the second stage of the process, is defined as the expression of the writer's thoughts in language. During the third stage, **evaluating,** the writer judges a draft to determine what changes would improve content and organization, word choice, and sentence structure. In the fourth stage, **revision,** the writer makes the changes needed to improve content, organization, and style. In the fifth stage, the writer **proofreads** to identify and correct errors in grammar, usage, and mechanics. In the last stage, the writer **prepares a final version** of the work that complies with the standards for correct manuscript form.

THE WRITING PROCESS

PREWRITING

The writer discovers and selects a subject for writing.
The writer limits the subject to an appropriate topic.
The writer establishes a point of view: an attitude and tone.
The writer evaluates the topic in terms of purpose, audience, and tone.
The writer gathers information.
The writer records specific details.
The writer evaluates and classifies these details.
The writer arranges information in a logical order.

WRITING A FIRST DRAFT

The writer expresses ideas in sentences and paragraphs.

EVALUATING

The writer evaluates the first draft in order to decide what changes in content, organization, word choice, and sentence structure would improve it.

REVISING

The writer improves the first draft by making changes in content, organization, and style.

PROOFREADING

The writer checks the revised draft to correct inaccuracies in grammar, usage, mechanics, and spelling.

WRITING THE FINAL VERSION

The writer prepares and proofreads the final version of the paper.

WRITING AS A RECURSIVE PROCESS

One insight gained from research into the writing process is the degree to which separate mental operations recur and interact with one another over and over during the composing process. The writing process is often presented as a neat linear progression from prewriting to revising. However, what actually takes place in the writer's mind is a rather untidy process in which planning, thinking, collecting of data, evaluating, rethinking, and revising of previous work occur frequently and concurrently. The writer who is brainstorming possible topics may simultaneously be making predictions about audience interests and evaluating a topic in relation to these interests. The writer who is organizing supporting material may also be evaluating material, judging the amount of support necessary to convince a specific audience, or pausing to gather new material.

Sondra Perl's work with unskilled college writers led to the discovery of two mental operations that seem to underlie this recursive process. The first, "retrospective structuring," refers to the frequency with which writers stop and review what they have produced either to reorient themselves before proceeding or to readjust previous work. The second behavior, "projective structuring," refers to the frequent pauses writers make to think through their next step. While evidence suggests that both these processes occur regularly in the mind of the good writer, beginning writers often have difficulty applying and balancing the two operations.

Beginning writers' problems with this recursiveness usually fall into two categories. Some students erroneously assume that once they have limited their topic or gathered information, these steps are behind them and don't need to be reviewed. Others become so involved in looking back and rethinking that they lose track of where they are headed, experience writer's block, or only progress slowly and painfully.

The classroom teacher, then, faces several tasks. The first is to help students understand that writing is an experimental, recursive process and that moving back and forth to reevaluate or readjust earlier work is a natural aspect of writing. The second task is to help immature writers make sound judgments about when to look back to evaluate and revise and when to push ahead so that they achieve a healthy, rewarding balance between free, uninhibited expression and critical reappraisal of their work.

The Value of Collaborative Writing

One way to open up the writing process and allow students insight into how and when recursiveness occurs is to carry out several writing assignments from start to finish as a class or in small groups. For example, early in a unit on descriptive writing, you might involve students in planning and writing a descriptive paragraph about a familiar local scene, a distinctive television character, or an unusual object. Use the chalkboard or transparencies to record work on each stage of the writing process and lead students in gathering details, organizing information, and developing a central idea. Clarify the various thinking processes students use and draw attention to points at which the class naturally stops to review and evaluate previous thinking.

Share Your Own Writing

Another effective way to demonstrate the recursive nature of the writing process is to share a writing project of your own with your classes. Use transparencies to present your prewriting, writing, evaluating, and revising. Explain your purpose for writing and the thinking and rethinking you do as you encounter obstacles, and draw attention to the points at which you evaluate and rework your material. Periodically, you may also want to complete writing assignments along with your students, following the same explanations and directions you provide for students.

Allow Time for Students to Apply the Process

Awareness of recursiveness in the writing process has additional implications for the scheduling and evaluating of writing. While it is important to foster responsibility by asking students to meet assignment deadlines, thinking carefully about a piece of writing or recycling to gather more data or to reorganize ideas takes time that may not be available to students who must submit a final draft on a specific date. Whenever possible, allow students enough time to evaluate their writing thoughtfully. You may also want to balance assignments due on a specific date with assignments that students revise until they are completely satisfied.

Provide Publishing Opportunities for Students

Many English educators believe that students should have many opportunities to write for a variety of real audiences—that is, audiences that include but also go beyond the English teacher. Enabling students to publish their writing is one way to assure them a variety of real audiences. *Publishing,* in this case, is broadly defined: it means that students' writing should be made available for others to read. Publishing students' writing can therefore take many forms: class, school, and community newspapers; class exhibits placed throughout the school; letters; mobiles; class or school literary (or any other) magazines; oral sharing; dramatic presentations to the class, school, parents, and community; and contests for student writing. With access to a range of audiences, students should come to understand two important ideas about writing: one, that different audiences and purposes affect what writers say and how they say it; and two, that school-sponsored writing can be meaningful.

THE WRITING PROCESS AS A MODEL

Unlike a mathematical or scientific formula which never varies and inevitably leads to the desired outcome, the writing process is a theoretical model of what we currently understand to happen in the mind of the writer. The value of a model is that it breaks down and clarifies the process followed by most writers, isolating individual skills that teachers can then assist students in mastering. However, it would be inaccurate to view the composing process as an inflexible series of steps or required procedures that must always be consciously carried out.

Variables That Affect the Writing Process

How an individual writer uses the writing process is affected by numerous factors; besides audience and purpose, these include the formality or consequence of the writing, the complexity of form and/or content, and the writer's previous experience or familiarity with a particular form or content. In formal writing situations or situations of consequence—a teen-ager writing a graduation speech or a biographical sketch for a college application—the writer benefits from conscious application of the writing process. In informal or insignificant situations—the same teen-ager tacking a reminder on the refrigerator door—the writer composes with little regard for prewriting, revising, or proofreading his or her work. In fact, in situations where time and efficiency are factors, conscious application of the writing process may hinder the writer. Most teachers have encountered one illustration of this—the student who is unable to complete an essay test because he devotes too much time to planning and organizing ideas.

Other variables—the form of the writing, the writer's familiarity with that form, and the complexity of the content—also affect how the writing process is implemented. Writers dealing with familiar form and content—the business manager writing a monthly report or the experienced teacher writing a simple lesson plan—often leap over phases of the prewriting process or carry them out unconsciously. On the other hand, the writer working with an intricate form or complicated content may adopt a highly recursive pattern of conscious recycling through phases of the writing process. The novelist Saul Bellow, for example, is said to have written twenty-five drafts of the novel *Herzog* before he was satisfied.

The Process Varies from Writer to Writer

The final variable is the writer. The act of writing is highly idiosyncratic and writers often have very different composing styles. Some take careful, detailed notes before they write; others know that their ideas will not really take shape until they begin writing. Some leap to conclusions and then seek details to support the conclusion. Some talk out loud. Some write conclusions first and introductions last. The writing process also varies *within* a writer. Someone who writes with ease one day may find it difficult, or even impossible, to write the next day.

What these variations suggest is the student writer's need to experiment. Just as they would not presume to tell a Hemingway or Jane Austen how to go about the act of composing, teachers should not dictate that the developing writers in their own classes follow exactly the same procedures or use the same methods. What teachers can do is acquaint students with numerous techniques and help them make perceptive decisions about those which work for them. Depending on your students' needs and abilities, you may want to discuss the writing processes of published writers. A series useful for this purpose is *Writers at Work—The Paris Review Interviews* (New York: Viking, 1958, 1963, 1967, 1976, 1981, 1984, 1986).

Implications for Classroom Instruction

Use this knowledge of variables that affect the writing process to build a composition program that will foster students' success. For example, if your class will be working with an unfamiliar form of writing, such as the persuasive essay, you may want to reduce the complexity of the task by limiting their choice of topics to familiar, less-complicated issues such as teen concerns. Or, you might direct the class in completing prewriting activities on a topic of mutual interest so that students can focus their attention on mastery of the new form without the complication caused by unfamiliar, complex content.

Try to balance challenging assignments (longer, formal papers involving unfamiliar form or content) with simpler or more familiar assignments that will bolster students' confidence. Also, consider these variables as you evaluate students' work; the student who consistently tackles challenging, complicated topics may not produce papers that are quite as polished or finished as the student who works with less demanding content.

Writing Task Analysis

How familiar is the student with the form of writing?
How familiar is the content?
How complex is the form of writing?
How complex is the content?
What is the importance/consequence of this writing?
How much time is available?

B. IMPLEMENTING THE WRITING PROCESS

The following suggestions may be helpful in developing a writing program geared to your students' needs and abilities.

TECHNIQUES AND STRATEGIES

PREWRITING

Avoid presenting the prewriting techniques outlined in the text as "rules" writers must follow. Such an approach often has a negative effect: rather than recognizing the value of brainstorming, clustering, or outlining, students perceive these techniques simply as additional steps they are required to complete. Instead, your goal should be to help students reach a point where they choose to spend time on prewriting, feel confident using various techniques, and voluntarily carry these out.

Too many students who have difficulty with writing jump to the conclusion that they just can't write or that they aren't yet inspired. Unfortunately, these individuals often believe the cure for their apprehension is to delay beginning. Point out that beginning the writing process by engaging in some prewriting activity, no matter how unformed or tentative the results, will help them clarify their ideas. They can, then, use the principle of recursiveness to recycle through various activities until they have a clear idea of what they want to accomplish.

Use Prewriting Techniques Frequently

If techniques such as brainstorming or clustering are new to your students, seize every opportunity to demonstrate their usefulness in both writing and nonwriting situations. If your classes are discussing the traits of a character in a novel or drama, use clustering to gather details about that character on the chalkboard. Point out that many psychologists recommend clustering, or mapping as an effective way to take notes from a textbook or to review notes before a test. Suggest that students use brainstorming in their extracurricular activities—to generate ideas for a Homecoming float, fund-raising projects, or solutions to school problems.

Vary Prewriting Activities

Help students discover which techniques work best for them and in what situations. Some educators, for instance, feel that brainstorming is a linear, rational approach to a topic, while clustering provides a visual "map" of the topic. This may explain why some writers find brainstorming more effective with persuasive topics but prefer clustering for expository writing. Encourage students to vary the techniques they use and to discuss their reactions to different activities. Help them discover both the applications and limitations of a single activity: that clustering can be used not only to gather information, but to limit a topic, to organize information, to clarify relationships; that the *5 W-How?* questions work well with narrative topics, but other techniques are better for exploring a persuasive topic; that the *5 W-How?* questions can be used over and over to explore a topic in depth.

Encourage Journal Writing

Another productive prewriting activity is maintaining a writer's journal. A writer's journal can take any convenient form, be it a looseleaf or spiral notebook or a collection of entries kept in a student's writing folder. Regardless of its form, a writer's journal provides students with an opportunity to record their thoughts, feelings, and experiences—perhaps in response to open-ended writing starters provided by the teacher. Through maintaining a writer's journal, students are able to write freely and comfortably about personally meaningful and significant concerns in a nonjudgmental context. Thus, the writer's journal serves as an important prewriting activity, by being a rich source of subjects and ideas that students can tap when they are searching for something to write about or when they are gathering information about a subject.

To fulfill this prewriting role, use of the writer's journal must be approached carefully and thoughtfully. It is first necessary for students to understand that a writer's journal may be a source of ideas and information for *public* writing which will be shared with others. At the same time, students should feel that they are in fact writing in a nonjudgmental setting. To be effective prewriting aids, students' journals therefore should not be evaluated. Teachers may note positive comments about students' willingness to record and share various ideas or experiences, or they may offer praise for students' faithful consistency in making journal entries; but evaluating spelling, grammar, usage, and mechanics or the content of entries can seriously impede the free expression of the ideas, feelings, and experiences students are willing to share with others.

Students may also use journals to record progress on their writing assignments. In this kind of writer's journal, or log, students note where they are in the writing process as they address a writing task. Using journals in this way generally makes students more aware of the recursive nature of their individual writing processes.

Allow Students to Experiment

Encourage your classes to adapt techniques to a specific writing task or to invent new techniques. Most teachers have encountered the student who writes an outline after completing the final draft. Sometimes this occurs because the writer finds the traditional form of outlining a cumbersome or ineffective means of organizing content for a particular paper. While you should continue to emphasize the need to organize information effectively, you might discuss alternative methods of organizing with your classes. Students writing short narrative papers, for example, might gather and organize details along a time line. For a descriptive paragraph about a familiar place, students might draw a simple diagram of the scene and record details directly on the diagram.

Allow Adequate Time for Prewriting

Student compositions display greater depth and more thoughtful development when ample time is allowed for prewriting. With major assignments students may benefit from what experts on creative thinking call "incubation," a period of time after their initial thinking about a project when they carry out other tasks. Classes preparing to write research papers might benefit from this approach. For a week before beginning the unit, have students spend five minutes of each class writing a journal response to open-ended statements: I am curious about ______, One thing I have always wanted to study is ______, I have often wondered why ______. At the end of the week, students can review their journal entries, using their comments to discover possible research paper topics.

WRITING THE FIRST DRAFT

Research into the writing process still provides only limited insight into what happens as the writer composes. What is commonly acknowledged is that successful writers have an inner voice that both guides and judges what they write. Some writers call this voice their internal critic. Depending on where the writer is in the composing process and how critical and insistent this inner voice is, it either helps or hinders the writer. During the evaluating, revising, and proofreading stages, the internal critic is a valuable guide because it draws the writer's attention to strengths and weaknesses in the work or helps the reader identify misspelled words and grammatical errors. However, if this inner voice appears during the composing stage, rather than during evaluating, revision, and proofreading, and constantly draws the writer's attention to minor errors or tears apart what has already been written, the writer feels defeated and overwhelmed. This may be the basis for what is commonly known as writer's block. The problem can appear either as a complete inability to begin drafting or as a damaging form of recursiveness in which the writer begins, pauses to evaluate, crosses out or throws away what has already been written, and begins again.

Teachers can aid their classes by drawing attention to this phenomenon so that students recognize and consciously control this internal critic. The following techniques have also proved successful in helping students to overcome problems that affect them while composing.

1. Use the tape recorder as an aid to writing. Some students are highly articulate speakers but encounter problems when they try to translate their thoughts into print. Some describe their problem as an inability to write fast enough to keep up with their thoughts. Others seem to lack an inner voice. They will tell you that they know what they want to say but can't put it into words. Frequently these students find it easier to talk through their papers, recording ideas with a cassette tape recorder; they can then replay the tape and use it as a guide in developing the first draft for a paper.

2. Urge students to confront and give shape to their internal critic by drawing a picture of this hypercritical monster. Visualizing the internal critic and then symbolically controlling it by turning the picture face down or crumpling it up and throwing it away also seems to provide an unconscious release that enables writers to proceed. Experts who treat the problem of writer's block in professional writers often use this technique.

3. Replace an inhibiting internal critic with a supportive, caring audience. This can be done in several ways. Students might imagine that someone who cares about them is looking over their shoulder and encouraging them as they write. Another possibility is to ask students to write the first draft of a paper as if it were a letter to a close friend or relative.

4. Encourage students to identify the problem that inhibits their work on a particular paper and help them to develop a solution. Students who have difficulty ordering and transcribing their thoughts or lose track of what they want to say sometimes benefit from writing the first draft of a paper in short telegraphic sentences that present ideas clearly and simply. Once this is accomplished, the student has a framework that can be evaluated for organization and then revised, first, by fleshing out barebone ideas and, then, by varying sentence structure and word choice.

EVALUATING

When writers evaluate, they look closely and critically at their papers. This requires the ability to perceive a problem in what they have written. Some research studies suggest that students do not revise effectively because they are unable to diagnose the problems in their drafts—that is, they cannot determine what the weaknesses in their papers are. Not knowing what to improve of course affects students' efforts to revise.

Using the Guidelines for Evaluating

English Composition and Grammar addresses the difficulty of identifying writing problems by focusing on standards students can use to judge their writing. Guidelines for Evaluating in each composition chapter present criteria, stated as questions, that students can apply to judge their drafts. These questions, specific for a particular form or mode, emphasize the key features of that form or mode. Review these guidelines with your students (in small groups or as a class) when they complete their first drafts. For small-group or class discussion, you may also want to apply these guidelines to anonymous student papers or to short pieces of writing published in newspapers or magazines. In this way, students should gradually become more skilled at noticing and diagnosing problems in their own writing. This should make them better writers and, by extension, more critical and discerning readers of others' writing. You may also consider applying a specific set of guidelines when you evaluate students' writing.

Techniques for Evaluating

Students can evaluate their writing more easily by using four techniques. Take time to discuss each technique, and remind students to use these approaches throughout the school year.

1. Allow students to put their first drafts aside for a day or so before evaluating them. By letting some time pass between drafting and evaluating, students should gain the distance that will help them to see their papers in a new, fresh perspective.

2. Urge students to focus on evaluating just one aspect of a draft at a time. They should reread each draft several times. One reading could focus on aspects of content, one on organization, and one on style (word choice and sentence structure). This breaks the task of evaluating into smaller, more manageable parts. Students might not then be so easily overwhelmed with the prospect of considering an entire draft all at once.

3. Encourage students to read their drafts aloud, listening for places where ideas are not clearly expressed or sufficiently developed, or where language is awkward or stilted. By reading their own writing as others might hear it or read it, students should gradually gain and refine the sense of audience that underlies effective writing and evaluating.

4. Allow your students to evaluate each other's writing, providing the constructive criticism every writer needs. To do so, students should use the particular set of Guidelines for Evaluating for a form or mode, just as they would to evaluate their own writing. You might also give your students any of the forms appropriate for peer evaluation that are found on pages T37–T39 of this introductory material and in the *Teacher's Resource Book.*

REVISING

Be sure all your students understand the term *revision,* since some of them may not have encountered the term before. Ninth-grade students, for example, may be accustomed to "correcting" their first draft. Explain that the word *revise* means to "re-see". When writers revise, they look again at their papers to make changes which improve the content, structure, organization, and style. As you discuss revision, stress that there is no single, correct way to solve problems in a draft. Remind students that different writers often apply different—but equally valid—solutions to the same writing problem.

Emphasize the Difference Between Revising and Proofreading

Research studies indicate that most of the changes high-school students make between the first and final drafts of a paper involve the correction of errors in spelling and mechanics. Students need to become more aware of revision as a process separate from proofreading and more skillful at making changes that significantly improve content, organization, and style. In an essay on the writing process, Jon Ramsey urges teachers to "discourage premature editing for surface correctness and shift attention to the larger structure which the essay gradually brings into being." For this reason, revising and proofreading are presented as separate operations in *English Composition and Grammar* and numerous revising charts which guide students in a thorough revision of their own papers are included in the text.

Recognize That Revision Is a Sophisticated Skill

Even in its simplest form successful revision requires the ability to work out a solution to a problem identified by evaluating. Too often students can recognize an ineffective introduction or faulty organization in their own writing but are crippled by their own lack of knowledge of alternative ways to handle content. In its more sophisticated form, as practiced by the professional writer, revision involves the juggling of numerous factors and considerations—clarity, word choice, logical organization, adequate development, sentence variety, etc. The beginning writer, who lacks this ability, often finds revision a bewildering process and, therefore, approaches the task in a haphazard fashion, catching some weaknesses, ignoring others, or inventing problems where they don't exist.

English Composition and Grammar bases its instruction in revision on four techniques students can use to revise their writing. These techniques are *adding* words, sentences, or paragraphs; *cutting,* or deleting, words, sentences, or paragraphs; *replacing,* or substituting, one thing with another; and *reordering,* or rearranging, the elements in a piece of writing. These four techniques are presented in charts for each form and mode in the composition chapters. Each chart includes a problem to be solved, the particular revision technique(s) to apply, and a specific way to use the technique for revising that element of a paper. Review these revising charts with your students, and encourage them to refer to the specific chart for a form or mode whenever they write. These charts are not intended to be all-inclusive—rather, they present *some* suggestions students can use to improve their drafts. You or your students may suggest other approaches that will also work well.

Use Models to Teach Revision Skills

Experts recommend that the classroom teacher present any new skill or concept in the following manner: (a) tell students in simple terms the value of the skill and how they will use it, (b) demonstrate, or model, use of the skill, (c) guide students' initial practice of the skill in simple situations and monitor their work, and (d) have students apply the skill on their own.

Close examination of models is an effective way to apply this procedure to the teaching of revision. Papers written by students in previous classes are excellent for this purpose since they usually contain representative examples of both strong and weak writing. For example, using a model on a transparency, you might (a) explain the value and importance of revision, (b) show, or model, how you would evaluate that paper, (c) explain each change as you make it, (d) provide a similar model for students to revise, and finally (e) ask students to revise their own papers.

One word of caution: While this procedure illustrates the in-depth revision process used by professionals and can be a valuable learning activity for older students, it may confuse beginning writers who have little or no experience with revision. Rather than devoting a lengthy period of time to a thorough revision of the content, structure, style, and organization in one model, teachers working with younger or less-advanced students often find it more effective to focus on one or two aspects of revision, such as logical organization or a clear statement of the central idea, and to examine these features in several models. This method allows inexperienced students to master a specific aspect of revision and to learn the art of revision one skill at a time.

The composition chapters in *English Composition and Grammar* also include model paragraphs with handwritten revisions. Often, annotations with these paragraphs identify the revision technique the writer used to make a specific change. Encourage your students to analyze the revisions in these models by discussing why the writer probably made a change and why this change solves or does not solve a particular problem. Students can also exchange papers and analyze each other's revisions. Small-group and class discussions can focus on other possible revisions the writer could use to correct a particular problem.

Peer Revision Groups

Dividing students into groups to revise one another's writing can be an extremely valuable activity. Students have an opportunity to see how other writers handled the same assignment. They can compare their judgments with those of other students and discover, within the give and take of small-group discussion, whether they are being too critical or not critical enough. As they debate how best to improve a particular aspect of a paper, they engage in problem solving and critical thinking.

Before you begin any form of peer revision, be sure students understand that their goal should be to assist one another. Emphasize that the purpose of the activity is not to point out everything that is wrong with a specific paper but to provide positive, constructive feedback and suggestions for improvement. Some teachers precede peer revision with one or two activities that heighten students' sensitivity to the difference between a constructive comment and a harsh or damaging one. You might, for example, put a list of possible comments on the chalkboard and ask students to consider how they would feel if a particular comment was made about their work. Would the comment encourage or discourage them? Would it hurt their feelings? Does the comment point out some specific thing they can improve or simply make a general negative judgment?

Formats for Peer Revision Vary

There is no established format for peer revision. A format that works well for one teacher may not work for another. The number of students in the class, the adaptability of the classroom for small-group work, students' revision skills, and the question of whether multiple copies of students' work can be produced are variables to consider in developing an effective revision format. In spite of these obstacles, most teachers discover that the benefits of peer revision outweigh the problems and inconvenience they encounter.

Some teachers prefer to divide the class into groups of five to seven students to ensure that authors obtain a broad range of feedback on their papers. Each paper is read aloud twice by the author. During the first reading, members of the group listen carefully. During the second reading, they offer comments, which one member of the group records.

One advantage of this format is that all reactions are shared with the author, discussed, and if necessary modified in the group setting. Another advantage is that reading their work aloud forces authors to attend closely to what they have written and often leads to new insights. However, some teachers find that students have difficulty following an oral reading and that comments are more perceptive when members of the group have copies of the paper in front of them.

Some teachers prefer not to set guidelines for the comments students offer on one another's papers; they feel open, unstructured discussion produces more authentic, complete reactions to student papers. This kind of open-ended revision can be exciting and quite successful with mature writers who have some skill at revision. However, teachers working with younger students or students who have little experience with revision are often disappointed. They find that their students, who are still learning how to articulate their reactions and how to distinguish a subjective response to content from a valid, objective remark, work best in groups that provide some kind of structure. This structure can be a checklist that calls attention to aspects of the paper or a list of specific questions to which students respond. You might also want to refer students to the revising charts in the composition chapters of the pupil's textbook; or, you might distribute the appropriate evaluation forms found in this introductory material and in the *Teacher's Resource Book*. In any case, students work within a framework that helps them formulate specific suggestions.

Another format that has proved effective in many classrooms involves rotating papers around the group for silent reading and consideration. Each person reads a paper independently and writes comments on a worksheet. When all papers have been read, they are returned to the writers with each reader's suggestions. Writers, then, take some time to read over the comments and ask members of the group for clarification.

Regardless of the format you use, students should always realize that final decisions about how to revise a paper are up to the author. Emphasizing this will defuse potentially explosive situations in which authors feel compelled to argue in defense of their work. Remind authors that they are always free to accept or reject suggestions and do not necessarily need to gain approval from their peers. Sometimes it is helpful to point out that the defensive author who argues with every criticism discourages the group from offering any valid criticism or suggestion for improvement; members of the group eventually realize that agreeing with the author or offering praise is much easier than trying to present honest reactions.

Additional Suggestions for Revision

1. Variations of the following technique can be used to focus students' attention on a particular feature of their first drafts. If the goal for a particular assignment is for writers to organize content coherently, you might ask students to underline the topic sentence in each paragraph of their papers once and to underline all transitional devices twice. If students cannot do this on their papers, they may need to critically evaluate and revise the structure of their paragraphs. With a class of ninth-graders working on adequate development of descriptive paragraphs, you might direct students to circle all sensory details they use. Again, suggest that students who find very few words they can circle might want to add more specific detail before they submit their papers.

Draw students' attention to the organization and development of the central idea in longer papers by asking them to write a brief one-paragraph gloss of their paper. This summary should begin with their thesis statement and be followed by the topic sentence of each paragraph in the body of the paper. Point out that if the resulting paragraph does not express what they intended, they may have wandered from the central idea in the body of the paper or neglected the development of a clear topic sentence for each paragraph.

Another possibility is to have students exchange papers and perform these operations on one another's work. This will give writers insight into how readers perceive their work.

2. To gain a better understanding of how students approach revision and what skills they already possess, you might ask students, working in small groups, to compare the first and final drafts of a model paper. Ask students to list the changes they find, to determine a reason for each change, and to decide whether each change improves the final draft.

3. Students may be able to identify a problem such as a weak introduction or an inadequate development, but they can't solve the problem if they lack awareness of alternative methods of handling content. Occasionally, you may want to deal with this need by planning lessons that will increase the number of writing options available to your students. For example, you might give students a model essay with a weak introduction and ask them to write two interesting alternative introductions. You might also ask students to revise a paragraph for two different audiences, varying sentence structure and word choice appropriately. Encourage students to share their work and to discuss the techniques they use.

PROOFREADING

In order to carry out this phase of the writing process, students will need to become familiar with how to use the textbook to answer questions about spelling, grammar, usage, and mechanics that arise when they are proofreading. A proofreading checklist, which includes references to appropriate pages in the text, appears on page

39 in the "Writing and Thinking" chapter of this book. (Individual copies of this checklist can be made from the copying master in the *Teacher's Resource Book*.)

Early in the year, you may want to schedule one or more activities that will acquaint students with the textbook's format and organization. One possibility is to doctor a paper written by a former student so that it includes examples of the kinds of errors students will be expected to correct in their writing. Ask students not only to find and correct the errors in the paper but also to locate information in the textbook that supports the corrections they made.

Set Realistic Standards for Accuracy

Few writers consistently produce flawless manuscripts; even professional writers make mistakes in their work. Try to set realistic expectations for accuracy. While you should not foster a careless lack of attention to proofreading, you should also remember that high-school students often create varied, interesting sentences that involve complicated questions of usage or punctuation. Teachers who place undue emphasis on accuracy may unwittingly create situations in which students avoid experimentation or consciously simplify their vocabulary and sentence structure to avoid errors. One way to handle this problem is to encourage students to underline or circle words, phrases, or punctuation they are not sure of on their first draft. These uncertainties can then be addressed and resolved before students submit their final drafts.

Encourage Students to Keep a Record of Errors and to Set Goals for Improvement

Marking student errors has little educational value unless students learn from these corrections. Asking students to correct their papers, perhaps by making the necessary change above the error on their final draft, is a good first step. However, students also need to analyze the kinds of errors they consistently make while writing. Often, they discover that many of their errors are related, and, rather than dealing with ten or fifteen discrete errors per paper, they are really facing only one or two problems, such as subject-verb agreement or comma splices. The *Teacher's Resource Book* includes a Writing Errors Record form that students can use to record and analyze errors in their own writing. You may want to reproduce individual copies of this form for your students. Another option is to ask students to keep a list of frequent errors in their English notebooks or writing folders and to write a brief statement explaining why they think they are making each kind of error. (Hint: Urge students to review this list before they proofread their next paper.) Another good follow-up to this recordkeeping is to require students to set a goal for improvement on their next paper. You might ask students to write a brief comment at the bottom of their final drafts explaining their goal. This can be as simple as the following note: My goal is to eliminate pronoun agreement errors; I had four on my last paper.

Provide Proofreading Practice Sessions

Proofreading depends both on students' knowledge of standard English and on their ability to perceive situations in their own writing where these standards are incorrectly applied. Sometimes, the problem students face is not a lack of knowledge but an inability to see errors in the context of their own writing. One way to strengthen students' perceptions is to use papers from previous classes for proofreading practice. Select papers with a variety of common errors or doctor the papers to include errors that appear frequently on students' writing. Reproduce individual copies of the model or present it on a transparency and ask students to identify and correct the errors. You can vary this activity by setting up an informal game in which students in different rows compete to identify the most errors.

WRITING THE FINAL VERSION

Be sure to give students clear, complete instructions on the format and criteria for their final drafts; nothing is more discouraging to students who have put sincere effort into their work than the discovery that they have neglected to follow a simple direction to write on every other line or not to write on the back of a sheet of paper. Generally accepted standards for manuscript form appear on pages 33–35 in the "Writing and Thinking" chapter of this text. However, you will probably want to supplement these guidelines with specific directions suited to your classroom situation. Write these directions on the board and ask students to copy them into their English notebooks or writing folders for future reference. It is also a good idea to post these instructions on the bulletin board as a reminder.

WRITING AND THINKING

Research into the writing process reveals the high degree to which effective writing depends on sound thinking. Underlying the sequence of prewriting, writing, and revising is a far more intricate network of mental operations, involving most of the critical thinking skills. For instance, carrying out even a simple task, such as writing a short expository paragraph, often involves higher-level thinking skills. These might include translation of facts, statistics, or observations about a topic into the writer's own words; interpretation of relationships between details and generalization; extrapolations, or predictions, about the audience's background and bias; application of knowledge about language, about the form and characteristics of the expository paragraph, and about audience to the current writing situation; anlaysis of relevant and irrelevant details, unstated assumptions, or the order inherent in the topic; synthesis of all previous thinking into a new structure, a piece of writing that combines the writer's awareness of audience, content, and paragraph form; and evaluations or judgments about the effectiveness of the final product.

Emphasize the Importance of Thinking Skills

Students should understand that sound thinking is an implicit part of good writing. Techniques such as brainstorming, clustering, or outlining are merely tools that help writers gather, clarify, and organize their thoughts. The physical act of brainstorming or outlining, by itself, does not insure good writing. Since every teacher has encountered the student who mechanically grinds out an assignment to please the instructor or meet the requirements of the course, it is important to emphasize that such techniques have value only when they are accompanied by careful, critical thinking. Demonstrate to your students the degree to which the writing process is a continuum by showing them how sound judgments in early phases of the writing process eliminate problems later on. Students should be aware, for example, that the writer who does not limit a topic appropriately or begins writing with inadequate supporting information, like the apprentice cabinetmaker who cuts shelves that are too short for the frame of a bookcase, overlooks problems that inevitably affect the quality of the final product.

The Benchmark Edition discusses and includes exercises in critical thinking in order to demonstrate the relationship between thinking and the writing process. These explanations are based on the taxonomy developed by Benjamin Bloom, et al. (See: Benjamin S. Bloom, ed., *Taxonomy of Educational Objectives; Book 1: Cognitive Domain* [New York: Longman, 1954, 1956].) In this widely accepted taxonomy, Bloom and his colleagues delineate educational objectives in terms of several thinking skills (knowledge, comprehension, application, analysis, synthesis, and evaluation). The clear relationship of thinking skills to educational activities also provides a rationale for making connections between thinking skills and the writing process.

As you present the critical thinking sections to students, keep two points in mind. First, remember that the thinking skills in Bloom's Taxonomy are arranged hierarchically—that is, mastery of one skill depends on satisfactory mastery of its predecessor. Second, notice how relating writing and thinking can simplify the teaching of writing. Critical thinking sections are generally placed where students might encounter some difficulty in the writing process. For example, to help students limit broad subjects to narrow topics, the thinking skill of analysis is emphasized. Similarly, the pupil's textbook connects the thinking skill of synthesis with writing a first draft and the thinking skill of evaluation with judging a draft's effectiveness. Making this connection between writing and thinking thus helps to explain why students often find writing difficult: As they work through the writing process, students often use the higher—and, consequently, the more complex—skills in Bloom's taxonomy, such as analysis, synthesis, and evaluation. The additional instruction and practice provided in the critical thinking sections helps students to deal with these crucial and difficult aspects of the writing process.

C. GENERAL PRINCIPLES AND TECHNIQUES

The following principles of composition teaching hold true for all grade levels.

PREPARE THOROUGHLY FOR EACH WRITING ASSIGNMENT

The easiest but least effective way to assign a composition is merely to say to a class, "Write a composition on anything you wish." Almost as ineffective is simply providing a list of topics and asking the class to choose one and write a theme on it. The amount of preparation desirable varies with the type of assignment and the ability level of the class, but it will often take the major part of a class period, and it may sometimes involve activities extending over a period of one or two weeks.

Clarify Major Learning Objectives

The suggested assignments for a year's program in composition on pages T44–T55 of this *Annotated Teacher's Edition* show the kinds of specific writing goals that teachers should define ahead of time. Consider students' current skills and ability levels in setting goals for a particular assignment. Usually, it is a good idea to focus on one or two important objectives. Be sure that students understand these objectives when you introduce the assignment and keep these central objectives in mind as you plan activities and develop evaluation criteria.

Teach or Review Important Skills

Analyze the skills students will employ to complete a particular assignment, and, if necessary, plan appropriate instruction or review. For example, if students will be writing an informal descriptive essay, you may want to plan one or more activities that will increase students' awareness of sensory detail.

The Benchmark Edition of *English Composition and Grammar* includes several features designed to simplify writing instruction. These features, found throughout the composition chapters, include the Critical Thinking sections, Guidelines for Writing, Guidelines for Evaluating, and revision charts. The pupil's textbook also includes techniques for prewriting (and for writing, evaluating, revising, and proofreading), labelled "Before You Write," and so on. This boxed and shaded material summarizes or highlights key ideas about the writing process. As your students work through the composition chapters, review these techniques and remind students to refer to them whenever they write. Also remind students to refer to "Part 3: Tools for Writing and Revising" when they have questions about grammar, usage, and mechanics in their writing.

Build Lessons Around the Writing Process

The writing process should be the framework for all major assignments in composition. Plan a schedule of appropriate lessons and activities that allows adequate time for prewriting, writing, evaluating, and revising. Each of the composition chapters in the text includes prewriting activities, evaluating guidelines, and revision charts that relate directly to the kind of writing covered in that chapter. In addition, copies of prewriting worksheets, evaluating guidelines, revision charts and evaluation sheets can be reproduced from the copying masters available in the *Teacher's Resource Book*. These materials will provide a sound basis for classroom instruction.

FOLLOW THROUGH AFTER EACH ASSIGNMENT

Few writing skills can be mastered in a single assignment. Improvement in writing requires regular review and frequent practice.

Teach a Corrective Lesson the Day the Papers Are Returned

The corrective lesson may be less than a class period in length, and it need not be confined to the skills the class has been taught. Of course, the first consideration should be given to those faults which prevented the compositions from achieving the learning purpose for which they were written. After this, take up any errors in technique which appeared often enough to make them suitable topics for study by the entire class or by small groups.

Make Composition Work Cumulative

During prewriting lessons, remind your class of the composition techniques they have learned in preceding compositions. Hold them responsible, for example, in their fifth composition for the applicable techniques learned in the first four. It may be advisable to assign two or three compositions to teach the same skill; in this event, variety should be achieved through different subject matter. The important thing is that through your careful planning, students gain a sense of growth from composition to composition. They should be conscious of the accumulation of skills.

In the areas of mechanics and usage, concentration on a few recurring errors is likely to be more effective than an attempt to explain all errors found in the students' papers. Write on the board two or three examples of such persistent errors, with corrections or explanations. Leave the errors there for a few days as reminders to all classes using the classroom.

Many teachers devote a few minutes daily, preferably at the beginning of the class period, to correcting one or two errors taken from student papers. The sentences are on the board when the class comes into the room. You discuss them with the class and require all students to write an improved version of each. This method, of course, may be used to teach any skill from punctuation and spelling to parallelism.

Have Students Keep a File of Their Writing

Composition work should give the writer a feeling of growth and real accomplishment. This feeling can be fostered by making it possible for students to see their writing accumulate and to have evidence of their improvement. If you have filing space in your classroom, have the students keep manila writing folders in which they will file their papers after they have revised and proofread them. Some teachers also have the students keep their "old" compositions in their notebooks.

Let students have an opportunity to look through their writing folders occasionally. Ask them to note weaknesses or mistakes which have appeared more than once. Also ask them to note writing problems they are overcoming. This should instill confidence in their steady, gradual progress in learning to write better. Students should benefit from taking a good look at their latest composition before they start work on the next one.

Sometimes in teaching (or in the school magazine) you may wish to use compositions written several weeks before. The file assures that these will be available.

Remember that a student's writing folder is private property, and that this privacy should be respected by the other members of the class.

VARY YOUR TEACHING METHODS

There are many devices you can use in teaching composition which not only will provide variety in the class routine but also will put your points across more effectively. The following methods have been successfully used by a great many teachers.

Use Student Writing as a Learning Aid

Many teachers keep a file of both strong and weak papers written by former students to use as classroom models or teaching aids. If you adopt this approach, ask students' permission to use their work and explain that you will remove the names from any papers that you use with later classes. Materials from this file can be used in a variety of ways:

1. Change a student paper to include several examples of common grammar, punctuation, and spelling errors. Early in the year, this can be used as a proofreading pretest to diagnose students' ability to detect and correct specific kinds of errors. Throughout the year, similar models in which you have purposely embedded errors can be reproduced and used to provide practice in proofreading.

2. Use portions of a paper or a single paragraph to illustrate a common weakness in students' writing. For example, you might prepare a transparency of a model that illustrates one of the following problems: overuse of the passive voice, unnecessary shifts in verb tense, or confusing shifts in point of view. Explain the problem to the class and demonstrate how you would revise the paper. Students then might be asked to make similar revisions in a second model.

3. If three or more papers dealing with the same topic but differing in quality are available, you can use these to gain valuable insight into how your classes evaluate writing. Reproduce copies of all three papers for each member of the class. Then divide the class into small groups and hand out copies of the three essays. Ask students to identify the strengths and weaknesses of each paper. It should become apparent which paper is the most effective. Ask each group to explain their judgments to the class. While this activity requires time and effort, it can reveal significant misconceptions students have about what constitutes good writing.

4. Use models to develop lessons that will increase students' repertoire of composition techniques. For example, reproduce copies of a well-written essay but eliminate the conclusion. Divide students into groups and ask each group to write two different conclusions for the essay. The same procedure can be used with introductions.

5. Use examples of effective student writing as models whenever possible. This will demonstrate that good student writing is possible and is valued.

Use Writing to Learn in Other Courses

Increasingly, secondary-school teachers are recognizing the value of writing as a tool for learning in all content-area subjects. This view promotes two general advantages for using writing in classes other than English. First, students can use writing to discover what they do or do not understand about a subject and its essential processes. For example, students can keep journals in which they track their activities for and reactions to a science experiment (much like keeping a writing process log). Second, students can apply what they know about the writing process and about writing specific forms and modes to all their school writing, such as writing research papers in history or social studies classes. Urge your students to use their knowledge of the writing process *whenever* they write. You might also collaborate with colleagues from other subject areas to develop activities that enable students to use writing as a tool for learning. To this end, the pupil's textbook includes material on using writing in other courses (see pages 707–709).

Make Frequent Use of Good Models

The model is an effective teaching device because it is the clearest means of showing a class what you are trying to teach them to do. Whether the model is taken from professional writing or from student writing does not matter so long as it helps students become aware of what constitutes effective writing. Some students might even be inspired to equal or to surpass the models you provide. For further suggestions, see "Use Models to Teach Revision Skills" on pages T15–T16 of this teacher's resource material.

Make Use of Sentence-Combining Exercises

Practice in the building of mature sentences from groups of short, choppy sentences which are provided by the teacher or the textbook will help students establish confidence in their writing ability. More suggestions for improving students' sentence dexterity through sentence combining may be found on pages 241–62 of this *Teacher's Edition.*

Make Use of Community Resources

The people, places, and organizations in your area can provide assistance and creative ideas for your composition program. A local history museum, for example, may have information on how to write a family history that could be used as the basis for a narrative writing assignment. Museums often have old photographs that can be reproduced or borrowed and used as a stimulus for writing. Rather than asking students to describe familiar objects, some teachers borrow nineteenth-century kitchen and farm utensils from museums for this purpose. Art museums often have collections of art slides or framed prints that are available for classroom use. These are excellent stimuli for both narrative and descriptive writing assignments, but they can also function in other ways. For instance, you might use similar works of art by different artists (two portraits, two rural landscapes, two still lifes) to illustrate the concept of style. Students who do not grasp the meaning of this abstract concept from a textbook definition or written models often catch on quickly when it is presented in visual terms.

The local newspaper can also be a rich source of possible topics for writing. Some teachers keep a classroom file of articles about local celebrities, clubs, and businesses to spark students' interest. One teacher who noticed an announcement for the meeting of a clown club arranged to have several clowns visit the classroom. As a follow-up, students wrote short papers describing the clowns' appearance, explaining the rewards of being a clown, or detailing how clowns apply makeup for a performance.

Develop Writing Situations That Involve a Real Purpose and a Real Audience

Students who know that no one but the teacher will read their writing are often unmotivated. Involving your classes in writing that has a purpose and will be read by others is a sure way to revive students' concern for effective communication.

Stretch your imagination or work in conjunction with other teachers to provide a real audience and purpose for writing done by your classes. Teachers from different schools sometimes develop exchange programs whereby students at the same grade level write about teen concerns or school-related issues that are of mutual interest and react to one another's papers. Successful exchanges can also occur between different grade levels within the same school district. High-school students, for example, might write short stories for a middle-school class. The middle-school class might then submit a set of their papers to the high-school class for revision suggestions. Some teachers have had success in involving their classes in the writing of booklets that outline the best part-time jobs in the community, serve as a guide to the school's extracurricular activities, explain service organizations that welcome teen volunteers, or advise freshmen on how to make the most of their high-school years. Other classes write monthly newsletters to parents about school activities or produce an annual review of the best books, films, and records of the year.

Use Photographs to Stimulate Writing

English teachers often note the importance of making students visually literate—that is, of enabling students to grapple with the flood of images in television programs and commercials, in movies, and in print advertisements. Many English teachers also find it valuable to use photographs as a stimulus for student writing. As an aid to teachers who use this approach, each book in the *English Composition and Grammar* series includes a portfolio of photographs entitled "Picture the Possibilities: Ideas for Writing." In this section, which follows the writing process chapters in the pupil's textbook, students learn how to probe pictures to discover ideas for writing—both for topics to write about and for ideas and details to develop a topic. Using photographs as springboards, explanations and exercises in the textbook treat each mode and form of writing. Summary guidelines also present questions students can use to probe *any* picture for writing ideas. In addition, each part opener page in the pupil's textbook includes photographs students might write about before and after they study the material in that part. The *Teacher's ResourceBank*™ also includes overhead transparencies of photographs and posters you can hang in your classroom to stimulate writing.

Depending on your students' needs and abilities, you might supplement the photographs in the textbook with ones you gather. You might also ask students to collect photographs to write about. In this way you can build a file of photographs that particularly suit your students. Remember, too, that paintings and prints can also be used to stimulate writing. (Many community libraries include works of art in the materials they circulate.) Student work from art classes can also be a source of images for student writing. Regardless of the specific stimulus you choose, you can still apply the approaches and guidelines presented in the pupil's textbook. Also remind students that photographs can be a source of ideas for writing in any content-area subject.

Use Audio-Visual Materials

The use of appropriate audio-visual equipment and materials not only enlivens classroom activity but can often assist students' learning. This list touches on only some of the methods creative teachers have used to improve writing instruction.

1. Slides are excellent stimuli for descriptive or narrative writing. Although commercially prepared slide series are available, many teachers prefer to develop their own material. Some teachers ask students to volunteer slides of vacation scenes, parades, picnics, children's parties, etc. If your school has a photography course or club, you might obtain more unusual slides from those sources or locate a talented student who can produce slides from photograph books.

Individual slides also are an excellent basis for prewriting activities. Students can hone their observation skills by listing details about a slide, or look for details that suggest what has occurred before a particular scene and what might occur after. To emphasize the importance of detail in writing, show several slides out of focus and ask students to guess the subject matter. Then, gradually bring each slide into focus. This activity will clearly demonstrate the role specific details play in defining a subject. Another possibility is to ask students to determine a central impression for a particular slide and to list details that do or do not support that impression.

2. Often used in connection with literature study, films and videotapes can also be valuable learning aids in the writing class. Short silent comedies by Chaplin, Keaton, or Laurel and Hardy, which are often available through local or school libraries, generate student interest and are adaptable to various writing situations. Younger students can describe the distinctive appearance, walk, and gestures of one of the comedians or write dialogue for a short silent film. Older or advanced students might compare the film personas of Chaplin and Keaton or analyze the comic techniques in several Laurel and Hardy films.

Before assigning a paper explaining a process, use a short film or videotape of a craftsman, scientist, or mechanic carrying out a process as the basis for in-class prewriting activities. Students can take notes on the process, compare their notes, determine key steps in the process, identify unfamiliar terms or equipment that needs explanation, and, if appropriate, write a paragraph or paper explaining the process.

The availability of videotape in most high schools solves many of the problems teachers once faced in arranging for outside speakers to meet with their classes. Videotaping allows a speaker to make a single presentation, which can then be replayed for other classes during the day and used over from year to year. Students frequently respond more enthusiastically to advice gained from adults or other educators, and a videotaped interview with a professional writer can have more impact than dozens of exhortations from you. Even if your community lacks a noted novelist or magazine freelancer, interviews with feature reporters, editors, or columnists from the local newspaper can provide valuable information about the writing process. Find out how these professionals discover and evaluate ideas for feature articles, collect information, avoid bias, and revise their work.

Since students also respond positively to advice

gained from peers, some teachers have videotaped panel discussions in which recent graduates talk about the kind of writing they do for college courses, the problems they have faced, and how their high-school writing experiences prepared them for these assignments.

3. The cassette tape recorder can be an especially useful device in helping less-advanced students who have difficulty punctuating their own writing. Punctuation is simply an established system for encoding the verbal cues, long and short pauses, that we use to clarify meaning in speaking. Suggest that students read and record their papers; they can, then, replay the tape and use their own natural pauses as an aid in determining where to place punctuation.

Abstract concepts such as tone, attitude, formal and informal language, or standard and nonstandard English can be difficult to grasp even for advanced students. Often, listening to brief recorded segments of formal and informal language, colloquial speech, or dialect is a more effective learning experience than looking at printed models.

Using Word Processors to Teach Writing

In recent years, microcomputers equipped with sophisticated software programs—such as word processing—have become increasingly available for educational purposes. Many students now have access to word processors, either at school or at home. Thus, using a word processor to teach writing is both feasible and desirable. While research in this area is still limited, findings suggest that using a word processor both facilitates writing and improves students' attitudes toward writing.

If you have access to a word processor, you might consider incorporating it into your writing instruction. In particular, you might want to use the software programs that aid prewriting. For instruction in ways to facilitate revision, your students might profit from using a word processor to enter and then to revise their first drafts. Professional journals, such as *School Library Journal* and *English Journal*, often discuss software suitable for teaching writing. Recent books also suggest ways you can incorporate word processing in the teaching of writing. (See: William Wresch, ed., *The Computer in Composition Instruction: A Writer's Tool* [Urbana: NCTE, 1984]; and, Dawn Rodrigues and Raymond J. Rodrigues, *Teaching Writing with a Word Processor, Grades 7–13* [Urbana: NCTE and ERIC, 1986].)

Use Peer Response Groups to Provide an Audience for Compositions

The group method is one way to ensure that students are writing for a specific audience, in this case for their classmates and the teacher. To implement this method, divide the class into groups of five or six students each, and have the students read their own compositions to their own group. This works best when you have movable desks and a room large enough to permit some separation of the groups. Arrange the grouping yourself, announcing where in the room each group will sit and which students will be in each group. Appoint a group leader, who will decide in what order the papers should be read and will conduct the discussion after each paper. If you wish, the group may select the best composition for reading to the entire class.

Advise the class in advance that, in selecting the best composition, they should keep in mind the learning purpose of the lesson. This will prevent the selection of a humorous composition simply because it is funny, even though the writer may have ignored the requirements of the assignment.

During the reading in groups, make a point of joining each group for a few minutes. Always stay long enough with a group to permit the reader to finish reading a paper. Getting up and moving in the middle of a composition will seem rude to the reader. Praise particular aspects rather than the whole composition, but be aware that your praise may sway the vote.

Some assignments—personal narratives, anecdotes, controversial issues—are better suited to the group method than are others, e.g., formal paragraphs, summaries, etc. If for any reason it seems better to have the members pass their papers around the group to be read silently by each student, this affords a variation in procedure. After reading, ask students to write a short, honest reaction to the paper, perhaps pointing out what they learned, what they already knew, what aroused their interest, or what confused them.

Use Small Groups to Enhance Learning

Small-group work provides opportunities for students to interact, to exchange ideas and formulate their own solutions, and to compare their conclusions with those of other students.

Small-group work produces the best results in a cooperative setting of open communication, mutual respect, and consideration of others. Students who are accustomed to teacher-directed learning may need some guidance in learning to function productively in small-group situations. Plan small-group activities carefully, monitor the results, and, if necessary, supplement students' skills with instruction that will improve students' listening, discussion, and problem-solving abilities.

Plan small-group activities carefully. If your classes are unaccustomed to working in small groups, begin with structured assignments that include: (a) a clearly defined task, (b) specific instructions on how to accomplish the task, and (c) a definite time limit. Unless students are quite mature or self-disciplined, vague directions to break into groups and comment on one another's papers will lead to little more than group gab sessions or heated and unproductive debates over inconsequential matters. On the other hand, an assignment to identify and correct all the grammar and spelling errors in a model paper or to brainstorm a list of twenty-five questions a reader might ask about a particular topic can lead to rewarding small-group learning.

Specific suggestions on how small groups can be utilized in various phases of the writing process appear on pages T16–T17 of the teacher's resource material.

D. MOTIVATION AND CLASS PROCEDURE

The teacher, rather than the textbook, is the key factor in motivation. A composition assignment should be adopted to a particular class at a particular time. You know your class. If you wish, you can make effective use of your students' recent experiences, of current events in school and outside school, of the literature they are reading, of controversial issues in which they are interested. The textbook provides the rules, teaching materials, and suggested assignments, but you must provide the motivating spark and adapt the assignments to appeal to your students.

The customary way to explain a composition assignment is to develop in class a sample composition similar to the one you are assigning. In doing this, you accomplish two things at once. You help students with the often frustrating task of thinking of something to write about, and you show them how to select and arrange their materials.

For example, if you wish to sharpen your students' descriptive powers, you may assign a one-paragraph description of a lively scene. The class will think of several such scenes: an amusement park, a public swimming pool, a sports stadium, a busy intersection, etc. Select one of these for development, and ask students to suggest things which might be included in the word-picture. List all the suggestions on the board. Then have the class choose those items they think would best convey the impression of color and movement. Discuss with the class possible ways of arranging the parts of the picture. Finally, discuss vivid words and phrases that might apply to this scene. Even the less-advanced students will emerge from a classroom experience of this kind with a clear idea of what is expected of them and of how to proceed. Ordinarily, of course, the students will not use in their papers the scene that was developed in class.

Every experienced teacher has a special bag of tricks and favorite writing assignments, ones which have produced the best results in the classroom. The inexperienced teacher, however, often needs ideas for composition assignments. The following suggestions, which have been tested in many classrooms and found effective, are intended to supplement the assignments in the textbook.

NARRATIVE ASSIGNMENTS

Narrative writing usually plays an important part in the eighth-grade composition program. Youngsters find it more interesting and less difficult than most other kinds of writing. As a rule, student "narratives" will be accounts of their personal experiences; therefore, it is a good idea to begin the year with autobiographical compositions. Following these assignments are several other kinds of assignments that can be given to eighth-graders which will involve some imaginative writing.

First-of-the-year Letter of Introduction

Explain that you would like to have a personal letter from your students telling those things about themselves that they think you would be interested in. Perhaps you will first write such a letter about yourself, introducing yourself to the class, and have copies mimeographed to pass out at the time of this assignment. Your letter can serve as a model for the student letters.

Make it clear that this is not a full autobiography. Explain also that you are not going to grade these first papers, but that you would like students to show their best writing. At some point, review the form of the friendly letter, textbook pages 203–205.

The following possible topics for the letter may be drawn from the class and listed on the board.

My family: background, brothers and sisters, parents' occupations, etc.
My home: location, size, my room, etc.
My personal likes and dislikes: TV programs, books, sports, etc.
My achievements: school, camp, sports, etc.

Explain that you do not expect a student to cover more than two or three of these topics, or to write more than one or two pages. When the list is complete, discuss the problem of organization. Then discuss ways of making the letter interesting: by using an original beginning or telling an anecdote, for example. You will receive honest self-appraisal if you tell the class that nobody but you will read these letters.

The Autobiography

In many schools the major writing assignment in the seventh or eighth grade is an autobiography. Children are always interested in themselves. They must be shown, however, that there are things to tell about themselves and their experiences which will be interesting to others. The autobiography should include several compositions. Bound in booklet form and illustrated by snapshots or drawings of people and places, the finished product should be something in which the students will take pride.

The autobiography might consist of three or more separate compositions. Most teachers tie in the autobiography project with the teaching of specific skills—e.g., if students are assigned to write a "chapter" describing their homes, they study the techniques of descriptive writing (textbook pages 118–123) in connection with this assignment.

Note: The autobiography should not be repeated in the eighth grade if students have done a similar project in the sixth or seventh grade.

Personal-Experience Narratives

This kind of topic can be made specific by asking students to think of a happy experience, a disappointment or decision they faced, a good day, a bad day, etc. Like most composition topics, these are best approached in class, where some students tell their experiences, thus suggesting to others the possibilities in their own experiences.

Ask the class what they think would be a good beginning for a composition of this kind. Make it clear that they should avoid the "One day . . ." beginning, which is trite and dull.

Emphasize the opportunity to show originality and to stir interest by creating an arresting title. Advise them to avoid the title which merely reflects the assignment—"A Happy Experience," "My Greatest Disappointment," "A Hard Decision." Better and more colorful are "Greener Pastures," "Crybaby," "I Should Have Said Yes."

Stories of Family Life

Some students may at first protest that nothing interesting ever happens in their family, but a little discussion of the following list of situations will suggest times when similar problems occurred in their own family group.

The time when:

1. The little boy in the family, tagging unwanted after his big brother, got hurt.
2. The girls' mischief-making spoiled a party that their older brother was having in the house.
3. The youngest child, playing with a neighbor child who was ill, got mumps and gave it to others in the family.
4. During a big storm, the electricity was cut off and the family had to cook in the fireplace and use candles for light.
5. A parent had to go to the hospital, and the children had to run the house.
6. The family got a big surprise for Thanksgiving.
7. The family had trouble with unpleasant neighbors.

Stories about Pets and Animals

Young people get deeply involved with pets and animals they've raised or seen in the woods and fields. This emotional attachment or interest provides strong motivation for witing. Suggest to the group that they write about their pets or stock they have raised or "wild animals they have known." The following topics may suggest ideas to your group:

1. The time my dog got lost
2. Trying to give away kittens
3. Hamsters have funny ways
4. Dogs get into mischief
5. Squirrels are acrobats
6. Teaching a parrot to talk

A Story Suggested by a Picture

A well-known and usually effective means of motivating narrative writing is a bulletin board display of two or three pictures which depict interesting situations. Illustrations from magazine stories, full-page advertisements, or photographs from magazines will serve. The students may be asked to write a story built around the illustrated event, or they may write a narrative about a personal experience of which the picture reminds them.

Completion of an Unfinished Story

The unfinished story technique is almost always a successful motivation for writing. The writing it produces, however, is imagined narrative as distinguished from personal-experience narrative, and the results will vary in quality as greatly as the imagination and creative ability of students.

Select a story in which a character is confronted with a dilemma. Read to the point at which the character must get out of the situation—stop just before the method for solving the problem is revealed. Remind the class that the way characters act must be consistent with their personalities as presented during the first part of the story.

Make clear that the students are to complete the story just as though they had written it from the beginning. They are the authors. Otherwise, they may simply write an essay-like conclusion beginning. "I think Marie should give the coin to Bryan because . . ."

The unfinished story printed below may be used as follows:

1. After reading the story to the class, discuss the issues involved in the unsolved problem and the alternate choices the person in the story faces.
2. Ask whether anyone in the class knows someone who faced a similar problem. If anyone does, ask that student to state the problem and tell what the person did about it.
3. Pass out mimeographed copies of the unfinished story, and assign the writing of an ending for it.

In the following story, "Trick or Treat," the issue is the responsibility of older children in their relations with younger children. The choices facing the older boys are to save Ronnie from full blame and severe punishment for an action into which they led him, thereby admitting their full guilt, or to be silent and escape punishment.

Trick or Treat

Pete's father, who insisted on accompanying the boys on their trick-or-treat route, agreed to allow them to knock at each door by themselves. However he was very firm on one point: "I want this clearly understood, Pete. No damage this Halloween. Ordinary trick or treat, okay. But keep it just fun. I want your word on this."

"Okay, Dad, I promise."

After Pete got dressed in his cowboy rig and he and his father met Pete's friend Sandy outside, they marched from door to door in their neighborhood, saying "Trick or treat!" and collecting handfuls of jellybeans and homemade cookies. Nothing unusual happened until they ventured into the big trailer camp several blocks away. A couple of younger boys had started tagging after them. Pete recognized one of them as eight-year-old Ronnie Hites, who lived a couple of blocks away.

"Quit following us!" Sandy ordered them. They hung back for a few moments but came on again.

While Pete's father waited at the entrance to the camp, Pete and Sandy started knocking on trailer doors and were given treats. But at the fifth trailer, a sour-faced man opened the door and at the sight of them, he flew into a rage.

"Go on, beat it! Get out of here or I'll throw dishwater on you!" he shouted. As they backed away, he slammed his door shut.

"What a crab!" Pete said surprised.

"No treat," Sandy said, "So he gets a trick."

Sandy noticed that a car stood in front of the next trailer, lights on and motor running. Somebody evidently was planning to leave in a moment or two. Sandy also noticed that, beside the trailer, there was an old towrope lying on the ground. He picked up the rope, hurried back, and started tying one end of it to the front hitch of the house trailer.

"Sandy," Pete whispered angrily, "no rough stuff. I promised my dad."

"That's right," Sandy said. "You promised *you* wouldn't play any rough tricks. So okay. *You* won't."

"You're included! I meant *we* wouldn't!"

"Okay. Hey, you!" Sandy called, low-voiced. The two younger boys, Ronnie and his pal, were hovering nearby, watching. Ronnie came forward. Sandy handed the end of the rope to the eight-year-old. "Can you tie a good knot?"

I can tie a square knot," Ronnie said proudly.

"Fine! Just tie this rope around the bumper of that car."

"What for?"

"To play a trick, that's all. You chicken?"

"That car'll tow the trailer away," Pete started to object.

"No, it won't," Sandy said. "It's just an old rope—it'll break. It'll just give the trailer a jerk."

Ronnie finished his knot—then ran, for the door of the nearby trailer opened and a man came out. Pete and Sandy also crouched back in the darkness as the man got into his car.

The car moved forward—and the rope lifted taut and broke with a violent twang; but it held just long enough to give a jerk to the house trailer—a strong, unexpected, forward jerk. Pete discovered something, then, that he had not noticed before. He had thought that the trailer would roll forward a few feet. But the trailer had been set up on permanent supports, on wooden blocks. And now it was jerked off those blocks; it lunged forward and crashed down onto the ground.

"Pete, come on!" Sandy whispered, and started running. Pete followed after him.

Behind them, the car had stopped. The trailer door had opened. Somebody was shouting angrily, *"Grab those kids!"*

The next day was Saturday, so Pete slept late. When he finally arose and went to the kitchen for some breakfast, his mother was in the backyard talking to the next-door neighbor over the back fence.

"It was the Hites kid," the neighbor was saying. "Just eight years old! The trailer was badly damaged. The poor man'll have to pay a couple of hundred dollars, maybe, to get it fixed up."

"I'm sure glad Pete stayed out of trouble," his mother said. "His father had really laid down the law to him."

Pete's appetite for breakfast vanished. As soon as he could leave, he went to Sandy's house.

"Sandy, what're we going to do about Ronnie Hites?"

"Nothing."

"He may tell the cops that a couple of older boys told him to tie that rope to the car!"

"So what? Ronnie doesn't know who we are. We were wearing costumes and masks. He can't give us away."

"But he's being blamed for it all!"

"Sure. He tied that rope to the car."

"But it wasn't really his fault. He didn't know what might happen. A little kid like that—he just did what we told him to do."

"Now he knows better."

"We can't let him take all the blame!"

"So what do you want to do?" Sandy demanded. "Tell your father that it was all *your* fault? After you promised him? And you want him to pay for all that damage!"

Pete gulped. He wanted to do the right thing, but—

A Series of Stories Relating the Adventures of the Same Imaginary Character

If you have a class interested in narrative writing, suggest that they plan a series of adventures of an imaginary character. Each week, for perhaps a month, the students will write a story in which this character is the protagonist. Familiar with TV serials and series of juvenile and detective fiction, many youngsters will take hold of this assignment and enjoy it more than any other composition work of the year.

The stories will probably be amusing rather than profound. The invented character may be a ship captain, a space explorer, a hunter, a boy or girl who is constantly getting into and out of difficulties, a melodramatic hero who always arrives in the nick of time. The class will enjoy parodying or satirizing some of the juvenile series they have read.

This assignment should not be allowed to go so long that it sinks of its own weight. You may prefer to have students write the stories at widely spaced intervals throughout the year rather than in a series of three or four in the month. These stories will provide pleasant relief from the more exacting and less entertaining assignments in expository writing.

Students with less creative ability should be permitted to choose to write another kind of narrative (personal experiences, family stories, character sketches, etc.) while other students develop serial adventures.

ONE-PARAGRAPH ASSIGNMENTS

Paragraph structure is usually an aspect of composition that receives special emphasis in the eighth grade. For the teacher who plans to give one-paragraph assignments frequently throughout the year, the following suggestions can be used to supplement the assignments in the textbook.

A Narrative Paragraph

Help the class to think up a number of provocative opening sentences which will require explanation in the form of telling an incident. The following sentences will suggest ideas:

1. The day I tried out for the Little League, everything seemed to go wrong.
2. I discovered, on my first job, that baby-sitting required a good sense of humor and a strong back.
3. Once, Friday the thirteenth turned out to be my lucky day.
4. I was warned that it was a mistake to shop for clothes in a hurry—but I had to learn the hard way.
5. For years my brother and I had wondered whether the old house on the corner was haunted—and one day last summer we decided to find out.

The Description of a Person

Begin the study of description by comparing a writer to a camera. In this sense, the eye of the writer, like the camera, records only what it sees. It is not concerned primarily with character or personality, although these may show through the picture as they do in a portrait. The writer is concerned only with appearance. Have the class turn to description of this kind in their literature books.

Tell them to choose for description a person they know— a coach, a teacher, a member of their family, a friend. The purpose is to make the reader *see* this person. Details of coloring, hair style, complexion, figure, and dress are necessary, but it is not enough to say "well-dressed" or "tall" or "handsome." It is the details you see when you look at a person that are necessary.

Assign a paragraph—no more than 100 words—for this kind of word picture. It is the quality, not the quantity, of words which counts.

The Description of a Favorite Place

Most students can tell of a favorite place they know. Given guidance and encouragement, they enjoy writing about it. The place may be a road, a spot in the woods, a beach, a room, a store, a restaurant, a church. Warn against trying to describe too large a place. Suggest a stationary point of view, like that of a photographer. Ask the students to try to show by describing—giving the facts vividly—what there is about the place that makes it appealing. The topic sentence should make clear what the place is and where it is. The purpose is not to conduct a guessing game.

Emphasize that all description appeals to the senses. Ask the students, in planning their description of a place, to figure out what appeals they can make to the senses of touch, smell, sound, and taste in addition to the obvious one of sight. Turn to examples in the literature they have read.

This assignment should be a brief paragraph. Too long a description is often dull.

A One-Paragraph Description of a Type Character

One kind of brief character sketch which most eighth-graders can write successfully is the single paragraph showing a "type character" in action. By describing the character's appearance and actions in a typical situation, the students should be able to make it clear what "type" they are describing without directly stating it. (The character should be given a name—*José, Rosemary, Professor Gonzales*—rather than a type designation.) The paragraphs will be read to the class to see if they can guess which type the author had in mind.

Here are some suggestions for type characters: the lazy person, the scholar, the tease, the hot-tempered person, the braggart, the snob, the self-important person.

A Paragraph of Indirect Characterization

This assignment requires the student to characterize a person indirectly through describing the person's home or car or locker or clothing, etc. The room of a child interested in science will be different from the room of a boy or girl interested in sports. The class can supply details—articles in the room, general appearance, etc. By outward appearances, by dress, one may judge whether a person is wealthy or poor, meticulous or slovenly, vain or humble. Bear in mind that in these descriptive assignments your teaching purpose is not only to teach students to describe effectively, but also to teach them always to select details for writing which will further the single effect they have in mind.

Two Contrasting Paragraphs of Description

You can demonstrate the importance of selecting the right descriptive details by placing the following list on the board and asking the class to select those details they would use to describe the corridors during the passing of classes and those they would select to describe the corridors when classes are in session. The exercise is easy and obvious, but it will help many students to see that if they write with a purpose and gather details that will achieve the purpose, the task of writing becomes much easier than if approached haphazardly without a clear intention.

Echoing footsteps
Shouting and laughter
Scuffling of feet
Glint of light on the floor
Horns of traffic passing the school
Lockers banging
Clatter of typewriters in typing room
Reverberating slam of a door
Hubbub of conversation
Patterns of sunlight from open classroom doors
Telephone ringing in an office
Bumping into others

Then have the class suggest details for contrasting descriptions of the main street in town on a busy weekday and on a quiet Sunday. After they have developed together a list of details to bring out the desired effect, assign a two-paragraph description in which the paragraphs bring out opposite effects. They may write either a description of the main street or a similar description of their own choice, such as one of the following:

The beach on a hot, sunny afternoon and the same beach at night or on a bleak winter day
An airport at noon and at midnight
The county fair on a sunny afternoon and on a rainy afternoon

Less-advanced students should probably be assigned to write only one descriptive paragraph, instead of two contrasting descriptions.

A Paragraph Inspired by a Short Film or a Piece of Music

For a creative assignment that will vary the formal study of paragraph structure, show students a five-minute segment of a film on a subject like the Grand Canyon, Redwood National Park, strange sea animals, or forest fires. Run the film without using the sound track. Then ask students to write a "mood" paragraph which—like "mood music"—will capture or reflect the feeling of the film. The paragraph should not be a factual description, and it need not even be about the film at all. A five-minute excerpt from a piece of music such as Debussy's *Nuages* or Rimski-Korsakov's *Scheherezade* may also be used for this assignment. The experiment is likely to lead to impressionistic writing or flowery description, but it can produce some very interesting compositions.

ESSAY ASSIGNMENTS

The following essay assignments represent types of expository writing that most students can handle adequately without a great amount of preliminary training.

An Essay Explaining a Shop or Art Project

If your students are taking shop or art, they are making things. A composition explaining how a student made something will be fairly easy to plan and, if clearly done, will interest the class. The thing made can be brought to class and put on display.

This assignment puts a premium on clarity and organization. The arrangement will probably be chronological. The process must be organized into a few major operations, each to be so clearly described that anyone can understand it. You will get better writing if you tell the class *not* to use the cookbook style, "Mix flour and butter, add water, and stir," but rather to use the first person, as though they are writing narrative, the authors telling exactly what *they* did.

The Essay Based on a Big "If"

Students usually respond to the possiblities in "wish-fulfillment" situations. For impromptu in-class writing, you can assign a composition detailing what the students would do—

1. *If* they had been given $1,000
2. *If* they could be proficient in any one skill they desired
3. *If* they could fix up their room at home any way they wished
4. *If* they could spend a month visiting any one place in the world they wished
5. *If* they could run the house for just one day
6. *If* they could teach the class for one day

Make the purpose of this assignment to give four or five specific reasons for liking or disliking something, or to give four or five specific details and examples.

The Argumentative Essay—an Essay that Grows Out of Class Discussion of a Controversial Topic

Pose a problem to your class and ask for their opinions about it. Continue the discussion until it reaches a point of great interest or indignation and then assign the writing of an essay giving the students' point of view and explaining why they think they are right. The best topics for this purpose are topics trhat arouse strong feeling. The hotter the discussion, the more easily the students will write. You may wish to use one of the following topics:

The school week should be six days long, including Saturday or Sunday.
Young people should turn their after-school earnings over to their parents.
Summer vacations are a waste of time; students should go to summer school.

Every young person should take music lessons.
Students should be required to study three languages other than English.

COMPOSITIONS BASED ON LITERATURE STUDY

Frequently throughout the year you should use the class's work in literature as the basis for their composition work. Sometimes a passage in a story they are reading can serve as a model for their own work. More often, a literary work will provide topics for essays or for reports.

Using Narrative: A New Episode for a Story

If your class has been reading together a novel such as Robert Louis Stevenson's *Treasure Island*, Majorie Kinnan Rawlings' *The Yearling*, or Jessamyn West's *The Friendly Persuasion*, they know the characters and the setting very well. A creative exercise in narrative writing can be motivated by asking the class to write an incident which might have happened in the story. Let them imagine such an incident which might have happened in the story. Let them imagine such an incident involving characters they know well. The students can specify where their "story" might fit into the book.

Explain to the class the difference between telling a story by *showing* what happened and telling a story by merely summarizing the action. Tell them to pretend that they are the author adding an incident to the book, merging it into the larger story.

A variation on this assignment is to have the students write a different ending for a story they have recently read.

Using Description: A Character Sketch

From the literature they have read, students remember many characters. The problem of characterizing one of these in 150–200 words can be challenging. They may begin by defining the character and personality of the person and then by listing the traits that support this definition. Each trait should be illustrated by reference to the character's actions in the story. A personality sketch of Charlie in Daniel Keyes's *Flowers for Algernon*, or of Anne In *The Diary of Anne Frank*, for example, can be planned in this way. Students will respond to such an assignment if you ask them to imagine that they are characterizing the person for someone who has absolutely no acquaintance with the book. Physical description of the person is less important here than evidence supporting the impression given in the topic sentence.

Using Exposition: A Report on a Subject Related to Literature Study

Three kinds of reports may be assigned in connection with literature study. These assignments will be especially appropriate when the class is working on Chapter 6, "Writing Exposition: Summaries and Reports."

1. *The report on a topic encountered in the reading:*

Pirates of the Spanish Main (*Treasure Island* by Robert Louis Stevenson)
Animals of the Florida Scrub (*The Yearling* by Marjorie Kinnan Rawlings)
Farm Life in Indiana (*The Friendly Persuasion* by Jessamyn West)
Mississippi Steamboats (*Life on the Mississippi* by Mark Twain)
Early History of the Mohawk Valley (*Drums Along the Mohawk* by Walter Edmonds)
The Strength of the Family (*Farewell to Manzanar* by Jeanne Wakatsuki Houston and James D. Houston)
Everyday Life in an Indian Tribe (*The Light in the Forest* by Conrad Richter)
Raising and Training a Horse (*The Red Pony* by John Steinbeck)

2. *The report on the life and work of an author.* Students will find help in gathering material for this kind of report in the section on reference books (pages 618–623) in Chapter 27, "Using the Library."

Biographical reports are likely either to be stereotyped and dull or else to be word-for-word copies of a reference book article. Warn your students against these dangers. If you wish them to avoid the trite beginning "______ was born in London, England, on January 1, 1920," have them clip a separate sheet of "vital statistics" to the front of their reports. This sheet will give in outline form the following data: *Name of subject; dates of birth and death; place of birth; names and occupations of parents; early schooling.* The written report will then review the author's achievements or one specific achievement, and it may begin by telling a revealing anecdote or an unusual fact. Emphasize that the class will be interested in learning what kind of person the author is, as well as in learning about the author's career.

Although you probably do not want to require that students turn in a formal bibliography with their reports, you should insist that they list their sources at the end of the papers.

3. *The general book report.* Book reports are often the kind of composition which students write most frequently—but least carefully. The class should be prepared for writing their first book reports as thoroughly as they are prepared for other composition assignments. Book reports should frequently be read aloud to the class and discussed from the point of view of organization and style, as well as from the point of view of content.

E. EVALUATION

In reading a student's composition, focus your attention on what the student is trying to say, rather than on superficial matters like punctuation or penmanship. Although usually you will want to mark some mechanical errors for correction, your grade and your written comments should be related chiefly to the *content* of the paper—not to its mechanical correctness.

MARKING A COMPOSITION

Marking papers will be easier if you decide in advance what you are looking for. For instance, when you are teaching the paragraph, you will want to concentrate largely on the paragraph structure in a student's theme. You may decide in advance to limit your comments entirely to remarks on paragraph development and unity.

The Grade on the Composition

Every composition assignment should have a specific objective which is clearly spelled out to the class and for which students will be held responsible. Compositions should then be graded chiefly according to how well they fulfill the objective of the assignment. For example, if the objective is to develop a paragraph by giving reasons, you should judge the composition according to whether the student chooses good reasons and presents them well. A composition which contains no reasons, even though it may be interesting and well written, should not receive full credit.

Mechanical skills are important, but they are never as important as content. Some teachers keep the two matters distinct by using the double grade—"B/C + "—the first grade representing content, the second one representing mechanics. Whether or not you use a double grade, it is essential to show the students that what they say—not how they spell it—is your chief concern. Avoid giving an "A" to a trite, dull composition which happens to be free from mechanical errors.

Your Written Comments

Students are interested in your reaction to what they have written. Encourage their eagerness to read your comments by making them as personal as possible, directed to an individual student as you have come to know that student's strengths and weaknesses. Since one is always more interested in repeating a pleasant experience than an unpleasant one, go out of your way to find things to praise even in poor papers, provided you feel the student has made a sincere effort.

Your comments in the margin should make the students think. They will appreciate this evidence that you have given their papers a careful and appreciative reading. They will be helped by questions such as the following: "Is this clear?" "Is this what you *really* mean?" "Can you *prove* this?" "Your ending might be your beginning. Why?" "Would an ordinary reader understand this?" They will be encouraged by positive comments: "I agree." "You support your arguments well." "With such a beginning, anyone would want to read on." "Fine phrase." "Good word."

Your Corrections

Every mark you put on a student's paper should have teaching value. Mark only those errors, therefore, which you are sure the student will be able to understand and correct. Students should not be held responsible for errors they have not been taught to avoid. If they fail to use the subjunctive where it would be expected in adult writing, ignore this fault; but if they have recently been taught to make verbs agree with subjects, check errors of this kind.

Bear in mind the age and ability of the writer. Since the student who makes the most errors is usually the one who is least able to understand and overcome mistakes, it is often helpful to pick out one or two errors that the student makes frequently—for instance, confusing *its* and *it's*—and assign individual drill, instead of asking the student to go over the composition and correct a dozen different unrelated errors at one sitting. If the same mistake occurs on the next composition, you may then ask the student to correct it, rewriting the sentence in which the mistake occurs. By the end of the year you may see good progress in overcoming errors through using this one-at-a-time approach.

Most teachers expect students to correct all errors checked on their papers and to revise all passages marked for revision. Unless students are required to return to you all papers with corrections properly made, your effort in checking the composition has been in vain. However, make sure at the beginning of the year that students understand your correction symbols. (Following is a list of standard correction symbols. It is also included as a copying master in the *Teacher's Resource Book.*) Go over the symbols in class, explaining what each one means and how to make the correction called for. Second, when a student has corrected a paper and returned it to you, read it over rapidly to see that all of your suggested improvements have been made. If a student has omitted any or "corrected" any incorrectly, return it to be corrected a second time. This will be time-consuming and possibly frustrating at first, but once the students realize that they must make corrections carefully, they will do so, and you will seldom have to return papers (and possibly reduce grades) after the first assignment or two.

Most Frequently Used Correction Symbols

Symbol	*Meaning*	*What to Do*
¶	paragraph needed	Start a new paragraph
no ¶	no paragraph	Join the following paragraph to the one before it
frag	sentence fragment	Supply a subject or verb—or both, if needed—to make a complete sentence
r-o	run-on sentence	Supply end punctuation, capitals, conjunctions, or semicolons to separate independent clauses
the american way	capital needed	Change the lower-case letter to an upper-case letter
my three Uncles	no capital needed	Change the upper-case letter to a lower-case letter
awk	awkward	Rephrase to make the section flow smoothly
//	not parallel	Rewrite so that "linked" parts are the same part of speech or the same structure
sp	spelling	Correct spelling
s-v	subject-verb do not agree	Change number (sing/pl) or form of subject or verb
ref	pronoun reference error	Change number (sing/pl) or case of pronoun to match noun to which it refers
∧	word, phrase, letter(s), or punctuation missing	Insert missing element into indicated space
s.s.	sentence structure error	Revise sentence
shift	unnecessary shift in person (point of view) or tense	Change any pronouns that do not maintain 1st, 2nd, or 3rd person; change tense of verb
t	wrong tense used	Change tense of verb
ℊ	word, words, or punctuation not needed	Delete word(s) or punctuation
wc	word choice	Substitute more precise or appropriate word

Continued

METHODS OF EVALUATION

Teachers of writing currently use a variety of techniques to evaluate students' composition skills.

Holistic Scoring

Holistic scoring procedures grew from the need of organizations such as the NAEP (National Assessment of Educational Progress) and ETS (Educational Testing Service) to develop a reliable and efficient procedure for scoring student writing samples. In holistic evaluation, no corrections or comments are made on the paper; instead, the evaluator reads each paper quickly and uses some form of scoring guide to respond to the work as a whole.

The reliability of holistic scoring is based on careful preparation of the scoring guide and training sessions which assist evaluators in ranking papers consistently.

One holistic procedure used nationally is the *Holistic-General Impression* scale. For this procedure, sample papers known as "range finders" are used to bring scorers to a point of agreement on what constitutes a high, average, or low ranking. General characteristics of high, average, and low papers are outlined on the scale. Since no specific characteristics are considered, no specific information is gleaned from this method.

Personal Experience Narrative —General Impression Scale	
Assignment: To write a narrative essay based on a personal experience with a clear central conflict	
4	Interesting and effective narrative topic; strong organization that enhances the central conflict; rich and specific supporting detail; writing style that appeals to audience; fresh, effective word choice; very few errors in mechanics
3	Effective narrative topic; clear organization that focuses on central conflict; sufficient supporting detail; writing style appropriate to audience but uninspired; accurate word choice; errors in mechanics occasionally interfere with reading
2	Less interesting or unclear narrative topic; organization flawed but focuses on central conflict; inadequate or less specific supporting detail; ordinary style marred by some awkward passages; imprecise word choice; errors in mechanics sometimes interfere with reading
1	Poor choice of narrative topic; confusing organization and/or lack of central conflict; unrelated or weak supporting detail; awkward, difficult style with little awareness of audience; careless or inexact word choice; frequent errors in mechanics that interfere with reading
0	No discernible attempt to develop narrative

A second common procedure, often referred to as *Holistic-Primary Trait* scoring, can be used to gain information about students' mastery of specific objectives. This method involves development of a rubric, a collection of definitive statements, which describes the primary traits (characteristics evaluators feel are significant to mastery of a particular form of writing) and some secondary traits. Primary trait scales involve careful analysis of the learning objectives for a mode of writing (narration, description, exposition, etc.) or a particular form or assignment (narrative paragraph, character sketch, or research paper). A rubric describing the primary traits of a narrative paragraph, for example, would differ significantly from a rubric for a persuasive paragraph. Once these desired traits, or characteristics, are identified, the evaluators develop succinct statements that describe how these traits appear in papers exhibiting a range of competency from very high to very low. The sample below shows a primary trait scale for a personal experience writing assignment.

Personal Experience Essay —Primary Trait Scale
A. Choice of Topic:
☐ Topic is a sound response to the assignment—writer has an apparent purpose, arouses readers' interest, and clearly suggests the significance of the event
☐ Topic is a good response to the assignment—writer's purpose is not as well-defined but the event is interesting to the reader
☐ Topic is a good response to the assignment but holds less interest for readers; significance of the event is not as clearly presented
☐ Topic responds to the assignment but holds little interest for readers; significance of the event is unclear
B. Development:
☐ Strong development of the experience that "puts the reader there"; the writer focuses on key details and includes little or no unrelated explanation or description
☐ Adequate development of the experience; the writer includes some details that "put the reader there," but includes unneeded passages of explanation or description
☐ Sketchy development of the experience; the writer develops only a few key details and includes too much unnecessary explanation or description
☐ Little or no development of the experience, or numerous unrelated details
C. Organization:
☐ Strong organization with an interesting beginning, middle, and conclusion
☐ Organized paper with a clear beginning, middle, and conclusion, but too much emphasis or too little emphasis is placed on some part of the experience

Continued

Personal Experience Essay —Primary Trait Scale

C. Organization:

- ☐ Paper lacks a clear beginning, middle, and conclusion
- ☐ No apparent attempt at organization

D. Details:

- ☐ Writer uses concrete sensory details to make the experience vivid for the reader
- ☐ Writer uses some good concrete sensory details
- ☐ Writer uses some concrete sensory details, but sometimes these do not add to the experience
- ☐ Writer uses few or no sensory details

E. Word Choice:

- ☐ Fresh, vigorous words that strengthen readers' understanding
- ☐ Interesting and vivid word choice in some spots; word choice is usually appropriate
- ☐ Word choice is appropriate but not particularly vivid or specific
- ☐ Word choice is often vague or inappropriate

F. Sentence Structure:

- ☐ Correct and varied sentence structure makes the paper interesting and easy to read
- ☐ Sentence structure is correct but lacks variety
- ☐ Sentence structure lacks variety and is sometimes incorrect
- ☐ Frequent errors in sentence structure make the paper difficult to read

G. Mechanics:

- ☐ Very few errors in punctuation, capitalization, or spelling; errors involve less familiar rules
- ☐ Some errors with unfamiliar rules; few errors with common rules for punctuation, capitalization, or spelling
- ☐ Some errors with familiar rules
- ☐ Numerous errors with familiar rules for punctuation, capitalization, and spelling

A third scoring procedure, called the *Analytic Scale,* is perhaps the most widely used method of holistic evaluation. Although many variations of the analytic scale exist, the most common one lists elements found in any piece of writing: ideas, organization, word choice, tone, grammar and usage, punctuation and capitalization, spelling, and handwriting. Readers rank papers on a continuum from high to low in each of these areas.

Analytic Scale

	Low	*Middle*	*High*	
General Impression				
Ideas	2	4 6 8	10	
Organization	2	4 6 8	10	
Word choice	1	2 3 4	5	
Tone	1	2 3 4	5	______
Specifics				
Grammar and usage	1	2 3 4	5	
Punctuation, cap	1	2 3 4	5	
Spelling	1	2 3 4	5	
Handwriting	1	2 3 4	5	______
			Total	______

Adapted from Paul B. Diederich, *Measuring Growth in Writing* (Urbana, Ill.: NCTE, 1974).

In the simplest form of analytic scoring, the *Dichotomous Scale,* readers evaluate each of the selected features by checking either a "yes" or "no" column. The dichotomous scale on the next page shows how this evaluation procedure might be adapted for a narrative essay based on a personal experience.

Personal Experience Narrative —Dichotomous Scale		
	YES	*NO*
Paper develops effective narrative and clearly suggests significance of event		
Organization is clear and focused on central conflict		
Narrative is adequately developed with appropriate specific details		
Style enhances narrative and shows awareness of reader		
Word choice is precise and appropriate		
Sentence structure is varied		
Spelling, grammar, and usage errors do not interfere with reading		

Conscientious teachers accustomed to responding personally with specific comments and corrections to every piece of writing generated by their students sometimes view holistic evaluation as a convenient solution to more time-consuming evaluation procedures. They may gain some reassurance about the value of holistic scoring from studies indicating that procedures limited to evaluation of a few features of students' writing are often more beneficial learning experiences than procedures which call attention to every error or weakness.

Self-Evaluation

Successful writers are those who can perceive the strengths and weaknesses in their own writing and make appropriate revisions. Self-evaluation, when thoughtfully carried out, fosters the kind of objective internal judgments made by mature writers.

In addition, self-evaluation gives teachers insight into the thinking processes of students. A simple self-evaluation task is to have the students rank their own papers high, low, or average and then write a paragraph explanation of the criteria they used to rank their work. Students' responses often reveal some startling misconceptions about the relative importance of factors such as grammar, spelling, and organization and provide teachers with an excellent opportunity to clear up misunderstandings. Teachers can also use this technique to identify and assist students who are overly critical of their own work.

It's important to note that self-evaluation need not be used in isolation. In fact, it is perhaps most valuable as an adjunct to holistic scoring and other methods of evaluation. Many teachers, for example, ask students to complete a brief self-evaluation based on open-ended statements similar to the ones shown below and to submit these with the final draft of their papers. Such forms give teachers further insight into the writers' ability to critically evaluate their own work and provide students with an opportunity to explain what aspects of the composing process pose problems for them.

Sample Self-Evaluation Items

1. I think one strength or one thing that works well in this paper is ________
2. I think the weakest aspect of my paper is ________
3. One problem I faced in this paper and wasn't sure how to solve was ________

Peer Evaluation

Because students become directly involved in close examination, analysis, and discussion of one another's essays, peer evaluation can be a highly effective and rewarding procedure. At its best, peer evaluation results in significant learning for both the writer and the evaluator. However, successful peer evaluation requires that students have some sensitivity to the writer's effort and share both an impartial, objective attitude and common understanding of the criteria for a particular assignment. Without these, peer evaluation can breed frustration, lead to angry confrontations between writers and evaluators, and be extremely painful for the writer whose work is evaluated in a subjective or arbitrary manner.

Most teachers find that peer evaluation is most effective in a cooperative classroom setting with older students who have a sound understanding of what constitutes good writing. In-class discussion and evaluation of papers similar to the ones students will write and evaluate are excellent ways to insure that students will react to one another's work fairly and objectively. Begin by showing how you would evaluate one or two papers; then, ask the class to explain how they would evaluate another model. Another procedure that eliminates some of the subjectivity from peer evaluation is use of a carefully prepared evaluation form.

EVALUATION FORMS

The following forms may be used as aids in evaluating student papers. They also appear as copying masters in the *Teacher's Resource Book.*

Name ______________ Date ________ Class _____ Score _____

Analytic Scale		
	Points Possible	**Points Given**
Main idea clearly stated in the introduction	5	
At least four significant pieces of information presented	4	
Transitions smooth from one paragraph to the next	3	
No more than two errors in subject-verb agreement	3	
Concluding statement made	2	
Legible handwriting	1	
	Total 18	

For use with multi-paragraph papers.

Name ______________ Date ________ Class _____ Score _____

Analytic Scale

1. The thesis statement is clearly expressed.

NOT ACCEPTABLE_ ACCEPTABLE_ IMPRESSIVE_ COMMENDABLE_

2. Ideas within the paragraphs are fully developed by specific examples and details.

NOT ACCEPTABLE_ ACCEPTABLE_ IMPRESSIVE_ COMMENDABLE_

3. Transitions are smooth and effective.

NOT ACCEPTABLE_ ACCEPTABLE_ IMPRESSIVE_ COMMENDABLE_

4. Sentences vary in structure.

NOT ACCEPTABLE_ ACCEPTABLE_ IMPRESSIVE_ COMMENDABLE_

5. The writer avoids common errors in grammar, usage, and mechanics.

NOT ACCEPTABLE_ ACCEPTABLE_ IMPRESSIVE_ COMMENDABLE_

6. The writer's style is not stiff or dull but reflects a sincere attitude and a highly personal involvement.

NOT ACCEPTABLE_ ACCEPTABLE_ IMPRESSIVE_ COMMENDABLE_

For use with longer papers written by students who have mastered the basic skills.

Name ______________ Date ________ Class _____ Score _____

Analytic Scale				
Circle the statement that fits best.				
Sentence Structure	Many errors	Some errors; not much variety	Some variety; minimum of errors	Variety in structure; error-free
Word Choice and Use	Simple words; a number of mis-spellings	Simple words; a few mis-spellings	Some in-teresting words; no more than two misspell-ings	Interest-ing words; no spell-ing errors
Clarity	Hard to follow idea	Basic idea is there but does not come through too clearly	Basic idea is clear but not fully developed	Easy to under-stand; fully developed

For use with shorter pieces of writing.

Writer's Name ______________ Reader's Name ______________

Title of Paper ______________

Peer Evaluation

Instructions:

Read the paper straight through. Do not reread. Give the paper a score of 1 (low), 2, 3, or 4 (high).

READER #1 ________

READER #2 ________

READER #3 ________

For use with pieces of writing of any length for basic comparison only.

Name________________ Date______ Class___ Score______

Dichotomous Scale		
	Yes	No
Sentences are complete.		
Each paragraph is indented.		
Handwriting is legible.		
Each sentence begins with a capital and ends with the proper punctuation mark.		
All details relate to the topic or main idea.		
No slang is used.		
Word choice is interesting.		
The main idea or purpose is clear.		

For use with shorter pieces of expository writing by students who lack mastery of basic skills.

Writer's Name________________ Reader's Name________________

Title of Paper______________________________

Peer Evaluation	Dichotomous Scale
1. The writer stays on the subject.	Yes ____ No ____
2. The writer uses some colorful words or phrases.	Yes ____ No ____
3. There are fewer than 3 errors in comma use.	Yes ____ No ____

For use with a shorter piece of writing.

Peer Reaction Sheet

Writer's Name: ________________

Reader's Name: ________________

Title of Paper: ________________

Superlatives

1. The most effective sentence:

____

____

____

2. The four most effective words or phrases:

1. __________________________
2. __________________________
3. __________________________
4. __________________________

3. The most interesting idea:

____

____

____

____

For use with shorter pieces of writing.

Writer's Name ____________ Reader's Name ____________

Title of Paper ____________

Peer Evaluation			
Circle the appropriate number.			
	Low	**Average**	**High**
Thesis Statement	1 2	3 4	5 6
Development of Ideas	1 2	3 4	5 6
Conclusion	1 2	3 4	5 6
Word Choice	1 2	3 4	5 6
Transitional Devices	1 2	3 4	5 6
Usage	1 2	3 4	5 6
Mechanics	1 2	3 4	5 6
Tone (the writer's attitude)	1 2	3 4	5 6

For use with longer pieces of writing by students who have analyzed and discussed one or more model papers.

Peer Editing Sheet

Writer ____________

Reader ____________

Title ____________

Line #	**Comment or Suggestion**
	____________ Reader's Signature

For use by students who have mastered basic writing elements.

Writer's Name ____________ Date ____________

Title of Paper ____________

Self-Evaluation **Analytic**

Sentence Structure Analysis

	Subject	**Verb**
Subject/ Verb (Choose four)	______	______
	______	______
	______	______
	______	______
Prepositional Phrases Used as Adjectives (Choose up to four)	______	______
	______	______
	______	______
	______	______
	______	______

Conjunctions (Choose up to four)

Coordinate: ______ ______

______ ______

Subordinate: ______ ______

______ ______

For use with shorter pieces of writing by students who need to gain mastery of basic skills.

Writer's Name ______________ Date ________

Title of Paper ______________

Self-Evaluation Form

1. Summary of main idea:

2. "to be" verb | line # | replacement action verb

3. Simple sentences combined into 1 sentence
   1.
   2.
   3.
   4.

For use with shorter pieces of writing.

Writer's Name ______________ Date ________

Title of Paper ______________

Self-Evaluation—Commentary

On the left side of this "double entry" form, write your final draft of the assignment. On the right side, write some personal comments on what you have written. Include at least three comments on how you wrote and at least one comment on how you feel about this piece of writing.

Final Draft	Personal Commentary

For use with students of all ability levels in writing. Can be used in the early stages of teaching self-evaluation techniques. Provide extra forms for longer pieces of writing.

Writer's Name ______________ Date ________

Title of Paper ______________________

Teacher-Student Conference	**Analytic**

Spelling

Number of Errors (circle 1) 0 1 2 3 4 4+

Corrections for up to four misspelled words

1. ________
2. ________
3. ________
4. ________

For use with students who need extensive work in basic skills with an intensely focused objective.

Writer's Name ______________ Date ________

Title of Paper ______________________

A Writer's Checklist		
	Yes	**No**
1. Have I expressed the main idea clearly?		
2. Have I written a strong topic sentence or thesis statement?		
3. Is there a clear-cut beginning, middle, and end?		
4. Have I included enough details to support my ideas?		
5. Have I used a style or language suitable to my purpose and my audience?		
6. Have I checked my spelling? capitalization? punctuation?		
7. Have I used the basic manuscript rules and format?		
8. Have I read my paper aloud to myself or to someone else?		

Writer's Name ____________ Reader's Name ____________

Title of Paper ____________

Composition Evaluation Form

Objectives	Level of Mastery		
	High	Average	Low
1. The topic is limited enough for development in an essay.			
2. The composition is well developed. Interesting or informative details are used. Tone is consistent.			
3. The purpose of the paper is clearly stated in the thesis.			
4. The introduction identifies the composition topic and arouses the reader's interest.			
5. Each paragraph in the body of the composition develops the topic of the composition.			
6. The writing is well organized; the paragraphs in the body follow a logical order.			
7. Each paragraph has a clear topic sentence or topic and restriction sentences.			
8. All the illustration sentences in each paragraph relate to the paragraph's central idea.			
9. The writer uses transition words or repeated phrases to make the composition coherent.			
10. The conclusion of the composition brings the paper to a close, restates the paper's central idea, and keeps the reader's interest.			

Comments:

Writer's Name ____________ Date ____________

Title of Paper ____________

Checklist for Proofreading

Directions: Check your paper carefully against each of the following points. When you have checked through your entire paper for that item, place a check mark in the blank before it.

____ **1.** The paper is neat.

____ **2.** Each sentence begins with a capital letter.

____ **3.** Each sentence ends with a period, question mark, or exclamation point.

____ **4.** Each sentence is complete. Each has a subject and a predicate and expresses a complete thought.

____ **5.** Complete sentences are separated by an end mark of punctuation or by a comma and a conjunction.

____ **6.** A singular verb is used with each singular subject and a plural verb with each plural subject.

____ **7.** Nominative case of pronouns is used for subject; objective case of pronouns is used for objects.

____ **8.** Singular pronouns are used to refer to singular nouns, and plural pronouns are used to refer to plural nouns.

____ **9.** Each word is spelled correctly.

____ **10.** Frequently confused verbs, such as *lie/lay, sit/set,* and *rise/raise,* are used correctly.

____ **11.** Frequently confused words, such as *all ready/already, farther/further,* and *fewer/less,* are used correctly.

____ **12.** Double negatives are avoided.

____ **13.** All proper nouns and proper adjectives are capitalized.

____ **14.** Word endings such as *–s, –ing,* and *–ed* are included where they should be.

____ **15.** No words have accidentally been left out.

____ **16.** No words have accidentally been written twice.

____ **17.** Each paragraph is indented.

____ **18.** Apostrophes are used correctly on contractions and possessive nouns.

____ **19.** Dialogue is punctuated and capitalized correctly.

____ **20.** Any correction that could not be rewritten or retyped is crossed out with a single line.

Writer's Name ____________ Date ____________

Title of Paper ____________

Individual Proofreading Record										
Directions: When your teacher returns a corrected writing assignment, write the topic in the appropriate box. Under the topic, record the number of errors you made in each area. Use this sheet when you proofread your next assignment, taking care to check those areas in which you make frequent mistakes.	**Assignment/Topic**									
	1	2	3	4	5	6	7	8	9	10
Error										
Sentence Fragments										
Run-on Sentences										
Subject–Verb Agreement										
Pronoun Agreement										
Incorrect Pronoun Form										
Use of Double Negative										
Comparison of Adjectives and Adverbs										
Confusing Verbs										
Irregular Verbs										
Noun Plurals and Possessives										
Capitalization										
Spelling Rules										
End Punctuation										
Apostrophe										
Confusing Words										
Quotation Marks and Italics										
Comma or Paired Commas										

STEPS TO RELIEVE THE BURDEN OF THE PAPER LOAD

First, dispel some of the myths teachers of writing have treasured and fostered traditionally: The teacher must personally evaluate each student's paper; all assignments are due on Friday and must be returned to the students on Monday; each paper must be corrected and marked for each discrete error; students should not be allowed to seek outside help in writing a paper; students are too embarrassed to share their papers; classroom discipline will fall apart if students break into small groups.

Some Suggestions to Try:

1. Check the school's activity schedule before deciding on a type of writing assignment and when it will be due. Students who are involved in preparing for a big event will not have the mental concentration demanded by a writing activity which will be vying with the big event. If necessary, design an assignment which will take advantage of what is happening. An experiential or reaction/opinion topic may succeed.
2. Vary the type of writing and the evaluation method from one assignment to the next. Experimenting with these two factors may not always achieve grand results but will avoid the monotony which gleans mostly boredom.
3. Rather than correcting every error on a paper, place a check mark in the margin of every line that contains an error. Hand the papers back and have the writers determine what each error is and make an appropriate correction. This method is quite successful with advanced students who know the rules but miss errors when they proofread. An added benefit of this approach is that it requires students to reexamine their work and analyze their own mistakes.
4. Occasionally, grade papers only for content. Look closely at what students have to say and ignore all mechanical errors. For students who have sound ideas but make frequent mistakes, having a paper returned without a host of correction marks is often a big boost.
5. Evaluate only a portion of each paper. For example, you might mark errors only on page one of each paper, or you might comment on the structure and development of one paragraph in the body of a paper.
6. If you find yourself making the same marginal comments over and over, develop a shorthand for these comments and acquaint your students with this system.

For instance, you might draw a vertical line in the margin to set off portions of the paper that are illogical or need further development. You might use a wavy line to set off words or phrases that are exceptionally strong. Brackets can be used to indicate nonstandard English or poor word choice.

7. Use random grading of minor assignments. Some teachers have worked out an effective system in which they select only five or six papers from each class to evaluate in depth. The teacher never lets students know whose papers will be selected and, to keep students on their toes, they occasionally grade the same students' work for two consecutive assignments. If you experiment with this method, be sure that you grade enough assignments by each student to make a fair and accurate evaluation of the writer's work at the end of the marking period.

A TEACHER'S BIBLIOGRAPHY ON THE WRITING PROCESS

Applebee, Arthur N. *Contexts for Learning to Write: Studies of Secondary School Instruction.* Norwood: Ablex Publishing Corporation, 1984.

Beach, Richard, and Lillian Bridwell. *New Directions in Composition Research.* New York: Guilford, 1983.

Britton, James, et al. *The Development of Writing Abilities (11–18).* London: MacMillan Education, 1975.

Clay, Marie M. *What Did I Write?* Exeter: Heinemann, 1975.

Cooper, Charles R., and Lee Odell. *Evaluating Writing: Describing, Measuring, Judging.* Urbana: NCTE, 1977.

Emig, Janet. *The Composing Processes of Twelfth Graders,* Urbana: NCTE, 1971.

Graves, Donald H. *A Researcher Learns to Write.* Exeter: Heinemann, 1984.

Hays, Janice N., et al., eds. *The Writer's Mind: Writing as a Mode of Thinking.* Urbana: NCTE, 1983.

Moffett, James. *Teaching the Universe of Discourse.* Boston: Houghton Mifflin, 1968.

Murray, Donald M. *Learning by Teaching: Selected Articles on Writing and Teaching.* Upper Montclair: Boynton/Cook, 1982.

---.*A Writer Teaches Writing: A Practical Method of Teaching Composition.* Boston: Houghton Mifflin, 1968.

---.*A Writer Teaches Writing.* 2nd ed. Boston: Houghton Mifflin, 1985.

Myers, Miles, and James Gray, eds. *Theory and Practice in the Teaching of Composition.* Urbana: NCTE, 1983.

Pooley, Robert C. *The Teaching of English Usage.* Urbana: NCTE, 1974.

Shaughnessy, Mina P. *Errors and Expectations: A Guide for the Teacher of Basic Writing.* New York: Oxford UP, 1977.

Smith, Frank. "Myths of Writing." *Language Arts* 58 (1981): 792–98.

Stanford, Gene, ed. *Classroom Practices in Teaching English, 1979–1980: How to Handle the Paper Load.* Urbana: NCTE, 1979.

Weaver, Constance. *Grammar for Teachers: Perspectives and Definitions.* Urbana: NCTE, 1979.

Wresch, William, ed. *The Computer in Composition Instruction: A Writer's Tool.* Urbana: NCTE, 1984.

F. SEQUENCE OF COMPOSITION ASSIGNMENTS

The assignments suggested below can serve as a foundation for the year's work in composition. Assignments 5–13 constitute a *growth program* that leads students by gradual steps from writing paragraphs to writing full reports using library resources. Assignments 14 and 15 present a *special type of writing that can be taught at any point in the year* that seems best to the teacher.

Assignment	Length	Suggested Time
1. A writer's log	• variable	• throughout • the school • year
2. Gathering ideas for writing	• variable	• throughout • the school • year
3. Writing for an audience	• variable	• throughout • the school • year
4. Evaluating and revising writing	• variable	• throughout • the school • year
5. A paragraph developing a topic sentence	• 1 paragraph	• 1 week

continued

Assignment	Length	Suggested Time
6. A narrative paragraph	• 1 paragraph	• 1 week
7. A descriptive paragraph	• 1 paragraph	• 1 week
8. An expository paragraph developed with facts and statistics	• 1 paragraph	• 1 week
9. A persuasive paragraph	• 1 paragraph	• 1 week
10. A short story (narrative) using vivid details	• 250-300 words	• 2 weeks
11. An expository composition	• 250-300 words	• 2 weeks
12. A summary	• one-third the length of an article	• 1 week
13. A report based on reference sources	• at least 400 words	• 2 weeks
14. A friendly letter	150-200 words	• 1 week
15. A business letter	• body 50-75 words	• 1 week

Note that each assignment on the list presents a *different* writing skill, and that ordinarily a teacher will want to provide additional practice in some of these skills. For example, a teacher may well give two or three assignments involving one-paragraph compositions that develop topic sentences (see Assignment 5); these additional compositions can be written in class or assigned as a day's homework. You should feel free to add extra assignments whenever they seem necessary, or to change the suggested assignments in any way you see fit to meet the needs of your own class.

SUGGESTED SEQUENCE OF COMPOSITION ASSIGNMENTS

Assignment 1 A writer's notebook (length will vary)

Time: Throughout the school year

Objective: To keep a writer's notebook in which the students record and describe their thoughts as they plan and develop a piece of writing.

Course work: *English Composition and Grammar,* page 14

Suggested model: *English Composition and Grammar,* page 14

Suggested topic: Topics to come from students' own writing and observations

Presentation: Throughout the school year, students should be encouraged to keep a writer's notebook in which they describe their thoughts as they move through the writing process. Many of your students may have had experience keeping the type of journal in which they record observations as possible sources of subjects and ideas for writing, but few will have had practice in actually writing about the writing process itself—the thinking and planning that actually goes on as they develop a piece of writing. Use the sample notebook entries on pages 4–5 to point out, first of all, how writers generally move back and forth from one stage of the writing process to another. This is also a good time to point out to students that there is no one particular way in which all writers write. If possible, bring to class selections in which various professional writers describe how they write. One writer may say, for example, that he or she writes very slowly, trying to perfect each phrase as it goes down on paper. Another writer may describe getting words down on paper as quickly as possible and then going back to revise the entire piece.

With students, complete Exercise 1, pages 4–5. Point out to students that the writer describes finding a subject, the process of gathering information to develop the subject, problems in making the first draft, and so on. The main purpose of the sample entries on pages 4–5 is to illustrate how writers move back and forth through the writing process. You may want students to keep their logs in somewhat greater detail. For example, you might give students specific questions to address in their logs such as the following ones: "What is my goal in writing this paper? Who is my audience? What do I need to remember about my audience's age, background, and interests that will affect the way that I write? Do I need to limit my topic? What methods for gathering information can I use? How can I organize that information?" Encourage students especially to write about problems that they encounter while writing and what they do to solve those problems. In the sample writer's log on pages 4–5, for example, the writer realized that there was not sufficient information to develop the topic and so developed a strategy for finding additional details.

Evaluation: Rather than grade students' writing logs, many teachers prefer to use them as a way of gaining insight into how their students think and plan as they write. This knowledge can be used to plan a more effective composition program.

Assignment 2 Gathering ideas for writing
(length will vary)

Time: Throughout the school year

Objective: To sharpen students' observation skills and to provide students with practical methods for gathering ideas for writing.

Course work: *English Composition and Grammar,* pages 20–25

Suggested model: *English Composition and Grammar,* page 14 (a sample journal entry), page 20 (brainstorming), page 21 (clustering), pages 22–23 *(5 W-How?* questions), and pages 23–24 (point-of-view questions)

Suggested topic: A topic suggested by Exercises 11–13, text pages 22, 23, and 25, or a topic of teacher's or student's choice

Presentation: Many teachers feel that perhaps the biggest problem students have with writing is their inability to use specific detail. Students seem unable to observe closely the world around them and to record those observations for use later as details for writing. The textbook sections "Using a Writer's Notebook," page 14, and "Using Your Powers of Observation," pages 15–16, give students instruction and practice in these areas. Encourage students to get in the habit of keeping a daily observation journal throughout the school year. Some teachers, as a way of respecting their students' privacy, make a distinction between a diary, kept by the student at home, where private thoughts and feelings are recorded, and a public journal, where observations about people, places, and events that one is willing to share with others are noted.

An especially effective method for helping students learn to observe concrete, sensory details is through the use of photographs (or posters you might have displayed in the room). As a class exercise, list five headings on the board: *Sight, Sound, Touch, Taste, Smell.* Then have students imagine they are part of the photograph (distribute copies of the same photograph) or poster and have students brainstorm a list of sensory impressions. Typically, they will come up with more sight than other kinds of sensory words. You can encourage other responses by asking such questions as, "What do you smell?" "What do you taste?" and so on. You might want students to keep a notebook of sensory words that describe different sensory impressions.

The methods for gathering ideas described on textbook pages 20–25 take advantage of the fact that most people have more knowledge of different subjects than they realize. Each of these methods, then, is in one way simply a drawing out of what the student already knows. Another advantage of these methods, however, is that they often help the students realize what they do not know and need to find out about a subject. Throughout the composition chapters of this textbook, students are reminded of these various methods of gathering ideas for writing and encouraged to use them with various forms of writing. It will be especially helpful to students later to have had adequate practice using the various methods at this point.

Assignment 3 Writing for an audience
(length will vary)

Time: Throughout the school year

Objective: To adapt writing to audience as necessary

Course work: *English Composition and Grammar,* pages 9–11

Suggested model: *English Composition and Grammar,* page 9 (paragraph 2)

Suggested topic: A topic suggested by Exercise 4, textbook pages 10–11, or a topic of teacher's or student's choice

Presentation: The ability to adapt one's writing to a particular audience is a basic writing skill. To reinforce this concept, you might begin by discussing with students ways in which audiences differ—in age, knowledge, interests, and so forth—and particular ways in which those differences affect choices the writer makes. Vocabulary and sentence length and complexity are two obvious variables. Other choices also dependent on audience include choice of subject, background information to supply about the subject, and terms, if any, to define. An interesting approach is to bring to class an article from a magazine for very young children such as *Jack and Jill,* an article from a magazine for slightly older children such as *National Geographic World,* and then an article from a magazine your own students might read such as *Teen.* Without telling the students the sources for the articles, let them guess the ages of the intended audience. Have them support their guesses with specific reasons such as choice of subject, vocabulary, sentence length, and so forth.

Another interesting activity is to have students write on the same subjects for different audiences. Have students begin by developing (perhaps brainstorming as a class) a list of details about a typical day at their school. Then have them use the list of details to write two letters—one to a group of first-grade students who will be coming on a field trip to visit the school, the other to a cousin of the same age and sex who lives in a different state. Have students work in small groups to exchange papers and compare ways in which they adapted their writing for the intended audience.

Evaluation: As you evaluate this type of assignment, concentrate primarily on how well students adapt their writing to the intended audience.

Additional practice: Throughout the composition section of this textbook, students will have additional practice in adapting various forms of writing to different audiences.

Assignment 4 Evaluating and revising writing
(length will vary)

Time: Throughout the school year

Objective: To evaluate and revise writing as appropriate for content, organization, and style.

Course work: *English Composition and Grammar,* pages 31–38

Suggested model: *English Composition and Grammar,* pages 36–37

Suggested topic: A topic suggested by the Review Exercise, page 29, or a topic of teacher's or student's choice.

Presentation: Although evaluation and revision are generally taught as separate stages in the writing process, most professional writers do not see them as separate from writing itself. In fact, there are only one or two known instances of professional writers who did not evaluate and revise their writing. Indeed, for most writers, the reverse is true—much more time is spent on evaluation and revision than on the initial drafting. However, many students, even today, think that "good" writing simply flows from the writer's pen (or word processor) without any conscious effort on the writer's part. You can help students understand how most writers really work by sharing with them facsimiles of writers' first and later drafts, showing the many changes that were made. It is often interesting to discuss with students why the writers made the particular changes that they did. For example, in one draft of "Stopping by Woods on a Snowy Evening," Robert Frost referred to the horse as "she." By the final draft, however, the horse had become a "he."

Students should also realize that writers use different techniques for revision. Some writers begin with the very first sentence they write, or even the first phrase, evaluating and then polishing it until they are satisfied. Other writers, however, move quickly through the first draft and only then begin making changes. Although your students may certainly make changes as they do the initial draft, they should be encouraged to go back through the entire piece at least once. Also, very often a writer's goals may change during the initial draft. A writer may begin, for example, by trying to convince readers that soap operas are a worthwhile genre. Writing the first draft, however, the writer might decide that soap operas are really a waste of time and thus change the initial goal. Before students begin to evaluate, therefore, ask them to write their goals for writing, in as specific terms as possible, on a slip of paper. If possible, meet with each student to discuss how the goal has changed or not changed since the initial draft and how the change will affect their revisions.

It is also important that students do not confuse revising with proofreading. A useful technique for helping students to understand this distinction is to use drafts of papers that you have saved from earlier classes. Distribute copies of the initial drafts and then discuss with students the content changes that were made and possible reasons for those changes. As students evaluate and revise their own writing, allow them, whenever possible, to work with partners or in small groups so that they have at least one other person as an audience.

Throughout the composition sections of this textbook, there are evaluating guidelines and revising charts specific to different forms of writing. Help students to become familiar with these tools by looking up the entries "Evaluation" and "Revision" in the index. Turn with them to the pages in the textbook where the various guidelines and charts are found.

Evaluation: Rather than grading students' initial drafts, you might prefer to evaluate changes they make during revision. Depending on the time available to you, you might allow students to prepare any number of drafts.

Additional practice: Throughout the composition sections of this textbook, students will be receiving additional practice in revising different forms of writing.

Assignment 5 A paragraph developing a topic sentence
(approximately 150–200 words)

Time: 1 week

Objective: To write a unified paragraph in which all the other sentences support the topic sentence.

Course work: *English Composition and Grammar,* pages 43–48

Suggested models: *English Composition and Grammar,* pages 44 and 47

Suggested topic: Help students find suitable topics by writing topic sentences such as the following ones on the board and having students fill in the blanks:

> ____ is more complicated than it seems.
> Learning to ____ is easy, if you follow a few simple steps.
> The trouble with cats (dogs, snakes, hamsters, etc.) is that ____.
> ____ is the worst place I have ever been.

Presentation: You may want to begin by having students practice identifying topic sentences. (See Exercise 1, page 45.) The textbook also provides ample practice by having students rewrite weak paragraphs by supplying details to further develop the topic sentence. (See Exercise 2, page 46.)

As a way of having students begin to write their own paragraphs, ask them to suggest three or four ways of completing each of the topic sentences (see *Suggested topic* above) on the board. List students' answers on the board. Then have them choose one of the completed sentences and ask them to suggest specific statements that would develop this topic sentence. Write the statements on the board as they are suggested. Then have the class tell you how to revise or reorganize the set of statements to make a good paragraph.

Another interesting approach to reinforcing the concept that a topic sentence is an idea developed with specific details is to have students make a collage around a topic sentence with pictures, words, and/or phrases and sentences cut from old magazines and newspapers. For example, a student might write a topic sentence such as "A police officer's job is a varied one." The student might then have pictures showing police officers pursuing a speeding driver, directing traffic, and comforting a lost child in a shopping center.

Depending upon your students' ability to work with paragraphs, you may want to spend more or less time on the concept that topic sentences do not always appear at the beginning of the paragraph and, indeed, many paragraphs do not have topic sentences at all. If you choose to develop this concept with your students, you might examine with them different types of writing, such as articles from newspapers, nonfiction books, teen-agers' magazines, and so on, looking for paragraphs that have no topic sentences or for paragraphs with topic sentences in various positions. Help students to realize that even when paragraphs do not have topic sentences, the writer generally has a controlling idea in mind that shapes and tightens the paragraph. You might also point out how paragraphs are sometimes used for effect or for transition, so that a writer might use simply a one-sentence paragraph between longer paragraphs.

Evaluation: Assign grades according to how well students meet the specific objective of writing a paragraph in which all the other sentences clearly support the topic sentence.

Additional practice: *English Composition and Grammar,* Chapter 2 Writing Review, pages 77–78

Assignment 6 A narrative paragraph
(approximately 150–200 words)

Time: 1 week

Objective: To write a narrative paragraph that (1) is developed with a single incident, (2) is adequately developed with specific details arranged chronologically, and (3) has other characteristics of an effective paragraph.

Course work: *English Composition and Grammar,* pages 79–84

Suggested model: *English Composition and Grammar,* page 80

Suggested topic: A topic suggested by Exercise 2, page 82, or a topic of teacher's or student's choice

Presentation: During the *prewriting* stage for this assignment, you may want to be certain that students understand the concept of incident—a single episode with a beginning, middle, and end. Have students bring in articles from magazines or newspapers that are about such incidents. Discuss with students the events that make up the incident and how they build to a climax. For example, in the summer of 1985 an explorer found, deep in the waters off the coast of Florida, a rich trove of gold and silver from sunken Spanish ships. A single incident from that experience might be the actual dive when the first piece of treasure was found. Events in the incident would then be the diver preparing for the dive, reaching the ship, and bringing up the first piece of gold or silver.

Exercise 1, page 81, supplies students with specific details to use in developing a narrative paragraph. You might prefer to do this exercise as a class activity, having students suggest suitable topic sentences and additional narrative details. You might, at this time, also discuss with students the concept of point of view in narrative paragraphs. As a class, have students write the entire paragraph from one point of view (a student volunteer can copy the paragraph on the board), and then have them rewrite the paragraph from a different point of view. Help students realize how changing point of view has affected the paragraph. (A first-person narrator, for example, cannot read another character's mind or see farther into the distance than physical sight allows.)

A problem for many students is using sufficient narrative details to recreate the incident for the reader. Review carefully the paragraph weak in narrative detail on page 80 and its revision on page 81 before students write their own paragraphs. Students can also practice supplying narrative details for weak drafts of narrative paragraphs that you have saved from previous classes. Have students work in small groups to use the *5 W-How?* questions to elicit detail. Then have students exchange papers and use the lists to develop the weak paragraphs.

As students work to *evaluate* and *revise* their narrative paragraphs, refer them to the Guidelines for Evaluating Narrative Paragraphs on page 83 and the revising chart on pages 73–75.

Evaluation: Evaluate this assignment based on parts of the objective given above that you have stressed with your students.

Additional practice: *English Composition and Grammar,* Review Exercise A, page 84.

Assignment 7 A descriptive paragraph
(approximately 150–200 words)

Time: 1 week

Objective: To write a descriptive paragraph that creates a mental image for the reader through the use of concrete, sensory details.

Course work: *English Composition and Grammar,* pages 84–89

Suggested models: *English Composition and Grammar,* pages 85, 86, and 87–88

Suggested topic: An object, place, or person, preferably one the student can observe firsthand before beginning to write

Presentation: Perhaps the most important skill in writing descriptive paragraphs is that of close, careful observation. If you have worked with students on Assignment 2 above ("Gathering ideas for writing"), you might want to begin this assignment by reviewing with students the importance of concrete, sensory details. If possible, send students to a place, such as a corner of the school cafeteria, or simply their own backyards, where they can sit quietly and record for perhaps fifteen minutes a list of sensory impressions. Remind them of the importance of using all their senses, rather than relying primarily on their sense of sight. Have student volunteers share their lists of details with the class or in small groups. As a class or group activity, then, students can use these lists to develop drafts of descriptive paragraphs. (If students work in groups in this manner, each group might develop a single draft.) As additional practice in supplying concrete, sensory details, you may prefer to momentarily skip to Review Exercise B, page 89. In this exercise, students are given a weak descriptive paragraph followed by a list of questions that should help them think of additional details. You may want to use this activity as a class exercise, and, for additional practice, reproduce drafts of weak paragraphs that you have saved from previous classes.

In the *prewriting* stage, another important skill is the ability to develop a main impression that is then supported with specific details (see the sample paragraph on pages 87–88), an impression that is often most strongly conveyed in the topic sentence. Other important skills include the use of precise and vivid language and the use of comparisons and figurative language. The section "The Descriptive Paragraph" is organized so that students have instruction and practice with each of these skills before the first paragraph assignment (Exercise 6, page 86). If you have used Review Exercise B, page 89, for additional practice in the use of sensory details, students should be well equipped to handle the remaining assignments in this section in which they are asked to write descriptions of places, objects, and people.

As students begin to *evaluate* drafts of their original paragraphs, refer them to the Guidelines for Evaluating Descriptive Paragraphs, page 89.

Evaluation: Paragraphs should be evaluated on how well the writer meets the goal of creating a mental image for the reader through the use of concrete, sensory detail. If you have emphasized the development of a main impression, you may want to evaluate for that objective also.

Additional practice: *English Composition and Grammar,* Chapter 3 Writing Review, item number 2, page 103

Assignment 8 An expository paragraph developed with facts and statistics
(approximately 150–200 words)

Time: 1 week

Objective: To write an expository paragraph that (1) is adequately developed with facts and statistics and (2) has other characteristics of an effective paragraph.

Course work: *English Composition and Grammar,* pages 90–92

Suggested model: *English Composition and Grammar,* page 90

Suggested topic: A topic in which the student has a particular interest and one that lends itself to development with facts and statistics

Presentation: To prepare students for this assignment, you might consider reviewing with them the characteristics of an effective paragraph as they were presented in Chapter 2, "Writing Paragraphs," text pages 43–58. These characteristics include a limited topic, a topic sentence in which the main idea of the paragraph is stated, adequate development of the topic sentence through the use of specific detail, and unity and coherence. You might review these concepts simply by discussing the elements as they are illustrated by sample paragraphs in Chapter 2. An alternate method of review is to reproduce drafts of weak paragraphs saved from previous classes and discuss with students specific strategies for improving the paragraphs so that they meet the criteria for effective paragraphs.

As you proceed through the *prewriting* stages for this assignment, you may want to make certain that students understand the definitions of the terms *fact* and *statistics* (see page 90). To test their understanding of these concepts, you might try giving them a list that is a mixture of facts, statistics, and personal opinions (that cannot be proved to be true), such as the following one: (1) Robert Frost is a well-known American poet. (2) *Raiders of the Lost Ark* is the best movie ever made. (3) Water boils at 100 degrees Celsius. (4) The country known today as Ethiopia was once known as Abyssinia. (5) Chemistry is the hardest course in school. (6) Albert Einstein developed the theory of relativity. (7) John Glenn, a former astronaut, was elected to the U.S. Senate in 1974. (8) *Funky Winkerbean* is a comic strip about the lives of high school students. (9) "M*A*S*H" is the best television series that has ever been developed. (10) Life as an only child is much easier than life with younger brothers and sisters.

If students are familiar with the use of reference sources (see the chapter "Using the Library," pages 613–625), you might assign them the task of using reference books to confirm such statements as the ones in the above list. Students should quickly realize that statements using words such as "best," "worst," "easiest," and so forth, are rarely facts that can be proved.

You want to proceed from this point by having students complete Exercise 9, pages 90–91, in which students are given a list of facts and statistics with which to develop a paragraph. (Refer them to library sources to find additional facts and statistics with which to develop the paragraph.) As students begin writing their own paragraphs, check that they have selected a topic sentence that lends itself to development with facts and statistics. As students begin *evaluating* and *revising* their paragraphs, refer them to the Guidelines for Evaluating Expository Paragraphs on page 97 and the revising chart on pages 73–75.

Evaluation: Check for students' use of adequate and currect facts and statistics. If you have reviewed before this assignment other characteristics of an effective paragraph, evaluate also for such criteria as main idea, unity, and coherence.

Additional practice: *English Composition and Grammar,* Review Exercise C, page 97, and Chapter 3 Writing Review, item number 3, page 103.

Assignment 9 A persuasive paragraph
(approximately 150–200 words)

Time: 1 week

Objective: To write a persuasive paragraph developed with reasons that build a logical argument.

Course work: *English Composition and Grammar,* pages 98–102

Suggested model: *English Composition and Grammar,* page 100

Suggested topic: A proposition that the student has to defend, such as those suggested under Review Exercise D, page 101.

Presentation: To write persuasive paragraphs, students must have, among other skills, the ability to choose topics that express opinions about serious issues and to support those opinions with accurate facts, examples, and other information. These and other *prewriting* steps necessary for developing persuasive paragraphs are presented on pages 98–101. You might begin by reviewing these steps with your students and then complete as a class activity Exercise 15, page 99, in which students are asked to identify effective topic sentences for persuasive paragraphs.

After students have read and discussed the model paragraph on page 100, write on the board a sentence such as "All eighth-grade students should be required to take band" (or "public speaking" or "typing" or another course that is now an elective in your school). Ask the class to give reasons that could be used *in favor* of this hypothetical proposal. Write these reasons in rough form beneath the topic sentence; then, with the aid of the class, write a paragraph based on the plan. You may wish to point out at this time that it is good to put the strongest reason either first or last, instead of burying it in the middle. (The model paragraph on page 100 is arranged with the most important reason last.)

As an additional activity, before students select and develop their own topic sentences and paragraphs, you might want them to complete Exercise 16, pages 100–101, in which they analyze the model paragraph. As students begin *evaluating, writing,* and *revising* their own paragraphs (based on Review Exercise D, page 101), refer them to the Guidelines for Evaluating Persuasive Paragraphs, page 102, and the revising chart, pages 73–75.

Evaluation: Evaluate students' paragraphs on the basis of their ability to support an opinion on a serious issue with sufficient and convincing reasons.

Additional practice: *English Composition and Grammar,* Chapter 3 Writing Review, item number 4, page 103.

Assignment 10 A short story
(approximately 250–300 words)

Time: 2 weeks

Objective: To write a short story (narrative), using vivid details

Course work: *English Composition and Grammar,* pages 104–33

Suggested model: *English Composition and Grammar,* pages 112–13

Suggested topic: A topic based on Exercise 11, page 113; Exercise 21, page 124; Exercise 22, page 125; and Exercise 23, page 126; or a topic of teacher's or student's choice

Presentation: Students should understand that stories usually begin with a problem or conflict and then tell what happens as a result, and that stories also have a clear beginning, middle, and end. To review this concept, you might use a well-known story from the students' literature textbook or use sample stories that you have saved from previous classes.

Working through the exercises in this part of the chapter will give students instruction and practice in such *prewriting* skills as finding appropriate topics for narratives, using specific details, and using dialogue. If you have completed Assignments 6 and 7 with your students (writing descriptive and narrative paragraphs), students may not need to cover all of the material contained in this section. However, if your students need additional help in developing the skill of using vivid, concrete details, you might want to cover with them the section of the chapter "Writing Description" on pages 118–23.

If students have problems thinking of ideas for stories, the use of "story starters" is particularly effective. A "story starter" may be the beginning of a story that sets the stage for action to come, leaving the reader at a moment of suspense. The following story starter is one such example.

> For several hours a heavy fog had gradually settled in over the Denver airport. Sitting in the boarding area, Ralph half expected to hear an announcement that the flight to San Francisco had been cancelled. Much to his surprise, however, the flight boarded and backed away from the runway on time. Ralph had always enjoyed the sense of power as the large plane lumbered down the runway and, with a giant thrust, lifted into the sky. Once he was in the air, Ralph settled back to enjoy the flight. At that moment, however . . .

Story starters might be ones that you have made up yourself, or you might have students try writing them, exchanging them with classmates, and then finishing each other's stories. Beginnings of newspaper and magazine articles, or even advertisements, can sometimes make good story starters. Yet another idea is to find a professional writer's story your students are not likely to know. Give the students the first two or three paragraphs and then have them finish the story. They will be interested in comparing their results not only with each other's, but also with those of the professional writer.

In some cases, especially when you work with story starters, you may not ask for much in the form of *evaluation* and *revision* from your students. In other cases, however, you will want students to work through separate drafts of their stories just as they would do with other forms of writing. In these instances, refer students to the Guidelines for Evaluating Narratives and the chart for revising stories on pages 127 and 128–30.

Evaluation: Many teachers prefer to treat this assignment as a "fun" assignment, not giving grades as they do with other types of writing. If you do evaluate your students' work, base your evaluation on the skills you have emphasized in your instruction.

Additional practice: *English Composition and Grammar,* Chapter 4 Writing Review, page 133

Assignment 11 An expository composition
(approximately 200–250 words)

Time: 2 weeks

Objective: To write an expository composition that (1) accomplishes the writer's goal of explaining information to a specific audience, (2) has a suitably limited topic, (3) has an effective introduction and conclusion, and (4) is unified and coherent

Course work: *English Composition and Grammar,* pages 134–69

Suggested model: *English Composition and Grammar,* pages 158–60

Suggested topic: A topic related to a student's hobbies or special interests, perhaps a topic suggested by Exercises 1–5, pages 135, 136, 137, 138, and 139

Presentation: By the time students begin to write expository compositions, they will already have had instruction and practice in many of the skills basic to this type and other types of writing: selecting and limiting a subject, gathering details, considering the audience, and so forth. If you have worked with students on Assignment 8 (writing expository paragraphs), students will also have had experience in developing topics that inform and explain. At this time, you might review with students the basics of writing an effective expository paragraph, perhaps using sample paragraphs you have saved from previous classes.

In the *prewriting* stage for this assignment, you will want to be certain that students understand the purpose of exposition: to inform or to explain. Have the class brainstorm possible topics for expository compositions, based on their hobbies and interests, and write these topics randomly on the board. Then discuss with students why the topics are or are not suitable for an expository composition.

Many teachers prefer to teach the expository composition in the form of a five-paragraph essay: one paragraph of introduction, three paragraphs to develop the topic, and a final paragraph that concludes the essay. Of particular importance to students in developing this type of composition are the arrangement of details and the transition from one paragraph to another. Students should understand that a composition is more than five paragraphs randomly strung together. The sections "Grouping Ideas and Details" and "Arranging Ideas and Details," pages 147–51, and "Using Transitional Words and Phrases," pages 156–57, give students instruction and practice with the arrangement of details and with transition. An interesting activity to illustrate the importance of unity and coherence in a composition is to have the class agree on a topic for an expository composition. Then divide the class into five groups. Have each of the members in one group write an introductory paragraph for a composition on that topic; each of the members of the second group write the first developmental paragraph for that topic; each member of the third, the second developmental paragraph; and so on. Then select one of the introductory paragraphs at random and have a volunteer write it on the board; then select one of the second, the third, fourth, and concluding paragraphs to write on the board until you have what seems to be a five-paragraph essay. Students will realize that, even though each paragraph develops the same topic, the composition does not work because the paragraphs do not develop particular parts of the topic. You can then discuss with students the value of an outline (pages 151–54) to ensure that each paragraph does indeed develop a part of the topic.

In presenting this assignment, have the students follow carefully the *prewriting, writing, evaluating,* and *revising* steps as they are presented in the chapter. You might find Exercise 30, text page 160, in which students are led through an analysis of a sample composition, particularly helpful.

Evaluation: Evaluate this assignment, basing your evaluation on the objective listed above.

Additional practice: *English Composition and Grammar,* Review Exercise A, page 160, and Chapter 5 Writing Review, pages 167–68

Assignment 12 A summary
(no longer than one third the length of the original article)

Time: 1 week

Objective: To write a summary that presents the important points of an article in the student's own words

Course work: *English Composition and Grammar,* pages 170–78

Suggested model: *English Composition and Grammar,* page 175

Suggested topic: A summary of the paragraphs in Exercise 2 (pages 173–74) or a summary of a magazine or newspaper article

Presentation: Begin the *prewriting* stages for this assignment by writing on the board the five requirements for a summary:

1. It should present only the main ideas of the original article.
2. The ideas should be presented in the same order as in the original.
3. The summary should be written in the writer's own words.
4. The summary should be suitable for its audience.
5. It should be one third or less the length of the original.

The material in this section is organized so that students first have practice in deciding on the main ideas in an article (Rule 6a and Exercise 1, pages 171–72), in taking notes about an article (Rule 6b and Exercise 2, pages 173–74), in writing the first draft (Rule 6c and Exercise 3, page 176), and then in evaluating and revising the draft (Rule 6d and Exercise 4, page 178). In addition to having students complete the exercises in this section, you might also want them to follow the same *prewriting, writing, evaluating,* and *revising* steps in preparing summaries of newspaper or magazine articles or summaries from textbook materials in other subjects. You might also wish to assign, for each summary, a different type of audience, thus giving students additional practice in adapting their writing to their readers.

As students work on *evaluating* and *revising* their summaries, either individually or in revision groups, refer them to the Guidelines for Evaluating a Summary and the revising chart, page 176–77.

Evaluation: Evaluate students' summaries on the basis of the five characteristics of effective summaries you have written on the board.

Additional practice: *English Composition and Grammar,* Review Exercise, page 178.

Assignment 13 A report based on reference sources
(at least 400 words)

Time: 2 weeks

Objective: To write a report, based on library reference sources, that (1) fulfills the writer's goal of informing the reader about factual information, (2) is based on a limited topic, (3) is developed with specific details organized in a logical manner, and (4) has other characteristics of an effective expository composition

Course work: *English Composition and Grammar,* pages 178–95

Suggested model: *English Composition and Grammar,* pages 190–93

Suggested topic: A topic suggested by Exercise 6, page 181, or a topic of the teacher's or student's choice

Presentation: If your students have already written expository compositions, they will have had instruction and practice in such important *prewriting* skills as limiting and developing topics and using various methods to gather ideas for developing the topics. They will also have had experience in writing compositions in which each paragraph develops an aspect of the topic and is clearly related to the other paragraphs. For this assignment, therefore, you might want to concentrate on those skills with which most students will be least familiar: using library sources to gather information, recording information on note cards, and developing outlines. They will also probably need help in learning to paraphrase, summarize, or quote material.

As a class activity, you might want to complete Exercise 5, page 180, in which students practice choosing limited topics suitable for library reports. In Exercise 6, page 181, students actually select the topic on which they will write the report. From this point on, you will forestall problems if you check students' work at each stage. For example, you should approve the students' topics individually before they begin their research, being certain that they select topics for which they can find adequate information in the school library. Under Rule 6g (pages 182–85), students are given instruction and practice in recording, on source cards, sources of information they find about their topics. The form suggested here is one of many suitable forms; you may have another you wish your students to follow, but, here again, students' work should be checked at this point. Be certain that they have enough sources and that the sources are sufficiently current for the selected topic. Under Rules 6h and 6i (pages 185–87), the students are given instruction and practice in developing a working outline and taking notes from their sources. In checking students' notes, be certain that they are either writing the material in their own words or properly paraphrasing, summarizing, or quoting, and that they are gathering sufficient material with which to develop their topics.

Then you should probably devote at least one class period apiece to each of the remaining steps of writing the report: organizing the notes into an outline, *writing* the rough draft, and *evaluating* and *revising* the report. By checking outlines, you can tell whether students have stuck to their topics and arranged their material in the best possible order. Before students begin revising their reports, you might find it helpful to complete, as a class activity, the section "Critical Thinking: Analyzing a Model," pages 190–93. Students will also find helpful the Guidelines for Evaluating Factual Reports, pages 194–95. In addition to reading the rough draft yourself, consider allowing students to work in either pairs or small evaluation groups as a way of getting additional feedback on their initial drafts. The importance of proofreading the final draft and preparing it in final form should also be stressed.

Evaluation: Some teachers prefer to give individual grades on each separate part of the report-writing process—the source cards, note cards, outline, rough draft, final draft, and so on.

Additional practice: *English Composition and Grammar,* Chapter 6 Writing Review, item number 2, page 200.

Assignment 14 A friendly letter
(150–200 words)

Time: 1 week

Objective: To write an interesting friendly letter using correct form

Course work: *English Composition and Grammar,* pages 201–207

Suggested model: *English Composition and Grammar,* page 202

Suggested topic: In preparation for this assignment, students might be told to keep a diary for a week. This preparation is especially useful for students who would otherwise claim "I have nothing to write about." Other specific suggestions may be found in Exercise 4, page 207.

Presentation: Have the class study the model friendly letter and discuss the questions directly above it.

To give students practice in using correct letter form, you may wish to have them write a skeleton letter like the one on page 204. Then make the composition assignment. Tell students that they should think of a real person to write to—a friend, a classmate, or a relative—and include items that would interest this person.

Evaluation: Grade on (1) the correctness of the letter form and (2) the content of the letter. Although you may wish to point out a blunder in usage or spelling, you should comment principally on form, interest, and style.

Additional practice: *English Composition and Grammar,* Exercise 4, page 207 (Students, of course, should select a situation different from the one they chose for the original letter.)

Assignment 15 A business letter

(The body of the letter should be 50–75 words.)

Time: 1 week

Objective: To write a clear, brief letter of request, using correct business-letter form

Course work: *English Composition and Grammar,* pages 211–20, 221–25

Suggested model: *English Composition and Grammar,* page 213 (form) and page 219 (request letter)

Suggested topic: A topic suggested by Exercise 10 or 11, pages 219–20, or a topic of teacher's or student's choice

Presentation: In the *prewriting* stages for this assignment, review with the students the steps for planning a business letter, page 212, in which such important points as audience, tone, conciseness, and brevity are discussed. Impress also upon your students the importance of using correct form and of writing business letters that are error-free. Before students write an actual letter, have them practice correct business-letter form by writing skeleton letters like the one on page 213.

For students of this age, the most practical letter for them to write is the letter of request (pages 218–19). You might first want students to complete Exercise 7, page 216, in which students are given all the information needed to write the letter. Also, if you want them to have additional practice in writing request letters, have students look in magazines for advertisements from such agencies as state tourist bureaus that will send free information on vacation sites and other tourist information in their states. You may also want to send for a quarterly publication titled *Consumer Information,* published by the General Services Administration of the U.S. Government. Many of the consumer publications are on subjects interesting to students, and most of them are free. To get a copy, write to Consumer Information Index, Pueblo, CO 81009. Another exceptionally helpful publication is one titled *All About Letters,* published jointly by the United States Postal Service and the National Council of Teachers of English. This book is filled with interesting and practical advice on writing all kinds of letters. It also has numerous addresses where students can write to receive free information on such appealing topics as bicycling, career exploration, dieting, stargazing, and so on.

As students move on to *evaluating, revising,* and *proofreading,* point out again the importance of correct form and error-free writing. Have students use the Guidelines for Evaluating Business Letters and Forms, pages 221–22, and the revising chart, pages 222–23.

Evaluation: Because form, neatness, and correctness are so very important in business letters, insist that students continue to draft their letters until they have written one suitable for mailing (whether or not they actually mail it).

Additional practice: *English Composition and Grammar,* Chapter 7 Writing Review 2, item number 2, pages 223–24

SECTION III

Suggested Teaching Procedures

PART ONE:

COMPOSITION: The Writing Process

pages 3–225

Before planning your composition program for the year, you may want to read the section on "The Teaching of Composition," pages T7–T55 of this *Teacher's Edition.* There you will find a great many suggestions concerning the nature of the writing process, techniques and strategies for implementing the writing process, motivation and class procedure, and evaluation of student papers. On pages T44–T45 there is also a list of suggested assignments that can provide the basis for a year's composition work.

At the beginning of the school year, you may find it wise to lay out a composition program for your class similar to that suggested on pages T44–T55 of this *Teacher's Edition.* Explain the program in general terms to your students so that they will understand what will be expected of them. They will cooperate more willingly and knowingly if they understand that their composition assignments are coming at regular intervals, with each assignment representing a specific advance in the gradual accumulation of skills necessary for competence in writing.

Ideally, you should start your composition program the first week of school. Take full advantage of your students' first-of-the-year willingness to work. Make clear the standards you expect to apply at this grade level.

Cross references to *Teaching Tests* and to tests and worksheets in the *Teacher's Resource Book* are listed at the end of each chapter.

CHAPTER 1

Writing and Thinking

(pages 3–42)

Chapter Objective

Students will recognize the stages of the writing process and their relationship to thinking, and will also practice the techniques and strategies related to each stage of the writing process.

PREWRITING (pages 5–29)

Objectives

1. Students will recognize that there are four basic purposes for writing: to describe, to narrate, to explain, and to persuade.
2. Students will determine their own purpose for writing.
3. Students will identify the audience for their writing.
4. Students will consider their own experiences as they choose a subject to write about.
5. Students will use brainstorming to discover ideas for writing.
6. Students will use a writer's notebook to gather ideas for writing.
7. Students will use critical thinking to observe and interpret details in order to discover subjects for writing.
8. Students will use the critical thinking skills of observing and interpreting to attend to specific sensory details for their writing.
9. Students will consider their attitude toward their subjects.
10. Students will limit their subjects to appropriate topics.
11. Students will use the critical thinking skill of analysis to divide broad subjects into suitable topics.
12. Students will gather information about their topics, using brainstorming and clustering, asking the *5 W-How?* questions, and asking the point-of-view questions.
13. Students will organize their information by eliminating irrelevant ideas and details and by using the critical thinking skill of classifying to group related ideas and details.
14. Students will arrange ideas and details in a logical order.

WRITING (pages 29–30)

Objectives

1. Students will develop first drafts on topics of their own.
2. Students will use the critical thinking skill of synthesis to develop their first drafts.

EVALUATING (pages 31–33)

Objective

Students will evaluate their final drafts for content, organization, and style, using the Guidelines for Evaluating Your Writing.

REVISING (pages 34–38)

Objectives

1. Students will analyze a writer's revisions.
2. Students will revise their own first drafts.

PROOFREADING (pages 38–40)

Objective

Students will proofread their revised drafts for errors in grammar, usage, and mechanics.

MAKING THE FINAL COPY (pages 40–42)

Objective

Students will follow correct manuscript form to prepare final copies of their revised and proofread drafts.

CHAPTER 2

Writing Paragraphs: Structure and Development

(pages 43–78)

Chapter Objective

Students will identify the basic elements composing the paragraph and will follow the steps of the writing process to develop paragraphs.

PREWRITING (pages 58–70)

Objectives

1. Students will develop a limited topic that is suitable for a paragraph.
2. Students will determine their purpose for writing the paragraph.
3. Students will consider how audience will affect their writing.
4. Students will gather information for the limited topics of their paragraphs.
5. Students will develop working plans for their paragraphs by writing topic sentences and listing specific details to develop them.
6. Students will use the critical thinking skill of generalizing to write a topic sentence.
7. Students will use the critical thinking skill of analyzing to decide which details support a main idea.

WRITING (pages 70–71)

Objective

Students will recognize that writers use their working plans to develop first drafts.

EVALUATING (pages 71–72)

Objective

Students will evaluate a first draft by reconsidering the draft's content, organization, and style.

REVISING (pages 73–76)

Objective

Students will revise a previously evaluated first draft by adding, cutting, reordering, and replacing.

PROOFREADING AND MAKING A FINAL COPY
(pages 76–77)

Objective

Students will proofread revised drafts of paragraphs to correct errors in usage and mechanics.

CHAPTER 3

Writing Paragraphs
Four Types of Paragraphs

(pages 79–103)

Chapter Objective

Students will use the writing process to compose four types of paragraphs: narrative, descriptive, expository, and persuasive.

CHAPTER 4

Writing Stories

(pages 104–33)

Chapter Objective

Students will use the writing process to write stories using narration and description.

PREWRITING (pages 104–13)

Objectives

1. Students will choose subjects that are appropriate for their narrative purpose.
2. Students will limit their subjects to a specific problem or experience.
3. Students will consider their purpose and audience.
4. Students will identify action details and gather information for their stories.
5. Students will arrange details and information for their stories.
6. Students will develop a story plan.

WRITING (pages 113–26)

Objectives

1. Students will use specific details to make their narratives vivid.
2. Students will use dialogue and description to make their stories lively and convincing.
3. Students will write first drafts with a beginning, a middle, and an ending.

EVALUATING (pages 126–27)

Objectives

1. Students will evaluate their own descriptions for content, organization, and style.
2. Students will use the Guidelines for Evaluating Narratives, page 127, to evaluate their writing.

REVISING (pages 128–32)

Objectives

1. Students will analyze a writer's revisions.
2. Students will revise sentences by replacing overused adjectives and adverbs.
3. Students will revise a paragraph by omitting unnecessary adjectives and adverbs.
4. Students will use a revising chart to revise the draft of their evaluated narratives.

PROOFREADING (pages 132–33)

Objectives

1. Students will proofread their stories for errors in usage and mechanics.
2. Students will prepare clean, accurate final copies of their narratives.

CHAPTER 5

Writing Exposition

(pages 134–69)

Chapter Objective

Students will identify the various functions of exposition and will successfully use the writing process to write expository compositions.

PREWRITING (pages 134–54)

Objectives

1. Students will choose a subject for their expository compositions by examining their personal resources, observing the world around them, keeping a writer's journal, brainstorming, and clustering.
2. Students will consider their audience.
3. Students will limit their subject to a manageable topic.
4. Students will state the purpose of their expository compositions.
5. Students will gather information for their expository compositions by listing ideas and details, using a writer's journal, and asking the *5 W-How?* questions.
6. Students will arrange their ideas and details into topic outlines or informal plans.

WRITING (pages 154–60)

Objectives

1. Students will write drafts of their expository compositions: the introduction, the body, and the conclusion.
2. Students will use transitional words and phrases.
3. Students will study a sample composition.
4. Students will refer to the Guidelines for Writing Expository Compositions, pages 168–69.

EVALUATING (pages 161–63)

Objectives

1. Students will evaluate their drafts for content, organization, and style.
2. Students will refer to the Guidelines for Evaluating Expository Compositions, pages 161–62.

REVISING (pages 163–65)

Objectives

1. Students will recognize that revision involves cutting, adding, reordering, or replacing words, phrases, sentences, or paragraphs.
2. Students will analyze a revised paragraph.
3. Students will use the revision chart to revise their own compositions.

PROOFREADING (page 166)

Objectives

1. Students will proofread their expository compositions.
2. Students will refer to the Guidelines for Proofreading, page 39.

WRITING THE FINAL VERSION (pages 166–67)

Objective

Students will prepare and proofread the final copies of their expository compositions.

CHAPTER 6

Writing Exposition

(pages 170–200)

Chapter Objective

Students will use the writing process to develop summaries, research reports, and book reports.

WRITING SUMMARIES (pages 170–78)

PREWRITING (pages 170–74)

Objectives

1. Students will consider the purpose and audience for their summary.
2. Students will gather information by taking notes.

WRITING (pages 174–76)

Objective

Students will write a first draft of their summary that is one third or less the length of the original article.

EVALUATING AND REVISING (pages 176–78)

Objective

Students will evaluate and revise the first draft of their summary, following the Guidelines for Evaluating a Summary.

WRITING LONGER REPORTS

(pages 178–95)

PREWRITING (pages 179–88)

Objectives

1. Students will develop a limited topic.
2. Students will consider the purpose and audience for their report.
3. Students will consider available library resources.
4. Students will find sources of information.
5. Students will record the sources used.
6. Students will develop a working outline.
7. Students will take notes on their reading.
8. Students will organize their notes according to headings.
9. Students will make a final outline based on their notes.

WRITING (pages 189–93)

Objectives

1. Students will write first drafts based on their final outline and notes.
2. Students will use critical thinking skills in analyzing a sample report.

EVALUATING AND REVISING (pages 194–95)

Objective

Students will evaluate and revise their reports, using the Guidelines for Evaluating Factual Reports.

WRITING A BOOK REPORT

(pages 195–200)

PREWRITING (pages 195–96)

Objectives

1. Students will consider the purpose and audience for their book report.
2. Students will gather specific information from the book and determine their opinion of it.
3. Students will summarize information about the book.

WRITING (pages 196–99)

Objective

Students will write first drafts of their book reports.

EVALUATING AND REVISING

(pages 199–200)

Objective

Students will evaluate and revise the first draft of their book report using Guidelines for Evaluating a Book Report.

CHAPTER 7

Writing Letters and Completing Forms

(pages 201–25)

Chapter Objectives

1. Students will correctly write social letters, including the bread-and-butter note and thank-you note.
2. Students will correctly write business letters.
3. Students will accurately complete a form supplied by the teacher.

SOCIAL LETTERS AND NOTES

(pages 201–11)

PREWRITING (pages 201–202)

Objective

Students will decide what to say in their social letters.

WRITING (pages 203–10)

Objectives

1. Students will choose appropriate stationery and ink for a friendly letter.
2. Students will follow generally accepted rules for the form of a friendly letter and its envelope.
3. Students will write prompt, courteous social notes, including bread-and-butter notes and thank-you notes.
4. Students will recognize the different purposes of the various kinds of social letters.

EVALUATING AND REVISING (pages 210–11)

Objective

Students will evaluate, revise, and proofread their social letters, using the Guidelines for Evaluating Social Letters.

PREWRITING (pages 211–12)

Objective

Students will plan business letters, considering purpose, audience, tone, and necessary ideas.

WRITING (pages 212–21)

Objectives

1. Students will follow generally accepted rules for the form of a business letter.
2. Students will become familiar with the order letter and the request letter.
3. Students will complete forms, supplying the information needed as accurately and thoroughly as possible.

EVALUATING AND REVISING (pages 221–23)

Objective

Students will revise and proofread their business letters and forms, using the Guidelines for Evaluating Business Letters and Forms.

PICTURE THE POSSIBILITIES:

Ideas for Writing
(pages IW1-IW16)

Section Objectives

1. Students will recognize that pictures are a source of ideas for writing.
2. Students will follow the steps of the writing process in writing about pictures.
3. Students will write a dialogue.
4. Students will write a story.
5. Students will write an expository paragraph of comparison or contrast.
6. Students will write a persuasive paragraph.
7. Students will write a descriptive paragraph.
8. Students will write an expository composition.

PART TWO

COMPOSITION: Writing and Revising Sentences

pages 229–62

This section is composed of two chapters on sentence writing that cover sentence fragments, run-on sentences, sentence combining and sentence revising.

The greatest single problem that many eighth-graders have with sentence structure is learning to recognize and use complete sentences. Do not expect that Chapter 8, "Writing Complete Sentences," offers a miracle cure for this problem. The work in this chapter has to be backed up by the study of sentence structure in the grammar chapters, by the work on punctuation in the mechanics chapters, and by continual practice in composition. Chapter 8 offers examples of the most common types of sentence fragments and run-on sentences and simple methods for correcting these.

Chapter 9, "Writing Effective Sentences," is an introduction to *style* in writing prose. Make it clear that there is nothing wrong with the grammatical structure of the sentences in the models and in the exercises; what is wrong is the awkward way the sentences follow one another.

Note on testing: The Sentence Structure and Composition Pretest (a diagnostic tool); a final test on each chapter, and two Sentence Structure and Composition Mastery Tests that cover the entire sentence-structure section are provided in *Teaching Tests, Second Course,* the test booklet that accompanies *English Composition and Grammar, Second Course.*

Cross references to *Teaching Tests* and to tests and worksheets in the *Teacher's Resource Book* are listed at the end of each chapter.

CHAPTER 8

Writing Complete Sentences

(pages 229–40)

Chapter Objective

Students will recognize sentence fragments and run-on sentences and correct them through several methods.

FRAGMENTS

(pages 229–36, rules 8a–8d)

Objectives

1. Students will identify sentences and fragments and correct the fragments.
2. Students will revise subordinate clause fragments to make them complete sentences.
3. Students will revise verbal phrase fragments to make them complete sentences.
4. Students will revise appositive phrase fragments to make them complete sentences.

RUN-ON SENTENCES

(pages 236–40, rule 8e)

Objective

Students will identify and revise run-on sentences.

CHAPTER 9

Writing Effective Sentences

(pages 241–62)

Chapter Objective

Students will write effective sentences through a variety of sentence combining and revising activities.

CORRECTING A CHOPPY STYLE BY COMBINING SENTENCES

(pages 241–56, rules 9a–9g)

Objectives

1. Students will combine sentences by inserting adjectives, adverbs, or prepositional phrases.
2. Students will combine sentences by using participial phrases and appositive phrases.
3. Students will combine sentences by using compound subjects and compound verbs.
4. Students will combine simple sentences by making them into compound sentences.
5. Students will combine sentences by using adjective clauses and adverb clauses.

CORRECTING A MONOTONOUS STYLE

(pages 256–59, rule 9h)

Objectives

1. Students will revise sentences by beginning them with adverbs, adverb clauses, prepositional phrases, or participial phrases.
2. Students will write original sentences beginning with given prepositional or participial phrases.

CORRECTING RAMBLING SENTENCES

(pages 259–62, rule 9i)

Objective

Students will correct rambling sentences by combining ideas and avoiding the overuse of *and, but,* or *so.*

PART THREE

TOOLS FOR WRITING AND REVISING

pages 263–593

GRAMMAR

(pages 265–416)

The study of English grammar helps students in two ways. First, it familiarizes them with sentence structure: the sentence base (subject—verb—complement) and the elements that modify the base. Understanding these concepts will enable students to vary sentence structures and to avoid fragments and run-on sentences in their writing. Second, grammar provides the terminology for talking about language. The names of the parts of speech and the parts of the sentence are often used in the English class. While some aspects of usage can be taught without reference to grammar terms, most instruction in usage and rhetoric is made more efficient by the use of traditional terminology.

Teaching Grammar as a New Subject

Some schools do not introduce formal study of grammar until the eighth grade. If this is the case in your school, you will probably want to devote most of your grammar teaching to the basic concepts. Attempting to teach all of the grammar chapters to a beginning class might mean taking too much time away from the study of composition and literature. (Writing applications, however, are included throughout the chapters on grammar.)

Teaching Grammar to Less-advanced Students

Your approach to grammar with a class of less-advanced students will be different from the approach used with an average class. You may find the following suggestions helpful.

1. Use short, clear sentences to illustrate grammatical points. (You might sometimes use as your first exam-

ples some of the sentences that appear in diagraming exercises later in the chapter. These sentences are usually very short and simple.)

2. Before assigning an exercise, go over it and change or leave out the sentences that you think may prove too difficult. You can then either put the exercise on the board or have it copied.

3. Simplify grammatical explanations and terminology whenever possible.

4. Use visual demonstrations: write sentences on the board, use diagrams, act out words. These students usually enjoy drawing sentence diagrams if the sentences are short and easy.

5. If, despite your best efforts, the class seems unable to grasp a particular concept, do not doggedly continue to work on it. Go on to something that the class *can* understand.

Teaching Grammar to Students Who Have Studied It Before

Eighth-grade students who have already studied grammar should review early in the year all items covered in the seventh grade. This review provides a connection with the work covered the preceding year, and it assures a grammar foundation on which to build the skills involved in good usage and writing. After a quick review, give a diagnostic test on the fundamentals of grammar. (If you test too soon after the summer vacation, many students who are potentially good in grammar may do poorly, not from ignorance, but rather as a result of their having been away from the subject.) Thus you will know very early in the year how much your students have retained, and you can plan your program accordingly.

Note: Many English teachers like to teach grammar because, unlike many other areas of English, it is definite, logical, and easily testable. As a result grammar is sometimes overtaught; that is, teachers spend more time on it than they need to or, indeed, can afford to. Keep your course balanced.

See pages T72–T76 and T76–T79 of this Teacher's Edition for comments on the usage and mechanics sections of Part Three.

Note on testing: Each chapter in this section includes not only a Diagnostic Test but also two Chapter Review Posttests. In addition, a Grammar Pretest (another diagnostic tool), a final test on each chapter, and Grammar Mastery Reviews that cover the entire grammar section are provided in *Teaching Tests, Second Course*.

Cross references to *Teaching Tests* and to tests and worksheets in the *Teacher's Resource Book* are listed at the end of each chapter.

CHAPTER 10

The Sentence

(pages 265–89)

Chapter Objective

Students will identify complete sentences and subjects and predicates, and they will classify sentences according to purpose.

THE SENTENCE

(pages 267–69, rule 10a)

Objectives

1. Students will identify complete sentences.
2. Students will write complete sentences using correct capitalization and punctuation.
3. Students will revise groups of words to form complete sentences.

THE SUBJECT

(pages 269–71, rules 10b and 10c)

Objective

Students will identify simple and complete subjects.

THE PREDICATE

(pages 271–76, rules 10d and 10e)

Objectives

1. Students will identify complete predicates.
2. Students will identify verbs and verb phrases.

3. Students will revise groups of words, adding either subjects or predicates to form complete sentences.
4. Students will identify subjects and verbs in their own writing.

THE SENTENCE BASE
(pages 276–77)

Objective

Students will add words and phrases to sentence bases to expand sentences.

COMPOUND SUBJECTS AND COMPOUND VERBS
(pages 277–81, rules 10f and 10g)

Objectives

1. Students will identify compound subjects and their verbs or verb phrases.
2. Students will identify compound verbs, their connecting word or words, and their subjects.
3. Students will write sentences with compound subjects or compound predicates.

CLASSIFYING SENTENCES BY PURPOSE
(pages 281–83, rule 10h)

Objective

Students will classify sentences according to purpose.

DIAGRAMING THE SUBJECT AND VERB
(pages 283–89)

Objective

Students will use diagrams to visualize the function of subjects and verbs.

CHAPTER 11

The Parts of Speech Noun, Pronoun, Adjective
(pages 290–308)

Chapter Objective

Students will identify common and proper nouns, pronouns, and adjectives and will use these parts of speech effectively in their own writing.

THE NOUN
(pages 291–94, rule 11a)

Objectives

1. Students will identify nouns in sentences.
2. Students will identify compound nouns.
3. Students will identify common and proper nouns.

THE PRONOUN
(pages 294–99, rule 11b)

Objectives

1. Students will identify pronouns in sentences.
2. Students will complete a paragraph by adding appropriate pronouns.

THE ADJECTIVE
(pages 299–304, rule 11c)

Objectives

1. Students will add appropriate and interesting adjectives to sentences.
2. Students will identify adjectives and the words they modify.
3. Students will identify proper nouns and proper adjectives.
4. Students will distinguish between pronouns and adjectives.

DIAGRAMING NOUNS AND ADJECTIVES

Objective

Students will use diagrams to visualize the function of nouns and adjectives.

CHAPTER 12

The Parts of Speech Verb, Adverb, Preposition, Conjunction, Interjection

(pages 309–35)

Chapter Objective

Students will identify and use these parts of speech effectively in their own writing: verb, adverb, preposition, conjunction, interjection.

THE VERB

(pages 310–17, rule 12a)

Objectives

1. Students will identify action verbs in a passage.
2. Students will add linking verbs to sentences.
3. Students will distinguish between action verbs and linking verbs.
4. Students will identify linking verbs and the words that the verbs link.
5. Students will identify verbs and verb phrases in a passage.
6. Students will distinguish between verbs and other parts of speech.

THE ADVERB

(pages 317–22, rule 12b)

Objectives

1. Students will identify adverbs that modify verbs.
2. Students will identify adverbs that modify adjectives.
3. Students will write a variety of adverbs to modify adjectives.
4. Students will identify adverbs that modify other adverbs.

DIAGRAMING VERBS AND ADVERBS

(pages 322–23)

Objective

Students will use diagrams to visualize the function of verbs and adverbs.

THE PREPOSITION

(pages 323–27, rule 12c)

Objectives

1. Students will identify prepositions, including compound prepositions, in sentences.
2. Students will identify prepositional phrases.
3. Students will write sentences using specified words first as adverbs and then as prepositions.

THE CONJUNCTION

(pages 327–29, rule 12d)

Objective

Students will identify coordinating and correlative conjunctions.

THE INTERJECTION

(page 330, rule 12e)

Objective

Students will identify interjections.

DETERMINING PARTS OF SPEECH

(pages 330–35, rule 12f)

Objective

Students will identify words as different parts of speech on the basis of the way the words function in a sentence.

CHAPTER 13

Complements

(pages 336–51)

Chapter Objective

Students will identify the following grammatical concepts and use them in their own writing: direct object, indirect object, predicate nominative, and predicate adjective.

THE SENTENCE BASE

(pages 336–39, rule 13a)

Objective

Students will identify subjects, verbs, and complements.

DIRECT AND INDIRECT OBJECTS

(pages 339–45, rules 13b and 13c)

Objectives

1. Students will identify action verbs and their direct objects.
2. Students will identify direct objects and indirect objects.
3. Students will diagram sentences containing direct and indirect objects.

SUBJECT COMPLEMENTS

(pages 345–51, rule 13d)

Objectives

1. Students will identify predicate nominatives and predicate adjectives.
2. Students will diagram subject complements.
3. Students will identify both subject complements and object complements.

CHAPTER 14

The Phrase

(pages 352–80)

Chapter Objective

Students will identify and use effectively in their own writing prepositional phrases, verbal phrases, and appositive phrases.

THE PREPOSITIONAL PHRASE

(pages 354–61, rules 14b–14d)

Objectives

1. Students will identify prepositional phrases.
2. Students will identify adjective phrases.
3. Students will identify adverb phrases.
4. Students will write sentences with prepositional phrases.
5. Students will diagram prepositional phrases and sentences with adjective and adverb phrases.

VERBALS AND VERBAL PHRASES

(pages 362–75, rules 14e–14j)

Objectives

1. Students will identify participles and the nouns or pronouns they modify and classify these participles as present participles or as past participles.
2. Students will identify participial phrases and the nouns or pronouns they modify.
3. Students will write sentences with participial phrases.
4. Students will identify gerunds and gerund phrases.
5. Students will write sentences with gerund phrases.
6. Students will identify infinitives.
7. Students will identify infinitive phrases and their use as different parts of speech.
8. Students will write sentences with infinitive phrases and identify them as nouns, adjectives, or adverbs.
9. Students will diagram sentences with verbal phrases.

APPOSITIVES AND APPOSITIVE PHRASES
(pages 375–80, rules 14k and 14l)

Objective

Students will identify appositives and appositive phrases.

CHAPTER 15

The Clause

(pages 381–400)

Chapter Objective

Students will identify independent and subordinate clauses—adjective, adverb, and noun—and will use these clauses effectively in their own writing.

THE INDEPENDENT CLAUSE
(page 383, rule 15b)

Objective

Students will identify independent clauses.

THE SUBORDINATE CLAUSE
(pages 384–86, rule 15c)

Objectives

1. Students will distinguish between independent clauses, subordinate clauses, and phrases.
2. Students will identify subordinate clauses and their subjects and verbs.
3. Students will write sentences with independent and subordinate clauses.

THE ADJECTIVE CLAUSE
(pages 386–90, rule 15d)

Objectives

1. Students will identify adjective clauses.
2. Students will write adjective clauses to make complete sentences.

THE ADVERB CLAUSE
(pages 390–93, rule 15e)

Objectives

1. Students will identify adverb clauses and the subordinating conjunctions that introduce them.
2. Students will add original adverb clauses to sentences.

THE NOUN CLAUSE
(pages 393–400, rule 15f)

Objective

Students will identify and classify noun clauses.

Diagraming Subordinate Clauses
(pages 395–400)

Objective

Students will use diagrams to visualize the function of subordinate clauses in sentences.

CHAPTER 16

The Kinds of Sentence Structure

(pages 401–16)

Chapter Objective

Students will identify simple, compound, complex, and compound-complex sentences. They will use these sentence structures to give variety to their own writing.

THE SIMPLE SENTENCE
(pages 402–404, rule 16a)

Objective

Students will identify subjects and verbs in simple sentences.

THE COMPOUND SENTENCE

(pages 404–407, rule 16b)

Objectives

1. Students will identify subjects, verbs, and conjunctions in compound sentences.
2. Students will distinguish between compound sentences and compound subjects and verbs.
3. Students will use diagrams to visualize compound sentences.

THE COMPLEX SENTENCE

(pages 407–11, rule 16c)

Objectives

1. Students will identify independent clauses and subordinate clauses in complex sentences.
2. Students will use diagrams to visualize complex sentences.

THE COMPOUND-COMPLEX SENTENCE

(pages 411–16, rule 16d)

Objective

Students will identify and classify clauses in compound-complex sentences.

USAGE

(pages 417–510)

Levels of Usage

> Good English is that form of speech which is appropriate to the purpose of the speaker, true to the language as it is, and comfortable to speaker and listener.
>
> —ROBERT C. POOLEY, *Grammar and Usage in Textbooks on English,* Madison, University of Wisconsin, 1933, p. 155

This widely quoted definition of good English has been adopted in many schools as the basis for the teaching of usage. Most teachers do not believe that the English used in formal essays is the only "correct" English—or that highly formal English is "correct" at all in ordinary conversation. In the *English Composition and Grammar* series, two levels of usage are distinguished: standard English and nonstandard English. Standard English is subdivided into standard formal and standard informal levels. The goals for the class in studying the chapters on usage should be, first, to overcome habits of nonstandard usage (such as *he don't, you was, me and him did,* and the double negative) and, second, to learn to use standard informal English in their speech and writing. For many classes there will be a third goal: learning certain standard formal usages that are usually observed in written English, though they are not necessarily observed in casual conversation (*it was he, neither of them is*).

Teaching Usage in the Eighth Grade

While the eighth grade is too early for any elaborate study of the different levels of usage, students can understand that playground English is different from classroom English, and that the English we use in dashing off a note to a friend is different from the English we use in business letters. Point out that we choose our English to fit the occasion, just as we choose our clothes to fit a wide range of occasions.

The five chapters in this section cover the errors in usage most frequently found in eighth-grade writing and speaking. No individual student—and usually no individual class—will make all these errors. *Concentrate on correcting the most important errors in your students' own speaking and writing.* Do not waste time drilling your students on a form that most of them already use correctly or on a form that they never use at all.

Most teachers spotlight their students' mistakes as a basis for instruction in usage. The best time for this instruction is the day that a set of papers is handed back or the day after the class has finished giving oral reports. Put on the board a number of examples taken from their work that show similar errors. Have the class find the errors and tell you why and how to correct them. With a little help from the teacher, many eighth-graders will be able to discover for themselves the principles of standard usage.

Some teachers have their students keep individual "improvement records" listing the mistakes made in each theme, with corrections. A glance at your students' records will show which usage problems they have overcome and which ones they still need to work on. During the year you may want to go through the records and make a list for each student of two or three rules to be studied. They can find these rules in the textbook and complete the accompanying exercises.

Students Who Speak Nonstandard English

Your approach to usage will be different with students who habitually use expressions like "them boys" and "we was." Much of the time you spend on usage will probably be devoted to oral drill with standard English forms. Select the most frequent nonstandard usages in your students' English and concentrate on them one at a time. Have students start a page in their notebooks with a title like "This Is How We Say It" and give them three or four items for this page every week. Ask them as homework to make up three good sentences for each item, have them checked, and enter them on the page as examples.

Many students express themselves in black English —the linguistic system of all blacks in a given community. Help these students learn standard English. Your approach must include a sensitivity to a different language pattern, an understanding of how systematic that language pattern can be, and the ability to handle the teaching of standard English in a practical and positive way.

See pages T66–T73 and T76–T79 of this manual for comments on the grammar and mechanics sections of Part Three.

Note on testing: The Diagnostic Tests will help you determine how much instruction your students need in usage. Posttests are provided at the end of each chapter. In addition, a Usage Pretest (another diagnostic tool), a final test on each chapter, and Usage Mastery Reviews that cover the entire usage section are provided in *Teaching Tests, Second Course,* the test booklet that accompanies *English Composition and Grammar, Second Course.*

Cross references to *Teaching Tests* and to tests and worksheets in the *Teacher's Resource Book* are listed at the end of each chapter.

CHAPTER 17

Agreement

(pages 417–40)

Chapter Objective

Students will practice two general usage rules for standard English: (1) a verb agrees with its subject in number and (2) a pronoun agrees with its antecedent in number and gender. Students will use verb forms and pronouns correctly to make their writing clear.

AGREEMENT OF SUBJECT AND VERB

(pages 419–34, rules 17a–17m)

Objectives

1. Students will classify nouns and pronouns according to number.
2. Students will identify the verb that agrees with a given subject.
3. Students will use the correct number for verbs in sentences with phrases following the subjects.
4. Students will identify verbs that agree with indefinite pronouns used as subjects.
5. Students will proofread sentences for correct subject and verb agreement.
6. Students will choose verbs that agree with singular and plural compound subjects.
7. Students will write sentences with collective nouns.
8. Students will follow rules of subject and verb agreement in sentences that begin with *here* or *there*.
9. Students will use *doesn't* and *don't* correctly with given subjects.

AGREEMENT OF PRONOUN AND ANTECEDENT

(pages 434–40, rule 17n)

Objectives

1. Students will proofread sentences for pronoun-antecedent agreement.
2. Students will identify antecedents and write pronouns that agree with them.

CHAPTER 18

Using Verbs Correctly

(pages 441–63)

Chapter Objective

Students will form the past and past participle forms of regular and irregular verbs and will be consistent in using verb tenses.

REGULAR VERBS

(page 445, rule 18b)

Objective

Students will correctly form and pronounce the past and past participle of regular verbs.

IRREGULAR VERBS

(pages 445–50, rule 18c)

Objectives

1. Students will write from memory the past and past participle forms of listed irregular verbs.
2. Students will identify the correct forms of irregular verbs in sentences.
3. Students will complete sentences by writing the correct past and past participle forms of verbs.
4. Students will proofread sentences for correct verb forms.

SPECIAL PROBLEMS WITH VERBS

(pages 450–57)

Objectives

1. Students will use the forms of *sit* and *set* correctly.
2. Students will use the forms of *lie* and *lay* correctly.
3. Students will write original sentences using the forms of *lie* and *lay* correctly.
4. Students will use the correct forms of *rise* and *raise*.

CONSISTENCY OF TENSE

(pages 457–63, rule 18d)

Objectives

1. Students will proofread a paragraph to make the tenses of the verbs consistent.
2. Students will be consistent in using verb tenses in their own writing.

CHAPTER 19

Using Pronouns Correctly

(pages 464–75)

Chapter Objective

Students will use the nominative and objective forms of personal pronouns correctly in both speaking and writing.

THE NOMINATIVE CASE

(pages 466–69, rules 19a and 19b)

Objectives

1. Students will use pronouns as subjects, including compound subjects.
2. Students will write pronouns in the nominative case to complete sentences.
3. Students will identify correct pronoun usage for predicate nominatives.

THE OBJECTIVE CASE

(pages 469–75, rules 19c and 19d)

Objectives

1. Students will use pronouns as objects, including compound objects.
2. Students will write pronouns as direct and indirect objects in sentences.
3. Students will write pronouns as objects of prepositions in sentences.
4. Students will identify correct pronoun usage in sentences.

CHAPTER 20

Using Modifiers Correctly

(pages 476–94)

Chapter Objectives

Students will use comparatives and superlatives of adjectives and adverbs correctly. Students will correct dangling and misplaced modifiers and will use modifiers correctly in their own writing.

GOOD AND WELL

(pages 487–79, rule 20a)

Objective

Students will identify the correct use of *good* and *well* in sentences.

COMPARISON OF MODIFIERS

(pages 479–84, rules 20b–20d)

Objectives

1. Students will form the comparative and superlative degrees of specific modifiers.
2. Students will proofread sentences for errors in the forms of comparison.

THE DOUBLE NEGATIVE

(pages 484–87, rule 20e)

Objective

Students will revise sentences by eliminating double negatives.

PLACEMENT OF MODIFIERS

(pages 487–94, rule 20f)

Objectives

1. Students will revise sentences that contain misplaced modifying prepositional phrases.
2. Students will revise sentences that contain dangling participial phrases.
3. Students will write sentences using introductory participial phrases.
4. Students will revise sentences with misplaced clauses.

CHAPTER 21

Glossary of Usage

(pages 495–510)

Chapter Objective

Students will use correctly words that are often confused and will identify and correct nonstandard usages and informal usages that are usually avoided in written English.

USAGE GLOSSARY

(pages 498–510)

Objectives

1. Students will identify correct usages.
2. Students will correct errors in usage.

WORDS OFTEN CONFUSED BECAUSE OF SIMILAR SOUND OR MEANING

a, an
accept, except
affect, effect
already, all ready
bad, badly
could
might
must **of** (for *have*
ought to or *'ve*)
should
would

good, well
its, it's
kind, sort, type
lie, lay
rise, raise
sit, set
than, then
their, there, they're
use to, used to
your, you're

NONSTANDARD USAGES

ain't
anywheres, everywheres, nowheres
bust, busted
can't hardly, can't scarcely
good for *well*
had of
had ought, hadn't ought
he, she, they in double subjects
hisself, theirself, theirselves
learn for *teach*
them for *these* or *those*
this here, that there
which for *who* or *that*, referring to persons
without for *unless*

INFORMAL USAGES USUALLY AVOIDED IN WRITTEN ENGLISH

between for *among*
bring for *take*
how come for *why*
kind of, sort of for *somewhat* or *rather*
less for *fewer*
like for *as* or *as if*
of with prepositions such as *inside, off, outside*
real for *very*
reason is because
some for *somewhat*
try and for *try to*
ways for *way*
when, where used to introduce definitions
where for *that*

Note: You can find interesting full discussions of many of these points of usage in a book such as Margaret M. Bryant's Current American Usage.

MECHANICS

(pages 511–93)

The section on mechanics includes four chapters: one on capital letters, two on punctuation, and one on spelling. This section can be taught as individual chapter units. Whenever possible, however, mechanics should be taught as the need arises: the commas in the heading of a letter when students are studying letter writing, quotation marks in connection with writing dialogue in stories, capital letters for place-names when they are writing about a trip. *English Composition and Grammar, Second Course,* because of its clear arrangement of rules and examples, can be an efficient reference for work throughout the school year.

Teaching Mechanics in the Eighth Grade

During the middle-school or junior-high years, capitalization, punctuation, and spelling should receive heavy emphasis. The quantity of these students' writing, both expository and creative, should be increasing. It is important for them to form good habits in the mechanics of written English.

Note on testing: Diagnostic Tests and Chapter Review Posttests are included in the student text for the chapters on capitalization and punctuation. In addition, a Mechanics Pretest, a final test on each chapter, and Mechanics Mastery Reviews covering the entire section are provided in *Teaching Tests, Second Course.*

Cross references to *Teaching Tests* and to tests and worksheets in the *Teacher's Resource Book* are listed at the end of each chapter.

CHAPTER 22

Capital Letters

(pages 511–27)

Chapter Objective

Students will recognize correct capitalization and will apply seven rules of capitalization to their own writing.

Proper Nouns
(pages 513–18, rule 22d)

Objective

Students will write common nouns and proper nouns using correct capitalization.

Proper Adjectives
(pages 518–519, rule 22e)

Objective

Students will correct sentences by capitalizing proper nouns and proper adjectives.

Names of School Subjects
(page 519, rule 22f)

Objective

Students will check for and correct capitalization errors in phrases containing the names of school subjects.

Titles
(pages 519–27, rule 22g)

Objective

Students will proofread sentences for errors in the capitalization of titles.

CHAPTER 23

Punctuation End Marks, Commas, Semicolons, Colons

(pages 528–51)

Chapter Objective

Students will use end marks, commas, colons, and semicolons correctly in their writing.

END MARKS
(pages 529–31, rules 23a–23e)

Objective

Students will correct paragraphs by adding end marks.

COMMAS
(pages 531–46, rules 23f–23m)

Objectives

1. Students will correct sentences by adding commas to separate items in a series.
2. Students will add commas to separate two or more adjectives preceding a noun.
3. Students will correct compound sentences by adding commas.
4. Students will correct sentences by adding commas to set off nonessential participial phrases and adjective clauses.
5. Students will correct sentences by inserting commas after introductory participial phrases and adverb clauses.
6. Students will correct sentences by adding commas to set off appositives and appositive phrases.
7. Students will correct sentences by adding commas to set off words in direct address.
8. Students will correct sentences by adding commas to set off parenthetical expressions.
9. Students will correct dates, addresses, and parts of letters by adding commas.

SEMICOLONS
(pages 546–48, rules 23n–23p)

Objective

Students will correct sentences by using semicolons.

COLONS
(pages 548–51, rules 23q and 23r)

Objective

Students will correct sentences by adding colons.

CHAPTER 24

Punctuation Italics, Quotation Marks, Apostrophes, Hyphens

(pages 552–71)

Chapter Objective

Students will use italics, quotation marks, apostrophes, and hyphens to make their writing clear.

UNDERLINING (ITALICS)

(pages 554–55, rule 24a)

Objective

Students will correctly use underlining (italics) to indicate titles.

WRITING QUOTATIONS

(pages 555–61, rules 24b–24k)

Objectives

1. Students will punctuate and capitalize sentences that contain direct and indirect quotations.
2. Students will punctuate and paragraph dialogue.
3. Students will correct sentences by inserting quotation marks and other punctuation marks and by underlining words that should be in italics.
4. Students will write a one-page narrative, using dialogue.

APOSTROPHES

(pages 562–67, rules 24l–24o)

Objectives

1. Students will form the possessive case of singular and plural nouns.
2. Students will write the singular possessive form, the plural form, and the plural possessive form of nouns.
3. Students will use apostrophes correctly in contrac-
4. Students will use apostrophes correctly to form the plurals of letters, numbers, and signs, and of words referred to as words.

HYPHENS

(pages 567–71, rules 24p and 24q)

Objective

Students will use hyphens correctly for word division, compound numbers, and fractions used as adjectives.

CHAPTER 25

Spelling

(pages 572–93)

Chapter Objective

Students will demonstrate good spelling habits, observe spelling rules, and correctly spell words that are often confused or commonly misspelled.

Notes on Teaching Spelling

Teach spelling frequently and regularly. Plan your work so that once or twice a week students concentrate on mastering the words in this chapter and on their own spelling lists. If you make spelling a frequent, regular lesson, your students will develop a better "spelling sense" than if you work at spelling for a week and then neglect it for two or three weeks.

Teach the spelling of words in context. Give a sentence with each new word. Have students make up other sentences. In drills and tests, use complete sentences whenever practicable. Experiments have shown that learning to spell a word as an item on a list is not the same thing as learning to spell it in context.

Review constantly. In each spelling lesson, bring up words already studied. Select for review the words that have proved most troublesome.

Give frequent short tests. Two tests of ten words each are more helpful than one test of twenty-five words. In giving a test, pronounce each word distinctly, use it in a sentence, and then pronounce it again.

Vary your lessons and tests. Sometimes you may dictate sentences containing the words under study. Occasionally you may have your students play a game: Give them a few words (e.g., *American stores* or *Washington's Birthday*) and from these have them make as many other words of four or more letters as they can. The class may be divided into teams to compete with each other, and they should be allowed to use the dictionary. Even less-advanced students enjoy finding words; they often become quite excited by the competition, willingly searching in the dictionary for additions to their lists.

Teach your students that the best way to study spelling is to write the words. Many students make the mistake of merely reading the words on a list over and over, repeating the spelling again and again, aloud or to themselves. What they learn in this way is not likely to be retained for long, and it often has no effect whatsoever on their spelling when they use the word in their writing. (For this reason the spelling bee, though entertaining, is usually not very effective for teaching students to *write* words correctly.)

SPELLING RULES

(pages 573–77, rules 25a–25i)

Objectives

1. Students will spell words with *ie* and *ei* and words with *-cede*, *-ceed*, and *-sede* correctly.
2. Students will follow the rules for adding prefixes and suffixes to words.

THE PLURAL OF NOUNS

(pages 577–79, rule 25j)

Objective

Students will correctly spell the plural of nouns.

PART FOUR

RESOURCES FOR WRITING AND STUDYING

pages 595–668

Chapter 26, "Using the Dictionary," Chapter 27, "Using the Library," and Chapter 29, "Studying and Test Taking," are usually taught as individual units at some point in the year's course. Chapter 28, "Vocabulary," however, contains a word list that is meant to be presented in regular weekly lessons throughout the year, even though you will probably want to set aside a week or two for special attention to the chapter.

Cross references to *Teaching Tests* and to tests and worksheets in the *Teacher's Resource Book* are listed at the end of each chapter.

CHAPTER 26

Using the Dictionary

(pages 597–612)

Chapter Objective

Students will use the various features of the dictionary effectively.

ARRANGEMENT

(pages 598–99, rule 26a)

Objective

Students will skillfully use alphabetical order and guide words.

FINDING THE RIGHT MEANING

(pages 599–601, rule 26b)

Objective

Students will find word meanings that fit the context.

CONTENT
(pages 601–606, rule 26c)

Objective

Students will identify and locate the different kinds of information in dictionary entries.

SPELLING,
CAPITALIZATION, and
SYLLABLE DIVISION
(pages 606–609, rule 26d)

Objective

Students will use the dictionary to check the spelling, capitalization, and syllable division of words.

PRONUNCIATION
(pages 609–12, rule 26e)

Objectives

1. Students will recognize accent marks and pronunciation symbols.
2. Students will use the dictionary to find the pronunciation of words.

CHAPTER 27

Using the Library

(pages 613–25)

Chapter Objective

Students will use the library and its reference materials.

THE ARRANGEMENT OF A LIBRARY
(pages 613–15, rules 27a and 27b)

Objectives

1. Students will locate books of fiction.
2. Students will understand the Dewey decimal system of arranging nonfiction.

THE CARD CATALOG
(pages 615–17, rule 27c)

Objective

Students will use the card catalog.

REFERENCE BOOKS
(pages 618–23, rules 27d and 27e)

Objective

Students will use the following reference books: encyclopedias, atlases, almanacs, biographical reference books, and the *Readers' Guide*.

CHAPTER 28

Vocabulary

(pages 626–46)

Chapter Objective

Students will increase their vocabularies.

LEARNING NEW WORDS
(pages 628–30, rules 28a and 28b)

Objectives

1. Students will use context clues to define words.
2. Students will use the dictionary to find word meanings that fit the context.

PREFIXES, ROOTS, AND SUFFIXES
(pages 631–35, rules 28c and 28d)

Objectives

1. Students will use prefixes to define words.
2. Students will use suffixes to define words.

USING EXACT WORDS
(pages 635–40, rule 28e)

Objective

Students will use exact adjectives, verbs, and adverbs in their writing and will recognize synonyms and antonyms.

SPECIAL VOCABULARIES
(pages 640–46, rule 28f)

Objective

Students will recognize and use specialized vocabulary words.

CHAPTER 29

Studying and Test Taking
(pages 647–68)

Chapter Objective

Students will use a variety of study and test-taking skills and strategies that can apply to a wide range of assignments in school.

STUDY SKILLS
(pages 647–60, rules 29a–29h)

Objectives

1. Students will apply the SQ3R (Survey, Question, Read, Recite, Review) Study Method.
2. Students will adjust their reading rates according to their purposes.
3. Students will identify main ideas (stated and implied) and supporting details in passages.
4. Students will distinguish between fact and opinion.
5. Students will take brief but clear study notes.
6. Students will summarize material they have read.
7. Students will use their studying and writing skills for other classes such as social studies or history.

PREPARING FOR AND TAKING TESTS
(pages 661–68, rules 29i–29k)

Objectives

1. Students will apply test-taking skills to objective information in this chapter.
2. Students will analyze sample questions for essay tests.

PART FIVE

SPEAKING AND LISTENING

pages 669–96

Because speaking and listening skills involve critical thinking as well, you may want to present the two chapters of Part 5 early in the year, when you introduce the critical thinking skills related to writing.

CHAPTER 30

Speaking

(pages 671–90)

Chapter Objective

Students will compose and deliver oral presentations, evaluate speeches, and participate in group discussions.

MAKING ANNOUNCEMENTS

(pages 671–72, rule 30a)

Objective

Students will prepare and deliver announcements.

PREPARING AN ORAL REPORT

(pages 672–78, rule 30b)

Objectives

1. Students will select subjects for oral reports.
2. Students will limit these subjects to manageable topics.
3. Students will gather information for their talks.
4. Students will prepare outlines and note cards for their oral reports.
5. Students will plan interesting introductions and strong conclusions.

DELIVERING AN ORAL REPORT

(pages 678–84, rules 30c–30e)

Objectives

1. Students will recognize nonverbal communication and use it effectively when they give talks.
2. Students will pronounce their words clearly when speaking before a group.
3. Students will speak with expression—appropriate emphasis and tone.

EVALUATING A SPEECH

(pages 684–86, rule 30f)

Objective

Students will deliver prepared talks and will evaluate talks given by others.

PARTICIPATING IN GROUP DISCUSSIONS

(pages 686–90, rule 30g)

Objective

Students will participate in and evaluate group discussions.

CHAPTER 31

Listening

(pages 691–96)

Chapter Objective

Students will improve their listening skills.

LISTENING TO MEDIA

(pages 691–92, rule 31a)

Objective

Students will select their radio and television programs and movies carefully.

LISTENING TO INSTRUCTIONS and **LISTENING TO OTHERS**

(pages 692–96, rules 31b–31e)

Objectives

1. Students will follow oral directions.
2. Students will determine their purposes for listening to oral reports.
3. Students will listen for the speaker's purpose, the main ideas, and specific details.
4. Students will evaluate nonverbal signals.
5. Students will distinguish fact from opinion in talks and speeches.

SECTION IV

Model Lesson Plans

MODEL LESSON PLANS

1. A MODEL LESSON PLAN IN GRAMMAR:

For an Average or Above-average Class

Note: The following lesson plan is suitable for use with students who studied verbs in the seventh grade and who will remember some of what they learned then. A class that has never studied this material before should proceed more slowly (see Model Lesson Plan 2).

OBJECTIVE

To teach students to identify action verbs, linking verbs, helping verbs, and verb phrases (rule 12a, page 310).

MATERIALS

English Composition and Grammar, Second Course, Chapter 12, pages 309–17.

PREPARATION

For homework, the class is to have read pages 310–11 and to have written Exercise 1 (page 311).

Write the following on the board:

1. Jack appeared at the door.
2. Our guests remained until 10 o'clock.
3. The child looked for his lost dog.

a. Jack appears healthy.
b. The pine tree remains green all year.
c. The child looked sad.

PROCEDURE

1. Stare into space for a moment or two, and then ask: "What unseen actions might I just have been performing?" (Since the reading assignment covered mental-action verbs, the class should readily give answers like "thinking," "dreaming," "deciding," etc). Ask: "Why do you think it is necessary when identifying verbs to remember that some actions are unseen?" (Answer: So that students will identify *all* verbs and not skip those in which the action expressed is not obviously "action.")

Go over the answers to Exercise 1 (homework assignment). Ask students to tell whether each verb expresses physical action or mental action.

2. Call attention to the sentences on the board. Ask: "Why are the underlined words verbs?" (Answer: They express action.) Call attention to the verbs in the second group of sentences and ask the following questions:

Question: In sentence a, is Jack *appearing* someplace, as he does in sentence 1?
Answer: No.
Q. In sentence b, does the tree perform the action of *remaining* in a place, as the guests do in sentence 2?
A. No.
Q. In sentence c, is the child actually *looking* for something?
A. No.
Q. Then, do the verbs in sentences a, b, and c express action?
A. No.

3. Go over the explanation of linking verbs and the example sentences, pages 311–12. The sentences on the board may be used as additional examples. Emphasize the fact that the verb most commonly used as a linking verb is *be.* Call on students to recite the various forms of *be.*

4. Have the class write Exercise 2, page 312. However, first tell students that in order to readily identify linking verbs, they should become familiar with the list on page 312. Therefore, in filling in the blanks with linking verbs, they should use as many verbs from that list as possible.

Go over answers orally and emphasize the basic pattern of all sentences with linking verbs—subject plus linking verb plus noun or adjective.

5. Ask, "Can some of the linking verbs that you used in this exercise also be used as action verbs?" (Yes. The example sentences on the board may be used as proof.) Have the class write Exercise 3, page 313.

6. Ask if this sentence sounds correct: "We listening to the music." (No.) Call on students to supply a word or words to "help" this poor sentence. Using one of the answers, explain that these "helping" words plus the

action word *listening* make up the verb of this sentence (for example, *had been listening*). Tell the class that *had* and *been* are *helping verbs.* Explain that the verb of this sentence is comprised of more than one word, and that such a multi-word verb is called a *verb phrase.*

7. Ask: "How many words are there in a verb phrase?" (Answer: The number varies from phrase to phrase.) Demonstrate this by using the verb phrases given by the students when they corrected the sentence in Procedure 6 (for example, *are listening* and *should have been listening*).

Ask: "What are the two parts of a verb phrase?" (helping verb or verbs and the main verb.) Supply a few main verbs (such as *crawl, found, tasting*) and ask students to add helping verbs to each in order to construct verb phrases. Have students refer to the list of helping verbs on page 64. Ask for two-word phrases, three-word phrases, and four-word phrases. Write several of the phrases on the board.

Have the class write Exercise 5, page 316. Go over answers orally.

8. Summary:
   a. Ask the class to define each of the following terms: *action verb, linking verb,* and *helping verb.*
   b. Have students identify the two parts of each verb phrase on the board (from Procedure 7).

Assignment

Write Exercise 4, pages 313–14. Read the section on how other parts of speech may interrupt the verb phrase (between Exercise 5 and Review Exercise A, page 316). Begin the Writing Assignment on page 314.

2. A MODEL LESSON PLAN IN GRAMMAR:

For a Below-average Class

OBJECTIVE

To teach students to identify action verbs and linking verbs (rule 12a, page 310).

MATERIALS

English Composition and Grammar, Second Course, Chapter 12, pages 309–17.

PREPARATION

Write the following on the board:

1. Mother's pies ______ good.
2. My dog ______ sad.
3. George Washington ______ our first president.
4. My name ______ Henry.
5. The new student ______ lonely.

The cat *tasted* its food.
That tree *grows* taller each year.

PROCEDURE

1. Have the class read the definition of a *verb,* page 310, (rule 12a). Tell them they will now study the first kind of "job" done by a verb: expressing action. Walk across the room and then ask, "What word will express what I just did?" Write *walk* on the board. Ask the class what you did just now. Put *write* under the word *walk.* Complete the list by asking students for some of the actions they performed today. Label this list PHYSICAL ACTION. Then demonstrate mental-action verbs in the following manner:
   a. Ask: "Has anyone ever *dreamed* in class without the teacher's seeing it?" (Yes.) "Does someone have to move in order to perform an action like dreaming?" (No.)
   b. Write *dream* on the board under the heading MENTAL ACTION. Complete this list by asking students for other mental-action verbs.
   c. Ask: "What are the two types of action verbs?" (Mental action and physical action.)

2. Have the class do Exercise 1, page 311. When going over the answers, have the students individually identify their action verbs as showing either mental or physical action. Emphasize the fact that action is not necessarily visible.

3. Tell the class they will now meet some verbs that do not express action. Call the class's attention to the numbered sentences on the board, and call on students to fill in each blank with a single word. Then demonstrate that these words are not actions performed by the subject. (For example: Mother's pies *taste* good. Ask: "Are the pies actually *tasting* anything?") Go over the explanation of linking verbs and the example sentences, pages 311–12. Ask: "Can anyone tell me why these verbs are called linking verbs?" Then demonstrate the "linking" process in the following manner:
   a. Show that the linking verbs in the sentences on the board join the subject to a word in the predicate.

b. Ask the class to look over all the words in the predicate that are joined to subjects, both in the textbook example sentences and in the board sentences. Ask: "In sentences with linking verbs, what parts of speech will the words that are joined to the subjects be?" (Nouns or adjectives.)

4. Tell the class that the verb most commonly used as a linking verb is *be*. Have the class read aloud the different forms of *be* on page 312, and ask the students to memorize these forms. Do the same for the list of linking verbs on the same page. Then have the class write Exercise 2, pages 312–13. Ask students to use a different linking verb for each blank so that they will become familiar with all of them.

5. Call attention to the two unnumbered sentences on the board. Ask: "Are *tasted* and *grows* linking verbs?" (No. The cat is performing the action of *tasting;* the tree is actually *growing.*) Go over the six example sentences on text page 313. Have the class write Exercise 3, page 313.

6. Summary:

a. Ask: "What are the two types of verbs we studied today?" (Action verbs and linking verbs.) Ask for definitions.

b. In the time remaining, have students identify orally some of the verbs in Exercise 4, pages 313–14. When students identify a linking verb, make sure that they know which words are linked and that they can identify them as the subject and a noun or adjective in the predicate.

Assignment

Finish Exercise 4, pages 313–14.

3. A MODEL LESSON PLAN IN USAGE:

For an Average or Above-average Class

OBJECTIVE

To teach students to avoid some common errors in subject-verb agreement (rules 17a–17f, pages 419–22.)

MATERIALS

English Composition and Grammar, Second Course, Chapter 17, pages 417–22.

PREPARATION

For homework, the students were to have read pages 419–20 and to have written Exercises 1 and 3 (pages 419–20).

Write the following on the board:

The book about the early explorers (is, are) on the teacher's desk.

1. Her guests
2. The lions
3. Some
4. The average
5. Any

PROCEDURE

1. Ask, "What important fact, or facts, about the subject and verb did you study in your assignment?" (Answer: A verb agrees with its subject in number; singular subjects take singular verbs and plural subjects take plural verbs.) Call on students to read some of the answers they wrote for Exercise 3 (homework assignment).

2. Point to the sentence on the board and ask, "Which verb form is correct, *is* or *are?*" Perhaps some students will think *are* is correct. In any case, do not give the correct answer immediately; instead, allow the class to arrive at an understanding or why *is* is correct by asking the following questions:

Question: What does the sentence say is on the desk, the *book* or the *explorers?*
Answer: The book.
Q. Then what is the subject of the verb?
A. *Book.*
Q. Is *book* singular or plural? Why?
A. Singluar. There's only one book.
Q. Therefore, which verb form is correct?
A. *Is.*
Q. Furthermore, what did we learn during our lessons on the subjects of sentences that tells you *book,* and not *explorers,* determines the verb number?
A. The object of a preposition is never the subject. (If this answer is not quickly given, you may prompt the class by asking, "Are there any prepositional phrases in the complete subject?")

3. Reinforce the point above about subjects and prepositional phrases, in the following manner:

a. Read aloud Sentences 3–7 in Exercise 4, page 421. Point out that any confusion over subject and verb agreement disappears when a sentence is read without the prepositional phrase. (For example, Sentence 6: The cucumbers . . . grow very quickly.)

b. Have the class write the answers to Exercise 4, page 421. Correct the answers orally.

4. Ask, "What are some of the indefinite pronouns?" As each student gives a correct pronoun, write it on the board. After a list is compiled, tell the class that these pronouns cause many errors in agreement because often a student does not know whether they are singular or plural. Ask if each of the following takes singular or plural verbs: *everybody, neither, some, any.* The class will probably disagree as to the correct answers. (It is possible that no one in the class will know that *some* may take either a singular or a plural verb.) Have students find the correct answers themselves by reading through rules 17d, 17e, and 17f, page 422.

5. Allow the class to study these rules and examples for three minutes. Then tell students to close their books. Point to a pronoun on the board and ask a volunteer to use it in a sentence. Do this for several of the pronouns. If a student makes an error in agreement, allow another member of the class to point out the mistake and make the necessary correction.

Have the class write the answers to Exercise 5, page 423. Go over the answers orally. If someone answers incorrectly, allow this student to correct the mistake by finding and then reading aloud the rule or example on page 422 which might have been applied in answering the question.

6. Summary:

a. Ask, "What common errors in subject and verb agreement did we learn to avoid in this lesson?" Tell the class that in the next lesson they will learn to avoid other common errors in agreement.

b. Call the class's attention to the subjects written on the board. For each, call on a volunteer to add words to complete the sentence. Stipulate that each subject must be followed by a prepositional phrase. If a student makes an error in agreement, allow another member of the class to point out the error and make the necessary correction.

Assignment

Write the answers to Review Exercise A, pages 424–25. Read through Rules 17g and 17h on the agreement of verbs and compound subjects, pages 425–26. Do Exercises 6 and 7.

4. A MODEL LESSON PLAN IN USAGE:

For a Below-average Class

OBJECTIVE

To teach students to avoid a common error in subject-verb agreement (rules 17a–17c, pages 419–21).

MATERIALS

English Composition and Grammar, Second Course, Chapter 17, pages 417–22.

PREPARATION

Write the following on the board:

1. The scores on the last test
2. The cathedrals in France
3. The teachers in our school
4. The owner of the hotels
5. The mountains of that area

The first one of the little piggies go to market.

PROCEDURE

1. To engage the students' interest and to review the meaning of singular and plural, allow a few minutes of debate on the question "Is a pair of scissors singular or plural?"

Tell the class that *all* nouns and pronouns are either singular or plural. Explain that although most of us use the correct singular or plural form without thinking about it, sometimes it is necessary to think carefully about the number of a noun or pronoun subject. Then tell the class that before the lesson is over, they will find out why.

Have the class write Exercise 1, page 419. Go over the answers orally. Ask, "How do we generally form plural nouns?" (By adding *-s* to the singular.) Use words in Exercise 1 as illustrations. Then ask: "Which plurals in Exercise 1 do not end in *-s*?" (*Feet, them, passersby.*) Ask for volunteers to contribute other plural nouns or pronouns which do not end in *-s* (for example, *women,* *geese, oxen*). Ask, "Therefore, can we always identify plurals by looking for the *-s* ending?" (No.) Point out that some words, such as *friendliness,* end in *-s,* yet are singular.

2. Have the class do Exercise 2, page 419, orally. Ask the following questions:

Question: How does the verb for *lion* (Exercise 2, Item 1) end?
Answer: In an *-s.*
Q. Is *lion* singluar or plural?
A. Singular.
Q. If we changed *lion* to *lions* would the verb ending change? How?
A. Yes. The *-s* would be dropped.

3. Go over rules 17b(1) and 17b(2) and the examples, page 420. Have the class write Exercise 3, page 420. Go over answers orally. Use Item 5, "the men *were,*" to show how *be* is conjugated differently from other verbs. Have various students read aloud the examples on page 420. Ask, "If someone were to say 'the men *is,*' how would you explain the mistake?" (Answer: The verb does not agree with the subject in number; *men* requires the plural verb *are.*)

4. Point to the sentence on the board and ask, "Does the verb *go* agree with its subject *piggies?*" (*Piggies* is not the subject. If no student corrects your error, call attention to the prepositional phrase "of the piggies" and ask if any word in a prepositional phrase is ever the subject.) Emphasize that the verb must agree with *one,* which is the subject, not with *piggies,* which is the object of a preposition. Go over rule 17c and the NONSTANDARD and STANDARD examples, page 421.

5. Summary.
   a. Ask, "Who knows why it is often necessary to think carefully about the number of a noun or pronoun subject?" (Answer: To avoid making errors in subject-verb agreement.)
   b. Call the class's attention to the complete subjects written on the board. For each complete subject, ask volunteers to add words to finish the sentence. (For example, "The scores on the last test *were much higher than our teacher had predicted.*") If a student makes an error in agreement, ask if the verb agrees with the subject or with the object of the preposition.

Assignment

Do Exercise 4, page 421.

5. A MODEL LESSON PLAN IN SENTENCE STRUCTURE:

For an Average or Above-average Class

OBJECTIVE

To teach students to combine short, choppy sentences into compound or complex sentences (rules 9f and 9g pages 249 and 251) and to utilize the sentence-combining techniques they learned in rules 9a–e.

MATERIALS

English Composition and Grammar, Second Course, Chapter 9, pages 241–56.

PREPARATION

For homework, the class was to have reviewed pages 241–49, including their work on Exercises 1–5 and Review Exercise A. Students were to have read pages 249–50 and to have written Exercise 6 (pages 250–51).

Write the following on the board:

1. Our houseplants have started to turn brown. We bought shrubs last year.
2. The speech was informative. The discussion after the speech was boring.

PROCEDURE

1. Direct attention to the sentences on the board, and ask, "Why might you want to revise sentences such as these in your compositions?" (Because a long series of short, choppy sentences would sound monotonous.) To demonstrate the combining of simple sentences into compound sentences, have various students read some of the sentences they wrote for homework (Exercise 6). Then ask the class to explain why they would or would not combine each pair of simple sentences on the board into a compound sentence. (The first pair should not be combined, because the ideas are not closely related. The second pair may be combined.) Have the class go over orally the remaining answers to Exercise 6, emphasizing the fact that only sentences with closely related ideas should be combined.

2. Ask, "Besides the compound sentence, what other type of sentence can be used to join related ideas?" (Complex.) Review the complex sentence by asking the following questions:

Question: What are the two parts of a complex sentence?
Answer: An independent clause and a subordinate clause.
Q. What are the two kinds of subordinate clauses that we have studied?
A. Adjective clauses and adverb clauses.

3. Go over the examples of how to make a complex sentence out of two simple sentences by using an adjective clause, pages 251–252. Emphasize the fact that in combining two ideas into a complex sentence, the more important idea should be put in the independent clause while the less important one is subordinated. Have students write Exercise 7, page 253. Go over the answers orally.

4. Go over the examples of how to make a complex sentence out of two simple sentences by using an adverb clause, pages 253–54. Have the class write Exercise 8, pages 254–55, and go over answers orally. Then go over the examples of how a false or meaningless relationship can be made by using a poorly chosen subordinating conjunction, page 254. (If any students have used poorly chosen conjunctions in answers to Exercise 3, use these answers too as examples.)

5. For practice in combining sentences without changing the meaning of the revised sentences, have the class do Review Exercise B, page 255, orally.

6. Summary:
   a. Remind the class that in this lesson both compound and complex sentences have been used to combine short sentences. Ask, "When can two simple sentences be combined into a compound sentence?" (When the ideas expressed in the sentences are closely related and of equal importance.) "What happens when you combine two simple sentences into a complex sentence?" (One idea is subordinated to the other.)
   b. Ask, "What are some of the subordinating conjunctions used to introduce subordinate clauses?" (See list on page 253.)
   c. Ask, "What are the relative pronouns usually used to introduce adjective clauses?" (*Who, whom, whose, which,* and *that.*)
   d. Turn to the example paragraphs on page 242. Have students explain how the sentences were rewritten in the second paragraph. (For example, the first four sentences in the original version have been combined into one sentence containing a compound subject and two prepositional phrases.)

Assignment

Write the answers to Review Exercise C, pages 255–56.

6. A MODEL LESSON PLAN IN SENTENCE STRUCTURE:
For a Below-average Class

OBJECTIVE

To teach students to recognize and correct run-on sentences (rule 8e, page 236).

MATERIALS

English Composition and Grammar, Second Course, Chapter 8, pages 236–40.

PREPARATION

Write the following on the board:

1. I became annoyed by the chatter at the party I went home.
2. Because I stuffed myself with too much chicken.
3. The engine of our car began making funny noises, the mechanic had to take it apart.
4. Jerry and I will leave tomorrow we will pack our lunches tonight.
5. Watching the automobile show. I lost track of the time.
6. The new road opened last week, traffic has been heavy.
7. Many days passed nobody came to visit me.

PROCEDURE

1. Ask, "Who remembers what a sentence fragment is?" Call attention to the board, and ask, "Do any of these

groups of words contain fragments?" (Yes, numbers 2 and 5.) Emphasize the fact that there is not enough written in a sentence fragment. Ask, "If it is possible to write an incorrect sentence by not writing enough, what other kind of error can we make in writing a sentence?" (Writing too much.) Point to the first example on the board and ask, "Does this sentence have too much in it? Why?" (Yes. There are really two sentences here.) Then ask the class how they would correct this example. (By placing a period after *party.*) Tell the class that they have just corrected a *run-on sentence.* Write this term on the board. Tell students that the main object of today's lesson is to learn how to eliminate run-on sentences from their writing. Point out that before they can eliminate run-ons, they must, of course, learn to identify them.

2. Go over rule 8e and the examples on pages 236–37. Point to the examples on the board and ask, "Why are most of these sentences run-ons?" (They consist of two or more sentences separated by a comma or by no mark of punctuation.) For each run-on, ask a student to go to the board and, using chalk and eraser, make it into two sentences. If a student places the period incorrectly, allow another student to point out the error and make the necessary corrections at the board.

3. Point out that many run-on sentences occur because the writer has used a comma in place of a period or a question mark. Use the example sentence for Exercise 6, pages 237–38, to demonstrate this point. Have the class write Exercise 6. Warn them first, however, to watch out for commas that are used in place of periods. Check the answers orally.

4. Point out that, thus far, the class has been correcting only single run-on sentences. Ask, "What did we say the main objective of learning to identify run-ons was?" (To eliminate them from our writing.) Point out that any run-ons in student writing will occur as parts of a paragraph rather than as isolated examples. Go over the example paragraph for Exercise 7, page 238. Have the class do the first paragraph in the exercise orally. Then have all the students except two write the answers for the second and third paragraphs. Send these two students to the board, one to write answers for the fourth paragraph, the other to do the fifth paragraph. Go over all the answers with the class.

5. Summary:
   a. Tell the class that for homework they will be writing a paragraph about a comic strip character, and that the main purpose of this assignment will be to write a paragraph free of run-ons and fragments.
   b. Tell students that the following exercise will help them with their homework assignment because it will give them practice in determining whether a sentence is correct or whether it is a fragment or a run-on. Have the class write answers to Review Exercise B, pages 239–40. Check the answers orally, reviewing the reasons why groups of words are fragments or run-ons. (For example, Number 9, "A young, handsome warrior," has no verb and therefore must be a fragment.)

Assignment

Do Review Exercise C, page 240.

7. A MODEL LESSON PLAN IN COMPOSITION:

For a Below-average Class

OBJECTIVE

To teach students how to write a paragraph using chronological order.

MATERIALS

English Composition and Grammar, Second Course, Chapter 2, pages 50–51.

PREPARATION

Write on the board the list of ingredients and the following steps (they are purposely out of order) for making French toast.

Ingredients: one egg, two tablespoons milk, one teaspoon margarine, one slice of bread
1. Put dipped bread into pan
2. Serve warm
3. Beat the eggs and the milk
4. Put margarine into frying pan
5. Fry on one side
6. When brown, turn over and fry on the other side
7. Dip slice of bread into mixture

Ask the students to explain why the steps for making the French toast are difficult to follow. (They are out of order.) Call on a volunteer to put the steps in order. Next Write *chronological order* on the chalkboard. Explain to the class that the steps are now in chronological order —the order in which the steps logically occur.

PROCEDURE

1. Read through rule 2f, subrule (1), and the text that follows them on page 50. Then read the model paragraph on pages 50–51.
2. Ask the students to explain why the ideas in the model paragraph are easy to follow. (The ideas are arranged according to a definite plan, that is, chronological order. The reader learns what occurred first, next, etc.)
3. Read through Exercise 5, with the students following along. Depending on your class's abilities, you might want to have them gather additional information on the topic. Begin the Prewriting part with them; that is, have the students put the details in chronological order. You might want to have the students follow these steps for completing the Prewriting part: (1) write the topic sentence at the top of a sheet of paper, (2) Number from 1–8, below the topic sentence, and (3) write the details in order as they are given (by volunteers).

Assignment

Complete Exercise 5. Be prepared to share your paragraphs with the class.

8. A MODEL LESSON PLAN IN COMPOSITION:

For an Average or Above-average Class

OBJECTIVE

To review coherence in a paragraph, in particular spatial order and order of importance.

MATERIALS

English Composition and Grammar, Second Course, Chapter 2, pages 51–53.

PREPARATION

Students are supposed to have read pages 51–53.

PROCEDURE

1. Review rule 2f (page 50) and subrule (2) (page 51) with the students. Explain that they will use spatial order as an arrangement in a paragraph when they write description, that is, when they describe a place, person, or thing.
2. Ask the students to describe the different kinds of spatial orders (near to far, right to left, top to bottom, outside to inside.) Ask students to describe the arrangement of ideas in the model paragraph on page 52 (from outside to inside).
3. Call on volunteers to read the paragraphs they wrote for Exercise 6 aloud.
4. Explain to the students that another kind of arrangement in a paragraph is order of importance. Read aloud the rule on page 53 and the text following it on page 53. Have a volunteer read the model paragraph on page 53. Then read the text below the model paragraph and call on another volunteer to answer the question: *What are the four reasons?* You might want to ask these questions in addition: *What is the most important reason? Is it effective at the end of the paragraph? Why?*

Assignment

Complete Exercise 7. Refer to page 15 for information-gathering techniques that will help you gather reasons to support your topic sentence.

Answer Key

ANSWER KEY

CHAPTER 1

Writing and Thinking

p. 10 EXERCISE **4**

Details you would include in a letter to a Japanese pen pal:

1. In winter I ride the bus, because we have a lot of snow and temperatures that are often below zero.
2. School starts at 7:30 in the morning and ends at 3:15.
3. Every day I have five classes, each taught by a different teacher.
4. Our town has two high schools and three junior high schools.
5. In nice spring and fall weather, I ride my bicycle to school.

Details you would include in a letter to a former classmate who has just moved to a town fifty miles away:

1. We watched the breakdancing on the river walk.
2. We took a field trip to the farm museum and watched a demonstration of plowing with horses.
3. The junior high band will perform at the Spring Festival.
4. Saturday I played a new video game with Enrique and his sister at the arcade in the mall.
5. Thursday there was a tornado warning. A siren went off, but nothing happened.

p. 27 EXERCISE **14**

Facts about comets
- Comets only visible as they approach the sun
- Two kinds: those with straight, gaseous tails and those with curving, dusty tails
- Have a small nucleus, a coma, or head, and a tail
- Composed of icy particles
- Usually look pink

The history of Halley's comet
- 1577—Queen Elizabeth I forbade anyone to look at comet
- Halley's comet—first observation recorded by Chinese in 240 B.C.
- Middle Ages—thought Halley's comet would bring famine and plagues
- 1910—Earth passing through tail of Halley's comet; anti-comet pills taken for protection

The latest appearance of Halley's comet
- In November 1985, tail 50 million miles long
- On latest orbit first visible to naked eye in November, 1985
- Comet at brightest from February to March 1986

CHAPTER 2

Writing Paragraphs

p. 62 EXERCISE **10**

(Answers will vary. Sample answers are given.)

1. To describe
2. To persuade
3. To explain or inform
4. To explain or inform
5. To describe

p. 77 EXERCISE **22**

(Answers may vary somewhat.)

In the creation myth of the Iroquois tribe, the earth began when the mother of earth fell *through* a hole in the sky. She fell into an endless lake, but fortunately with her fell a cosmic tree *that* had some magical earth around *its* roots. The young woman who fell from the sky was saved from drowning by two swans. Then *four* animals—Otter, Beaver, Muskrat, and Toad—each dived to the bottom of the lake to try to get some of the magical earth on the *tree's* roots. Otter, Beaver, and Muskrat *drowned, but* Toad was able to get a single mouthful of the earth. *It* grew first into an island for the mother of earth to stand on. *Then* it grew and grew and kept right on growing until it became the *whole* world.

CHAPTER 3

Writing Paragraphs

p. 85 EXERCISE **4**

(Answers will vary. Sample answers are given.)

1. Shiny, deep green, waxen, shriveled stem, sculptured sides
2. Dull brown, edges worn smooth, dated 1975, letter D (Denver mint) beneath the date, back lettering is upside down when you turn the coin over
3. Red-handled, white bristles, bristles beginning to spread apart and look frayed, whitish deposit of toothpaste at base of bristles, toothbrush marked "soft" in white letters beginning to blur
4. Yellow-orange "Velvet" brand, number 2, letters stamped in blue, no eraser left, dull point
5. White running shoe with silver-blue wing-shaped decorations on side, gray rubber cleats, shoelaces dirty at ends, one lace frayed with tip gone

CHAPTER 5

Writing Exposition

p. 149 EXERCISE **19**

1. School activities
    Athletic activities
        football
        baseball
        gymnastics
    School clubs
        glee club
        science club
        drama club
2. Model planes
    Materials
        balsa wood
        sharp knife
        blueprints
        paint
        glue
    Procedures
        cutting out parts
        gluing parts together
        painting

p. 154 EXERCISE **24**

Taking a Camping Trip

Purpose: To explain how to prepare for and take a safe camping trip

I. Planning
    A. Selecting equipment
        1. Knives, hatchets, and axes
        2. Food, pans, plates, spoons, etc.
        3. Bedding
        4. Tents
    B. Selecting clothing
II. Setting up camp
    A. Choosing a campground
        1. Presence of fuel
        2. Dry ground
    B. Setting up tents
    C. Making a fire
        1. Chopping wood
        2. Arranging the wood
    D. Purifying water
III. Camp health and safety
    A. Personal health
    B. Safety tips
        1. Safety when hiking
        2. Safety in the water

p. 162 EXERCISE **31**

(Answers will vary somewhat in wording.)

1. Yes, the word *also* is a transition, but it is not very visible.
2. Yes, it develops II. B., "Post office."
3. No, the sentence on buying or ordering foreign stamps should tell where. The sentence about foreign stamps being unusual is not related to the topic and should be omitted.
4. No, the sentence about large post offices should follow the first sentence.
5. *Places* needs to be made more specific. *Local* should be *domestic,* the opposite of *foreign.*
6. Answers will vary but should include the recommendations made in numbers 3, 4, and 5.

CHAPTER 6

Writing Exposition

p. 193 EXERCISE 12

(Answers will vary.)

1. The limited topic is the lost colony of Roanoke—how it began and what happened to it. Yes, it is suitable for a short, factual report. The topic involves a mystery that is intriguing to most eighth-grade students.
2. The first paragraph captures the interest of readers by announcing a daring adventure the colonists are about to undertake.
3. The conclusion points out that, even though the original colony—Roanoke—was lost, it helped the colony of Jamestown, recognized as the first colony in the New World, to succeed.
4. The first sentence of paragraph 2 is the topic sentence. The remaining details explain why earlier groups of English people sailed to the New World, and with what result.
5. The topic sentence of paragraph 7 is the first sentence. Remaining details in the paragraph tell why John White thought he knew where the missing colonists had gone.
6. Paragraph 4 tells how the Roanoke colonists worked to make the New World their home but also how they remained dependent for a long time on getting supplies from England. It was for that reason that John White agreed to return to England.
7. Paragraph 9 gives some of the possible explanations for the disappearance of the colonists.
8. In paragraph 3, the settlers arrived at Roanoke Island. By paragraph 6, the settlers had disappeared.
9. The transition word "although" connects these sentences.
10. The word "now" connects these sentences.

CHAPTER 7

Writing Letters and Completing Forms

p. 206 EXERCISE 3

1.

(Student's name
and address)

Ms. Ellen Craig
111 Orchid Way
Butte, Montana 59601

2.

(Student's name
and address)

Dr. N. T. Bain
P.O. Box 753
Winamac, Indiana 46996

p. 216 EXERCISE 7

Judy Muller
32 Brenda Drive
Flagstaff, Arizona 86001

Acme Outfitting Company, Inc.
P.O. Box 289
Milwaukee, Wisconsin 53248

p. 216 EXERCISE **7** Continued

32 Brenda Drive
Flagstaff, Arizona 86001
December 2, 1988

Acme Outfitting Company, Inc.
P.O. Box 289
Milwaukee, Wisconsin 53248

Customer Service Department:

Kindly send me your mail order catalog on sporting goods and hunting and fishing equipment. Thank you.

Yours truly,
Judy Muller
Judy Muller

CHAPTER 8

Writing Complete Sentences

p. 232 EXERCISE **2**

(Answers may vary slightly.)

Fifteen very young dinosaurs were waiting in a nest while their mother went looking for food. Before the adult dinosaur could return, disaster struck. The small prehistoric creatures all perished when a volcano buried the nest in debris.

Scientists recently uncovered the fossils of these small dinosaurs, which lived 70 million years ago. After they studied the remaining fragments of bones, scientists reconstructed the appearance of the dinosaurs. The name given to these extinct lizards was *hadrosaur,* which means "duck-billed lizard." Adult hadrosaurs were plant eaters that could scoop up vegetation from watery swamps.

The discovery of these fossils was important because it shed light on one of the mysteries about dinosaurs. Before this recent discovery was made, scientists debated whether dinosaurs were coldblooded or warmblooded. Fossil evidence shows these tiny hadrosaurs were living in a nest. They were likely warmblooded because few coldblooded animals are fed by their parents or protected in nests.

p. 234 EXERCISE **4**

(Answers will vary.)

Alice's Adventures in Wonderland is a literary classic read by college students as well as elementary-school students. Every child enjoys this story, missing some of the fun but laughing at many of the comic incidents. When children grow up, they read the story again, finding more humor in it.

In one of the most famous episodes in the book, Alice finds herself at an unusual tea party given by the Hatter. The Hatter and his companions, the March Hare and the Dormouse, being very lazy, have allowed dirty dishes to pile up all over. The Dormouse tells a long story, falling asleep in the middle. The March Hare offers Alice wine. After accepting the offer, she is told that there is no wine. For a while the three creatures ask her riddles having no answers. Then they ignore her, carrying on a ridiculous conversation among themselves. Finally, Alice, thoroughly exhausted, manages to escape.

p. 235 REVIEW EXERCISE **A**

(Answers will vary.)

1. As I was driving home, I saw a turtle on the highway.
2. While trying to cross the road, it had been rolled over on its back by a car.
3. Now it was lying there in the middle of the highway, helplessly moving its feet back and forth.
4. Because I remembered that a turtle cannot get off its back on a smooth surface, I stopped the car and picked the animal up.
5. It immediately drew its feet and head under its shell, so that I could see no more than two eyes staring at me from inside the shell.

6. The turtle was a box turtle, a very shy land dweller.
7. Because I wanted to observe it for a while, I took it to Tall Oaks, my parents' cottage in the mountains.
8. Arriving there, I put the turtle down on a rug which covers most of the living room floor.
9. After being still for almost ten minutes, the turtle slowly began to stick its feet and head out from its shell.
10. As soon as if felt safe, it crawled very awkwardly but quickly across the rug, heading for a corner of the room.

CHAPTER 9

Writing Effective Sentences

p. 249 REVIEW EXERCISE **A**

(Answers will vary.)

The deep Majestic River runs swiftly between high mountains. Lush, green vegetation crowds the river's shores and grows up the mountain slopes. Campers and day hikers fish in the clear pools beneath the river's rapids. Canoes and rubber rafts can navigate the river from High Falls to Bolt's Landing.

CHAPTER 10

The Sentence

p. 284 EXERCISE **16**

1. Midas | is
2. He | was
3. One | gave
4. Midas | could turn
5. This | could be done

6. gift | pleased
7. it | became
8. you | Do know
9. (you) | Read
10. people | can make

p. 285 EXERCISE **17**

1. 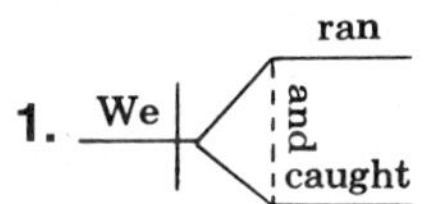

2. 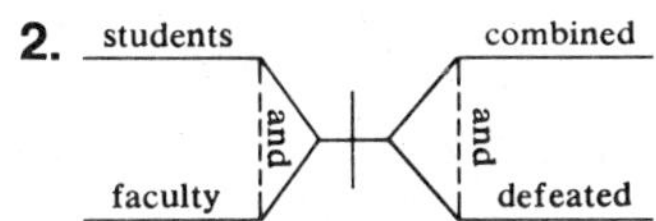

3. 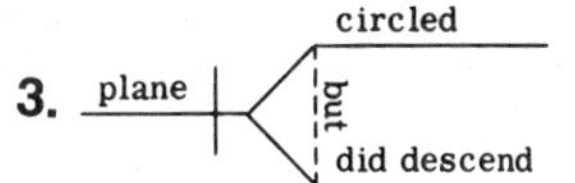

4. 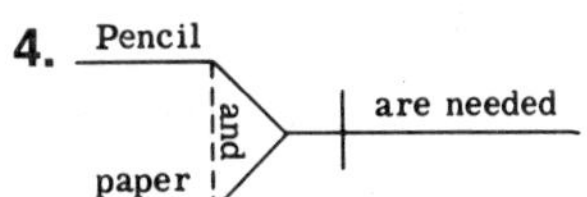

5. 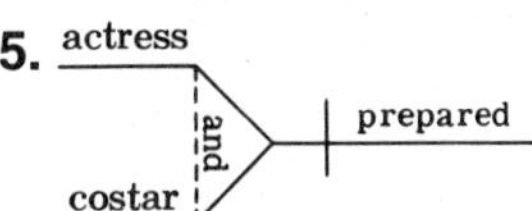

CHAPTER 11

The Parts of Speech

p. 294 REVIEW EXERCISE **A**

PROPER NOUNS	COMMON NOUNS
Lincoln Memorial	day*
Washington	people
Henry Bacon	monument
Memorial Day	hall

PROPER NOUNS	COMMON NOUNS
West Potomac Park	statue
Lincoln Memorial	figure
Abraham Lincoln	blocks
Daniel Chester French	marble
Lincoln	sculptor
Gettysburg Address	armchair
	meditation
	wall
	passage
	address
	wall

* *In this sentence, day is a noun used as an adverb; some teachers call it an adverb.*

p. 306 EXERCISE **10**

1. 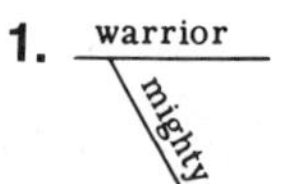

2. ox | big | blue

3. 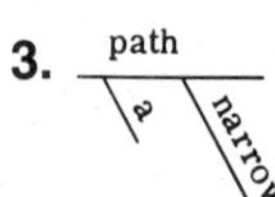

4. movie | long | exciting

5. 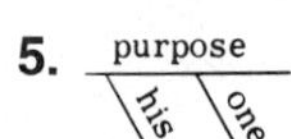

6. one | the | last

7. 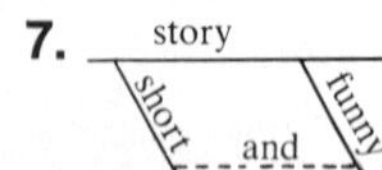

8. others | many

9. offer | my | final

10. turtle | the | slow | but | persistent

p. 306 EXERCISE **11**

1. 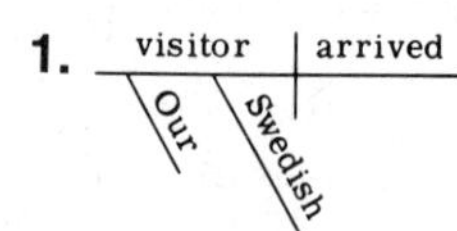

2. answers | were given | Several

3. 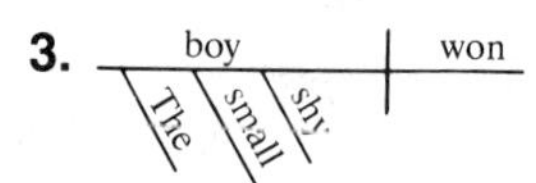

4. 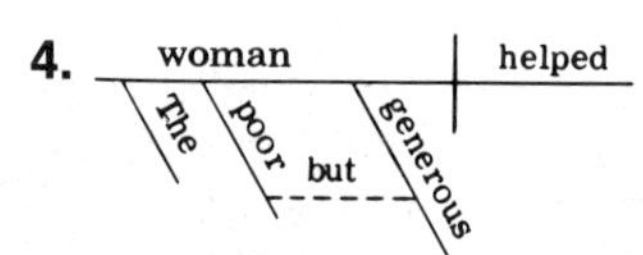

5. 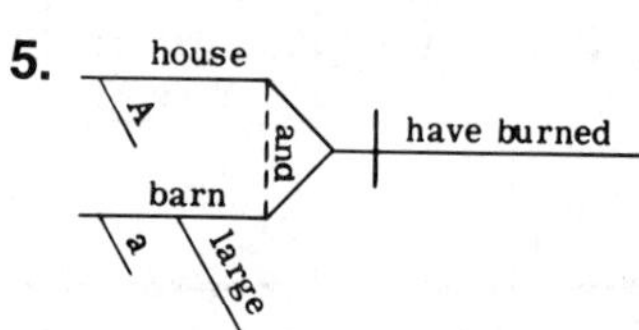

p. 307 REVIEW EXERCISE **E**

1. 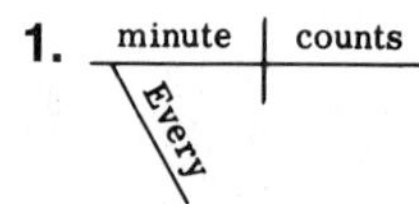

2. 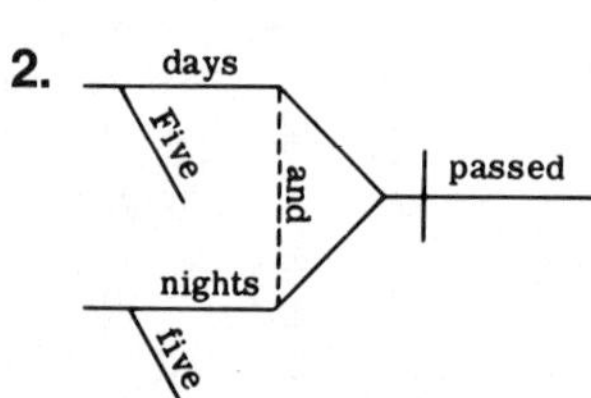

3. 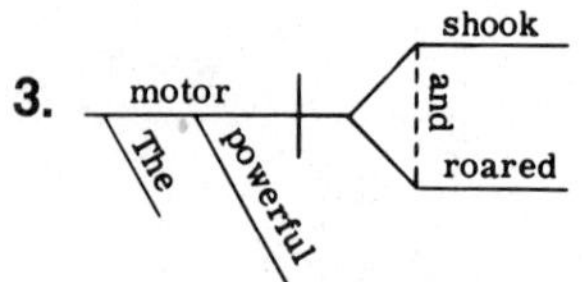

4. 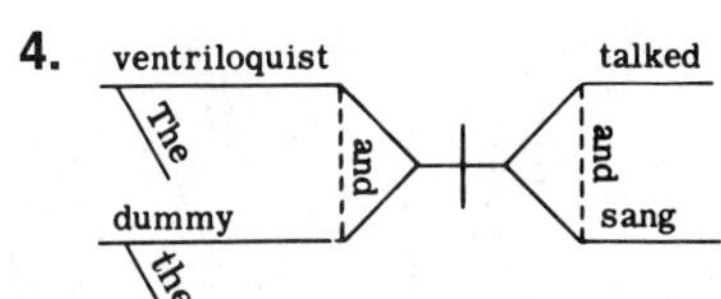

5. 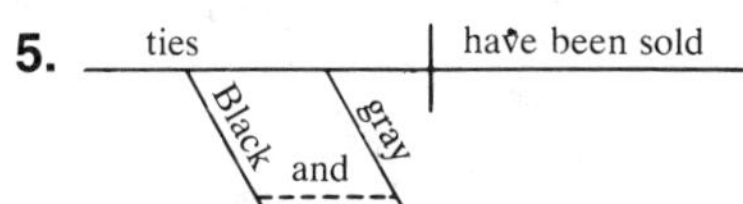

CHAPTER 12

The Parts of Speech

p. 323 EXERCISE 10

1. 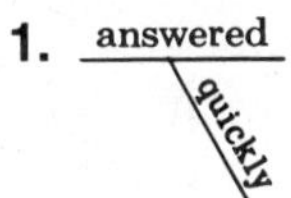

2. 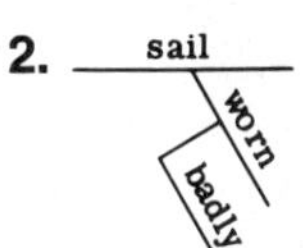

3. 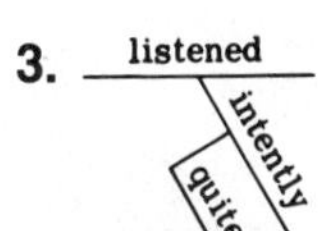

4. 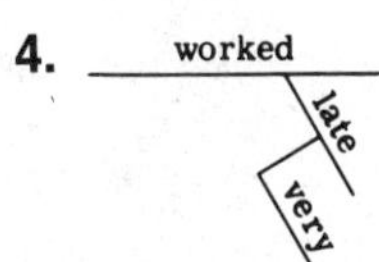

5. 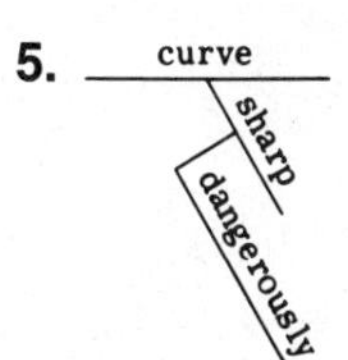

6. 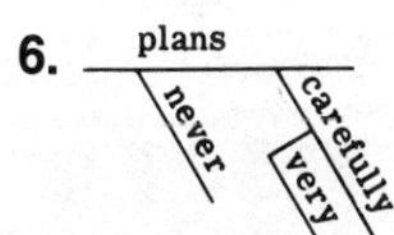

7. walked
proudly
away

8. 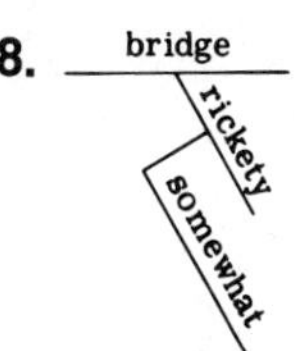

9. may happen
possibly

10. drove
slowly
rather

p. 323 EXERCISE 11

1. 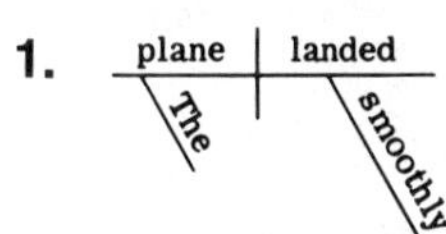

2. 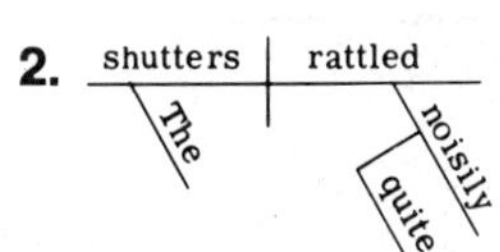

3. 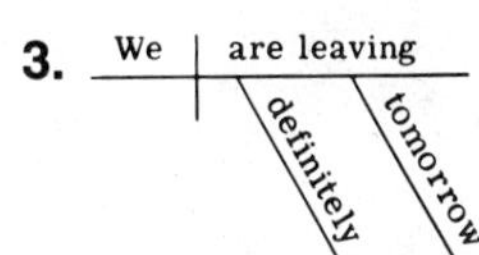

4. 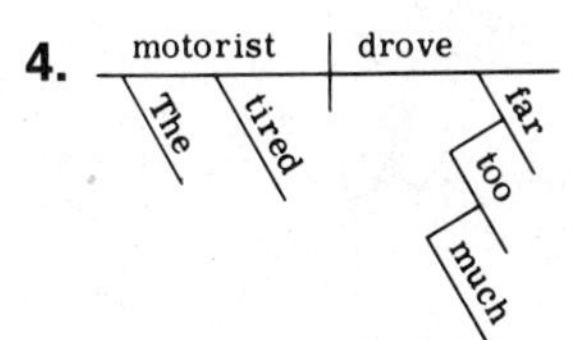

5. 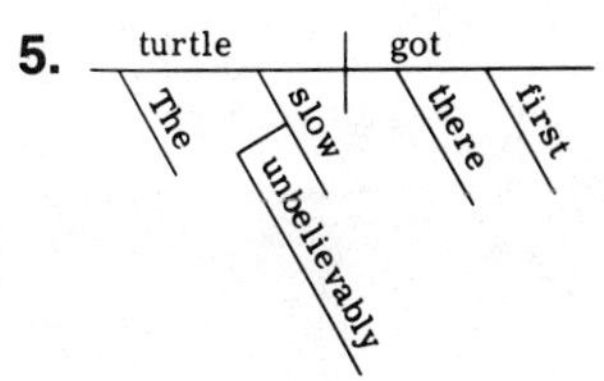

6. 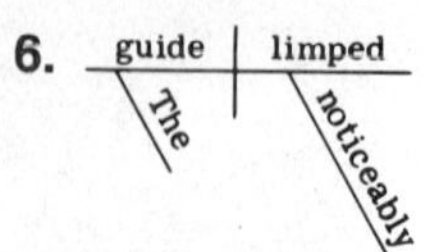

7. 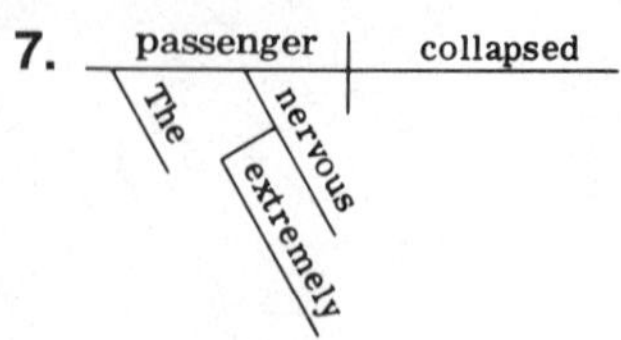

8. 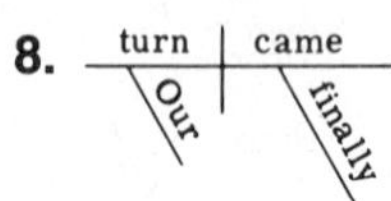

9. 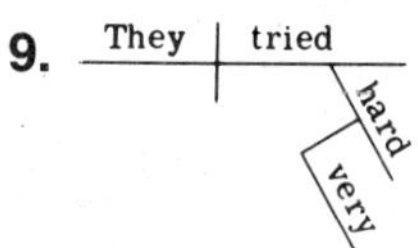

10. 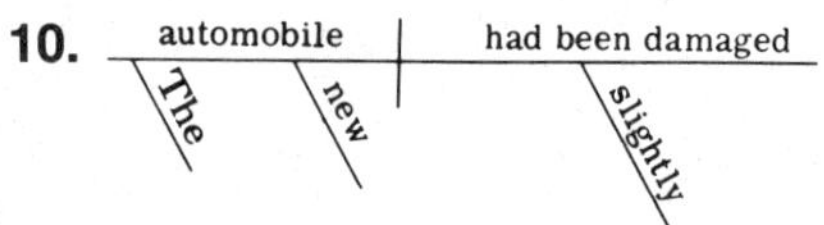

CHAPTER 13

Complements

p. 343 EXERCISE 5

1. 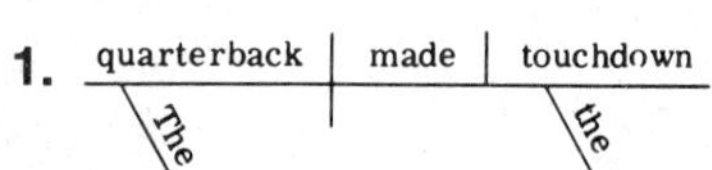

2. 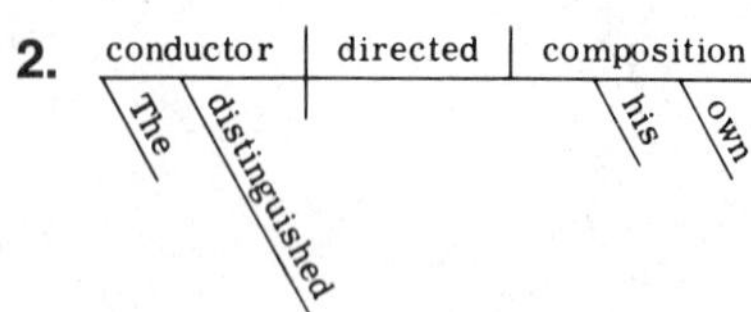

3. 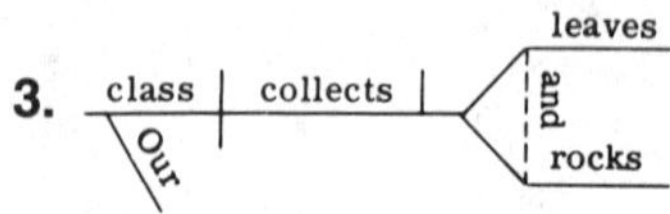

4. 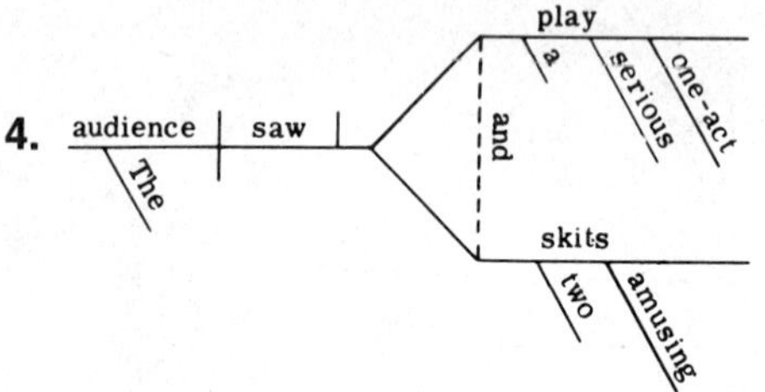

5. 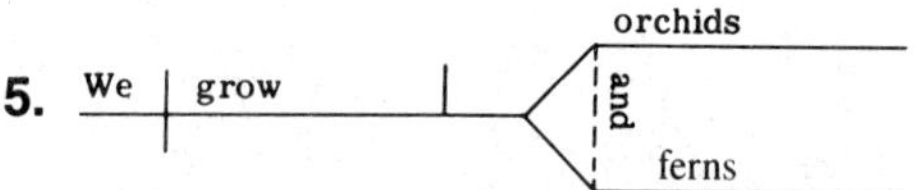

(Note: one-act play *may also be diagramed as one noun.)*

p. 344 EXERCISE 6

1. 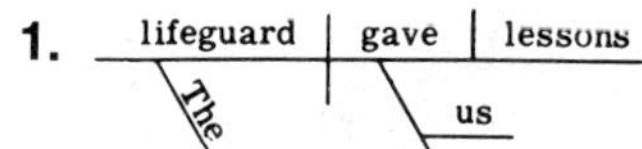

2. 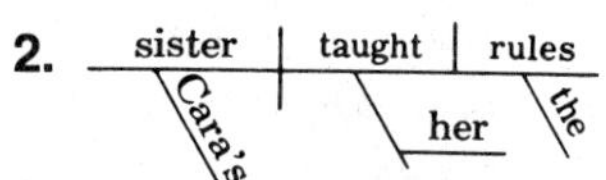

3. 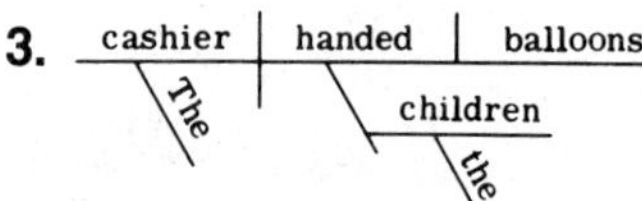

4. 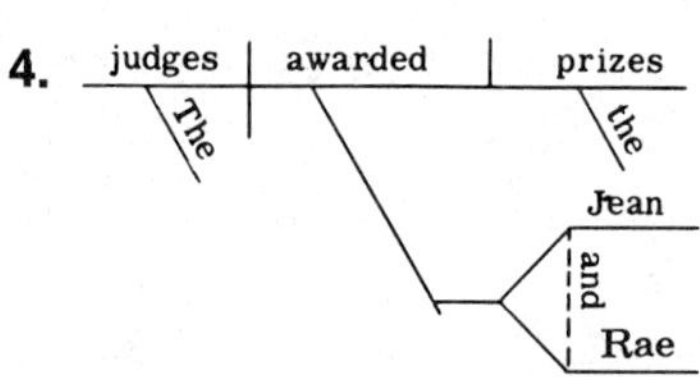

5. 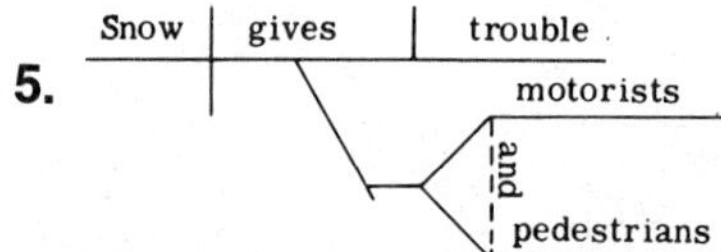

p. 349 EXERCISE 8

1. 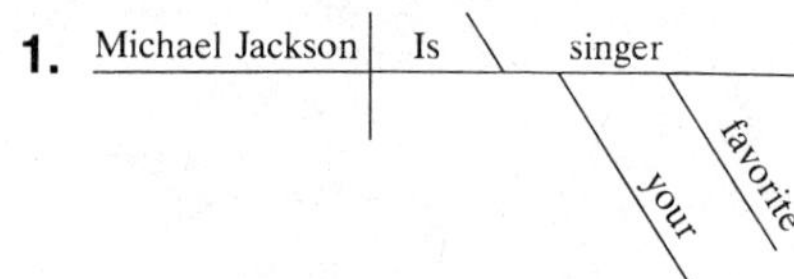

2.

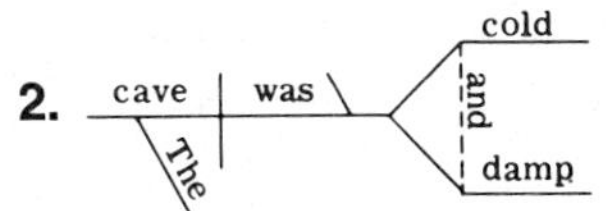

3.

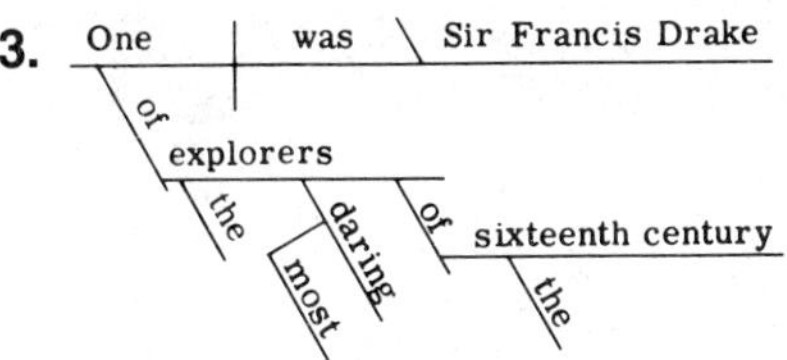

(Note: sixteenth *may also be diagramed as a modifier of* century.*)*

4.

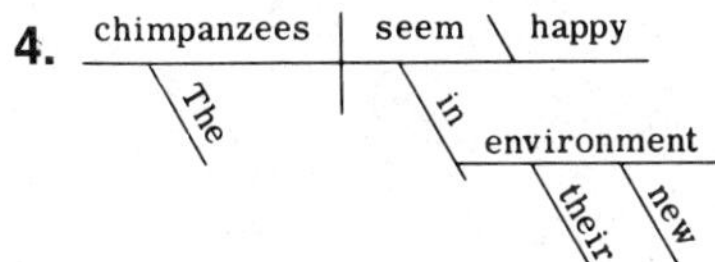

5.

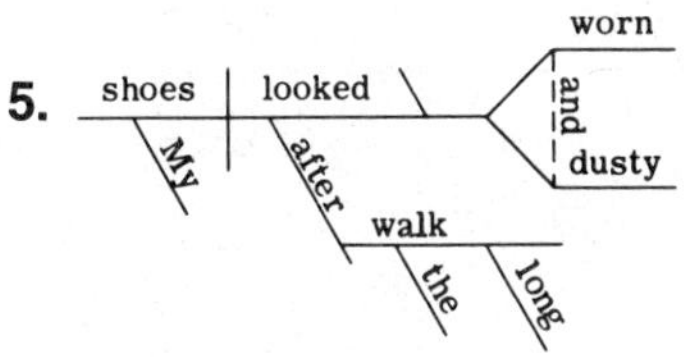

p. 350 REVIEW EXERCISE D

1.

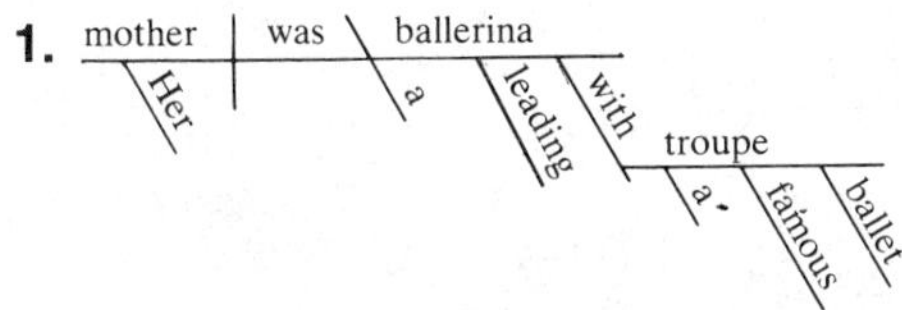

(Note: ballet troupe *may also be diagramed as one noun.)*

2.

3.

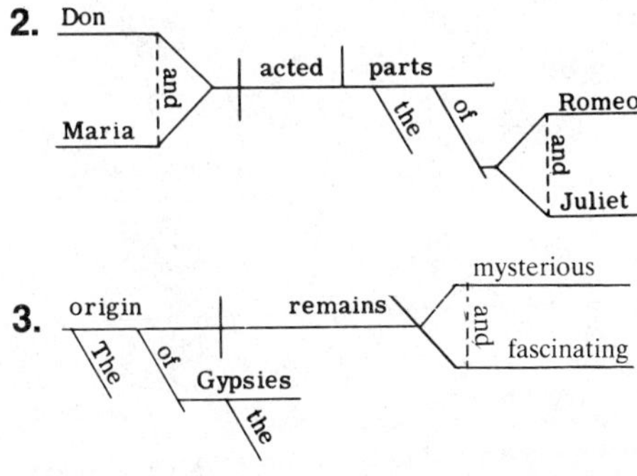

4.

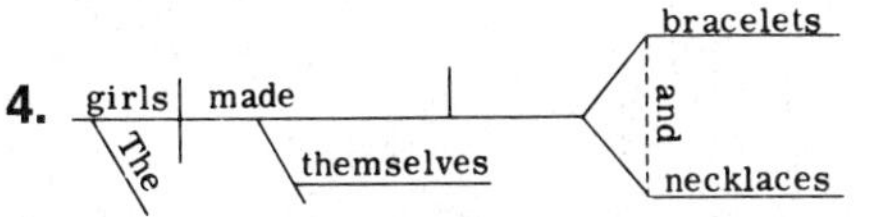

5.

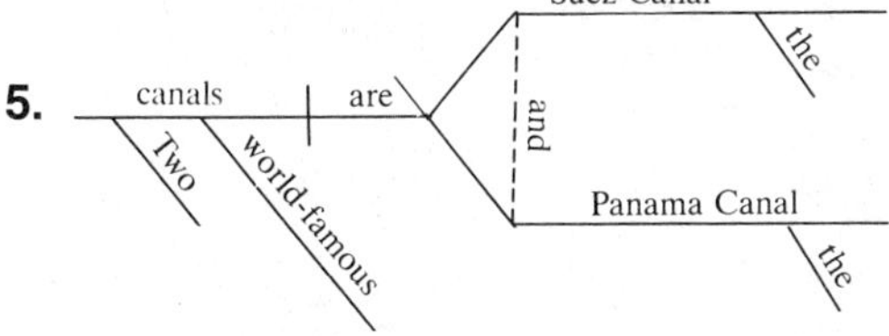

CHAPTER 14

The Phrase

p. 360 EXERCISE 7

1.

2.

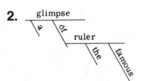

glimpse

a

of

ruler

the

famous

3.

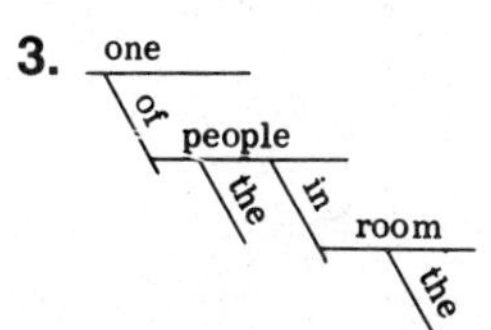

4.

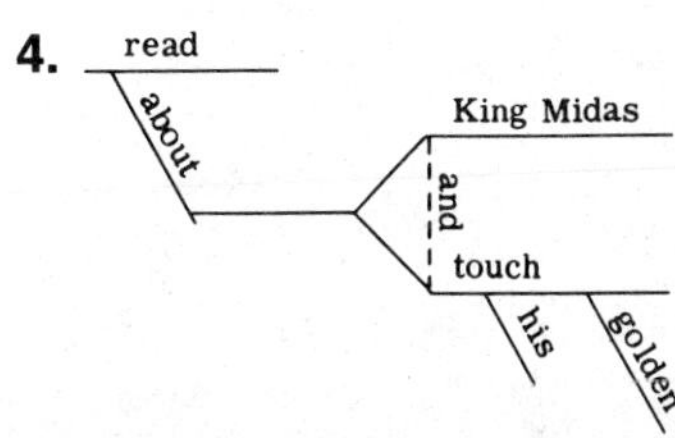

5.

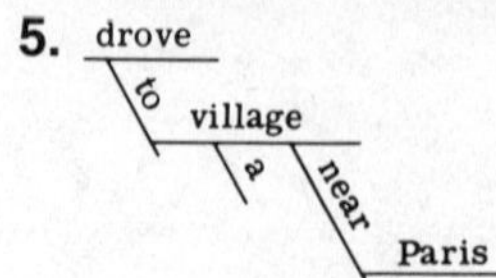

p. 360 EXERCISE 8

1.

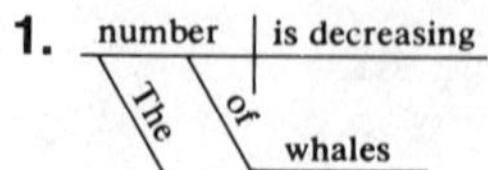

2.

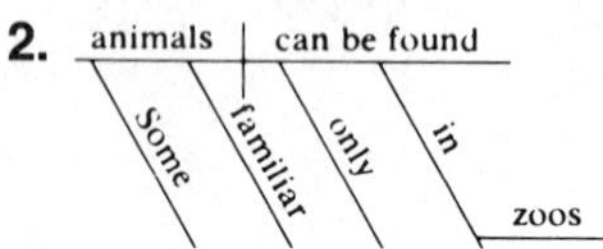

3.

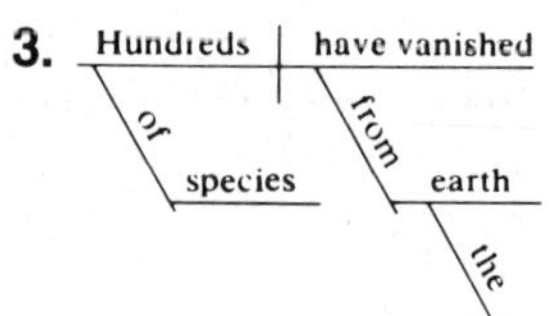

4.

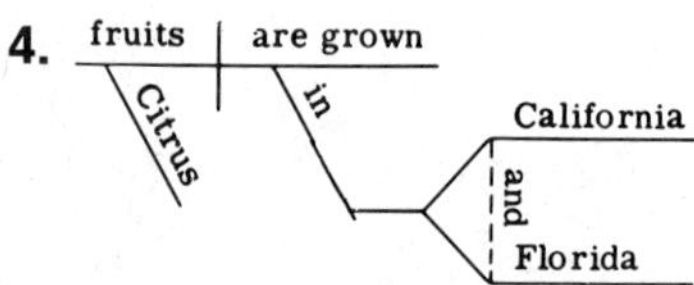

5.

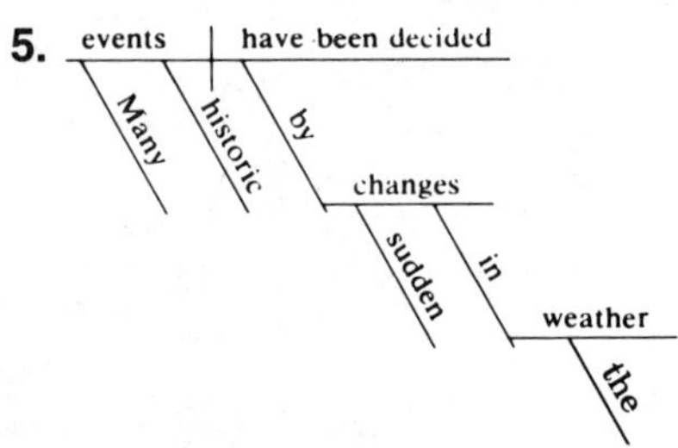

6.

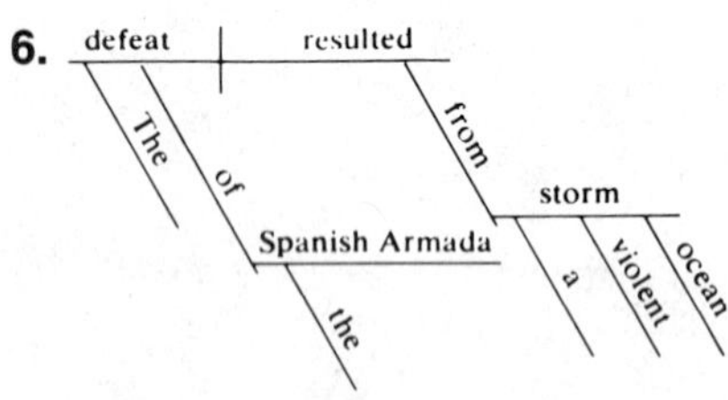

p. 375 EXERCISE 18

1.

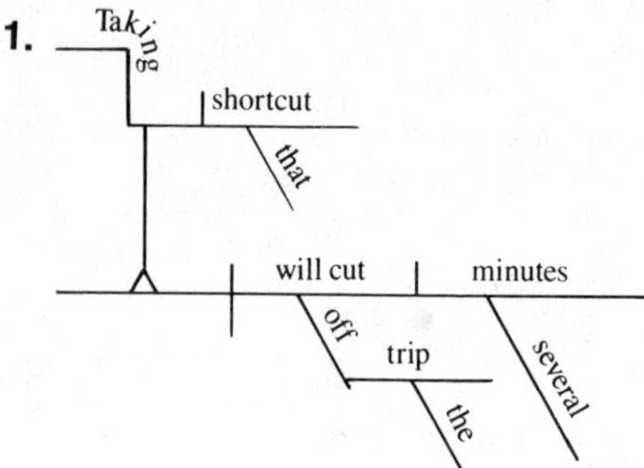

2.

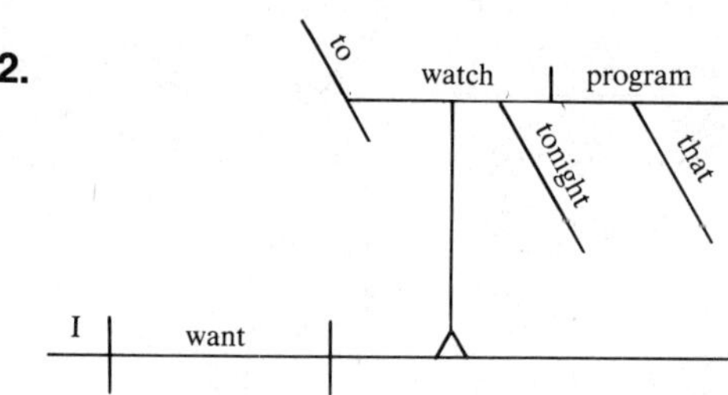

3.

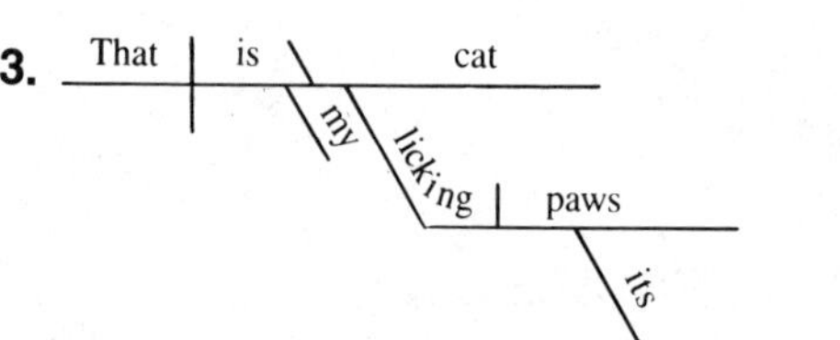

4.

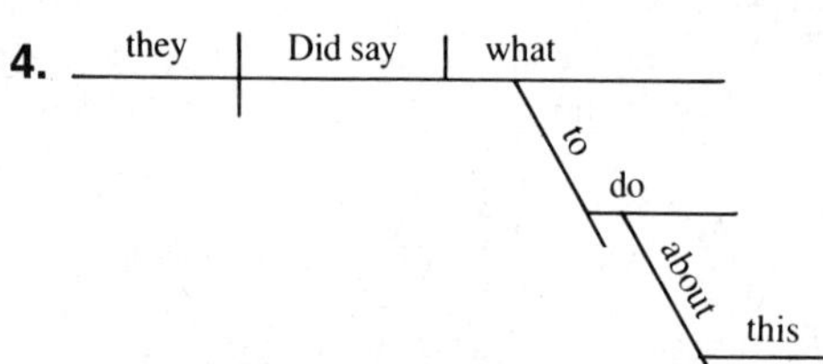

5.

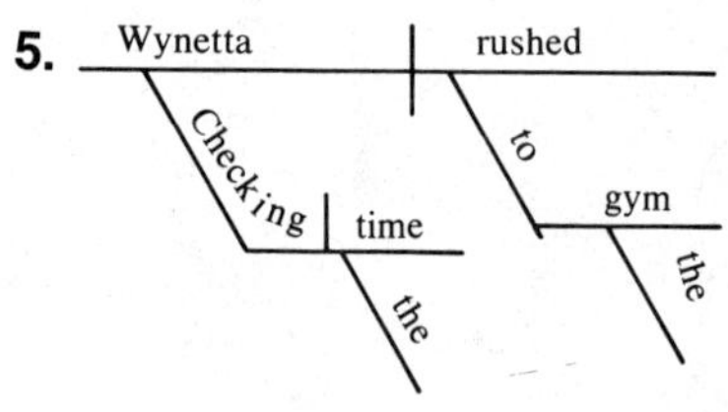

CHAPTER 15

The Clause

p. 397 EXERCISE 10

1.

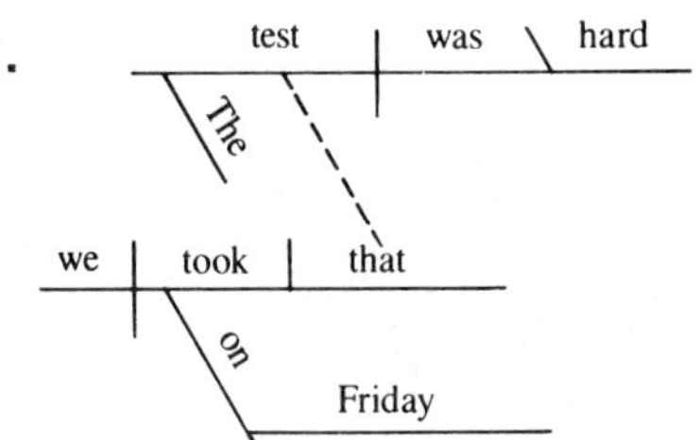

2.

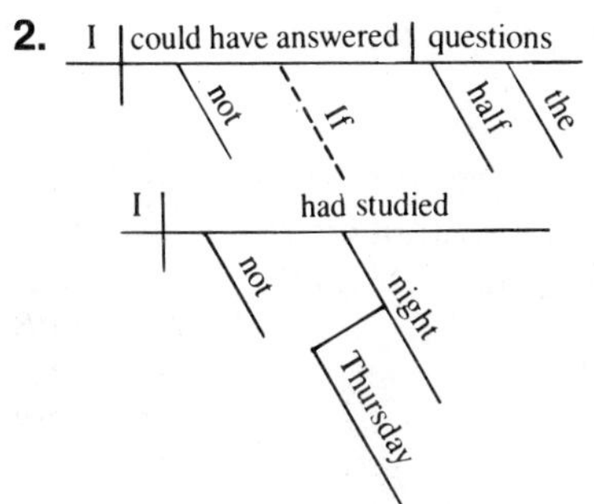

3.

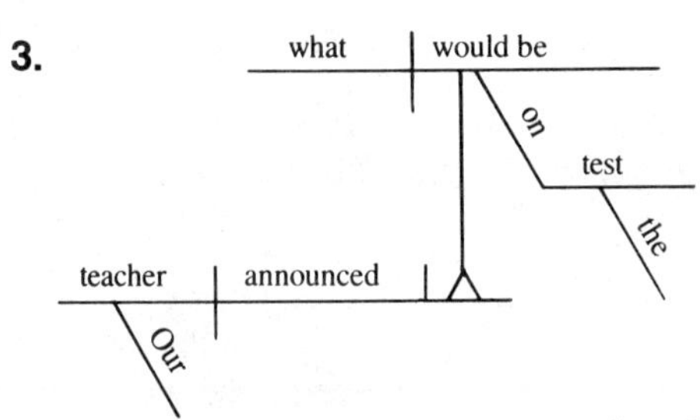

4.

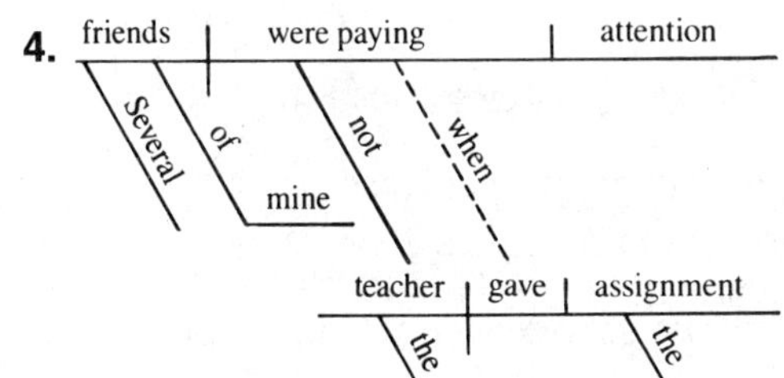

5.

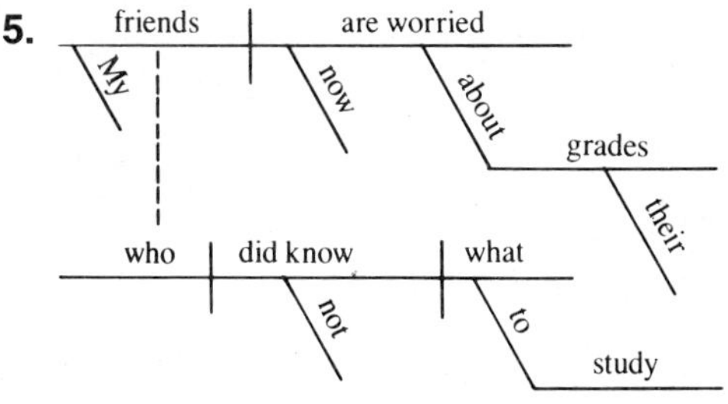

CHAPTER 16

The Kinds of Sentence Structure

p. 407 EXERCISE 4

1.

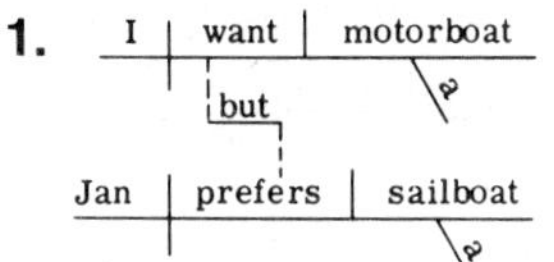

2.

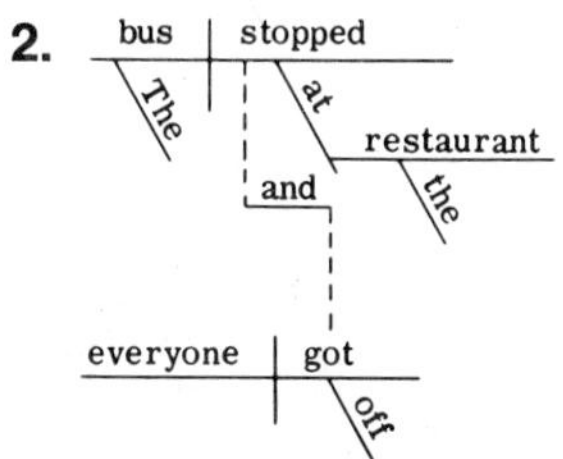

3.

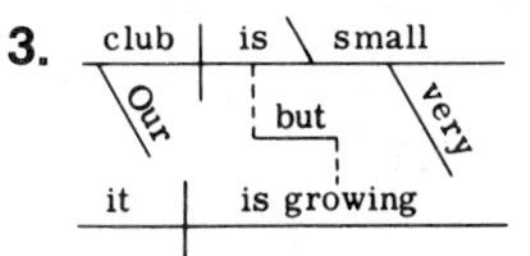

4.

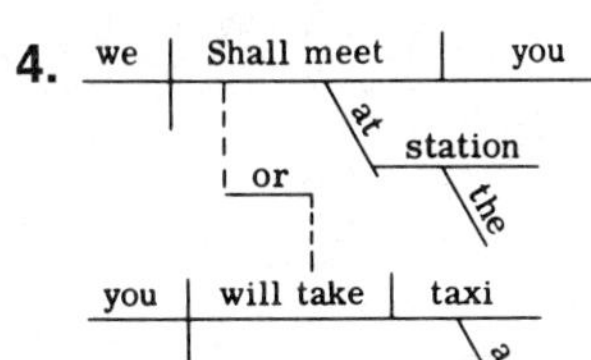

5.

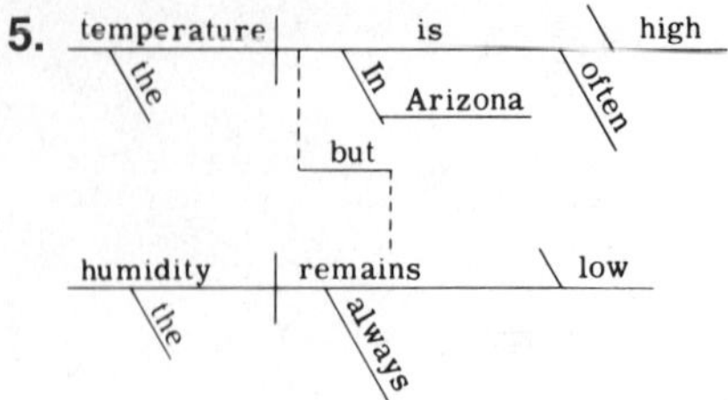

p. 411 EXERCISE 6

1. 2.

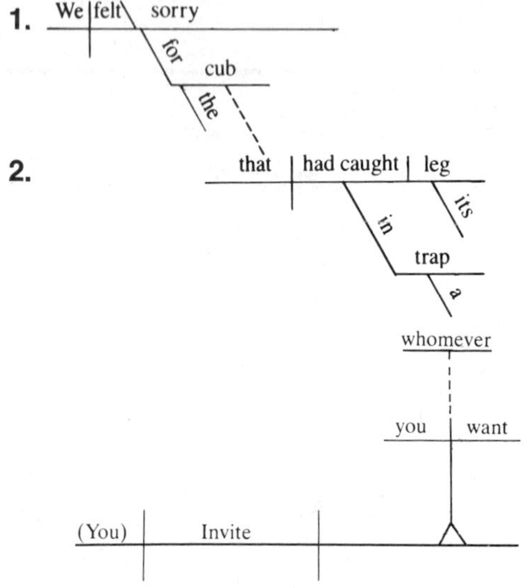

3.

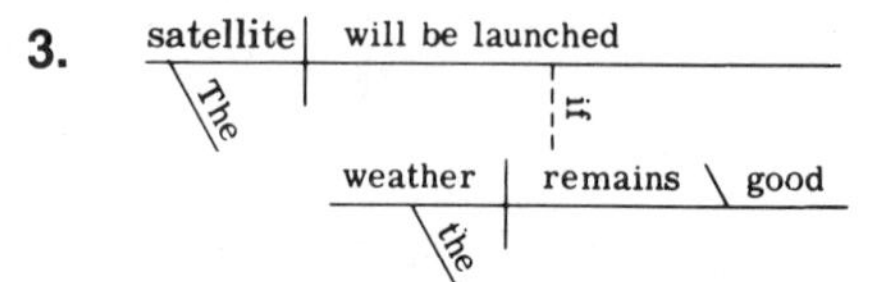

4.

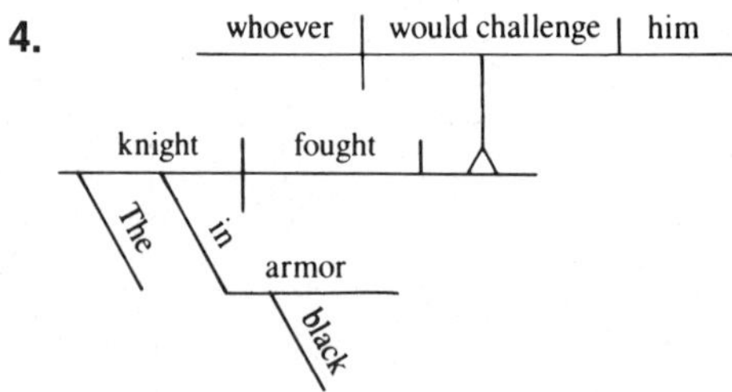

5.

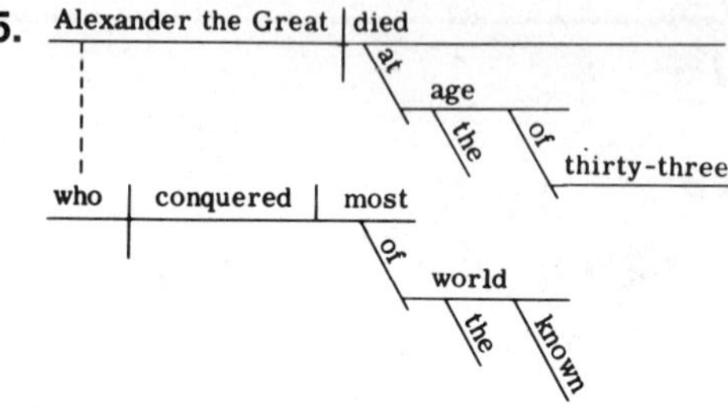

CHAPTER 18

Using Verbs Correctly

p. 458 EXERCISE 13

At my grandparents' house that morning, I *woke* up before anyone else and quietly grabbed the fishing pole and *headed* for the pond. Across the water, I saw ripples. "I have to catch the fish," I *said* to myself. I threw my lure near where I *saw* the ripples and reeled in the line. The fish *didn't* seem interested. I saw more ripples and *threw* the line in the water again. "I've got a strike!" I *shouted* to the trees around me. As I reeled in the line, a beautiful trout *jumped* out of the water and spit out the hook. Discouraged, I *went* back to the house. Grandpa was sitting at the table with a bowl of hot oatmeal for me. I *said,* "Maybe tomorrow we'll have trout for breakfast."

CHAPTER 20

Using Modifiers Correctly

p. 477 DIAGNOSTIC TEST, PART B

(Answers may vary. The following are possibilities.)

11. I looked for the key under the doormat.
12. The library in our school has several books about dinosaurs.
13. When supper was ready, Howard woke his father, who was sleeping soundly.
14. The book that I wanted to read is not in the library.
15. Aunt Joan sent away a magazine coupon for a free recipe book.

16. The band that will perform next week is my favorite.
17. Left alone for the first time in his life, my little brother was scared by strange sounds in the night.
18. We put the cats outside after they had eaten all their food.
19. Many African nations prohibit the hunting of elephants, which are often slaughtered only for their tusks.
20. Sitting in the bleachers, we were right in front of the outfielder who caught the ball.

p. 485 EXERCISE 5

(Answers may vary slightly.)

1. Josie has never been to Tennessee. (*or* hasn't ever)
2. Because of the heavy rain, we could scarcely find our way home.
3. He never had any problem with public speaking. (*or* He had no)
4. The athletes hardly have a break between events in the meet.
5. Don't use forks to get toast out of the toaster.
6. By the time I had made sandwiches for everyone else, I didn't have anything left for me. (*or* I had nothing)
7. I hardly listen to gossip.
8. Your answer doesn't make any difference to me. (*or* makes no difference)
9. Don't ever say *not* and *scarcely* together. (*or* Never say)
10. The goalie doesn't have any excuse. (*or* has no excuse)

p. 488 EXERCISE 6

(Answers may vary slightly.)

1. In class today the nature photographer told us about filming a herd of water buffalo.
2. We watched the antics of a dancing bear inside the ring.
3. The mannequins in the window display drew a huge crowd.
4. Hundreds of people in their cars were watching the show.
5. The assignment required three articles on the Statue of Liberty from magazines. (*or* The assignment on the Statue of Liberty required three articles from magazines.)
6. On Saturday my aunt promised that she would take me to the symphony. (*or* My aunt promised that she would take me to the symphony on Saturday.)
7. There is one gymnast on the gymnastics team who can tumble as well as vault.
8. The marathon runner with the blue T-shirt twisted his ankle.
9. The model in the designer gown posed gracefully in front of the statue.
10. Through our field binoculars we saw the trapeze artist swinging dangerously.

p. 491 EXERCISE 9

1. The soldiers who had volunteered for the mission were far from their base camp.
2. We tiptoed over the ice, which had begun to crack, in our heavy boots.
3. The spaniel that won the dog show belongs to Bernie.
4. Several gospel songs that were often sung by Mary Lou Williams were presented at yesterday's assembly.
5. The telethon that ran for thirty-six hours had achieved its goal.
6. The game that was scheduled for tomorrow was canceled by the two schools.
7. The strange messenger who was dressed as a chicken gave Mr. Johnson a dozen balloons.
8. The sweater that I have lost belongs to my best friend.
9. My married sister Becky who lives in Michigan came for the weekend to see me.
10. The documentary which will be broadcast in the fall was filmed at several locations.

p. 492 REVIEW EXERCISE C

(Answers will vary somewhat.)

1. During last night's concert, the singing group was protected by guards from being swarmed.
2. Attempting to raise money for the homeless, the group sang many sad songs.
3. Years ago the singers wore strange costumes and makeup so that fans could hardly tell what their faces really looked like.
4. When the fans began to tire of these gimmicks, the singers, who were also tired of the gimmickry, tried out a new look.
5. They finally chose the more simply tailored look of the two they had considered.
6. Warned about the fickleness of fans, the group also practiced a different style of singing.
7. Few fans could tell how nervous the singers were the first time they appeared in public after changing their style.
8. "That was the scariest performance of my career," one singer remarked.

9. When the audience cheered heartily, the singers' fears were relieved.
10. Both the concert and the fund raising ended exceptionally well.

p. 494 CHAPTER 20 REVIEW: POSTTEST 1 PART **B**

(Answers will vary.)
16. In class today our teacher told us that she had been a nurse.
17. The woman who runs the store helped us.
18. The man looked sadly at the charred house destroyed by the fire.
19. After missing the bus, I had my mother give me a ride in the car.
20. With a crafty maneuver, the fox escaped from the hounds pursuing it.
21. The squirrels chattered at me while I was walking through the park.
22. My uncle who is in the Army lives in Germany.
23. Preserved in formaldehyde, the squid fascinated the students.
24. Keeping track of the race with binoculars, we saw the blue car with a yellow roof pull into the lead.
25. From inside our warm house we watched the snow pile up in drifts.

CHAPTER 24

Punctuation

p. 553 DIAGNOSTIC TEST, PART **B**

11. Uncle Ned reads the *Wall Street Journal* every day.
12. "Fill in all the information on both sides of the form," the secretary said.
13. How many times have you seen the movie of Margaret Mitchell's novel *Gone with the Wind*?
14. Many of the students enjoyed the humor and irony in O. Henry's short story "The Ransom of Red Chief."
15. My little sister asked, "Why can't I have a hamster?"
16. Please don't sing "I've Been Working on the Railroad."
17. Over the summer my older sister played in a band on a Caribbean cruise ship named *Bright Coastal Star.*
18. "Read E. B. White's essay 'The Decline of Sport,' and answer the study questions," the teacher announced.
19. Dudley Randall's poem "Ancestors" questions why people always seem to believe that their ancestors were aristocrats.
20. "Wait here," the clerk said, "while I go to check the price."

p. 559 EXERCISE **4**

"Lynette, did you enjoy reading *The Yearling*?" Miss Bishop asked.

"I think it's the best book I have ever read, Miss Bishop."

"Can you tell us why you liked it?"

"The characters seemed so real," Lynette replied, "and their struggles made me like them even more."

"What were some of the struggles Jody and his family faced?"

"They struggled to raise crops and to gather food to get through the winter. Jody was lonely until he found Flag."

"What conflicts did keeping the deer as a pet cause?"

"Flag ate some of the crops, and Jody struggled with his father to keep the deer. Jody loved his pet and had trouble admitting it couldn't live with the family."

"Good, Lynette."

p. 564 EXERCISE **8**

SINGULAR POSSESSIVE	PLURAL	PLURAL POSSESSIVE
1. stove's	stoves	stoves'
2. puppy's	puppies	puppies'
3. donkey's	donkeys	donkeys'
4. mouse's	mice	mice's
5. calf's	calves	calves'
6. potato's	potatoes	potatoes'
7. elephant's	elephants	elephants'
8. tooth's	teeth	teeth's
9. school's	schools	schools'
10. valley's	valleys	valleys'

p. 569 REVIEW EXERCISE **D**

1. "I'll see you tomorrow at the sale at Sport World," said Vera. "It's on the corner of Thirty-ninth and Vine."
2. Today's *Geneva Gazeteer* has a story about the fire at the Pattersons' home; its roof was destroyed.
3. Belinda, Bill, Don, and Vickie have each read at least twenty-one books since last year's book fair.
4. "I can't imagine," remarked Judy, "a more terrifying short story than 'The Most Dangerous Game.' "
5. Seventy-three percent of the legislators voted to extend the school day.

6. Lisa reported that one third of the students interviewed said they usually had no homework, while a two-thirds majority said that they had too much.
7. "Although I offered to help with the cleanup," Renee explained, "Brian said that he could manage alone."
8. Augusta Savage's *Lift Every Voice and Sing* is the sculpture I'd most like to see for myself.
9. Larue's eyes twinkled as he replied, "Why, I've no idea what you're talking about; nobody's planning a party."
10. She'll ride to today's meeting with us.

p. 570 CHAPTER 24 REVIEW: POSTTEST, PART **B**

11. The best chapter in our vocabulary book is the last one, "More Word Games."
12. "I answered all the questions," Todd said, "but I think that some of my answers were wrong."
13. There is a legend that the band on the *Titanic* played the hymn "Nearer My God to Thee" as the ship sank into the icy sea.
14. Mr. Washington asked Connie, "What flag included the slogan 'Don't Tread on Me'?"
15. *Star Wars* was more exciting on the big movie screen than it was on our small television set.
16. "Play the Gene Autry tape again, Mom," Jonathan said, grinning at his mother.
17. Wendy wrote an article called "Students, Where Are You?" for our local newspaper, the *Morning Beacon.*
18. In the short story "The Tell-Tale Heart," Edgar Allan Poe explores the theme of guilt.
19. "Can I read *Treasure Island* for my book report?" Carmine asked.
20. Every Christmas Eve my uncle recites "The Night Before Christmas" for the children in the hospital.

CHAPTER 26

Using the Dictionary

p. 608 EXERCISE **11**

(Answers will vary according to which dictionary is used. The following answers are based on Webster's Seventh New Collegiate Dictionary.*)*

1. *Cupid* is capitalized when it is used as the name of the Roman god of love. It is not capitalized when it refers to the small, winged figures often seen in pictures (as on valentines).
2. *Democrat* is capitalized when it refers to a member of a particular political party. It is not capitalized when it refers simply to a believer in democratic government.
3. *Nativity* is capitalized when it refers to the birth of Jesus. It is not capitalized in other uses.
4. *Senate* is capitalized when it refers to the United States Senate or to the upper legislative body of a particular state. It usually is not capitalized in other uses.
5. *West* is capitalized when it is the name of a particular geographical section, or when it is a last name. It is not capitalized when it refers to a compass direction.

p. 612 REVIEW EXERCISE

1. *(Answers will vary in wording.)*
   a. A *synonym* is a word having a meaning the same or nearly the same as another word.
   b. A *macron* is a diacritical mark used to indicate a long vowel.
   c. A *guide word* is a word appearing at the top of the page of a dictionary to indicate the page's alphabetical contents.
   d. The *schwa* is a vowel symbol ( ) used to represent the unstressed vowel sound sometimes represented as "uh."
2. *(Answers will vary; consult the sections in the textbook chapter.)*
3. It would occur after *mother* and *motherhood.*
4. *(Answers will vary in wording.)*
   The label *slang* indicates a word is used in certain informal situations but is not usually used in written English except in written dialogue.
   The label *informal* indicates that a word is generally used in informal or conversational speech, but not in formal writing.
   The label *archaic* indicates that a word which was used by earlier speakers or writers is no longer in ordinary use in speaking or writing.
5. definition
   companion forms (run-on entry)
   synonym
   illustration and illustrative example
   part of speech
   usage
   origin
   capitalization
   syllable division

CHAPTER 27

Using the Library

p. 621 EXERCISE **6**

1. a. April 13, 1909, Jackson, Mississippi
b. December 18, 1947, Cincinnati, Ohio
c. December 21, 1954, Fort Lauderdale, Florida
d. August 18, 1937, Santa Monica, California
e. October 8, 1941, Greenville, North Carolina

2. a. Henry Clay
b. Daniel Webster
c. Jeremiah S. Black and William H. Seward
d. Robert Bacon and Philander C. Knox
e. Charles E. Hughes

3. 1923—Robert A. Millikan
1938—Enrico Fermi
1946—Percy W. Bridgman
1970—Louis E. Néel and Hannes O.G. Alfvén
1976—Burton Richter and Samuel C.C. Ting

4. 1926—Sinclair Lewis, *Arrowsmith*
1928—Thornton Wilder, *The Bridge of San Luis Rey*
1947—Robert Penn Warren, *All the King's Men*
1955—William Faulkner, *A Fable*
1959—Robert Lewis Taylor, *The Travels of Jamie McPheeters*
1980—Norman Mailer, *The Executioner's Song*

CHAPTER 28

Vocabulary

p. 641 EXERCISE **13**

(Definitions may vary depending on the dictionary available. Student sentences will, of course, vary.)

acute—of less than 90 degrees
bisect—to divide into two equal parts
diameter—a straight line passing through the center of a circle; the length of such a line
exponent—Albegra—a small figure or symbol placed above and at the right of another figure or symbol to show how many times the latter is to be used as a factor
intersection—the set containing all the points common to two or more given sets
numeral—a figure, letter, or word, or group expressing a number
obtuse—greater than 90 degrees and less than 180 degrees
quotient—result obtained when one number is divided by another
radical—the indicated root of a quantity or quantities, by an expression written under the radical sign
radius—any straight line extending from the center of to the periphery of a circle or sphere; the length of such a line

p. 641 EXERCISE **14**

(Definitions may vary depending on the dictionary available. Student sentences will, of course, vary.)

History
blockade—a shutting off of a port or region of a belligerent state to prevent passage in or out
capitalism—economic system in which all means of production and distribution are privately owned
depression—a period marked by slackening of business activity, unemployment, and falling prices and wages
filibuster—to engage in unauthorized warfare as a freebooter; to obstruct the passage of a bill
gerrymander—to divide (a voting area) so as to give one political party a majority in as many districts as possible
initiative—the right of a group of citizens to introduce a matter for legislation
recall—the process of removing, or the right to remove, an official from office by popular vote
referendum—the submission of a law, proposed or already in effect, to a direct vote of the people
totalitarian—government or state in which one political party or group maintains complete control under a dictatorship and bans all others
vassal—a subordinate, subject, servant or slave

Geography
arid—lacking enough water for things to grow; dry and barren
fiord—narrow inlet or arm of the sea bordered by steep cliffs
fissure—a long, narrow, deep cleft or crack
meridian—a great circle of the earth passing through the geographical poles and any given point on the earth's surface
monsoon—any wind that reverses its direction seasonally or blows constantly between land and adjacent water

plateau—an elevated tract of more or less land
peninsula—a land area almost entirely surrounded by water and connected with the mainland by an isthmus
precipitation—a depositing of rain, snow, sleet, etc.
topography—the accurate and detailed description of a place; the study or description of a region or system
tributary—flowing into a larger one (a tributary stream)

p. 641 EXERCISE **15**

(Definitions may vary depending on the dictionary available. Student sentences will, of course, vary.)

antibody—a protein produced in the body in response to contact of the body with an antigen, and having the specific capacity of neutralizing, hence creating immunity
condensation—the act of condensing, as the reduction of a gas to a liquid
electron—any of the negatively charged particles that form a part of all atoms
embryo—an animal in the earliest stages of its development in the uterus
friction—the resistance to motion of two moving objects or surfaces that touch
fulcrum—the support or point of support on which a lever turns in raising or moving something
nebula—any of several vast, diffuse, cloudlike patches seen in the night sky, consisting of stars too far away to be seen singly
radiation—energetic nuclear particles, as neutrons, alpha and beta particles, etc.
satellite—a small planet revolving around a larger one; a man-made object put into orbit around the earth
spectrum—the series of colored bands diffracted and arranged in the order of their respective wave lengths by the passage of white light through a prism and shading continuously from red to violet

---

CHAPTER 29

Studying and Test Taking

p. 653 EXERCISE **4**

(Answers will vary in wording.)

1. (a) St. Catharines was a cold place, unlike what Harriet had ever experienced before.
(b) Harriet had to make a home for herself.
(c) Harriet worked in the forest felling trees. In addition, she sometimes cooked or cleaned house for other people.
(d) Harriet tried to find work for the new fugitives.

2. (a) Elephants could trample an army or tear down the walls of a city.
(b) One elephant carrying armed men had the power of a modern tank.
(c) Soldiers who saw these elephants for the first time became frightened and ran away.
(d) Horses were also frightened by the elephants and refused to fight.

p. 668 EXERCISE **10**

(Answers will vary somewhat in wording.)

1. Compare—point out likenesses (or differences) between the Versailles Treaty and President Wilson's Fourteen Points
2. Interpret—explain the significance of the poem; give reasons—back up explanation with quotes from poem and discussion of poetic devices
3. Explain—give reasons for the struggle between Antigone and Creon
4. Describe—give an account of the geography and climate of Costa Rica
5. Show—provide examples, giving ways the selections illustrate American beliefs; identify—make note of or list

English Composition and Grammar

BENCHMARK EDITION

John E. Warriner

Second Course

Harcourt Brace Jovanovich, Publishers

Orlando San Diego Chicago Dallas

THE SERIES:

English Composition and Grammar: Introductory Course
English Composition and Grammar: First Course
English Composition and Grammar: Second Course
English Composition and Grammar: Third Course
English Composition and Grammar: Fourth Course
English Composition and Grammar: Fifth Course
English Composition and Grammar: Complete Course

Annotated Teacher's Edition and Teacher's Resource Book for each above title.

CORRELATED SERIES:

English Workshop: Introductory Course
English Workshop: First Course
English Workshop: Second Course
English Workshop: Third Course
English Workshop: Fourth Course
English Workshop: Fifth Course
English Workshop: Review Course

Composition: Models and Exercises, First Course
Composition: Models and Exercises, Second Course
Composition: Models and Exercises, Third Course
Composition: Models and Exercises, Fourth Course
Composition: Models and Exercises, Fifth Course
Advanced Composition: A Book of Models for Writing, Complete Course

Vocabulary Workshop: Introductory Course
Vocabulary Workshop: First Course
Vocabulary Workshop: Second Course
Vocabulary Workshop: Third Course
Vocabulary Workshop: Fourth Course
Vocabulary Workshop: Fifth Course
Vocabulary Workshop: Complete Course

John E. Warriner taught English for thirty-two years in junior and senior high schools and in college. He is chief author of the *English Composition and Grammar* series, coauthor of the *English Workshop* series, general editor of the *Composition: Models and Exercises* series, and editor of *Short Stories: Characters in Conflict*. His coauthors have all been active in English education.

ii

For permission to reprint copyrighted material, grateful acknowledgment is made to the following sources:

Isaac Asimov: From *Asimov on Numbers* by Isaac Asimov. Copyright © 1977 by Isaac Asimov.

Atheneum Publishers, Inc.: From "Attitude" in *Happy to Be Here* by Garrison Keillor. Copyright © 1982 by Garrison Keillor.

Banyan Books, Inc.: From *Florida by Pack and Paddle* by Mike Toner and Pat Toner. Copyright © 1979 by Mike Toner and Pat Toner.

The Curtis Publishing Company: From "How to Make Champions" in *The Saturday Evening Post.* © 1956 by The Curtis Publishing Company.

Benjamin Franklin Literary & Medical Society, Inc.: From "Nature's Medicines: Spearmint" by Lois Wickstrom in *Child Life* Magazine. Copyright © 1981 by Benjamin Franklin Literary & Medical Society, Inc., Indianapolis, IN. From "Magnificent Failure—Or Was He?" by Eleanor Anderson in *Young World* Magazine. Copyright © 1978 by The Saturday Evening Post Company, Indianapolis, IN.

Friends of Animals, Inc.: From "Do You Really Want a Pet?" by Alice Herrington in *Family Circle* Magazine, January 25, 1983.

Harcourt Brace Jovanovich, Inc.: From *Concepts in Science,* Third Edition, Level Purple by Paul Brandwein, et al. From *American History* by John A. Garraty. Copyright © 1982 by Harcourt Brace Jovanovich, Inc. From *American Civics,* Fourth Edition by William H. Hartley and William S. Vincent. Copyright © 1967, 1970, 1974, 1979, 1983 by Harcourt Brace Jovanovich, Inc. From *Strategies in Reading C* by Ethel Grodzins Romm. Copyright © 1984 by Harcourt Brace Jovanovich, Inc. From Tests to accompany *AMERICA: Its People and Values,* Heritage Edition by Leonard C. Wood, Ralph C. Gabriel, and Edward L. Biller. Copyright © 1985 by Harcourt Brace Jovanovich, Inc. Graphics for the letter "M" from *HBJ School Dictionary.* Copyright © 1985 by Harcourt Brace Jovanovich, Inc. Entries "smart," "dexterous," and "lovely" from *The HBJ School Dictionary.* Copyright © 1977 by Harcourt Brace Jovanovich, Inc.

Harper & Row, Publishers, Inc.: Specified excerpt from p. 45 in *Weapons and Hope* by Freeman Dyson. Copyright © 1984 by Freeman J. Dyson. Originally published in *The New Yorker.*

Houghton Mifflin Company: Entries "offensive" and "credit" from the *American Heritage Student Dictionary.* © 1986 by Houghton Mifflin Company.

Jon R. Luoma: From "Troubled Skies, Troubled Waters" by Jon R. Luoma.

The Nature Conservancy News: Adapted from "Remembrances of a Rain Forest" by Paul Colinvaux in *The Nature Conservancy News,* Vol. 29, No. 4, July/August 1979.

The New York Times Company: From "7 Days on the Yangtze" by Barbara Goldsmith in *The New York Times,* March 17, 1985. Copyright © 1985 by The New York Times Company. From "What's New in Laser Technology" by Gordon Graff in *The New York Times,* April 7, 1985. Copyright © 1985 by The New York Times Company. From "Technology: Helping Driver Feel at Home" by John Holusha in *The New York Times,* February 28, 1985. Copyright © 1985 by The New York Times Company.

Outdoor Life Books: From *Bears* by Ben East. Published by Outdoor Life Books.

Prentice-Hall, Inc., Englewood Cliffs, NJ: From *The Amateur Naturalist's Handbook* by Vinson Brown. © 1980 by Prentice-Hall, Inc.

Random House, Inc.: From *Losing Battles* by Eudora Welty. Copyright © 1970 by Eudora Welty.

Russell & Volkening, Inc., as agents for Ann Petry: From *Harriet Tubman* (Titled: "They Called Her Moses") by Ann Petry. Copyright © 1955, renewed 1983 by Ann Petry.

Saturday Review: From "The Great American Barbe-Queue" by Charles Kuralt in *Saturday Review* Magazine, June 26, 1976. © 1976 by Saturday Review Magazine.

Scholastic Inc.: From "How Do They Make Snow?" by Brian McCallen in *Science World* Magazine, November 5, 1982. Copyright © 1982 by Scholastic Inc.

Simon & Schuster, Inc.: Entry for "Franklin Pierce" from *Webster's New World Dictionary of the American Language,* Second College Edition. Copyright 1970, 1972, 1974, 1976, 1978, 1979, 1980 by Simon & Schuster, Inc.

Smithsonian Institution Press: From "An old Africa hand fights to keep his lions wild and free" by Dick Houston in *Smithsonian* Magazine, July 1983.

iii

Sports Illustrated: From "On Sturdy, Light Off-Road Bicycles, Racers Can Handle Tough Terrain" in "On the Scene" by Dan Levin in *Sports Illustrated,* April 29, 1985. © 1985 by Time Inc. From "Grandeur and Torment" by Kenny Moore in *Sports Illustrated,* April 8, 1985. © 1985 by Time Inc. From "On the Road Again and Again and Again" by William Nack in *Sports Illustrated,* April 22, 1985. © 1985 by Time Inc.

Straight Arrow Publishers, Inc.: From "Here Comes the Son" by Elizabeth Kaye in *Rolling Stone,* June 6, 1985. © 1985 by Straight Arrow Publishers, Inc. All rights reserved.

University of Notre Dame Press: From *Barrio Boy* by Ernesto Galarza. Copyright © 1971 by University of Notre Dame Press, Notre Dame, IN 48558.

Viking Penguin Inc.: From "The World's Biggest Membrane" in *The Lives of a Cell, Notes of a Biology Watcher* by Lewis Thomas. Copyright © 1973 by The Massachusetts Medical Society. Originally published in *The New England Journal of Medicine.*

Franklin Watts, Inc.: From *The Lost Colony* by Dan Lacy. Copyright © 1972 by Franklin Watts, Inc.

Western Publishing Company, Inc.: From *Geology* by Frank H. T. Rhodes. © 1972 by Western Publishing Company, Inc.

The H. W. Wilson Company: From *Readers' Guide to Periodical Literature.* Copyright © 1978, 1979 by The H. W. Wilson Company.

World Book, Inc.: From article "Halley's Comet" in *The World Book Encyclopedia.* © 1985 by World Book, Inc.

PHOTO CREDITS

Key: T,Top; B,Bottom

Cover: HBJ Photo

Page 1,Ed Cooper; 2,Ed Cooper; IW1,Richard Howard; IW2,William Thompson; IW4T,HBJ Photo; IW4B,Ann Hagen Griffiths/Omni-Photo Communications; IW5,Clyde H. Smith from F/Stop Pictures; IW6T,Denver Public Library Western Collection; IW6B,William Thompson; IW8,George Ancona/International Stock Photo; IW9,Steve Elmore; IW10,General Biological Supply House, Inc.; IW12T,John R. McCauley/Photri; IW12B,Peter Fronk from Click/Chicago; IW13,John Moran; IW14,Frank Niemeir; IW16,Ed Cooper; 227,W. Metzen/H. Armstrong Roberts, Inc.; 228,Ed Cooper; 263,David Lissy from Click/Chicago; 264,Gianni Tortoli/Photo Researchers; 595,Phil Degginger/H. Armstrong Roberts, Inc.; 596,H. Armstrong Roberts, Inc.; 669,ZEFA/H. Armstrong Roberts, Inc.; 670,J. Smith/Leo De Wys, Inc.

Printed in the United States of America
ISBN 0–15–311732–X

iv

To the Student

A long time ago when education did not have to be so complicated as it must be today, the main subjects in school were referred to as the three R's: reading, 'riting, and 'rithmetic. As a familiar song says, they were "taught to the tune of a hickory stick." The hickory stick, fortunately, is not much used any more, but the three R's remain. Two of them, reading and writing, make up a large part of the school subject called English.

If someone were to ask you the unlikely question, "What do you do in English?" your reply might be something like this: "In English we read stories and poems and stuff like that. We write our own stories and poems and themes. We learn about nouns and verbs and, well, subjects and predicates, I guess. And we give talks in front of the class." This answer is a fairly good account of what you do in English.

A teacher, however, would use different terms in answering the same question. Instead of mentioning just stories and poems, a teacher might say you study *literature.* Writing stories, poems, and themes is practicing written *composition.* Noun, verb, subject, and predicate are terms used in the study of *grammar.* Talks in front of the class are a means of improving your *speech.* The four main areas of English, then, are literature, composition, grammar, and speech.

This book deals mainly with the last three of the four areas, composition, grammar, and speech. To use a language well, you need to know how it works. By studying grammar, you learn how the language works. This knowledge will help you to improve both your writing and your speech.

Although you write much less often than you speak, written composition demands a large amount of English time because writing is hard to learn. Each year in school you will be expected to do more written work in most of your classes, but it is only in English class that you learn how to write.

By writing well, you communicate with others. By speaking (and listening) well, you also communicate with others. Speech skills are a vital part of your education because you spend so much of every day talking with others.

v

Mastering the three areas in this textbook—composition, grammar, and speech—is not an easy task. However, you can do it if you have sound guidance. Your teacher is your most helpful guide, but your textbook is also an important guide. Study it, follow the rules, do the practice exercises, and whenever you write or speak, put to use what you have learned. You will find your work will improve steadily.

J. W.

vi

CONTENTS

vii

Part Two: COMPOSITION: Writing and Revising Sentences

Part Three: TOOLS FOR WRITING AND REVISING

GRAMMAR

PART ONE

COMPOSITION:
The Writing Process

PART ONE:

COMPOSITION:

The Writing Process

pages 1–225

USING THE PICTURES

The pictures on this and the next page, along with those in the section "Picture the Possibilities" following page 226, provide students with sources of ideas for writing. The following suggestions will help you show students how to use the pictures, either singly or in combination, to generate ideas and gather information.

Grand Canyon/Watchtower

- Help students list details of size, shape, color, texture, etc., for a description of the scene. To help them arrange the details in spatial order, suggest that they direct the reader's eye from the tower in the foreground to the farthest point visible in the scene. Advanced students might attempt to describe the scene from the vantage point of the top of the tower.
- Another possibility would be to have students write library reports on the Grand Canyon. Using the *5 W-How?* questions would help them gather facts and statistics to include. Among the questions such a report might answer are *What is the Grand Canyon? Where is it? How was it formed? How many acres does it cover? How long is it? What is its greatest depth? Width?* Students might instead write about Grand Canyon National Park or about a national or state park near your community.
- Other subjects the picture might

suggest include erosion, the Colorado River, the National Park Service, towers, and stone buildings.

Sunset/Cannon Beach, Oregon

- Students could use this scene as the setting for a story. They might begin by using their imaginations to brainstorm answers to questions such as *Where am I? What month, day, and time of day is it? Am I alone, or is someone with me? Why am I* (or *are we*) *here? What problem do I* (or *we*) *face?*
- Another possibility would be to have students imagine themselves in the scene and use questions such as these to gather concrete and sensory details: *What colors do I see in the rocks? In the water? In the sky? What shapes do I notice? What material is the beach made of? How does it feel beneath my feet? How does the air feel on my skin? How does it smell? What sounds do I hear?* They could use their answers to write a description or incorporate the details into a narrative.
- The reflection of the sunset in the water could lead students to the idea of writing a paper explaining what reflection is and how various surfaces reflect light.
- The natural beauty of this scene might remind students of scenic areas in their own community that should be preserved in a natural state. They could select one such area and write letters to the editor explaining why they believe the area should not be commercially developed.

Connecting the Pictures

Have students write paragraphs comparing the shape of the tower with that of the rock formations.

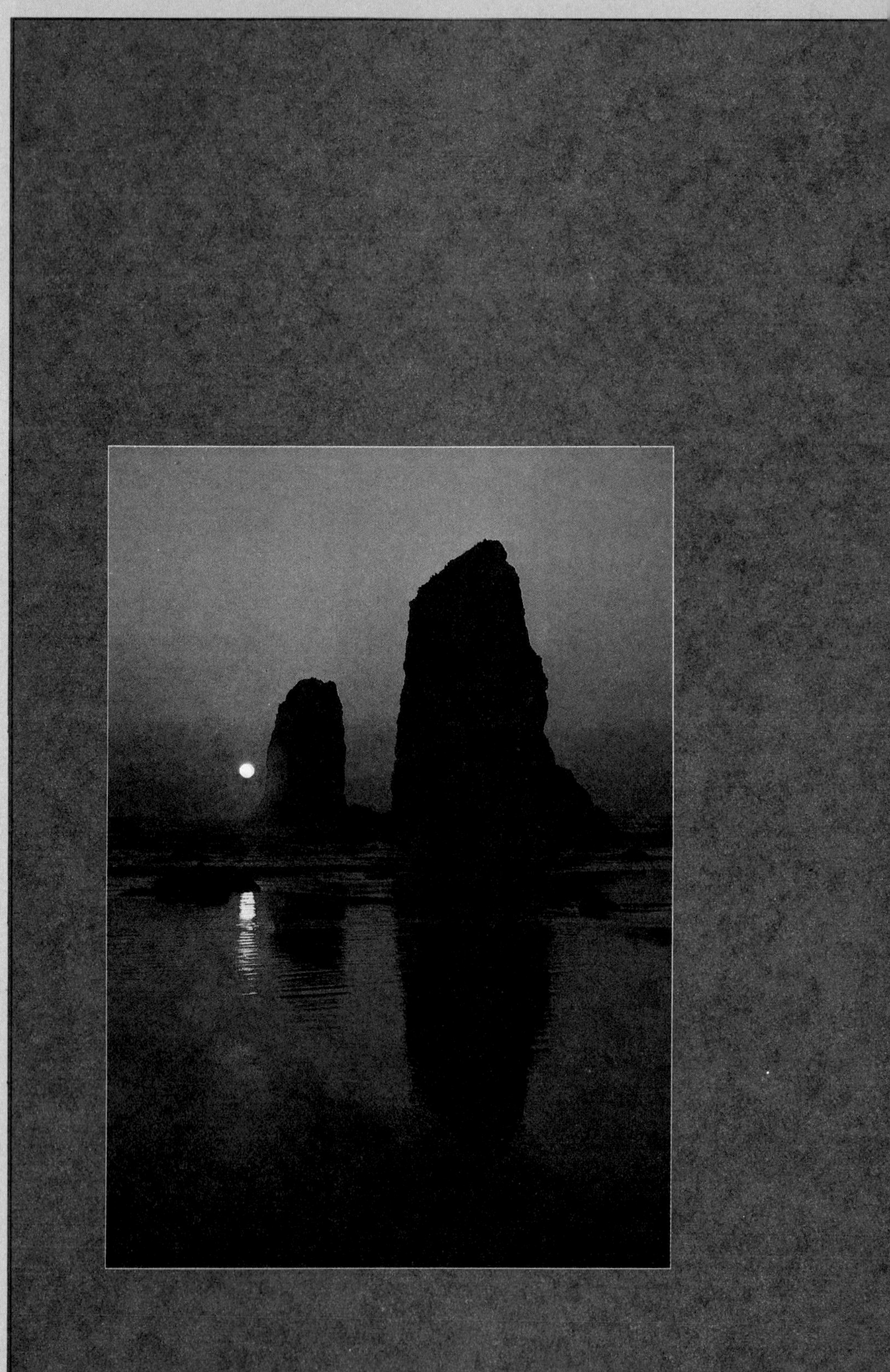

CHAPTER 1

Writing and Thinking

THE WRITING PROCESS

A *process* is a series of actions carried out to produce or create something. Writing is a process—it involves several stages of thinking and putting words on paper. Thinking, in fact, is a big part of the writer's job. In this chapter you will learn and practice all steps of the writing process, including the *critical thinking* that you must do at every stage.

THE WRITING PROCESS

The following list shows six stages in the writing process. Notice that the *prewriting* stage includes several steps.

PREWRITING

1. Deciding on a purpose, or reason, for writing
2. Thinking about the audience's needs and interests
3. Choosing a subject for writing
4. Limiting the subject to a suitable topic
5. Gathering information on the topic
6. Organizing the information

WRITING THE FIRST DRAFT

7. Expressing your ideas in sentences and paragraphs

Chapter Overview

Given the demands for clear written expression that students encounter in secondary school, it is important for eighth-graders to develop specific skills and techniques in writing. By learning about the stages of the writing process and about how writers can communicate effectively, students should become better able to organize and express their own ideas. As they practice skills and techniques in the writing process, students will also be exercising the critical thinking skills that underlie the writing process.

Chapter Objective

Students will recognize the stages of the writing process and their relationship to thinking, and will also practice the techniques and strategies related to each stage of the writing process.

PRESENTING THE CHAPTER

LESS-ADVANCED STUDENTS Less-advanced students may have had little experience with the writing process, and those experiences may often have been frustrating or dissatisfying. It is therefore important for less-advanced students to become comfortable with using the writing process. To this end, concentrate on helping your students develop a sense of the whole process and of its recursive nature, rather than stressing the fine points and details of each stage in the writing process. You may also want to assign exercises selectively, complete exercises orally whenever possible, and use small-group activities liberally. Because evaluation can be intimidating to beginning writers, you may want to avoid assigning grades to exercises students complete in this chapter. Keep as your goal helping students to recognize the dynamic and individual nature of the writing process. Using the writing process can enable students to discover that they have something to say and that they can express their ideas effectively.

ADVANCED STUDENTS Advanced students have often already had successful and rewarding writing experiences. Try to build on this positive background by focusing on the particular writing skills these students need to practice. You should also emphasize the critical thinking skill sections in this chapter, as your advanced students should have little difficulty grasping the relationship between writing and thinking. *(See listing of Alternative Worksheets on page 42.)*

THE WRITING PROCESS

This introductory section outlines the five major stages in the writing process: prewriting, writing, revising, proofreading, and preparing the final copy. It is important for students to understand what each stage entails, as these stages will be the basis for this chapter and for subsequent composition chapters in this text. As you present this introduction, stress also the recursive nature and individual nature of the writing process. All writers develop their own habits for approaching a writing task. At the same time, the writing process does not involve only forward movement—writers can move back and forth, skip stages, and complete two steps at the same time.

EXERCISE 1. Use this exercise to

EVALUATING

8. Reexamining the ideas, organization, and word choice in your first draft

REVISING

9. Making changes to improve the first draft

PROOFREADING

10. Checking for errors in grammar, usage, and mechanics
11. Correcting errors

MAKING THE FINAL COPY

12. Copying the final draft in a correct form
13. Correcting any copying errors

As you learn these steps, keep in mind that you will not always follow them in a rigid order. How you apply the process depends on what you are writing and on your habits as a writer. For example, if you are writing a quick note, you may spend only a minute or two planning your message. For an important report, you may spend several days in the prewriting stage. On some occasions, you may be revising a paper and find that you need to return to a prewriting step. Every time you write, you face a different situation and make different decisions.

EXERCISE 1. Understanding the Writing Process. The following entries from a writer's notebook show how one student used the writing process to prepare an article for the school newspaper. Use the list of writing stages on pages 3–4 to answer the questions following these entries.

Tuesday—I've spent an hour brainstorming subjects for my next article for the school newspaper. I think kids would be interested in the summer space-camp Brian attended. I can talk to Brian tomorrow and find out more about the camp.

Wednesday—Wow! Brian really had a lot to say about the model rockets they launched, their experiments with weightlessness, and the simulated space shuttle mission. I think I have plenty of information. All I have to do is write it up.

Thursday—I wrote half of my first draft, but when I read over it I wasn't thrilled. It's too disorganized. I thought I could tell what happened at camp day by day, but I got off the track. Maybe I should stop and organize my notes.

Friday—I finished writing my second draft and started revising. I decided I needed more details about the simulated space shuttle mission; I called Brian and got more information.

Saturday—Finished proofreading and correcting mistakes in the article. I can write the final copy.

1. What stage was the writer at on Tuesday? What step did the writer complete? 1. Prewriting, choosing a subject
2. On what day did the writer move to the *writing* stage? 2. Thurs.
3. On Thursday the writer moved from the *writing* stage back to *prewriting*. Why? 3. Her first draft was disorganized.
4. Why did the writer move from *revising* back to *prewriting* on Friday? 4. She needed more information.
5. What step in the process should the writer devote more time to when writing the next article? 5. Organizing ideas

PREWRITING

Prewriting includes all the thinking and planning that you do before you begin to write. What you put on paper during this stage will guide your writing.

Before You Write. Ask yourself:

- Why am I writing? (purpose)
- Who will read what I write? (audience)
- What will I write about? (topic)
- What will I say about the topic? (details)
- How will I organize my ideas? (order)

prompt discussion of students' own writing processes. Try to enable them to see the similarities and differences that exist among members of the class (including you) as writers. Also try to prompt students to realize what their own writing processes are.

PREWRITING

Section Overview

The techniques and strategies of the prewriting stage of the writing process, which students can apply to all types of writing, enable them to discover what they have to say about a topic. It is important for students to learn these techniques and strategies and to practice them in their own writing.

IDENTIFYING YOUR PURPOSE (rule 1a)

As you present this section, remind students that they also write for these four basic purposes. You may want to ask your students to catalog the kinds of writing they have recently done, discussing the purpose for each. Also, remind your students that the four basic purposes for writing often overlap; for example, when writers describe as they attempt to explain how something works or tell a story as they attempt to persuade an audience. Students should carefully consider their purpose for writing as they undertake any writing task.

Understanding and making sound decisions about each of these questions will help you produce strong writing.

You do not have to answer these questions in the same particular order every time you prepare to write. Begin with what you know about the writing task. If your English teacher asks you to write a description that will interest your classmates, you know your purpose (to describe) and audience (your classmates). With these in mind, you can search for an appropriate topic and gather interesting details.

IDENTIFYING YOUR PURPOSE

1a. Determine your purpose for writing.

When you think about *why* you are writing, you think about your *purpose.* You will find that having a clear purpose in mind will help you decide what ideas to present to your readers.

Most writing has one of four basic purposes:

1. To tell a story, or what happened (*narrative* writing)

EXAMPLE We had just finished our picnic lunch when my uncle hollered, "Look at that!" Lumbering down the path toward us was an elephant. We thought the animal was loose until we saw one of the zookeepers walking beside her. The zookeeper explained that the elephant, named Tiny, was simply out for a stroll. As we talked, Tiny stood quietly waving her huge gray ears back and forth like fans, curling and uncurling her trunk. When the zookeeper tapped Tiny's front leg, she rose up on her hind legs and turned in a circle almost as if she were dancing.

2. To describe (*descriptive* writing)

EXAMPLE Tiny was at least three or four feet taller than the zookeeper. Her bulky gray body was covered with wrinkled, tough skin that hung in loose, baggy folds around her short, thick legs. In contrast, her ears were like two paper-thin palm leaves attached to each side of her head.

3. To explain or inform (*expository* writing)

EXAMPLE An elephant uses its trunk the way we use our hands. Because the trunk is strong and flexible, an elephant can lift and carry a six-hundred-pound log simply by curling its trunk around the log. Using the delicate knob at the end of its trunk, an elephant can locate and pick up an object as small as a dime. In the jungle heat an elephant cools off by filling its trunk with water and shooting the water across its back. An adult elephant can store a six-gallon shower in its trunk.

4. To persuade (*persuasive* writing)

EXAMPLE Many wildlife experts predict that the elephant —along with the cheetah, the Siberian tiger, and the rhinoceros—will disappear within the next twenty-five years. Few people realize that more than a thousand varieties of wild animals are threatened with extinction. The threats to these animals include the clearing of more than 100,000 acres of jungle every day, illegal hunting, and the poisoning of the environment with pesticides and powerful fertilizers. Unless people around the world support conservation groups such as the World Wildlife Fund and the zoo's Save the Animals program, seeing a live elephant or tiger may become as difficult as seeing a live dinosaur.

Occasionally, it may seem that the writing you are planning does not fit these four purposes. For example, you may decide to entertain your readers with humor. If you look closely at your plan, you will probably discover that you really have one of the four basic purposes. Perhaps you will entertain readers by *persuading* them to do something silly, by *telling a* funny *story,* or by *describing* an amusing scene.

EXERCISE 2. This exercise is useful as an oral activity. You may want to supplement the exercise with additional examples of writing for a variety of purposes.

Sometimes, part of a long piece of writing has a purpose separate from the basic purpose. For example, the main purpose of a newspaper article may be to persuade students to attend a workshop on bicycle safety. The reporter might begin by telling about a bicycle accident that happened because someone did not follow the safety rules. Most of the writing you do will have a single major purpose.

Before You Write. Decide whether your main purpose is to

- tell a story (tell what happened).
- describe.
- explain or inform.
- persuade.

Defining your purpose for writing will help you make decisions about the kinds of details you gather. Descriptive writing includes details about how something looks, tastes, smells, sounds, or feels when touched. Narrative writing emphasizes events and action. Expository writing gives readers new and specific information. In persuasive writing, you support an opinion with reasons and evidence.

Understanding your purpose can also help you decide on your topic. Some topics are more appropriate for one purpose than another. If you recently saw a magician's performance, you might describe the magician's appearance or tell what happened during the act. It would be more difficult, based only on your observations, to write a persuasive paper or to explain how each trick was performed.

EXERCISE 2. Identifying Purposes for Writing. Read each of the following paragraphs. Decide if the writer's purpose is to describe, to tell a story, to explain, or to persuade.

1. It was a perfect Halloween night. From behind the gray edges of the clouds, a round orange moon lit up a starless sky. The

moonlight outlined the bare twisted limbs of the apple tree in the yard. The wind whistled and moaned, scattering dead leaves and rattling in the dry weeds along the fence. Somewhere in the distance an owl hooted. 1. descriptive

2. Several Halloween customs can be traced back to the Celts, who lived in England over a thousand years ago. The Celts believed dangerous spirits were allowed to roam the countryside on October 31, the night before their new year. To protect themselves from these wandering spirits, the Celts stayed at home and put good things to eat outside their doors. If they had to go out, they dressed up in unusual disguises, hoping any evil spirit they encountered would mistake them for other wandering spirits. 2. explanatory

3. Some students and parents want to do away with trick-or-treating because candy or fruit can be tampered with—but marching around town in costumes is half the fun of Halloween! I think we should continue to trick-or-treat but accept only donations for UNICEF. We could all meet at school and divide into groups with one adult in each group. Later we could come back to the gym for a community Halloween party with games and refreshments. We could even turn the locker room into a "haunted house." 3. persuasive

EXERCISE 3. Identifying Purposes for Writing. Imagine that you will write a one- or two-page paper about each of the following topics. For each one, tell what your major purpose for writing would be.

1. The sights and sounds of a hayride on a crisp autumn evening 1. to describe
2. Why your school needs a larger gymnasium 2. to persuade
3. What happened at last Friday's pep rally 3. to narrate
4. The training required to become a veterinarian 4. to explain
5. The time your aunt, a veterinarian, was knocked over by a cow 5. to narrate

KNOWING YOUR AUDIENCE

1b. Always consider the needs and interests of your readers.

EXERCISE 3. This exercise can be used as an oral activity, particularly in small groups for your less-advanced students.

KNOWING YOUR AUDIENCE (rule 1b)

Students should be reminded to consider their audience's age, knowledge, interests, and opinions as they work through the prewriting stage of the writing process.

EXERCISES 4 and 5. These two exercises focus on adjusting writing for specific audiences. Use Exercise 4 as an introductory oral activity before you assign Exercise 5 for individual or small-group work. Or you may want to complete Exercise 4 in small groups before students complete Exercise 5 individually. Allow students to compare their rewritten paragraphs in Exercise 5, and ask them to discuss how they adjusted their writing to suit different audiences in each case.

Another important step in prewriting is thinking about your *audience*—the person or persons who will read your writing. Good writers plan their writing to fit their audience's age, knowledge, interests, and opinions. Last week one student completed three pieces of writing:

A letter to Exotic Pets, Inc., about food for her new parrot
A one-page science report about the habits of tropical birds
A letter to her six-year-old cousin, who has the measles

When she wrote to her young cousin, she used simple words and short sentences that he could understand. To amuse him, she told a funny story about her new parrot. In her letter to Exotic Pets, Inc., she stated clearly what seeds and bird food she wanted. Because this was a business letter, she included only the information needed to fill her order. Since her teacher is interested in what she has learned about parrots, she wrote a report about their habits and behavior. She included scientific terms to show that she knew their meanings. In each situation, what she knew about her readers' age, education, interests, and opinions influenced how she handled her topic.

Before You Write. Consider your audience by asking yourself:

- Will the topic and details interest the readers?
- What background information do they need?
- How simple or complex should my language be?
- Do the readers have special feelings about the topic?

EXERCISE 4. Choosing Details to Fit the Audience. Imagine that the following items are details about your school and recent activities. Decide which details you would include in a letter to a new Japanese pen pal who has never been to the United States. Then decide which details you would include in a letter to a former classmate who has just moved away. See Answer Key.

1. In winter I ride the bus, because we have a lot of snow and temperatures that are often below zero.

2. We watched the breakdancing on the river walk.
3. We took a field trip to the farm museum and watched a demonstration of plowing with horses.
4. The junior-high band will perform at the Spring Festival.
5. Saturday I played a new video game with Enrique and his sister at the arcade in the mall.
6. School starts at 7:30 in the morning and ends at 3:15.
7. Every day I have five classes, each taught by a different teacher.
8. Thursday there was a tornado warning. A siren went off, but nothing happened.
9. Our town has two high schools and three junior high schools.
10. In nice spring and fall weather, I ride my bicycle to school.

EXERCISE 5. Rewriting to Fit the Audience. The paragraph about Halloween customs on page 9 was written for an eighth-grade audience. Read it carefully; then rewrite it for an audience of third-grade students. Answers will vary.

CHOOSING A SUBJECT

Do not overlook your own experiences when you search for a writing subject. Experienced writers know they often produce their best work when they write about what they know well. In the following paragraph, the writer used her experience with ice skating to explain how skates should fit.

> Beginners who wobble around the rink or can't balance on their blades often assume they have weak ankles. Actually, the problem is usually skates that are too big. When you rent skates, remember that skate sizes normally run larger than shoe sizes. Ask for skates that are a half size smaller than your shoe size. Lace the bottom two or three eyes of the skate loosely. Then lace the skate tightly up to your ankle and tie a half knot. Lace the rest of the skate loosely and stand up. You should be able to wiggle your toes, but if you can move your heels up and down inside your skates, your skates are too big.

CHOOSING A SUBJECT
(rules 1c–1f)

This section presents four specific methods students can use to discover subjects to write about. Each method is based on students' exploring their own experiences to discover subjects for writing. To introduce this section you may want to ask students to outline or inventory their hobbies, favorite school subjects, reading and viewing favorites, and so on. This quick inventory can serve as a reminder and as a starting point when students select subjects to write about in this chapter. Depending on your students' needs and abilities, you may want to focus on only one or two of these discovery techniques. Just be sure that each student can use at least one discovery technique to find subjects to write about.

Starting with Yourself

1c. Consider both direct and indirect experiences.

Direct experiences are those you experience yourself: places you visit, people you know, your hobbies, and sports you participate in. What interesting places could you describe? What is special about a person you know? What memorable events can you share with your readers?

EXAMPLES *Places:* sitting under the oak tree at the end of the cornfield, the waiting room at my dentist's office
People: how my cousin copes with her handicap
Hobbies: restoring a Model T Ford, raising rabbits as a 4-H project
Sports: tobogganing at the forest preserve, trying out for the swimming team
Work: stocking shelves at my aunt's hardware store

Indirect experiences are those you gain from reading, watching films or television, or listening to another person. If you have read several articles about experiments during flights of the space shuttle, you probably know enough to write about this subject. If your great-uncle has told you about the hardships his family faced during the Depression, you might write about his experiences.

EXAMPLES *Reading about the Loch Ness monster:* how scientists have searched for the monster
Tour of the local hospital: how a heart monitor works, why the community needs a trauma center
Nature program you heard on the radio: how animals communicate

Using Brainstorming

1d. Use brainstorming to discover ideas for writing.

Brainstorming encourages a free flow of thinking. It can help writers recall experiences they may have forgotten. When you

EXERCISE 6. Students may profit from talking their answers over with other students in small groups.

brainstorm, you concentrate on a broad subject and record all the ideas that come into your mind, even those that seem far-fetched. A weak idea often leads to a good one. You can brainstorm alone or in a group. Find a quiet spot, write your subject at the top of a sheet of paper, and let your mind relax. Record all the ideas that occur to you. When you run out of ideas, go over your list. Circle any items that might be good writing subjects. If you have more ideas as you read through the list, add these.

Here are some of the notes one student made while brainstorming about his own experiences:

Places
- the tree house my sister and I built when I was six
- the hayloft of the farm

People
- canoeing with my grandfather
- my sister's struggle to make the gymnastics team

Part-time Work
- giving my aunt's terriers a bath
- the pros and cons of a paper route

Hobbies/Crafts
- how to do simple calligraphy
- collecting unusual bumper stickers
- making art objects out of old tin cans

Sports
- junior-high football—is it dangerous?
- skateboarding—picking the right skateboard

Clubs and Activities
- raising a seeing-eye dog as a 4-H project
- starting a music group with friends

EXERCISE 6. Using Brainstorming. Choose three of the following areas of experience. For each of these, spend at least five minutes brainstorming possible subjects for writing. When you have run out of ideas, exchange papers with at least two of your classmates. Ask them to tell you which subjects on your list interest them the most. Answers will vary.

EXERCISE 7. Remind students to record in their notebooks ideas and experiences that they are willing to share with others.

1. When I was seven . . .
2. Interesting places
3. People I know well
4. Sports and recreation
5. Chores and part-time jobs
6. Moments I'll never forget

Using a Writer's Notebook

1e. Keep ideas in a writer's notebook.

Many writers keep notes about their experiences in a special notebook, or journal. They express thoughts and feelings about people, events, and books or articles they have read. They may add newspaper clippings, quotations, cartoons, advertisements, or photographs that interest them. Some writers simply talk to themselves on paper or list questions for which they would like to find answers. Your writer's notebook can include anything that interests, puzzles, or impresses you—anything you want to remember or explore as a possible subject for writing and that you feel comfortable sharing with others. Here is an example entry from one student's journal.

> Jill is so funny. She's only three, but she tries so hard to be grown up. Yesterday in church she decided she should sing the hymns with everyone else. Of course, she can't read, so she just hums or goes "la-la-la-da." I couldn't help laughing. When she saw me, she got very serious, scowled and said, "Jimmy, I not funny." It's odd. Even when Jill messes up my room, I'm amused. When my nine-year-old sister does something silly or bothers me, I'm annoyed. I know I'm too hard on her. Maybe it's easier to understand brothers and sisters if they're much younger than you are. I wonder if other kids my age have the same feelings.

EXERCISE 7. Keeping a Writer's Notebook. For the next week, collect at least one item a day to put in a writer's notebook. (You may want to use a folder.) The daily entry might be a few sentences you write about an experience. It might also be a newspaper or magazine article, cartoon, comic strip, advertisement, picture, or a letter to an editor or advice columnist. Use your imagination in deciding what to include in your notebook.
Answers will vary.

Using Your Powers of Observation

1f. Use your powers of observation to find subjects.

Rather than waiting to be inspired, good writers use their powers of observation to discover subjects in the world around them. They train themselves to look closely, to notice details, and to explore the meaning of events and problems.

Here is a paragraph one student wrote about the school cafeteria. This writer not only used powers of observation to record a variety of details but also thought about the relationship of certain things in the scene.

> Twenty minutes after one. The last lunch hour ended fifteen minutes ago. Right now the only sound in the cafeteria is a muffled conversation coming from the kitchen. I'm sitting at a gray formica table near the door to the main hall. A pool of chocolate milk from an overturned carton has worked its way to the edge of the table, where it's dripping slowly to the floor. Under the table on the right, I can see three crumpled napkins, a plate smeared with half-eaten spaghetti and green beans, several forks, a spoon bent into a U, two grease-stained paper bags, and a half-eaten banana. This isn't unusual. All the tables are dotted with abandoned brown plastic trays, lunchbags, and spills. The Pep Club has taped "school spirit" posters on the walls around the room. Behind me a large orange-and-blue sign proclaims, "Be proud of your school." It's hard to be proud of this mess! Why can't school spirit include the lunchroom?

CRITICAL THINKING:
Observing and Interpreting Details

Writers train themselves to be observant. They begin by paying careful attention to the details that make up an experience. Often these are *sensory details*—ones that describe the sight, sound, feel, smell, or taste of something. Then they search for words and phrases that will help their readers understand what they have

CRITICAL THINKING:
Observing and Interpreting Details

This section encourages students to use their critical thinking skills to develop a keen ability to observe and describe details. Explain to your students that this ability takes time to develop. You might help them learn how to begin by describing something that you have observed carefully and listing the details on the board.

EXERCISE 8. Allow the students to share their details with each other either in a whole-class activity or in small groups.

CONSIDERING YOUR ATTITUDE (rule 1g)

This section introduces the difficult concept of tone, or the writer's attitude toward a subject. To make the text's point about adopting a new or unusual attitude, you may want to contrast the model by Garrison Keillor on pages 16–17 with a technical explanation of how to prepare to bat. Some students may also appreciate the attitude evident in the writings of Mark Twain or Tom Wolfe.

observed. A keen ability to observe and describe details takes practice. For that reason, writers make frequent sensory observations in their notebooks. One day they may record the posture and expressions of people waiting in a long line. Another day they might write about all the sounds they hear in a quiet library or about the taste of a spicy Mexican dinner.

EXERCISE 8. Observing Sensory Details. Choose two of the following experiences or images and describe each one in several sentences. Try to experience or observe directly each detail before you translate it into words. Answers will vary.

1. The taste, smell, and feel of eating a spoonful of peanut butter
2. The expression on the face of someone who is angry
3. The look and sound of ice cubes in a glass of water
4. The inside of your school locker and the sounds of using it
5. The posture and expressions of two students waiting to catch the school bus

Considering Your Attitude

1g. Consider your attitude toward a subject.

Attitude is the feeling a writer has about a subject. This feeling is expressed in the *tone* of the writing: the kinds of words the writer chooses to talk about a subject. Good writers do not always search for unusual subjects. Instead, they may express a new or unusual attitude that makes even a common subject interesting. For example, probably thousands of writers have written about playing baseball. The following comments on this overworked subject are appealing because of the writer's amusing attitude. Rather than offering serious advice, he gives his readers some tips on how to act like a pro.

> 1. When going up to bat, don't step right into the batter's box as if it were an elevator. The box is your turf, your stage. Take possession of it slowly and deliberately, starting with a lot of back-bending, knee-stretching, and torso-revolving in

the on-deck circle. Then, approaching the box, stop outside it and tap the dirt off your spikes with your bat. You don't have spikes, you have sneakers, of course, but the significance of the tapping is the same. Then, upon entering the box, spit on the ground. It's a way of saying, "This here is mine. This is where I get my hits."

2. Spit frequently. Spit at all crucial moments. Spit correctly. Spit should be *blown,* not ptuied weakly with the lips, which often results in dribble. Spitting should convey forcefulness of purpose, concentration, pride. Spit down, not in the direction of others. Spit in the glove and on the fingers, especially after making a real knucklehead play; it's a way of saying, "I dropped the ball because my glove was dry."

3. At the bat and in the field, pick up dirt. Rub dirt in the fingers (especially after spitting on them). Toss dirt, as if testing the wind for velocity and direction. Smooth the dirt. Be involved with dirt. If no dirt is available (e.g., in the outfield), pluck tufts of grass. Fielders should be grooming their areas constantly between plays, flicking away tiny sticks and bits of gravel.

GARRISON KEILLOR

Before You Write. Choose a subject that

- is interesting to you.
- is interesting to your audience.
- draws on your experiences.

LIMITING THE SUBJECT

1h. Limit your subject to a topic that fits your writing task.

When you write, you are limited by space and time. You may have two hours and the space of a paragraph or a week and the space of a three-page report. Your writing will be easier, more enjoyable, and more interesting to readers if you make sensible decisions about how much of a subject you can cover.

LIMITING THE SUBJECT (rule 1h) and

CRITICAL THINKING:
Analyzing a Subject

This section and its accompanying critical thinking skill section discuss how to limit a broad subject to a manageable topic. This is an important concept for beginning writers, who often tackle large subjects and are then frustrated by their difficulties in managing them. Be sure to stress how a broad subject can be analyzed, or divided into its constituent parts, by using the various divisions mentioned in the text.

A *subject* is a broad area of knowledge. The subject "science," for example, includes all kinds of science throughout history. Even in a very long book, it would be difficult to cover every aspect of this subject.

A *topic* is a limited subject. Working with a topic means that you can give readers the kind of specific information that makes writing interesting.

How much you need to limit a subject depends on the *form* of your writing. The form might be a paragraph, a two-page composition, or a ten-page report. Usually, shorter forms of writing require more limited subjects. If you are writing a paragraph, you will have to limit your subject to a topic that can be developed in several sentences. For a ten-page report you can select a topic that covers more information.

Before You Write. To limit your subject

- consider the *form* of your writing.
- choose a *topic* to fit the form.

CRITICAL THINKING: Analyzing a Subject

To discover smaller parts of a subject, you can use the critical thinking skill of *analysis*. When you analyze something, you break it down into separate parts and think about how these parts are related. You can divide a subject into parts such as examples, features, time periods, places, events, causes, or uses; these divisions may be suitable topics for writing.

EXAMPLE *Subject:* Monsters

Places: Loch Ness (the monster), Frankenstein's castle, the Himalayas (the Yeti)

Time periods: Greek mythology (monsters in), the 1950's (monster movies of), the Middle Ages (dragons of), today's science fiction (monsters in)

Examples: sea monsters, vampires, King Kong, trolls

People: Mary Shelley (creator of Frankenstein), Dr. Seuss's Grinch, children and the monsters they imagine, scientists who have studied Loch Ness
Processes: how special effects are used to create film monsters, how to live in a house with a troll under the stairs

If your first analysis of a subject does not uncover topics that are limited enough, continue the process. Analyze, or break down, these topics into smaller and smaller parts.

EXAMPLE *Topic:* Movies about monsters
People: Bela Lugosi as Dracula, Boris Karloff as Frankenstein's monster, Steven Spielberg and monsters
Places: the planet of the apes, Transylvania, *Lost World*
Examples: silent films, slapstick monster films, 3-D films
Time periods: the Edison Company's first Frankenstein film, teen-oriented monster films of the 1950's, monster films of the 1980's
Processes: how special effects were used in *King Kong,* how makeup artists designed a face for Frankenstein's monster

EXERCISE 9. Recognizing Subjects and Topics. Number your paper 1–10. For each of the following items, write whether it is a subject or a topic suitable for a short composition.

1. Railroads 1. subject
2. Caring for a gerbil 2. topic
3. How a pencil is made 3. topic
4. Famous Americans 4. subject
5. Snoopy, the all-American dog 5. topic
6. The development of the first railroad 6. topic
7. Airplanes 7. subject
8. How a small plane is checked for safety before takeoff 8. topic
9. Stranded in a blizzard on Christmas Eve 9. topic
10. Safety precautions for skateboarding 10. topic

EXERCISE 9. This exercise, which asks students to differentiate between subjects and topics, can be used as an oral activity.

EXERCISE 10. This exercise directs students to analyze a broad subject to find appropriate topics. You may want to complete one or two items in small groups or with the entire class before students complete an item individually. It is important for students to recognize the many possibilities for limiting a broad subject.

GATHERING INFORMATION (rule 1i)

The text presents the following methods for gathering information about a topic: using brainstorming and clustering, asking the *5 W-How?* questions, and asking the point-of-view questions. These methods vary in difficulty, so you may want to present them selectively, according to your students' needs and abilities. Your less-advanced students, for example, may find brainstorming and asking the *5 W-How?* questions useful, whereas your advanced students can concentrate on clustering and asking the point-of-view questions. At any rate, be sure your students can capably use at least one method to gather information about their topics.

EXERCISE 10. Analyzing Subjects to Find Topics. Select one of the items in Exercise 9 that you recognized as a *subject.* List at least four divisions that you can break the subject into, such as time periods, events, and so on. Then write all the topics you can think of for each division. Underline answers that could be topics for a short composition. Answers will vary.

GATHERING INFORMATION

Writers know they can write more effectively when they have many details to choose from. Before they write, they explore their topics thoroughly, gathering all the information they can.

Using Brainstorming and Clustering

1i. Use brainstorming or clustering to gather information.

Earlier in this chapter you used *brainstorming* to recall experiences that you could write about. You can also use brainstorming to remember details of an experience that lie buried in your memory. When you brainstorm, you relax and allow your mind to wander over the topic. One thought leads to another to unlock memory and flood the mind with once-forgotten details. For example, here are details the writer gathered for the paragraph about a school cafeteria on page 15:

varied sounds	overturned milk cartons
muffled conversation	crumpled napkins
unusually quiet	list of spelling words
mess	bent spoon
food	grease-stained paper bags
half-eaten banana	tables
pool of chocolate milk	formica tops
spaghetti and green beans	several forks
Trash spills over.	plastic trays

Notice that some details are words or phrases; one is a sentence. How you record your thoughts when you brainstorm is not important; you want to capture all ideas as they come to mind.

Clustering is another way to tap bits of information stored in your memory. To use clustering, write your topic in the center of a sheet of paper and draw a circle around it. Now let your mind wander freely over the topic. As details come to mind, write them down and circle them. Use lines or arrows to show how one detail is related to another. You will probably discover branches of related ideas growing out from the center. A cluster about the writer's school cafeteria might look like this:

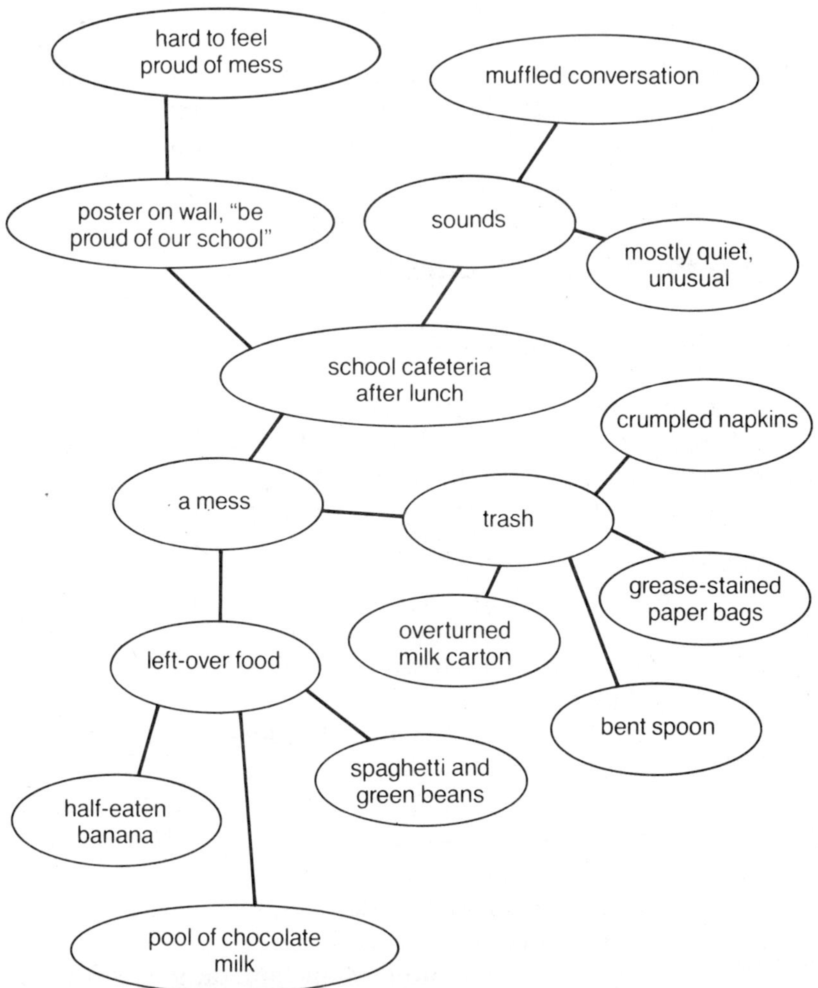

EXERCISES 11 and 12. These two exercises provide practice in the information-gathering methods. Assign these exercises selectively, according to your students' needs. Each exercise can be used for small-group work before students attempt an exercise item individually.

EXERCISE 11. Using Clustering. Choose a topic from the list in Exercise 12, or another topic. Write your topic in the center of a blank sheet of paper and circle it. Begin to add ideas around it as they come to mind. Continue to add, circle, and connect details until you are sure you have run out of ideas. Save your work.
Answers will vary.

Using the Library

1j. Use your library to gather information.

When you are interested in a topic but do not have much direct experience with it, you can use the library to find more information. Refer to Chapter 27 to review how to find information in magazines, newspapers, and reference books.

Asking the 5 *W-How?* Questions

1k. Use the *5 W-How?* questions to gather information.

To gather information for news stories, reporters use six basic questions: *Who? What? Where? When? Why?* and *How?* You can use this technique, too, when you want to gather details from the experiences of others or from your own experiences.

EXAMPLE *Topic:* Observing bald eagles
Who? I and my uncle, a photographer; plus about seven hundred other people
What? A field trip to observe bald eagles; almost three hundred live in the area
Where? On land owned by Nature Conservancy near Keokuk, Iowa; where Des Moines River joins the Mississippi River
When? Last weekend, at dawn, when birds are feeding on fish in the river
Why? To see and help photograph the eagles; carried some of my uncle's equipment
How? Used telephoto lens on camera; binoculars

You can gather even more information by asking additional questions. Notice in the next example how the writer used variations of the six basic questions to go further into the topic.

Where? On land owned by Nature Conservancy near Keokuk, Iowa
Why do the eagles come here? To escape the frozen rivers in Canada and to feed on the gizzard shad
What is the gizzard shad? Small boneless fish
How? Used a telephoto lens; binoculars
Why? It's difficult for a human to approach a bald eagle.
Why is it difficult? Eagles have keen eyesight and will leave an area if they sense anything out of the ordinary.

EXERCISE 12. Asking the 5 *W-How?* Questions. Use the *5 W-How?* questions to gather information on one of the following topics or on another topic. Write down the questions you ask and your answers. (You may need to research some questions.)
Answers will vary.

1. An interesting relative
2. A special community event
3. An ideal weekend outing
4. A problem in your school
5. A hobby you enjoy
6. A childhood memory
7. A lesson from television
8. Your community in 1930
9. A recent teen fad
10. A violent storm

Asking Point-of-View Questions

1l. Use point-of-view questions to gather information.

Like a photographer, you can see a topic from different perspectives, or points of view. You can "zoom" in to look closely at special features. You can set a "time-lapse" view to reveal how something changes over time. Or you can step back for a "wide-angle" view to see how a topic fits into its natural background. To examine your topic from these three perspectives, you ask certain questions.

1. *What is it?*

From this point of view, you are looking closely at the topic, asking questions about its definition, appearance, and function.

EXAMPLE *Topic:* Statue of Liberty

How large is the statue? About 151 feet tall and weighs 225 tons

What is it made of? Iron framework covered with hundreds of copper plates; thickness of each plate about one-third inch

What does it look like? Tall woman in long gown with graceful folds, holding torch over her head

What is its function? Symbol of freedom, called "Liberty Enlightening the World"

2. *How does it change or vary?*

This point of view helps you focus on how your topic has changed or will change over a period of time.

EXAMPLE *Topic:* Statue of Liberty

When was the statue built? Built in France, then disassembled and shipped to New York in 214 boxes; arrived on June 19, 1885, but pedestal wasn't ready

What changes occurred? At first a bright copper; slowly acquired a green color (patina). Flame of the torch copper at first, then gold. In 1916, six hundred pieces of yellow glass installed to make light of torch brighter

Why did the statue need restoration? Torch in danger of collapse; much of the copper corroded. Braces inside the statue weakened; some parts of copper skin nearly worn through

How has restoration changed the statue? New double-decker glass elevator in base of statue. New railing on old circular stairway of 171 steps and a sturdier platform in the crown

3. *What are its relationships?*

This perspective reveals how the topic fits into a larger system and how parts of the topic relate to each other.

EXAMPLE *Topic:* Statue of Liberty

How does the statue relate to New York City? On Bedloe's Island (Liberty Island) at entrance to New York Harbor. Tallest structure in the city in 1885.

What meaning does the statue have for Americans today? Close to Ellis Island, where twelve million immigrants landed; first thing many of them saw from decks of the ships that brought them to America

EXERCISE 13. Asking Point-of-View Questions. Using the three different points of view, ask questions to gather information about one of the following topics. Write the questions you ask and your answers. Answers will vary.

1. A job such as yardwork or baby-sitting
2. A room in your house or apartment
3. A kind of music
4. A nearby tourist attraction or park
5. An abstract concept such as teamwork or school spirit

ORGANIZING INFORMATION

Once you have gathered information about a topic, you must arrange your notes in an order that will be easy for readers to understand and follow. This prewriting step will give you a plan for your writing.

1m. Eliminate any notes not related to your purpose.

A first step in arranging information is to cross out any items that clearly do not relate to your purpose. Look at the following notes for a short paragraph. Its purpose is to inform readers about the man for whom Halley's Comet is named. Which item would you eliminate?

The comet was named after the astronomer Edmund Halley.
My great-grandfather, who is ninety, saw the comet in 1910.
Halley developed the theory that paths of comets are controlled by gravity.
He became interested in comets when he saw a brilliant one over England in 1682.
Halley also discovered the 75-year orbit of the comet that is named for him.

EXERCISE 13. You may wish to do the first item orally before you assign the rest of this exercise.

ORGANIZING INFORMATION (rules 1m–1o) and

CRITICAL THINKING:
Classifying Information

This section discusses how students can organize the information they have gathered by first eliminating irrelevant information, then classifying related ideas and details into groups, and finally arranging these groups into a logical order. Stress that students organize their information by following these three steps in order. This should simplify the task of dealing with sometimes large (and often overwhelming) amounts of information.

The second item should be crossed out because it does not give information about the astronomer Edmund Halley. Keep in mind that if you have gathered as much information as possible, you are likely to have more details than you need.

1n. Classify your notes by grouping related details.

The next step is to put related items into groups. Your purpose may suggest how to group your notes. For example, if you want to tell about amusing events at a wedding, you would probably group details by the time at which they happened: before the wedding, during the ceremony, and at the reception. If you want to describe three antique cars that a wedding party rode in, you would probably put details about each car in a separate group.

CRITICAL THINKING:
Classifying Information

When you *classify,* you identify items that have something in common. Then you group these items under a heading that explains how they are related. Here is how one writer classified notes about the Statue of Liberty:

Design of the Statue
- by French sculptor Bartholdi
- his wife posed as model, but statue has mother's face
- made four-foot clay model first, then larger models
- each model—more than 9000 measurements

Construction of Statue
- wooden molds built from pieces of full-size plaster model
- copper sheets hammered into shape over mold
- internal framework designed by Gustave Eiffel
- frame is four iron piers, ninety-seven feet tall with hundreds of struts and cross-braces

Transportation to New York
- statue presented to U.S. ambassador on July 4, 1884
- statue carefully taken apart and packed in boxes
- 214 boxes loaded aboard the *Isère*
- reached New York on June 19, 1885

EXERCISE 14. You may want to do this exercise orally with less-advanced students.

EXERCISE 14. Classifying Information. Classify the items in the following list under these three main headings: See Answer Key.

Facts about comets
The history of Halley's comet
The latest appearance of Halley's comet

comets only visible when they approach the sun
in November 1985, tail 50 million miles long
two kinds: those with straight, gaseous tails and those with curving, dusty tails
on latest orbit first visible to naked eye in November, 1985
1577—Queen Elizabeth I forbade anyone to look at comet
have a small nucleus, a coma, or head, and a tail
composed of icy particles
Halley's Comet—first observation recorded by Chinese in 240 B.C.
Middle Ages—thought Halley's comet would bring famine and plagues
1910—Earth passing through tail of Halley's comet; anti-comet pills taken for protection
usually look pink
comet at brightest from February to March 1986

1o. Arrange your notes in a logical order.

After you have sorted your notes into groups, the next step is to decide in what order you will present these details. Usually, your purpose will suggest an order. For example, the writer's purpose for using the following items is to tell what happened over a period of time. Such details are usually arranged chronologically —in the order in which they happened.

EXAMPLE *Topic:* How makeup artist turned Karloff into Frankenstein's monster

Details: a. Wax applied to eyelids
b. Invisible wire clamps to pull down corners of his mouth
c. Corners of forehead and brow built up with layers of cotton strips and adhesive

EXERCISE 15. This exercise provides practice in classifying and arranging ideas and details. It can be used for a class oral or small-group activity.

d. Gray-green makeup applied
e. Scar and fake metal clamps added to forehead
f. Took over three hours for whole process

The writer's purpose for the next group of details is to persuade readers by giving reasons. Details for persuasion are often arranged from least important to most important.

EXAMPLE *Topic:* Student council should volunteer to clean writing off lockers

Details: a. If everyone helps, won't take long
b. Bring radios and have a party when finished
c. Graffiti unattractive; and suggest lack of concern about our school
d. If students know lockers are cleaned, may stay clean longer
e. Money saved in fund for another computer

Details that explain how to do or make something are usually arranged in the order in which they should be carried out. Details that describe are arranged to guide the reader's eye—from right to left, top to bottom, or near to far. If your purpose does not suggest an order, choose an arrangement that will be clear and easy for readers to follow. For example, you may decide that the notes under one heading should be presented first because your readers will need this information to understand the material under another heading.

Before You Write. To organize your notes,

- remove unrelated ideas.
- group related ideas.
- put ideas in a logical order.

EXERCISE 15. Arranging Details. Copy the following details, putting them in an order you think is logical. Be prepared to explain your arrangement. Answers will vary.

1. At 5:13 A.M. on April 18, 1906, a severe earthquake struck the city of San Francisco.

2. In three days nearly five square miles of the city had been destroyed.
3. Rain fell on April 21 and extinguished the fires still smoldering in thousands of buildings.
4. The first severe shock was followed by two lesser earthquakes.
5. On April 19, the fire department had to dynamite buildings in the fire's path.
6. After the three earthquakes, fires broke out across the city.
7. On April 20, shifting winds pushed the fire into new areas, threatening the mansions on Nob Hill.
8. The city's six hundred firefighters sprang into action.
9. Broken water pipes throughout the city hampered the firefighters' efforts.
10. Within the week, the city started to rebuild.

REVIEW EXERCISE. Following the Steps for Prewriting. Plan a paragraph on a topic of your choice. Decide on your purpose and audience. Then choose a subject and limit it to a topic that can be covered in a single paragraph. Use at least one of the techniques for gathering information to make a list of specific details. Classify the details and arrange them in a logical order. Answers will vary.

WRITING

The second stage of the writing process is writing a first *draft,* or first version, of your paper. Students sometimes think that good writers write exactly what they want to say the first time. Actually, most writers produce many drafts before they are completely satisfied.

WRITING A FIRST DRAFT

1p. Write a first draft based on your organized notes.

REVIEW EXERCISE. This exercise directs students to follow the steps of prewriting to develop a paragraph on their own topic. To complete this exercise well, students should have ample time to make their prewriting decisions. Some students may also profit from individual conferences with you as they progress through the steps in prewriting.

WRITING

Section Overview

Student writers often believe they can produce a polished piece of writing in a single writing session. What beginning writers need to recognize is that writing generally involves developing a series of drafts. These drafts allow writers to explore and refine their thoughts. Students also need to practice using the critical thinking skill of synthesis as they develop drafts of any piece of writing.

To encourage students to develop several drafts of a piece of writing, you might allow them to write drafts on a word processor. Because the word processor responds quickly, its use can reinforce ideas about the recursive nature of the writing process and can help students create a free flow of writing. This can especially help students who experience writer's block. For students already interested in microcomputers, this approach extends their skill to another language activity.

WRITING A FIRST DRAFT
(rule 1p) and

CRITICAL THINKING:
Synthesis

This section discusses the nature of a first draft—that it is not a polished piece of writing, but rather an exploration of the writer's thoughts on a topic. Stress the tentative nature of any first draft as you present this section to your students. If possible, you may want to invite local journalists, poets, novelists, and other writers to discuss how they develop drafts of their work. Explain that developing a draft involves synthesis: bringing together different elements into a whole.

EXERCISE 16. This exercise directs students to write their own first drafts. Be sure to allow students ample time to complete the drafts capably, and, if possible, arrange individual conferences with students who experience difficulty.

Before you begin your draft, take a few moments to review your organized notes. Then refer to them as you put your ideas into sentences and paragraphs. Remember that your first draft is only a beginning. You should have time later to make improvements.

Also, keep in mind that writing is a process of discovery. As your first draft takes shape, you may discover that you need more information, or you may decide that some details do not fit your topic. Perhaps the way you planned to present information is not as clear as you thought it would be. When these situations occur, remember that the writing process is flexible. You can always stop to gather more information or reorganize your ideas. You can even start over.

CRITICAL THINKING: Synthesis

Whenever you decide how to put together separate elements to create something new, you use the critical thinking skill called *synthesis*. Pioneer families used synthesis when they combined logs, clay, and straw to build frontier cabins. They used synthesis again when they collected scraps of fabric, cut them into interesting shapes, and fit them together to create patchwork quilts. Writers use synthesis when they collect and combine ideas or information to create paragraphs, compositions, letters, and stories.

When You Write. In a first draft, remember to

- use your prewriting plan as a guide.
- write freely.
- consider your purpose.
- keep your readers in mind.

EXERCISE 16. Writing a First Draft. Using the prewriting notes you developed for the Review Exercise (page 29), write a first draft of a paragraph. Answers will vary.

EVALUATING

In any draft, there is room for improvement. To improve a draft, you first must *evaluate,* or make judgments about, the strengths and weaknesses of the draft.

EVALUATING YOUR WRITING

1q. Evaluate the content, organization, and style of your draft.

To judge your writing, consider three aspects: *content, organization,* and *style. Content* refers to what you have said. *Organization* concerns the way you have arranged your ideas. *Style* deals with your choice of words and sentences.

As you evaluate each aspect, you will be deciding what works and what does not work in your draft. You may realize that you do a little of this thinking while you are writing. Be careful not to let your judging block the free flow of your writing. Keep in mind that you will have this stage of the process in which to consider areas for improvement. Evaluation is often easier and more effective with a complete draft in hand.

When You Evaluate. Try these techniques:

- Set your draft aside for a while so you can come back to it with the fresh eye of a reader.
- Read the draft several times, considering just one aspect each time.
- Read your draft aloud, to hear any awkward language.
- Ask someone to read the draft and comment on its strengths and weaknesses.

Many professional writers ask someone to read their drafts and comment on them. Your teacher may occasionally ask you to exchange papers with one or more of your classmates and make

Section Overview

Students need to learn that developing a draft is not the final step in the writing process. They also need to learn how to evaluate; that is, to reconsider what they have written and to determine how to improve their drafts. Students should evaluate for content, organization, and style; they should also recognize that evaluating, revising, and proofreading are three distinct steps.

EVALUATING YOUR WRITING (rule 1q)

As you present this section, stress that evaluating is an important *separate* stage of the writing process, one that allows writers to refine how they have expressed their ideas. Stress, too, that evaluating does not represent failure; rather, writers evaluate because self-expression often requires more than one attempt. Because the notion of style is a difficult one for some students to grasp, you may want to stress evaluating for content and organization with your less-advanced students.

CRITICAL THINKING:
Evaluation

Explain that evaluation is a skill that takes a great deal of practice to develop. Review the Guidelines for Evaluating, and remind students to refer to them whenever they evaluate a piece of writing.

comments about the writing. This exchange gives you a chance to learn how someone else handles a similar writing situation. Whenever you make suggestions about another person's writing, try to be specific and helpful. Before you say something, think about how you would feel if someone made the same comment about your writing. Would you understand what they meant? Would the comment help you improve your work or leave you feeling confused or discouraged?

CRITICAL THINKING:
Evaluation

When you evaluate your writing, you make judgments about it. To make good judgments, you need well-thought-out *standards,* or principles, by which to measure your writing.

The following guidelines can help you decide where your draft needs improvement. You can apply these standards to almost any form of writing. In other composition chapters, you will also find evaluation guidelines that apply to particular kinds of writing. Use those guidelines and always feel free to refer back to these guidelines when you judge your writing.

GUIDELINES FOR EVALUATING YOUR WRITING

Content

Purpose	1. Do all the ideas help to achieve a main purpose (explain or inform, tell a story, describe, or persuade)?
Topic	2. Is the topic suitably limited for the form of writing?
Audience	3. Are the topic and details suitable for the audience?
Topic Development	4. Is enough information given to understand the topic? Is too much given—does it all "belong"?

Organization

Order	5. Does the order of ideas fit the purpose? Will this order make sense to the reader?
Transitions	6. Are ideas clearly connected, with words such as *also, first, these, however,* and *therefore*?

Style

Word Choice	7. Are exact and vivid words used?
	8. Does the vocabulary fit the audience and purpose?
Sentence Structure	9. Do the sentences vary in length and how they begin?

EXERCISE 17. Evaluating a First Draft. Read the following first draft and answer the questions that follow it.

If it weren't for the whims of an Egyptian ruler, the figure we know as the Statue of Liberty might be standing on the banks of the Suez Canal. It's kind of a neat story; here's what happened. In 1867 Ismail Pasha, the khedive of Egypt, asked Frédéric Bartholdi, a French sculptor, to design a lighthouse to be built at the entrance to the Suez Canal. The canal was started in 1859 and finished in 1869. Impressed with the colossal Sphinx and obelisks he had seen on an earlier trip to Egypt, Bartholdi prepared drawings and architectural specifications for a lighthouse in the shape of a titanic human figure holding aloft a large torch. For unknown reasons, the khedive did not respond to Bartholdi's design. In 1869, Bartholdi abandoned the project, but he revived it in 1872 when he was asked to submit plans for a monument commemorating the ties between France and America.

1. Is the purpose of this paragraph (a) to persuade, (b) to describe, or (c) to tell what happened?
2. If this paragraph were intended for an audience of third-graders, what words would you change? 2. Answers will vary. Possible answers are underscored.
3. Is this topic limited enough for a paragraph? 3. yes
4. Which sentence in this paragraph is not related to the topic?
5. Do you think the second sentence adds anything to the paragraph? Would you advise the writer to keep this sentence?

4. "The canal was started in 1859 and completed in 1869." 5. no

EXERCISE 18. Evaluating Your Draft. Using the guidelines on page 31, evaluate the draft you wrote for Exercise 16. Read your draft several times. Consider carefully the answer to each guideline question. Answers will vary.

EXERCISES 17 and 18. These two exercises focus on evaluating. Exercise 17 asks students to analyze one writer's evaluation of a first draft; use this exercise as a class oral activity or for small-group work before students begin to evaluate their own drafts in Exercise 18. As students evaluate their own writing, remind them to refer to the evaluation guidelines in the text. Depending on your students' needs and abilities, you may want to select three items or so from the evaluation guidelines on which students should focus their efforts. This should be less overwhelming for some students than evaluating their drafts for each item listed in the guidelines.

Section Overview

The revision stage is the natural outgrowth of evaluation. Now that students have uncovered problems in content, organization, and style, they should use specific procedures to revise them.

If your students have access to a word processor, you might encourage them to use it to revise their drafts. Word-processing programs, such as *Warriner's Writer's File,* enable students to insert, delete, move, and replace text easily. Thus, revising on a word processor frees students from rewriting or retyping entire papers. In this way, its use might encourage students to make major substantive changes to improve a draft. Revising with the word processor can also help to reinforce the important distinction between revising and proofreading.

REVISING YOUR FIRST DRAFT (rule 1r)

As you present this section, stress the directions in *When You Revise.* Once the students master the techniques, they should be able to understand Revising a Draft, pages 35–36, without too much difficulty. Do go over this chart carefully, however, even with more advanced students, to make sure they understand that for each problem there are specific revision strategies.

REVISING

Once you have identified problems, experiment with changes that will improve your work. When you move around words, phrases, and ideas, you are *revising*—the next stage in the writing process.

REVISING YOUR FIRST DRAFT

1r. Revise your draft to improve its content, organization, and style.

Consider the aspects of content, organization, and style. Whichever aspect you want to work on, you can usually improve your writing with a combination of four basic techniques.

When You Revise. Use these techniques:

TECHNIQUE	EXAMPLE
• *Add* words, sentences, or even paragraphs that will make the meaning clearer.	The War of the Whiskers between France and England raged from 1152 to 1453.
• *Cut,* or remove, words, phrases, sentences, or paragraphs that are unnecessary or unrelated to the topic.	The successful Grand Prix race driver Jackie Stewart ~~speaks with a Scottish accent and~~ retired from racing at age thirty-four.
• *Reorder,* or rearrange, words, ideas, or paragraphs so that the flow of ideas is logical and easy to follow.	Our plans are to visit Vienna in September, London in November, ~~and~~ Lisbon in October.
• *Replace* words or details that do not work with wording or ideas that better fit the topic or audience.	The ~~really huge~~ carefully constructed Great Wall of China is the largest single structure of the ancient world.

The following chart gives examples of problems you might have found through your evaluation. It then shows how you use the four revision techniques to make improvements. Notice that these problems are the kind that might turn up in any kind of writing task. In other composition chapters, you will find revising charts for particular kinds of writing. Remember that you can refer to this chart anytime you are revising a draft.

REVISING A DRAFT

PROBLEM	TECHNIQUE	REVISION
The purpose is not clear.	Add/Cut	Make sure you know your purpose. Add details that fit it. Remove comments that do not fit it.
The ideas are too general.	Replace	Make general ideas more specific. Do more research, if needed. Be sure the topic is not too broad for the form of writing.
Some information is "extra" or not related to the main idea.	Cut	Remove "padding" and unrelated ideas. Keep only the background needed by the particular audience.
It is hard to follow the ideas.	Reorder/Add	Move sentences or paragraphs to fit what a reader needs to know first, second, and so on. Add linking words such as *this, when, then, these.*
Some terms are too complex or too simple for the audience.	Add/Replace	Add definitions to explain unfamiliar terms. Change the wording to fit the audience's age and background.

EXERCISE 19. You may decide to have your students work on this exercise in small groups. Be sure to go over the answers to the questions.

PROBLEM	TECHNIQUE	REVISION
The beginning is dull.	Add	Add examples, incidents, or other details that will interest the audience. Be sure the topic will interest the audience.
Some words are vague or overused.	Replace	Replace words that stand for a group of things with more exact words. Use exact, vivid adjectives, adverbs, and verbs.
Some wording seems very informal.	Cut/Replace	When light, informal expressions do not fit the purpose and audience, remove slang, contractions, and so on or replace them with standard formal words.
The sentences are monotonous.	Replace/ Reorder	Combine choppy sentences. Split rambling sentences. Change the word order so sentences begin in different ways.

EXERCISE 19. Analyzing a Writer's Revisions. Read the following first draft with the writer's revisions and answer the questions that follow it. If you are not sure what one of the revision symbols means, refer to the chart on pages 39–40.

For thirty dollars, car owners in our state can order ~~really neat~~ [meaningless] "prestige" license plates. Instead of a ~~bunch~~ [jumble] of letters and numbers ~~with no meaning,~~ these plates carry a message of six or seven letters. ~~I kept a list of the messages I've seen on these special plates. The messages fall into several categories.~~ [For Convenience,] Some individuals, like my grandfather, simply have their initials and year of birth (HGD 1918) printed on their plates. ~~I guesse that's convenient~~. My aunt, ~~who works as~~ a veterinarian, has a plate that advertises her profession (DVM 146). I've also seen plates that read BARBER, THE DOC, TEACH, and PHOTOG, but I'm still wondering about a plate that read KGB SPY. A small group of friendly folks have plates with ~~messages~~ greetings like LOVE YA, SMILE, or HELLO. For sports fans, of course, a license plate is another way to show their team loyalty: GO SOX, ILLINI, and METS FAN are examples of this. I haven't figured out one thing. is why Some drivers have plates that read A KLUTZ, DIZZY, or FAT BOY. Maybe they like to laugh at themselves. Maybe someone gave them the plate as a gag? My favorite plates are the ones that state the obvious. THE CAR, BACK END, BUMPER, VEHICLE, or MY AUTO fall into this category. Finally, one word of advice: watch out for the car with A GRUMP on the plate. That's my sister and she's not kidding.

1. What do you think is the writer's purpose? 1. to explain
2. Do you think this paragraph was written for an audience of young children, an audience of experts, or students your age? Explain your answer. Answers will vary.
3. The writer crossed out three sentences. Why do you think these were taken out? 3. not relevant
4. Where did the writer make a change to vary the beginning of a sentence? Is this change an improvement? 4. "For convenience";—"One thing"—yes
5. Where did the writer change a general word to a more specific word? How does this improve the draft?
5. "bunch"—"meaningless jumble"; "messages"—"greetings"

EXERCISE 20. Revising a First Draft. Using the four revision

EXERCISE 20. Remind your students that a careful job of revising will help them produce a much clearer composition. Encourage them to continue to evaluate and improve their writing even during revision.

Section Overview

Students often confuse proofreading and revising, so it is important for them to learn that proofreading is a distinct stage of the writing process. Students should also recognize that correcting their errors will make their writing clearer to their potential audiences.

PROOFREADING YOUR WRITING (rule 1s)

When you present this section, remind students of the value of setting their writing aside for a while before they proofread, and demonstrate how they can "read" their papers backward to proofread. Review the Guidelines for Proofreading on page 39, and remind students to refer to them whenever they need to proofread a piece of writing. This section also includes a list of Revising and Proofreading Symbols. Present these symbols selectively, as they can be confusing to some students.

techniques and the chart on pages 35–36, revise the first draft that you evaluated for Exercise 18. Answers will vary.

PROOFREADING

The term *proofreading* comes from publishing. After the printer has made press plates for a book or article, a set of trial pages, called proofs, is run off. These proofs are checked carefully to correct all mistakes before thousands of copies roll off the press.

PROOFREADING YOUR WRITING

1s. Proofread your writing.

Proofreading is another important stage of the writing process. Errors in spelling, grammar, usage, or mechanics can distract the reader from the ideas in your paper.

When You Proofread. Use these techniques:

- Set your revised draft aside for a while so it is easier to see mistakes.
- If you made any revisions, recopy the draft before you proofread.
- Cover with blank paper all lines except the one you are reading (to help you concentrate).
- Check all doubtful spellings in the dictionary.
- Look in the index of this book to find a point of grammar, usage, or mechanics that you want to review.

The chart on pages 39–40 shows common proofreading symbols. You can save time by learning to use these marks. Also, refer to the following Guidelines for Proofreading. The questions will help you identify common errors.

EXERCISE 21. This exercise directs students to proofread their own revised drafts. You may want to allow students to exchange papers and double-check each other's work as part of this exercise.

GUIDELINES FOR PROOFREADING

1. Does every verb agree in number with its subject? (pages 419–32)
2. Are verbs in the right form and tense? (pages 443–47, 457–58)
3. Are troublesome verbs such as *sit/set* and *rise/raise* used correctly? (pages 450–54)
4. Are all pronouns in the right form? (pages 465–71)
5. Are the comparative forms of adjectives and adverbs used correctly? (pages 479–84)
6. Are double negatives avoided? (pages 484–85)
7. Do all sentences and proper nouns and adjectives begin with a capital letter? (pages 512–21)
8. Are all words spelled correctly? (pages 572–93)
9. Is the punctuation correct at the end of sentences and within sentences? (pages 528–68)
10. Is every sentence a complete sentence? (pages 229–37)

EXERCISE 21. Proofreading a Revised Draft. Proofread the draft you revised for Exercise 20. Be sure to check each of the points in the Guidelines for Proofreading. Answers will vary.

REVISING AND PROOFREADING SYMBOLS

Symbol	*Example*	*Meaning of Symbol*
≡	at Waukeshaw lake	Capitalize a lower-case letter.
/	a gift for my Uncle	Lower-case a capital letter.
∧	cost fifty cents	Insert a missing word, letter, or punctuation mark.
∧	ate two much	Change a letter.
℘	What day is is it?	Leave out a word, letter, or punctuation mark.
	rakeing leaves	Leave out and close up.
⁀‿	any body	Close up space.
∾	recieved	Change the order of letters.

Section Overview

Students should recognize the importance of form and appearance in the final copy of any written work. They should also know that there are standards for manuscript preparation that they should follow to prepare final copies of their writing.

PREPARING A FINAL COPY (rule 1t)

As you present the nine standards for manuscript preparation, try to provide an example of a correctly prepared manuscript to which students can refer. You may also want to provide an example of a poorly prepared manuscript to illustrate how form and appearance can detract from the way a writer conveys ideas. Depending on your students' needs and abilities, you may choose to focus on a few standards for manuscript preparation rather than on the entire list.

tr.	The girl with the dog in the red dress	Move the circled words to the place marked by the arrow. (Write *tr* in nearby margin.)
¶	¶ The last step is	Begin a new paragraph.
⊙	Please be patient⊙	Add a period.
^,	Yes^, that's right.	Add a comma.
#	figure#skating	Add a space.
(:)	all of the following items(:)	Add a colon.
(;)	It's not hard(;) I'll help you.	Add a semicolon.
=	his great=grandfather	Add a hyphen.
∨'	Linda∨' s work	Add an apostrophe.
stet	a ~~bitterly~~ cold day	Keep the crossed out material. (Write *stet* in nearby margin.)

MAKING THE FINAL COPY

PREPARING A FINAL COPY

1t. Write your final version in standard manuscript form.

A manuscript is any handwritten or typed composition. Sometimes you can hand in a manuscript on which you have neatly made some corrections. Most of the time, however, you will want to prepare a clean, correct final copy. Certain rules for the form of a final version are widely used and accepted.

Using Correct Manuscript Form

Unless your teacher gives you other specific directions, follow these rules:

1. Use 8 $\frac{1}{2}$ x 11-inch paper, plain white for typed manuscripts or ruled white for handwritten ones.
2. Write only on one side of each sheet.
3. Write in blue or black ink, or type. If you type, double-space the lines.
4. On each page, leave one-inch margins at the top, the sides, and the bottom. Keep the left margin straight; make the right margin as straight as possible.
5. Indent the first line of each paragraph about one-half inch from the left margin.
6. Write your name, the class, and the date on the first page, as your teacher directs.
7. If your paper has a title, write it in the center of the first line. Do not enclose the title in quotation marks. Skip two lines between the title and the first line of your composition.
8. Number all pages. Place the number in the upper right corner, about one-half inch down from the top.
9. Write neatly, forming your letters carefully. Do not let *n*'s look like *u*'s, *a*'s like *o*'s, and so on; dot the *i*'s and cross the *t*'s. If you have to erase, do it neatly.
10. When you have finished preparing the final revision, proofread it again to correct any copying errors.

Using Abbreviations

In compositions, you rarely use abbreviations. Acceptable ones are *Mr., Mrs., Ms., Dr., Jr.,* and *Sr.,* when they are used with a name; *A.M.* (*ante meridiem*—before noon)—8:00 A.M., and *P.M.* (*post meridiem*—after noon)—3:00 P.M.; *A.D.* (*anno Domini* —in the year of our Lord)—A.D. 1986, and *B.C.* (before Christ) —200 B.C. (Note that A.D. precedes the number, but B.C. follows it.)

A few abbreviations for well-known organizations are also acceptable and may be used without periods. Examples are *YWCA, PTA, FBI,* and *UN.* If you are in doubt, spell it out.

Dividing Words

EXERCISE 22. In this exercise students prepare final copies of their writing. Remind them to proofread once again. If possible, encourage your students to exchange their papers to read and to respond to each other's writing.

CHAPTER 1 WRITING REVIEW

This exercise provides students with an additional opportunity to develop a piece of writing following the steps in the writing process. Assign this exercise according to your students' needs. You may also want to compile your students' work into a class anthology.

Additional Practice

Teacher's Resource Book, Worksheet pages 3–15, Alternative Worksheet pages (for less-advanced students) 511–13

Testing

Teaching Tests booklet, pages 1–4, 13–18
Teacher's Resource Book, Test pages 371–74, 375–76, 377–78, 407–412

Follow these rules:

1. Divide a word only between syllables (thus, you can never divide a one-syllable word). If you are unsure of the syllables, look up the word in the dictionary.
2. Never divide a word so that only one letter is left on a line.

Writing Numbers

In compositions, spell out numbers of one or two words; write longer numbers in numerals. If you write several numbers, some short and some long, write them all the same way. Always spell out a number that begins a sentence.

EXAMPLES **twenty-one, 201**
Karen had **90** baseball cards yesterday and now has **120.**
Two hundred and fifty-seven people were there.

Write out numbers like *seventh* and *fifty-third,* unless they stand for a day of the month, as in June **14.**

EXERCISE 22. **Preparing a Final Copy.** Prepare the final copy of the paragraph you proofread for Exercise 21.
Answers will vary.

CHAPTER 1 WRITING REVIEW

Applying Your Knowledge of the Writing Process. Write a one- or two-page composition on a topic of your choice. Use your knowledge of the writing process to complete the following steps:
Answers will vary.

1. Decide on a purpose, audience, and subject.
2. Limit the subject to a suitable topic.
3. Gather details and organize them.
4. Write a first draft.
5. Evaluate and revise the draft.
6. Proofread and prepare a final copy.
7. Correct any copying errors.

2 a

CHAPTER 2

Writing Paragraphs

STRUCTURE AND DEVELOPMENT

A *paragraph* is a group of closely related sentences. Together, the sentences make one main idea clear.

In this chapter you will study the structure and development of paragraphs. You will also learn to use the stages of the writing process to write your own paragraphs.

THE STRUCTURE OF A PARAGRAPH

Well-written paragraphs have certain common qualities. Learning to recognize these qualities will help you write effective paragraphs of your own.

THE MAIN IDEA

2a. A paragraph is a series of sentences that presents and develops one main idea about a topic.

The sentences in a well-written paragraph work together to make one main idea clear. Often, this main idea is stated in a single sentence. In the following paragraph, for example, the topic is

Chapter Overview

This chapter presents material on topic sentences, supporting sentences, clincher sentences, unity and coherence, and the steps of the writing process applied to paragraph development. Eighth-graders might already be familiar with some of these concepts and skills, but they still need a great deal of practice in writing fully developed, well-organized paragraphs.

One point that frequently puzzles eighth-graders is the fact that very few paragraphs in the stories and articles they read seem to have the kind of structure which they are taught a paragraph "should" have —beginning with a topic sentence, developing the topic fully, and so forth. You may wish to explain to the class that in a long piece of writing, paragraphing is used to break the material up into smaller units, but naturally each new paragraph unit does not always introduce a completely new topic. You might remind students, for instance, that in written dialogue a new paragraph begins every time there is a new speaker, and so a one-word remark such as "What?" or "Oh!" is sometimes the whole paragraph.

Then you might explain that a *one-paragraph theme,* by contrast, is a whole composition in itself. Therefore, like any other composition, it usually begins with an introduction (the topic sentence) and then goes on to cover its topic fully. If you want to have your students bring in examples of professional paragraphs which are comparable to the kind of paragraphs they will be writing in this chapter, advise them to look for complete-in-one-paragraph editorials on the editorial page of a newspaper or single-paragraph anecdotes in a magazine like *Reader's Digest*.

Chapter Objective

Students will identify the basic elements composing the paragraph and will follow the steps of the writing process to develop paragraphs.

PRESENTING THE CHAPTER

LESS-ADVANCED STUDENTS With this class, concentrate on the topic sentence, the use of specific details and examples, and logical arrangement. It is probably not necessary to require such a student to learn the difference between the various methods of paragraph development or the various types of arrangement *as such;* you can approach the matter instead by teaching that the information given in a paragraph "should be appropriate to the topic" and "should be arranged in a sensible way." Wherever possible, use student paragraphs (taken perhaps from the school magazine) as models for a less-advanced class; models by professional writers are often not simple enough. *(See listing of Alternative Worksheets on page 78.)*

ADVANCED STUDENTS If these students already write well-organized and coherent paragraphs, you may wish to omit some of the work on unity and coherence (pages 48–58).

dishonest sales practices. The main idea, that wise consumers learn to recognize such practices, is stated in the first sentence. Each of the other sentences helps make that idea clear by giving details (specific information). The details *develop,* or support, the main idea.

> **Wise consumers learn to recognize dishonest sales practices.** Store owners who offer large discounts such as "30 percent off," for example, may first have raised the original price of the merchandise. Another dishonest offer is called "bait and switch." A store advertises an item at a much lower price than usual (the bait). Customers asking for this item are told that it is inferior in quality and are pressured to buy another brand, one that costs more (the switch).

THE TOPIC SENTENCE

2b. The topic sentence states the main idea of a paragraph.

Often, as in the paragraph above, the topic sentence is the first sentence. In this position, it tells the reader immediately what the paragraph is about. It also helps the writer keep to the point.

The topic sentence may instead appear in the middle or at the end of a paragraph. In the following paragraph, for example, the details are given first, and the topic sentence concludes the paragraph.

> Coal miners once worked with pick and shovel and hand drill. Now they use power cutters, drilling machines, mechanical loaders, timbering machines, and roof bolters. Electric locomotives, which have replaced mules, pull larger cars that carry heavier loads. Conveyor belts, too, move coal in a continuous flow through mine tunnels to the cleaning, washing, and loading machines. **In every way, mechanization has vastly increased the efficiency of coal mining.**

In your reading, you will notice that some paragraphs do not have topic sentences. Until you have more writing experience, however, plan to begin your paragraphs with a topic sentence that states your main idea. This will give you valuable practice in identifying your main idea and developing it clearly.

EXERCISE 1. Identifying Topic Sentences. Identify the topic sentence in each of the following paragraphs. Be prepared to discuss how the other sentences develop the main idea.

1. Many people think that the rocket is a recent invention, but it was used as a primitive weapon many centuries ago. The Chinese had rockets in the thirteenth century and called them "arrows of fire." In the fifteenth century, the Italians used animal-shaped rockets that traveled over the ground on rollers. These Chinese and Italian rockets were probably not very destructive. They were designed to frighten enemies, not to kill them.

2. All lasers contain some material—a gas, crystal, or dye—that emits light waves when an electrical voltage or a light source is applied to them. These waves, unlike those in ordinary light, are perfectly aligned, resulting in a beam with such concentrated energy that it can cut through a 4-inch steel plate. Lasers are classified by the materials that emit the light—for example, carbon dioxide gas or yttrium-aluminum (YAG) crystal.

   GORDON GRAFF

3. Michigan was once called *Michigama,* an Algonquian name meaning "great water." Missouri comes from another Algonquian name for "people of the big canoes," and Wyoming comes from *Mecheweami-ing,* which means "large plains." Both North and South Dakota are named for a tribe, the Dakota, whose name means "to think of as a friend." Nearly half of the states have names based on words from Native American languages.

SUPPORTING SENTENCES

2c. Other sentences in a paragraph give specific information that supports the main idea in the topic sentence.

THE MAIN IDEA, THE TOPIC SENTENCE, SUPPORTING SENTENCES, and THE CLINCHER SENTENCE (rules 2a–2d)

These sections present the basic elements that constitute the paragraph: the main idea and topic sentence, the supporting sentences, and the clincher sentence. As you present this section, encourage students to locate examples of paragraphs that have these separate components, and ask students to identify these parts. You may also want to point out that not all paragraphs include a clincher sentence. Emphasize the role of the topic sentence, especially with your less-advanced students.

EXERCISE 1. You may want to use Exercise 1 as an oral activity before students complete Exercises 2 and 3 individually.

EXERCISES 2 and 3. Your less-advanced students may especially profit from completing these exercises in small groups.

A paragraph should have enough specific information to make the main idea clear. Usually, three or more supporting details are necessary for an effective paragraph.

WEAK **Members of a group called the Animal Liberation Front "rescued" 260 animals in a middle-of-the-night raid on a university research center.** They claimed the animals were being mistreated. A university spokesman said they were not.

IMPROVED **Members of a group called the Animal Liberation Front "rescued" 260 animals in a middle-of-the-night raid on a university research center.** The group claimed that they had rescued 80 rats, 70 gerbils, 35 rabbits, 38 pigeons, 21 cats, 9 oppossums, and a baby primate from cruel experiments. Vicky Miller, the group's spokesperson, said that the animals were in "safe" shelters and homes. A university official denied that the animals had been mistreated and said that they were now in worse hands.

EXERCISE 2. Revising a Weak Paragraph. The following paragraph is weak in supporting details. Study the paragraph and answer the questions. Use your answers to revise the paragraph so that it has enough information to make the main idea clear. Write your revised paragraph on a separate sheet of paper.
Answers will vary.

Last night's crucial match between Fairview and Ridgemont was decided in the final thirty seconds of the game. The gym was very crowded, and the fans were excited. The score had been close all through the game, but in the last minute the home team pulled ahead by four points.

1. What kind of game was it?
2. Why was the game important? Which side was the home team?
3. What sounds could you hear?
4. Exactly what happened during the last thirty seconds of play? Who scored the winning points?
5. What did the players do when the game ended? The fans?

THE CLINCHER SENTENCE

2d. A paragraph may end with a clincher sentence.

A *clincher,* or *concluding, sentence* may be used to give a paragraph a sense of completeness. Such a sentence may emphasize the main idea by restating the idea in different words. It may instead summarize the details given or suggest a course of action.

In the following paragraph, notice how the concluding sentence summarizes the details given to support the topic sentence (the first sentence).

> **There is still some good outdoor cooking going on in this country, but none of it needs machinery.** The first meal that comes to mind is a clambake last summer in Maine. Here is the authentic recipe for a clambake: dig a big hole in a beach. If you have a Maine beach to dig your hole in, so much the better, but any beach will do. Line the hole with rocks. Build a big fire on the rocks and take a swim. When the fire is all gone, cover the hot rocks with seaweed. Add some potatoes just as they came from the ground; some corn just as it came from the stalk; then lobsters, then clams, then another layer of seaweed. Cover the whole thing with a tarp and go for another swim. Dinner will be ready in an hour. It will make you very happy. **No machine can make a clambake.**
>
> CHARLES KURALT

Not every paragraph needs a clincher sentence. Such a sentence is usually not needed in a short paragraph. Also, a clincher sentence should not just be tacked on to a paragraph that is effective without it.

EXERCISE 3. Writing Clincher Sentences. For each of the following paragraphs, write a clincher sentence. Try writing two or three versions for each paragraph, and tell which one you think is most effective. Answers will vary.

1. Many movie stars changed their names when they went into show business. John Wayne's real name, for example, was

UNITY (rule 2e)

To check students' comprehension of the concept of unity, you may want to provide examples of paragraphs in which there are sentences that do not support the paragraph's main idea. You may obtain such examples from anonymous student papers.

Marion Morrison, and Judy Garland's was Frances Gumm. Before he became Cary Grant, the dimpled movie star was Archibald Leach. Lauren Bacall was once Betty Perske, and Fred Astaire was Frederick Austerlitz. It's hard to tell where Woody Allen got "Woody"; his real name is Allen Stewart Konigsberg.

2. Surprisingly, in these days of ballpoint pens and computers, old-fashioned quill pens made from bird feathers are still in use. Lloyd's of London, which was founded in the eighteenth century to insure ships, uses swan quill pens for entering marine accidents into its record book. Lloyd's gets its swan quills from Abbotsbury, England, home of the largest swan flock in the world. During molting season each year, every one of the adult swans loses eleven quill feathers from each wing.

UNITY

2e. Every sentence in a paragraph should be directly related to the main idea.

All of the sentences in a paragraph should work together as a unit to make one main idea clear. Sentences that do not directly support the main idea confuse the reader; they should be removed. In the following paragraph, the crossed-out sentence is not directly related to the main idea in the topic sentence (the first sentence).

> **According to psychologists, certain adult personality traits are a result of a child's place in the family.** Adults who were only children are likely to be high achievers, verbal, and self-confident. They like to work alone and tend to be perfectionists. Firstborn children have most of these same characteristics. My sister Sheila, who is a firstborn, is finishing her second year in medical school. Middle children must compete for their parents' attention, and as adults they are skilled in dealing with people. Adults who were youngest children tend not to be high achievers but work hard to be liked.

EXERCISE 4. Use Exercise 4 as an oral activity or for small-group work.

The best way to achieve unity in a paragraph is to check each supporting sentence against your topic sentence, as you draft your paragraph and again as you evaluate it.

EXERCISE 4. Identifying Sentences That Destroy Unity. Read each of the following paragraphs carefully. If all of the sentences in the paragraph are directly related to the main idea, write *U* (for unity) after the proper number. If the paragraph contains one or more sentences that destroy the paragraph's unity, write the sentence or sentences you think should be omitted.

1. Among the Chinese, there are surprisingly few last names. Almost all Chinese last names have only one syllable, and in Shanghai, China's largest city, only 408 one-syllable last names appear in the city's records. The most common are Zhang, Wang, Liu, and Li. Because there are so few last names, many people in China have exactly the same names. For example, almost 5,000 people in Shenyang, Manchuria, are named Li Shuzhen ("fair and precious"). In that same city, 4,300 people have the name Wang Yulan, and more than 3,000 are named Wang Wei. In the United States, the most common last names are Smith, Jones, and White. How many Robert Smiths can you find in your city's phone book?

2. Migrating birds travel at heights far above the 50 to 100 feet at which small birds usually fly. Flocks of thrushes and warblers have been sighted at heights of up to 20,000 feet. Bar-headed geese fly at almost 30,000 feet as they wing their way over Mount Everest, earth's highest mountain. Mount Everest is in the Himalayas on the border of Nepal and Tibet. Highest-flying of all is the Ruppell's griffon, a type of vulture, one of which collided with a plane at 37,000 feet over Africa. At this height, humans would die because of lack of oxygen, but birds have air sacs in addition to lungs. These air sacs enable them to get oxygen even at heights where there is very little oxygen.

3. A newly formed company is offering to broadcast messages into space. For a $30.00 fee, the company will send your message to any of the planets in our solar system. Just suppose

COHERENCE (rule 2f)

This section discusses arranging ideas in chronological and spatial order and by order of importance. Depending on your students' needs, you may want to present only one method of arrangement—your less-advanced students, for example, should easily grasp the idea of chronological order, whereas order of importance could be too difficult for them. You may, once again, choose to supplement the text's examples with examples of your own choosing.

that you could actually broadcast your own message into space. What would you say? For an additional fee, the company will assist you in writing a message that is appropriate for the planet you have chosen. A brochure describing the service is available from Intraplanet, Inc., 4202 Woodlynne Avenue, Indianapolis, Indiana, 43201.

COHERENCE

2f. The ideas in a paragraph should be arranged in a clear order and connected smoothly.

A paragraph in which the ideas are easy to follow has *coherence;* its sentences flow smoothly and clearly from one to the next.

Order of Ideas

In this section you will learn four ways of arranging ideas in a clear order. The order you use for a particular paragraph will depend partly on your purpose and partly on your main idea.

Chronological Order

(1) Ideas may be arranged in chronological order.

Chronological, or *time, order* makes clear the order in which events happened. This order is usually used in paragraphs that tell a story or tell about a historical event. It is also used to make clear the order in which the steps in a process should be carried out. In the following paragraph, for example, the writer uses chronological order to tell how to ride a wave on a surfboard.

> **A new swell approaches, and you decide to ride it in.** This is a much trickier feat. You turn your body toward shore and glance coolly over your shoulder to note how big the wave is, how fast it is coming and, most crucially of all, when it will break. Your judgment, let's say, is just right. You are already planing toward the beach when the wave reaches you. It bears you surgingly up and forward, and just then the threatening tracery along its crest breaks, not over you but under you.

EXERCISE 5. You may want to do the first part of the exercise orally before the students write the paragraph.

You can feel its chaotic turbulence beating all along your body. It goes on and on, like some rolling hydraulic engine beneath you, shooting you wildly toward shore. At last it beaches you, with a certain grudging gentleness. Victory.

JOHN KNOWLES

EXERCISE 5. Writing a Paragraph Using Chronological Order. Arrange sentences a–h in chronological order. Then write the paragraph, beginning with the topic sentence given.

A, E, H, F, G, D, B, C Answers will vary.

Topic sentence: In 1872 Susan B. Anthony led a group of women who challenged the laws that kept them from voting.

a. 1870—Fourteenth and Fifteenth Amendments added to the Constitution; gave black men the right to vote, but not women

b. After trial Anthony continued working for amendment giving women right to vote

c. 1920—Nineteenth Amendment ratified, giving women right to vote

d. At trial, Judge Ward Hunt told jury to find Anthony guilty; then dismissed jury before they could vote; trial helped movement for women's vote

e. October 1872—Anthony led group of fifteen women; registered to vote in Rochester, New York; insisted that wording in Fifteenth Amendment giving right to vote to "citizens of the United States" applied to women too

f. November 28, 1872—Anthony and other women arrested for having voted

g. U.S. government prosecuted only Anthony; trial began June 17, 1873

h. November 5, 1872—Anthony and other women cast their ballots in Rochester

Spatial Order

(2) Ideas may be arranged in spatial order.

Spatial order makes clear the location of the parts of a scene. Suppose you are describing a room. You might imagine yourself

EXERCISES 6 and 7. These exercises provide practice in writing paragraphs in a logical order. Assign these exercises selectively, according to the methods of arrangement you have stressed in class. Encourage your students to share the paragraphs they write using spatial order in Exercise 6.

standing in the doorway and begin by mentioning the objects immediately to your left. You could then mention other objects in the order in which you see them as you move your eyes around the room from left to right. Other spatial orders include near to far, right to left, top to bottom, and inside to outside.

The following paragraph uses spatial order to describe the layers of the earth. Notice how the writer moves the reader's attention from the outer layers to the inner layers.

Earth scientists have discovered that the earth is composed of a number of layers. The outside layer, called the crust, is hard rock, which varies in thickness. In many places it is twenty or thirty miles thick, but beneath some parts of the sea it has a thickness of only three miles. Inside the crust, there is a layer about eighteen hundred miles deep called the mantle, which is composed of flowing rock. Beneath the mantle is the outer core, a layer about thirteen hundred miles thick and thought to be liquid iron. Finally, there is the inner core, which is a ball of hot, solid metal.

topic sentence

four layers described in spatial order (outside to inside)

EXERCISE 6. Writing a Paragraph Using Spatial Order. Use the following topic sentence and details to write a paragraph. Arrange the details in a spatial order from near to far.

Answers will vary.

Topic sentence: From where he sat on the beach, Sam had a clear view of the people and the ocean.

Details:

a. Directly in front of him—family with three young children, umbrella, portable crib, blankets
b. Far out at sea—two ships
c. Elderly couple on chairs reading magazines
d. At water's edge—children building sand castle
e. Close to shore—people bobbing in waves
f. Colorful sails of sailboats beyond the swimmers

Order of Importance

(3) Ideas may be arranged in order of importance.

In paragraphs that give information or persuade, ideas are often arranged in *order of importance.* Usually, the ideas are arranged from least important to most important. With this arrangement, the most important idea stays with the readers because it is the last thing they read. However, the opposite order may also sometimes be effective. In either case, the reader should be able to tell which of the ideas is the most important.

In the following paragraph the writer gives four reasons to explain why a school newspaper is needed. The reasons are arranged from least important to most important. What are the four reasons?

> **Our school needs a student newspaper.** A newspaper can entertain the school by printing interesting news about students. It can announce important events like a basketball game or a Halloween party. The money raised from sales can be donated to a worthy cause or used to buy a gift for the school. Most important, a student newspaper can provide valuable writing practice for students.

EXERCISE 7. Writing a Paragraph Using Order of Importance. Arrange sentences a–c in order of importance. You may use either most-to-least important or least-to-most important order, and you may add other related details. Then write the paragraph, beginning with the topic sentence given.

Answers will vary.

Topic Sentence: Every child over six should be responsible for a pet.

Reasons: a. teaches discipline
b. develops concern for other living things
c. provides companionship

Comparison or Contrast

(4) Ideas may be arranged in an order that shows comparison or contrast.

EXERCISE 8 and REVIEW EXERCISE

A. Your students may enjoy completing Exercise 8 in small groups. When your students complete Review Exercise A individually, have them discuss and defend their answers.

Answers: Exercise 8

(Answers will vary somewhat in wording.)

1. ATBs are lightweight and have eighteen speeds, while bicycles of the 1940's were heavy and had one speed. Both types of bicycles have fat tires and upright handlebars, can go over curbs, and are "plain and strong."
2. ATBs have fatter tires and more speeds than the bicycles of the 1960's and 1970's. ATBs have upright handlebars rather than downturned ones, and they can go over curbs. The similarity lies in the light weight of both types of bicycles.

A *comparison* shows how two people, places, or things are alike. A *contrast* shows how they are different. Some paragraphs use both comparison and contrast.

In the following paragraph, the writer compares and contrasts ATBs (all-terrain bikes) with earlier models.

> Once, when Harry Truman was President and Joe Louis ruled the ring, bicycles were bicycles the way men were men—plain and strong. In those days, you could ride bikes over curbs. They had fat tires and wide, upright handlebars. So what if they only had one speed? Pushing 46 pounds of rubber and steel up a hill would have been very good exercise—if exercise had been invented yet. But then the '50s brought lighter, three-speed English bikes, and the '60s and '70s brought 21-pound ten-speeds, with downturned handlebars and skinny tires, bikes that could *go,* even up hills, but not over curbs. Then, as the '70s waned, there was another development. Out of California came all-terrain bikes. The ATBs have eighteen speeds, weigh 25 to 32 pounds, and are something of a throwback: they are plain and strong, with fat tires and upright handlebars, and you can ride them over curbs. But you can also ride them up hills, and they are light enough to carry up stairs.
>
> DAN LEVIN

EXERCISE 8. Analyzing a Paragraph of Comparison and Contrast. Answer these questions about the paragraph above.

1. Name two ways in which ATBs are different from bicycles of the '40s (when Truman was President). Name two ways in which ATBs are like bikes of the '40s.
2. Name three ways in which ATBs differ from bikes of the '60s and '70s. Name one way in which they are alike.

REVIEW EXERCISE A. Choosing an Order for Arranging Ideas. Number your paper 1–10. For each of the following topics, tell what kind of order you would use. Write *Chr* (chronological), *S* (spatial), *I* (order of importance), or *C-C* (comparison or contrast). Be prepared to explain your answers.

1. A typical Saturday morning in your home 1. Chr
2. How being in the eighth grade is different from being in the seventh grade 2. C-C
3. What the school cafeteria looks like after lunch 3. S
4. Your favorite pair of shoes 4. S
5. Why people should have hobbies 5. I
6. How mopeds are different from motorcycles 6. C-C
7. How to load a dishwasher 7. Chr
8. A time when you laughed a lot 8. Chr
9. Why everyone should wear a seat belt 9. I
10. Why you should be the first student to go on a space flight 10. I

Connections Between Ideas

To link the ideas within and between sentences, you can use *direct references* and *transitional expressions.*

Direct References

Direct references are words and phrases that remind the reader of something mentioned earlier in the paragraph. They may be pronouns, key words and phrases, or rewordings.

(1) Use pronouns to refer to nouns and ideas mentioned earlier.

Using pronouns lets you avoid repeating the same words over and over. Compare the following two examples.

UNNATURAL Jenny gets up at 6:00 A.M. every morning to shampoo and blow-dry Jenny's hair so that Jenny's hair looks shiny, soft, and clean.

NATURAL Jenny gets up at 6:00 A.M. every morning to shampoo and blow-dry *her* hair so that *her* hair will look shiny, soft, and clean.

(2) Repeat key words or phrases from earlier sentences.

A key word or phrase is one that is part of the main idea. For example, in the paragraph about Jenny, the key word *hair* is

CONNECTIONS BETWEEN IDEAS

This section demonstrates how students can show connections between ideas in their paragraphs. For your less-advanced students you may want to stress using transitional expressions. You may also want to point out five to ten transitional expressions they can use rather than reviewing the extensive lists on page 57 of the pupil's edition. Advanced students should practice using direct references: pronouns, key words and phrases, and rewording.

repeated. Repeating such terms not only links the sentences, it also emphasizes the main idea.

(3) Use words or phrases that mean the same thing as words or phrases in earlier sentences.

In the following paragraph, the boldfaced words or phrases are reworded in later sentences; the rewordings are underlined.

> Another project involving ergonomics (a word derived from the Greek "work" plus "law" or "customs") was conducted by the **design staff** of the General Motors Corporation. The designers studied **how a driver adjusts the seat** in response to various distances and angles between the steering wheel and foot pedals. With space at a premium in new, smaller cars, the designers hoped to be able to reduce the leeway of front-seat adjustment, thus providing more room for rear-seat passengers.
>
> JOHN HOLUSHA

Transitional Expressions

Words and phrases that show how ideas are related to one other are called *transitional expressions.* Notice how each underlined transitional expression in the following paragraph shows the relationship between the idea in the sentence and the idea in the preceding sentence.

> **The first plastic was invented as the result of a contest.** After the Civil War, the game of billiards became very popular. Billiard balls had always been made of ivory, but now there was not enough ivory to meet the demand. Consequently, one firm offered a prize of ten thousand dollars for a good substitute. Hoping to win this prize, John Wesley Hyatt mixed cellulose, nitric acid, and camphor to produce a substance called "celluloid." Since this new substance was not suitable for billiard balls, Hyatt did not win the prize. However, the invention turned out to be worth a great deal more than ten thousand dollars. Soon many articles were being made from this plastic. As a result, Hyatt became extremely wealthy.

Different transitional expressions show different kinds of relationships.

Transitional Expressions

To show chronological order

after	finally	next
afterward	first (second, etc.)	now
before	later	presently
eventually	meanwhile	soon

To show spatial order

above	below	in the distance
across	beyond	near
ahead	here	next to
around	in front of	outside
behind	inside	to the right (left)

To link similar ideas

again	for example	likewise
also	for instance	moreover
and	furthermore	of course
another	in addition	similarly
besides	in a like manner	too

To link ideas that are dissimilar or seem contradictory

although	in spite of	otherwise
as if	instead	provided that
but	nevertheless	still
even if	on the contrary	yet
however	on the other hand	

To indicate cause, purpose, or result

as	for	so
as a result	for this reason	then
because	hence	therefore
consequently	since	thus

Not every sentence requires a transitional expression. A paragraph that contains too many transitional expressions sounds awkward. Direct references, which are more natural, should be used whenever possible.

REVIEW EXERCISES B and C. These two exercises provide practice in achieving logical order, first by arranging ideas in logical order and then by using transitional expressions, pronouns, key words and phrases, and rewording to show relationships between these ideas. Your students may enjoy completing each exercise in small groups; after students complete their work, ask them to share the paragraphs they write in Review Exercise C with the entire class.

PREWRITING

Section Overview

To write an effective paragraph, students should carefully plan what they want to say and how they intend to say it. Following the steps in the prewriting stage of the writing process should enable students to develop effective paragraphs.

CHOOSING AND LIMITING A SUBJECT (rule 2g)

Introduce this section by reminding your students to consider their own knowledge, interests, and experiences as they try to find something to write about. You may wish to review Limiting the Subject, page 17 of the pupil's edition. Go over the material on brainstorming, clustering, and asking the *5 W-How?* questions carefully before assigning Exercise 9. Make certain that your students are able to use at least one technique to develop a suitably limited topic to write about.

REVIEW EXERCISE B. Arranging Ideas in a Clear Order. On a separate sheet of paper, write the sentences a–g in an order that will make the main idea in the topic sentence clear. Save your paper. Answers will vary. Possible answers are given.

Topic Sentence: Here are some ways to keep houseplants healthy.

3. a. Don't overwater.
4. b. Too much water causes root rot and kills houseplants.
7. c. Fertilize once a month from early spring through early fall.
6. d. You can test to see whether the soil is dry by pushing your finger into the top layer of soil.
1. e. Use the correct soil mixture so that plants have air and water around the roots.
5. f. Water thoroughly, but let the surface soil dry out thoroughly between waterings.
2. g. You can add one-third sand or perlite to a soil mixture.

REVIEW EXERCISE C. Writing a Coherent Paragraph. Using your paper from Review Exercise B, write a paragraph. Use direct references and transitional expressions to link the ideas in the paragraph. Answers will vary.

THE DEVELOPMENT OF A PARAGRAPH

In Chapter 1 you learned about the writing process. Now you will learn how to use the writing process to write effective paragraphs.

PREWRITING

CHOOSING AND LIMITING A SUBJECT

2g. Choose a subject, and limit it to a topic that is suitable for a paragraph.

A *subject* is a broad area, one that has too many parts to cover in the 100–150 words in a paragraph. The subject "computers," for example, includes all of the different kinds of computers as well as their history, their uses, and so on. (See pages 11–17 for help with choosing a subject.)

To find a suitable *topic* for a paragraph, you begin by dividing the subject into its smaller, more specific parts. Three techniques for limiting a broad, or general, subject are brainstorming, clustering, and asking the *5 W-How?* questions.

Brainstorming

To brainstorm, begin by writing your subject at the top of a sheet of paper. Then jot down whatever ideas come to your mind, without stopping to judge them.

The following list shows the ideas one writer found by brainstorming on the subject "movies" for two minutes. Notice that the list is made up of narrower parts of the general subject.

Subject: Movies
Ideas: history of movies
silent films—silent film stars
how movies are made
my favorite movies—favorite movie stars
Oscars—history of Academy Awards
kinds of movies—Which are most popular?
movie classics—all-time great movies
rating systems for movies
watching movies at home with a VCR—pros and cons
special effects
movies of the future—What will they be like?

Although all of these topics are more limited than "movies," they are still too broad for a paragraph. The writer decided to use brainstorming to limit "history of movies" further, as follows:

Limited topics:
First motion picture
First movie theater
First sound film
First film in three colors

Clustering

Clustering produces a diagram instead of a list. First write your subject in the middle of a sheet of paper and circle it. Then, as you think of smaller parts of the subject, write each one down around the subject, circle it, and draw a line connecting it to the idea that made you think of it.

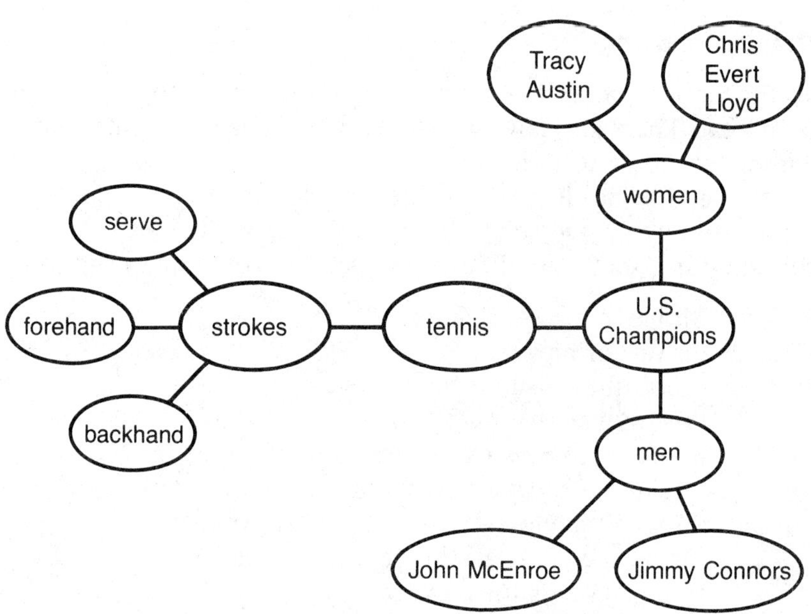

Asking the 5 *W-How?* Questions

The *5 W-How?* questions are *Who? What? When? Where? Why?* and *How?* The following example shows how one writer used these questions to limit the subject "kites."

General subject: Kites
5 W-How? questions: *What* is the history of kite flying?
Who invented kites? *Who* flies kites?
When were kites invented?
Where do people fly kites?

Why are kites so popular?
How do kites work? *How* do you build a kite? *How* do you fly a kite?

Changing the questions into phrases can help you decide whether the parts are limited enough for a paragraph. For example, you could change "Who invented kites?" to "The inventor of the kite," and "How do you build a kite?" into "How to build a kite." Either of these topics would be suitable for a paragraph.

If a part that you discover is too broad, you can use the *5 W-How?* questions to divide it further. "The history of kite flying," for example, is too broad for one paragraph because it covers hundreds of years and many countries. You could limit it further as follows.

General subject: The history of kite flying
5 W-How? questions: *What* is kite flying?
Who invented kites?
When were kites invented?

Before You Write. To limit a subject to a topic that is suitable for a paragraph:

- Use brainstorming, clustering, or the *5 W-How?* questions.
- Divide and subdivide the subject according to time periods, examples, features, places, uses, or causes.

EXERCISE 9. Choosing and Limiting a Subject. Choose one of the following subjects or a subject of your own. Limit the subject to find three topics that are suitable for a paragraph. Keep a record of the questions, lists, or diagrams that you use to limit the subject. Answers will vary.

bicycling	drawing	gymnastics	raising livestock
camping	football	music	science fiction
cars	gardening	photography	skating

EXERCISE 9. This exercise directs students to select and limit topics of their own. Students may use any one of the limiting techniques to develop a narrow topic to write about. You may want to develop one limited topic with the entire class before students work on this exercise individually.

CONSIDERING PURPOSE (rule 2h)

This section directs students to decide whether their writing is to explain or inform, persuade, tell a story, or describe. Many topics will imply one of the four basic purposes.

EXERCISE 10. You may wish to use this exercise for a small-group activity. Have the students explain their answers.

CONSIDERING PURPOSE

2h. Determine your purpose for writing.

Determining your purpose for writing will help you choose details to include in your paragraph. It will also help you set the *tone* of your writing—the attitude you reveal toward your subject and your audience. (See pages 6–9 for more information about purpose.)

EXAMPLES

Purpose: To persuade
Limited Topic: Why our state should pass a seat belt law
Details:
a. Wording of proposed bill
b. Reasons for passing bill
c. What citizens can do to support bill's passage

Purpose: To inform
Limited Topic: Results of seat belt law in one state
Details:
a. Statistics on deaths and serious injuries from automobile accidents during year *before* law went into effect
b. Statistics from same state during year *after* law went into effect
c. Conclusions based on two sets of statistics

Before You Write. Determine your purpose:

- to explain or inform
- to persuade
- to tell a story
- to describe

EXERCISE 10. Choosing a Purpose. Number your paper 1–5. For each of the following limited topics, write an appropriate purpose: to describe; to tell a story; to explain or inform; or to persuade. (For some topics, more than one purpose is appropriate.) See Answer Key.

1. *Limited topic:* The launching of a rocket
2. *Limited topic:* Why every student should take a computer course

3. *Limited topic:* Your community's first settlers
4. *Limited topic:* What you like most about your best friend
5. *Limited topic:* Your favorite place outdoors

CONSIDERING AUDIENCE

2i. Consider how your audience will affect your writing.

Your *audience* (the people who read what you write) affects your writing in three ways:

1. *The topic you choose.* Your classmates, for example, would probably be more interested in the story of the curse written on the wall of the Egyptian King Tutankhamen's tomb than in an explanation of the king's foreign policy.

2. *The details you include.* For a class of fourth-graders, for example, you might tell when and why mockingbirds sing. For an older audience, you might include additional details such as the bird's scientific name and the results of a study on how females choose their mates.

3. *The language that you use.* You would need to use shorter, simpler sentences and easier words for a young audience than for adults. You would also need to avoid difficult concepts or explain them in simple terms.

Before You Write. To consider how your audience will affect your writing, ask yourself:

- What topic will my audience find most interesting?
- What details about this topic will my audience find most interesting?
- What ideas, words, and kinds of sentences will my audience be able to understand?

EXERCISE 11. Identifying Purpose and Audience. Bring to class three different paragraphs from newspapers, magazines, or books. Be prepared to identify the writer's purpose and audience.
Answers will vary.

CONSIDERING AUDIENCE (rule 2i)

This section discusses three ways in which audience affects writing. Introduce this important concept by drawing upon students' experiences. You might ask students to consider how differently they would discuss a class party with friends in the neighborhood as opposed to how they would discuss it with the school principal. Be sure to stress the three points the text makes about audience considerations.

EXERCISE 11. This exercise directs students to bring in examples from outside sources. You may wish to have them attach their examples to notebook paper. They can write the purpose and audience below each example.

GATHERING INFORMATION (rule 2j)

Students can use brainstorming, clustering, asking the *5 W-How?* questions, interviewing, and researching at the library to gather information about their limited topics. Have students select one topic to gather information on and apply two or three of these methods to it. Be sure that each student can capably use at least one method to gather information on his or her own topic.

EXERCISE 12. This exercise directs students to gather information for one of the limited topics from Exercise 9. You may want to allow your students to gather information on topics of their own as well. Your less-advanced students may profit from your assistance with this exercise.

DEVELOPING A WORKING PLAN (rule 2k)

This section shows students how to develop a working plan for their paragraphs by writing a topic sentence and selecting details to support it.

With a less-advanced class or with students who have not been formally introduced to paragraph structure in previous grades, you may find that the concept of the topic sentence is difficult to grasp. There are several approaches you can use to make the idea clearer to them.

GATHERING INFORMATION

2j. Gather information about your limited topic.

You can use a number of different techniques to gather information for a paragraph. If you are writing about a topic you know well, you can use brainstorming, clustering, or the *5 W-How?* questions to think of possible details to include. (See pages 20–25 for more information on these techniques.) If you are writing about an unfamiliar topic, you will need to do some research by interviewing someone who knows the topic well, or by using library sources. In any case, be sure to take detailed notes as you gather information, and save them to use as you organize and draft your paragraph.

EXERCISE 12. **Gathering Information.** Choose *one* of the limited topics you found for Exercise 9 (page 61). Using one or more of the techniques discussed above, gather information about your topic. Save your notes. Answers will vary.

DEVELOPING A WORKING PLAN

2k. Develop a working plan for your paragraph.

A *working plan* for a paragraph is made up of a topic sentence and a list of supporting details arranged in a clear order.

EXAMPLE *Topic sentence:* Japanese folk tales include many stories of animals that help or reward people.

Details:

a. Kindness to animals; Japanese idea of divine spirit, *kami,* in all nature
b. Animals sometimes become human beings
c. Story of sparrow whose tongue was cut by washerwoman —punishment for eating woman's rice
d. Old couple (neighbors) found and cared for sparrow
e. Sparrow transformed to human—offered elderly couple two boxes; they chose small box that contained unending money

Writing an Effective Topic Sentence

An effective topic sentence states a single main idea clearly and precisely. It covers all of the supporting details and *only* those details. It also catches the readers' attention and makes them want to keep reading.

One writer gathered the following list of details about a computer game. Which of the suggested topic sentences would be most effective for a paragraph based on these details?

Details:

a. Computer software game—called "Synthetic Adventure —The Flask of Doom"
b. Created by chemistry professor, Fred D. Williams —teacher at Michigan Tech
c. Teaches organic chemistry
d. Player visits planet Organo—people who live there are organic compounds
e. Player's "mission" goal of game—finding a DNA molecule
f. DNA—basic material in all living matter; transmits inherited characteristics specific to each kind of plant or animal
g. Players, accompanied by chemicals (Organo residents), visit more than 50 locations; combinations of chemicals produce compounds to solve game's problems

Possible topic sentences:

a. Students can learn organic chemistry more easily.
b. A new computer game called "Synthetic Adventure—The Flask of Doom" helps make learning the chemical compounds of organic chemistry easier and more interesting.
c. "Synthetic Adventure—The Flask of Doom" is one of several new computer games.

Sentence b is the most effective. It covers all of the details, it is clear and precise, and it catches the readers' attention. Sentence a is not only too general—it does not mention the specific game that is the topic of the paragraph—it is dull. Sentence c is misleading because it suggests that the paragraph will be about more than one game.

1. Show the class that they are already in the habit of using topic sentences, even though they may never have heard the term before. Already in the third or fourth grade they were writing little compositions beginning with sentences such as "Our vacation was really fun" or "I love to play the piano." These are topic sentences. Every time they begin a conversation with a remark such as "Let me tell you about a scary thing that happened on our camping trip," they are using a kind of topic sentence. Have students give you examples of similar topic sentences that they might use in speaking or writing—sentences that tell what it is they are going to talk about.

2. Help students make up simple, clear topic sentences for their first paragraph-writing assignments. If they are going to write paragraphs, for instance, on "My Ambition," it is perfectly appropriate to begin with the topic sentence "My ambition is to become a jazz pianist." Some students will be able to write far more imaginative openings for their paragraphs, but for the purpose of explaining what a topic sentence is, it is best to begin with the clearest possible examples. Help the less-gifted writers arrive at a clear statement such as the previous one; encourage good writers to exercise their imaginations.

3. Give the class some practice in completing paragraphs for which they are given ready-made topic sentences and a list of appropriate details that they can use in writing succeeding sentences. You can make up the exercises yourself and either have them mimeographed or put them on the board for the class to copy. Such exercises will help give students a clear idea of the nature and function of the topic sentence.

4. Have the class clip paragraphs with good topic sentences from newspapers and magazines and bring them in for an exhibit on the bulletin board. Ask them to underline the topic sentences. (Be sure to explain to them in advance that not all paragraphs in newspapers or magazines will have topic sentences.)

EXERCISE 13. With less-advanced students, you may decide to do Item 1 orally. Then assign Item 2 as individual work.

Answers: Exercise 13

(Answers will vary. Sample topic sentences are given.)

1. Voting in elections is both a privilege and a responsibility for American citizens.
2. For many Americans, especially in the West and in the Sunbelt area, home is a mobile home or trailer.

Before You Write. As you write your topic sentence:

- Make sure that it covers all of the details you plan to include and *only* those details.
- State one main idea as clearly and precisely as you can.
- Try to catch the reader's attention.

EXERCISE 13. Writing Topic Sentences. Write a topic sentence for each of the following lists of details. (You may decide not to cover all of the details.) Try writing several different versions, and choose the one that you think is most effective.

1. a. More than one third of the approximately 60 million potential voters in the United States not registered
   b. About 80 percent of registered voters vote in Presidential elections
   c. Reasons people don't register: don't care; don't think a single vote can make a difference; don't want to be called to jury duty (voter registration rolls used for jury pool)
   d. Voting in elections a citizen's responsibility; can't vote if you're not registered
   e. Countries that have no free elections; many Americans take right to vote and other freedoms for granted
   f. Importance of registering to vote
   g. Necessity of making a special effort to get groups that traditionally have low voter-registration count to register
2. a. Mobile homes (trailers); way of life for many Americans
   b. Wyoming—18.3 percent of homes are mobile homes; Montana and Arizona—13 percent; Nevada—12.8 percent; New Mexico—12.5 percent
   c. National average—5.3 percent of all homes mobile homes
   d. More in Rocky Mountain states because of "boom and bust" jobs; temporary, immediate homes
   e. More trailers also in Sunbelt states; inexpensive and easily maintained homes
   f. Lowest percentage in Washington, D.C.—1 percent; low percentage of mobile homes in urban Northeast
   g. Feeling of rootlessness

CRITICAL THINKING:
Forming a Generalization

A *generalization* is a general conclusion about a group of people, events, objects, places, or ideas.

EXAMPLES Soccer is the most popular sport in the world.
Mammals give birth to live young.
Airplane travel is safer than automobile travel.

To be *valid* (reasonable), a generalization must be based on a fairly large number of facts or on many observations made without prejudice. A valid generalization suggests that additional facts or observations will probably also support the conclusion.

A *hasty generalization* is one that is based on too few facts or on prejudiced observations.

EXAMPLES Snakes are dangerous.
Athletes are poor students.

The topic sentence of a paragraph may state a generalization. The other sentences present evidence such as facts, examples, or reasons to support the generalization. In the following paragraphs from a handbook for foreigners who plan to study in the United States, for example, the boldfaced topic sentences are generalizations. What evidence is given to support each generalization?

> **Americans are very informal.** They like to dress informally, entertain informally, and they treat each other in a very informal way, even when there is a great difference in age or social standing. Foreign students may consider this informality disrespectful, even rude, but it is a part of U.S. culture.
>
> **Americans are achievers.** They are obsessed with records of achievement in sports, and they keep business achievement charts on their office walls and sports awards displayed in their homes.
>
> **Americans value punctuality.** They keep appointment calendars and live according to schedules. To foreign students, Americans seem "always in a hurry," and this often makes

CRITICAL THINKING:
Forming a Generalization

As you present this section of the chapter, be sure to stress that the critical thinking skill of forming a valid generalization underlies writing an effective topic sentence.

EXERCISES 14 and 15. These exercises provide practice in analyzing paragraphs. Go over the two sections on Critical Thinking (pages 67–68) before assigning these exercises.

CRITICAL THINKING:
Deciding Which Details Support a Main Idea

As you discuss supporting topic sentences, ask students to support the generalizations they may have already developed in your class discussions.

them appear brusque. Americans are generally efficient and get a great many things done, simply by rushing around.

UNITED STATES INFORMATION AGENCY,
BUREAU OF EDUCATIONAL AND CULTURAL AFFAIRS

EXERCISE 14. Analyzing Paragraphs Based on Generalizations. Answer these questions about the paragraphs above about Americans. Answers will vary.

1. Are these generalizations reasonable? Explain your answers.
2. What other valid generalizations can you make about Americans? List your generalizations and a sentence or two to support each one.

Choosing Details

Before you write your first draft, look again at your list of details. If any of them do not directly support your main idea, remove them. If you do not have enough details to make the main idea clear, either gather more information, revise your topic sentence, or select a new topic.

Once you have enough details to make your main idea clear, arrange them in the order in which you will present them. You may also want to give your paragraph a title that identifies your topic and catches the attention of your audience.

CRITICAL THINKING:
Deciding Which Details Support a Main Idea

To decide which details best support your main idea, you use the critical thinking skill of *analysis.* You decide how each detail is related to your main idea. Including only those details that are *directly* related to your main idea helps you write a unified paragraph.

EXAMPLE
Topic sentence: Too few American citizens take the privilege and responsibility of voting seriously.

Possible details:

a. More than one third (approximately 60 million) of those eligible to vote not registered
b. Only about 80 percent of registered voters vote in Presidential elections.
c. Can't vote if you're not registered
d. Many countries have no free elections
e. Where do you register to vote?
f. Everyone in my family registered to vote
g. Some people don't register because they don't think a single vote can make a difference; don't want to be called to jury duty (voter registration rolls used for jury pool)
h. Voter registration card—useful as identification
i. Registering to vote is not as complicated or as time consuming as many people think it is.

Details e, f, and h are not directly related to the paragraph's main idea. Therefore, these three details should not be included in the paragraph.

Before You Write. Use the following guidelines to decide which details to include and which ones to leave out.

- Is this detail *directly* related to the paragraph's main idea as it is stated in the topic sentence?
- How will this detail function within the paragraph? Is it an example?
- Will this detail help the reader understand the main idea, or will it confuse or distract the reader? Will the paragraph be easier to understand with the detail or without it?

EXERCISE 15. Analyzing Possible Details for a Paragraph. Decide which of the following details support the main idea in the topic sentence given, and write them on a separate sheet of paper. Be prepared to explain your choices. Answers will vary.

Topic sentence: Running for office in a class election is a lot of work, but it can also be a lot of fun.

REVIEW EXERCISE D. This exercise directs students to choose details to develop a working plan for the topic from Exercise 12. You may wish to give less-advanced students individual help at this stage of the writing process.

WRITING

Section Overview

Students need to learn how to develop a first draft based on their working plan. They need to learn to include the details that support the main idea or generalization stated in the topic sentence and to arrange these details as clearly as possible. Students also need to recognize that a first draft represents the writer's first attempt to express his or her ideas about a particular topic. Students should work to express their ideas as clearly as possible in this first draft.

WRITING A FIRST DRAFT (rule 2l)

This section directs the students to write their first drafts using their working plan, keeping their purpose and audience in mind, and adding related ideas as they think of them. Encourage your students to write freely, leaving evaluation, revision, and proofreading for a later time.

Possible details:

a. Qualifying for nomination—past grades and conduct examined
b. Writing campaign speeches—broadcast over radio
c. Candidates running for same office sometimes best friends: Pat and I both candidates for vice-president of Student Council
d. Fun preparing campaign posters, writing slogans, and handing out buttons
e. In city, state, and national elections, electioneering not permitted near polls
f. Suspense while votes counted
g. Day of elections—candidates exhausted, voters still trying to decide
h. Candidates talk to students: try to make themselves known, try to understand the concerns of their classmates
i. Responsibilities of class officer

REVIEW EXERCISE D. Developing a Working Plan. Develop a working plan for the topic on which you gathered information for Exercise 12. Write a topic sentence. Then list the details you have gathered, as well as any other details you can think of, and arrange them in a clear order. Save your paper. Answers will vary.

WRITING

WRITING A FIRST DRAFT

2l. Write the first draft of your paragraph.

As you write your first draft, use your working plan that includes your topic sentence and list of supporting details as a guide. Keeping your purpose and audience in mind, begin with your topic sentence, and shape each of your supporting details into sentences. You may want to devote several sentences to one detail. You may combine several details into a single sentence, and you may include related details as you think of them.

Remember that you will have time later to improve your writing. Simply try to write your ideas down at this point.

When You Write. As you write your first draft:

- Use your working plan as a guide.
- Keep your purpose and audience in mind.
- Write freely, adding related ideas as you think of them.

EXERCISE 16. Writing a First Draft. Use the working plan you prepared for Review Exercise D (page 70) to write the first draft of your paragraph. Keep the above *When You Write* guidelines in mind as you write your draft. Remember that you will evaluate and revise your paragraph later. Save your paper.
Answers will vary.

EVALUATING

EVALUATING YOUR PARAGRAPH

2m. Evaluate the first draft of your paragraph.

When you *evaluate,* or judge, your paragraph, you read it carefully several times. You look for strengths and weaknesses in the content, organization, and style (word choice and sentence structure).

If possible, let some time pass between writing your first draft and evaluating it. You should try to read your draft as if you were seeing it for the first time. This will help you notice areas that need to be improved. You may also want to ask a classmate to evaluate your paragraph.

The following Guidelines for Evaluating Paragraphs will help you evaluate any paragraph you write. In Chapter 3 you will find specific guidelines for evaluating the four basic types of paragraphs (expository, persuasive, descriptive, and narrative).

EXERCISE 16. This exercise directs students to write their first draft. If you have them write in class, you may wish to walk around the room, answering questions or just offering encouragement.

EVALUATING

Section Overview

It is important for students to recognize that all writers evaluate their work, looking for ways to improve it. With this understanding, students should learn that writing a draft also entails both evaluating and revising. When these steps are complete, then students should proofread.

EVALUATING YOUR PARAGRAPH (rule 2m)

Emphasize that students should focus on content, organization, and style in *separate* readings of any first drafts they write. It would be difficult to focus on all three aspects at once, even for very skilled writers. Remind students, too, to allow some time to pass before they begin evaluating; this may enable them to approach their evaluating with a new perspective. Review carefully the Guidelines for Evaluating Paragraphs on page 72.

EXERCISES 17 and 18. Exercise 17 gives students practice in evaluating a paragraph using the Guidelines for Evaluating Paragraphs. You may have them do this exercise in small groups. In Exercise 18, the students evaluate their own paragraphs using the same guidelines. You may decide to have them exchange papers with another student when they have finished evaluating their own work.

Answers: Exercise 17

1. Yes, the first sentence of the paragraph identifies a limited topic (stories about animals in Japanese folktales) and states one main idea (that the animals in these stories help or reward people).
2. Yes, the paragraph discusses one story at length in order to make the main idea clear.
3. No, the last two sentences in the paragraph do not support the main idea.
4. No, the paragraph does not include a clincher sentence.
5. No, the second and third sentences in the paragraph are not in a clear order. These sentences might be moved to the end of the paragraph to give it a strong conclusion. (Students might also note that the second sentence is a run-on sentence that should be corrected in the proofreading stage of the writing process.)
6. Beginning with the fourth sentence, ideas in the paragraph flow smoothly. Nevertheless, the writer could add transitional expressions (such as *first, then,* and *finally*) to show more clearly how ideas are related.
7. Yes, the language of the paragraph is specific, although the writer could add adjectives and adverbs to make it more vivid.

GUIDELINES FOR EVALUATING PARAGRAPHS

Topic Sentence	1. Does the topic sentence identify a limited topic and clearly state one main idea?
Topic Development	2. Are enough supporting details and sentences given to make the main idea clear?
Unity	3. Does the paragraph have unity? Does each sentence directly support the main idea?
Concluding Sentence	4. Does the clincher sentence, if any, give the paragraph a strong ending?
Order of Ideas	5. Are the ideas arranged in a clear order? Does the order help make the main idea clear? Should any sentences or ideas be moved?
Relationships Between Ideas	6. Do the ideas flow smoothly from one sentence to the next? If appropriate, are transitional expressions used to show how ideas are related?
Word Choice	7. Is the language specific and vivid? Is it appropriate for the purpose and audience? Are difficult words defined or explained?
Sentence Variety	8. Do the sentences vary in structure and length? Are they appropriate for the audience?
Tone	9. Is the tone suitable for the purpose and the audience? Is the same tone used throughout the paragraph?

EXERCISE 17. Evaluating the First Draft of a Paragraph. Number your paper 1–9. Read the following first draft of a paragraph written for an eighth-grade audience. Then use the Guidelines for Evaluating Paragraphs on pages 71–72 to evaluate it. Answer each question on the guidelines by writing *yes* or *no* after the appropriate number on your paper.

Japanese folk tales include many stories of animals that help or reward people. These stories increase the Japanese belief of kindness to animals, it is based on the believe that *kami* is found in all of nature. *Kami* is a divine presence. One story is about a sparrow, a washerwoman, and an old couple. The washerwoman cuts the sparrow's tongue because the sparrow ate some of her rice. The old couple found and cared for the sparrow. They had been kind to the sparrow even before this happened. The sparrow became a human being. The sparrow offered the couple a choice of two boxes. They chose the smallest box, they found in it unending money. In these folk tales the animals become human beings. I think everyone should be kind to animals.

EXERCISE 18. Evaluating Your Paragraph. Use the Guidelines for Evaluating Paragraphs on pages 71–72 to judge the first draft of the paragraph you wrote for Exercise 16. Save your paper for later use. Answers will vary.

REVISING

REVISING YOUR PARAGRAPH

2n. Revise the first draft of your paragraph.

Making changes to improve your writing is called *revising*. Four strategies for improving your writing are *adding, cutting, reordering,* and *replacing*. The following chart shows how you can use these four strategies to revise paragraphs.

REVISING PARAGRAPHS

PROBLEM	STRATEGY	REVISION
The paragraph does not have a topic sentence.	Add	Add a sentence that identifies the topic and clearly states the main idea.
The topic sentence is too broad.	Cut	Remove words, phrases, or clauses that do not keep to one main idea.
The topic sentence is too narrow.	Add	Add words, a phrase, or a clause that will make the sentence cover all the details in the paragraph.

8. No, the sentences do not vary in length and structure (note that most sentences follow a subject/verb pattern). Students will probably note that the sentences are nevertheless appropriate for the intended audience.
9. Yes, the tone is consistent and suitable for both purpose and audience.

REVISING

Section Overview

It is important for students to recognize that revision is a specific step that follows the evaluation stage of the writing process. With this understanding, students should learn that revising entails four strategies which can be applied to revising paragraphs.

REVISING YOUR PARAGRAPH (pages 73–76, rule 2n)

Emphasize that revision is not a haphazard procedure. Each problem uncovered in the evaluation stage can be revised in an orderly way by use of the chart Revising Paragraphs.

PROBLEM	STRATEGY	REVISION
The topic sentence is dull.	Add/Replace	Add vivid details. Replace general words with specific ones.
One or more of the sentences are not directly related to the main idea.	Cut	Remove the sentence(s).
The paragraph does not contain enough details to make the main idea clear.	Add	Add facts, statistics, examples, reasons, concrete or sensory details, or an incident.
The paragraph trails off or ends abruptly.	Add	Add a clincher sentence: Restate the main idea, summarize the information given, or suggest a course of action.
The ideas are not arranged in a clear order.	Reorder	Rearrange the sentences to make the order of ideas clear.
The ideas do not flow smoothly.	Add/Replace	Add direct references and transitional expressions. Substitute more appropriate transitional expressions.
The language is dull.	Add/Replace	Add vivid nouns, verbs, adjectives, or adverbs. Replace general words with specific ones.
The language is too difficult for the audience.	Add/Replace	Add definitions and explanations. Substitute easier words.
The sentences are monotonous.	Replace	Combine sentences. Vary sentence beginnings. Vary sentence length.
The tone is not appropriate or does not stay the same throughout the paragraph.	Replace	Substitute words that are more formal/informal, serious/humorous, etc.

EXERCISE 19. Analyzing a Writer's Revisions. Study the following revised draft. (The notes in the margin show the revision strategies that the writer used.) Then answer the questions that follow the paragraph.

Japanese folk tales include many stories of
animals that help or reward people. These — add
stories increase the Japanese belief of kindness — replace
to animals, it is based on the believe that *kami* — replace; add; replace
is found in all of nature. *Kami* is a divine — add; cut
presence. One story is about a sparrow, a — cut; add
washerwoman, and an old couple. The washerwoman cuts the sparrow's tongue because — add
the sparrow ate some of her rice. The old — replace
couple found and cared for the sparrow. They — add; reorder
had been kind to the sparrow even before this
happened. The sparrow became a human
being. The sparrow offered the couple a — replace
choice of two boxes. They chose the smallest — replace
box, they found in it unending money. In these — replace; reorder
folk tales the animals become human beings. I — add; replace; cut
think everyone should be kind to animals. — cut

1. Why did the writer add the word *grateful* and the clause *who are kind to them* to the topic sentence (the first sentence)?
2. What specific information did the writer add to the paragraph?
3. Find two places where the writer reordered information. Why do you think the writer made these changes?
4. How did the writer vary the sentence structure?
5. Why did the writer remove the last sentence?

EXERCISE 19. You may wish to go through the entire paragraph several times. The first time ignore the revisions. Then discuss with the class the changes, using the questions following the paragraph.

Answers: Exercise 19
(Answers will vary somewhat in wording.)

1. The topic sentence was too narrow. The additions make the sentence cover the main idea of the paragraph more completely.
2. The writer added the facts that the animals reward those who are kind to them, and that they transform themselves into humans in order to do so.
3. The sentence about animals becoming humans was moved up to logically follow the other sentence describing the general nature of these stories. The two sentences about the old couple were combined for smoothness.
4. The writer has used complex sentences and sentences with compound predicates. There are also sentences with phrases used as adverbs, adjectives, and appositives.
5. The last sentence is not related to the main idea.

EXERCISES 20 and 21. Exercise 20 directs students to revise an easy paragraph. This will prepare them to proceed to the revision of their own paragraph in Exercise 21. If your students worked in pairs or in small groups, you may wish to allow them time to share their revisions with the same peers before going on to Proofreading and Making a Final Copy.

PROOFREADING AND MAKING A FINAL COPY

Section Overview

Students need to learn that their revised drafts should conform to the forms and conventions audiences recognize. By proofreading their paragraphs for errors in usage and mechanics, students will prepare their writing for their audiences. Students should also learn to recopy carefully as they prepare final copies of their writing.

PROOFREADING YOUR PARAGRAPH AND MAKING A FINAL COPY (rule 2o)

As you present this section, remind students to refer to the Guidelines for Proofreading on page 39 of Chapter 1. Emphasize that the goal of proofreading is to locate and correct errors that may confuse or distract the writer's audience.

EXERCISE 20. Evaluating and Revising a Paragraph. Use the Guidelines for Evaluating Paragraphs on pages 71–72 to evaluate the following paragraph. Then revise the paragraph, using the paragraph revision chart on pages 73–75. Answers will vary.

Jason is my best friend. He has been my best friend since he moved next door last summer. My family stayed home last summer because our car broke down and it cost a lot of money to get it fixed. Jason has a lot of talent. He plays the clarinet. He is in a youth symphony. He is also in the school band. Jason likes sports, too. He writes well, and he likes to tell jokes. He makes friends easily. Jason has a great sense of humor.

EXERCISE 21. Revising Your Paragraph. Using your answers for Exercise 18 and the chart on pages 73–75, revise the paragraph you wrote for Exercise 16. Save your paper. Answers will vary.

PROOFREADING AND MAKING A FINAL COPY

PROOFREADING YOUR PARAGRAPH AND MAKING A FINAL COPY

2o. Proofread your revised paragraph and make a final copy. Then proofread again.

When you proofread, you read letter by letter to find and correct mistakes in usage, spelling, capitalization, and punctuation. You check for each kind of error separately, so that you do not overlook anything.

Once you have corrected such mistakes, recopy your paper neatly. Proofread this final copy also, to make sure you did not make any new errors in recopying.

EXERCISE 22. Proofreading a Paragraph. Using the Guidelines for Proofreading on page 39, proofread the following paragraph. Write the corrected version on a separate sheet of paper. You may need to reword the paragraph to correct run-on sentences and sentence fragments. See Answer Key.

In the creation myth of the Iroquois tribe, the earth began when the mother of earth fell threw a hole in the sky. She fell into an endless lake but fortunately with her fell a cosmic tree, it had some magical earth around it's roots. The young woman who fell from the sky was saved from drowning by two swans. Then three animals—Otter, Beaver, Muskrat, and Toad—each dived to the bottom of the lake. To try to get some of the magical earth on the trees roots. Otter, Beaver, and Muskrat drownded; Toad was able to get a single mouthful of the earth, it grew first into an island for the mother of earth to stand on, and then it grew and grew and kept right on growing. Until it became the hole world.

EXERCISE 23. Proofreading Your Paragraph. Proofread the paragraph you revised for Exercise 21. Then make a final copy and proofread it. Answers will vary.

CHAPTER 2 WRITING REVIEW

Writing an Effective Paragraph. For this assignment, your teacher may give you a topic. If not, you may choose and limit one of the following subjects or a subject of your own.
Answers will vary.

Athletes	Clothing
Dreams	Games
Science	Health

PREWRITING Make sure that your topic is limited enough to cover in one paragraph. After you have decided on your purpose and your audience, gather possible details to include. Then make a working plan: write a topic sentence, choose the details you will use to support it, and arrange the details in a clear order.

EXERCISES 22 and 23. These exercises direct students to proofread paragraphs. You may want to assign Exercise 22 only to your less-advanced students; also be sure to review students' responses to this exercise orally. Your students may help each other proofread the paragraphs that were revised in Exercise 21 before they make a final copy.

CHAPTER 2 WRITING REVIEW

This review exercise provides an additional opportunity for students to use the writing process to develop a paragraph. Assign this exercise if your students would profit from this extra practice. Remind students to refer to the Guidelines for Evaluating Paragraphs, the chart Revising Paragraphs, and the Guidelines for Proofreading.

Additional Practice

Teacher's Resource Book, Worksheet pages 16–32, Alternative Worksheet pages (for less-advanced students) 514–16

Testing

Teaching Tests booklet, pages 1–4, 5–6, 13–18
Teacher's Resource Book, Test pages 371–74, 379–84, 407–412

WRITING As you write your first draft, follow your working plan. Write freely, and be sure to keep your purpose and audience in mind.

EVALUATING AND REVISING Use the Guidelines for Evaluating Paragraphs (pages 71–72) to judge your writing. Then use the paragraph revision chart (pages 73–75) as you revise your writing.

PROOFREADING AND MAKING A FINAL COPY Proofread your paragraph (see the Guidelines for Proofreading on page 39). Then make a clean copy and proofread it.

CHAPTER 3

Writing Paragraphs

FOUR TYPES OF PARAGRAPHS

Most paragraphs can be grouped into four types, according to the writer's main purpose, or reason, for writing.

TYPE OF PARAGRAPH	PURPOSE	EXAMPLE
Narrative	To tell a story	A paragraph telling what happened in the school cafeteria today
Descriptive	To describe	A paragraph describing what you had for lunch today
Expository	To explain or give information	A paragraph explaining how the cafeteria manager plans balanced meals
Persuasive	To persuade	A paragraph persuading students to keep the school cafeteria clean

In this chapter you will learn methods of developing these four types of paragraphs. Each method uses a different kind of *detail.*

THE NARRATIVE PARAGRAPH

A narrative paragraph tells a story or relates a series of events. It may illustrate a point, or it may simply entertain.

Chapter Overview

Besides understanding the paragraph's basic structure and development, students should learn that paragraphs can be written for four basic purposes. They should learn, too, that each of the basic kinds of paragraphs has its own unique features and appropriate methods of development. Being able to illustrate and identify each type of paragraph—narrative, descriptive, expository, and persuasive—will help students successfully complete composition assignments.

Chapter Objective

Students will use the writing process to compose four types of paragraphs: narrative, descriptive, expository, and persuasive.

PRESENTING THE CHAPTER

LESS-ADVANCED STUDENTS You may want to concentrate on one or two types of paragraphs with your less-advanced students rather than presenting all four types discussed in the chapter. These students may especially enjoy writing narrative paragraphs based on incidents from their own experiences. Here you should emphasize using chronological order to present narrative details. You may also want to present expository paragraphs, as students will often be required to write them in their content-area classes. Stress developing an expository paragraph with facts and statistics. Review carefully the Guidelines for Evaluating that accompany each section, and remind your students to refer to these guidelines whenever they write paragraphs. *(See listing of Alternative Worksheets on page 103.)*

ADVANCED STUDENTS Advanced students should easily grasp the four types of paragraphs discussed in this chapter. You may, nevertheless, choose to emphasize writing any one or two of these types, depending on your students' interests. For example, advanced students may especially enjoy using figurative language in descriptive paragraphs and developing persuasive paragraphs about school-related issues. You may also want to supplement the chapter by asking your advanced students to locate examples of each kind of paragraph in their own reading.

THE NARRATIVE PARAGRAPH

Narrative paragraphs are developed following the basic steps in the writing process; nevertheless, students should learn to focus on the unique features of narrative—especially incidents and narrative details—as they plan their narrative paragraphs.

DEVELOPING A NARRATIVE PARAGRAPH (rule 3a)

In these pages students encounter three aspects of writing a narrative paragraph: relating events in an incident by chronological order; including narrative details; and choosing a point of view. As you discuss developing a narrative paragraph with an incident, remind students to use transitional words and phrases that indicate time order. Stress that narrative details enliven a paragraph by taking the reader beyond a mere recounting of basic events in an incident.

Developing a Narrative Paragraph

3a. Develop a narrative paragraph with the details of an incident.

An *incident* is an event that takes place in a short time. The following paragraph uses the details of an incident to develop the main idea in the topic sentence (the first sentence). Notice that the writer arranges the ideas in *chronological* (time) order. The italicized words help the reader keep track of the order of events.

> Not all of Adamson's encounters with his liberated lions have been so uneventful. *Several years ago,* he was out on patrol *when* he met up with two of his ex-charges, a male named Suleiman and his sister, Sheba. They playfully bounded straight at Adamson. Suleiman grabbed him from behind and the two of them crashed to the ground. *When* Adamson squeezed off a warning shot with his pistol, the animal—no longer playful—growled and bit deeply into his neck. Adamson *then* jammed the weapon into a fleshy area above the lion's shoulder and fired. *With that,* the lion retreated and Adamson hobbled off, bleeding profusely. He made it back to camp where doctors in Nairobi were radioed to fly up and repair the damage. "I worried *all night* about Suleiman," he recalled sheepishly. "I was relieved *the next morning when* he showed up looking little the worse for wear except for a bullet lodged under his skin."
>
> DICK HUSTON

Using Narrative Details

Narrative details are specific pieces of information—action verbs, specific nouns, and precise adjectives and adverbs. They help the reader picture the actions and answer the question *What happened?* Compare the following two versions of a paragraph.

WEAK The boy was riding a bicycle. He didn't see the barrier and hit it. He fell, and the bicycle fell on top of him. He picked himself up and rode away.

IMPROVED The sandy-haired boy in cutoff shorts and a yellow T-shirt was riding a rusty green Raleigh. As he rode across the narrow wooden footbridge, the boy turned to watch a tern dive-bomb into the water for a fish. Looking over his shoulder, he crashed into the metal barricade at the end of the bridge. For a moment he struggled to keep his balance. Then he fell beneath the bicycle, landing on his elbow and crashing against his funny bone. He looked around; no one had heard the crash or seen him fall. The boy rocked and moaned, cradling his elbow. As the terrible pain subsided, he picked up his bicycle and rode slowly away.

EXERCISE 1. Writing a Narrative Paragraph. Arrange the following details in order. Then write a narrative paragraph. You may add other related details. Answers will vary.

Details:

a. Began to smell burning
b. Had to pay for repairing window
c. Nobody in family home, nobody could be reached
d. Left vegetables cooking on stove
e. Last summer—finally learned not to get locked out
f. Neighbor helped; broke bathroom window and climbed through
g. Went out of house for just a minute—left keys on kitchen table; door locked behind

Choosing a Point of View

In the *first-person point of view,* the storyteller (narrator) participates in the action. As you read the following paragraph from an article about a skiing trip through the Grand Canyon, notice that the writer uses the first-person pronouns *I, myself, my,* and *we* to show that he took part in the trip.

We clipped on our skis, slung on our packs, ducked under a gate and stepped onto the snow. It was ice. The morning was sunny, but there had been no fresh snow for more than a

Depending on your students' abilities, you may want to omit the discussion on choosing a point of view, a difficult concept to master. To illustrate point of view, you may want to tell the same story from the perspective of two different participants. Your advanced students should, however, be encouraged to experiment with both first- and third-person points of view. This section concludes with Guidelines for Evaluating Narrative Paragraphs; review them carefully with your students.

EXERCISE 1. This exercise provides the details for a narrative paragraph. The students must put these details in order and then write the paragraph. You may want to ask volunteers to read their paragraphs aloud.

EXERCISE 2. Review carefully the five points in *Before You Write* before you assign this exercise. With less-advanced students, review also the steps of the writing process included directly below the exercise.

week, and the surface was solidly frozen. *We* set off at a modest pace, with Quiroz up front. *I* charged up a few hills to assure *myself I* could handle this, then dropped in behind Babbitt and Warner. *My* pack was already heavy.

KENNY MOORE

In the *third-person point of view,* the storyteller does not take part in the story. Instead, the writer uses the third-person pronouns *he, him, she, her, they,* and *them* to refer to the people in the story. The paragraphs about George Adamson (page 80) and about the boy on the bicycle (pages 80–81) are written from the third-person point of view.

Before beginning a narrative paragraph, decide which point of view you will use. Do not mix first- and third-person points of view in the same paragraph.

Before You Write. To develop a narrative paragraph:

- Select an incident that takes place in no more than a few hours.
- Use the *5 W-How?* questions to gather details.
- Arrange the important events in chronological order.
- Choose first-person or third-person point of view.
- Write a topic sentence that sums up the incident, tells how it came about, or states the general idea the incident illustrates.

EXERCISE 2. Writing a Narrative Paragraph. Write a narrative paragraph using the details of an incident. You may use one of the following ideas or one of your own. Answers will vary.

1. An experiment that didn't work
2. Overcoming a fear
3. A time when I laughed a lot
4. A chore that turned out to be fun
5. A promise that was hard to keep

PREWRITING Use one or more of the techniques on pages 12–15 to find possible incidents to use. Select an incident that will interest your audience, and use the *5 W-How?* questions to gather details. Arrange the important events in chronological order. Then write a topic sentence that sums up the incident, tells how it came about, or states the general idea that the incident illustrates.

WRITING As you draft your paragraph, include only those details that will help the reader understand what happened. Try not to get sidetracked into details that are not needed and may confuse the reader.

EVALUATING AND REVISING Ask yourself: Have I arranged the events in the order in which they took place? Have I included only details that will help my readers understand what happened? Then use the Guidelines for Evaluating Narrative Paragraphs below and the paragraph revision chart on pages 73–75 to judge and improve your writing.

PROOFREADING AND MAKING A FINAL COPY After using the Guidelines for Proofreading on page 39 to correct your paper, make a final copy and proofread it.

Evaluating and Revising Narrative Paragraphs

You can use the following guidelines to evaluate, or judge, the narrative paragraphs you write. The paragraph revision chart on pages 73–75 will help you improve your writing.

GUIDELINES FOR EVALUATING NARRATIVE PARAGRAPHS

Topic Sentence	1. Does the topic sentence sum up the incident, tell how it came about, or state a general idea?
Topic Development	2. Are enough details included so that the audience can understand what happened?
Unity	3. Have unrelated details been left out?
Order of Ideas	4. Are the actions arranged in the order in which they took place?
Relationships Between Ideas	5. Do the ideas flow smoothly? Are they linked with direct references and with transitional expressions (*then, in the meantime,* etc.)?
Word Choice	6. Is the language specific rather than general? Is it appropriate for the audience?

EXERCISE 3. This exercise directs students to evaluate and revise a narrative paragraph. Note that the exercise first directs students to evaluate the paragraph with the guidelines on page 83. Their evaluation should make students notice that the paragraph lacks narrative details. Using the five questions that follow the sample paragraph, students can generate the narrative details needed to revise and improve the paragraph. Students may enjoy completing this exercise in small groups and then sharing their revisions with the entire class.

Answers: Exercise 3
(Answers will vary somewhat in wording.)

1. The topic sentence introduces the incident and sets the time of the event.
2. The main events of the incident are present, but details are missing.
3. Depending on how the writer might have more fully developed the story, the facts that Amy locked the doors and that she cried may or may not be relevant.
4. Yes, the actions are in order.
5. No, the ideas do not flow smoothly; they lack transitions.
6. The language is mostly general, except for the specific verb *coasted.* The language is probably too simple for the audience.

REVIEW EXERCISE A. This review exercise provides an additional opportunity for students to write narrative paragraphs. As an alternative, you may allow students to select their own topics to write about for this exercise. Encourage students to share their paragraphs with small groups or with the rest of the class.

EXERCISE 3. Evaluating and Revising a Narrative Paragraph. Number your paper 1–6. Use the guidelines above to evaluate the following first draft written for an eighth-grade audience. Answer each question on the guidelines in writing. Then revise the paragraph on a separate sheet of paper, using the paragraph revision chart on pages 73–75. The questions following the paragraph may help you think of narrative details to add to improve the paragraph. Answers will vary.

> When Amy was very little, she learned something important about driving a car. She got in her father's car. She locked the doors and released the emergency brake. The driveway was on a hill, so the car coasted backward down the hill. Amy cried. The car stopped moving. It was blocking the street. Amy's father came and got her out.

1. How old was Amy?
2. What did she learn from this experience?
3. How did Amy feel when the car began to move?
4. How did Amy's father find out what had happened?
5. How did he get Amy out of the car?

REVIEW EXERCISE A. Writing a Narrative Paragraph. Write a paragraph based on one of the following incidents or on an incident of your own choice. Answers will vary.

1. You become lost on a wilderness hike.
2. You are taking your little sister for a walk when you meet a dangerous-looking dog.
3. You look out your window and see black smoke pouring from a neighbor's house (or apartment).
4. You help an elderly neighbor who lives alone.
5. You work very hard on a science project.

THE DESCRIPTIVE PARAGRAPH

A descriptive paragraph creates a picture in the reader's mind. It focuses on one person, place, or object. The details are usually arranged in spatial order.

Developing Descriptive Paragraphs

3b. Develop a descriptive paragraph with concrete and sensory details.

Concrete details mention specific objects, places, or people. *Sensory details* appeal directly to the senses: sight, hearing, taste, touch, and smell. Notice how the writer of the following paragraph uses concrete details and sensory details that appeal to smell, hearing, and sight to describe a place.

> I remember my first walk in a Nigerian rain forest. It is moist and the air is soft, a comforting warm smell actually made by the fungi underfoot. The trunks of the great trees rise straight up and tall, set out like pillars along the nave of a great Gothic cathedral. Clouds float between the branches, drifting patches of vapor that come and go. The trees branch out at about a hundred feet. Where there is a break in the canopy, light streams through against the rising mist in rays that you can see. I remember how an ugly dead growth on the branch of one tree suddenly opens in at the middle and says, "Gronk." It is a giant yellow casque hornbill. I remember, too, how the silence that makes me place my feet so carefully is broken as frogs begin to sing, then more frogs and more until the song sweeps into the distance and stops as suddenly as it began.
>
> PAUL COLINVAUX

EXERCISE 4. Gathering Sensory Details. Spend at least five minutes carefully observing each of the following objects. Write three sensory details that you could use to describe each object.
See Answer Key.

1. A green pepper
2. A penny
3. A toothbrush
4. A pencil
5. A shoe

Using Precise Language

A descriptive paragraph should be vivid. Specific nouns, action verbs, and carefully chosen adjectives and adverbs are needed to give the reader a clear picture.

THE DESCRIPTIVE PARAGRAPH

Developing Descriptive Paragraphs (rule 3b)

This section outlines several hints students should consider as they plan their descriptive paragraphs. Of particular importance are deciding on a main impression, listing and arranging concrete and sensory details, and considering how to use figurative language effectively. The text also discusses the distinction between concrete and sensory details. You may want to supplement the text's models —perhaps with paragraphs from the work of Annie Dillard, Lewis Thomas, or Joan Didion.

EXERCISE 4. As an alternative to this exercise, you may want to ask students to use only one sense to gather sensory details about these common objects. Students could, for example, gather details about a green pepper using only their sense of touch. Allow students to share the details they gather; this could lead to a lively class discussion.

EXERCISES 5–7. You may want to do Exercise 5 orally. Before assigning Exercise 6, be sure the students have had time to find a photograph. You could ask them to search for one as a homework assignment. Be sure to have some extras in case someone forgets to bring in a picture. Students will probably enjoy sharing their paragraphs from Exercises 6 and 7.

The following paragraph is a character sketch of Julian Lennon, the rock musician whose father, John, was a member of the Beatles. Notice how the writer of the paragraph uses precise language to describe Julian.

> He is beginning to look more like his father. His pale face displays soft and sensuous features and sparkling eyes. His personality is an odd contradiction between depression and energy, self-doubt and triumph of spirit. Contemplating the demands of a new tour, he is extremely nervous. He sits for a while drumming his fingers, then jumps up and dashes around the room on a skateboard, then stops to fake a sob and moan, "I want me mommy!" But as rehearsals progress, the nervousness leaves him. He sings with abandon. His tentative movements on stage become a strut. In the first performance, the audience screams with delight. He is clearly in command of the stage and everyone on it, the hall and everyone in it.

EXERCISE 5. Making Descriptions Vivid. Revise each of the following sentences. Add specific nouns, action verbs, and precise modifiers to create a clear picture. Answers will vary.

1. A woman answered the door.
2. The student sat at the desk.
3. Someone was using a machine that made a lot of noise.
4. The singer sang a sad song.
5. The audience applauded.
6. The basketball player scored two points.
7. The kitchen was filled with a good smell.
8. The baby cried loudly for a long time.
9. Lou felt bad about the news.
10. The driver got in the car and drove away quickly.

EXERCISE 6. Writing a Paragraph Describing a Person. Find a photograph in a newspaper or magazine that clearly shows a person's face and body. Observe the photograph carefully, and write a paragraph describing the person. Answers will vary.

Using Comparisons and Figurative Language

Comparisons and figurative language help make a description vivid. In the following paragraph, Lewis Thomas compares the "dead" moon with the "living" earth. To say that the earth is alive is to use a figure of speech called a *metaphor.* Notice the other italicized figurative language.

> Viewed from the distance of the moon, the astonishing thing about the earth, catching the breath, is that it is alive. The photographs show the dry pounded surface of the moon in the foreground, *dead as an old bone.* Aloft, *floating free* beneath the moist, gleaming *membrane of bright blue sky,* is the rising earth, the only *exuberant thing* in this part of the cosmos. If you could look long enough, you would see the swirling of the great drifts of white cloud, covering and uncovering the half-hidden masses of land. If you had been looking for a very long, geologic time, you could have seen the continents themselves in motion, drifting apart on their crustal plates, *held afloat* by the fire beneath. It has the organized self-contained look of *a live creature, full of information, marvelously skilled in handling the sun.*
>
> LEWIS THOMAS

EXERCISE 7. Writing a Paragraph Describing an Object. Write a paragraph describing one of the objects in Exercise 4 or an object of your own choosing. Answers will vary.

Creating a Main Impression

A descriptive paragraph may create a single main impression of a topic. Often, that main impression is revealed in the topic sentence. In the following paragraph, for example, the topic sentence gives the writer's main impression of the way she saw a harbor in China: as a speeded-up movie. Each supporting detail she includes helps reinforce that impression.

> As our bus draws up at the wharf in Chongqing, once known as Chungking, we seem to enter a speeded-up movie. Hordes of people scramble down a crazy-quilt pattern of steps that saw-tooth steeply in two opposing directions, criss-crossing

Creating a Main Impression

As you present this section, stress first that students should decide upon the main impression they wish to convey about the place, object, or person they are describing. Then they should concentrate on selecting words that will convey this impression: specific verbs, precise modifiers, comparisons, and figurative language. Your less-advanced students may have some difficulty with the description by Barbara Goldsmith. Go over this description orally with them. Advanced students should be especially encouraged to write descriptions of people. This section ends with *Before You Write* on page 88. You may want to point out these suggestions before your students do Exercises 6–8.

EXERCISE 8. You may wish to give students a chance to gather details for this exercise several days before they write. You might also permit those who plan to write about the same place (for example, the cafeteria during lunch) to talk together in a group as a prewriting strategy.

in the middle. It is low tide, and there are more than 300 steps swarming with men, women, and children all scampering down toward the river, carrying bamboo poles balancing baskets of cabbages, apples, mandarin oranges, tangerines, persimmons, radishes, grain, spices, chickens, ducks, fish. Children carry stoves, old men fishing poles and nets, Mao-suited businessmen briefcases. Beside a gangplank, people squat in small groups like coveys of birds, counting producc, rcarranging cargo and finally funneling into a green, triple-decked ferryboat with a bright red star at the top. When the boat pulls away an hour later, we have observed more of life and human interaction than at any previous time in China.

BARBARA GOLDSMITH

EXERCISE 8. Writing a Paragraph Describing a Place. Write a paragraph describing one of the following places or a place of your own choosing. Answers will vary.

1. The cafeteria during lunch hour
2. An empty football stadium
3. A park during a snowfall (or heavy rainstorm)
4. The street outside your home at 5:00 A.M.
5. A classroom during a test

Before You Write. To create a main impression in a descriptive paragraph:

- Use the *5 W-How?* questions to gather precise concrete and sensory details.
- Select only those details that will create a single impression.
- Arrange the details in spatial order.
- Write a topic sentence that gives the main impression you want to create.

Evaluating and Revising Descriptive Paragraphs

Use the guidelines on the next page to evaluate the descriptive paragraphs you write. Once you have decided which areas need to be improved, refer to the paragraph revision chart on pages 73–75 to revise your writing.

GUIDELINES FOR EVALUATING DESCRIPTIVE PARAGRAPHS

Topic Sentence	1. Does the topic sentence identify the topic? If it creates a main impression, does it do so clearly?
Topic Development	2. Are enough concrete and sensory details included to create a vivid picture of the topic?
Unity	3. Does each sentence reinforce the main impression?
Order of Ideas	4. Are the details arranged in spatial order?
Relationships Between Ideas	5. Do the ideas flow smoothly? Are they linked with direct references and with transitional expressions (*above, to the left,* etc.)?
Word Choice	6. Is the language specific rather than general? If figurative language is used, is it appropriate and effective?

REVIEW EXERCISE B. Evaluating and Revising a Descriptive Paragraph. Use the guidelines above to evaluate the following paragraph. Then revise the paragraph, adding specific details and replacing general words with specific ones. You may make up any additional information you need. The questions following the paragraph may help you think of details to add.
Answers will vary.

> The girl walked to the door of the house. She had long hair. She wore ordinary clothes. She looked worried and nervous. She carried something in her right hand. She waited next to the door.

1. What does the girl look like? How old is she? How tall? Is she slim or heavy? What color is her hair? How does she wear it?
2. What exactly is the girl wearing? What color are her clothes? Is the girl's appearance neat or sloppy?
3. How can an observer tell that she is worried and nervous? What is she carrying in her right hand? How does she move?
4. What does the house look like? Why is the girl waiting at the door? What does she do while she waits?
5. What sounds can the girl hear? What can she smell?

REVIEW EXERCISE B. To evaluate and revise the descriptive paragraph in this exercise, students should refer to Guidelines for Evaluating Descriptive Paragraphs that precede the exercise. Students can also apply the evaluation guidelines to their own descriptive paragraphs from Exercises 6, 7, and/or 8 after you have discussed their evaluations and revisions for this review exercise.

THE EXPOSITORY PARAGRAPH (rules 3c–3f)

This section presents four methods for developing expository paragraphs: using facts and statistics, using examples, using definitions, and using the details of a process. Of these four methods, students most often use facts and statistics and definitions in writing expository paragraphs for their content-area classes; accordingly, you may want to stress these two methods of paragraph development. Be sure your students understand the difference between facts and opinions; also stress that a paragraph developed with a definition first places the word in its general class before its distinguishing characteristics are discussed. You may want to ask your students to find additional examples of each type of paragraph development, either from textbooks or from their extracurricular reading. Your less-advanced students may enjoy explaining processes with which they are personally experienced, whereas your advanced students may enjoy explaining complex scientific processes.

EXERCISES 9 and 10. Encourage your students to share their paragraphs orally with the rest of the class or a small group.

THE EXPOSITORY PARAGRAPH

The purpose of an expository paragraph is to give information or to explain. Expository paragraphs may be developed with facts and statistics, with examples, by definitions, with the details of a process, or by a combination of these methods.

The order in which you arrange the ideas in an expository paragraph depends on the specific purpose of the paragraph. A paragraph explaining how to do something, for example, uses chronological order to help the audience understand what to do first, second, and so on. (See pages 25–28 for more information.)

Developing with Facts and Statistics

3c. Develop an expository paragraph with facts and statistics.

A *fact* is information that can be proved to be true; a *statistic* is a numerical fact. The following paragraph uses facts and statistics to give information about a professional basketball.player.

> Marques Haynes was on the road again, just as he has been every season since he left Langston nearly 40 years ago. He won't admit to his exact age—"I'm 37 $\frac{1}{2}$ and holding," the man says—but he figures to be 60 or thereabouts, assuming he was 21 when he graduated from Langston in '46. That was about 12,000 basketball games ago, Haynes estimates, played during an odyssey of more than four million miles with the Globetrotters (1947–'53); the original Harlem Magicians ('53–72); the Globetrotters again ('72–79); Meadowlark Lemon's Bucketeers ('79-81); the Harlem Wizards ('81–83); and finally his own Harlem Magicians again. It is an odyssey that has taken him to 97 countries and to so many American cities, towns, and hamlets that he is hard put, glancing at a map, to find a place he hasn't been.
>
> WILLIAM NACK

EXERCISE 9. Writing a Paragraph Using Facts and Statistics. Write an expository paragraph based on the following information. You need not use all of the information.

Answers will vary.

Details:

a. Roberto Clemente, one of baseball's all-time great outfielders and hitters
b. Tried to help others, especially young people in Puerto Rico, where he was born and grew up
c. Humanitarian—person who tried to help others
d. In 1972 after earthquake in Managua, Nicaragua, Clemente appealed to Puerto Ricans on radio and TV: contribute food and supplies for Managuans
e. Raised more than $150,000; 26 tons of supplies
f. New Year's Eve, 1972—Clemente on flight from San Juan, Puerto Rico, to Managua to deliver supplies
g. Plane took off at 9:00 P.M.; crashed at sea—no survivors
h. Clemente mourned as "*un gran hombre—un hombre de buen corazón*" (a great man—a man of good heart)

EXERCISE 10. Writing a Paragraph Using Facts and Statistics. Write an expository paragraph on one of the following topics or on a topic of your own. Answers will vary.

1. Redwood trees
2. Blue whales
3. The Lincoln Memorial
4. The most recent Super Bowl
5. The Mississippi River

PREWRITING Use reliable reference works (See Chapter 27.) to gather accurate facts and statistics. As you select details to include, remember that too much information may confuse or bore your audience. Arrange your notes in an order that will be easy to follow, and then write a topic sentence stating your main idea.

WRITING Evaluate your choice of details as you write your draft. Remember to define unfamiliar terms for your audience.

EVALUATING AND REVISING Ask yourself: Does every piece of information directly support my main idea? Have I included neither too few details nor too many? Then use the evaluation guidelines on page 97 and the paragraph revision chart on pages 73–75 to judge and improve your writing.

EXERCISES 11 and 12. Assign one or both of these exercises if you taught the method of developing a paragraph through examples.

PROOFREADING AND MAKING A FINAL COPY First make sure that you copied the information from your notes correctly. Then use the Guidelines for Proofreading on page 39. Remember to proofread your final copy as well.

Developing with Examples

3d. Develop an expository paragraph with examples.

An *example* is a person, thing, or event that stands for others of the same kind. Using examples that your audience is familiar with can help you make a general idea clear in the limited space of a paragraph. In the following paragraph, the writer uses examples to develop the main idea. What is that idea?

> The story of David with his slingshot slaying the clumsy giant has delighted children for at least three thousand years. David was an early example of a common type of folk hero—the one who fights with skill and daring against superior force and wins. Sometime before David's triumph in the valley of Elah, Odysseus was in Sicily winning his battle of wits against the Cyclops. Similar stories are found in the folklore of nations all over the world.
>
> FREEMAN DYSON

EXERCISE 11. Writing a Paragraph Using Examples. Write an expository paragraph developed with examples. You may use one of the following topics or a topic of your own. Answers will vary.

1. Home accidents caused by carelessness
2. Ways of preserving foods
3. Skills needed to be an effective quarterback
4. The popularity of sports in America
5. Free or inexpensive spare-time activities

PREWRITING First decide how your topic can be explained through the use of examples. Then use an information-gathering technique (pages 20–25) to find examples that are familiar to your audience. Arrange the material in an easy-to-follow order, and write a topic sentence that states your main idea.

WRITING Keep your audience and purpose in mind as you write. Remember that you will have another chance to consider the examples when you evaluate your paragraph.

EVALUATING AND REVISING Ask yourself: Have I included enough examples to make my main idea clear? Will the examples be familiar to my audience? Then judge and improve your writing, using the evaluation guidelines on page 97 and the paragraph revision chart on pages 73–75.

PROOFREADING AND MAKING A FINAL COPY Proofread your paper, using the Guidelines for Proofreading on page 39. Then make a final copy and proofread it.

EXERCISE 12. Writing a Paragraph Using Examples. Write an expository paragraph developed with examples. You may use one of the following topics or a topic of your own. Answers will vary.

1. Popular cartoon characters
2. Ways to keep healthy
3. Conveniences that were unknown fifty years ago
4. Words based on people's names
5. Study skills

Developing by Definition

3e. Develop an expository paragraph by definition.

A definition is a clear and detailed explanation of the meaning of a word. The first step in writing a definition is to identify the general class (group) to which the object or idea belongs.

EXAMPLE A *skunk* is a *mammal* of the weasel family.

The second step is to point out the characteristics that set the object or idea apart from all other members of its class.

EXAMPLE *Skunk*—bushy tail; small (about size of cat); black fur, generally with two white stripes down back; gives off foul-smelling liquid when attacked; nocturnal (active during night, sleeps during day)

EXERCISE 13. If these topics seem too difficult, allow your students to choose their own. A definition may be developed through descriptive details, facts, examples, and comparison or contrast.

The following paragraph defines the term *Impressionism* as it applies to painting. Notice that the topic sentence identifies the class and mentions two important characteristics (where Impressionism began and when). The supporting sentences list other characteristics and give examples and related information.

Impressionist painting began in France during the 1870's. The Impressionists tried to capture the impression of an object in nature with short brush strokes of pure color. They were especially concerned with the effects of sunlight and often painted outdoors. Impressionist painters include Claude Monet, Camille Pissaro, Alfred Sisley, and Edgar Degas. Impressionism had a profound effect on painting. Before Impressionism, artists painted their subjects almost photographically. After Impressionism, artists felt free to express themselves however they wished.

topic sentence

characteristics

examples

importance of Impressionism

EXERCISE 13. Writing a Paragraph of Definition. Write a paragraph defining one of the following terms. **Answers will vary.**

1. Bat (the animal)
2. Success
3. Diamond
4. Microwave oven
5. Responsibility

PREWRITING Identify the class to which the object or idea belongs and list as many distinctive characteristics as you can think of or find in reference books. You may also want to include several examples. Decide what information to use and how to arrange it. Then write a topic sentence that identifies the class and mentions one or two of the most important characteristics.

WRITING Write freely, adding transitions that will help your audience follow your ideas. Avoid using other terms for which you would need to provide definitions.

EVALUATING AND REVISING Ask yourself: Have I identified

the general class to which my topic belongs? Have I included enough details to show how it is different from other members of that class? Use the evaluation guidelines on page 97 and the revision chart on pages 73–75 to judge and improve your writing.

PROOFREADING AND MAKING A FINAL COPY Use the guidelines on page 39 to proofread your paragraph. Then make a final copy and proofread it.

Developing with Details of a Process

3f. Develop an expository paragraph with details of a process.

A *process paragraph* explains how to make or do something. The process should be limited enough to be explained fully in a paragraph. For example, "how to maintain a ten-speed bike" has too many parts to explain fully in one paragraph. You could, however, explain a limited topic such as "how to check the brakes on a ten-speed bicycle."

The details in a process paragraph are the supplies and equipment needed and the steps to be carried out. The steps are arranged in chronological order.

In the following paragraph, the writers explain how to do the basic forward stroke in paddling a canoe.

> In the flat waters of Florida, most of your effort will go into strokes designed to move the canoe forward in as straight a line as possible. **Even people who have never been in a canoe before seem to know instinctively how to execute the forward cruising stroke.** Bring the paddle forward, plant the entire blade in the water, and draw it back slightly past your shoulders. Simple. And by observing a few more points, it can become the kind of stroke you can repeat a thousand times a day without tiring. Be sure to reach forward slightly at the start of each stroke. The power comes when the blade is perpendicular to the surface, not at the end of the stroke as it flattens out in the water. And be sure to draw the paddle back parallel to the center line of the canoe, not the side. Otherwise, your partner will wind up fighting your efforts.
>
> MIKE TONER and PAT TONER

EXERCISE 14. You may want your students to exchange papers and evaluate the clarity of the instructions.

EXERCISE 14. Writing a Process Paragraph. Write a paragraph explaining how to make or do something. You may use one of the following topics or one of your own. Answers will vary.

1. How to take a photograph
2. How to make a salad
3. How to study for a test
4. How to do a somersault
5. How to make a long-distance telephone call

PREWRITING To gather information, carry out the process yourself. Take notes on all of the details involved: materials, amounts, tools and equipment, time required, and the size, shape, texture, etc., of the end product. Then arrange the steps in chronological order, and write a topic sentence that identifies the process and catches the attention of your audience.

WRITING As you write your first draft, remember that your audience is probably not as familiar with the process as you are. Use specific words rather than general ones, and add transitions where they are needed.

EVALUATING AND REVISING Ask yourself: Have I included all of the necessary details? Have I arranged the steps in chronological order? Then use the Guidelines for Evaluating Expository Paragraphs on page 97, and refer to the paragraph revision chart on pages 73–75 as you improve your writing.

PROOFREADING AND MAKING A FINAL COPY Read your paragraph carefully, using the Guidelines for Proofreading on page 39. Proofread again after you make a final copy.

Before You Write. In planning an expository paragraph:

- Decide which method of development you will use: facts and statistics, examples, definition, details of a process, or a combination of methods.
- Arrange the information in an order that will be easy for your audience to follow.
- Write a topic sentence that identifies your topic and states your main idea clearly.

Evaluating and Revising Expository Paragraphs

The following guidelines will help you evaluate the expository paragraphs you write. Once you have found areas that need to be improved, you can use the paragraph revision chart on pages 73–75 to revise your writing.

GUIDELINES FOR EVALUATING EXPOSITORY PARAGRAPHS

Topic Sentence	1. Does the topic sentence identify a limited topic and clearly state one main idea?
Topic Development	2. Is the method of development (or combination of methods) appropriate for the main idea and for the audience? Are enough details given to make the main idea clear? Is the information accurate?
Unity	3. Is each sentence directly related to the main idea?
Conclusion	4. Does the clincher sentence, if any, provide a strong ending for the paragraph?
Order of Ideas	5. Are the ideas arranged in an order that will be easy for the audience to follow?
Relationships Between Ideas	6. Do the ideas flow smoothly? Are they linked with direct references and appropriate transitional expressions (*first, since, for example,* etc.)?
Word Choice	7. Is the language specific rather than general? Is it appropriate for the audience? Are technical terms and difficult words defined or explained?

REVIEW EXERCISE C. Writing an Expository Paragraph. Write an expository paragraph on one of the following topics or on a topic of your own. Answers will vary.

1. Equipment and supplies for one-night campout
2. Mummies
3. How to save money on groceries
4. How to wash a car
5. What a termite is

REVIEW EXERCISE C. This review exercise provides an additional opportunity for students to write expository paragraphs. Assign this exercise according to your students' needs. Students may also find it helpful to write an expository paragraph under your guidance for one of their other content-area classes.

Developing Persuasive Paragraphs (rule 3g)

This section discusses three basic aspects of developing a persuasive paragraph: distinguishing fact from opinion; building an argument; and writing a clincher sentence. Remind your students of the purpose of persuasive writing, and be sure to provide individual assistance to your less-advanced students.

THE PERSUASIVE PARAGRAPH

The purpose of a persuasive paragraph is to convince the reader to agree with an opinion, and, sometimes, to perform a certain action. The paragraph presents an *argument*, which is a well-thought-out explanation for the opinion. It uses language that creates a serious, unemotional *tone,* or expressed attitude.

Developing Persuasive Paragraphs

3g. Develop a persuasive paragraph with reasons.

In a persuasive paragraph, the topic sentence states the writer's opinion. The supporting sentences present *reasons,* statements that explain the opinion. Each reason is supported with *evidence* —details such as facts, statistics, or examples.

Distinguishing Fact from Opinion

The topic for a persuasive paragraph should be a debatable issue—one about which people can reach different conclusions. The topic sentence (sometimes called the *position statement*) states the writer's opinion on the issue. Statements of fact are not debatable because they can be proved to be true. Therefore they are not suitable topic sentences for persuasive paragraphs.

FACT Four out of ten high-school students in this country drop out of school without graduating.

OPINION To help keep students from dropping out of school, the school system should start a counseling program run by and for students.

The issue should also be one about which people have differing opinions, and it should not be just a personal preference.

NOT SUITABLE Students should learn to write well. [Most people would agree.]

SUITABLE Every eighth-grade student should be required to write two compositions a week.

NOT SUITABLE Pizza tastes best with mushrooms and onions. [personal preference]

SUITABLE The school cafeteria should not sell junk foods such as soda, candy, and other sweets.

The topic sentence for a persuasive paragraph should state the writer's opinion precisely and make a specific suggestion.

WEAK Something needs to be done about the long lines in the school cafeteria.

WEAK People have to wait too long to buy their lunches in the school cafeteria.

IMPROVED To relieve crowding in the cafeteria, students should be allowed to eat lunch outside of school.

Before You Write. In choosing a topic and writing a position statement for a persuasive paragraph:

- Make sure that the topic is a debatable issue that is not just a personal preference.
- State your opinion clearly and precisely.

EXERCISE 15. Identifying Effective Topic Sentences. Number your paper 1–10. If the topic sentence is suitable for a persuasive paragraph, write *S.* If it is not suitable, write *NS.* Be prepared to explain your answers.

1. Every eighth-grade student should be required to participate in at least one after-school activity. 1. S
2. Something should be done to reduce crime in this community. 2. NS
3. Handicapped people should be treated fairly. 3. NS
4. Living in the country is better than living in the city. 4. NS
5. Automobile drivers and passengers should be required to wear seat belts. 5. S
6. The media should not be allowed to advertise alcoholic drinks. 6. S
7. Vandalism must be stopped. 7. NS
8. Bicycling is better than jogging. 8. NS

EXERCISE 15. Remind students that the position statement is a topic sentence, just like the topic sentences found in other kinds of paragraphs. Stress that the reasons used to develop or support this position statement can be facts, statistics, examples, or incidents —whatever evidence the writer can present to develop a logical argument to support his or her opinion.

EXERCISE 16. This exercise presents skills used in writing persuasive paragraphs. Students may complete this exercise individually and then share their responses with a small group or the entire class.

Answers: Exercise 16
(Answers will vary somewhat in wording.)

1. The issue is whether students should be required to maintain a certain grade level in order to participate in extracurricular activities. It is a debatable issue and therefore a suitable topic for a persuasive paragraph.
2. The writer feels that grades of 70 or more should be a requirement for eligibility.
3. The writer gives three reasons.

9. All students in physical education classes should do aerobic exercises three times a week. 9. S
10. Dog owners should be required to leash their dogs. 10. S

Building an Argument

Usually, at least three reasons are needed to explain an opinion in a persuasive paragraph. The reasons should be specific, and they should not simply repeat the opinion in different words.

Each reason should be supported with accurate details such as facts, statistics, or examples. For instance, statistics on successful student-run counseling programs would strengthen the argument for starting such a program in your school.

The reasons in a persuasive paragraph are usually arranged from least important to most important. Readers tend to remember best what they read last.

As you read the following paragraph, notice how the writer makes the argument build.

> All students who participate in extracurricular activities should be required to have grades of 70 or above in all of their academic subjects. First, many students devote so much time to extracurricular activities that they neglect their academic studies. Fifty-two percent of the freshmen at one high school are failing one or more courses. Second, academic subjects prepare students for jobs. Employers often examine school records to decide whom to hire. Most important, having to pass academic subjects will help students learn to balance work and leisure. People who can both work hard and play hard have skills for dealing with a rapidly changing world.

EXERCISE 16. Analyzing a Persuasive Paragraph. Use the paragraph above to answer the following questions in writing.

1. What is the issue? Is it suitable for a persuasive paragraph? Why or why not?
2. What is the writer's opinion?
3. How many reasons does the writer give to support the opinion in the position statement?

4. In what order does the writer give the reasons? Do you think the last reason is the most important? Why or why not?
5. What is your opinion on this issue? List your reasons briefly, in order from least important to most important.

Writing a Clincher Sentence

A *clincher* (concluding) *sentence* can provide a stong ending for a persuasive paragraph. It may (1) summarize the writer's argument or (2) suggest that the audience perform a specific action.

TO SUMMARIZE AN ARGUMENT	For these reasons, tobacco smoking should be banned in public places.
TO SUGGEST AN ACTION	To help defeat this proposal, attend the meeting of the city commission at 7:30 P.M.

Before You Write. To develop a persuasive paragraph:

- Give at least three reasons that explain your opinion.
- Gather details (facts, statistics, or examples) to support each reason.
- Arrange the reasons and supporting details from least important to most important.

REVIEW EXERCISE D. Writing a Persuasive Paragraph. Write a persuasive paragraph on one of the following topics or on a topic of your own. Answers will vary.

1. An eleven-month school year for all students
2. An optional extra period at your school
3. A dress code for students at your school
4. A counseling program run by and for students at your school
5. A law banning tobacco smoking in public places

Evaluating and Revising Persuasive Paragraphs

You will find the following guidelines helpful for evaluating the persuasive paragraphs you write.

4. The reasons are given in what the writer feels is the order from least important to most important. Answers will vary.
5. Answers will vary.

REVIEW EXERCISE D. This exercise directs students to write a persuasive paragraph. Go over *Before You Write* before they begin to work. Point out the Guidelines for Evaluating Persuasive Paragraphs on page 102.

WRITING A LETTER TO THE EDITOR

This section discusses a familiar form of persuasive writing, the letter to the editor. As you present this section, remind students that the letter to the editor adheres to the principles for developing a persuasive paragraph, although different publications may require writers to submit their letters in different formats. You may want to ask students to locate examples from local newspapers, national magazines, or school publications, and to use these examples as the basis for class discussion of the basic aspects of persuasive writing. You may also want students to view television newscasts or radio broadcasts to determine that editorials in these media also adhere to the principles of developing persuasive paragraphs.

GUIDELINES FOR EVALUATING PERSUASIVE PARAGRAPHS

Topic Sentence	1. Is the topic a debatable issue that is not just a personal preference? Does the position statement present an opinion clearly and precisely?
Topic Development	2. Are at least three reasons given to explain the opinion? Is each reason supported by accurate details?
Unity	3. Is each sentence directly related to the opinion in the position statement?
Conclusion	4. Does the clincher sentence sum up the argument or suggest an action for the reader to take?
Order of Ideas	5. Are the reasons arranged from least important to most important?
Relationships Between Ideas	6. Are the ideas easy to follow? Are direct references and transitional expressions (*first, most importantly,* etc.) used to link the ideas?
Word Choice	7. Is the language specific rather than general?
Tone	8. Is the tone serious and unemotional?

Writing a Letter to the Editor

Letters to the editor appear on the editorial pages of newspapers and in special columns in magazines. The writer may comment on a debatable issue or on an earlier story or article. The writer may instead praise or criticize the work of a group or an individual.

A letter to the editor should be brief, but it should present enough reasons and supporting details to be convincing. It should be written in business letter form (see Chapter 7) and follow the publication's guidelines, which appear in the letters to the editor section.

Here is an example of a letter to the editor.

To the Editor:

This community should have middle schools for grades 6 through 8. Currently, students attend elementary schools from kindergarten through grade 6 and junior high schools from grades 7 through 9. Seventh- and eighth-grade students require the close supervision of the middle-school structure. These students are too big for elementary school but too young for the independence of junior high. In a middle school they would be less likely to be influenced by those older teen-agers who are trouble-makers. They would also be more likely to receive individual attention from teachers and administrators. Finally, teachers who know the specific needs of seventh- and eighth-graders would be better able to provide the leadership and guidance these students require.

A CONCERNED PARENT

EXERCISE 17. Writing a Letter to the Editor. Write a letter to the editor in which you agree or disagree with the opinion in the letter above. Give at least three reasons and details to support your opinion. Answers will vary.

REVIEW EXERCISE E. Writing a Letter to the Editor. Write a letter to the editor of your local or school newspaper. You may use one of the topics in Review Exercise D or a topic of your own. Support your opinion with at least three reasons and specific information. Answers will vary.

CHAPTER 3 WRITING REVIEW

Writing Different Types of Paragraphs. Write each of the following paragraphs: Answers will vary.

1. A narrative paragraph about something funny that happened to you or to someone you know
2. A descriptive paragraph about a place (house, apartment, community) where you would like to live someday
3. An expository paragraph giving information about a topic you are interested in
4. A persuasive paragraph or letter to the editor suggesting a way to improve your school or community

EXERCISE 17 and REVIEW EXERCISE E. These two exercises direct students to write letters to the editor. You may want to assign only one exercise, depending on your students' needs. Whenever possible, encourage students to write sincere letters that they can actually submit to a publication; seeing their letters in print may be very rewarding to students and will serve as a reminder of the importance of writing responsible persuasive paragraphs or letters.

CHAPTER 3 WRITING REVIEW

This review exercise directs students to write each of the four kinds of paragraphs studied in this chapter. Depending on your students' needs, you may choose to assign fewer than four paragraphs. Remind students to refer to the evaluation guidelines for each kind of paragraph as they complete this exercise. You may want to compile students' work for this exercise into a class anthology. You may consider including paragraphs they have written for other content-area classes.

Additional Practice

Teacher's Resource Book, Worksheet pages 33–45, Alternative Worksheet pages (for less-advanced students) 517–19

Testing

Teaching Tests booklet, pages 1–4, 13–18
Teacher's Resource Book, Test pages 371–74, 385–94, 407–412

Chapter Overview

Writing stories provides excellent practice in writing compositions. At the same time, students who have followed the writing process to develop their stories may also begin to experience a greater appreciation and understanding of the fictional literature they read.

The narratives that students write for this unit will usually recount incidents from their own experiences, but if you have some students who want to write fiction, you can certainly allow them to do so.

You will find two types of exercises in this chapter. One type provides practice in the skill that is being developed. The other type provides a strand of exercises. Each exercise in the strand can build upon the work completed in a previous exercise, allowing students to take a subject selected at the beginning of the chapter completely through the writing process to the final copy.

Note: Many teachers have found it effective to combine writing stories with a literature unit on the short story.

Chapter Objective

Students will use the writing process to write stories using narration and description.

PRESENTING THE CHAPTER

LESS-ADVANCED STUDENTS Your less-advanced students may be intimidated by the prospect of having to write an entire story by themselves. To alleviate this stress, you could have the entire class choose and limit a subject, determine audience and purpose, gather information, and arrange story details.

CHAPTER 4

Writing Stories

USING NARRATION AND DESCRIPTION

Have you ever heard of a "natural storyteller"? This person can hold everyone's attention telling about a personal experience. The use of gestures, facial expressions, and tone of voice makes his or her stories vivid and interesting. Of course, the stories must also be organized so that they lead somewhere and end at a definite point. The "natural storyteller" is skilled in the art of *narration.*

Written narratives do not have the storyteller's facial expressions or personal contact. The words, alone, must create an interesting, funny, or thrilling story. It is therefore very important for the writer of narratives to have a plan and use effective devices. In this chapter, you will learn to plan a written story and use some devices to make it vivid and interesting.

PREWRITING

CHOOSING A SUBJECT FOR A STORY

4a. Choose a subject that is appropriate for your purpose.

The purpose of any narrative is to tell *what happened.* Whether the story is true or fictional, it usually begins with a problem or a conflict and then tells what happens as a result of that problem. The problem or conflict does not have to be serious nor does it have to be physical. It may be a humorous situation, such as being frightened by your younger brother looking for his pet hamster. It may be an internal problem, such as a teen-ager's embarrassment after doing poorly in class or on the soccer field. The subject for your story may be your own experience, one of someone you know, or the fictional experience of a person you create out of your imagination. Be sure the subject is one that you are willing to share with others.

Before You Write. To find a subject for a story,

- Look through your writer's notebook for exciting or moving experiences.
- Talk with friends or family members about experiences they have shared with you or events from the past.
- Brainstorm, searching your mind for events that stand out because of a problem or struggle and someone's attempt to solve it.
- Ask yourself questions: What was my most exciting day? What was the most serious problem I ever had to face? What was a hard decision for me? What was the best or worst thing that ever happened to me? What "firsts" —such as the first time I water-skied, snow-skied, gave a speech, performed in a play—would make an interesting story?

EXERCISE 1. Identifying Appropriate Subjects. Some of the following subjects are appropriate for a narrative purpose and some are not. Number your paper 1–10. For the appropriate subjects, write *A*. For the inappropriate ones, write *I*. Be prepared to discuss your answers.

1. How my illness spoiled our trip to Washington, D.C. 1. A
2. Finding your way around the Smithsonian Institution 2. I

After this prewriting is complete, you could divide the class into small groups to write specific parts of the narrative. *(See listing of Alternative Worksheets on page 133.)*

ADVANCED STUDENTS Advanced students should enjoy the creative challenge of writing stories using narration and description. In each case, stress the importance of language choices and of the arrangement of narrative and descriptive details. Your advanced students should be encouraged to write other stories during the year.

PREWRITING

Section Overview

Planning is important in writing stories as it is in other forms of writing. The material in this section of the chapter provides practice in the thinking process writers go through before writing a draft.

CHOOSING A SUBJECT FOR A STORY (rule 4a)

Also remind students that when they search for subjects, they are not limited to their own experiences. Encourage them to interview others—parents, grandparents, or neighbors—about an incident from their past. Although the event may be true, encourage writers to use their own details to make the story interesting.

EXERCISE 1. To make sure your students understand the concept of writing stories, you may do Exercise 1 as an oral activity. Ask why some subjects are appropriate for a story and others are not. How can the subjects that are not appropriate be changed? Number 2, for example, could be altered to read "Getting lost among the dinosaurs at the Smithsonian Institution."

EXERCISE 2. This exercise could be done as a small-group activity. Write a few of the story subjects from each group on the board.

EXERCISE 3. Make sure that each student has picked a workable subject.

LIMITING SUBJECTS TO MANAGEABLE TOPICS (rule 4b)

Students often need help in focusing on a limited part of a broad subject. Remind them that their goal is to select a topic that can be developed in a short narrative composition.

3. The importance of participating in athletics 3. I
4. How I learned a lesson from a younger person 4. A
5. Why students should spend at least one hour studying each night 5. I
6. How to cook eggs sunny side up 6. I
7. My quarrel with Julian about the class party 7. A
8. The difference between reading a science fiction story and watching a science fiction movie 8. I
9. The time our car stalled in a blizzard 9. A
10. How I took the wrong plane and ended up in the Caribbean Islands 10. A

EXERCISE 2. Searching for Story Subjects. Using the suggestions in the preceding "Before You Write," make a list of at least ten problems or conflicts you could use as the basis for a story. Save your work. Answers will vary.

EXERCISE 3. Choosing a Subject for a Story. From your list of problems or conflicts in Exercise 2, choose the one you think is the most interesting. If possible, talk over several choices with a small group to get their reactions. Answers will vary.

LIMITING SUBJECTS TO MANAGEABLE TOPICS

4b. Limit your subject to a topic that is a specific problem or experience.

A topic for a brief story, one that can be handled in a few paragraphs or pages, must be limited. An appropriate topic for a short narrative is a *specific* problem or a *specific* conflict.

For example, a story about all the problems and conflicts you have faced with your best friend would be vague and unfocused. You would be forced to tell about several experiences—the time you were not invited to your friend's party, the time the two of you got into trouble for going to a movie after school, the time your friend loaned you a new tape player, and so forth. As a result, you would not be able to include any of the specific details that make a story interesting. If you limited your subject to one experience (the time your friend loaned you the new tape player), you could add precise details, developing your story in an interesting way.

EXERCISE 4. Limiting a Subject for a Brief Story. Some of the following subjects are too broad for a brief story. Others are suitably limited for a story of two or three pages. Number your paper 1–5. Write *B* if the subject is too broad and *L* if the subject is appropriately limited. Be prepared to discuss your answers.

1. The history of the English monarchy 1. B
2. An encounter with a runaway horse 2. L
3. Flying a balloon across the United States 3. B
4. How I lost a race and won a friend 4. L
5. My father's childhood in Maryland 5. B

EXERCISE 5. Limiting Your Subject for a Brief Story. Decide whether the subject you selected for Exercise 3 (or any other subject of your choice) is limited to a *specific* problem or experience. If it is not, rewrite it, making it suitable for a brief story that you will write later. Answers will vary.

THINKING ABOUT PURPOSE AND AUDIENCE

4c. Think about the purpose and audience of your story.

Throughout the writing process—planning, writing, evaluating, revising—you should be aware of your purpose in writing and your audience. In a story, the purpose is to tell what happened in a way that will interest the reader (*audience*). Keeping that purpose in mind will help shape your story and make it more interesting.

Your audience may be your teacher and your classmates or another audience. All audiences, no matter who they are, have special needs and interests that you must identify and keep in mind to write effectively.

EXERCISES 4 and 5. Complete Exercise 4 as an oral activity. For each subject that is too broad, ask the students to tell how the subject can be sufficiently limited to make an appropriate topic for a brief story. Number 1 could be "Queen Victoria's love for Prince Albert"; number 5 could be "My father's first try at milking a cow." Exercise 5 should be done as individual work. Check each student's topic.

THINKING ABOUT PURPOSE AND AUDIENCE (rule 4c)

Creative writers may either write a story and then decide what audience would be interested in it, or they may write with a certain audience in mind. This text stresses the latter procedure, but students may work either way as long as they maintain a sense of writing for readers. An audience of classmates would probably be the most enjoyable for students.

CRITICAL THINKING:
Analyzing the Needs and Interests of an Audience

Focus on the five questions as you present this section. These questions, for which students can write out answers, should guide students' thinking about their audience and their stories.

CRITICAL THINKING:
Analyzing the Needs and Interests of an Audience

Analysis is the critical thinking skill you use when you divide something into its parts and study the relationships among the parts. The needs and interests of your audience will affect what you can write. To analyze these needs and interests, ask yourself the following questions:

1. What background information does my audience already have?
2. What background information will my audience need to understand my story?
3. What kinds of problems and experiences will interest my audience?
4. What can I do to make the problem or experience interesting to my audience?
5. How will my audience's knowledge and background affect the words I use?

Suppose you are writing a story about an alligator climbing your back fence to chase your dog. Your readers will be your classmates in your new school in Minnesota. Using the five questions above, your analysis of your audience might be as follows:

1. They know that alligators live in warm climates and that they sometimes attack small animals and people.
2. They need to know that I used to live in Florida. They need to know that an alligator can move fast on land and can climb a wire fence.
3. They are interested in daring adventures of people their own age and in adventures with happy endings.
4. I need to get them interested in the danger to the dog and in the idea that an alligator can climb a fence. I should wait until the end of the story to let them know that the dog was saved.
5. They will understand almost any word I use. If I use difficult words such as "interceded" and "assault," they may be confused or think I am showing off.

EXERCISE 6. Analyzing an Audience. Choose one topic and one audience from the following lists. Write this topic and audience at the top of a sheet of paper. Using the five questions on page 108, analyze the audience. Number each item and write your answers. Be prepared to discuss your answers.
Answers will vary.

Topics	*Audiences*
1. The night we saw a spaceship over the our house	a. readers of a local newspaper
2. Why I came in second in the contest	b. seven-year-old children in Japan
3. How I saved my cousin from the ocean's undertow	c. eighth-graders in your school

EXERCISE 7. Analyzing Your Audience. Using your topic from Exercise 5 (or any topic of your choice), answer the five questions on page 108. If your teacher has not assigned a specific audience, your readers will be your teacher and classmates. Save your work. Answers will vary.

GATHERING INFORMATION FOR YOUR STORY

4d. Identify action details, and gather information for your story.

To gather information for a narrative, you must focus on the question *What happened?* The *5 W-How?* questions used by reporters will help you collect the details you need. In the following example, notice how a writer uses the *5 W-How?* questions to gather information.

Who was involved in this experience? My mother and I
What happened? Mother left me at home alone while she went to help a sick neighbor. I got scared. I hid under the bed and fell asleep. My mother couldn't find me and was afraid I had drowned in the well. She was angry when she found me.
Where did the experience take place? In our home
When did the actions occur? They started when my mother went to visit a sick friend. They ended when I woke up and crawled out from under the bed.

EXERCISES 6 and 7. These exercises should be written. Exercise 6 could be used to begin class discussion on audience. If your circumstances permit, you may want to discuss students' work in Exercise 7 in small groups or individually.

GATHERING INFORMATION FOR YOUR STORY (rule 4d)

Asking the *5 W-How?* questions is one way students can gather information for their narratives. To demonstrate its usefulness, you may want to bring in newspaper human interest stories and have students analyze the *5 W-How?* content in the articles.

EXERCISE 8. Students could discuss the *5 W-How?* questions in small groups to gain insight into perception of audience. Then the exercise should be written out and placed in student folders (or whatever storage system you have devised) for possible future uses.

ARRANGING DETAILS AND DEVELOPING A STORY PLAN (rules 4e and 4f)

You may want to introduce this section by reviewing the concept of chronological order. Students may enjoy relating the order of events in favorite television programs, movies, or books. Similarly, students may profit from working in small groups to develop story plans for their favorite television programs, movies, or books. This would be a good time to show a film of a short story and analyze it as a class activity.

Another popular activity is to cut apart panels of Sunday comic strips, put each set in an envelope, and give each student a different envelope. Have the students arrange the comics in a logical order. This may be especially enjoyable to less-advanced students.

Why is this experience and its outcome interesting? I discovered how easily concern and relief can turn into anger.

How did I feel? I was afraid of being caught by a ghost or a kidnapper. I wondered why my mother was angry.

Before You Write. To gather information for a narrative, ask yourself:

- Am I writing about a problem or conflict of my own? (If so, review your writer's notebook, talk to friends or relatives, or brainstorm.)
- Am I writing about an experience or problem that is being faced by someone else? (If so, interview that person, if possible.)
- Am I writing about an imaginary event? (If so, allow your imagination to create what *might* have happened. Jot your ideas down; you can organize them later.)

EXERCISE 8. Gathering Information for a Narrative. Using your topic and audience analysis from Exercise 7 (or another topic of your choice), gather action details and information for your narrative. Refer to the *Before You Write* suggestions above, and use the *5 W-How?* questions. Write down the details you gather; you will use them later. Answers will vary.

ARRANGING DETAILS AND DEVELOPING A STORY PLAN

4e. Arrange the information for your story.

The actions in a narrative are usually arranged in the order in which they happened (*chronological* order). Notice the chronological order of the action details below:

mother was called to take care of a sick person
left me at home alone

no problems before dark
sat outside
as darkness came, decided to go in house
felt sleepy
afraid to sleep on top of bed
crawled under the bed
fell asleep
awakened to sound of voices
heard them searching for me
crawled out from under bed and told them I was there
was surprised because my mother was angry with me rather than happy to see me

EXERCISE 9. Arranging Action Details for a Story. On a sheet of paper, list the following actions in the order you think they might have happened. Answers may vary.

6. felt surprised
5. car suddenly started rolling
1. Aunt Ann left me in her car while she ran back into the house for something
7. went through a fence
3. pretended I was driving
8. sideswiped a tree
4. released the brake
9. smashed into neighbor's house
2. turned on the car radio

EXERCISE 10. Arranging Action Details for Your Story. Arrange the list of action details you gathered for Exercise 8 in chronological order. Save your list. Answers will vary.

4f. Plan your story before you write it.

Before writing any narrative, work out a rough plan to guide your thinking. Your plan will help you to include all the necessary details. The information gathered with the *5 W-How?* questions can be used to create a story.

EXERCISES 9 and 10. Exercise 9 can be used as a group oral activity before students complete Exercise 10.

Before You Write. To create a story plan, include:

- *When* (My mother left me alone and went to visit a sick friend; I was a small child.)
- *Where* (I was at home.)
- *Who* (My mother and I)
- *What happened* (It became dark and I was afraid. I went into the house and crawled under the bed to hide. I fell asleep. Mother came home. She couldn't find me. She was afraid I was in the well. I woke up. I told her where I was. She was angry rather than happy.)
- *How I felt* (Puzzled that she was angry with me rather than happy to see me)

Read the following personal experience narrative taken from *Barrio Boy.* Does it tell *when, where, who, what happened,* and *how the writer felt*?

> A neighbor who lived at the other end of the block, across from the orchard, came to our cottage in distress. There was a sick person at their house and help was needed. It was a situation in which I would clearly be in the way. My mother did something unusual; she decided to leave me alone in the cottage. . . .
>
> While the twilight lasted I had no problems. I sat by the back door facing the orchard, thinking of many things, alert for the footsteps of Doña Henriqueta. But as night fell and the darkness deepened, I decided that since I was taking care of the house I might as well be inside of it. . . .
>
> My mother had said that if I felt sleepy I was to get into bed. That would have been very well if she had been there and it was still light outside. Now it was certainly the wrong thing to do. The back door would be open and I might be caught asleep on top of the bed by a ghost or a kidnapper.
>
> I crawled under the bed wrapped in my sarape and wedged myself on the floor as close to the door as possible. I intended to stay awake and crawl out as soon as my mother was home.

I was awakened by voices in the room. By the candlelight I could see feet shuffling by me. People were calling my name. I heard my mother say, "The well. Please look in the well again."

I wormed my way from under the bed, stuck out my head, and said, "Here I am."

I could not understand why a mother should not be overjoyed to find that her son had not fallen into the well and drowned but had only been asleep under the bed. She wanted to know since when I had forgotten that I was to answer instantly when I was called.

ERNESTO GALARZA

EXERCISE 11. Creating a Story Plan. Using the list of details you organized in Exercise 10 (or another topic and list of details), prepare a story plan. Save it for later use. Answers will vary.

WRITING

CHOOSING DETAILS

4g. Choose specific details and specific verbs to make the action vivid.

The use of specific details makes a story vivid by telling the reader exactly what happened. If such details are missing, the reader may lose interest. Compare the following two paragraphs. Which is more interesting?

1. When the canoe touched the river bank, I told John to push us off. Instead he panicked. He got up, tried to climb to the shore, and overturned the canoe. I fell into the water.

2. The canoe glided toward the river bank. I felt a bump as it touched land. "Use your paddle. Push us away," I told John. He put his hand on the side of the canoe and pushed himself to

EXERCISE 11. Try to review the story plans in Exercise 11 to see if students' plans can actually guide their first drafts. You might do this in group discussions or individual student conferences, depending upon your class schedule.

WRITING

Section Overview

Students must learn to base their drafts on the planning they have done in the prewriting stage of the writing process. They also need to consider specific features of narrative writing: using specific details and specific verbs, using dialogue, and writing a beginning, a middle, and an ending. Regarding a draft as a beginning is also an important concept for students to grasp.

CHOOSING DETAILS (rule 4g)

This section discusses a complex writing skill: how to include vivid details without at the same time including unnecessary details. Students can easily grasp the importance of omitting unnecessary details if you remind them that they lose interest in long-winded stories. Ask students to include vivid details that will help their audience feel that they are present at the scene of the narrative.

EXERCISES 12 and 13. Both of these written exercises could be evaluated in class in small groups. Have students consider the suggestions in *When You Write.*

his feet. I yelled at him to sit down, but he wasn't listening. His hands trembled. Awkwardly he teetered on one foot as he reached out to grab a branch that was hanging over the bank. The canoe began to rock. "Sit down!" I yelled. The canoe rocked violently. Suddenly I was thrown from my seat and hit the water with a splash.

You will probably think that the second paragraph is more effective. The first paragraph gives only general information. The second paragraph tells how John used his hand to push himself up and how he looked (teetering awkwardly) as he tried to leave the canoe. Instead of the general statement *I fell into the water,* the second paragraph gives two specific details: being thrown from the seat and the splash of hitting the water. Also, the second paragraph does more than tell what happened; it *shows* what happened. Instead of directly stating *he panicked,* a detail, John's trembling hands, reveals his nervousness.

Specific verbs also make a story vivid. Some verbs describe actions more specifically than others. The verb *walk,* for example, gives a general idea of an action; the verbs *amble, stroll, swagger,* and *shuffle* give more specific impressions. Specific verbs can help the reader clearly picture the action. Of course, you should not try to use a vivid verb in *every* possible situation. If you are simply telling how you get to school in the morning, it would be better to use *walk* than *stroll* or *amble.* If the point is *how* you walk, a more specific verb may be better.

When You Write. To write an effective story,

- Give specific details to make the action vivid.
- Avoid general statements; instead let the readers draw their own conclusions from the details.
- Use enough specific details so that the readers feel they are participating in or witnessing the action.
- Use specific verbs.

EXERCISE 12. Identifying Specific Verbs. List the specific verbs in the following paragraph. Be prepared to explain how these verbs make the action vivid.

The circus was a blend of movement, color, and noise. In the center ring, a bareback rider performed. As her horse pranced around the ring, the rider tensed, whirled in the air, and landed neatly on the horse. In another ring, a seal held a large ball in its flippers. A clown dressed in orange, green, and purple tiptoed up and reached out for the ball. The seal yelped. The clown staggered back, threw up his hands, and flopped to the sawdust floor. Above the crowd, aerialists performed their dangerous work. A man swung out on a trapeze, holding a woman by the wrists. Suddenly he released her. As she plunged into space, a third aerialist swooped down just in time and caught her by the wrists.

EXERCISE 13. Using Specific Details. Using the suggestions above, rewrite one of the following paragraphs. Answers will vary.

1. When the principal called on me, I was very nervous. I grew calmer as I explained why our class should be permitted to take a class trip out of town. At the end of my speech, my classmates applauded.

2. The two boys clenched their fists. Each wanted to appear brave but did not really want to fight. After the crowd watching them left, each muttered a final insult and left.

REVIEW EXERCISE. Writing a Paragraph Using Specific Details and Verbs. Write a paragraph of fifty to seventy-five words about one of the following situations. Include specific details and specific verbs. Answers will vary.

1. Being caught in a violent storm
2. Winning (or losing) a race (for example, three-legged race at a picnic)
3. After riding for twenty minutes, discovering you are on the wrong bus
4. Trying to keep a young child from crossing the street against the traffic light
5. Making a report to the class

REVIEW EXERCISE. Help less-advanced students get started by reviewing carefully the directions for prewriting on the top of page 116. All students should concentrate on specific details and specific verbs.

USING DIALOGUE (rule 4h)

If you are going to encourage the class to use dialogue, you should decide now how much time you want to spend teaching them to punctuate quotations. Teaching all the rules for the punctuation of quotations (text pages 555–60) will probably take several days and will require much drill. Most teachers, however, do not require eighth-graders to do a professional job in the area of punctuation. You may wish to present only a few of the most important points and then encourage students to use their textbooks for reference when they have further questions. With a less-advanced class, you might give only the following rules:

1. Quotation marks come in pairs. Do not leave out the second half of the pair.
2. In writing dialogue, begin a quotation with a capital letter.

PREWRITING Draw on your experience or your imagination to plan your paragraph. Use the *5 W-How?* questions, brainstorming, or clustering to gather specific details about the situation. After you have identified several actions and specific details, arrange them in chronological order.

WRITING, EVALUATING, AND REVISING Review your plan and write a first draft that includes specific details and verbs showing how the actions occurred. Write freely without stopping to make corrections. Use the evaluation guidelines on page 122 to evaluate your work, and revise your paragraph by referring to the chart on page 73. Use the proofreading guidelines on page 39 as you proofread your paragraph and make a final copy.

USING DIALOGUE

4h. Use dialogue to make your story lively and convincing.

If you present the direct speech of people, your narrative will be more interesting and realistic than if you merely describe their thoughts and feelings indirectly. Dialogue helps to tell the story in a more exciting way. Using peoples' exact words also helps to reveal their personalities.

In the following passage, the characters are conversing, but what they say is described. The result is a dull, uninteresting paragraph.

> My friends Sue and Edie went abalone fishing at Hondo Beach. When I met them, I asked where they had been. They told me. I asked what an abalone was. Sue said it was a shellfish. I asked how they caught abalone. Sue said they waded out into the water and pried them off the rocks. Edie said the water was very cold.

In the following paragraphs, the conversation is written as dialogue. Notice how lively and convincing this second version is. Notice that the dialogue also indicates the distinct personalities of the speakers.

I ran into Sue and Edie on the street.

"Where'd you go yesterday?" I asked them.

"Abalone fishing at Hondo Beach," Sue said.

"What's abalone?" I wanted to know.

"A shellfish."

'Like oysters?"

"No more like oysters," Edie snorted, "than a wheelbarrow is like a motorcycle."

Sue explained, "An abalone has just one top shell, like a snail. It's open at the bottom."

"You fish for 'em with hook and line?"

"Gosh, are you ignorant!" Edie said.

"They stick to the rocks, underwater," Sue said, "and you wade out—"

"In water that's so cold you turn blue," Edie interrupted.

"—and you pry them off the rocks. It's easy."

"Sure," Edie said, "as easy as prying names off plaques."

One goal in writing conversation is to keep the reader aware of who is talking. How many different ways are shown in the passage above? Notice where the speaker is identified—at the beginning, at the end, or in the middle of the speech. With several speeches there is no identification, yet the author has made it clear.

When You Write. In writing dialogue,

- Make sure the dialogue has a purpose; that is, ask yourself if it reveals something about the characters or the action.
- Keep the reader aware of who is talking. Occasionally use the names of the speakers so the reader will not be confused.
- Place quotation marks around the words that are spoken.
- Use commas to separate a person's speech form the rest of the sentence. (See pages 555–60 for the rules on punctuating dialogue.)
- Start a new paragraph when the speaker changes.

EXERCISE 14. After students have finished writing this exercise, allow them to share their dialogues in small groups. They can use the suggestions in *When You Write* (page 117) to evaluate each other's work.

WRITING DESCRIPTION (rule 4i)

It is helpful to use models when you are teaching descriptive writing. *Composition: Models and Exercises, Second Course* presents a number of suitable models. Models can also be found in the class's literature books.

EXERCISE 14. Writing Dialogue. Review the suggestions above. Select one of the following situations, and write a short conversation to fit it. Answers will vary.

1. Two teen-agers are bragging about their athletic skills (or grades in school, etc.).
2. Two friends argue about a hero (from sports, television, movies, etc.).
3. A teen-ager insists that he or she is old enough and capable enough to have a part-time job.
4. An eighth-grader tries to convince his or her parents that an allowance must be increased.
5. A girl is helping a boy with his algebra, but he would rather talk about sports.

WRITING DESCRIPTION

4i. Use description to make your story vivid and convincing.

A good description makes the reader see, hear, or otherwise experience something. A description of a *scene* can help the reader visualize it. A description of a *person* can familiarize the reader with that person. Description can convince the reader that *what is happening* in a story is real. Even a sentence or two of vivid detail can make a story more effective. In this part of the chapter, you will learn how to use description to improve your stories.

(1) Use details that appeal to the senses.

To write a good description, you must be a keen observer. As you notice the sights, sounds, and smells around you, make a mental list of them. (For example, in the school halls, you might *see* the students milling around on their way to classes; you might *hear* them talking or shouting; finally, you might *feel* some of them jostling you.)

You can make a story lifelike by using these details that appeal to the senses. The senses you will use most often are *sight* and *hearing,* but many times you will also use *touch, taste,* and *smell.*

Notice where the writer appeals to various senses in the following description.

I pushed up the high steps into the aisle of the bus. The shrill screaming, shouting, and laughing were a wall of noise in front of me. Because we had been waiting in the rain, the air in the bus was steamy and smelled of wet wool. As I tried to squeeze past the boy ahead of me, my books began to slide out of my arms. When I grabbed for them, my right hand struck a hockey stick and was twisted backward painfully. The books slipped away. I saw that every seat was taken, but nobody seemed to be sitting down. The aisle was jammed. Everywhere arms were waving and pushing.

EXERCISE 15. Observing Details. Test your powers of observation on your way home from school. How many details can you observe? To which senses do they appeal? List at least ten details and indicate the senses to which they appeal. Answers will vary.

EXERCISE 16. Writing a Description. Organize the list of details you observed for Exercise 15 in chronological order (see the model above) or spatial order (pages 51–52). Using this list, write a one- or two-paragraph description of your trip home. Answers will vary.

EXERCISE 17. Adding Descriptive Details. The addition of vivid details would improve the following paragraphs taken from stories. Revise two of the three paragraphs, using the directions in parentheses. Answers will vary.

1. At the end of the debate an elderly man stood up. "I've attended many town meetings," he said, "and I've never heard such nonsense as I've heard tonight." Angrily he tore the meeting's agenda into pieces. (Insert two or three sentences to follow the first. Describe how the man looked and spoke.)

2. My sister had worked on the model boat for months. It had occupied most of her spare time. Carefully she had carved, sanded, and painted it. Now she displayed it to us proudly. (Write two or three sentences about the boat.)

EXERCISES 15 and 16. When you assign Exercise 15, make sure the students understand that they will use these details in a writing assignment. This may encourage them to take the assignment more seriously. You may want to have the students share their paragraphs or compositions for Exercise 16 with the rest of the class.

EXERCISE 17. This exercise could be used as a small-group activity. Assign one paragraph to each group. You may wish the students to underline the new sentences they add.

EXERCISE 18. This would be an appropriate time to give more advanced students the opportunity to use a thesaurus or a dictionary of synonyms.

3. It was a very unpleasant trip. I was relieved when the plane finally arrived at the airport in San Francisco. (Insert several sentences after the first. Show how the trip was unpleasant. Appeal to at least three of the senses.)

(2) Select adjectives and adverbs carefully, and use them sparingly.

You recall that an adjective describes a noun or a pronoun and tells *what kind, which one, how many,* or *how much.* An adverb describes a verb, an adjective, or another adverb and tells *when, where, how,* or *to what extent.* Adjectives and adverbs are called *modifiers.* (See pages 299 and 317.) Modifiers can be overused. Notice the dull, tired modifiers in the following example:

> We had a swell time, because the speaker was very interesting. He made some tremendously good remarks. After he finished, the applause was absolutely fabulous. We all agreed that he was a terrific speaker.

The speaker was *interesting* and *terrific,* but these overused words tell little about the speaker or his speech. Was he *stimulating? Thought-provoking? Witty? Persuasive?* Similarly, the applause is described as *absolutely fabulous,* a phrase that is vague. Was the applause *energetic? Deafening?* Avoid such words as *swell, terrible,* and *terrific.* When you evaluate and revise your own writing, replace them with more exact modifiers.

Some vague, overused adjectives and adverbs are

absolutely	grand	swell
awful	great	terrible
cool	horrible	terrific
cute	neat	tremendous
fabulous	nice	very
funny	really	wonderful

EXERCISE 18. Using Fresh, Exact Adjectives and Adverbs. Write the following sentences. In the first five, use fresh, exact *adjectives.* In the second five, use fresh, exact *adverbs.* If you wish, use a dictionary or a book of synonyms.

Answers will vary. Possible answers are given.

1. She refused to give him a(n) —— answer. 1. flattering
2. In spite of his —— suit, he looked well-dressed. 2. shabby
3. They ate an enormously —— dinner. 3. rich
4. The actress had a strikingly —— hair style. 4. fashionable
5. The general handled his troops with —— skill. 5. utmost
6. A frightened child —— asked a question. 6. hesitatingly
7. My new sweater is —— scarlet. 7. bright
8. After cleaning house, I flopped —— on the sofa. 8. wearily
9. It was chilly outside, but we sat —— around the fire. 9. snugly
10. Talking —— , I began to unwrap the presents. 10. excitedly

(3) Use description to make characters seem real and interesting.

The people in a story are called *characters.* A writer usually focuses on a major character. Through description the character becomes more realistic. For example, the author focuses attention on one important character at the beginning of *Treasure Island.*

> I remember him as if it were yesterday, as he came plodding to the inn door, his sea chest following behind him in a handbarrow; a tall, strong, heavy, nut-brown man; his tarry pigtail falling over the shoulders of his soiled blue coat; his hands ragged and scarred, with black, broken nails; and the saber cut across one cheek, a dirty, livid white.
>
> ROBERT LOUIS STEVENSON

When You Write. To write a description of a character,

- Determine the interesting features of this character.
- Decide if anything about this character would affect the action of the story. (For example, is the character's quick temper important?)
- If the character is a real person, observe him or her. Take notes about appearance, mannerisms, etc.
- Use brainstorming or clustering to gather details.
- Select adjectives and adverbs that are fresh and exact.
- Use words that appeal to the reader's senses.
- Arrange details in a logical order.

EXERCISES 19 and 20. Writing a description of a character and a setting will prepare students for writing a first draft. Give students time to consider and possibly take notes on the suggestions in *When You Write* on page 121 and *When You Write* on this page. This work should be checked, either by you or by peers.

EXERCISE 19. Writing a Description of a Character. Review the story plan you developed for Exercise 11. Select a character you plan to include in your story. Using the preceding suggestions, write a short description of the character. Answers will vary.

(4) Use description to make the setting vivid.

The *setting* is where a story happens. If you were writing about a night spent in a supposedly haunted house, a specific description of the house (setting) would make your story more effective. In the following description from the novel *Losing Battles,* the description of dawn suggests the importance of the rural setting.

> When the rooster crowed, the moon had still not left the world but was going down on flushed cheek, one day short of the full. A long thin cloud crossed it slowly, drawing itself out like a name being called. The air changed, as if a mile or so away a wooden door had swung open, and a smell, more of warmth than wet, from a river at low stage, moved upward into the clay hills that stood in darkness.
>
> Then a house appeared on its ridge, like an old man's silver watch pulled once more out of its pocket. A dog leaped up from where he'd lain like a stone and began barking for today as if he meant never to stop.
>
> EUDORA WELTY

When You Write. To write the description of a setting,

- Brainstorm for details. (See page 20.)
- If your setting is a real place you can visit, go there and observe as many details as you can.
- Try to recall or observe specific sights, sounds, smells, tastes, and feelings related to the setting.
- Select details that reflect the *mood* of the setting —mysterious, dreary, pleasant, etc.
- List the details, using vivid, fresh adjectives and adverbs.
- Arrange the details in a logical order. (Review spatial order, pages 51–52.)

EXERCISE 20. Writing a Description of a Setting. Review the story plan you developed for Exercise 11. Using the suggestions above, write one or two paragraphs describing the setting of your narrative. Answers will vary.

WRITING A FIRST DRAFT

4j. Write a first draft of your story.

Most good narratives include five basic story elements: interesting start, beginning explanation, action, climax, and ending. Many good stories may omit one or more of the five elements. Keeping them in mind, however, will help you organize your story.

Interesting Start and Beginning Explanation

If you do not interest your readers in the first one or two sentences, they may stop reading—and never discover the rest of your story. Note the beginning of the following narrative.

> Some years ago my friend Chip and I tried to go to the moon, but some apples and pears got in our way. Both Chip and I had seen a television program about reaching the moon. When we talked about the program, we agreed that the important thing was to get up enough speed to overcome the earth's gravity. The rest would be easy. We decided to try an experiment. There was a long block in our neighborhood that ran downhill and then uphill. If we took Chip's wagon and got up enough speed going downhill, we might be able to leave the earth going uphill.

The first sentence contains an *interesting start* because it arouses the reader's curiosity. It also introduces the subject and the characters in addition to telling when ("some time ago").

The rest of the paragraph is the *beginning explanation*. Notice that the paragraph does not supply unnecessary information (for example, how Chip and the writer became friends). It does, however, include an important description of the setting, "There

WRITING A FIRST DRAFT (rule 4j)

This section of the chapter emphasizes that a good narrative must have an interesting start, a beginning explanation, action, a climax, and an ending. This section should build on previous exercises in which students prepared story material for the actual writing.

For other examples of the five elements listed above, supplement the text with models from literature books. Read extracts to the class to have them identify the part of the story represented. This activity could be augmented by having students supply some of the other elements. For example, after you read the start of a story, the class would create the action.

EXERCISES 21 and 22. These exercises must be written. If at all possible, give class time for each.

was a long block in our neighborhood that ran downhill and then uphill."

This paragraph avoids a common problem in story writing: beginning in the wrong place. The writer should not begin the story with getting up that morning or going to school or even with meeting Chip. The real beginning of the story is the decision by Chip and the writer to make the trip.

When You Write. In writing the beginning of your story,

- Make the start interesting; make your reader want to keep reading.
- Identify the time, place, and people, if this information is important.
- Include any background information the reader will need to understand the action of the narrative.

EXERCISE 21. Writing the Beginning of Your Story. Using your topic and the plan you developed for Exercise 11, write a story beginning. Answers will vary.

Action and Climax

The middle of a narrative is made up of the action and the climax. The *action* is the series of step-by-step events that happen after the beginning explanation, and the *climax* is the high point of the story. In the story about the trip to the moon, the second paragraph gives the step-by-step account of the action. Notice how it tells specifically what happened the morning of the attempted trip.

> The next morning we got up very early. We wanted to reach the block before people started coming out of their apartment houses to go to work. I sat in the front of the wagon. Chip gave a push and jumped on behind me. The wagon went faster and faster. Chip and I cheered. We were sure that we would leave the earth's gravity and would be on our way to the moon. I began to daydream about newspaper headlines and being interviewed on television.

In this story the climax, in the third paragraph, is the wagon crashing into Mrs. Clark's fruit stand. Notice the way in which this climax is made vivid by the use of specific details and effective verbs.

> Suddenly Chip yelled, "Watch out!" Going uphill had made our wagon change direction. We were headed straight for Mrs. Clark's fruit stand. I grabbed the handle of the wagon to steer, but it was too late. We crashed into the fruit stand and almost hit Mrs. Clark. Mrs. Clark shouted, as the fruit spilled in all directions.

When You Write. In writing the middle of your story,

- Allow enough time to write the entire middle section in one sitting.
- Keep your story plan nearby. Make any necessary changes as you write.
- Let your thoughts flow freely, concentrating on actions that build toward the climax, the high point of the story.
- Use chronological order.
- Include dialogue if it is appropriate.
- Use vivid, specific details that appeal to the reader's senses.

EXERCISE 22. Writing the Middle of Your Story. Using the suggestions above, write the middle section of the story you started to write in Exercise 21. Answers will vary.

Ending

The ending of a story ties up the loose ends. The ending may state how the writer felt about the events of the story, or it may merely suggest the writer's feelings. In this story, the ending tells what happened after the wagon hit the fruit stand. Although we are not told directly, the details about the dented wagon, being grounded, and paying for the damaged fruit give us a good idea of how Chip and the writer must have felt. We are not surprised that they did not plan another trip to the moon for a while.

EXERCISE 23. Be available for individual conferences with those who need extra help writing the ending of their story.

EVALUATING

Section Overview

Students must learn that evaluating is a complex stage of the writing process that is separate from writing and revising.

EVALUATING A NARRATIVE (rule 4k)

To evaluate their narratives well, students need time to think about their writing. Try to allow a day or two to pass before students begin evaluating their drafts. Encourage students to refer to the Guidelines for Evaluating Narratives, page 127 of the text, whenever they write narratives.

The story has a sad ending. Out of our allowances we paid $3.40 for the fresh fruit that Mrs. Clark lost. Chip's wagon had a big dent in it. I was grounded for sneaking out of the house in the early morning. Chip and I postponed our plans for the next moonshot indefinitely.

What happened in this ending? Can you tell how the writer felt? What clues are given to tell you the writer's feelings?

When You Write. To write the ending of your story, ask yourself:

- What has happened so far in the opening and the middle?
- What is the outcome of these events?
- How can I tie up all the loose ends?
- What are my feelings about the story? Should I state these feelings directly or just suggest them?
- Will my ending satisfy my reader that the story is over? (Some stories are *open-ended;* that is, they do not tell the reader what finally happens.)

EXERCISE 23. Writing the Ending for Your Story. Using the questions above as a guide, write an ending for the story you began in Exercises 21 and 22. Answers will vary.

EVALUATING

EVALUATING A NARRATIVE

4k. Evaluate the first draft of your story.

Many writers feel that the evaluation stage is the most important part of the writing process. Here, once the first draft is on paper, the writer can decide which changes would shape and polish the story. Try to set your draft aside. Then, when you evaluate, carefully consider content, organization, and style. Use the following guidelines to evaluate your draft.

GUIDELINES FOR EVALUATING NARRATIVES

Start	1. Does the start grab the audience's attention immediately?
Beginning Explanation	2. Are the characters and setting introduced in the beginning explanation? Is necessary background information included?
Action	3. Do specific details make the action vivid? Are any important actions missing? Should any actions be omitted because they could distract the reader by not being directly related to the story?
Climax	4. Is the story's high point obvious?
Ending	5. Does the ending tie up the loose ends? Are the writer's feelings about the story expressed or suggested?
Order	6. Are the actions arranged in chronological order?
Characters	7. Are the characters' most important features or traits obvious? Are details arranged to emphasize these features?
Dialogue	8. Is the dialogue lively and natural-sounding? Are sentences fairly short, as they are in normal conversation? Does the dialogue tell something about the characters or action?
Setting	9. Do details of setting reflect the right mood for the story? Are they arranged in spatial order?
Word Choice	10. Are words and sentences appropriate for the audience? Are specific nouns, verbs, adjectives, and adverbs used to create vivid pictures? Are there any unnecessary adjectives and adverbs? (Remember that too many could spoil your descriptions.)

EXERCISE 24. Evaluating Your Story. Using the preceding guidelines, evaluate your first draft. Make notes on the draft to remind you where to revise. If possible, have another reader help you evaluate. Perhaps you can read your story to a small group and then discuss whether it follows each guideline. Answers will vary.

EXERCISE 24. After students have evaluated their own stories, you may wish to have them trade stories for peer evaluation. Be sure to be available so that students can check with you on whether a suggested evaluation will improve their story or not.

Section Overview

Students must learn that revising is the natural outgrowth of the evaluating stage in the writing process. Since they have learned to uncover problems in their writing during the evaluation stage, they should also learn to concentrate efficiently and productively on how to eliminate these problems.

REVISING A NARRATIVE
(rule 4l)

Remind students that revising may be done more than once and that writers have been known to revise a section of a story dozens of times. Suggest to students that they revise their stories for content and then revise them for organization. Discuss the techniques for revising short stories in the chart on pages 128–30.

REVISING

REVISING A NARRATIVE

4l. Revise the first draft of your story.

After you evaluate your draft, you are ready to revise those areas that need improving. Very few writers are satisfied with their first effort, so they evaluate and revise with care. To revise, you can cut out words or sentences. You can add new ideas and details, or you can reorder what you have already written. You can also replace one word or sentence with another. The following chart suggests how to use these techniques to revise your story.

REVISING STORIES

PROBLEM	TECHNIQUE	REVISION
The start is not interesting.	Replace	Replace the beginning with an opening situation or dialogue that will grab the reader's attention or arouse curiosity.
The characters are not introduced clearly.	Add	At an appropriate place in the beginning explanation, add more details about the characters. Use vivid, lively language.
The setting is vague or missing.	Add	If the setting is important, add descriptive details early in the story. Use details that reflect the mood of your story (exciting, mysterious, etc.).

PROBLEM	TECHNIQUE	REVISION
Specific details about what happened are missing.	Add	Review your story plan; then add missing details to the first draft.
Some actions or details are not directly related to the story.	Cut/Replace	Cut any details that are not related to the story or the characters. Replace unrelated details with ones that will make the story's events clear.
The climax is lost.	Add	Add details that will make the climax stand out or that will make it more exciting, vivid, etc.
The ending is not satisfying.	Replace/Add	Replace the ending with one that is more interesting, logical, or realistic. Add your feelings about the story either directly or indirectly to the ending of your story.
The order of the events is not clear.	Reorder	Reorder details or actions that are confusing, out of order or are not clear to the reader.
The characters' personality traits are not clear.	Add/Reorder	Add details that emphasize the characters' most important features. Rearrange details so the most important ones stand out.
The dialogue is not natural-sounding.	Replace	Ask someone to read the dialogue aloud. Replace any dialogue that does not sound natural. Remember that people usually speak in very short sentences or even parts of sentences.

EXERCISE 25. You should go over the model carefully to show students how the chart, Revising Stories, is applied to revisions of narratives.

PROBLEM	TECHNIQUE	REVISION
Some dialogue does not reveal anything about the characters or the action.	Cut/Add	Cut dialogue that fails to tell something about events or characters. Add dialogue about important actions or people.
The setting doesn't seem to fit the story.	Replace/ Reorder	Replace details of setting that do not reflect the right mood. Reorder details so they help to tell the story.
Some words are not appropriate for the audience.	Replace	Review the characteristics of your audience; then replace the inappropriate words.
There are too many adjectives and adverbs.	Cut/ Replace/ Add	Cut unnecessary adjectives and adverbs. Replace them with comparisons (something is *like* something else) or reword sentences to make nouns and verbs do the work of describing. (*He darted,* for example, instead of *He suddenly ran.*) Add specific, exact words.

EXERCISE 25. Analyzing a Writer's Revisions. Read the following revised draft of two paragraphs from the personal experience narrative on pages 123–26. Then answer the questions that follow the paragraphs.

The next morning we got up very early. We wanted to reach the block before people started coming out of their apartment houses to go to work. ~~My dad always leaves early, too~~. I sat in the front of the wagon. Chip gave a push and jumped on behind me. The wagon went faster and faster. Chip and I cheered. We were sure that we would leave the earth's gravity and would be on our way to the moon. I began to daydream about newspaper headlines and being interviewed on television. cut

add

We were headed straight for Mrs. Clark's fruit stand. Suddenly Chip yelled, "Watch out!" Going uphill had made our wagon change direction. I grabbed the handle of the wagon to steer, but it was too late. We ~~ran~~ crashed into the fruit stand and almost hit Mrs. Clark. Mrs. Clark ~~was angry~~ shouted. The fruit spilled in all directions.

reorder

replace

replace

1. Why did the writer add a sentence to the first paragraph?
2. Why did the writer cut one sentence?
3. Why did the writer reorder some sentences?
4. Why did the writer replace "ran" with "crashed" and "was angry" with "shouted"?
5. What other changes should the writer make? Why do you think so?

EXERCISE 26. Replacing Overused Adjectives and Adverbs. Number your paper 1–10. For each item, replace the overused adjectives and adverbs in italics with words that are fresher and more exact. Answers will vary.

EXAMPLE 1. I wanted to paint the room purple, but Geraldo thought it would look *funny*.
1. *peculiar*

Answers: Exercise 25
(Answers will vary somewhat in wording.)

1. The writer added a sentence that gives more insight into the main character's personality.
2. The sentence about the writer's father was unrelated to the story.
3. In the second paragraph, reordering put the events into logical sequence.
4. The more specific verbs make the narrative more colorful.
5. Some of the sentences in the first paragraph should be combined for smoothness and for variety in sentence structure.

EXERCISE 26. If thesauruses and dictionaries of synonyms are available in your classroom, encourage your students to use them. Perhaps you can, at least, find enough of these books for small-group work.

EXERCISES 27 and 28. Exercise 27 should prepare students to cut out unnecessary adjectives and adverbs in their own writing. You may wish to have volunteers share their revised paragraphs in Exercise 27 before you have students work individually on revisions of their stories in Exercise 28.

PROOFREADING

Section Overview

Students should recognize that proofreading plays a distinct role in the writing process; it focuses on the mechanical aspects of writing and therefore follows the revising stage.

PROOFREADING YOUR STORY AND MAKING A FINAL COPY (rule 4m)

Remind students why proofreading is a vital part of the writing process: it eliminates careless errors that may distract or confuse their audience. Students should also understand that many readers are unwilling to tackle a messy, illegible manuscript, thus making it important to prepare a clean, accurate final copy.

1. Sabrena, your birthday party was *nice.*
2. I had an *absolutely terrible* time at the dentist's.
3. It is a *cute* little puppy that often does *cute* tricks.
4. Paul Simon has recorded a *terrific* new song.
5. Just as we ran out of ideas, Wanetta made a *neat* suggestion.
6. Kim gave a *swell* performance in the class play.
7. Margie's hair looks *horrible* this morning.
8. The homework Mr. Rubin assigned is *really* difficult.
9. Jonathan plays the clarinet *awfully* well.
10. We had an *awfully wonderful* weekend at your home.

EXERCISE 27. Omitting Unnecessary Adjectives and Adverbs. The following paragraph has too many adjectives and adverbs. Rewrite it by eliminating unnecessary modifiers, by using comparisons, and by replacing a verb and an adverb with an exact verb. Answers will vary.

The shabby, pathetic-looking little man shuffled timidly and fearfully along the dingy, cracked, uneven sidewalk. His old, battered hat jiggled precariously on his head. When he saw Mr. Abercrombie, the banker, coming up the street, he cautiously sidled up to him. Mr. Abercrombie walked haughtily past.

EXERCISE 28. Revising Your Own Story. Using the revising chart on pages 128–30, revise the draft of the narrative you evaluated in Exercise 24. Answers will vary.

PROOFREADING

PROOFREADING YOUR STORY AND MAKING A FINAL COPY

4m. Proofread your story and make a final copy.

If possible, put your paper away for a few days and come back to it with a fresh eye. The Guidelines for Proofreading (page 39) will remind you of the things to look for. If you have used dialogue in your narrative, pay particular attention to the punctuation and paragraphing of each speaker's words.

Remember that your aim is to have people enjoy what you have written. Readers may be unable or unwilling to read a paper that does not follow correct manuscript form. Review those standards (page 41) or your teacher's directions before making your final copy.

EXERCISE 29. Proofreading and Making a Final Copy of Your Narrative. Using the Guidelines for Proofreading on page 39, proofread the narrative you revised for Exercise 28. Then make your final copy. Proofread it again to check for any mistakes made in recopying. Answers will vary.

CHAPTER 4 WRITING REVIEW

Writing a Story About an Imaginary Experience. Write a story about an imaginary experience, such as your or someone else's first day in a new school or first attempt at some athletic or artistic task. Using the process you practiced in this chapter to choose a subject, consider your purpose and audience, gather and arrange information, write, evaluate, revise, proofread, and make a final copy of your narrative. Answers will vary.

EXERCISE 29. This exercise directs students to proofread and make a final copy of their narrative. Once again papers should be passed around small groups to check for mechanical errors before the final copy is submitted for grading. Some of the finished products should be read aloud to the class, either by the writer or by you. Let the students know that you are proud of their hard work and its results. If your students participated in peer evaluation, recognize their efforts in this area also.

CHAPTER 4 WRITING REVIEW

If your students are capable of writing another narrative, assign this exercise now. Otherwise, it could be used as an extra-credit assignment at any time. It is important to allow and encourage your students to write throughout the year. Some stories could be distributed in an eighth-grade anthology and perhaps traded with eighth-graders from another school.

Additional Practice

Teacher's Resource Book, Worksheet pages 46–52, Alternative Worksheet pages (for less-advanced students) 520–21

Testing

Teaching Tests booklet, pages 1–4, 13–18
Teacher's Resource Book, Test pages 371–74, 395–96, 407–412

Chapter Overview

This chapter focuses on writing exposition. The emphasis here is on having students write compositions that clearly provide information. This chapter guides students through each step of the writing process and ends with the final copy of an expository composition. Keeping a notebook of work from this chapter might be helpful to students

Chapter Objective

Students will identify the various functions of exposition and will successfully use the writing process to write expository compositions.

PRESENTING THE CHAPTER

LESS-ADVANCED STUDENTS With these students, you may want to emphasize those topics with which students feel most comfortable. For example, a "how-to" expository composition on their favorite sport or hobby could give them the self-confidence they will need to tackle the research paper in the next chapter. To give students practice in limiting subjects, you might have them write shorter compositions than the text suggests.

As an additional activity, you could ask students to bring in "how-to" articles from newspapers or magazines. You could ask them to identify the purpose, audience, details, the *5 W-How?* questions, etc. You may want to schedule a lot of class time for this chapter to ensure that students are successful in each step of the writing process. You might consider teaching the use of an informal outline instead of a formal one with this group. *(See listing of Alternative Worksheets on page 169.)*

CHAPTER 5

Writing Exposition

THE WHOLE COMPOSITION

In this chapter you will use the steps in the writing process to write expository compositions—compositions whose purpose it is to explain or inform. A composition is a group of closely related paragraphs that, together, present a single main idea about a topic. Most compositions can be divided into three main sections —the introduction, the body, and the conclusion.

PREWRITING

SEARCHING FOR SUBJECTS

5a. Search for subjects for your expository compositions.

Many of the compositions you write this year will be on subjects assigned by your teachers. Sometimes, however, you may have to find a subject of your own. For example, your teacher might ask you to write one of the following expository compositions:

A composition explaining how to make *something* or how to do *something*

A composition giving directions to *some place*
A composition giving information about *someone, something,* or *some place*

To find a subject for an expository composition, begin by examining your personal resources—your interests, your knowledge, and your experiences. In your search, you can use any of the methods described below.

(1) In your search for subjects, consider what you know about and what you like to do.

Perhaps you know a great deal about collecting stamps or coins: how to start a collection, where to obtain specimens, what pleasures and advantages this hobby offers. You may like to hike on nearby nature trails or play tournament chess. These are all possible subjects for an expository composition.

Before You Write. To examine your personal resources for an expository composition, ask yourself:

- What are my interests? What do I especially look forward to doing in my free time?
- What do I know about through my hobbies, reading, participation in sports and other after-school activities, TV viewing, and movie-going?
- What experiences have I had that might interest someone else?

EXERCISE 1. Examining Your Personal Resources. Using the questions in Before You Write (above), examine your interests, knowledge, and experiences. Save your answers for use later in this chapter. Answers will vary.

(2) In your search for subjects, observe the world around you.

Suppose that you have been asked to write a composition explaining how to do something. To find a subject to write about, you can observe the world around you. For example, you may

ADVANCED STUDENTS Your advanced students will probably feel fairly comfortable with most of the prewriting stages in this chapter if they choose subjects for which they will not have to do *any* research. These students can be expected to write an expository composition about three to five paragraphs in length, as suggested by the text. If they choose a subject on which they need to do some research, they should be able to gather and organize the material.

You may want to confer with teachers in the social studies department for a list of subjects they will cover in that class. Students might write a composition on some aspect of the Revolutionary War, for example.

PREWRITING

Section Overview

Using the steps of the prewriting stage of the writing process will enable students to choose an appropriate subject for their purpose from their own resources, gather information about their limited topic, and organize this information into a draft.

SEARCHING FOR SUBJECTS (rule 5a)

This section gives students several ways to search for possible subjects from their own resources. You may find that your students feel comfortable with only one or two of these discovery techniques. If that is the case, you may want to emphasize only those techniques by providing class time for presentation and practice of each.

EXERCISE 1. You may want your students to use list form for this exercise. They can title the lists *Interests, Free Time Activities, Hobbies, Reading, Sports,* etc. Encourage them to keep their answers in a safe place so that they can refer to them later.

EXERCISE 2. You may want to supplement these subjects by assigning others, such as "giving information about after-school activities."

have noticed how a neighbor plants a vegetable garden, how a friend strings her guitar, and how a relative uses a computer. Thinking about your own resources, you may realize that using a computer interests you more than planting a garden or stringing a guitar. You have discovered a possible subject for your expository composition.

Before You Write. To find possible subjects for an expository composition by observing, ask yourself:

- What have I observed in the world around me—at home, in my neighborhood, in school, on a trip, etc.?
- Which of these observations are of interest to me?

EXERCISE 2. Using Your Observations to Search for Subjects. Using your observations of the world around you, list at least three broad subjects for each of the following expository writing assignments. For example, for a composition giving information about something, three broad subjects that might grow out of your observations are "sea creatures," "repairing a broken sidewalk," and "trees in my neighborhood."

Answers will vary.

1. Giving information about an event
2. Explaining how to do something
3. Giving information about a person
4. Explaining how to make something
5. Giving information about a place

(3) Use a writer's journal as a source of possible subjects.

Keep a writer's journal in which you record your feelings, thoughts, and experiences. Later, when you want to find something to write about, you can look through your journal for a possible subject.

For example, here is a sample entry from one student's journal:

> We had a speaker at school today—a stockbroker from New York. She explained how stocks are traded at the New

EXERCISE 3. You may wish for your students to keep their journal in their English notebook or folder so that they can refer to it when they are searching for subjects or details.

York Stock Exchange on Wall Street. In some ways it's much simpler than I expected. If I wanted to buy some stock in a company, I would call my personal stockbroker. This person would place my order with a telephone clerk at the stock exchange in New York. The clerk would talk to a broker there. This broker, who is on the floor of the stock exchange, would actually bargain with other brokers to get the amount of stock I want to buy at the best possible price. After the deal is made, the broker would tell the telephone clerk, who would call my personal broker. I would have to pay for the stock five days later.

If you read this entry in your writer's journal, it might suggest "buying stock" as a broad subject for an expository composition. Thinking about this entry might also lead you to other possible broad subjects such as "becoming a stockbroker" or "the New York Stock Exchange." Keeping a writer's journal not only lets you record things you can refer to later, but also suggests subjects for compositions.

EXERCISE 3. Keeping a Writer's Journal. Keep a writer's journal for three to five days. This journal can be a notebook or a file folder. In your journal, record the thoughts, feelings, and experiences you want to share with other people. Then, using your writer's journal as a source, list at least five broad subjects for an expository composition. (Remember that the purpose of exposition is to inform or to explain.) If you already keep a journal regularly, you may refer to any entries you wish.
Answers will vary.

(4) Use brainstorming in your search for subjects.

You can also use brainstorming to search for subjects to write about. When you brainstorm for subjects, you write down as many ideas as you can think of all at once. Your aim is to list as many subjects as possible, without stopping to judge their suitability. Deciding which subjects you can actually write about comes later in the writing process.

Suppose, for example, that your English teacher has asked you to write a composition giving information about someone or

EXERCISES 4 and 5. Theses exercises provide practice in using discovery techniques. You may divide the class into groups for Exercise 4. With less-advanced students, you may decide to provide other examples of clustering on the board before they begin to work individually.

something. To search for subjects, you might brainstorm for ideas by using the question "Who or what do I know about?" The list you come up with might look like this:

playing the piano
planting a vegetable garden
the local recreation program
being a day-camp counselor
my uncle's trip to Alaska
waltzing on ice skates
understanding my brother
snorkeling
types of cameras

After you brainstorm, you can select a subject from those on your list. These subjects are still too broad or general to be suitable for an expository composition, but you have discovered several possible subjects to write about.

EXERCISE 4. Using Brainstorming to Search for Subjects. Use brainstorming to search for at least ten subjects for an expository composition. Focus on your own knowledge. Think up as many answers as possible to the question "Who or what do I know about?" Keep your list of possible subjects. You may want to refer to this list later in the chapter. Answers will vary.

(5) Use clustering in your search for subjects.

You can also use clustering to search for subjects to write about. When clustering, you make a diagram instead of a list. You begin by writing a word or a phrase in the center of a sheet of paper. Then you write down as many ideas related to that word or phrase as you can. As you add each idea, circle it and connect these circled words and phrases with lines. Each line should connect an idea with the idea it came from. As in brainstorming, you do not take time to judge your ideas.

As with the other methods of searching for subjects, any one of the circled words or phrases can be a broad subject for an expository composition.

Suppose, for example, that your teacher has asked you to write a composition explaining how to make or do something. Your clustering diagram might look like this:

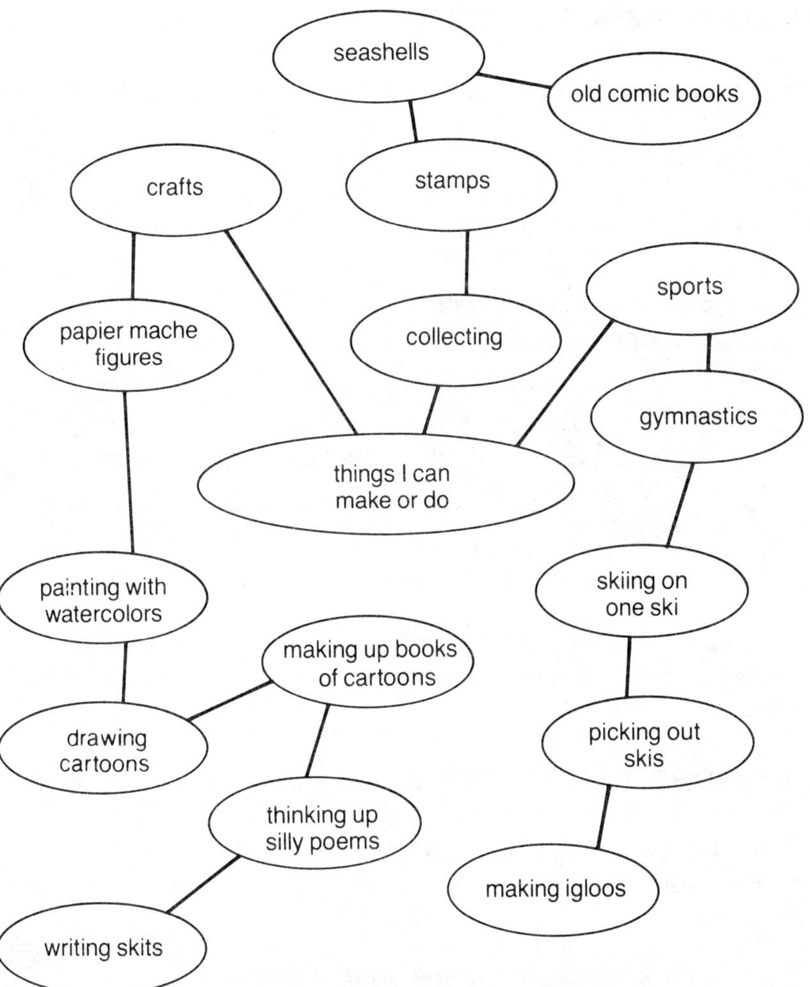

EXERCISE 5. Using Clustering to Search for Subjects. Use clustering to search for possible subjects for an expository composition. Use one of the following ideas to start your cluster diagram: Answers will vary.

Things I am interested in	Things I know about
Things I can make or do	Things I have experienced

Circle and connect the words or phrases you think of. Keep your work in your notebook for use later in this chapter.

CHOOSING A SUBJECT (rule 5b)

This section instructs students to select one subject that they can explain well.

EXERCISE 6. Some students may want to talk with you individually about their decision. In any case, encourage them to make a *firm* decision so that they will not vacillate as the chapter progresses.

THINKING ABOUT YOUR AUDIENCE (rule 5c)

Since the purpose of expository writing is "to inform *someone* about something or to explain something to *someone*," your students will need to consider audience through each step of the writing process. You may want to have them refer to the four questions on analyzing audience (*Before You Write*, page 141) throughout their work in this chapter.

CHOOSING A SUBJECT

5b. From your list of possible subjects, choose one to write about.

To choose a subject, review the subjects you discovered in Exercises 1–5 on pages 135–39. The subject you choose should be one you understand well enough to explain to someone else.

Before You Write. When choosing a subject, ask yourself the following questions:

- What subject interests me enough to want to explain it to someone else?
- What subject do I know enough about to explain it clearly to someone else?
- What subject do I have enough experience with to explain it to someone else?

Usually subjects that you understand well enough to explain to someone else will appear in your answers to at least two of these three questions.

EXERCISE 6. Choosing a Subject for Your Composition. Review the lists of possible subjects you made for Exercises 1–5. Using the questions above, choose one subject for an expository composition. Answers will vary.

THINKING ABOUT YOUR AUDIENCE

5c. Think about the audience for your expository composition.

Your audience is the person or people for whom you write. In expository writing the audience is especially important because the purpose of exposition is to inform *someone* about something or to explain something to *someone*.

Suppose, for example. that you chose "science-fiction movies" as a subject for your composition. How you explain this

EXERCISE 7. You may want to do this exercise as an oral activity to make certain that students know some characteristics of each audience.

broad subject will depend on who your audience is. If you are writing for fourth-graders, you might want to explain why certain movies are called science fiction. For an audience made up of your classmates, you might explain the differences between the special effects in two science-fiction movies. For an audience of parents, you might explain why science-fiction movies are good entertainment for people your age.

Your audience will also affect how you write your composition. For an audience of fourth-graders, for example, you will have to use simple vocabulary and easy-to-understand sentences. For an audience of parents, on the other hand, you can use more technical terms and more difficult sentences.

Before You Write. To think about your audience, ask yourself these questions:

- How can I best describe my audience? Is it made up of children? Adults? Classmates?
- Is this particular subject suitable for this audience?
- What does my audience already know about this subject?
- What does my audience want to know or need to know about this subject?

EXERCISE 7. Thinking About Audiences. Following are five audiences paired with five subjects. Answer the question about the audience that follows each pair. Answers will vary.

1. *Subject:* Microcomputers in math class
   Audience: Members of an eighth-grade class
   How can you describe this audience?
2. *Subject:* Safety with strangers
   Audience: First-graders
   What does this audience want to know or need to know about this subject?
3. *Subject:* William Shakespeare
   Audience: Eighth-grade English teachers
   What does this audience already know about the subject?

EXERCISE 8. You may want to have your less-advanced students write for their peers. This may eliminate confusion about selecting appropriate vocabulary words and sentence structure.

LIMITING YOUR SUBJECT (rule 5d) and

CRITICAL THINKING: Analyzing a Broad Subject

This section emphasizes the necessity of limiting a subject in order to achieve the purpose of exposition—that is, to provide precise, detailed information explaining a subject. The six questions should help your students limit their subjects.

4. *Subject:* Summer arts festivals
   Audience: Readers of the local newspaper
   How can you describe this audience?
5. *Subject:* Local elementary schools
   Audience: Tenth-graders
   Is this subject suitable for this audience? Why or why not?

EXERCISE 8. Thinking About Your Audience. Using the four questions in Before You Write on page 141, think about the audience for your expository composition. Write a brief answer for each question. Answers will vary.

LIMITING YOUR SUBJECT

5d. Limit your subject to a manageable topic.

A subject is a broad area with many different parts. Suppose, for example, you chose the subject "stamp collecting." To explain the different parts of this subject, you would have to write a long report. For a short expository composition, "stamp collecting" should be limited to one of its smaller parts, called a "topic." The limited topic "beginning a stamp collection" is an example of a manageable topic for a short expository composition.

CRITICAL THINKING: Analyzing a Broad Subject

To limit your broad subject to a manageable topic, analyze your subject by dividing it into its smaller parts. The following questions will help you analyze your subject:

1. What are *examples* of the subject?
2. What are *uses* of the subject?
3. What are *types* of the subject?
4. What are *activities* involving the subject?
5. What *time periods* does the subject include?
6. What *places, people,* or *events* does the subject include?

EXERCISES 9, 10, and 11. Since Exercises 9 and 10 are related, you may want to have your students complete them as one exercise. For each *NS* answer in Exercise 9, you may want to discuss with the class how the topic can be limited to become a good composition topic. This activity provides practice in critical thinking skills. Check work done for Exercise 11. This is an exercise that should be saved in students' files or notebooks as a possible basis of their expository compositions.

As you answer these questions about your subject, you will be dividing it into smaller, more limited, topics for your composition. Keep in mind, however, that you will probably not be able to use each question with every subject. The broad subject "stamp collecting," for example, can be limited by using questions 3 and 4:

Subject: Stamp collecting
Types: rare stamps, first day covers, commemorative stamps, specialized stamps (railroads, birds, ships, paintings, etc.)
Activities: trading with other collectors, joining stamp clubs or societies, attending exhibitions, beginning to collect and display stamps

Any one of the limited topics listed above could be a manageable topic for an expository composition.

EXERCISE 9. Identifying Limited Topics. Four of the subjects listed below are too broad to be manageable composition topics. Four are limited enough to be suitable topics. Number your paper 1–8. Write *S* after the number of each suitably limited topic. Write *NS* after the number of each subject that is not suitably limited.

1. The youth of an American President 1. S
2. Mystery stories 2. NS
3. Profile of a local disc jockey 3. S
4. Pioneer life 4. NS
5. Environmental pollution 5. NS
6. Starting a vegetable garden 6. S
7. Hunting for snakes 7. S
8. The women's rights movement 8. NS

EXERCISE 10. Developing Limited Topics. For each of the four broad subjects identified in Exercise 9, develop at least two limited topics. Remember to use the questions in Critical Thinking on page 142 to divide each broad subject into its smaller parts.
Answers will vary.

EXERCISE 11. Developing Your Own Limited Topic. Using the broad subject you chose for Exercise 6, develop a topic that is limited enough for a composition. Use the Critical Thinking questions to divide your subject into its smaller parts. Be sure to limit, or narrow, your subject enough so that it can be clearly explained in a short composition. Answers will vary.

STATING YOUR PURPOSE

5e. State the purpose of your expository composition.

The purpose of an expository composition is to explain or inform. For your statement of purpose, however, you should focus specifically on *what* your composition will explain to your audience, or *what* you will inform your audience about. To do so, use phrases such as *to explain, to inform, to show, to indicate,* or *to discuss* in your statement of purpose. For example, for the topic "beginning a stamp collection," the statement of purpose might read: *to explain how a beginner can collect and display stamps.*

Focusing on your topic in this way will help you later in the writing process. By clearly stating the purpose of your composition, you will know what kind of information you should gather for your composition. This statement of purpose can also be included in the introductory paragraph you write for your composition.

EXERCISE 12. Stating a Purpose. For each limited topic listed below, write a statement of purpose for an expository composition.

1. Muhammad Ali's prizefighting record
2. How Manhattan got its name
3. Making toothpick sculptures
4. Space achievements of the 1980's

EXERCISE 13. Stating a Purpose for Your Own Composition. Write a statement of purpose for the limited topic you have chosen for your expository composition. Save this statement of purpose in your notebook for possible use in the introductory paragraph of your expository composition. Answers will vary.

STATING YOUR PURPOSE (rule 5e)

This section directs students to determine a definite purpose for their compositions and to state it by using such phrases as *to explain, to inform, to show, to indicate,* or *to discuss.* This might be a good time to have students find examples of statements of purpose in expository writing in magazine and newspaper articles. This practice may help students adhere to their stated purpose while writing their drafts.

EXERCISES 12 and 13. These exercises give students practice in writing statements of purpose. You might want to do Exercise 12 as an oral activity. Ask students to think of other subjects and to volunteer statements of purpose for these subjects. When you feel certain that the class understands this exercise, assign Exercise 13. This will be the statement of purpose for their compositions and should be saved in their files or notebooks. Try to review their work here to determine whether the statement of purpose is usable.

Answers: Exercise 12

(Answers may vary slightly, but possibilities are given below.)

1. to discuss Muhammed Ali's prizefighting record
2. to explain how Manhattan got its name
3. to show how to make toothpick sculptures
4. to discuss space achievements of the 1980's

GATHERING INFORMATION

5f. Gather information for your expository composition.

The three strategies that follow will help you gather information for your expository composition.

(1) List ideas and details for your expository composition.

Listing ideas and details is very much like brainstorming and clustering. Your purpose is to jot down as many ideas and details as possible. Later you will decide which ones you should include in your composition and how they should be organized.

Study the following sample list of ideas and details for the topic "beginning a stamp collection." Notice that the information is listed as it occurred to the writer, rather than in an organized plan. Keep in mind that there may be some ideas and details the writer might eventually decide not to use in an expository composition on this topic.

Topic: Beginning a stamp collection
Purpose: To explain how a beginner can collect and display stamps
Ideas and details:

family mail
hobby stores
removing stamps from envelopes
fun of watching collection grow
learning locations of countries
appreciating beauty of stamps
stamp dealers
history of postage stamps
learning about people and customs of foreign lands
mounting stamps in album
supplies: tongs, hinges, album
post office
stamp packets
approval sheets
valuable stamps

EXERCISE 14. Listing Ideas and Details. For each limited topic that follows, list at least five ideas and details. (Your teacher may instead want you to select only one topic and list as many ideas as you can about it.) Answers will vary.

GATHERING INFORMATION (rule 5f)

Students will probably be impressed that they have three methods of gathering information from their own resources, without consulting one reference book. These methods are (1) listing ideas and details, (2) using a writer's journal, and (3) asking the *5 W-How?* questions. You might want to use a class period to present each technique and to allow students to practice each in class.

EXERCISE 14. Your less-advanced students should probably concentrate on one topic.

EXERCISES 15–17. Each of these exercises gives students practice in information-gathering methods. You may want to extend Exercise 16 by having students answer all questions on each topic. Of course, students could make the topics more specific, for example, by changing number 3 to "The easiest way to learn how to play tennis." Exercise 17 will need to be written and saved for the draft of the expository composition.

1. Differences between concerts and record albums
2. How to ride a bicycle safely
3. Why I watch television
4. The care and feeding of small animals

(2) Use your writer's journal as a source of information about your topic.

On pages 136–37 you learned about using a writer's journal to search for subjects for a composition. A writer's journal can also be a source of ideas and details about your topic.

The sample entry on page 136, for example, contains ideas and details about how stocks are traded. If you were writing a composition on this topic, you could use this particular journal entry as a source of information on how a stockbroker goes about buying stocks.

EXERCISE 15. Gathering Information from a Writer's Journal. If you keep a writer's journal, review it for any ideas and details related to the limited topic you developed in Exercise 11. Write these ideas and details in your notebook.
Answers will vary.

(3) Ask the *5 W-How?* questions to gather information on your topic.

Asking questions is often a useful way to find information about a topic. Newspaper writers ask the *5 W-How?* questions: *Who? What? When? Where? Why? How?* The answer to each of these questions will give you a piece of information—an idea or a detail—about your topic.

For example, study how one student used the *5 W-How?* questions to gather information on the topic "being a day-camp counselor."

Who? Who can be a day-camp counselor?
Young people with day-camp experience, good personal reputations, and some outdoor camping and crafts skills

What? What do day-camp counselors do?
Supervise children in day camps, give classes in craft projects and outdoor skills, assist the camp directors

When? When are jobs available for day-camp counselors?
Every summer, usually in one-week sessions in June, July, and August

Where? Where are jobs available for day-camp counselors?
Local communities, religious groups, community organizations, and groups like the Boy Scouts, Girl Scouts, and Camp Fire Girls sponsor day camps.

Why? Why would someone want to be a counselor at a day camp?
To work with young people, to make some money, and to spend the summer outdoors in an interesting environment

How? How can someone get a job as a day-camp counselor?
Call local religious groups, ask the local parks and recreation department, contact groups such as the Boy Scouts and Girl Scouts. See what jobs they have and what kind of people they like to fill them with.

EXERCISE 16. Asking the 5 W-How? Questions. Select a topic from the following list. Then ask the *5 W-How?* questions to gather information on the topic. For each question, write at least one answer. Answers will vary.

1. My favorite team's greatest accomplishment
2. What I really want to do this summer
3. Recreational opportunities in our community

EXERCISE 17. Gathering Information on Your Topic. Using one or more of the methods described on pages 145–47, gather information on the limited topic you have chosen for your expository composition. Keep the information you gather for use later in this chapter. Answers will vary.

GROUPING IDEAS AND DETAILS

5g. Group the related ideas and details you have gathered.

GROUPING IDEAS AND DETAILS (rule 5g)

This section presents the first step in organizing material: grouping related ideas and devising a heading for each group.

You are now ready to begin grouping, or classifying, the information you have gathered for your expository composition.

To classify information, you identify and group together closely related ideas and details. Then you give each group a heading that shows how the items are related. For example, the ideas and details listed for the topic "beginning a stamp collection" (page 145) can be classified into the following groups under four headings:

GROUP 1: Pleasure of collecting stamps
fun of watching collection grow
appreciating beauty of stamps

GROUP 2: Educational value
learning about people and customs of foreign lands
learning locations of countries

GROUP 3: Sources of stamps
family mail
hobby stores
post office
dealers: packets, approval sheets

GROUP 4: Displaying stamps
removing stamps from envelopes
supplies: tongs, hinges, album
mounting stamps in album

When you attempt to group the ideas and details you have gathered, you may find that some items do not fit anywhere. For example, two ideas in the list on page 145 have been eliminated from the above groupings.

history of postage stamps [eliminated because it does not contribute to purpose of composition]
valuable stamps [eliminated because a beginning collector would not ordinarily try to collect valuable stamps]

Remember that in exposition, as in most other kinds of writing, what you leave out can be as important as what you put in. By omitting an unrelated idea or detail from your list, you can often improve your composition.

EXERCISES 18 and 19. These exercises provide practice in arranging ideas and details. You may decide to have the students work on them in small groups.

Before You Write. To group ideas and details, ask yourself these questions:

- Which of my ideas and details are closely related?
- Which heading will show how each group of ideas and details is related?
- Which, if any, ideas and details should be eliminated because they do not fit anywhere?

EXERCISE 18. Eliminating Ideas and Details. The following list contains several ideas or details that do not fit the topic "repairing a bicycle." Decide ~~which items do not fit~~ and copy them on your paper. Be prepared to explain your choices.

Topic: Repairing a bicycle
Purpose: To show how to make simple repairs on a bicycle
Ideas and details:

adjusting the handlebars
~~long-distance bicycling~~
~~streets vs. dirt roads~~
removing the chain
locating a tire puncture
~~safety helmets~~
~~selecting a bicycle~~
~~locking the bicycle~~
measuring the height of the seat

EXERCISE 19. Grouping Ideas and Details. The ideas for each of the following topics can be grouped under two separate headings. First write down the topic. Then supply appropriate headings and list related ideas and details under each heading.
See Answer Key.

EXAMPLE 1. Baking bread
Mixing ingredients; flour; shortening; kneading dough; setting oven; yeast; salt; forming loaves; water; letting dough rise

1. *Baking bread*

Ingredients	*Procedure*
flour	*mixing ingredients*
shortening	*kneading dough*
yeast	*forming loaves*
salt	*letting dough rise*
water	*setting oven*

EXERCISE 20. You may wish to have students do this work in class so that you can check their listings quickly and offer suggestions. Ask students to evaluate whether they have more information than they can use in one paper. If any do, have them go ahead and eliminate one or more groups from their listing.

ARRANGING YOUR IDEAS AND DETAILS and **MAKING AN OUTLINE** **(rules 5h and 5i)**

The informal plan and topic outline are explained in this section. The informal plan may be the better choice for less-advanced students, while the topic outline could be a challenge for your advanced students. The emphasis is on placing information in a logical order. An additional teaching technique here is to have the students read a professional example of expository writing and together (in class discussion) trace the plan of the finished piece.

1. School activities
   Glee club; football; baseball; science club; drama club; gymnastics
2. Model planes
   Balsa wood; sharp knife; cutting out parts; gluing parts together; blueprints; paint; painting; glue

EXERCISE 20. Grouping Your Own Information. Sort into groups the ideas and details you gathered for a topic of your own in Exercise 17. First give each group a heading; then list related ideas and details under the headings. Answers will vary.

ARRANGING YOUR IDEAS AND DETAILS

5h. Arrange your ideas and details in logical order.

Often the ideas and details you have listed for your composition suggest the most logical arrangement. For example, the details for a composition about producing a play might follow the order of time: choosing the play, casting the play, and rehearsing the play. A composition on "our responsibilities," on the other hand, might call for an arrangement that builds from the most general to the most specific: responsibilities to our country, responsibilities to our community, responsibilities to our family, and responsibilities to ourselves.

As you arrange your ideas, experiment with the order until you find the arrangement that will present your ideas in the clearest possible way and will make the most sense to your audience.

Before You Write. To arrange your ideas in order, ask yourself:

- Does my list of ideas and details suggest the use of time order or of another order?
- Does the arrangement present my ideas in the clearest possible way?
- Will the arrangement make sense to my audience?

EXERCISE 21. Deciding on Order of Arrangement. For each of the following topics, indicate the order you would use to arrange the headings for a composition: order of time, general to specific, or specific to general.

1. How to assemble a telescope 1. time
2. The importance of being familiar with microcomputers 2. general to specific *or* specific to general
3. How to prepare for a math test 3. time
4. Directions to the Bijou Theater from Edgewater High School 4. time
5. The ambitions of my generation 5. general to specific *or* specific to general

EXERCISE 22. Arranging Your Own Ideas and Details. Arrange the ideas and details you grouped in Exercise 20 into the order most logical for your composition. Answers will vary.

EXERCISES 21 and 22. In Exercise 21 allow students to change details if they wish. For example, number 3 could be "How to prepare for a science test." If you are not planning to teach outlining to less-advanced students, be sure to check their work carefully in Exercise 22.

MAKING AN OUTLINE

5i. Make a topic outline for your expository composition.

By organizing and grouping your ideas and details, you have developed an informal plan for your composition. You are now ready to make a topic outline—a formal plan prepared according to a specific set of rules.

A topic outline is made up of main headings—the most important ideas—and subheadings. Subheadings are the details that support the idea expressed in a main heading. Each heading in a topic outline is expressed in a word or a phrase.

A topic outline should include a title. Although you may change the title later, be sure that it indicates your topic and appeals to the interest of your audience. Including your statement of purpose will help you keep that purpose in mind.

As you study the rules for outlining on pages 152–53, refer to the following topic outline for the composition about beginning a stamp collection.

Title: Beginning a Stamp Collection [title not part of outline]
Purpose: To explain how a beginner can collect and display stamps

I. Reasons for collecting stamps
   - A. Pleasure
     - 1. Fun of watching collection grow
     - 2. Appreciating beauty of stamps
   - B. Educational value
     - 1. Learning about people and customs of foreign lands
     - 2. Learning locations of countries

II. Sources for the collector
   - A. Family mail
   - B. Post office
   - C. Hobby stores
   - D. Stamp dealers
     - 1. Packets
     - 2. Approval sheets

III. Stamp display
   - A. Supplies
     - 1. Album
     - 2. Hinges
     - 3. Tongs
   - B. Procedure
     - 1. Removing from envelopes
     - 2. Mounting in album

IV. Specialization

Notice that a fourth main idea has been added to provide a conclusion for the composition.

Rules for Outlining

Observe the following rules when you make a topic outline:

(1) First, write the title and the purpose of your composition.

(2) Use a Roman numeral and a period before each main heading. Before each subheading under a main heading, use a capital letter and a period. Before each subheading under another

subheading, use an Arabic numeral and a period. For most short compositions, these levels of headings and subheadings are sufficient, as shown in the sample outline on page 152.

(3) Do not include a single subheading under a main heading or under another subheading. You cannot divide a heading into fewer than two subheadings.

(4) Indent subheadings so that all capital letters and numerals of the same kind are lined up directly under one another.

(5) Begin each main heading and subheading with a capital letter. Since the headings in a topic outline are not complete sentences, they should not be followed by periods.

EXERCISE 23. Completing a Topic Outline. Copy the incomplete outline given at the left. Then fill in the blanks with the appropriate items listed at the right.

Title: Our Science Club
Purpose: To explain how our science club began and to show its activities

I. Formation of club
  A. Choosing a club
  B. Recruiting members
  C. Electing officers
    1. Campaigning for office
    2. Holding elections
  D. Writing the club constitution
II. Club activities
  A. Tours of laboratories
    1. Government laboratories
    2. Industrial laboratories
  B. Projects
    1. Raising an ant colony
    2. Studying a bacterial mold
  C. Talks by eminent speakers
  D. Discussions of current scientific developments

Holding elections
Tours of laboratories
Recruiting members
Discussions of current scientific developments
Raising an ant colony
Choosing a name
Industrial laboratories
Electing officers
Club activities
Studying a bacterial mold

EXERCISE 23. You may wish to help your students get started by doing A. and B. under I. on the board.

EXERCISE 24. This exercise requires students to practice correct outline format.

EXERCISE 25. Emphasize to your students that this outline is temporary; that is, when they write their composition or even when they evaluate it later, they may make changes.

WRITING

Section Overview

The draft of an expository composition includes an introduction, body, and conclusion. Students should learn to write their expository compositions based on the work completed in the prewriting stage. They should realize that they may add details during this creative process.

WRITING A FIRST DRAFT (rule 5j)

This section of the chapter guides students through the writing of the first drafts of their expositions. It explains how to write the introduction, the body, and the conclusion and reminds students to focus attention on purpose, audience, and topic while writing. Although the draft is based on the prewriting steps, the text encourages students to continue to add information that will be suitable for their purpose and improve their compositions. Remind students that they may need to write several drafts before they are satisfied with their work.

The text supplies a sample composition (pages 158–60) in which students can identify elements that

EXERCISE 24. Developing a Topic Outline. Arrange the following ideas and details into a topic outline. Include a statement of purpose. The completed outline, like the one on page 152, should have three levels: Roman numerals, capital letters, and Arabic numerals. See Answer Key.

Title: Taking a Camping Trip
Major ideas:
- Camp health and safety
- Planning
- Setting up camp

Supporting ideas and details:

Selecting equipment	Dry ground
Making a fire	Safety when hiking
Safety tips	Arranging the wood
Setting up tents	Tents
Presence of fuel	Purifying water
Knives, hatchets, and axes	Safety in the water
Chopping wood	Choosing a campground
Selecting clothing	Bedding
Personal health	Food, pans, plates, spoons, etc.

EXERCISE 25. Developing a Topic Outline for Your Own Composition. Prepare an outline for the information you grouped and arranged in Exercises 20 and 22. Remember that this outline will guide you when you write your composition. Make certain, therefore, that it includes all the ideas you want to explain in your composition. Answers will vary.

WRITING

WRITING A FIRST DRAFT

5j. Write a draft of your expository composition. Include an introduction, a body, and a conclusion.

In Chapter 4 you learned that a narrative has a beginning, a middle, and an end. In the same way, a composition has three main parts: an introduction (the beginning); a body (the middle); and a conclusion (the end). Each of these parts has its own purpose in presenting your topic to your audience.

As you write the first draft of your expository composition, allow your writing to flow freely. Concentrate on putting down your ideas about your topic. Later you will be able to revise and proofread. Right now you should simply focus on writing down your thoughts about your topic.

Use your outline as a guide, but if new ideas about your topic occur to you, include them in your draft even though they do not appear in your outline. Later in the writing process, you will be able to decide which ideas to keep.

Writing the Introduction

The *introduction* to an expository composition should arouse the interest of your audience and indicate the purpose and topic of your composition. For example, the first sentence in the introduction to the sample composition on page 158 arouses interest by asking a question which is then answered. The introductory paragraph goes on to suggest the topic and the purpose of the composition—to explain how to begin a stamp collection. You may, if you wish, make your statement of purpose the last sentence in the introduction.

EXERCISE 26. Writing an Introductory Paragraph. Write an introduction for your expository composition. Be sure you include a sentence that states your composition's general purpose and topic; in this way, your audience will know what to expect when they read your composition. Answers will vary.

Writing the Body

The body is the longest part of a composition. In it, you develop the main ideas and supporting details shown in your topic outline. As a general rule, write at least one paragraph for each main heading. Sometimes, however, you may need more than one

they have been taught. This composition is based on the topic outline on page 152.

Review carefully the Guidelines for Writing Expository Compositions (pages 168–69). Encourage your students to refer to these guidelines whenever they write exposition.

EXERCISE 26. You may want to have students refer to the sample composition on page 158 as an example of an introduction. Your students' introductions may be much shorter, depending on their needs and abilities. Students will need to save this work in their files or notebooks.

EXERCISE 27. If you do not have a selection of published expository compositions in your classroom, you could ask students to bring in examples for this exercise in identifying transitional words and phrases. You could also once again refer to the sample composition on pages 158–60.

paragraph to explain an idea clearly and fully. In the sample composition on pages 158–60, for example, section II in the outline (page 152) is developed in three paragraphs; section III is developed in two paragraphs.

Using Transitional Words and Phrases

To help your audience follow the ideas developed in the body of your composition, use transitional words and phrases. In Chapter 2 you studied one use of transitional words and phrases—to connect *ideas* within a paragraph. In a composition, transitional words and phrases are also used to make smooth connections between *paragraphs*. By showing how one idea relates to another, transitional words and phrases enable your audience to follow your train of thought from sentence to sentence and from paragraph to paragraph.

Here are some commonly used transitional words and phrases.

next	moreover	furthermore	at the same time
then	besides	nevertheless	first (second, third)
thus	therefore	for example	on the other hand
in fact	finally	in addition	

Keep in mind that it is especially important to use transitional words and phrases in expository writing. When you are writing to inform or explain, you need to be sure your audience is following each point you make. This is particularly true of compositions that explain how to make or do something and of compositions that give directions. For each of these expository compositions, success depends on understanding how each step relates to the next. For example, if you were explaining how to make toast, you would probably use words or phrases that show time order: "*First* place the slice of bread in the toaster, *then* push the handle down, and *finally* remove the toast when it pops up."

EXERCISE 27. Identifying Transitional Words and Phrases. Find an expository paragraph in an encyclopedia, newspaper article, magazine article, how-to manual, cookbook, or textbook.

If you are permitted to cut the paragraph out, paste it to a sheet of paper; then circle all the transitional words and phrases in the paragraph. If you cannot cut the paragraph out, simply write down all the transitional words and phrases it contains. How do they help you follow the writer's train of thought? Be prepared to explain why these transitions are or are not effective.
Answers will vary.

When You Write. When you write the body of your composition

- use your topic outline as a guide.
- write at least one paragraph for each of the main headings in your outline.
- use transitional words and phrases to help your audience follow your ideas from sentence to sentence and from paragraph to paragraph.

EXERCISE 28. Writing the Body of Your Expository Composition. Using the topic outline you developed for Exercise 25, write the body of your expository composition.
Answers will vary.

Writing the Conclusion

The *conclusion* should bring your composition to a definite close. One way of concluding a composition is to sum up some of the points you made earlier in the composition. For example, notice that the last sentence of the sample composition on page 160 restates the main idea of the first paragraph. In a short composition, the conclusion can be only one or two sentences long.

When You Write. When you write your conclusion

- bring your composition to a definite close.
- leave your audience with something to think about.

EXERCISE 29. Writing the Conclusion. Think about the preceding *When You Write* as you write the conclusion for your expository composition. Answers will vary.

EXERCISE 28. You might want to provide class time for students to work on the body of their compositions. Encourage students to use their informal plans or topic outlines as guides, but also remind them that they may add information and details now. Ask them to check for smooth transition from one idea to the next.

EXERCISE 29. Remind students that a conclusion brings the composition to a definite close. Some conclusions restate the main idea of the composition, and others summarize previously made points. An effective conclusion need not be long, but it must be conclusive.

Studying a Sample Composition

The sample composition that follows was developed from the topic outline on page 152. The notes in the margin show how the outline and the composition are related. Notice how the introduction arouses interest and suggests the purpose of the composition. Each paragraph in the body then explains the main headings in the outline. Finally, notice that the conclusion brings the composition to a definite end.

BEGINNING A STAMP COLLECTION

introduction (reasons for collecting stamps—I, A-B in outline)

Have you ever wondered why people collect stamps? Stamp collecting is a popular hobby for several reasons. Collectors gain pleasure from the varied colors and designs of the stamps, while enjoying the fun of watching their collections grow. In addition, stamp collecting has educational value. *(transition)* Stamps often tell the collector a great deal about the customs, events, and famous citizens of a country. Furthermore, collectors soon learn to find out the exact location of a country and often become interested enough to find out other important facts about that country. *(transition)* Now that you know how interesting stamp collecting can be, you may want to begin a collection of your own.

body (acquiring stamps—II, A in outline)

Beginning collectors can start with family mail. A variety of stamps can be collected from the letters and packages the average family receives. If a relative or family friend happens to be living overseas, another valuable source is available.

(II, B-C in outline; transition)

In addition, the collector can buy domestic stamps at the post office. Some large post offices have special windows for new stamps, and all local post offices sell the new stamps when they are first issued. Foreign stamps can be bought in hobby stores or ordered from stamp dealers.

In fact, stamp dealers who advertise in magazines (often in magazines popular with young people) are an important source of stamps for all collectors. Most dealers offer beginners a packet of assorted stamps at a low price. After collectors have acquired many common stamps, they may be interested in dealers' approval sheets. Stamps on an approval sheet are usually less common than those in the packets; each is mounted and priced separately. Collectors keep any stamp they want and send their money and the remaining stamps back to the dealer.

(II, D in outline; transition)

Most collectors display their stamps in albums. Albums for beginners usually have pictures of some of the stamps and sections for the different countries. Besides an album, a collector needs stamp tongs—a sort of tweezers—and hinges—small bits of gummed paper that attach the stamp to the album page.

(displaying stamps—III, A in outline)

Stamps taken from the family mail, as well as some stamps included in the packets that come from dealers, have to be removed from the envelope to which they are still sticking. To remove a stamp, the collector first places it face down on a blotter and moistens the envelope paper with warm water. After the paper is thoroughly soaked, the stamp can

(III, B in outline)

transition

transition

EXERCISE 30. This exercise analyzes the sample composition provided in the text. You might want to do this exercise as an oral activity before you have students write Exercises 26, 28, and 29. If not, you might consider allowing students class time to apply the questions in this exercise to their own compositions, giving them time to write a second draft if necessary.

Answers: Exercise 30

1. A possible audience might be young people interested in beginning stamp collections. Students' explanations of their responses will vary.
2. Answers will vary.
3. The third paragraph could become part of the second paragraph and the topic would still be explained clearly.
4. The first sentence of each paragraph is a topic sentence, with subsequent sentences in each paragraph providing supporting details. The outline and the actual composition are similar in their main topics and supporting details.
5. Answers will vary.

REVIEW EXERCISE. This exercise provides an opportunity for students to write another expository composition. If you decide to assign this to some students, remind them to refer to the Guidelines for Writing Expository Compositions.

usually be removed easily. By working slowly and carefully with the tongs, the collector can avoid tearing or otherwise damaging the stamp. To mount the stamp in an album, the collector allows it to dry, then folds a hinge with the gummed side out, moistens it, and attaches the stamp to the page. *transition*

After beginners have had a taste of the pleasure of collecting, they are likely to want to specialize. For example, they may wish to concentrate on stamps of a particular country, or on those that have ships or certain animals on them. Whether they specialize or not, however, they are certain to gain much enjoyment and knowledge from their hobby. **conclusion** (specializing—IV in outline) *restates first sentence*

EXERCISE 30. Studying an Expository Composition. Answer each of the following questions about the sample composition on pages 158–60. Be prepared to explain your answers.

1. Who is the audience? Why do you think so?
2. If you were writing this composition, what information would you add? What information would you omit? Why?
3. How could the writer of this composition form paragraphs differently and still explain the topic clearly?
4. Select any one paragraph in the composition. Write down its topic sentence, and then list all the ideas and details that support this topic sentence. Also, compare these ideas and details to those listed in the outline. How are the composition and outline similar or different?
5. Do you think the writer successfully explained how to begin a stamp collection? Why or why not?

REVIEW EXERCISE. Writing an Expository Composition. Following the Guidelines for Writing Expository Compositions at the end of this chapter (pages 168–69) and the steps in the writing process, write a composition on a topic of your own.

EVALUATING

EVALUATING YOUR DRAFT

5k. Evaluate the draft of your composition for content, organization, and style.

When you evaluate something, you judge whether it measures up to certain standards. The standards you use to evaluate your draft are a measure of its content, its organization, and its style.

Content is what you say about your topic—the ideas and details you use to develop the major ideas about your topic. *Organization* is the arrangement of those ideas and details. *Style* concerns the words you use and the kinds of sentences you write; for example, short and simple or long and complicated.

The following Guidelines for Evaluating Expository Compositions provide standards for judging the content, organization, and style of your draft. These guidelines will help you identify the parts of your draft that should be changed to achieve the basic purpose of an expository composition: to explain something to a particular audience or to inform an audience about something. Read each guideline question and answer it honestly. When you answer no, you have identified something that needs to be changed. The labels at the left will help you focus not only on the part of your composition that should be changed but on the particular writing skill that should be improved.

GUIDELINES FOR EVALUATING EXPOSITORY COMPOSITIONS

Introduction	1. Does the introduction attract the attention of the audience?
Purpose	2. Does the introduction tell the audience what the composition will be about?
Development	3. Do the paragraphs in the body develop the main ideas and supporting details in the topic outline? Is there at least one paragraph for each main heading?

Section Overview

Evaluating is an important step in the writing process. Students should learn that their first drafts may be changed and refined many times and in many different ways.

EVALUATING YOUR DRAFT (rule 5k)

Evaluation may be a difficult concept for eighth-grade students. They may confuse evaluating with revising and proofreading, separate steps in the writing process. In evaluation, the emphasis is on judging content, organization, and style to produce a better, more understandable composition which fulfills the purpose for which it was written. This section of the chapter gives three strategies to make evaluating easier: (1) set the draft aside for a few days, (2) read the draft aloud, and (3) ask for comments from classmates. It also gives guidelines (pages 161–62) that students can use while going through the evaluation process.

This would be a good opportunity to bring out a collection of poorly written letters to the editor from your newspaper. You will probably want to cut off the writers' names. If you have the time and resources, you might want to duplicate several and distribute them to students for evaluation. Instruct students to refer to the guidelines on pages 161–62. This assignment would be a challenge to your advanced students, particularly if they do not agree with the viewpoint being expressed.

EXERCISES 31 and 32. Exercise 31 offers practice in evaluating. You may want to do this exercise as a class or small-group activity. After your students evaluate their own compositions in Exercise 32, you may have them exchange papers and evaluate another student's composition.

	4. Are enough details included to make the topic clear to the reader? Are there any details that should be omitted because they are not related to the topic?
Arrangement	5. Are the paragraphs in the body arranged in an order that will be clear to the reader and easy to follow?
Transitions	6. Do transitional words and phrases help the reader follow ideas from sentence to sentence and from paragraph to paragraph?
Conclusion	7. Does the conclusion bring the composition to a definite close?
Word Choice	8. Will the audience understand the language used in the composition? Are any unusual words defined or explained?

EXERCISE 31. Using the Guidelines for Evaluating Expository Compositions. Following is a draft of the third paragraph in the sample composition on pages 158–60. Read the draft and reread the guidelines. Then answer each question that follows the draft. Be prepared to give reasons for your answers. Not all the guidelines apply to the draft. See Answer Key.

> The collector can also get local stamps at the post office. Foreign stamps can be bought or ordered. Some really large post offices have places to buy new stamps, and all post offices have these stamps when they first come out. Some of the foreign stamps are unusual.

1. Is there a transition between this paragraph and the paragraph that precedes it?
2. Does the paragraph help develop one of the main headings in the topic outline on page 152?
3. Are enough details included to make the explanation clear to the reader? Should any details be omitted?
4. Are the details arranged in an order that is easy to follow?
5. Are the words and sentences appropriate for the topic?
6. Based on your answers to these questions, what specific changes do you think the writer should make in the draft?

EXERCISE 32. Evaluating Your Own Composition. Evaluate the draft you wrote for the Review Exercise on page 160 by

applying each of the Guidelines for Evaluating Expository Compositions. Mark places in your draft where you should make changes and keep the marked draft for use later in the chapter.
Answers will vary.

REVISING

REVISING YOUR DRAFT

51. Revise your draft, making any necessary changes to improve the content, organization, and style.

By evaluating your draft, you have identified those parts that should be changed. Using this information, you are now ready to revise your draft, making the changes that will improve it.

You can use four strategies to revise your draft:

1. You can cut—or omit—words, phrases, and sentences.
2. You can add ideas and details.
3. You can reorder—or rearrange—words, sentences, and paragraphs.
4. You can replace one thing with another.

The following chart shows how you can use these strategies to revise your expository composition.

REVISING EXPOSITORY COMPOSITIONS

PROBLEM	TECHNIQUE	REVISION
The introduction does not tell what the composition will be about.	Add	Include the statement of purpose or another sentence that suggests the purpose.

Section Overview

Students should learn that revising follows the evaluating stage in the writing process. At this point, they have evaluated their compositions, and now they are ready to use specific techniques to revise the problems they uncovered during evaluation.

PROBLEM	TECHNIQUE	REVISION
The introduction does not arouse interest.	Add	Begin with an appropriate question or with another means of attracting interest.
A paragraph discusses more than one main idea.	Cut/Add	Omit details that are not related to a single main idea. Make a new paragraph with these details, or add them to an existing paragraph on the same idea.
The order of ideas is not easy to follow.	Reorder	Find the sentence or paragraph where the flow of ideas is interrupted; then move it so that the order of ideas is clear to the reader.
It is difficult to follow ideas from sentence to sentence (or from paragraph to paragraph).	Add	Add transitional words or phrases to connect ideas (or paragraphs); for example, *besides, finally, on the other hand, thus.*
Some of the words are not appropriate to the topic (or the audience).	Add/Replace	Add definitions or explanations as needed. As appropriate, replace informal words with more formal vocabulary.
The composition does not come to a definite close.	Add	Add a summary of points made in the body of the composition, or restate the main idea indicated in the introduction.

Following is a revised draft of the paragraph you evaluated in Exercise 31. As you study the revisions, refer to the notes in the margin. They indicate the revision strategies used by the writer.

Revised paragraph	Revision
In addition, The collector can ~~also get local~~ buy domestic stamps at	add; replace
the post office. Foreign stamps can be	reorder
bought in hobby stores or ordered from stamp dealers. Some ~~really~~ large post	add; cut
offices have ~~places to buy~~ special windows for new stamps, and	replace
all local post offices ~~have these~~ sell the new stamps when they	add; replace
are first ~~come out~~ issued. ~~Some of the foreign stamps~~	add; replace; cut
~~are unusual.~~	cut

EXERCISE 33. Studying a Revised Paragraph. Answer each of the following questions by referring to the preceding paragraph.

1. In line 1 the writer added *In addition* to the first sentence in the paragraph. Why do you think the writer added this phrase?
2. In lines 1, 3, 4, and 5, the writer replaced certain words and phrases. Why do you think the writer made each of these changes in the paragraph? (In your answer consider clarity, accuracy, appropriateness.)
3. In lines 3 and 5 the writer added words and phrases. How do these additions help the reader?
4. In line 3 the writer omitted a word. In lines 6–7 the writer omitted a sentence. Why do you think these cuts were made?
5. The writer moved a sentence in line 2 to the end of the paragraph. Why do you think this change was made?
6. Does the revision correct the problems you identified in Exercise 31? Do you think the revision is better than the first draft? Why or why not?

EXERCISE 34. Revising Your Own Composition. Using the revision chart on pages 163–64, decide what strategies to use when revising your own composition. Then make the necessary revisions. For help with correcting monotonous or rambling sentences, refer to Chapter 9. Answers will vary.

EXERCISES 33 and 34. You may decide to have your students work on Exercise 33 orally, either as a class or in small groups. Students should use the revision chart to revise their own compositions individually. Be available to offer help as it is requested.

Answers: Exercise 33
(Answers will vary somewhat in wording.)

1. Coming at the beginning of the sentence, it provides a better transition from the previous paragraph than does *also,* which was "hidden" in the sentence.
2. The more specific substitutions add clarity and are more appropriate to the topic. "New stamps" is more concise than "when they first come out."
3. The added material provides detail needed for clarity.
4. The word *really* was omitted because it is imprecise and colloquial. The sentence was omitted because it does not relate to the main idea in the paragraph. The last sentence was irrelevant.
5. The sentence was moved so that the two about the post office could remain together, before a new idea was introduced.
6. Yes. Answers will vary.

PROOFREADING

Section Overview

Students should learn that proofreading is a separate and important stage in the writing process. At this point, they have made major revisions and should now look for spelling, capitalization, usage, and mechanics errors. They need to realize that these errors can confuse and distract the reader from the purpose of the composition.

PROOFREADING YOUR EXPOSITORY COMPOSITION (rule 5m)

When presenting this section, emphasize that students should reread their compositions several times, looking for different types of errors on each reading. You may want to suggest the Guidelines for Proofreading (page 39) as a checklist for the reading.

EXERCISE 35. This exercise directs the students to proofread their revised compositions. If at all possible, try to provide class time so that students can use grammar books, dictionaries, the teacher, and classmates' comments to check on any questionable items in their compositions.

WRITING THE FINAL VERSION

Section Overview

The final version of students' expository compositions should be in correct manuscript form, neat, and free of errors.

PROOFREADING

PROOFREADING YOUR EXPOSITORY COMPOSITION

5m. Proofread your expository composition.

After you revise your draft, check your composition for any mistakes in spelling, grammar, usage, and mechanics. By correcting these mistakes, you will make it easier for your audience to understand the ideas you are trying to communicate about your topic.

To proofread effectively, read over your composition several times, concentrating on a different item each time. In one reading, check for correct spelling and proper capitalization; in another check for correct punctuation; in another check for correct verb form and tenses, and so on. By focusing on one item at a time, you will notice errors more easily.

While you are proofreading, refer to the Guidelines for Proofreading on page 39 and the Revising and Proofreading Symbols on pages 39–40.

EXERCISE 35. Proofreading Your Expository Composition. Proofread the composition you revised in Exercise 34. Then exchange compositions with a classmate to double-check one another's proofreading skills. Answers will vary.

WRITING THE FINAL VERSION

MAKING THE FINAL COPY

5n. Make the final copy of your expository composition.

You are now ready to make the final copy of your composition. This is the version that you will pass along for your audience to read. When you prepare this copy, use correct manuscript form (see Chapter 1) or follow any special instructions your teacher may give you.

After you make this final copy of your composition, proofread it again. It is easy to omit words or to make accidental errors as you recopy your draft. Proofreading one more time will help you catch these mistakes before your audience reads your composition.

EXERCISE 36. Preparing a Final Copy. Prepare a final copy of any expository composition you have written, evaluated, and revised in this chapter. Proofread your final copy for mistakes in spelling, grammar, usage, punctuation, and capitalization before your audience reads it. Answers will vary.

CHAPTER 5 WRITING REVIEW 1

Writing an Expository Composition. Following the steps of the writing process, write an expository composition on a topic of your choice. As you plan, write, and revise your composition, be sure to refer to the Guidelines for Writing Expository Compositions at the end of this Review. Also refer to the Guidelines for Evaluating Expository Compositions (pages 161–62), to the revision chart (pages 163–64), and to the Guidelines for Proofreading (page 39). If your teacher allows, you may also want to share your composition with your classmates after you have revised and proofread. Answers will vary.

CHAPTER 5 WRITING REVIEW 2

Studying Your Expository Writing. What you have learned about writing exposition in this chapter applies to the expository writing you do in all your school subjects. Select and read over an expository paragraph or composition you have written for one of

MAKING THE FINAL COPY (rule 5n)

As you present this section, emphasize that the final copy must be in correct form. You may want to allow students some time in class to proofread again for any errors they may have made in recopying. Exchanging papers for one final reading may reveal minor errors.

EXERCISE 36. Encourage students to prepare a neat, error-free composition for their final copy. You might want to allow them to use correction fluid for minor errors. Consider compiling their work in a class or grade anthology.

CHAPTER 5 WRITING REVIEW 1

If you assign this exercise in writing another expository composition, remind students to use all the writing stages and to refer often to the guidelines for writing, evaluating, and proofreading expository compositions.

CHAPTER 5 WRITING REVIEW 2

In this review, students apply what they have learned in this chapter to a composition they have written for another class. This is an excellent way to have them transfer their knowledge directly to practical use in other course work. You may need to coordinate this review with teachers in other departments so that students will have such a composition available for analysis.

your other classes, such as a paper for a science or social studies class. Then answer the following questions: Answers will vary.

1. Who is your audience for this paper?
2. What did you do to adjust to your audience's needs when you wrote this paper?
3. Did you follow the steps in the writing process when you wrote this paper? Why or why not?
4. What part of the writing process would you use differently to improve your paper? Why?
5. How do you think knowing about the writing process can help you improve your writing in your other classes?

GUIDELINES FOR WRITING EXPOSITORY COMPOSITIONS

Prewriting

1. Select a topic you are interested in and understand well enough to explain to someone else.
2. Limit your topic so that you can discuss it clearly and thoroughly in a few paragraphs.
3. Ask yourself what someone unfamiliar with your topic might want or need to know about your topic. Then gather information for your composition with your audience in mind.
4. Determine whether you have used any technical or unusual words which need to be defined.
5. Group and arrange ideas and details so that your topic will make sense to your audience. Use this arrangement to help you prepare a topic outline for your composition.

Writing

6. Write an introduction that includes a statement indicating the general purpose and topic of your composition.
7. Use your topic outline as a guide when you draft the body of your composition. Be sure to connect your ideas by using transitional words and phrases.
8. Write a conclusion that brings your composition to a definite close.

Evaluating and Revising

9. After you write a draft of your composition, evaluate it for content, organization, and style. Make certain that you have included enough information to explain the topic to your audience. Ask yourself if you have presented ideas

and details in an order that will be clear to your audience. Check that the words and sentences you have used fit your audience. Then revise your draft, making necessary changes.

Proofreading and Preparing a Final Copy

10. Proofread your composition for mistakes in spelling, grammar, usage, punctuation, and capitalization *before* and *after* you prepare a final copy for your intended audience.

Additional Practice

Teacher's Resource Book, Worksheet pages 53–56, Alternative Worksheet pages (for less-advanced students) 522–23

Testing

Teaching Tests booklet, pages 1–4, 13–18
Teacher's Resource Book, Test pages 371–74, 397–98, 407–412

Chapter Overview

This chapter covers writing other forms of exposition—summaries, longer reports, and book reports. In each case, students will be reading, synthesizing material, and reporting on their subjects.

This chapter also guides students through the steps of the writing process for each of the forms of exposition.

Chapter Objective

Students will use the writing process to develop summaries, research reports, and book reports.

PRESENTING THE CHAPTER

LESS-ADVANCED STUDENTS You may feel that your less-advanced students are not quite ready to study all sections of this chapter. Book reports may be presented to these students, and oral reports are especially effective.

If you require your less-advanced students to write longer reports, you may want to have them choose topics directly related to their own experience. The papers can be short (about 250 words) and can be based on only two or three sources. Encyclopedias will probably be more useful than specialized reference books for reports of this kind. Students can also write for information to organizations such as chambers of commerce (see The Request Letter, text pages 218–19). *(See listing of Alternative Worksheets on page 200.)*

ADVANCED STUDENTS When advanced students have completed their prewriting, they may need to concentrate on writing interesting titles and introductions. You may

CHAPTER 6

Writing Exposition

SUMMARIES AND REPORTS

All through school, you will be asked to find information and to report on it in your own words. This is one of the most useful skills that you will study this year—not just in English class, but in your other courses as well.

WRITING SUMMARIES

The simplest kind of report is the *summary,* an account in your own words of a longer piece of writing. As with other forms of writing, preparing a summary involves using the writing process.

PREWRITING

CONSIDERING PURPOSE AND AUDIENCE

6a. Consider the purpose and the audience for a summary.

The *purpose* of a summary is to provide a short account of a longer piece of writing while retaining its essential meaning. To accomplish this purpose, include the main ideas of the original article. Leave out unimportant details, examples, and so on.

Your audience will affect the way in which you write the summary. If your summary is for a younger audience than the original audience, you may have to use shorter sentences and less difficult vocabulary. For some audiences, you may also need to define terms and to give some background information. For example, if you are summarizing an article on dangerous insects for students in your science class, you can assume they know what an insect is. For a class of second-graders, you might need to explain that an insect is "a small animal with three pairs of legs, such as a fly or mosquito."

EXERCISE 1. Deciding on Main Ideas. Read the following article carefully to decide which main ideas should be included in a summary. Then answer the question that follows the paragraphs.

> To get the full picture of what a swarm of army ants looks like, imagine a tide of them up to 33 yards (30 m) wide moving through the jungle at speeds up to 38 yards (35 m) an hour. A swarm this big makes a crackling and hissing sound in the jungle somewhat like rain coming through the trees.
>
> The eerieness of a swarm of army ants is increased by the fact that, en masse, they have—just as their name suggests—a distinctly military appearance. In fact, many species of army ants travel in a classic pincher formation that is shaped something like a *V*. This pincher formation allows an army—of people or ants—to encircle an enemy and fall upon it suddenly from all sides.
>
> A feature of army ants that makes them so dangerous is their constant hunger for fresh, live food. Unlike ordinary ants, which usually scurry about looking for bits of dead food, grains of sugar, fresh leaves, and so forth, army ants kill what they eat. Their diet includes anything that comes in their path—grasshoppers, baby birds in a low-hanging nest, lizards, snakes, and rats. There have even been reports of army ants attacking penned livestock and, within minutes, tearing whole cows to pieces.
>
> DONALD CAUSEY

want to have them write book reports at regular intervals throughout the year. Their book reports could be included in a class or grade anthology used to encourage other students to read the same books.

WRITING SUMMARIES

Summarizing information is an essential step not only in preparing research papers but also in mastering knowledge of any kind. The purpose of teaching the formal written summary in the eighth grade is chiefly to accustom students to (1) picking out essential facts and (2) giving these facts *in their own words.*

PREWRITING

Section Overview

Knowing how to distinguish the main ideas of an article or book and then determine the purpose and audience for which a summary is written will help students in the prewriting stage of the writing process.

CONSIDERING PURPOSE AND AUDIENCE (rule 6a)

This section defines a summary as "a short account of a longer piece of writing." It cautions students to omit details not necessary to express the main idea. Students must consider the appropriateness of kinds of sentences and vocabulary words used for their audience.

EXERCISE 1. This exercise gives students practice in reading an article and determining the main ideas. You may want to use this as a class or small-group activity to introduce the chapter.

GATHERING INFORMATION (rule 6b)

This section directs students to read the chosen article once for general understanding and again for taking notes on the main ideas. As an example, this section includes an article and notes on main ideas from the article.

Each of the following notes is from the article on army ants. Which of them should be included in a summary?

Notes:

1. Army ants can travel up to 35 meters an hour.
2. The swarm sounds like rain coming through the jungle.
3. Many army ants travel, like a military formation, in a V.
4. One reason army ants are so dangerous is that they are always searching for fresh, live food.
5. Examples of the kinds of food regular ants eat are grains of sugar and fresh leaves.

GATHERING INFORMATION

6b. Gather information for the summary by taking notes.

To write a summary, first read through the article carefully, looking for main ideas. During this first reading, do not take notes. Instead, concentrate on understanding what you read. Then read over the article again, this time jotting down the main ideas. In taking notes, be certain that you use your own words.

EXAMPLE

Original:

Halley's comet, *HAL eez,* is a brilliant comet named for the English astronomer Edmund Halley. Before Halley made his investigations, most people believed that comets appeared by chance and traveled through space in no set path. But Halley believed that comets belonged to the solar system and took definite paths around the sun at regular intervals. He found that the paths taken by certain comets in 1531 and 1607 were identical with the path of a comet observed in 1682. He decided that the same comet made all these paths. He predicted that it would reappear in 1758 and at fairly regular intervals thereafter. The comet was seen in 1758 and made its closest approach to the sun in 1759. It appears an average of every 77 years and was seen as long ago as 240 B.C.

JOSEPH ASHBROOK

Notes:

1. Comet named for English astronomer Edmund Halley
2. Before Halley's study, comets thought to appear by chance
3. Halley believed comets followed paths, appeared regularly
4. Proved comet named after him reappears every 77 years

Notice how the writer of these notes concentrates on what Halley learned about comets. The notes do not include details such as exact years.

Before You Write. To gather information for a summary:

- Think about these questions:
  1. What general topic is the article about? (*Hint:* Look carefully at the first and last paragraphs, which often introduce and sum up the general topic.)
  2. What are the most important ideas about this topic? (*Hint:* Subtitles or headings within the article often identify main ideas.)
  3. What supporting details (specific dates, examples, or descriptions) can be left out without changing the essential meaning?
- Use a dictionary to look up unfamiliar words or phrases.
- As you take notes, remember to:
  1. Follow the pattern of organization used in the article.
  2. Put ideas into your own words, or paraphrase.
  3. Copy the writer's exact words, if you use a direct quotation. Enclose the writer's words in quotation marks, and give the page number on which the quotation appears.

EXERCISE 2. Taking Notes. The following paragraphs are from an article about people who worked to improve the lives of others. First, read the article carefully, looking for main ideas. Then read the article again, making notes on the main ideas.

Answers will vary.

HELPING THE DISADVANTAGED

Many people were unwilling to live in isolated communities and abandon all the customs and patterns of ordinary life.

EXERCISE 2. This exercise instructs students first to read the article and then to reread it while taking notes on main ideas. Go over Before You Write orally before you assign this exercise.

Section Overview

Students should learn that a summary is one third or less the length of the original article, must be in the students' own words, and should follow the organization of the original article.

WRITING THE FIRST DRAFT (rule 6c)

This section gives an estimate of the length of a summary and directs students to use the organization of ideas of the original article. It also gives an example of an article and a summary of that article.

They were nonetheless sincerely interested in improving society. Some devoted their energies to helping people in need. Samuel Gridley Howe, a Boston doctor, specialized in the education of the blind. In the 1830s he founded a school, the **Perkins Institution.** He developed a method for printing books with raised type so that blind people could learn to "read" with their fingertips. Howe's greatest achievement was teaching Laura Bridgman, a child who was both blind and deaf, to read in this way and to communicate with others through signs called a manual alphabet. Another of his pupils, Anne Sullivan, learned the manual alphabet to communicate with Laura. She later became the teacher of Helen Keller, a remarkable woman who lost her sight and hearing as an infant.

Another Massachusetts reformer, Dorothea Dix, practically revolutionized the treatment of the mentally ill. Dix was a schoolteacher. One day in 1841 she was asked to teach a Sunday school class in a jail in Cambridge, Massachusetts. When she went to the jail, she discovered to her horror that insane and feeble-minded people were being kept there and treated like ordinary criminals.

Thereafter, Dix devoted her life to improving the care of the insane. She visited prisons all over the country and wrote reports describing conditions and exposing their faults. Dix insisted that insanity should be treated as a disease and that it could be cured. Through her efforts many states set up asylums for the care of the mentally ill.

JOHN A. GARRATY

WRITING

WRITING THE FIRST DRAFT

6c. Write the first draft of a summary.

Rely primarily on your notes to write the first draft of your summary. The summary must be in your own words, and should follow the organization of ideas in the original.

EXAMPLE

Original: AMERICAN ECONOMIC SUCCESS

The United States is one of the richest nations in the world. Most Americans enjoy a high standard of living. A nation's **standard of living** is the well-being of its population based on the amount of goods and services they can afford. On the average, we have more money to spend, and more goods to buy, than the people of most other nations. Our economic system produces more goods and services than any other in the world.

What makes all this possible? There are a number of reasons for our economic success. First of all, the United States is a land of great natural resources. We have timber, minerals, energy resources, a good climate, and fertile soil in abundance. In addition, we always have had energetic and inventive people. They have taken our resources and turned them into needed and desirable products.

Furthermore, our system of government has ensured the right of private enterprise—that is, the owning and operating of businesses by individuals rather than by the government. It has protected the right of individuals to own property and make a profit. Finally, the United States has developed an economic system in which most of its people can find work and earn financial success.

WILLIAM H. HARTLEY *and* WILLIAM S. VINCENT

Summary:

The United States is one of the wealthiest nations on earth. Americans, who provide more goods and services than any other people, have a high standard of living. They can afford to buy many goods and services. America is economically successful because it is rich both in natural resources and in industrious people. Our system of government, which ensures the individual's right to own businesses and to make a profit, also contributes to our economic success.

EXERCISE 3. This exercise gives students practice in writing a summary. After looking over their work, you might want to have students read their summaries to the class to provide examples of different but acceptable summaries.

EVALUATING AND REVISING

Section Overview

Students should evaluate and revise their draft, checking for main ideas, appropriate sentence length and vocabulary, and length of the summary.

EVALUATING AND REVISING THE SUMMARY (rule 6d)

Students should wait a few days after writing their summary before they evaluate and revise it. They should use the guidelines (pages 176–77) to check their work. Then they should use the chart Revising Summaries on page 177 to correct any problems they uncovered while evaluating.

When You Write. To write your summary

- State the main ideas clearly and briefly.
- Present ideas in the same order used in the original article.
- Keep your summary to one fourth or one third the length of the original article.
- Include all important ideas, but do not add ideas that are not in the article.

EXERCISE 3. Writing a First Draft of a Summary. Using your notes from Exercise 2, write a first draft of a summary. Your teacher may ask you to turn in your notes with the first draft of your summary. Answers will vary.

EVALUATING AND REVISING

EVALUATING AND REVISING THE SUMMARY

6d. Evaluate and revise the first draft of your summary.

Like any other first draft, the first draft of your summary can probably be improved. When you examine a first draft to locate its strong points and weak points, you are evaluating your work. If possible, put your first draft aside for several hours or a day before you evaluate it. Then reread your first draft and answer each of the questions in the Guidelines for Evaluating a Summary.

GUIDELINES FOR EVALUATING A SUMMARY

Main Ideas	1. Are only the main ideas of the original article included in the summary?
Audience	2. Is the summary suitable for the audience?

Paraphrasing	3. Is the summary written in the writer's own words?
Order	4. Does the organization of ideas in the summary follow that of the original?
Length	5. Is the summary one third or less the length of the original?

After you have evaluated your summary, revise it by using the four revising techniques: adding, cutting, reordering, and replacing. The chart below suggests how you can use these techniques to improve your draft. Keep the original article until you have completed your revision, as you may need to check details.

REVISING SUMMARIES

PROBLEM	TECHNIQUE	REVISION
The wrong details are included.	Cut/Add	Cut unimportant details that are not main ideas. Add important ideas.
The summary doesn't seem right for the audience.	Replace	Replace words and sentences to make them more suitable for the audience.
The summary is not written in your own words.	Replace/Add	Replace the author's words with your own. Add quotation marks to show where the author's exact words are used.
The order of ideas isn't the same as the original article.	Reorder	Reorder sentences or ideas until the organization follows the original.
The summary is too long.	Cut/Replace	Cut unimportant details in the summary. Replace long discussions with shorter ones.

EXERCISE 4. This exercise directs students to evaluate, revise, and proofread their summary. You may want students to exchange papers to check for omissions, wordiness, and errors. If at all possible, allow class time for the final revision so that students can consult with you on the appropriateness of their classmates' evaluations.

REVIEW EXERCISE. Depending on your students' needs and abilities, you may want to provide this additional opportunity to write, evaluate, and revise a summary. It might be enjoyable to read some especially interesting summaries to the class.

EXERCISE 4. Evaluating and Revising a Summary. Using your work from Exercise 3, evaluate and revise the first draft of your summary. Then recopy the summary. Before handing in your final draft, proofread it for errors. (See the Guidelines for Proofreading on page 39.) Answers will vary.

REVIEW EXERCISE. Writing a Summary. Using what you have learned in this chapter, prepare a summary of one of the selections listed below. Follow these steps: Answers will vary.

(a) Read the article, looking for main ideas.
(b) Read the article again, taking notes on the main ideas.
(c) Use your notes to write a first draft.
(d) Evaluate your first draft using the guidelines on pages 176–77.
(e) Revise, using the chart on page 177 to make necessary changes.
(f) Proofread the draft for errors.
(g) Make a final copy, proofreading again to catch any mistakes.

1. An article in a magazine or newspaper
2. An encyclopedia article
3. A magazine profile of a historical figure or a famous person
4. An editorial from your school or local newspaper
5. Part of a chapter in your science or social studies book

WRITING LONGER REPORTS

A more challenging kind of report, which you will often be asked to write, requires that you gather and organize information from a number of sources. To write this kind of report, you follow these basic steps:

1. Develop a limited topic
2. Gather information
3. Organize the information
4. Write a first draft
5. Evaluate and revise the report

PREWRITING

DEVELOPING A LIMITED TOPIC

6e. Develop a limited topic, keeping in mind your purpose, audience, and library sources.

Sometimes your teacher will assign a report topic; at other times you may be asked to develop your own topic. If you begin with a broad subject, such as "animals," "astronomy," or "computers," you must limit it in the same way you would a composition topic (see pages 142–43). Your factual report will probably be a short one, perhaps only several paragraphs long. The topic should be one about which you can give detailed information in that amount of space.

Before You Write. Use your library as a source for subject ideas.

- To gather subject ideas, skim articles in current magazines and newspapers, thumb through the subject cards in the library card catalog, or look at articles and pamphlets in the library's vertical file.
- Before you make a final decision about a subject, check your library to learn what sources are available. You will probably need at least four books, articles from magazines and newspapers, or pamphlets for your report. If your subject is very new or very technical, you may not find the information you need.

The purpose of a factual report is to present factual information. Select a topic about which you can find information in sources such as books and encyclopedias, not a topic based on personal experience. For example, you may have had an exciting

Section Overview

Students should learn how to write an effective, well-organized report.

DEVELOPING A LIMITED TOPIC (rule 6e)

This section of the chapter discusses how to develop a limited topic based on purpose, audience, and library resources. You may need to review the section on limiting subjects on pages 17–20 in Chapter 1. If possible, try to provide class time for library research to help determine whether there is enough available resource material to support the chosen topic.

EXERCISES 5 and 6. Exercise 5, on choosing appropriate topics, could be accomplished as a class oral activity. For each inappropriate topic, ask how the topic can be changed to support an effective report. For Exercise 6 you may want to allow students to develop their own topics, subject to your approval.

experience participating in a bike-a-thon to support diabetes research. Your experience riding in the bike-a-thon is a personal one; you will not find information about it in your library. However, you could write a factual report about some aspect of diabetes—its causes, effects, and possible cures. You would be able to find the needed information in the library.

The topic you develop should also be interesting to your audience. Most audiences are interested in new or unusual topics or in fresh information on well-known topics. For example, most eighth-graders have learned something about when, where, and how dinosaurs lived, but they may not know why skeletons of dinosaurs that lived in swampy marshlands are found today in dry, desert climates.

Before You Write. To develop a limited topic for a factual report:

- See pages 142–43 for more information on ways to limit a subject.
- Think about your audience and their interests when you develop a limited topic: What do they already know about the subject? What aspect, or part, of the subject will be new to them?
- Keep in mind both the number of available sources and the length of your report. A short report on a subject with many sources means limiting your subject more than you would for a longer report or a report based on fewer sources.
- Remember that the main purpose of a report is to present information you have gathered. Avoid limited topics for which you would rely on your own experiences or opinions: "why we need more computers in our school," "what it was like to be hypnotized."

EXERCISE 5. Choosing Report Topics. Some of the following topics are suitable for a factual report; others are not.

Number your paper 1–10. Write *S* for topics that are suitable and *U* for ones that are unsuitable. (Unsuitable topics may be based on personal experience or they may be uninteresting to the audience. They may also be too broad for a short report or too technical for available sources.) Be prepared to explain your answers. Answers may vary depending upon available sources.

1. How computers are used to help paralyzed people walk 1. S
2. The role of women in the settlement of the West 2. U
3. The first walk on the moon 3. S
4. Unicorns and other mythical animals 4. U
5. How and why hypnotism works 5. S
6. Why the class-sponsored carwash was a failure 6. U
7. UFO's 7. U
8. The feeding habits of the male strap-toothed whale 8. U
9. What I learned about crazy diets 9. U
10. Magnetic resonance readings for medical diagnosis 10. U

EXERCISE 6. Developing a Limited Topic. Develop a limited topic for your factual report. You may use a topic already mentioned in this chapter or a topic of your own. Review the *Before You Write* suggestions on pages 179 and 180 as you develop your topic. Save your work. Answers will vary.

GATHERING INFORMATION

6f. Find sources of information about your topic.

The reference section of your library is the best place to begin gathering information. An encyclopedia or other general reference work will usually provide you with a good introduction to your topic. However, this introduction is usually only a general one. Depending on your subject, you may also find additional information in more specialized reference books (pages 618–23). For more detail, you must find books and magazine or newspaper articles about your topic.

GATHERING INFORMATION (rules 6f and 6g)

This section gives suggestions on finding reference material and explains how to make source cards for encyclopedias, books, and magazines or newspapers. You may want to coordinate an introduction to reference material with "Using the Library," Chapter 27 of the text, and with the school librarian. A day or two in the library discovering the card catalog, the *Readers' Guide,* encyclopedias, and so forth should be helpful for further research.

If the three types of source cards confuse your less-advanced students, you may want to have them use only one type of reference resource and, therefore, one type of source card.

Before You Write. To locate sources of information on your topic:

- Write down the titles of any sources listed at the end of encyclopedia articles about your topic. Look for these sources in your library.
- Look under all possible subject headings in the card catalog and the *Readers' Guide to Periodical Literature.* Sources with information on the lost colony of Roanoke, for example, might be found under "Roanoke," "United States History," or "North Carolina—History."
- Check the bibliography (an alphabetical list of sources the author used) of any useful book you find to identify other possible sources.
- Examine both the index (an alphabetical list of topics covered in that book) and the table of contents (a list of chapter titles) to find how much information that source has about your topic.

6g. Record information about the sources from which you gather information.

Your readers will want to know where you found the facts used in your report. They may want to read more about your topic or check that you reported facts accurately. When you take notes from a source, prepare a separate card, called a *source card,* that gives information about the source.

Use 3 x 5-inch note cards or slips of paper as source cards. The source cards you prepare for books, magazine articles, and encyclopedia entries will be slightly different. On the source card for each, record the following information.

An encyclopedia source card:

1. The name of the author of the article, if there is one
2. The name of the article (in quotation marks)
3. The name of the encyclopedia (underlined)
4. The year of the edition

EXAMPLE

①

"Lost Colony." World Book Encyclopedia. 1985 ed.

Notice the punctuation on the card. A period comes at the end of the article's title, before the quotation marks. A period also follows the name of the encyclopedia. Note that *edition* is abbreviated as *ed.*

A book source card:

1. The name of the author (last name first)
2. The title of the book (underlined)
3. The place of publication
4. The name of the publishing company and the year of publication

EXAMPLE

②

Kupperman, Karen Ordahl. Roanoke: The Abandoned Colony. Totowa: Rowman & Allanleld, 1984.

Place a comma between the author's first and last names. A period comes after both the author's name and the book's title. Notice the colon after the place of publication and the comma

EXERCISES 7 and 8. These exercises direct students to gather information and prepare source cards. If you have decided to use only one type of reference resource, you could instruct students to find at least three of that one type.

between the name of the publishing company and the year of publication.

A magazine or newspaper source card:

1. The name of the author, if there is one
2. The name of the article (in quotation marks)
3. The name of the magazine or newspaper (underlined)
4. The date of the magazine or newspaper
5. The page numbers of the article

EXAMPLE

(3)

"Lost Colony: A Mystery Now Solved?" U.S. News & World Report, 9 July 1984: 61.

If the article begins on one page and then continues later in the magazine, put a comma between page numbers. A hyphen between page numbers means that the article is on all pages between the numbers. Notice how the date is written: day, month, year, with a colon following the year. Also notice that neither the word *page* nor its abbreviation *p.* is used, and that a period follows the page number.

Note that each source card has a circled number in its upper right-hand corner. As you fill out each source card, assign a number in this way to each source. Later, when you begin taking notes, you can mark each note card with this number, instead of writing out the name of the source on each note card.

EXERCISE 7. Gathering Information. Using your school library, locate four sources of information about the limited topic you developed for Exercise 6. Find at least one encyclopedia article, one book, and one magazine or newspaper article about your topic. Answers will vary.

EXERCISE 8. Preparing Source Cards. Using 3 x 5-inch note cards or slips of paper, prepare a source card for each source you found for Exercise 7, in the correct format. Give each source card a number, beginning with 1. Answers will vary.

DEVELOPING A WORKING OUTLINE

6h. As you read about your topic, develop a working outline.

Suppose you are preparing a report on the "lost colony," a settlement on Roanoke Island off the coast of North Carolina. Established by English settlers in the sixteenth century, the colony simply disappeared.

In the library, you have found an encyclopedia article, two books, and a magazine article about your topic. After reading the encyclopedia article, you decide that you will deal with three main points or ideas in your report:

I. Departure of colonists from England
II. Arrival of colonists on Roanoke Island
III. Disappearance of colonists

These points, or topics, are the beginning of a working outline that can guide your research. You now know, for example, that you need to find information on each of these three topics. You may discover other topics as your research continues. If a new topic seems important to your report, add it to your rough outline. If you are gathering many notes on one topic, consider breaking that heading down into two or more subdivisions. (For more information on outlining, see pages 151–53.)

EXERCISE 9. Developing a Working Outline. First, read one of the sources from Exercise 7 that gives general information for your report. Then write down three topics that you think you will cover. Use your working outline to guide your research.
Answers will vary.

TAKING NOTES

6i. Take notes on your reading.

DEVELOPING A WORKING OUTLINE, TAKING NOTES, and **ORGANIZING THE REPORT** (rules 6h–6j)

These sections explain how to develop a working outline, take notes, organize those notes according to their headings, and make an outline based on notes. Remind students that they can take notes by paraphrasing, summarizing, or quoting exactly, but they must credit their sources. If students will be quoting, you might want to review the section on quotations, pages 555–60.

You will probably want to devote quite a bit of class time to teaching this section and checking students' notes, outlines, and use of their own words. Although this material might be difficult for some students, they will need to use it throughout their academic years.

EXERCISE 9. This exercise directs students to select three topics from their reading that they will cover in their report. If possible, you may want to check topics to make sure that they will produce a unified report.

Your reading will include encyclopedia articles, parts of books, and magazine articles. You cannot hope to remember all of the details of information that you collect. Consequently, you will need to take notes.

The best way to take notes is to write them on note cards or slips of paper, using a different card for each note. Early in your reading, you will find that information for your report falls into a number of general divisions or topics. Once you have three or four divisions, you can use them as headings for your note cards. When you find information that relates to one of these headings, write the heading at the top of the card and underline it. Then write your notes under the heading. Underneath the note, write the page number(s) on which you found the information.

EXAMPLE

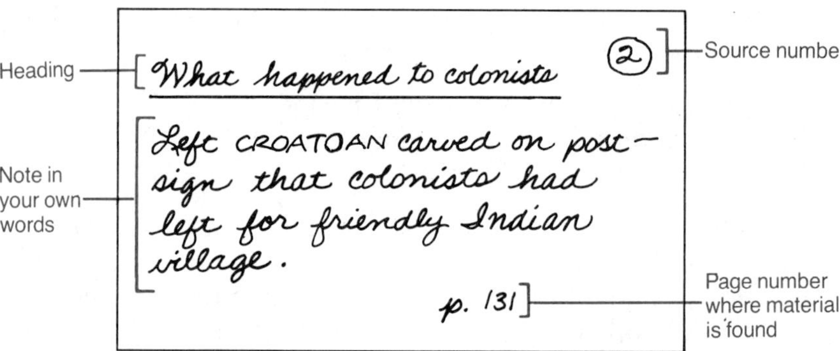

The number in the upper right-hand corner means this note is from source card 2 (*Roanoke: The Abandoned Colony*). Use separate note cards for each heading and for each source. For example, the note above is about what happened to the Roanoke colonists. You might also find information on that topic in an encyclopedia and a magazine article. You would then have three note cards with the same heading but different source numbers.

Before you begin taking notes, read over your source material, looking for main ideas. Then, as you read back over your material, jot down notes. There are three ways that you can take notes, illustrated in the following example.

1. You can *paraphrase,* putting material in your own words.
2. You can *summarize* by giving only the main ideas.
3. You can combine paraphrasing with direct quotation from the material.

Original:

If they did indeed go to Croatoan, the mist of history closes over them there. They may have stayed and intermarried with the Indians. Over a century later the explorer John Lawson, writing in 1709, said he saw the ruins of the fort on Roanoke and found some guns and coins there. And he said the surviving Indians of the Hatteras area claimed to have white ancestors.

DAN LACY

Paraphrase of information:

If colonists went to Croatoan, they were lost to history —may have intermarried with Indians there. One hundred years later, explorer named John Lawson saw ruins of fort on Roanoke, also guns and coins. Lawson said Hatteras Indians believed they had white ancestors.

Summary of information:

If colonists went to Croatoan, they were lost to history. Explorer later found evidence of colonists of Roanoke. Hatteras Indians believed they had white ancestors.

Paraphrase of information, with quotation:

If colonists went to Croatoan, "the mist of history closes over them there"—may have intermarried with Indians. One hundred years later, explorer named John Lawson saw ruins of fort of Roanoke, also guns and coins. Lawson said Hatteras Indians believed they had white ancestors.

EXERCISE 10. Taking Notes. Using your sources from Exercise 7, prepare at least ten note cards. On each note card, tell whether your note is a paraphrase, a summary, a quotation, or a combination of these. Answers will vary.

EXERCISE 10. This exercise directs students to prepare at least ten note cards, indicating the kind of notes taken. You may want to have students write some paraphrases, some summaries, and some quotations. Check their cards for each.

EXERCISE 11. This exercise instructs students to prepare a final outline based on their notes. If possible, check students' outlines for logical order of topics and to see that there are enough details to support a report.

ORGANIZING THE REPORT

6j. Organize your notes according to their headings, and make a final outline.

Now you must prepare to use the notes for your report. Eliminate notes that contain duplicate information or facts that do not fit your limited topic. Next sort the cards in piles according to their headings. Each pile will contain all the information on one main idea or topic. Review each pile to decide if you have enough notes to explain each heading, or if you should gather more. Also decide if a large number of notes should be divided into two headings.

After eliminating and sorting, you are ready to shape your final outline. Put your headings and subheadings in a logical order that will make sense to your audience. Then prepare a final outline, using correct outline form (see pages 151–53). Study this final outline for the report on the lost colony.

I. Departure of colonists from England
    A. Purpose of colonists
    B. Purpose of earlier explorers
II. Arrival of colonists on Roanoke Island
    A. Disappearance of earlier explorers
    B. Beginning of colony
        1. Need for food and supplies
        2. Return of leader to England
III. Disappearance of settlers
    A. John White's return to Roanoke
    B. Absence of settlers
        1. Missing houses and household goods
        2. Carved sign
    C. Ideas about disappearance
        1. Spanish ships
        2. Hostile Indians
        3. New life with friendly Indians

EXERCISE 11. Preparing an Outline. Using the note cards you made for Exercise 10, prepare an outline for your report.
Answers will vary.

WRITING

WRITING THE FIRST DRAFT

6k. Using your final outline and your notes, write the first draft of your report.

As you write the first draft of your report, consider the following suggestions.

1. Remember that a factual report is a kind of expository composition. As such, it has the same basic parts: *introduction, body, conclusion.* It should have an interesting, limited topic sufficiently developed with specific details. (See Chapter 5.)
2. Be certain that you understand all the terms you use. Look up difficult or unfamiliar words in the dictionary.
3. Use your own words in writing the report. Introduce quotations only when they are particularly apt or striking, and use them correctly.
4. Put every necessary detail into your report, and omit unnecessary items. Stick to your topic.
5. Using your outline as a guide, present information in a logical order, one that is easy for readers to follow.

6l. At the end of your report, list the sources for your material.

Study the list of sources at the end of the model report (page 193). Notice that sources are listed alphabetically by the last name of the author; when an author is not given, the source is listed alphabetically by the first word in the title ('"Lost Colony': A Mystery Now Solved?").

If you filled out your source cards correctly, making a list of your sources is easy. You can copy information directly from these source cards. However, before you begin, check each source card to be sure you have (a) included all the required

Section Overview

Writing a report based on resources involves many skills, including selecting a topic; finding information; taking notes; organizing information; writing; and using proper spelling, grammar, and mechanics. Students must use these skills in order to produce a unified, well-developed report.

WRITING THE FIRST DRAFT (rule 6k)

Have students follow the suggestions on page 189 while writing their drafts. When they have finished, ask them to check their papers with the list provided. You may want to have students exchange papers for peers' reaction to the first draft.

information for that source, (b) recorded information in the right order, and (c) used punctuation correctly.

CRITICAL THINKING:
Analyzing a Model

You use the critical thinking skill of *analysis* when you look closely at something to understand what its parts are and how they are put together. Carefully examining the parts and organization of a model report will help you write your own factual report. As you read the following model, notice how the writer introduces the topic and develops it further in each paragraph. Think about the writer's plan of organization, whether paragraphs are arranged in a logical order, and look for topic sentences in each paragraph.

ROANOKE: THE LOST COLONY

1 In May 1587 a group of 117 men, women, and children sailed from England, headed for the part of the New World they called Virginia. As the travelers said goodbye to their native land, they never expected to return home. Their purpose was to begin a new life across the ocean—to build houses and to plant crops. They were to be the first English settlers in that vast new land.

2 Although these settlers were the first English people who intended to make their homes in Virginia, they were not the first to reach the land. In both 1584 and 1585 groups of Englishmen had landed in the New World. These groups, however, had come for a much different reason. Their purpose was to find a base for English ships in the New World. From the base, English ships could easily attack the ships of England's great enemy, Spain, sailing in the nearby Caribbean. Both groups of explorers landed on Roanoke Island, off the coast of present-day North Carolina. To their disappointment, the early explorers found that the waters there were too shallow to be used as ports for their ships. All but fifteen of the men in these two groups returned to England.

3 On July 22 the ships carrying the third group of English people—the settlers—anchored off Roanoke Island. On the island, they found that the fifteen men left behind from the earlier group had disappeared. All that remained was the skeleton of one sailor lying across the path. The few huts that the men had built stood in ruins, overgrown with twisted vines. These new settlers would have to begin again.

4 The Roanoke colonists set to work to build new houses. By August 18, less than a month after they landed, they must have already felt a tie to their new home. On that day Virginia Dare became the first English child born in the New World. The colonists intended to plant crops and to learn to hunt and fish, but it would be a long time before they could take care of themselves. At the end of the year, they would need more supplies. John White, a leader of the expedition and the grandfather of Virginia Dare, agreed to return to England with a group of sailors. There he hoped to gather more supplies and to return to Roanoke Island before the year was out.

5 John White never saw his new granddaughter or the other settlers again. On his return to England, he found that England's enemy, Spain, was gathering a vast fleet of ships. With these ships, called the Armada, Spain intended to gain control of the seas and, in this way, to dominate England. To defend England, Queen Elizabeth ordered all ships to remain at home. It was not until three years later that John White was able to return to Roanoke with the promised supplies.

6 As White finally approached the shore of Roanoke, one day before his granddaughter's third birthday, he called out to the colonists through the dark night. There was no answer. The sailors landed and crossed the island looking for the colonists. In the sand were footprints that the sailors knew must have been made by Indians. The English colonists would have worn shoes. The colonists' houses had been torn down, the planks taken away. All of the colonists' clothes and household goods were gone also. Near the huts, carved in the bark of a tree, were the letters CRO. Nearby, on a post, the word CROATOAN had been carved.

7 Now, John White thought he knew where the colonists

might have gone. Before he had left three years earlier, he and the colonists agreed on some signs. If the colonists had to leave Roanoke for some reason, they were to carve the name of the place where they were going. Croatoan was a village of friendly Indians on an island fifty miles away. White thought that the colonists, probably near starvation after three years with no supplies, had gone there for help. White was comforted that there was no cross carved in the tree above CROATOAN. A cross was the colonists' signal that they were in danger.

8 The next day, White planned to sail from Roanoke to Croatoan to search for the colonists. Because of violent storms, however, the ships had no choice but to sail for England. John White never again returned to Roanoke.

9 What happened to the settlers on Roanoke Island remains a mystery. Some historians believe that Spanish ships may have landed and carried them away. Others believe that the settlers were captured and killed by hostile Indians. There is, however, another possible solution. In southeastern North Carolina, not far from the original Roanoke, live the descendants of a group of Indians called the Lumbees. Unlike most brown-eyed descendants of Native Americans, many of the present-day Lumbees have blue eyes. Many of them also have the English names of some of the English settlers, names like Bailey, Dale, and Cooper. Perhaps the colonists, in the three years of their isolation, began a new life with their Indian neighbors.

10 The next group of settlers to the New World came to Jamestown, Virginia. With them they brought records kept by John White about the experiences of the Roanoke colonists. Those records helped the new colony to succeed. That is why, even though Jamestown is recognized as the first English settlement in the New World, the Roanoke settlers will always be remembered for their important role in America's history.

Sources

Kupperman, Karen Ordahl. Roanoke: The Abandoned Colony. Totowa, NJ : Rowman & Allanheld, 1984.

Lacy, Dan. The Lost Colony. New York: Franklin Watts, 1972.
"'Lost Colony': A Mystery Now Solved?" U.S. News & World Report 9 July 1984: 61.
Smelser, Marshall. "Lost Colony." World Book Encyclopedia. 1985 ed.

EXERCISE 12. Analyzing a Model Report. Write your answers to the following questions about the model report.
See Answer Key.

1. What is the limited topic for this report? Is it a suitable topic for a short factual report?
2. How does the writer catch the audience's attention in the introductory first paragraph?
3. The conclusion does not simply repeat the ideas in the report. What does it do instead?
4. What is the topic sentence of paragraph 2? What details develop this main idea?
5. What is the topic sentence of paragraph 7? What details develop this main idea?
6. This report has unity because each paragraph develops the topic. What does paragraph 4 tell you about the topic?
7. What information does paragraph 9 give you about the topic?
8. This report has coherence because its ideas are arranged in a logical order. In paragraph 1, the English settlers leave England for the New World. What happens to the settlers in paragraph 3? In paragraph 6?
9. What transition word connects the last sentence in paragraph 1 with the first sentence in paragraph 2?
10. How does the writer connect the last sentence in paragraph 6 with the first sentence in paragraph 7?

EXERCISE 13. Writing a First Draft. Using your outline and your notes, write a first draft of your report. Answers will vary.

EVALUATING AND REVISING

EVALUATING AND REVISING YOUR REPORT

EXERCISES 12 and 13. Exercise 12 calls for an analysis of the model report included in the text. Students should consider many of these questions when writing their own reports in Exercise 13. Remind students to include additional information and details not included in their outlines if these would help produce an interesting, unified, well-written report.

EVALUATING AND REVISING

Section Overview

Evaluating is the stage for students to check not only content and organization but also style. They should look for smooth transitions from one idea to the next as well as for an interesting, informative report. In revising, the students should use specific strategies designed to improve the problems they uncovered in evaluating.

EVALUATING AND REVISING YOUR REPORT (rule 6m)

Review the Guidelines for Evaluating Factual Reports with your students. Remind them to use these guidelines when writing reports for other subjects.

EXERCISE 14. This exercise calls for the final draft of the report. Students may find it helpful for classmates to proofread their papers before handing them in to the teacher.

WRITING A BOOK REPORT

One important job of an English teacher is to *help students find books that they will really enjoy reading.* An inexperienced teacher can get ideas on this point by talking to the school librarian or to the young adults' librarian at the local library. Librarians know which books are currently popular with students of different ages and different interests, and they also know about many recent books that most adult readers (including many English teachers) may not yet have heard of.

It is always desirable to have a classroom library from which students can borrow books. You may be able to borrow books from the school library for this purpose, changing the selection every month or two. Or you may have a permanent library, to which students (and their parents) are occasionally asked to contribute books. The books should be chosen to appeal to a wide range of interests, and their degree of difficulty should also range considerably.

The second important job of the English teacher is to *encourage students to express their opinions*

6m. Evaluate and revise your report.

If possible, put your first draft aside for a few days. This time away from your writing will help you look at it more objectively. To evaluate your report, either alone or in a small group carefully examine your first draft. Decide how well it meets the guidelines for a factual report. As you reread your first draft, ask yourself each of the questions in the following Guidelines for Evaluating Factual Reports. Your answers to these questions will help you decide where you need to make changes in, or revise, your first draft.

You can revise your report by adding, cutting, replacing, or reordering. The chart on page 177 will help you decide which technique you should use to improve a particular part of your writing.

GUIDELINES FOR EVALUATING FACTUAL REPORTS

Topic	1. Does the report have a suitably limited topic? Is it suitable for the audience?
Introduction	2. Does the introduction catch the audience's attention?
Paragraph Development	3. Does each paragraph have a main idea expressed in a topic sentence? Is this main idea developed with details?
Conclusion	4. Does the conclusion signal that the report is ending, without repeating ideas in the body?
Unity	5. Are all details in the report related to the topic?
Coherence	6. Are details given in a logical order?
Topic Development	7. Does the report include enough factual information to develop the topic?
Source Material	8. Is the report written in the writer's own words? Is the material paraphrased or summarized as appropriate? Does quoted material use quotation marks for the writer's exact words?
Sources	9. Are sources listed at the end of the report?

EXERCISE 14. Evaluating and Revising Your Report. Use the guidelines on page 194 to evaluate the first draft of your report. Then revise it, referring to the chart on page 177. Proofread your paper, using the guidelines on page 39. Recopy

your report, and proofread it carefully before you hand it in. Your teacher might ask you to hand in your source and note cards, your outline, and your first draft, as well as your final draft. Answers will vary.

WRITING A BOOK REPORT

A book report gives two kinds of information: what the book is about and what you think of it.

PREWRITING

6n. Think about the purpose and audience for your book report. Think also about gathering specific information from your book.

Prewriting Hints for Writing a Book Report

1. *The purpose for writing a book report is to inform your audience about the book's content and about your opinion of the book.* In the first part of a book report, you usually tell what the book is about, identify the title and author, and explain whether the book is fiction or nonfiction. If you are reporting on a novel, indicate the background of the story—time, place, main characters, and conflict. For a nonfiction book, summarize the important information given. If you are reporting on a biography, indicate why the person written about is important, and mention chief incidents in that person's life.

In the second part of a book report, you usually explain your reaction to the book. This part of the report is important because it shows how carefully and thoughtfully you have read the book.

2. *Use specific details or examples from the book.* Whether you are telling about the book's content or your reaction to it, support what you say with specific details or examples from the book. You may want to quote words or sentences from the book. For example, notice the first paragraph of the sample book report (page 197). The writer says that the book is about eight people

of books honestly, backing up their opinions with reasons and facts. It is not necessary for students to say they like every book they read, even if the book appears on the approved reading list for the grade. In fact, reports panning books will probably be more thoughtful and interesting than ones in which the students hide their real feelings about them.

PREWRITING

Section Overview

Students will be required to write book reports throughout their school years. Knowing the prewriting steps for drafting a book report should make this assignment easier and more appealing.

PREWRITING HINTS FOR WRITING A BOOK REPORT (rule 6n)

This section explains three aspects of the book report to consider in the prewriting process: (1) informing the audience about the book's content and the student's opinion of the book; (2) using specific details from the book to describe the book or the student's opinion of the book; and (3) summarizing information about the book. Here students will use critical thinking skills, select details, and summarize—all very important and distinct skills.

EXERCISE 15. This exercise directs students to select a book (fiction or nonfiction), read it, and make notes about content and the student's opinion of it. Student are cautioned to include specific details. You may want to provide class time for students to select and read their books. You will probably want to give them a date on which class writing activities will begin so that they can adjust their out-of-class reading time accordingly.

WRITING

Section Overview

Writing a book report requires students to use several skills—reading, understanding, analyzing, summarizing, and, of course, writing. All of these are important skills for students to practice.

Writing a First Draft of a Book Report (rule 6o)

This section includes a sample book report and a list of questions students should be able to answer after reading the book report. As a related activity, you may want to have students bring in book reviews from newspapers and magazines for class or group discussion.

who have made important contributions to other people's lives. Then the writer mentions the specific contributions of two people. In the second paragraph of the report (page 198), the writer gives one reason for liking the book. In the rest of the paragraph, the writer gives details to support the reason.

In preparing a book report, use your note-taking skills (see pages 172–73). After you read the book, jot down notes about its content and your reaction. Look up details that you may have forgotten about the plot and the characters.

3. *Summarize information about the book.* Avoid getting bogged down in too many details. You cannot possibly give every detail of plot in a novel or every piece of information in a nonfiction book. Instead, concentrate on selecting important details about the plot and the main characters, or discuss the main ideas in a nonfiction book.

EXERCISE 15. Preparing a Book Report. Select a book for your report. Read the book and make notes about its content and your reaction to it. List specific details from the book. For a novel, jot down details about plot, setting, and main characters. For a nonfiction book, make notes about important information. For both types, note specific details to support your reaction to the book. Answers will vary.

WRITING

6o. Write a first draft of your book report.

In preparation for writing your own report, read the following sample report. As you read, ask yourself these questions:

1. What is the book about?
2. What specific details does the writer give about its content?
3. What is the writer's reaction to the book?
4. What specific details are included to support the writer's reaction?

A Report on *Shortchanged by History: America's Neglected Innovators,* by Vernon Pizer

1 *Shortchanged by History: America's Neglected Innovators,* by Vernon Pizer, is the story of eight Americans who have "fallen through the cracks of history." Each of these people has made an important contribution to the lives, health, and safety of millions of people, but each has been forgotten. Among these people is the man who designed and built the first flour mill. This same man also built, in the early 1800's, a steampowered vehicle that actually moved across roads under its own power and then left behind its land wheels to become a boat. Another one of these people discovered the process for separating red and white blood cells to make plasma. The plasma, which could be dried and safely stored, has saved the lives of countless burn and wound victims.

identifies title, author, and subject of the book

example helps reader understand content of book

second example

2 I like this book because each of the eight accounts reads like an exciting adventure story. James Eads, for example, worked on a Mississippi riverboat during the mid-1800's. Underneath the treacherous waters of the Mississippi, all up and down the river, were wrecks of riverboats. James Eads thought there should be a way to recover the cargo and the engines of the wrecks lying at the river's bottom. While in his early twenties, Eads invented a diving

writer's reaction and first reason for this opinion

specific example supports writer's opinion

bell that, carrying two men, could be lowered through the heavy currents. Through the open bottom of the diving bell, the men could attach lines to the submerged cargo. Air pumped from the salvage boat above kept water out of the bell. Before his first bell was ready, Eads was asked to recover a cargo of gold ingots. Unable to refuse the challenge, Eads fitted a huge wooden barrel with weights and descended through the raging current. Much to everyone's astonishment, the twenty-two-year-old Eads rescued the entire cargo.

3 Another reason I like *Shortchanged by History* is that each of the people described in the book had great moral courage. Sara Josephine Baker, for example, became a physician in 1898, a time when most people did not approve of women doctors. Because she wanted so much to help people, Dr. Baker became a health inspector for New York City. In her job, she was sent to the place with the worst living conditions in the city—a place called "Hell's Kitchen." Going by herself from tenement to tenement, Dr. Baker worked especially to improve the health of infants. When she began her work, as many as fifteen hundred babies were dying in New York City each week. Battling the constant prejudice against women doctors, she trained a team of nurses to go into the slums to teach health education. She established free clinics throughout the city for mothers and

second reason for writer's opinion

specific example supports writer's reaction

their babies. Before her work ended, she was responsible for reducing the death rate of infants in New York City by 50 percent.

4 In the world today, names like Alexander Graham Bell, Thomas Edison, and Wilbur Wright are remembered. The author of *Shortchanged by History* helps us recognize the important contributions of eight other Americans.

brief conclusion emphasizes book's value

EXERCISE 16. Writing the First Draft of a Book Report. Using your notes from Exercise 15, write the first draft of your book report. Answers will vary.

EVALUATING AND REVISING

6p. Evaluate and revise the first draft of your book report.

The following guidelines will help you evaluate the draft of your book report. Revise your report by referring to the chart on page 177. You should proofread your report, make a final copy, and then proofread again to catch any accidental errors (see the guidelines on page 39).

GUIDELINES FOR EVALUATING A BOOK REPORT

Title, Author	1. Are the book's title (underlined) and author mentioned early in the report? Is the title of the book underlined when it is mentioned?
Content and Reaction	2. Does the report give information about both the book's content and the writer's reaction to the book?
Development	3. Do specific details and examples support the writer's statements about the book? Do specific reasons explain the writer's reaction to the book?

EXERCISE 16. In this exercise, students write their book reports from the notes they made for Exercise 15. You may want to have them check the guidelines on pages 199–200 for inclusion of all necessary elements. Remind students to use transitional words and phrases to make their writing smooth. If possible, provide class time for writing the book reports so that you can check on students' progress.

EVALUATING AND REVISING

Section Overview

Students should learn to check for all elements of a good book report as they evaluate and revise their work.

Evaluating and Revising Your Book Report (rule 6p)

This section includes Guidelines for Evaluating a Book Report. You may want to go over each point on the list as students check their book reports. Remind students to use these guidelines whenever they write book reports.

EXERCISE 17. After students have revised their book reports, you might want to have them divide into small groups to read each other's work. This will not only help catch errors that writers missed but also expose classmates to the books being read by others and perhaps encourage them to read more. You might want to compile a list of books especially recommended by students and distribute it to all your classes.

CHAPTER 6 WRITING REVIEW

This review provides another opportunity for students to write a summary, report, and/or book report. Depending on your students' needs and abilities, you may not want to assign this to all students.

Additional Practice

Teacher's Resource Book, Worksheet page 57

Testing

Teaching Tests booklet, pages 1–4, 13–18
Teacher's Resource Book, Test pages 371–74, 399–400, 407–412

Novel	4. For a novel, are the setting and main characters discussed? Is enough of the plot revealed to give readers a general idea of the story?
Nonfiction	5. For a nonfiction book, does the report summarize important information?

EXERCISE 17. Evaluating and Revising a Book Report. Evaluate the first draft of your book report from Exercise 16. Revise to make changes that improve the first draft, using the chart on page 177. Using the guidelines on page 39, proofread your report. Then recopy your paper and proofread again.
Answers will vary.

CHAPTER 6 WRITING REVIEW

Applying Your Knowledge of Summaries, Reports, and Book Reports. Complete one or more of the following activities. Answers will vary.

1. Following the procedure you learned in this chapter, write a summary of the model report on the lost colony of Roanoke Island (pages 190–93). Remember that your summary should be no more than one third the length of the original report.
2. Develop another limited topic for a factual report. Using this new topic, follow the steps of the writing process to develop another report.
3. Choose a different type of book from the one you reported on in this chapter. For example, if you have already reported on a nonfiction book, choose a novel. Then follow the steps in the writing process to write a book report.

CHAPTER 7

Writing Letters and Completing Forms

SOCIAL LETTERS, BUSINESS LETTERS, AND FORMS

Letters from friends are enjoyable. It is interesting to learn about their experiences and thoughts, about general news of other friends. However, you will not receive many letters unless you write letters.

SOCIAL LETTERS AND NOTES

PREWRITING

DECIDING WHAT TO SAY

7a. In a friendly letter, write about the things that interest you and the person to whom you are writing.

Before you write, jot down your ideas. Include news that will interest your friend. Think of your friend's letter to you. Reply to

Chapter Overview

This chapter covers the two basic types of letters, the business letter and the social letter. It also includes a section on completing forms. In teaching the chapter, there are three points to emphasize: (1) mastering correct form for social letters and business letters; (2) learning that the content and tone of a letter should take into account the person to whom the letter is addressed; and (3) learning the importance of completing forms accurately and thoroughly.

Chapter Objective

Students will correctly write social and business letters and will accurately complete a form supplied by the teacher.

PRESENTING THE CHAPTER

LESS-ADVANCED STUDENTS You may want to teach only one type of social letter and one type of business letter to this group. Mastering one will make it easier to learn the others later. If you choose to teach the letter of request, you could assign students to send out letters for information on national parks or vacation resorts. Even if students can never go to any of these places, they might be able to use the information in a social studies class for a report. Making the purpose of these assignments more real to these students should probably hold their interest longer. Emphasize the section on completing forms correctly with these students.

ADVANCED STUDENTS Your advanced students may have mastered the social letter before eighth grade. A quick review is probably all that will be necessary. You may want to emphasize the business letter—in particular, the role of the business letter in helping students find information for reports in other classes.

SOCIAL LETTERS AND NOTES

PREWRITING

Section Overview

Students will learn that they should use the writing process in writing social letters. They should determine interesting subjects for their reader.

DECIDING WHAT TO SAY (rule 7a)

Remind students that their first step in the prewriting stage should be to determine purpose and audience. Remind students that they should not write about anything too personal to share with classmates and the teacher. If students are having difficulty with audience and purpose, you could write a letter to the entire class asking questions to which you expect answers. You could compose an entirely fictitious situation in which the students are now in the ninth grade and you have moved to another state. You could ask about school this year and what their plans are for spring break. You would, or course, want to mention your new teaching job and the area you live in. Your letter to them would serve as a model and also help to determine purpose and audience for their return letters.

questions or comments. As you write, keep in mind your audience—the receiver of your letter. You would not send the same kind of letter to a friend as you would send to a parent.

Study the following example of a friendly letter. Would you say that Bill is thinking of his friend Tom as he writes? Would this letter be different if it were written to Bill's grandmother?

1849 West Sixth Street
Los Angeles, California 90014
April 14, 1988

Dear Tom,

You asked what Carl and I have been up to lately. Well, Carl is taking care of a horse for friends of his parents, but he's afraid to ride it. I said I'd ride it. You know me—no brains.

That horse jumped suddenly high into the air and tried to throw me off. I stayed on, though, until it reared straight up and fell over backwards. Carl's dad ran over to me. He was mad, but all he said was that maybe we'd better put the horse back in the stable.

You asked what I'm doing for the Science Fair at school. Carl and I have taken photographs of cloud formations. We are mounting these photographs for an exhibit on weather forecasting.

How about letting me know what you're doing?

Sincerely,
Bill

A Friendly Letter

WRITING

WRITING A FRIENDLY LETTER

7b. Choose stationery and ink that are suitable for a friendly letter.

Use letter stationery. White is always appropriate, though other colors may be used.

Write in ink, never in pencil. (If you can type *well,* type your letters.) Avoid ink blots and erasures. Keep your writing neatly spaced and properly aligned; crowded lines that climb, stagger, or droop give a bad impression. Keep your margins wide and equal on the top and bottom as well as on the sides.

7c. Follow generally accepted rules for the form of a friendly letter.

The form of a friendly letter is easy to master. Study the following instructions and sample letter.

The Heading

The *heading* tells when and where the letter was written. It consists of three lines, placed at the upper right corner of the page. The writer's address is written on the first two lines, and the date of the letter is written on the third. A comma is used between city and state and between the day of the month and the year. The ZIP code number appears several spaces after the state and on the same line. There is no punctuation at the ends of the lines.

Two kinds of headings are appropriate in a friendly letter. The example on this page is in *block style.* All lines of the heading begin directly below the beginning of the first line. Another form

Section Overview

It is important for students to learn the form and purposes of social letters, as they will use this type of writing throughout their lives.

WRITING A FRIENDLY LETTER (rules 7b and 7c)

For most classes, studying the correct form for friendly letters will be a matter of review. To find out how much your students have retained from their previous training, ask them to give you directions as you put a "skeleton letter" on the board. (See the example of a skeleton letter on textbook page 204.) Have the class tell you what should come first in the letter. (The writer's address and the date; you can use your school's address and the current date.) Then have them tell you how to arrange these items on the page and how to punctuate them. Write the items on the board as the correct answers are given.

After the skeleton letter has been completed, have the students write similar skeletons of their own, using their own address and signature. Once you have checked the students' papers for correct form, they can keep their own skeleton outlines in their notebooks and refer to them in doing future letter-writing assignments. You can follow the same procedure in teaching the correct form for addressing envelopes.

often used for friendly letters is *indented style,* in which the heading looks like this:

2534 Polk Place
Portland, Oregon 97235
May 6, 1988

18 Prince Street
Houston, Texas 77008
April 14, 1988

Dear Bob,

Sincerely yours,
Jim

Form of a Friendly Letter

The Salutation

The *salutation* begins at the left-hand margin, is placed a short distance below the heading, and is followed by a comma.

The Body

The *body* of a friendly letter is the message, what you have to say. The first line of the first paragraph should be indented about an inch from the left margin. The first line of other paragraphs must be indented the same way.

The Closing

The *closing* for a friendly letter may be *Your friend, Sincerely, Sincerely yours,* or any similar phrase, except *Yours truly* and *Very truly yours,* which are used in business letters. The closing is placed below the last line of the letter, begins to the right of the middle of the page, and is followed by a comma. Only the first word of the closing is capitalized.

The Signature

The signature in a friendly letter is usually your first name. Center it under the closing and write it by hand, even if you have typed the entire letter.

EXERCISE 1. Writing a Friendly Letter. Write a letter to a friend your own age about the experiences you have had in the last few days. Remember to use the correct form. Answers will vary.

EXERCISE 2. Writing a Friendly Letter. Write a letter to a relative or an adult about the same experience you used in Exercise 1. Keep in mind the receiver, or audience, of your letter. Be prepared to discuss how your two letters differ.
Answers will vary.

Addressing the Envelope

The envelope of a letter should be addressed carefully, for the letter may not be delivered if the address is carelessly written. Always include the ZIP code number and a return address (so that the letter may be returned if your correspondent has moved).

EXERCISES 1 and 2. These exercises instruct students to plan and write two letters—one to a peer, another to a relative or an adult friend. These should help students to determine how various audiences affect their letters.

EXERCISES 3 and 4. Exercise 3 provides practice in addressing envelopes. Exercise 4 directs students to write a letter and address an envelope. If additional practice is needed, you may want to have students suggest situations and give addresses for the entire class to use as an exercise.

Susan Froelich
597 Spruce Street
Kansas City, Kansas 66143

Miss Astrid Addison
89 Kirkland Street
Cambridge
Massachusetts 02127

A Model Envelope

Study the example above and the following instructions.

1. Place the return address (your address) in the upper left corner of the envelope.
2. Place the address of the receiver just below the middle and to the left of the center of the envelope.
3. If the letter is going to an adult, write a title before the name: *Mr., Mrs., Ms., Dr.,* etc. Do not use a title in the return address.
4. Write the state on the same line as the city, with a comma after the city. Place the ZIP code number several spaces after the state.
5. If you use *Post Office Box, Rural Free Delivery,* or *Rural Route* in the address, you may use abbreviations: *P.O. Box, R.F.D.,* or *R.R.*

EXERCISE 3. Addressing Envelopes. Using your ruler, draw the outlines of two envelopes. Address each, using your own return address. See Answer Key.

1. Ms. Ellen Craig 111 Orchid Way
   Butte, Montana 59601
2. Dr. N. T. Bain P.O. Box 753
   Winamac, Indiana 46996

EXERCISE 4. Writing a Friendly Letter. Write a letter for one of the following situations, or for a situation of your own. Also address an envelope for your letter. Answers will vary.

1. You are visiting relatives in another city, and they have taken you to a World Series game. Write to your parents.
2. A next-door neighbor has moved away. Give her news about your neighborhood and ask questions about her new neighborhood.
3. You are a ham radio operator, and you have been exchanging messages with another ham radio hobbyist. Invite him or her to visit you. Tell him or her what to expect during the visit.

Folding the Letter

If your letter stationery is a folded page, fold it in half and insert it, fold first, into the envelope. If the stationery is a single sheet as wide as the envelope, fold it into thirds and insert it into the envelope, with the last fold first, as on page 216.

WRITING SOCIAL NOTES

7d. Write prompt, courteous social notes.

Social notes are written to extend or accept an invitation or to thank someone for a gift or favor. They follow the form of a friendly letter and are written on personal stationery, or if they are brief, on correspondence cards.

The Bread-and-Butter Note

Occasionally you visit friends or relatives who live out of town. After your visit, you should write a note to your host or your friend's parents to thank them for their kindness. This note, called a "bread-and-butter" note, should be written promptly. Tell your hosts how much you appreciated their efforts to make your visit pleasant. Mention some of the things they did for you. Your hosts may be interested, too, in your trip home, so you may also mention it briefly.

WRITING SOCIAL NOTES (rule 7d)

This section gives the purposes of the bread-and-butter note and the thank-you note and gives an example of each. These notes should be friendly, courteous, and prompt. When you introduce this section, you may want to ask students what they think the difference between a note and a letter is. You might also ask for definitions of *bread-and-butter.* Ask what occasions call for bread-and-butter notes and thank-you notes. A good time to teach these would be just before or just after winter or spring break when students may have visited friends or relatives and may have received gifts.

Study the sample bread-and-butter note. Notice that it follows the form of a friendly letter.

34 Casa Grande Drive
Berkeley, California 94713
August 6, 1988

Dear Mr. and Mrs. De Stefano,

Ever since I got home, I've been thinking about the wonderful week I spent with your family in Yosemite Park. The park had always been a sort of picture album place to me, and now I've got my own snapshots of it! But the outdoor scenery was only part of the pleasure of camping with your family. Waking up in the morning to the smell of frying bacon and eggs, hiking up the steep trails and coming back to cool off with a swim in the river, sitting around the campfire singing and telling stories – I'll remember these things for a long time. Thanks ever so much for having me as a guest.

Please tell Helen I'll send her some of my snapshots as soon as they are ready.

Sincerely yours,
Nora Davis

A Bread-and-Butter Note

The Thank-You Note

After receiving a gift or favor from someone you cannot thank in person, you should write a thank-you note. Always write promptly. A delay suggests that you do not appreciate the gift. A thank-you note will seem less like a duty if you also write about something else and give specific reasons for your gratitude. Notice how Tony thanks his uncle in the thank-you note below.

641 Ardmore Avenue
Philadelphia, Pennsylvania 19153
June 3, 1988

Dear Uncle Harry,

Thanks ever so much for the model plane engine. I'm having a lot of fun with it. The other boys tell me that a Junior Wasp model like this is very dependable. It starts easily and runs with no trouble. I've been running it on a breaking-in block. It's surprising how much roar such a tiny engine has! I'm eager to finish building my model. I know this engine will really make it zoom.

The folks gave me some fine birthday presents too, but I suspect that I'll remember this birthday most of all because of your wonderful gift.

Your nephew,
Tony

A Thank-You Note

EXERCISE 5. Writing a Bread-and-Butter Note. Write a bread-and-butter note for one of the following situations, or for a situation of your own. Answers will vary.

1. A friend's family has taken you on a camping trip.
2. You stayed for a week on your grandparents' farm.

EXERCISES 5 and 6. These exercises provide practice in writing social notes. Encourage students to choose a real or imaginary situation of their own. Look for courteous and short but friendly notes.

Section Overview

As with other forms of writing, students need to evaluate, revise, and proofread their social letters to check for content, style, form, and errors.

EVALUATING AND REVISING SOCIAL LETTERS (rule 7e)

This section includes five guidelines students can use to evaluate and revise their social letters. You may want to introduce these guidelines earlier in the chapter when students begin writing letters. If you want to wait, have students evaluate, revise, and proofread the collection of letters they have written from the social letter sections of this chapter.

BUSINESS LETTERS AND FORMS (pages 211–23)

Eighth-graders may rarely write business letters, but they will be interested to learn that there are a number of occasions on which they could write such letters. They may wish to obtain information from a company or a government agency; or, after reading a magazine article or viewing a television program, they may have definite questions about the subject of the article or program. Occasionally letters of opinion by twelve-year-olds appear in print. Suggest all these uses of the business letter to your class. Ask each student to think of a specific situation that might call for a business letter and to describe the situation on a slip of paper. The situation may require writing to a magazine or book publisher, an author, a company advertising a

3. An uncle has taken you on a trip to New York City, where you visited the Empire State Building and the Statue of Liberty.

EXERCISE 6. Writing a Thank-You Note. Write a thank-you note and address an envelope for one of the following situations, or for a situation of your own. Answers will vary.

1. An aunt, who owns her own company, has sent you a share of her company's stock for graduation.
2. Your grandfather, who lives in another town, has sent you ten dollars for your birthday.
3. An older cousin lives in Europe. He knows you have been collecting stamps since you were seven. He has sent you proof sets of stamps from various countries.

EVALUATING AND REVISING

EVALUATING AND REVISING SOCIAL LETTERS

7e. Evaluate your social letter; then revise it by making necessary changes.

To evaluate, read your letter several times to locate strengths and weaknesses in its content, organization, appearance, and form. Locate any items which need more explanation and any unnecessary points. You may want to make notes in pencil on your first draft. Use the following guidelines to evaluate your social letters.

GUIDELINES FOR EVALUATING SOCIAL LETTERS

Content	1. In a friendly letter, is there news the reader would like to know or find interesting? Are questions answered that may have been asked in the friend's last letter? In a note of thanks, is it clear what the writer appreciates?

Coherence	2. Is the letter organized so the reader can follow it easily?
Appearance	3. Is the letter neatly written in pen or typed?
Form	4. Is the form correct, with each of the parts complete and correctly placed? Are the address and date in the heading? Is the salutation suitable? Does a comma follow the salutation? Are the first line of the body and the first lines of any other paragraphs indented? Is the closing appropriate? Is the first word in the closing capitalized? Does a comma come at the end of the closing?
Envelope	5. Is the address on the envelope complete? Is it correctly placed?

You should revise your social letters to improve their content, organization, appearance, and form. Use the four revising techniques: cutting, adding, replacing, and reordering. Use the suggestions in the chart on page 222 to revise your social letters. Proofread your letters by referring to the Guidelines for Proofreading on page 39. Be sure to proofread again after you recopy your letters.

BUSINESS LETTERS AND FORMS

Business letters and forms are important in our daily lives. You may have already written to order merchandise or to request information. Later you may write business letters to apply for a job or a school. You will have to know how to complete forms correctly as you go through school and get a job.

PREWRITING

PLANNING A BUSINESS LETTER

When you plan your business letters, use the following steps.

product, a television station or network, a tourist agency, a well-known scientist, or a government official. It may ask a question or express an opinion. Choose five or six of the most interesting suggestions to discuss with the class.

Impress on the class the fact that they should not actually mail the business letters they write for school assignments, unless the letters request information that the students really need or order items they really wish to buy, etc. Never allow a business letter to be mailed before you have checked it for form and content.

In teaching the correct form for business letters, you can follow the same procedure that was suggested above for teaching the form of a friendly letter.

In teaching students how to complete forms, emphasize thoroughness, honesty, clarity, and accuracy. Assemble, ahead of time, sample forms that you will use when you present this section.

PREWRITING

Section Overview

Writers of all ages need to learn how to plan business letters that will accomplish their purposes. Eighth-graders might want to write letters of complaint to a manufacturer of an inferior product or letters to a camp requesting information on summer counselor opportunities.

PLANNING A BUSINESS LETTER

This section includes several hints for students to consider when planning their business letters.

Since many of these are the same as for writing other forms of composition, students need to focus on business letters' format and purpose. You may want to ask students to actually decide on a subject for a business letter and respond to the hints listed on page 212.

WRITING

Section Overview

Students should learn the format unique to the business letter in order to communicate adequately in this way. They should also learn to complete forms accurately and thoroughly.

WRITING A BUSINESS LETTER (rules 7f–7g)

This section explains all the elements of a standard business letter, the location of each element, and the proper punctuation to be used. It also explains the characteristics unique to the order letter and the request letter and gives an example of each. You may want to go over this section carefully in class, having students actually write, fold, and stuff a business letter in an envelope. It might be helpful to have students memorize the two-letter postal code included in this section.

1. *Consider your purpose.* Think about why you are writing the letter. Are you ordering something? Are you asking for information?
2. *Consider your audience.* Keep in mind your audience. What do they already know? What do they need to know?
3. *Consider your tone.* A business letter should sound courteous. If you must make a complaint in a letter, do so politely.
4. *Gather your ideas.* Jot down exactly what you want to say or whatever information you intend to convey. Include as much information as necessary to explain the situation fully.
5. *Be brief.* Check to see that you have not included any unnecessary information. However, do not leave out any important details; if you do, the reader of the letter will not be able to respond promptly.

WRITING

WRITING A BUSINESS LETTER

7f. Follow generally accepted rules for the form of a business letter.

You should use unruled white paper that is $8\frac{1}{2}$ x 11 inches. If you type well, it is always good to type your business letters. If you do not type well, it is acceptable to write carefully in black or blue ink.

Make your letter neat and attractive. Center it on the page, leaving equal margins on the right and left sides and on the top and bottom. Avoid ink blots, erasures, and crossed-out words. Write only on one side of the page.

The form of a business letter is somewhat different from that of a personal letter. A business letter always includes an *inside address,* as in the following example:

567 Hardwood Street
San Diego, California 92128
December 10, 1988

Mr. John Anders
Acme Sporting Goods Company
33 Norton Avenue
Cleveland, Ohio 44105

Dear Mr. Anders:

Very truly yours,

Donald Hayes

Donald Hayes

Form for a Business Letter

The Heading

A business letter always requires a complete heading: street address on the first line; city, state, and ZIP code number on the second line, with a comma between the city and state; date on the third line, with a comma between the day and the year. Block style, not indented style, should be used in the heading of a business letter.

The Inside Address

A business letter includes an inside address, which gives the name and the address of the person or the firm (sometimes both) to whom you are writing. A comma is used between the city and state, and the ZIP code number appears several spaces, or about one-quarter inch, after the state. Place the inside address four typewriter lines below the heading and on the other side of the page, flush with the left-hand margin.

The Salutation

The salutation is placed two typewriter lines below the inside address, flush with the left-hand margin. It is followed by a colon, not a comma as in a friendly letter. Salutations will vary. If you are writing to a person whose name you have used in the inside address, you say *Dear Mr.——:* (or *Dear Miss——:* or *Dear Mrs.——:* or *Dear Ms.——:*).

EXAMPLE Ms. S. E. Sorenson, Circulation Manager
Astronomy Magazine
67 East Eighth Street
New York, New York 10003
Dear Ms. Sorenson:

If you are writing to a person whose name you do not know, but whose official position you do know, say *Dear Sir:* or *Dear Madam:*

EXAMPLE Public Relations Director
State Oil Company
317 Bush Street
Dallas, Texas 75243
Dear Sir: (or Dear Madam:)

If, however, you are writing to a group or a company, you may use an impersonal salutation (*Customer Service:, Editors:, Personnel:*).

EXAMPLE Bradley Electronics Corp.
56 La Mesa Drive
Lafayette, California 94549
Mail Order Department:

The Body

The first sentence of the body begins two lines below the salutation. This first line should be indented and the first lines of all other paragraphs should be indented the same distance. (If you are using a typewriter, indent five spaces.) Keep the left-hand margin straight; keep the right-hand margin as straight as possible.

The Closing

The correct closing for a business letter is *Yours truly* or *Very truly yours* or *Sincerely yours.* The closing should begin a little to the right of the middle of the page. Only the first word is capitalized. A comma follows the closing.

The Signature

In line with and directly below the closing, sign your full name in ink. If you are typing the letter, type your name below your written signature. Do not put a title (Mr., Mrs., Miss, etc.) before your handwritten signature.

Yours truly,
Margaret Nolan

Very truly yours,
John Anderson
John Anderson

The Envelope

The return address and the address on the envelope of a business letter are written and placed exactly as they are on the envelope of a friendly letter. The "outside" address should be the same as the inside address.

Folding the Letter

If the letter is written on $8\frac{1}{2} \times 11$-inch paper and is to be put into a long envelope, fold the sheet up a third of the way from the bottom, then fold the top third down over it.

EXERCISE 7. This exercise directs students to write a business letter and address an envelope from information provided. If you are not sure students can correctly accomplish this yet, you may want to practice on the board a few other simple letters before assigning this exercise.

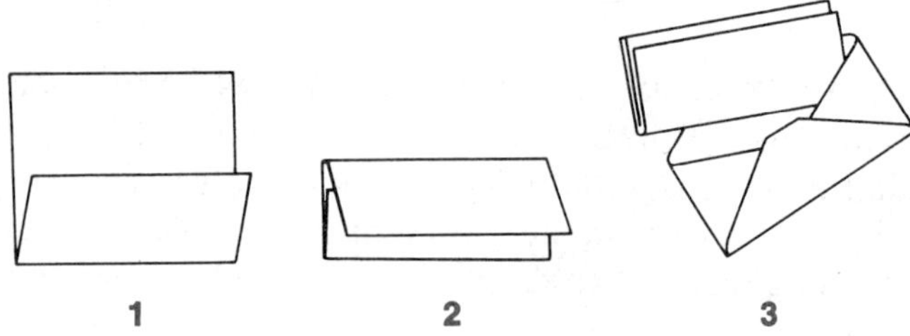

If the sheet is to go into a small envelope, fold the page up from the bottom to within a quarter of an inch of the top; then fold the right side over a third of the way, and fold the left side over it. Insert the letter into the envelope with the last fold at the bottom of the envelope.

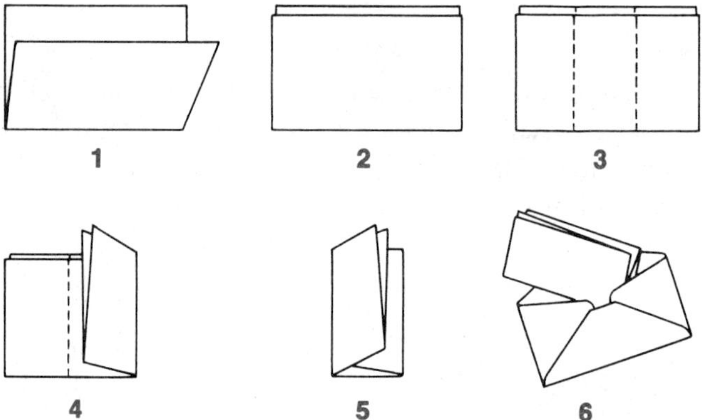

EXERCISE 7. Writing a Business Letter; Addressing an Envelope. The information needed for a business letter follows. Write the letter in correct form on a sheet of unruled white paper and address an envelope for it. See Answer Key.

32 Brenda drive, Flagstaff, Arizona 86001 december 2 1986 Acme outfitting company inc p.o. box 289 milwaukee wisconsin 53248 customer service department kindly send me your mail order catalog on sporting goods and hunting and fishing equipment thank you yours truly judy muller

Writing the Order Letter and the Request Letter

7g. Become familiar with the two common kinds of business letters: the *order* letter and the *request* letter.

The Order Letter

In an order letter, identify the merchandise you want by catalog number, by the place you saw it advertised, and by price. State how you are paying for the merchandise (cash, check, money order, C.O.D., or charge).

89 East First Street
Kankakee, Illinois 60901
March 10, 1988

Standard Equipment Company
448 Westwood Boulevard
St. Louis, Missouri 63107

Mail Order Department:

Please send me the field glasses, No. 791, which you advertised for $11.98, postpaid, in the February 17 issue of the <u>Farm Gazette.</u>

I am enclosing a money order for $11.98.

Very truly yours,

Rachel Beam

Rachel Beam

Model Order Letter

Sometimes you may need to return merchandise that was not exactly what you ordered. In your letter, indicate what merchandise you wanted. Be sure to use a polite tone.

EXERCISE 8. If you do not have enough mail-order catalogs available for all students, ask them to bring catalogs from home. Many are available that contain appropriate items—greeting cards, cheese, athletic clothing and equipment, Scandinavian sweaters, electronic equipment, museum posters, household goods, etc. You may want to look over the catalogs quickly in case someone brings in one that is not appropriate for a classroom.

EXERCISE 9. This exercise directs students to write a business letter about a problem with an order and to address an envelope for the letter. Have students evaluate their letters according to the criteria in Exercise 8 and check for wordiness. You may want to have them exchange papers for review.

> ☞ **NOTE** You will order many items of merchandise not by letter, but by order blank. When you use an order blank, follow the directions carefully and fill in all the blanks. No cover letter is necessary.

EXERCISE 8. Evaluating an Order Letter. Select an item you would like to order from the advertisements in a catalog, newspaper, or magazine, and write a letter ordering it. Exchange letters with a classmate to evaluate each other's letter. Check to see whether it (1) follows correct form; (2) it identifies the item wanted; (3) it states how the item is being paid for.
Answers will vary.

EXERCISE 9. Writing a Business Letter. Write a letter for one of the following situations. Also address an envelope for the letter. Answers will vary.

1. You ordered a pair of rabbits, New Zealand Giants, from Beyer's Mail Order Mart, 88 Hemingway Street, Augusta, Georgia 30915. Instead of live rabbits, you received a set of "rabbit ears" antennae for a television set. You enclosed full payment.
2. You ordered a cotton sweater from the Chic Shop, 49 Sierra Road, Philadelphia, Pennsylvania 19154. You received the wrong size and color.
3. For your mother's birthday, you ordered a sweater from Gifts Galore, 819 West Drive, Dubuque, Iowa 52018. In your letter you enclosed a money order. Your mother's birthday is a week away, and the sweater has not yet arrived.
4. You ordered (enclosing full payment) a pair of work gloves from Mercantile Mail Order Company, 97 West Ivy Street, Akron, Ohio 44153. You received twelve pairs of mittens.

The Request Letter

Occasionally you have to write a letter requesting information or sample materials. In such a letter you are asking a favor. Be brief, clear, and courteous.

34 Addison Place
Boise, Idaho 83742
December 2, 1988

Air-Industry, Inc.
10 West Norton Avenue
Los Angeles, California 90037

Publicity Department:

Our eighth-grade class at Brice Junior High School is studying the use of helicopters in farming operations. If you have a free brochure describing your helicopters and how they are used on farms, we would appreciate receiving ten copies.

Yours truly,

Martha Ames

Martha Ames

Model Request Letter

EXERCISE 10. Writing a Request Letter. Write to a government department, asking for free pamphlets about the duties and services of the department. Address an envelope for your letter, but do not mail the letter. **Answers will vary.**

EXERCISE 11. Writing a Business Letter. Write a letter for one of the following situations. Address an envelope, but do not mail the letter. **Answers will vary.**

1. Your class has been studying wildlife conservation. You would like some maps showing the great "flyways" on the North America continent used by migrating birds. Write to the Fish and Wildlife Service, United States Department of the Interior, Washington, D.C.

EXERCISE 10. This exercise gives students practice in writing a request letter. If students are not familiar with government departments, you may want to write a few on the board: parks and recreation, transportation, health, justice, planning, etc.

EXERCISE 11. This exercise gives additional practice in writing business letters with the general information provided. Advise students to use ZIP codes for all their correspondence.

COMPLETING FORMS
(rule 7h)

This section stresses the importance of filling out forms accurately and thoroughly. It also advises students to research carefully, if necessary, to locate the correct details requested on the form. Have ready, ahead of time, forms for Exercise 12. Be sure to go over the sample form with your students.

2. Your class wants to visit a famous museum in your area (or in another city). Write for information about visiting hours and fees. Ask whether a reduced rate is possible for your group. Inform the management of your purpose for making the visit.
3. Write to the United States Government Printing Office, Washington, D.C. Ask for publications on a particular subject and tell why you are interested in this subject.

COMPLETING FORMS

7h. Complete forms accurately and thoroughly.

Forms are an important source of information, used when you order magazines, join clubs, or apply for jobs or to schools. Knowing how to complete forms accurately and thoroughly is an important skill that can save you time and lessen certain errors.

STUDENT INFORMATION FORM

Pinewood Junior High School

(No Nicknames)
Name Zurich, Karen Lee
Last First Middle

Age 13 Male ____ Female X
Date of Birth 6/4/74
Place of Birth Tampa, Florida
City State
Home Address 111 Tice Place
Lakeland, Florida 33805
Phone# (813) 858-5040

Transported by bus Yes X No ____
Bus # 309

Last School Attended Lowery Elementary
Where Tampa, Florida
City State

Date Withdrew or Graduated 6/85

With whom do you live Jean & Phil Zurich
Relationship mother & father

Father
Zurich, Philip Mark
Last First Middle
Address 111 Tice Pl. Lakeland, Fl.
Place of Employment Eli Electric
Occupation Sales Manager

Mother
Zurich, Jean Mary
Last First Middle
Address 111 Tice Place
Place of Employment Cob Real Estate
Occupation Real Estate Consultant

NAME OF FAMILY DOCTOR Dr. M.H. Marte

Model Student Information Form

For any form, supply all the information requested and answer accurately. If you do not have the information requested, do not make up anything; do some research to locate the correct details. Study the sample form on page 220 and notice the type of information that forms usually require.

EXERCISE 12. Completing a Form. Supply the information needed to complete each blank in a form provided by your teacher. Answers will vary.

EVALUATING AND REVISING

EVALUATING AND REVISING BUSINESS LETTERS AND FORMS

7i. Evaluate and revise your business letters and forms.

Use the following guidelines to evaluate your business letters and forms for clarity and appearance. Use the revising chart on page 222 to make changes which will improve your work. Be sure to proofread your work, using the Guidelines for Proofreading on page 39. Also proofread again after you recopy your letter or form.

GUIDELINES FOR EVALUATING BUSINESS LETTERS AND FORMS

Content	1. Is the letter's purpose clear? Is all necessary information included?
Order Letter	2. In an order letter, is the letter brief and to the point?
Request Letter	3. In a request letter, is the request made courteously?
Form	4. Is the letter neat? Does the heading give the complete address and the full date? Is the inside address accurate, complete, and properly spaced? Is the salutation appropriate? Are the first lines of the body and other paragraphs

EXERCISE 12. You may wish to assemble a folder of forms relevant to your particular students. For example, look into the types of camps located in your area. They may have forms for students who wish to apply as counselors to fill out.

EVALUATING AND REVISING

Section Overview

Since business letters and forms are sent for specific purposes, usually with the expectation of a specific reply, it is important that students learn to communicate their message effectively. They should also check for neatness and format.

EVALUATING AND REVISING BUSINESS LETTERS AND FORMS (rule 7i)

This section directs students to check for clarity, appearance, and the items listed in the guidelines. You might want to have students evaluate and revise any of the business letters they have written for this chapter or assign another letter. Encourage students to mail letters for which they would like a reply. Allow some class time for students to share the replies. Some students may wish to send in the forms they completed. Before they revise, go over the chart Revising Social Letters, Business Letters, and Forms on pages 222–23.

indented? Is the closing appropriate? Is the form correct, with each of the parts correctly placed and punctuated?

Style — 5. Is block style used correctly in the letter?

Envelope — 6. Is the address on the envelope accurate, complete, correctly placed, and identical to the inside address? Has the letter been folded to fit the envelope? Is the return address on the envelope?

Forms — 7. Is all the requested information supplied? Is it accurate?

REVISING SOCIAL LETTERS, BUSINESS LETTERS, AND FORMS

PROBLEM	TECHNIQUE	REVISION
The content is not clear, or information is missing.	Add	Add details that make your message clear. Add a concluding sentence that sums up the letter. Add details that answer questions or provide requested information.
The order of ideas doesn't make sense.	Reorder	Rearrange sentences and paragraphs in a logical order that makes your point clear.
The letter or form looks messy.	Replace	Rewrite or retype the letter or form so there are no messy corrections.
The heading or inside address is not complete, or is incorrectly placed.	Reorder/Add	Move to the correct position. Add missing details about addresses or the date.
The salutation or closing doesn't sound right.	Replace	Use a salutation or closing that fits the purpose of the letter and the receiver.

PROBLEM	TECHNIQUE	REVISION
The body is not indented correctly.	Replace	Indent all paragraphs the same way.
The address on the envelope is incomplete.	Add	Add the return address and ZIP code numbers. Add missing items to the address.

CHAPTER 7 WRITING REVIEW 1

Writing a Friendly Letter. Write the letter for one of the following situations, or for a situation of your own. Evaluate, revise, and proofread your draft. Answers will vary.

1. You are a 4-H Club member. At a recent convention you made friends with another 4-H member. Write a letter to your new friend, telling about club activities and your exhibit for the 4-H Club county fair.
2. You have been elected secretary of your club. Write to a friend or relative, describing the club, its purpose, and its members.
3. Write to an older brother or sister at college or an out-of-town relative. Tell about your own progress at school, and ask questions about that person's life.

CHAPTER 7 WRITING REVIEW 2

Writing Business Letters. Write a letter for each of the following situations. Evaluate, revise, and proofread your letters, and address an envelope for each. Answers will vary.

1. Write an order letter to Travis Novelty Company, 18 Meadow Street, St. Louis, Missouri 63128, for the following merchan-

CHAPTER 7 WRITING REVIEWS 1 and 2

These review exercises direct students to write friendly and business letters. You might encourage students to write a letter to a friend or relative for the friendly letter. They might write a business letter for which they desire an answer instead of following the directions given. In both cases, remind students to refer to the guidelines for evaluating friendly and business letters and forms before and after they have written the letter. If students would enjoy sharing replies of either friendly or business letters, you might allow class time for this. Since these replies will be received after you have finished this chapter, you could allow the last few minutes of some future class periods for this activity.

dise: 2 giant balloons, at $.85 each; 18 pencils, with the name "Pat" printed in silver, at $.35 each; and 1 box of birthday candles, at $1.35. You are enclosing a money order to cover the total cost.

2. Write a request letter asking for the summer schedule of plays at the Beacon Summer Theater, Portsmouth, Rhode Island 02871; inform the theater that you represent a group and need information on group ticket rates.

☞ **NOTE** The United States Postal Service recommends using two-letter codes for states, the District of Columbia, and Puerto Rico. The service also recommends using nine-digit ZIP codes. When you use these codes, the address should look like this:

EXAMPLE Ms. Linda Ramos
6 Northside Dr.
St. Joseph, MO 64506–1212

The two-letter code is in capital letters and is never followed by a period. The following is a list of two-letter codes for states, the District of Columbia, and Puerto Rico.

Alabama AL
Alaska AK
Arizona AZ
Arkansas AR
California CA
Colorado CO
Connecticut CT
Delaware DE
District of Columbia DC
Florida FL
Georgia GA
Hawaii HI
Idaho ID
Illinois IL
Indiana IN
Iowa IA
Kansas KS
Kentucky KY
Louisiana LA
Maine ME
Maryland MD
Massachusetts MA
Michigan MI
Minnesota MN
Mississippi MS
Missouri MO
Montana MT
Nebraska NE

Nevada NV
New Hampshire NH
New Jersey NJ
New Mexico NM
New York NY
North Carolina NC
North Dakota ND
Ohio OH
Oklahoma OK
Oregon OR
Pennsylania PA
Puerto Rico PR
Rhode Island RI
South Carolina SC
South Dakota SD
Tennessee TN
Texas TX
Utah UT
Vermont VT
Virginia VA
Washington WA
West Virginia WV
Wisconsin WI
Wyoming WY

Additional Practice

Teacher's Resource Book, Worksheet pages 58–63

Testing

Teaching Tests booklet, pages 1–4, 7–8, 13–18
Teacher's Resource Book, Test pages 371–74, 401–402, 407–412

PICTURE THE POSSIBILITIES:

IDEAS FOR WRITING

Pictures can bring back memories, awaken strong feelings, and spark the imagination. In this section you will learn how to use pictures to discover ideas for writing.

Ideas for Writing

Section Overview:

Today's students live in an increasingly visual world. This section is designed to show students how they can use the images with which they are surrounded as a source of ideas for writing.

Four of the fifteen pictures are accompanied by detailed suggestions for generating ideas and gathering information. Two writing assignments are provided for each of these pictures, each focusing on a separate purpose.

Following the pictures is a set of questions useful for exploring any picture. The section concludes with an assignment directing students to write for a purpose and in a form of their own choosing. This assignment may be used with the remaining pictures in the text and with pictures from other sources.

PRESENTING THE LESSON

LESS-ADVANCED STUDENTS Allow these students to complete the assignments in small groups. Encourage them to make use of the questions in the text, and work closely with them throughout the prewriting stage.

ADVANCED STUDENTS These students will enjoy using the text suggestions as springboards for their own ideas and writing for audiences other than their classmates. Challenge them to find and write about pictures from other sources as well.

ASSIGNMENT: Dialogue

The questions in the text are designed to help students create an interesting situation for the dialogue they are to write. Go over the questions in class, emphasizing that there are no "right" or "wrong" answers and encouraging students to suggest possible answers. Other questions you might have them consider are: How well do the girls know each other? What day of the week is it? What time of day?

Less-advanced students might benefit from working in small groups, with each group developing a single situation and writing only one dialogue. Alternatively, you might have pairs of students role-play the characters and tape-record the conversation to use in writing their first drafts. If you use this approach, you may want to allow teams made up of two boys or of one girl and one boy to act out characters of their own gender.

To help students generate ideas, suggest that they have the characters talk about (1) what happened just before the picture was taken or (2) what they are planning to do next.

Be sure to let students know whether you plan to evaluate their papers for content only or for mechanics as well. Your decision will, naturally, be based on how extensively you have taught the punctuation of dialogue.

In reviewing students' papers, look especially for natural-sounding conversation; details that show personality; and clear indications of who is speaking.

ASSIGNMENT: Narration

Depending on the amount of practice your students have had with writing stories, you may need

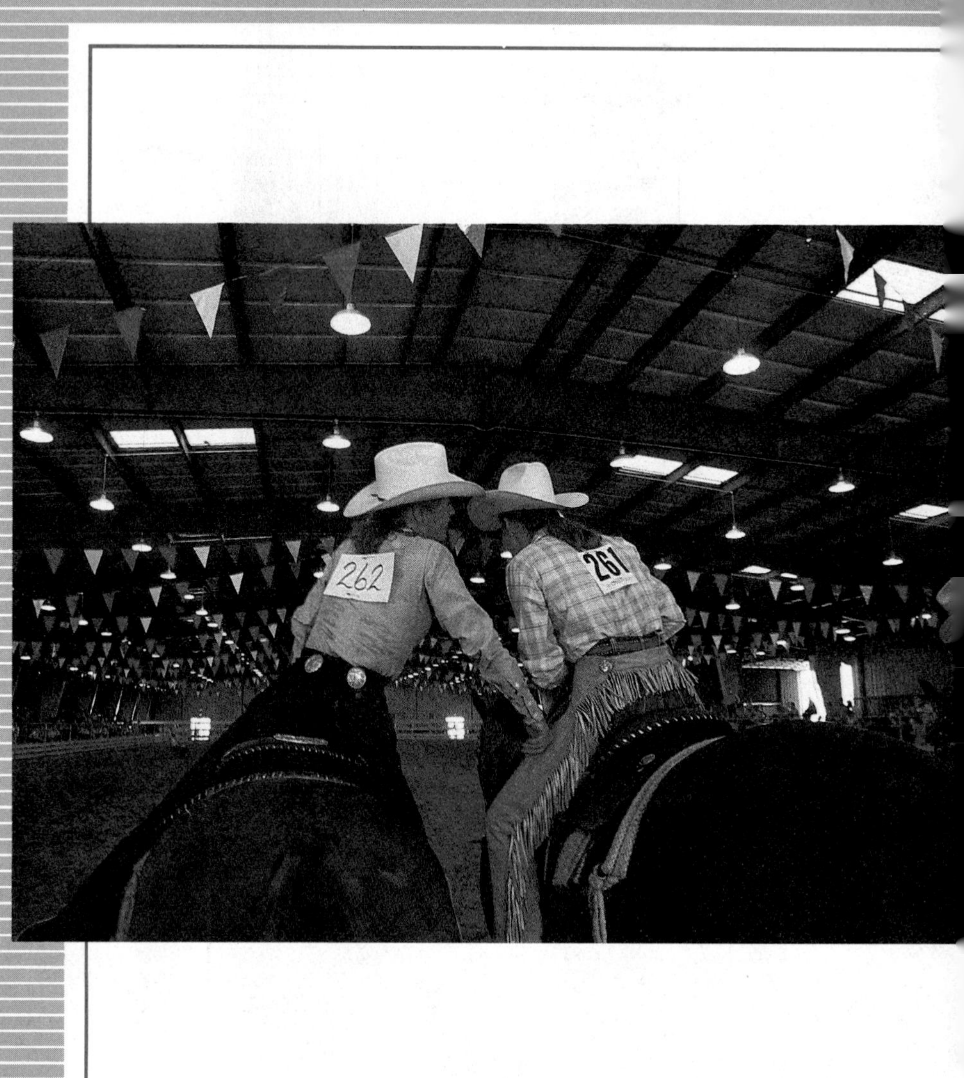

Probing the Picture

One way to use this picture would be to write a **dialogue** between the two girls. To create an interesting situation, you could brainstorm to develop questions such as *Who are the girls? How old are they? What part of the country do they live in? Why are they in the arena? Do the girls own the horses? Do they live on farms, or are they from the city? Why is the girl on the left smiling?* Your answers to these questions would help you create lively, natural–sounding conversation.

A second way to use the picture would be to write a **story**. If you have ever ridden a horse, you could brainstorm to discover a personal experience to write about. If not, you could use the *5 W-How?* questions to make up a story in which the girls are the main characters. For example, *What problem do the girls face? Where and when does the action take place? Who else takes part in or witnesses the events? How is the problem worked out?* Using your imagination to answer these questions would help you develop a plan for your story.

Writing Activities

Using the steps of the writing process, complete one of the following activities.

- Create a situation and write a short dialogue that shows the personalities of the girls in the picture.
- Use the picture to write either a personal experience narrative or a made–up story.

to review the five basic elements of a narrative before making this assignment: an interesting start; a beginning explanation; action; climax; and ending.

Remind students that the central question any narrative must answer is *What happened?* Emphasize the importance of using chronological order to avoid confusing the reader and of including only details that are directly related to the action.

You may need to point out to students who elect to write a personal-experience story that the experience should be one they will feel comfortable sharing with their classmates. Less-advanced students might benefit from working through the prewriting stage of a made-up story as a class and then meeting in three groups, with one group writing the beginning, one the middle, and one the ending.

Before students begin writing, remind them that the *5 W-How?* questions can be useful for gathering details for both personal-experience and imaginative stories. You may also need to review the use of first person and of third person. Encourage students who have completed the preceding assignment to incorporate their dialogues into the stories they write.

In evaluating students' stories, look for an interesting beginning, a middle that leads to a climax, and an ending that ties up the loose ends; the use of chronological order; and the exclusion of details not directly related to the action.

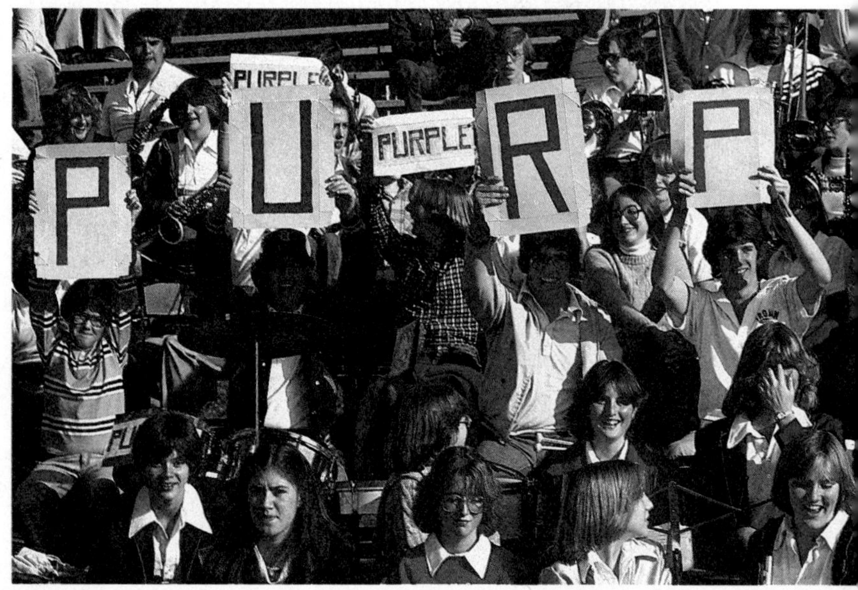
PURPLE
P
U
PURPLE
R
P

IW5

ASSIGNMENT: Exposition

Students will find this assignment easier to complete if you work with them as a class during the information-gathering stage. Begin by drawing on the chalkboard a chart like the one described in the text. Then ask students to identify the pictures' features and to suggest whether each feature is similar or different in the two pictures.

Since most students will probably focus on the differences between the pictures, you may need to point out the similarity between some of the items, such as the shapes of the rides and the safety bars on the chairs. You may want to allow students to copy the completed chart into their notebooks for use in writing their first drafts.

Advanced students might be encouraged to compile this information on their own. You may instead prefer to have them pursue the idea of comparing or contrasting free-time activities of earlier years with those of today. Note that papers on that topic might well result in compositions rather than paragraphs.

Unless you have taught the alternating and block methods of arranging details in a paragraph of comparison and contrast, you may want to discourage students from attempting such a paragraph. For most eighth-graders producing an effective paragraph of either comparison or contrast will be challenge enough.

As you review students' papers, look for the inclusion of at least three features and the use of appropriate transitional expressions.

ASSIGNMENT: Persuasion

Go over the questions in the text with students, showing them how

Probing the Pictures

This combination of pictures could serve as the basis for an **expository** paragraph of comparison or contrast. One approach would be to study both pictures carefully in order to develop a list of details showing how the scenes are similar and how they are different. To do this, you could make a chart with two columns at the top, one labeled "Similar" and the other labeled "Different." Then you could list the features of the pictures (rides, hair styles, clothing, etc.) down the left side of the chart. Once you had filled in the chart, you could decide whether to use comparison, contrast, or both. Another approach would be to use library sources to find out what free-time activities young people enjoyed in the 1900's and compare or contrast them with the ones you and your friends enjoy.

You could instead use the picture to write a **persuasive** paragraph. To find possible debatable issues, you could brainstorm on the subject "rides," developing questions such as *Should children under twelve be forbidden to go on certain rides without an adult? Should people who do not follow safety precautions on rides be required to leave the grounds? Should people be required to wear shoulder harnesses on certain rides? Should local inspectors make sure that rides are safe before the public is allowed to use them?*

Writing Activities

Using the steps of the writing process, complete one of the following activities.

- Write an expository paragraph comparing or contrasting the pictures.
- Write a persuasive paragraph on one of the issues suggested above or on another issue the pictures suggest.

each one can be converted into a declarative sentence that could serve as a position statement. Since most if not all of your students will have had at least some experience with amusement park rides, they should have little difficulty in choosing one of these positions to support or in coming up with position statements of their own.

Review with students the basic elements of a persuasive paragraph: at least three separate, specific reasons that support the opinion in the position statement; evidence, such as facts, statistics, or examples, that supports each reason; and, optionally, a clincher sentence that summarizes the argument or suggests a specific action.

Students may be able to draw on their own experience to build their arguments. Alternatively, your local newspaper's library staff might provide them with facts and statistics on accidents involving rides in your community, or you might arrange for them to interview a local official who inspects the rides.

To vary the assignment, you might have students write letters to the editor of the local newspaper. Explain that in persuasion, order of importance is determined largely by the importance the audience attaches to each reason.

In evaluating students' work, check for a clear and precise position statement; at least three reasons and relevant evidence; and an appropriate pattern of organization.

IW9

ASSIGNMENT: Description

The text questions are designed to elicit concrete and sensory details that will produce vivid descriptive writing. Allow ample time for students to go over the questions, either in small groups or as a class, and to generate lists of details to consider as they draft their papers. Some of your eighth-graders will enjoy locating and observing an actual spider web for this assignment.

Remind students that the topic sentence of a descriptive paragraph often conveys a main impression. Less-advanced students may need your help in understanding that the topic sentence should not only identify the topic but also make a general statement about it or summarize the details in the paragraph.

Review with students the use of specific verbs, precise modifiers, and comparisons in description. Remind them not to settle for the first word that comes to mind but to search for the word that most precisely communicates their meaning.

Help students understand that chronological order would be a logical order for a paragraph in which they describe the web as though they were observing it in person, while spatial order would be more appropriate for one in which they describe how the parts of the web are related to one another and to the web as a whole.

In reviewing students' work, look for the use of specific concrete and sensory details; precise words; and a clear organizational pattern.

ASSIGNMENT: Exposition

Go over the text with the class, pointing out that the first topic suggested is a *type* of spider, while

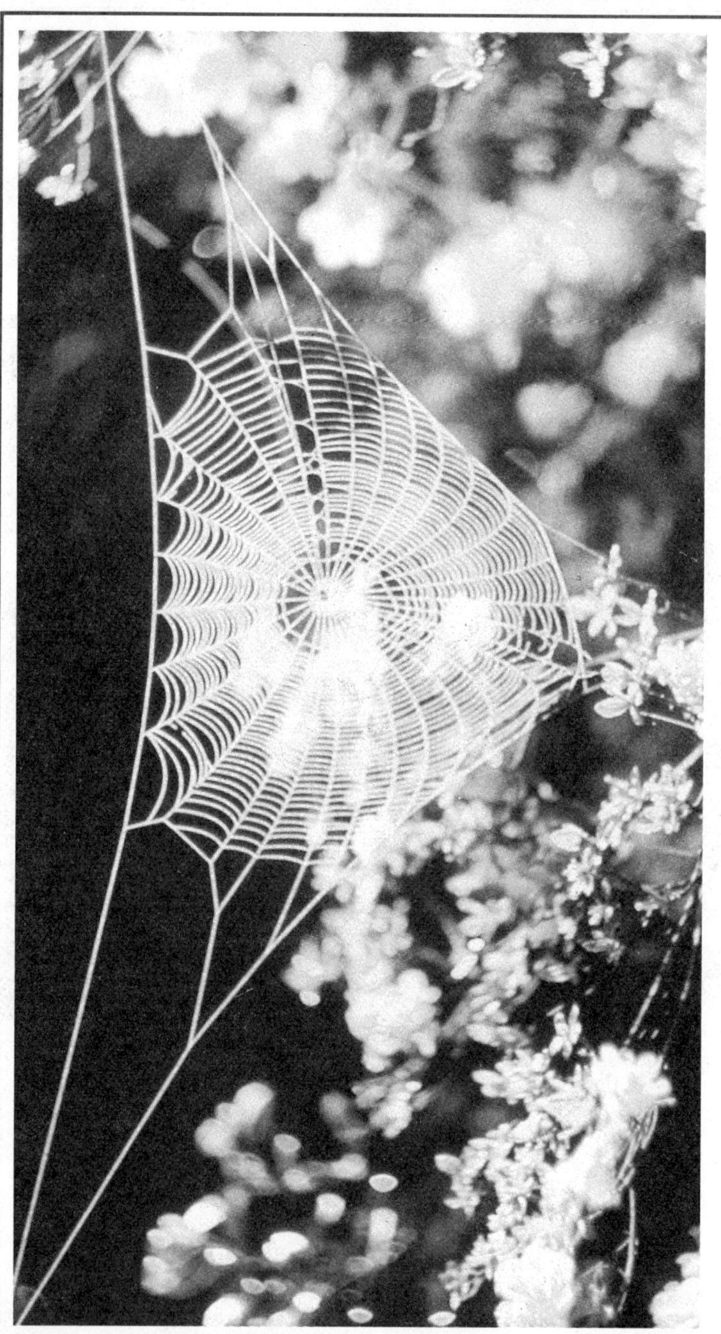

Probing the Picture

You could use this picture to write a **descriptive** paragraph. To create a main impression, you could focus on the picture's strongest features: the detailed circular pattern within the triangle and the reflection of light from the web's strands. You could instead imagine yourself observing the web in person and gather concrete and sensory details by asking questions such as *What other patterns do I see in the web? In the surrounding branches? What odors do I smell in this part of the woods? How does the web feel against my skin when I accidentally brush against it?*

Another possibility would be to use the picture to write an **expository** composition. You could begin by dividing the subject "spiders" into smaller parts to find possible topics. Then you could use the *point-of-view questions* to gather information from library sources. For the topic "tarantula," for example, you might ask questions such as *What other names are these spiders known by? Where do they live? What do they eat? How are they like other kinds of spiders? How are they different?* For the topic "spider webs," you might ask, *Do all spiders build webs? What function does a spider web serve? What material is it made of? What are the features (size, shape, strength, etc.) of a spider web?*

Writing Activities

Using the steps of the writing process, complete one of the following activities.

- Write a paragraph describing the picture.
- Write an expository composition on a topic you find by dividing the subject "spiders" into smaller parts.

the second is an *activity* that (some) spiders engage in. Encourage students to think of other questions they might ask about each topic.

Have students form small groups and brainstorm to discover their own topics and questions they might ask about them. Remind them that other possible ways to limit a subject (not all of which apply to the subject "spiders") are on the basis of examples, uses, time periods, and people, places, and events. You may want to specify a minimum and a maximum length for the assignment for students to use as a guide in limiting the subject.

Remind students to take their own interests into account when they choose a topic and to make sure that they can find enough information on the topic they select. You may want to have them clear their topics and lists of questions with you before they begin gathering information.

With less-advanced students, you might have small groups complete the assignment. Each group member could write a paragraph answering one question, and the students could work together to arrange the paragraphs in order, to write the introduction and the conclusion, and to revise the composition.

Check students' papers for an interesting introduction; clear organization; and a conclusion that sums up the main points or reinforces the introduction.

IW13

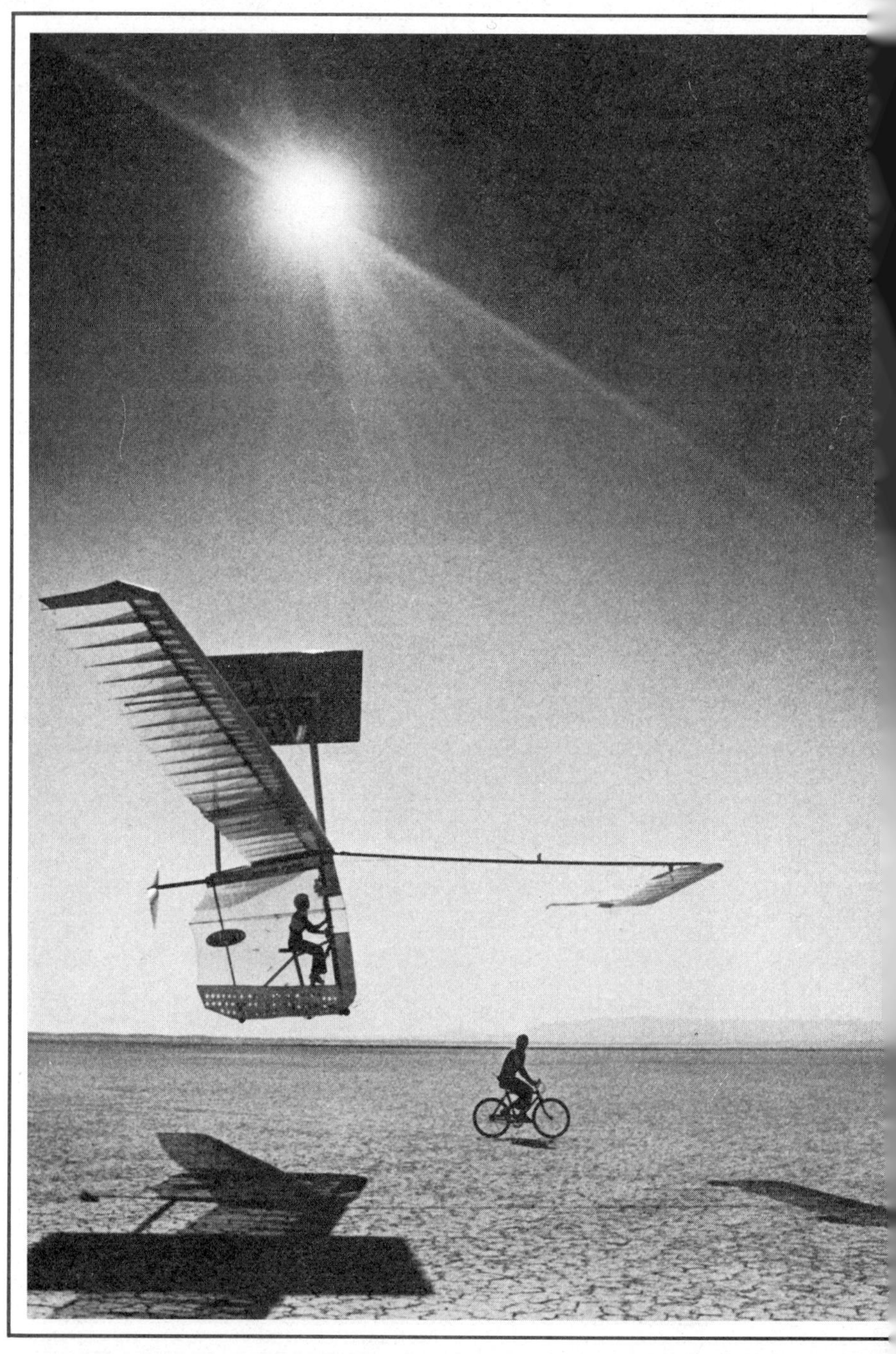

Probing Pictures to Discover Writing Ideas

The following questions will help you use any picture to discover ideas for writing.

1. What about this picture do I find most interesting? What idea does it suggest?
2. For what purpose could I use this idea?
3. What are the picture's strongest features? How could I use those features to achieve my purpose?
4. Would using the *5 W-How?* questions help me gather information to use?
5. What might have happened just before or just after the picture was taken? What might the person(s) have said?
6. What main impression do I get from this picture?
7. What concrete and sensory details do I observe as I study the picture? What details do I imagine when I think of myself as being in the scene?
8. Could I explain how to make or do what the picture shows?
9. Could I give information about what the picture shows by telling who or what the subject is, what its history is, or how it is similar to and different from others of the same kind?
10. What debatable issues does the picture suggest to me?

On Your Own

Write a paper for your classmates on any of the pictures you have not written about. You may choose the form (paragraph, report, story, letter-to-the-editor) and the purpose (to tell a story, to describe, to explain or inform, or to persuade). Follow the steps of the writing process.

USING THE QUESTIONS

These questions provide techniques for using pictures to discover writing ideas and for gathering information. Go through them carefully in class, making sure that students understand the kinds of ideas and details they are designed to elicit. You may also want to spend some class time discussing the remaining pictures in this section. If you plan to have students complete the assignment below independently, however, you will not want to allow the discussion to become too detailed.

ASSIGNMENT: On Your Own

This assignment gives students the opportunity to use the questions to discover their own ideas for writing. You may of course specify an audience other than their classmates for students to write for, or you may leave the choice of an audience to them. You may also prefer to make the assignment more structured by designating the form, the purpose, or both.

The assignment may be repeated or varied with pictures from other sources. Possible sources include local newspapers; magazines (e.g., *Audubon, Ebony, Life, National Geographic, Newsweek, Smithsonian, Sports Illustrated, Time*); books featuring the work of photographers; calendars; posters; school yearbooks; and family albums. Students might also enjoy taking and writing about their own photographs.

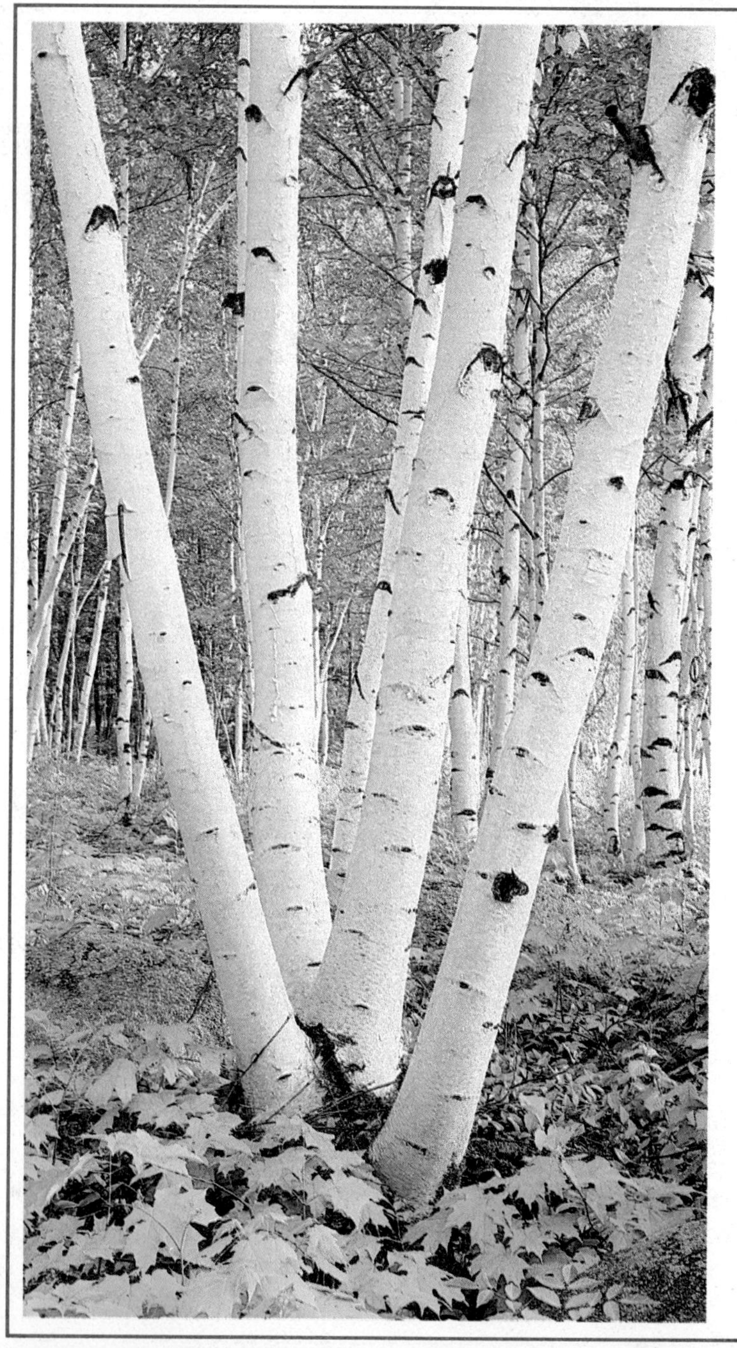

PART TWO

COMPOSITION: Writing and Revising Sentences

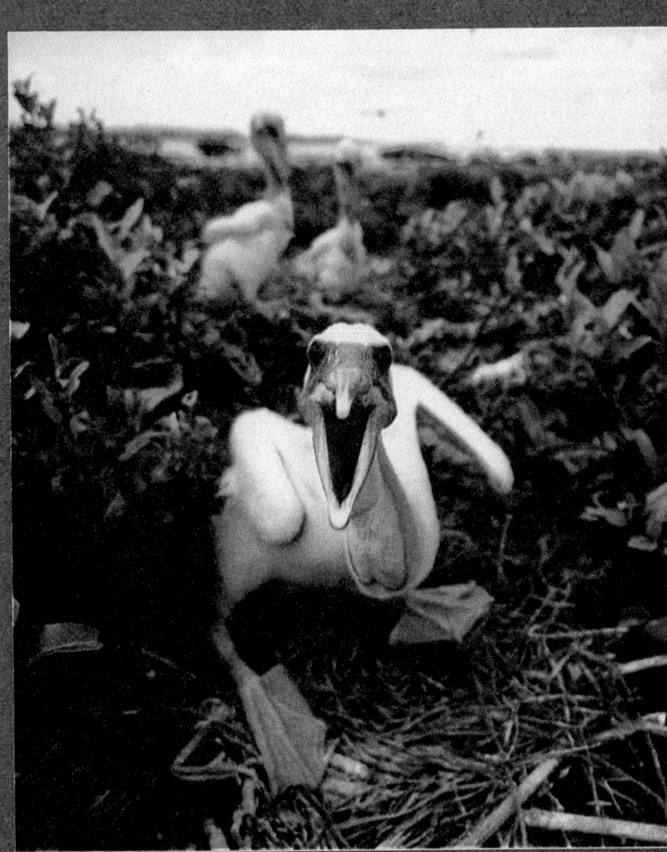

COMPOSITION: Writing and Revising Sentences

pages 227–62

USING THE PICTURES

The pictures on this and the next page, along with those in the section "Picture the Possibilities" following page 226, provide students with sources of ideas for writing. The following suggestions will help you show students how to use the pictures, either singly or in combination, to generate ideas and gather information.

Baby Pelican

- One way to use this picture would be to have students write a report on white pelicans. They could begin by brainstorming to develop questions such as these to guide their research: *What is the scientific name of the white pelican? Where does it live? To what other birds is it related? How big does it get? What does it eat? How does it gather its food? Where does it build its nest? How many eggs does the female lay at one time? How do the parents care for the chicks?*
- Have students write paragraphs contrasting three or more features of the white pelican (for example, appearance, habitat, range, food-gathering methods) with those of the brown pelican.
- Have students imagine that they took the picture and write narrative paragraphs telling what happened just before or just after they snapped the shutter. Remind them that

using narrative details will help their readers picture the actions and understand what happened.

SEAGULL ON SIGN

- To gather information for a library report on gulls, students could use questions similar to those listed under the first suggestion on the preceding page.
- Another possibility would be to have students write papers comparing or contrasting gulls and terns, the birds to which gulls are most closely related.
- Have students collect examples of signs in their neighborhoods that prohibit certain activities. They could then write paragraphs giving examples of the signs they found and telling where they observed each one.
- Have students form small groups and brainstorm to come up with signs they would like to see prohibiting a certain activity in the classroom, the lunchroom, or the halls. Students could then use that idea as the basis for a letter to the editor of the school paper or a persuasive paragraph.
- This picture was taken in the San Juan Islands in Puget Sound, Washington. You might provide copies of a magazine article on the islands, on Puget Sound, or on some aspect of life in Washington state and have students summarize the article. You could of course adapt this idea by providing an article on your own community or state.

Connecting the Pictures

Have students write paragraphs giving examples of other types of water birds. They might instead give examples of types of birds in their own neighborhoods.

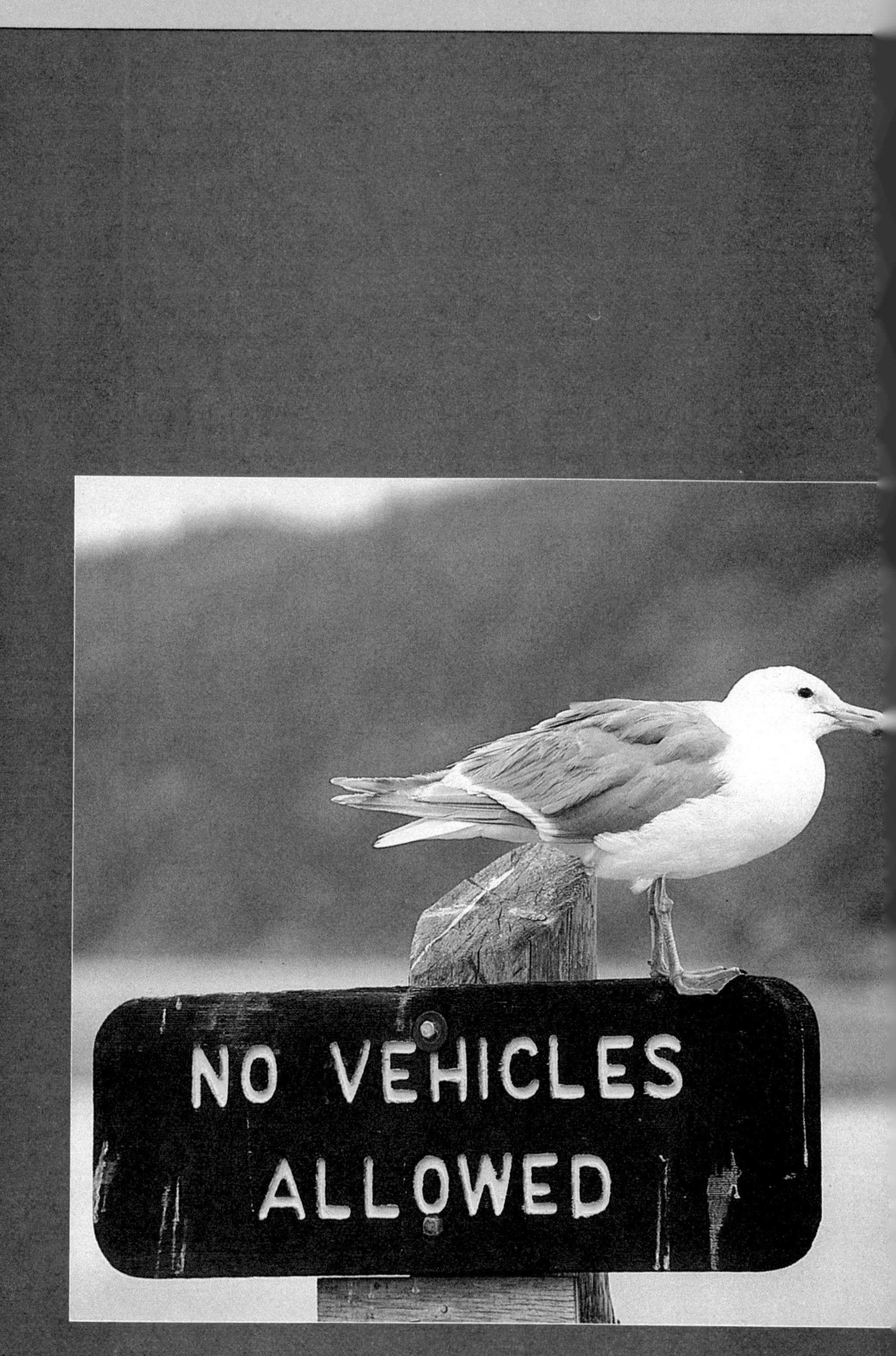

CHAPTER 8

Writing Complete Sentences

SENTENCE FRAGMENTS AND RUN-ON SENTENCES

When you speak, you signal the end of a sentence by making your voice rise or fall and by pausing. When you write, the signals you use are end marks: periods, question marks, and exclamation points. If you use these marks incorrectly, you give your reader the wrong signals. You can eliminate many punctuation problems by reading aloud what you have written, listening for the signals your voice gives. In this chapter you will learn to identify and avoid two frequent errors that occur in written composition: the *sentence fragment* and the *run-on sentence*.

FRAGMENTS

A sentence expresses a complete thought. When only a part of a sentence is punctuated as though it were a complete sentence, the resulting error is a *sentence fragment.* A fragment often belongs with the sentence that precedes it.

8a. A *fragment* is a separated sentence part that does not express a complete thought.

Chapter Overview

"Sentence sense" is a general term for the ability to recognize and use complete sentences. Through practice, students can develop the ability to tell a sentence from a sentence fragment or a run-on sentence.

Occasionally students will point out that professional writers do not always use complete sentences. You could discuss this matter with the class, covering situations such as these:

1. Written conversation.
2. First-person narratives that are written to sound as if the narrator is talking informally to the reader.
3. Places where a writer is trying to achieve a particular rhetorical effect (incomplete sentences broken off with a dash or a series of dots; sentence fragments used for repetition or emphasis). You may want to assure your class that you will not mark off for natural-sounding written dialogue that contains sentence fragments, or for other fragments or run-on sentences that are used deliberately to create an effect.

Chapter Objective

Students will recognize sentence fragments and run-on sentences and correct them.

PRESENTING THE CHAPTER

LESS-ADVANCED STUDENTS These students may not be able to tell complete sentences from fragments or run-ons until they hear the examples read aloud by the teacher. For such students, reading practice is as important as writing practice. *(See listing of Alternative Worksheets on page 240.)*

ADVANCED STUDENTS By now, these students should be doing a great deal of original writing. Naturally, they should get their ideas down freely in their rough drafts. Use the errors you find in their final versions to determine what exercises to assign from this chapter.

FRAGMENTS (rules 8a–8d)

To illustrate complete sentences and fragments, put on the board some items such as the following ones.

1. Listening carefully in class.
2. Rosa did her lessons early in the evening.
3. Which the teacher had assigned.
4. After night had fallen.
5. When the last bell rang.
6. She found her books under her desk.
7. At eleven o'clock.

Review the definitions of *sentence, phrase, clause, independent clause,* and *subordinate clause.* Then go over the items on the board, having students identify fragments.

EXERCISE 1. After your class completes this exercise, give them examples of sentence fragments taken from their own compositions. Have them revise these fragments to make complete sentences.

To decide whether or not a group of words is a sentence, ask yourself these two questions: (1) Does it have a verb and its subject? (2) Does it express a complete thought? If the answer to either question is "no," the group of words is not a sentence but a sentence fragment.

Each of the following examples contains a sentence and a fragment, which is printed in italics.

The newspaper staff worked late. *Putting out a special edition.* [The fragment contains no main verb or subject.]

We look forward to meeting Ms. Cox. *Our new teacher.* [The fragment contains no verb or subject.]

As the horses neared the gate. The excitement increased. [The fragment contains a verb and a subject, but it does not express a complete thought. It leaves the reader wondering what happened *as the horses neared the gate.*]

Since these fragments belong with the sentences they precede or follow, you can correct them by joining them to the sentences.

The newspaper staff worked late **putting out a special edition.**

We looked forward to meeting Ms. Cox, **our new teacher.**

As the horses neared the gate, the excitement increased.

EXERCISE 1. Identifying Sentences and Fragments; Correcting Fragments. Seven of the italicized groups of words that follow are fragments, while three are complete sentences. Indicate a complete sentence by placing a *C* after the proper number. Correct each fragment by writing the entire item and making the fragment part of the sentence.

EXAMPLES
1. Dolphins are intelligent animals. *That are being closely studied today.*
1. *Dolphins are intelligent animals that are being closely studied today.*
2. The study of this aquatic mammal has already shown surprising results. *The dolphin has been trained as a diver's seagoing partner.*
2. *C*

1. The man who has done the most research on the dolphin is Dr. John C. Lilly. *Who is attempting to devise a method of communication between humans and dolphins.* 1. Lilly who
2. *By putting a partially paralyzed dolphin into a tank with other dolphins.* Dr. Lilly discovered the dolphin's distress call.
3. The dolphin emitted its distress call. *When it began to sink.*
4. It was immediately assisted by two other dolphins. *They lifted it to the surface for air.* 2. dolphins, Dr. 3. call when 4. C
5. Dolphins usually stay in groups. *Helping each other out in times of trouble.* 5. groups, helping
6. A baby dolphin is looked after by two adults. *Its mother and an assistant mother serve as nurses.* 6. C
7. Even a deadly shark is no match for two angry mother dolphins. *Striking at their foe with their beaklike noses.*
8. *In addition to having unusual ability to mimic the human voice.* The dolphin is of extreme interest because of its streamlined body and its amazing built-in sonar system.
9. Nuclear-powered submarines have been designed in the same general shape as the dolphin. *It is the most perfectly streamlined animal known.* 7. dolphins striking 8. voice, the 9. C
10. The dolphin possesses a built-in sonar apparatus. *Which is as accurate as sonar equipment used by scientists.* 10. apparatus, which

Three Kinds of Fragments

The *subordinate clause,* the *verbal phrase,* and the *appositive phrase* are three common kinds of fragments.

The Subordinate Clause

8b. A subordinate clause must not be written as a sentence.

A subordinate clause is a group of words that contains a verb and its subject but does not express a complete thought (see page 384). It cannot stand by itself but must always be attached to an

THREE KINDS OF FRAGMENTS (rules 8b–8d)

For teaching purposes—to provide separate though similar discussions of fragments—this section is divided according to grammatical types of fragments: the subordinate clause, the verbal phrase, and the appositive phrase. Students, however, will probably not approach fragments through grammar. They will usually identify fragments by the fact that they "sound" incomplete. As long as they can do this accurately, less-advanced students should not be expected to label the kind of fragment. Students who cannot spot fragments by their incompleteness will not be able to spot them by applying grammar.

EXERCISE 2. Give students the hint that the fragments should be tied either to what precedes or to what follows.

independent clause (a group of words that contains a subject, a verb and does express a complete thought). *As she turned the corner* is a subordinate clause. If you read this word group aloud, you will hear at once that it is not a complete sentence. Read the following subordinate clauses aloud. Do they sound like complete sentences? Then notice the difference when they are joined to independent clauses.

When it rains during a football game [What happens then?]

Who directed us to our seats [If a question is intended, the word group is a sentence. If not, it is a fragment.]

When it rains during a football game, the stadium looks like a patchwork quilt of umbrellas.

We found an usher, **who directed us to our seats.**

Relative pronouns (*who, whom, whose, which, that*) or subordinating conjunctions (see the list on page 392) introduce subordinate clauses. These are very important words, for they can change a sentence into a fragment.

SENTENCE It rains during a football game.
FRAGMENT **When** it rains during a football game.
SENTENCE An usher directed us to our seats.
FRAGMENT An usher **who** directed us to our seats.

EXERCISE 2. Correcting Sentence Fragments. The following paragraphs contain ten fragments. Write the paragraphs, attaching the fragments to the related independent clauses.

See Answer Key.

Fifteen very young dinosaurs were waiting in a nest. While their mother went looking for food. Before the adult dinosaur could return. Disaster struck. The small prehistoric creatures all perished. When a volcano buried the nest in debris.

Scientists recently uncovered the fossils of these small dinosaurs. Which lived 70 million years ago. After they studied the remaining fragments of bones. Scientists reconstructed the appearance of the dinosaurs. The name given to these extinct lizards was *hadrosaur*. Which means "duck-billed lizard." Adult hadrosaurs were plant eaters. That could scoop up vegetation from watery swamps.

The discovery of these fossils was important. Because it shed light on one of the mysteries about dinosaurs. Before this recent discovery was made. Scientists debated whether dinosaurs were coldblooded or warmblooded. Fossil evidence shows these tiny hadrosaurs were living in a nest. They were likely warmblooded. Because few coldblooded animals are fed by their parents or protected in nests.

EXERCISE 3. Correcting Sentence Fragments. Make each of the following fragments into a complete sentence by adding an independent clause. Write each sentence on your paper, using punctuation and capital letters correctly. Answers will vary.

EXAMPLE 1. Because I missed the bus by seconds.
1. *I was twenty minutes late to school because I missed the bus by seconds.*

1. Who broke her glasses.
2. That are working on a clean-up campaign for the school.
3. If you want to own a pet.
4. Because the library closes at six o'clock.
5. Whom I met at your party.

The Verbal Phrase

8c. A verbal phrase must not be written as a sentence.

A verbal is a word that is formed from a verb but that is used as another part of speech. Present participles and gerunds are verbals that usually end in *-ing* (*coming, working, being*). Past participles are verbals that usually end in *-d, -ed, -t, -n,* or *-en* (*looked, slept, broken*). Infinitives are verbals that usually consist of *to* plus the verb (*to go, to play*).

A verbal phrase is a phrase (group of words working together as a part of speech) containing a verbal. It is often mistaken for a sentence because the verbal is often mistaken for a main verb. However, a phrase does not have both a subject and a verb and, therefore, cannot express a complete thought. By itself, a verbal phrase is a fragment.

EXERCISE 3. Students of all levels of ability can do this exercise, which requires them to produce original sentences. Have some of these sentences read aloud so that students can hear several correct ways to make the fragments into sentences.

EXERCISE 4. You may want to do this exercise orally, especially with a class of less-advanced students.

The Appositive Phrase

Your students should know what an appositive is, but they may not grasp the meaning of the term *appositive phrase* unless you explain it. Show them that such a phrase may be long and apparently intricate when the modifiers of the appositive include a clause. For example:

> The platypus, *a strange little animal that comes from Australia and can be seen in this country only in zoos,* is considered a mammal even though it lays eggs.

FRAGMENTS Lying lazily on the beach
Built of bamboo
Waiting at the doctor's office
To see a movie

Like subordinate clauses, verbals depend on independent clauses to make their meaning complete.

SENTENCES **Lying lazily on the beach,** I fell asleep.
A house **built of bamboo** cannot withstand a heavy wind.
Waiting at the doctor's office is difficult for me.
They wanted **to see a movie.**

EXERCISE 4. Correcting Sentence Fragments. The following paragraphs contain ten verbal phrases incorrectly used as sentences. Revise the paragraphs, joining the fragments to the proper independent clauses. See Answer Key.

Alice's Adventures in Wonderland is a literary classic. Read by college students as well as elementary-school students. Every child enjoys this story. Missing some of the fun but laughing at many of the comic incidents. When children grow up, they read the story again. Finding more humor in it.

In one of the most famous episodes in the book, Alice finds herself at an unusual tea party. Given by the Hatter. Being very lazy. The Hatter and his companions, the March Hare and the Dormouse, have allowed dirty dishes to pile up all over. The Dormouse tells a long story. Falling asleep in the middle. The March Hare offers Alice wine. Alice is told that there is no wine. After accepting the offer. For a while the three creatures ask her riddles. Having no answers. Then they ignore her. Carrying on a ridiculous conversation among themselves. Finally, Alice manages to escape. Thoroughly exhausted.

The Appositive Phrase

8d. An appositive phrase must not be written as a sentence.

An appositive identifies or explains the noun or pronoun it follows (see pages 375–76). An appositive phrase is an appositive with its modifiers. Neither an appositive nor an appositive phrase can stand alone; it should be set off from the rest of the sentence by a comma or commas.

FRAGMENT The eighteen sailors rowed 3,618 miles to Timor. *An island near Java.*

SENTENCE The eighteen sailors rowed 3,618 miles to Timor, **an island near Java.** [*An island near Java* is an appositive phrase explaining *Timor* and should be joined to the preceding sentence.]

FRAGMENT We had dinner at the Banana Tree. *A restaurant near Key West.*

SENTENCE We had dinner at the Banana Tree, **a restaurant near Key West.** [*A restaurant near Key West* is an appositive phrase explaining *Banana Tree.*]

EXERCISE 5. Correcting Sentence Fragments. Revise the following items, attaching the appositive phrases to the independent clauses from which they have been separated. Change punctuation and capital letters wherever necessary. Some of the appositive phrases belong in the middle of sentences.

1. Rachel and I enjoy playing *Parcheesi.* A game from India. *1. Parcheesi, a*
2. We saw two movies. A science fiction thriller and a western.
3. In 1818 Mary Wollstonecraft Shelley wrote *Frankenstein.* The famous horror novel. 2. movies, a 3. *Frankenstein,* the
4. The Battle of Marathon was won by the Greeks. One of the most famous battles in the history of the world. 4. Marathon, one . . . world, was
5. Coretta King has become as well known as her husband for the advocacy of civil rights. The widow of Dr. Martin Luther King, Jr. 5. King, the . . . Jr., has

REVIEW EXERCISE A. Correcting Fragments. Revise the following items, eliminating fragments by attaching them to independent clauses. See Answer Key.

EXERCISE 5. With a less-advanced class, complete the first item orally and put the answer on the board before you assign the rest of the exercise.

REVIEW EXERCISE A. Advanced students, in addition to revising the items, might be asked to name the kind(s) of fragments found in each one.

RUN-ON SENTENCES
(rule 8e)

Run-on sentences are usually easier for eighth-graders to spot and revise than sentence fragments. Students tend to write run-on sentences when they are working quickly and one idea flows naturally into the next. If they read what they have written aloud, they will usually be able to tell where sentences should end. When you present examples to the class, call on the students who are the best oral readers to read them aloud. More often than not, a student will stumble at the point where there should have been a period—and your teaching point will be made.

You can use the examples in the textbook as the starting point in discussing run-on sentences, but you should eventually show examples taken from your students' own writing.

1. As I was driving home. I saw a turtle on the highway.
2. It had been rolled over on its back by a car. While trying to cross the road.
3. Now it was lying there in the middle of the highway. Helplessly moving its feet back and forth.
4. Because I remembered that a turtle cannot get off its back on a smooth surface. I stopped the car and picked the animal up.
5. It immediately drew its feet and head under its shell. So that I could see nothing more than two eyes. Staring at me from inside the shell.
6. The turtle was a box turtle. A very shy land dweller.
7. I took it to Tall Oaks. My parents' cottage in the mountains. Because I wanted to observe it for a while.
8. Arriving there, I put the turtle down on a rug. Which covers most of the living room floor.
9. The turtle slowly began to stick its feet and head out from its shell. After being still for almost ten minutes.
10. As soon as it felt safe, it crawled very awkwardly but quickly across the rug. Heading for a corner of the room.

RUN-ON SENTENCES

Another common writing fault is the *run-on sentence.* Run-on sentences occur when the writer fails to recognize the end of a sentence and runs on into the next sentence without proper punctuation or, sometimes, without any punctuation at all.

8e. A *run-on sentence* consists of two or more sentences separated only by a comma or by no mark of punctuation.

RUN-ON Romare Bearden is a prominent artist his collage is in the museum.

CORRECTED Romare Bearden is a prominent artist**. H**is collage is in the museum.

RUN-ON Lee Trevino was playing in the golf tournament, I hoped I could go.

CORRECTED Lee Trevino was playing in the golf tournament**.** **I** hoped I could go.

A comma marks a pause in a sentence, not the end of the sentence, and thus should not be used between two sentences.

EXERCISE 6. Revising Run-on Sentences. Revise the following run-ons. Number your paper 1–10. After the proper number, write the last word in the first sentence and place a period after it; then write the first word of the next sentence, beginning it with a capital letter.

EXAMPLE 1. The Virgin Islands' weather is perfect, daytime temperatures are in the 80's year round.
1. *perfect. Daytime*

1. In nineteenth-century England there were two types of English pepper moths one type was all black, and the other had gray and white speckles. 1. moths. One
2. The black variety was extremely rare, most people had only seen speckled pepper moths. 2. rare. Most
3. The moths lived on the bark of surrounding trees, most trees in England had a gray moss covering them. 3. trees. Most
4. The speckled moths blended into this background the birds that ate pepper moths could not see them against the moss.
5. The black moths could be easily seen they were frequently killed by birds. 4. background. The 5. seen. They
6. The Industrial Revolution in England produced many factories, when the smoke and soot created by the factories filled the air, it covered the neighboring trees. 6. factories. When
7. The amount of soot, two tons per square mile, was enough to color the trees black, the speckled moths could now be easily seen by birds searching for food. 7. black. The
8. The black moths blended into the background of the black trees, the birds began to dine on the speckled variety. 8. trees. The
9. Within fifty years, the black variety outnumbered the speckled moths 99 to 1, the advantage of a particular color for protection had completely reversed. 9. 1. The

EXERCISE 6. Decide if this exercise is too easy for your average or above-average class. With a less-advanced class, however, go over the exercise carefully. Since these students do not always heed written punctuation marks in their oral interpretation, read the items aloud yourself to show how they sound when they are incorrectly punctuated.

EXERCISE 7. You may wish to use this exercise to find out which students need extra help. Noticeably poor scores usually will indicate either that students are not trying or that they have serious difficulties with reading (and probably with writing).

10. Other animals use protective coloration certain kinds of fish have the same color as their surroundings and can blend with the background to escape enemies. 10. coloration. Certain

EXERCISE 7. Revising Run-on Sentences. Each of the following passages contains several run-on sentences. You will find the passages hard to read because run-on sentences interfere with the clear expression of ideas. After you have decided where each sentence should end, write the last word of each complete sentence on your paper. Place the appropriate end mark after the word; then write the first word of the next sentence, beginning it with a capital letter.

EXAMPLE 1. *Jest* once had a different meaning than it does today, in medieval times the English used the word to refer to a brave act or the story of such a deed, by the sixteenth century it meant "to jeer or mock" now, of course, a *jest* is a joke.

1. *today. In*
deed. By
mock." Now

1. Our word *humor* has an interesting history, it comes from the Latin word for liquid, in the Middle Ages people believed that four liquids in the body made up one's character, thus a person with too much of one humor might be quite odd or eccentric. 1. history. It, liquid. In, character. Thus
2. Our word *paper* comes from the French word *papier*, this word can be traced back to the Greek *papyros*, which is the name of an Egyptian plant, part of this plant was sliced into strips and then soaked in water, finally, it was pressed and pasted into a writing material that was used by the Egyptians, Greeks, and Romans. 2. papier. This, plant. Part, water. Finally
3. The comma can be traced back to the Greek language, our word *comma* comes from the Greek word *komma*, which means "a piece cut off" when you use a comma, you cut off an expression from the rest of the sentence. 3. language. Our, off." When
4. The word *rigmarole* came from a group of documents called *ragman roll* written in 1291, Scottish lords signed these

documents to prove their loyalty to King Edward I of England since many of the documents were so full of signatures that they were confusing and hard to read, the word *rigmarole* came to mean "a series of confused or foolish statements."

5. Have you ever wondered about the origin of the word *sandwich*, it came into use during the eighteenth century, John Montagu, the Earl of Sandwich, was addicted to gambling, so addicted that he often would not stop for his meals, during one of his twenty-four-hour gambling sessions, he instructed someone to bring him slices of bread with roast beef inserted between them because the Earl of Sandwich did not want to stop gambling long enough to go to dinner, the world gained the sandwich. 4. 1291. Scottish, England. 5. *sandwich*? It, century. John, meals. During, them. Because

REVIEW EXERCISE B. Identifying Sentences, Fragments, and Run-ons. Some of the following expressions are sentences. Others are fragments or run-ons. Number your paper 1–20. After the proper number, write *S* (sentence), *F* (fragment), or *R* (run-on). Be prepared to tell how you would correct the fragments and run-ons.

1. Medusa and her two sisters were three horrible monsters who had at one time been beautiful women. 1. S
2. The most beautiful of the three, Medusa, was very proud, she boasted that she was even more beautiful than the goddess Athena. 2. R
3. Because of her pride, she and her two sisters were turned into monsters. 3. S
4. Who had hissing serpents for hair. 4. F
5. No one dared look upon Medusa and her sisters. 5. S
6. Because anyone who did turned to stone. 6. F
7. Lying all about them were stones that had once been men. 7. S
8. Medusa and her two sisters menaced the land for years finally they were challenged by Perseus. 8. R
9. A young, handsome warrior. 9. F
10. Having been given magic weapons by the gods. 10. F

REVIEW EXERCISE B. This exercise reviews the material covered in the chapter. The students must determine if groups of words are complete sentences, fragments, or run-ons. Decide ahead of time whether you will have them revise fragments and run-ons.

REVIEW EXERCISE C. This exercise requires original writing, emphasizing the skills covered in this chapter.

Additional Practice

Teacher's Resource Book, Worksheet pages 64–77, Alternative Worksheet pages (for less-advanced students) 528–29

Testing

Teaching Tests booklet, pages 1–4, 9–10, 13–18
Teacher's Resource Book, Test pages 371–74, 403–404, 407–412

11. Perseus set out to kill Medusa. 11. S
12. The only mortal one of the three sisters. 12. F 13. F
13. When he approached the area in which the monsters lived.
14. Perseus put on a magic cap that made him invisible, he held up a shield that had been given to him by Athena. 14. R
15. Studying the reflection of Medusa and her sisters in his shield. 15. F
16. Perseus slowly approached the monsters.
17. Luckily, they were sleeping. 17. S 18. R
18. Still using the shield as a mirror, he cut off Medusa's head with a single stroke he put the head into a special pouch. 16. S
19. Which had also been given to him by Athena. 19. F
20. The other sisters awoke but could not see him, therefore he escaped with the head of Medusa. 20. R

REVIEW EXERCISE C. Revising Fragments and Run-ons in Your Own Writing. Pretend that you are writing to a person who has never seen a comic strip. Write a paragraph in which you describe one of the main characters in your favorite comic strip. After you have finished writing the paragraph, read your sentences aloud, one by one, to be sure that you have not carelessly written a fragment or a run-on. Make any necessary corrections.
Answers will vary.

CHAPTER 9

Writing Effective Sentences

SENTENCE COMBINING AND REVISING

As your writing assignments become more demanding, you should develop the habit of writing at least two drafts of a composition. In the first draft, express what you have to say. In the revised draft, concentrate on writing clearly and on eliminating faults in style. Watch especially for groups of choppy, abrupt sentences and for rambling sentences held together by a string of conjunctions. Such sentences, while occasionally effective, become tiresome if used too often. This chapter will show how to recognize such poorly written sentences and how to revise them.

CORRECTING A CHOPPY STYLE BY COMBINING SENTENCES

Short sentences are often effective in a composition, but a long series of short sentences tends to irritate readers. They slow the reader down and make it difficult to focus on what is being said. Such choppy sentences are often similar in construction and thus are monotonous in their effect. The following passage of choppy sentences would irritate most readers.

Chapter Overview

Many eighth-graders still rely almost entirely on two kinds of sentences in their written work:

1. Simple subject-first sentences ("Our science class is studying rocks. We are going to visit a stone quarry. It is near Douglastown.")
2. Compound sentences that are little more than a series of simple subject-first sentences strung together with *and*'s and *so*'s ("Our science class is studying rocks and so we are going to visit a stone quarry, and it is near Douglastown.")

Although most students recognize that sentences like these sound childish, they may not know how to improve them. This chapter takes up specific methods of sentence improvement one at a time and provides separate exercises for each method.

Chapter Objective

Students will write effective sentences through sentence combining and revising activities.

PRESENTING THE CHAPTER

LESS-ADVANCED STUDENTS Students who write in a choppy style or a rambling style can usually learn to improve their sentences, but they may not have a firm enough grasp of grammatical ideas to benefit from the specific suggestions in this chapter. You may wish to present choppy style simply as "writing that needs more connecting words," and rambling style as "writing that has too many connecting words." *(See listing of Alternative Worksheets on page 262.)*

ADVANCED STUDENTS Use this chapter to help advanced students become more conscious of style in their own writing.

CORRECTING A CHOPPY STYLE BY COMBINING SENTENCES (rules 9a–9g)

Using the exercises here, you can assist students systematically in producing more complex, more mature sentences. Since the exercises provide the content of sentences to be improved, student attention is focused on problems of structure.

Introduce this section by putting on the board a sample passage, such as the one on text page 242, which consists entirely of simple subject-first sentences. Ask the class whether the passage seems to be "grown-up" writing or whether it sounds like something for (or by) elementary-school children. Then have students suggest revisions that will combine these sentences. Write their combined sentences on the board. When they have produced a revised version that satisfies them, have them point out the different techniques employed in the revision. List the techniques on the board as they are given.

> Victor visited Williamsburg, Virginia. Marsha also went. The visit took place during the summer. They both visited for the first time. They toured the buildings together. Marsha was studying the antiques collection. Victor was examining the architecture. They began to share each other's interest. The architecture was from the colonial period. The antiques were from the colonial period.

By combining sentences that are closely related, the passage could be revised as follows:

> During the summer, Victor and Marsha visited Williamsburg, Virginia, for the first time. As they toured the buildings together, Marsha was studying the antiques collection, but Victor was examining the architecture. They began to share each other's interest because both the architecture and the antiques were from the colonial period.

Several methods have been used in revising the passage. For example, the first four sentences in the original version have been combined into one sentence containing a compound subject and two prepositional phrases. You should be familiar with ways to combine short, related sentences.

9a. Combine short, related sentences by inserting adjectives, adverbs, or prepositional phrases.[1]

WEAK At half time, the coach gave the players confidence in themselves.
The players had been discouraged.

BETTER At half time, the coach gave the discouraged players confidence in themselves. [The adjective *discouraged* in the second sentence is inserted into the first sentence.]

WEAK In the second half, the team improved. They improved rapidly.

BETTER In the second half, the team improved rapidly. [The adverb *rapidly* in the second sentence is inserted into the first sentence.]

[1] If you need to review adjectives, adverbs, and prepositional phrases, see Chapters 11 and 12.

EXERCISE 1. You may want to review the rule on commas separating adjectives, text page 533, before assigning this exercise.

WEAK The solar-energy panels were installed yesterday. They are on the garage roof.

BETTER The solar-energy panels were installed yesterday on the garage roof. [The prepositional phrase *on the garage roof* in the second sentence is inserted into the first sentence.]

When you join short sentences by inserting adjectives, adverbs, or prepositional phrases, be sure the new sentence reads smoothly. (Review the rule concerning commas separating adjectives on page 533.)

EXERCISE 1. Combining Sentences by Inserting Adjectives, Adverbs, or Prepositional Phrases. Combine each group of short, related sentences into one sentence by inserting adjectives, adverbs, or prepositional phrases. There may be more than one correct way to combine the sentences. Add commas where they are necessary. Answers will vary.

EXAMPLE 1. The bird sings in the cage.
The bird is yellow.
It sings sweetly.
The cage is by the window.
1. *The yellow bird sings sweetly in the cage by the window.*

1. Conservation laws protect wildlife.
The laws are strong.
They protect wildlife inside state parks.
1. Strong conservation laws protect wildlife inside the state parks.
2. We will make the decorations.
We will do this shortly.
The decorations are for Flag Day.
2. Shortly, we will make the decorations for Flag Day.
3. Miguel wrote his letter.
He wrote it on Saturday.
It was a letter to the mayor.
3. Miguel wrote his letter to the mayor on Saturday.
4. Poland has one of the tallest structures.
It is one of the tallest structures on earth.
Poland is in northeastern Europe.
4. Poland, in Northeastern Europe, has one of the tallest structures on earth.

Using Participial Phrases (rule 9b)

Use the examples in the text to show students how two related sentences can be combined by making one of the sentences a participial phrase. Emphasize that a participial phrase must be near the noun or pronoun it modifies to prevent confusion.

5. The two parties argued their cases.
   The parties were angry.
   They argued in front of the judge.

5. The two angry parties argued their cases in front of the judge.

9b. Combine closely related sentences by using participial phrases.

A participle is a verb form that acts as an adjective, modifying a noun or a pronoun. A participial phrase (see page 363) is a group of related words that contains a participle. In the following examples, all the words in boldfaced type are part of the participial phrase.

EXAMPLES **Grinning from ear to ear,** Michelle trotted off the stage. [*Grinning* is a present participle.]

Battered by the high seas, the small ship limped into port. [*Battered* is a past participle.]

Two closely related sentences can be combined by making one of the sentences a participial phrase.

EXAMPLE The librarian answered our question.
He was whispering in low tones.

Whispering in low tones, the librarian answered our question.

A participial phrase must be placed close to the noun or pronoun it modifies. Otherwise, the phrase may confuse the reader.

MISPLACED Caught in the chicken coop, the farmer cornered the fox.

IMPROVED The farmer cornered the fox caught in the chicken coop.

> ☞ **NOTE** Use a comma after a participial phrase that begins a sentence.

EXAMPLE Embarrassed by our loss, our team sat in the locker room.

EXERCISE 2. Combining Sentences by Using a Participial Phrase. Combine each of the following groups of sentences into one sentence by using a participial phrase. Insert the participial phrase in the correct place and add commas where they are necessary.

EXAMPLE 1. The class worked quickly.
They divided up the job.
1. *Dividing up the job, the class worked quickly.* or *Working quickly, the class divided up the job.*

1. The referee signaled a score.
   She was standing beneath the basket.
2. The secretary called a meeting.
   He was troubled by the press reports.
3. The audience applauded loudly.
   They were interrupting the singer.
4. The town is safe and secure.
   It nestles beneath two mountains.
5. I was puzzled by the rules of the game.
   I decided not to play.

9c. Combine short, related sentences by using appositive phrases.

Appositive phrases (see page 376) are useful for explaining or identifying nouns or pronouns. The following sentence contains an appositive phrase in boldfaced type.

EXAMPLE At the movie theater I saw Mrs. Jacovina, **our next-door neighbor.**

Two related sentences can be combined by using an appositive phrase.

TWO SENTENCES Marlene won the competition.
She is an excellent tennis player.

ONE SENTENCE Marlene, an excellent tennis player, won the competition.

EXERCISE 2. You may choose to have students work together in pairs or small groups. Then have one person from each group write the group's answers on the board.

Answers: Exercise 2
(Answers may vary.)

1. Standing beneath the basket, the referee signaled a score.
2. Troubled by the press reports, the secretary called a meeting.
3. The audience applauded loudly, interrupting the singer.
4. Nestled beneath two mountains, the town is safe and secure.
5. Puzzled by the rules of the game, I decided not to play.

Using Appositive Phrases (rule 9c)

Review the appositive and the appositive phrase (pages 375–77) before you assign the next exercise. Make sure your students understand how to set off an appositive with commas.

EXERCISE 3. This exercise should be easy for most of your students. You can check the answers orally, but make sure students have used commas correctly.

Answers: Exercise 3

1. Lena Jackson, our new doctor, lived in Japan before moving here.
2. I finally spoke to Mr. Powell, the store manager.
3. Joan made the lasagna, the most popular dish at the picnic.
4. Bob, the sportswriter for our newspaper, was at the last baseball game.
5. *Carnival of Autumn,* a painting by Marsden Hartley, is in the Museum of Fine Arts in Boston.

Using Compound Subjects and Verbs (rules 9d and 9e)

Two other ways of combining short, related sentences are by (1) writing a single sentence with a compound subject and (2) writing a single sentence with a compound verb. When using a compound subject, students should be reminded that the subject must agree with the verb in the new sentence. When using a compound verb, students may need help deciding which connecting words best convey the meaning of the new sentence.

EXERCISE 3. Combining Sentences by Using an Appositive Phrase. Combine each group of sentences by using an appositive phrase. Place the phrase next to the noun or pronoun it explains or modifies. Put commas at the beginning and end of each appositive phrase to set it off from the rest of the sentence.

EXAMPLE 1. Karen bought me a sweater.
She is my good friend.
1. *Karen, my good friend, bought me a sweater.*

1. Lena Jackson lived in Japan before moving here.
   She is our new doctor.
2. I finally spoke to Mr. Powell.
   He is the store manager.
3. Joan made the lasagna.
   It was the most popular dish at the picnic.
4. Bob was at the last baseball game.
   He is the sportswriter for our newspaper.
5. *Carnival of Autumn* is in the Museum of Fine Arts in Boston.
   It is a painting by Marsden Hartley.

Another method of combining short, related sentences is to join the subjects to make a compound subject or to join the verbs to make a compound verb.

9d. Combine short, related sentences by using compound subjects.

A compound subject (see page 278) consists of two or more simple subjects joined by a conjunction and having the same verb.

EXAMPLE This **table** and that **chair** are ready for the movers.

Often two short sentences may contain similar verbs but different subjects.

EXAMPLE The radio report predicted rain.
The television news also predicted it.

You can combine these short sentences by writing a single sentence with a compound subject.

EXAMPLE **Both the radio report and the television news** predicted rain.

Words that connect (called *conjunctions*) a compound subject are *and, or, both—and, either—or,* and *neither—nor.* The choice of the conjunction depends on the meaning of the sentence.

Compound subjects must agree with the verb in the sentence.

EXAMPLES Paul has missed the bus.
His sister has missed it also.

Paul **and** his sister have missed the bus. [Subjects joined by *and* or *both—and* take a plural verb.]

An almanac gives the answer.
An atlas gives the answer.

Either an almanac **or** an atlas gives the answer. [Singular subjects joined by *or, either—or,* or *neither—nor* take a singular verb.]

EXERCISE 4. Combining Sentences by Using a Compound Subject. Combine each pair of sentences by writing one sentence with a compound subject. Be sure the subject and the verb agree in number. Answers will vary.

EXAMPLE 1. Arlene will not be at the party tomorrow.
Margery will not be there either.
1. *Neither Arlene nor Margery will be at the party tomorrow.*

1. ~~Rugby is~~ played in England. 1. Rugby and soccer are
~~Soccer is played there also.~~
2. My sister went to the zoo. 2. and I
~~I went there with her.~~
3. The sun ~~is a reliable source~~ of energy. 3. and coal are reliable sources
~~Coal is another reliable source.~~
4. ~~Engineering~~ might be Teng's career choice. 4. Either engineering or medicine
~~Medicine might be his career choice instead.~~
5. Cheating ~~is~~ not allowed in class. 5. and whispering are
~~Whispering is not allowed either.~~

EXERCISE 4. You may want to help the students combine the first two sentences. Focus on agreement of subject and verb in the newly formed sentence.

EXERCISE 5. Be sure to point out that the choice of connecting words depends upon the meaning of the sentence.

9e. Combine short, related sentences by using compound verbs.

A compound verb (see page 278) consists of two or more verbs that have the same subject and are joined by a connecting word. In the following example, the compound verb is printed in boldface.

EXAMPLE The senator **voted** for the conservation law but **lost** the election.

You can combine two sentences by writing one sentence with a compound verb.

EXAMPLE He backed the car down the driveway.
He lurched to a stop in the street.

He **backed** the car down the driveway and **lurched** to a stop in the street.

The connecting words used most frequently to join compound verbs are *and, but, or, either—or, neither—nor,* and *both—and.* The choice of the conjunction (or connecting word) depends on the sentence meaning.

EXERCISE 5. Combining Sentences by Using a Compound Verb. Combine each pair of short sentences into a single sentence with one subject and a compound verb. Use appropriate connecting words to clearly express the meaning.

EXAMPLE 1. In February Teresa visited her grandparents in Puerto Rico.
She also toured Everglades Park in Florida.
1. *In February Teresa both visited her grandparents in Puerto Rico and toured Everglades Park in Florida.*

1. He repaired the bicycle ~~yesterday.~~ 1. yesterday and raced
~~He raced~~ with it today.
2. I had heard of ~~polecats.~~ 2. polecats but had never
~~I had never~~ seen one before.
3. The guard did not hear the car ~~approaching.~~ 3. approaching and was
~~She was~~ taken completely by surprise.

4. The train was late leaving the ~~station~~. 4. station but still
~~It still~~ arrived on time.
5. Mr. Verris casually crossed the hall. 5. hall, entered the room,
~~He entered the room~~ and quietly handed out the tests.

REVIEW EXERCISE A. Revising a Passage by Combining Sentences. The following passage contains several short, related sentences. Revise the passage, combining the sentences by the methods you have learned thus far. Do not change the meaning of the original. Add commas where they are necessary.
See Answer Key.

The Majestic River runs between the mountains. It is a deep river. It runs swiftly. The mountains are high. Lush, green vegetation crowds the river's shores. The vegetation also grows up the mountain slopes. Campers fish in the river's pools. Day hikers also fish there. The pools are clear. The pools are beneath the rapids. Canoes can navigate the river. Rafts can also do this. The rafts are rubber. Canoes and rafts can navigate the river from High Falls to Bolt's Landing.

9f. Combine short, related sentences by making them into a compound sentence.

A compound sentence is really two or more simple sentences joined together. When simple sentences are joined together in a compound sentence, they are called independent clauses. (See pages 404–406 for more information on independent clauses and compound sentences.) The following sentence has two independent clauses.

EXAMPLE Tractor drivers (S) bulldozed (V) a barrier around the forest fire, and helicopter crews (S) drenched (V) the fire with chemicals.

Two simple sentences closely related in meaning may be joined into one compound sentence.

EXAMPLE The quarterback threw a long pass.
A defender intercepted the ball.

REVIEW EXERCISE A. Having students combine the sentences in this paragraph will show you how well they have understood rules 9a–9e.

Using Compound Sentences (rule 9f)

Note: Since many eighth-graders already overuse compound sentences, some teachers may want to omit this section and proceed directly to the work with complex sentences.

Students often fail to realize that ideas must be closely related if they are to be combined in a compound sentence. A board illustration will clarify this point:

I like fried chicken, and my birthday is next week.

Have students tell you that the sentence is compound because it contains two independent clauses connected by *and*. Then ask them whether this compound sentence is a sensible one. They should see that since the two clauses are not related, the resulting sentence is ridiculous. Have them suggest a more logical compound sentence, or write the following example:

I like fried chicken, and my mother will serve it for my birthday dinner next week.

They should see that when the ideas are more closely related, the combined clauses make a logical compound sentence.

EXERCISE 6. This exercise can be done orally to emphasize that different conjunctions affect meaning: *And* has the connotation of *too* or *in addition to; but* suggests contrast or opposites; *or* signifies a choice.

The quarterback threw a long pass, but a defender intercepted the ball.

The conjunctions (connecting words) used to join the parts of a compound sentence are usually *and, but, or,* or *nor.* The choice of the conjunction depends on the meaning of the sentence.

Be sure that the ideas you connect in the compound sentence are closely related and equal in importance. If you attempt to correct a choppy passage by connecting unrelated ideas, the result will be even worse than the original choppy version.

UNRELATED IDEAS I read the entire television schedule. I like to watch news documentaries.

RELATED IDEAS I read the entire television schedule. I could not find even one interesting program.

UNEQUAL IDEAS Lynn was elected class president. Cara didn't vote.

EQUAL IDEAS Lynn was elected class president. Peter became secretary.

NOTE Remember to put a comma before *and, but, or,* and *nor* when they join independent clauses (see page 534).

EXAMPLE Alice brought her new water skis, and Tina borrowed her parents' ski boat.

EXERCISE 6. Combining Sentences by Making Them into a Compound Sentence. Most of the following items consist of two or more closely related ideas. Combine these ideas into a single compound sentence, using *and, but,* or *or* as the connecting word. Add commas where they are necessary. A few items contain unrelated or unequal ideas. In such cases, write *U* after the proper number on your paper to show that the ideas are better expressed in two separate sentences.

1. Other nations use the metric ~~system~~. The United States has decided to use the same system. **1. system, and the**

2. International trade depends on a uniform system of weights and measures. 2. U
   The United States leads the world in scientific research.
3. The United States is slowly converting to the metric ~~system~~. ~~This~~ process is called metrification. 3. system, and this
4. We can resist the change in systems until the last possible ~~moment~~. 4. moment, or we
   ~~We~~ can learn to use the metric system now.
5. The metric system is actually very easy to use.
   A decimeter is one tenth of a meter. 5. U
6. Metric weights are based on the ~~kilogram~~. 6. kilogram, and metric
   ~~Metric~~ lengths use the meter as the basic unit.
7. Many citizens of the United States still use the old system of ~~measurement~~. 7. measurement, but many
   ~~Many~~ professions and corporations have switched to the metric system.
8. All metric measurements are based on the number 10. 8. U
   Some baseball parks measure their distances in meters.
9. Counting by tens is second nature to most ~~people~~. 9. people, but the
   ~~The~~ metric system still seems complicated to many.
10. Metrification will be a difficult ~~process~~. 10. process, but careful
    ~~Careful~~ planning will help.

Compound sentences can combine equal items from two separate sentences. When combining unequal ideas, however, it is best to use complex sentences.

9g. Combine short, choppy sentences into a complex sentence. Put one idea into a subordinate clause.

A complex sentence (see page 408) has an independent clause and at least one subordinate clause.

(1) Use an adjective clause to combine sentences.

An adjective clause (see page 386) is a group of words containing a subject and verb that, like an adjective, modifies a noun or a

Using an Adjective Clause (rule 9g–1)

Write on the board a few pairs of short sentences that can be combined into complex sentences containing adjective clauses:

1. I have a dog. His name is Stuart.
2. We looked at a new house. It is located on Young Street.

Before the students start to combine these short sentences, review with them the following facts about adjective clauses:

1. An adjective clause must contain a subject and predicate.
2. An adjective clause must modify a noun or pronoun.
3. An adjective clause usually begins with a relative pronoun (*who, whose, that, which, whom*).
4. An adjective clause must be subordinate in meaning to the main part of the sentence.

As each student combines a pair of sentences, have someone explain how the sentences are combined and why the resulting sentence is correct. If a student combines the sentences in an incorrect way, have others point out the errors. For example, a student may say, "I have a dog, and his name is Stuart," or, "My dog's name is Stuart." Have students identify the first of these as a compound and the second as a simple sentence. Point out that, even though there is nothing wrong with either of the sentences, they do not follow the directions to use an adjective clause.

pronoun. In the following example, the adjective clause is in boldfaced type.

EXAMPLE The girl **who just waved to me** is my first cousin. [The adjective clause modifies *girl.*]

Adjective clauses begin with one of the relative pronouns —*who, whom, whose, which,* or *that* (see page 387). Study the following examples of the relative pronoun used in a sentence.

EXAMPLES Mr. Allen praised Tom, **who** had written an excellent paper.
Mr. Bingley gave a slide show, **which** the entire class enjoyed.
The answer **that** she gave was an abrupt "no."

When two sentences are closely related, the second sentence may help to modify a noun, pronoun, or adjective in the first sentence.

EXAMPLE Nora played her favorite record.
I had given it to her. [This sentence modifies *record* in the first sentence.]

You can combine these two sentences by turning the second sentence into an adjective clause and inserting it into the first sentence.

Nora played her favorite record, **which I had given to her.**

> ☞ **NOTE** Use commas to set off adjective clauses that are not essential to the basic meaning of the sentence. Do not use commas with clauses that are essential to the meaning. (See page 536.)

EXAMPLES This is my favorite coin**, which I bought four years ago.** [nonessential clause]
This is the coin **that I told you about.** [essential clause]

EXERCISE 7. Combining Sentences by Using an Adjective Clause. Combine each of the following groups of sentences into a single sentence by putting one of the ideas into an adjective clause. Use commas where they are necessary.

Answers will vary somewhat.

EXAMPLE 1. Wendy Quon won the championship.
She is a great athlete.
1. *Wendy Quon, who is a great athlete, won the championship.*

1. The motion was passed by the Student Council.
~~I had stated it~~. 1. that I had stated
2. Julie dived in to help Jan. 2. , who is the best swimmer in our crowd,
~~Julie is the best swimmer in our crowd~~.
3. I helped with the campaign of Senator ~~Blake~~. 3. Blake, who
~~He~~ was the best candidate for the office.
4. "The Tell-Tale ~~Heart~~" is my favorite story. 4. Heart," which was written by Edgar Allan Poe,
~~It was written by Edgar Allan Poe~~.
5. She gave us some ~~advice~~. 5. advice that
~~It~~ hindered more than it helped.

(2) Use an adverb clause to combine sentences.

An adverb clause (see page 390) is a group of words containing a subject and verb that, like an adverb, modifies a verb, an adjective, or an adverb.

EXAMPLE She sings **whenever she is alone.**

Adverb clauses, like adverbs, may tell *how, when, where, why, to what extent,* or *under what condition* an action is done. They begin with a subordinating conjunction. In the example, *whenever* is a subordinating conjunction. Study the following list:

Subordinating Conjunctions

after	before	than	whenever
although	if	unless	where
as	since	until	wherever
because	so that	when	while

EXERCISE 7. Have the class do the first item orally before you assign the others as written work.

Using an Adverb Clause (rule 9g–2)

Teach the use of adverb clauses the same way you taught the use of adjective clauses: Review the characteristics of the adverb clause, and give the class pairs of sentences that can be combined by turning one sentence into an adverb clause.

For more information on subordinate clauses, see Chapter 15.

EXERCISE 8. Do the first item orally, writing students' answers on the board. Go over the punctuation of introductory adverb clauses (page 538) at this time. Then assign the rest of the exercise as written work.

Examine these two sentences:

The conductor stopped the orchestra.
The violins were not in tune.

You can combine these two sentences by turning the second sentence into an adverb clause and inserting it into the first sentence.

The conductor stopped the orchestra because the violins were not in tune.

When you combine two short sentences by turning one of them into an adverb clause, be careful to choose the correct subordinating conjunction. A poorly chosen conjunction will show a false or meaningless relationship between clauses. For example, a number of subordinating conjunctions could be used to join the following two sentences, but not all of them would show a relationship that makes sense.

EXAMPLE Mario is industrious.
He receives high grades.
UNCLEAR Unless Mario is industrious, he receives high grades.
CLEAR **Since** Mario is industrious, he receives high grades.

☞ NOTE A comma is used after an adverb clause placed at the beginning of a sentence.

EXAMPLE Although her head ached, she continued dancing.

EXERCISE 8. Combining Sentences by Using an Adverb Clause. Combine each of the following groups of sentences into a single sentence by putting one idea into an adverb clause. Refer to the subordinating conjunctions on pages 253 and 392.
Answers will vary. Suggested answers are given.

EXAMPLE 1. Rosa saw the fox near the tree.
She photographed it.
1. *When Rosa saw the fox near the tree, she photographed it.*

1. ~~Her ankle pained her sharply~~. 1. Although her ankle pained her sharply, she
   ~~She~~ She kept on playing.
2. ~~He saw the truck rolling down the hill toward him~~. 2. When he saw the truck rolling down the hill toward him, he
   ~~He~~ jumped onto the curb.
3. Jane's mother motioned to ~~us~~. 3. us as we
   ~~We~~ walked across the street.
4. Cathy held the tent up ~~straight~~. 4. straight while Jeannette
   ~~Jeannette~~ hammered down the stakes.
5. ~~Norm forgot the time of the party~~.
   ~~We~~ were late. 5. Because Norm forgot the time of the party, we

REVIEW EXERCISE B. Using Sentence-Combining Methods. Combine each of the following groups of sentences into one smooth, clear sentence by using the sentence-combining methods you have learned. Do not change the meaning of the sentences you combine. Add commas where they are necessary.

1. No one has ever solved the mystery.
   It is the mystery of the ship *Mary Celeste.*
   It set sail in 1872 bound for Europe.
   It set sail from New York.
2. The ship was found.
   It was floating in the Atlantic Ocean.
   It was found without a crew.
3. The crew may have been murdered.
   The crew may have deserted.
   No sign of a struggle was found.
4. A child's toys lay undisturbed.
   They lay on the bed.
   It was the captain's bed.
   The toys suggest that the child left suddenly.
5. People still look for clues.
   These people are curious.
   The clues may explain the crew's disappearance.

REVIEW EXERCISE C. Revising a Paragraph by Eliminating Choppy Sentences. Revise the following paragraph to elimi-

REVIEW EXERCISES B and C. Emphasize the importance of retaining the intended meaning of each sentence group. Go over the revisions orally.

Answers: Review Exercise B
(Answers will vary.)

1. No one has ever solved the mystery of the ship *Mary Celeste,* which set sail from New York in 1872 bound for Europe.
2. The ship was found floating in the Atlantic Ocean without a crew.
3. The crew may have been murdered, although there was no sign of a struggle, or they may have deserted.
4. A child's toys lay undisturbed on the captain's bed, suggesting that the child had left suddenly.
5. Curious people still look for clues that may explain the crew's disappearance.

CORRECTING A MONOTONOUS STYLE (rule 9h)

The exercises in this section encourage students to vary sentence beginnings. Unlike revisions that combine short sentences into compound or complex sentences, these revisions do not necessarily promote clarity: They provide stylistic variety. In presenting the section, review grammatical terms or punctuation rules that are relevant, but avoid turning your presentation into a grammar lesson. Simply emphasize that *a sentence need not begin with the subject*. Then offer grammatical alternatives.

nate choppy sentences, but be careful not to change the meaning of the original paragraph. Use the sentence-combining methods you have learned. Add commas as necessary. Answers will vary.

> Robert Frost wrote many poems. Frost grew up in New England. Many of his poems are about the countryside in winter. One poem has been popular with students. It is titled "Stopping by Woods on a Snowy Evening." In this poem a traveler pauses on a journey. The traveler pauses for a moment. The journey is by horse and wagon. The traveler watches the snow. It is falling in the woods. The woods are far from the nearest village. People disagree about the poem's meaning. They enjoy it immensely. It seems to touch on a deep truth about life. It describes a common experience.

CORRECTING A MONOTONOUS STYLE

If you look at the first passage on page 242, you will notice that each sentence in the paragraph begins in the same way, with a subject followed by a verb. In the revised passage, however, each sentence begins differently. The first sentence begins with a prepositional phrase, the second sentence begins with a subordinate clause, and so on. This was done to avoid monotony.

9h. Correct a monotonous style by varying the beginnings of sentences.

Young writers often write a paragraph of sentences all of which begin with the subject. To avoid such monotony, you can revise some sentences to begin with a modifier: an adverb, an adverb clause, a prepositional phrase, or a participial phrase. You will not need to revise them all, however. If all the sentences were changed to begin with an adverb, for example, the passage would be as monotonous as before. Moreover, you should never write an unclear or awkward sentence merely for the sake of variety. If a sentence sounds best with the subject first, you should leave it that way and try to revise some of the sentences near it, if necessary.

EXERCISE 9. This exercise asks students to change word order. Review the use of the comma after introductory expressions (pages 538 and 539) before assigning the exercise.

(1) Vary sentences by beginning them with adverbs.

EXAMPLES She paid her debts willingly.
Willingly she paid her debts.

She said sorrowfully, "We're leaving."
Sorrowfully she said, "We're leaving."

(2) Vary sentences by beginning them with adverb clauses.[1]

EXAMPLES The pain eased after the tooth was pulled.
After the tooth was pulled, the pain eased.

He was not afraid to fight, although he was small.
Although he was small, he was not afraid to fight.

EXERCISE 9. Beginning Sentences with an Adverb or Adverb Clause. Revise the following sentences by beginning them with either an adverb or an adverb clause.

1. She agreed to his proposal reluctantly. 1. Reluctantly, she
2. She lived in Mexico before she moved here. 2. Before . . . here, she
3. Tim was polite although they had angered him. 3. Although . . . him, Tim
4. She will wash the car if you wish. 4. If you wish, she
5. She wisely pretended not to hear. 5. Wisely, she pretended

(3) Vary sentences by beginning them with prepositional phrases.[2]

EXAMPLES A portrait of our mother hung on the wall.
On the wall hung a portrait of our mother.

A police officer sat in the car.
In the car sat a police officer.

Sometimes when you move a prepositional phrase, you may want to change the position of the verb also.

EXAMPLE A kettle hung above the fire.
Above the fire hung a kettle.

[1] See pages 390–92 for an explanation of adverb clauses.
[2] See page 354 for an explanation of the prepositional phrase.

EXERCISE 10. This exercise gives students an opportunity to begin *original* sentences with prepositional and participial phrases.

EXERCISE 11. Remind students to check the punctuation of their revised sentences.

Answers: Exercise 11
(Answers may vary somewhat.)

1. After she finishes her homework, Alice practices the piano.
2. To annoy me, she sang in her shrill voice.
3. Jumping from his chair, the rainmaker smiled with satisfaction as he pointed at the dark clouds massing overhead.
4. Around his neck the general wore a Medal of Honor.
5. Finally her parents said that she could go hiking on Saturday afternoon if she finished painting the fence.

(4) Vary sentences by beginning with participial phrases.[1]

A participial phrase is usually separated from the rest of the sentence by a comma.

EXAMPLES The fielder, **leaping up,** caught the ball.
Leaping up, the fielder caught the ball.
They stared at each other in bewilderment, **stunned by the news.**
Stunned by the news, they stared at each other in bewilderment.

(5) Vary sentences by beginning them with infinitive phrases.[2]

EXAMPLES **To get to Homer's Fish Market,** turn left at the next corner.
To stay on the team, you must attend every game.

EXERCISE 10. Writing Sentences with Introductory Phrases. Use the following prepositional and participial phrases to begin sentences of your own. Answers will vary.

1. On her day off,
2. Resisting temptation,
3. In shocked surprise,
4. Inside the old valise,
5. Delighted with the new coat,

EXERCISE 11. Beginning Sentences with an Adverb, a Phrase, or a Clause. All of the following sentences begin with the subject. For the sake of variety, revise them with an adverb, a phrase, or a clause at the beginning.

1. Alice practices the piano after she finishes her homework.
2. She sang in her shrill voice to annoy me.
3. The rainmaker, jumping from his chair, smiled with satisfaction as he pointed at the dark clouds massing overhead.
4. The general wore a Medal of Honor around his neck.
5. Her parents said, finally, that she could go hiking on Saturday afternoon if she finished painting the fence.

[1] See page 363 for an explanation of the participial phrase.
[2] See page 371 for an explanation of infinitive phrases.

REVIEW EXERCISE D. Combining Sentences; Varying Sentence Beginnings. Revise choppy and monotonous sentences in the following paragraphs by combining short sentences into longer sentences and by varying the beginnings of sentences. It may not be necessary to revise every sentence. Your aim should be a series of sentences that are clear, show variety, and are pleasing to read. Answers will vary.

A lens is different from an ordinary pane of glass. A pane of glass has a flat surface. A lens is curved. Rays of light go through a pane of glass without much change. Rays of light are bent, or refracted, in a lens. This refraction may change both the shape and the size of an image. The curve of the lens determines the size of the image. A concave lens curves inward. It is called a reducing glass. A convex lens curves outward. It is a magnifying glass. Lenses often combine the qualities of a concave and a convex lens. Lenses may be concave on one side and convex on the other. A lens may also have one flat surface. A planoconcave lens is flat on one side and concave on the other, for example.

An optical lens must be made from glass of high quality. It must be manufactured by highly trained experts. Optical glass is first tested for flaws. It is then molded into discs. A disc is first ground roughly, then precisely, to give it the correct shape. It is finally polished with ferric oxide. This substance is called rouge by glassmakers.

Two or more lenses are combined in a microscope so that we can see very small objects. One lens is called the objective. It produces the primary image. The second lens is the eyepiece, or ocular. It magnifies the primary image. A microscope is judged not only by its magnifying power. It is also judged by its resolving power. This is its power to show separation between things that are very close together.

CORRECTING RAMBLING SENTENCES

Sometimes you may try to avoid a choppy style by stringing many short sentences together, using the conjunctions *and, but,* and *so*

REVIEW EXERCISE D. Be sure to allow class time for a discussion of students' revisions. You may want to read aloud some good examples of revised sentence groups so that students can "hear" the improved style.

CORRECTING RAMBLING SENTENCES (rule 9i)

Requiring students to proofread their papers carefully before handing them in is often the best attack on rambling sentences. Most eighth-graders find the fault easy to spot and to correct.

EXERCISE 12. If only a few of your students still write in this style, you might assign this exercise and the preceding explanation as individual homework.

to join them. Such rambling sentences are just as irritating and monotonous to read as short, choppy sentences. Learn to avoid them in your writing.

9i. Correct rambling sentences by combining ideas and avoiding the overuse of *and, but,* and *so.*

Since rambling sentences are usually choppy sentences joined by conjunctions, the methods of correcting choppy sentences may also be applied to rambling sentences. Some of the clauses can be combined into compound or complex sentences. Study the following rambling sentence to see how it was revised.

RAMBLING I saw a television program last night, and it was about invaders from another planet and my little brother Ted became frightened so Mom calmed him down and told him that there is little evidence of life on other planets but that there may be life on Mars but few people believe that life exists there either.

REVISED Last night I saw a television program which was about invaders from another planet. When my younger brother Ted became frightened, Mom calmed him down. She told Ted that there is little evidence of life on other planets. Mom added that there may be life on Mars but few people believe that life exists there either.

As with choppy sentences, the first step in revising a rambling sentence is to recognize it as bad writing. When you review your compositions, watch for long sentences in which the conjunctions *and, but,* or *so* are used a great deal. Usually you will find that the independent clauses are not very closely related. These clauses should be rewritten to show a closer relationship, or, sometimes, they should be allowed to stand as complete sentences. The final step in revising rambling (or choppy) sentences is to read aloud what you have written. If the passage does not sound right, you have more revising to do.

EXERCISE 12. Revising a Rambling Style. Revise the rambling style of the following passages. Break the sentences down

REVIEW EXERCISE E. Remind students to keep the intended meanings of sentences as they recast them. Encourage them to proofread and read aloud their revised versions. Allow class time for a discussion of the completed work.

into clauses, and combine some clauses into compound or complex sentences. Let other clauses stand as complete sentences. To avoid a monotonous style, vary the beginnings of some sentences. Then read the passages aloud to see if the sentences flow smoothly and have variety. Answers will vary.

1. Paul bought some skis, and he decided he must systematically learn to ski, and so he asked himself what to do first. The answer was to consult an instructor, and the instructor pointed out that it was dangerous to ski if you didn't know how to fall down properly, and so Paul thanked her, and he went home, and he dressed in his new ski clothes, and he went down the slopes and practiced falling down all day. He sprained his wrist at 3:00, and he twisted his leg at 4:36, and he left the slopes at 4:38, and now the skis are mine. I bought them from Paul for a song, and so tomorrow I plan to take my first fall at 9:30 sharp.

2. Joan thinks she can speak French, but she made a funny mistake the other day when Lisa came limping into class with a bandage on her ankle, and she had sprained it while playing hockey, so Joan thought she would show off her French. She meant to say, "*C'est dommage,*" and it means "That's too bad," but she said, "*C'est fromage*" instead, and it means "That's cheese," but Joan was quite proud of herself until Mrs. Stevens pointed out the mistake.

REVIEW EXERCISE E. Revising a Passage by Eliminating Choppy and Rambling Sentences. There are both choppy and rambling sentences in the following passage. Revise it so that the sentences are clear, well written, and varied. Read your revised version aloud to see if the sentences flow smoothly.
Answers will vary.

The dam is not a modern invention. It was used in ancient times. It was used very early in Egypt. It was used to dam the Nile River. The first dam recorded in history was built about 2600 B.C. It was a large stone dam. It was located about eighteen miles south of Memphis. This dam was an engineering failure. Other Egyptian kings built other dams to store water. Their dams created Lake Moeris.

Additional Practice

Teacher's Resource Book, Worksheet pages 78–96, Alternative Worksheet pages (for less-advanced students) 530–531

Testing

Teaching Tests booklet, pages 1–4, 11–12, 13–18
Teacher's Resource Book, Test pages 371–74, 405–406, 407–412

The Babylonians also built dams to control the Tigris and Euphrates rivers, and the Romans built dams, and the dams lasted for centuries. Emperor Nero directed the building of a dam, and it lasted for 1,300 years, but the Arabians built a dam that lasted more than 1,000 years, and it was two miles long and 120 feet high so it was the greatest dam ever built.

Two of the largest dams in the world today are in the United States. One is the Hoover Dam, and it is near Las Vegas, Nevada. The other is the Grand Coulee Dam, and it is in the state of Washington. Each dam is an important source of electrical power. Both serve American cities. They produce over 10,000 megawatts of power each year.

PART THREE

TOOLS FOR WRITING AND REVISING:

Grammar ▪ Usage ▪ Mechanics

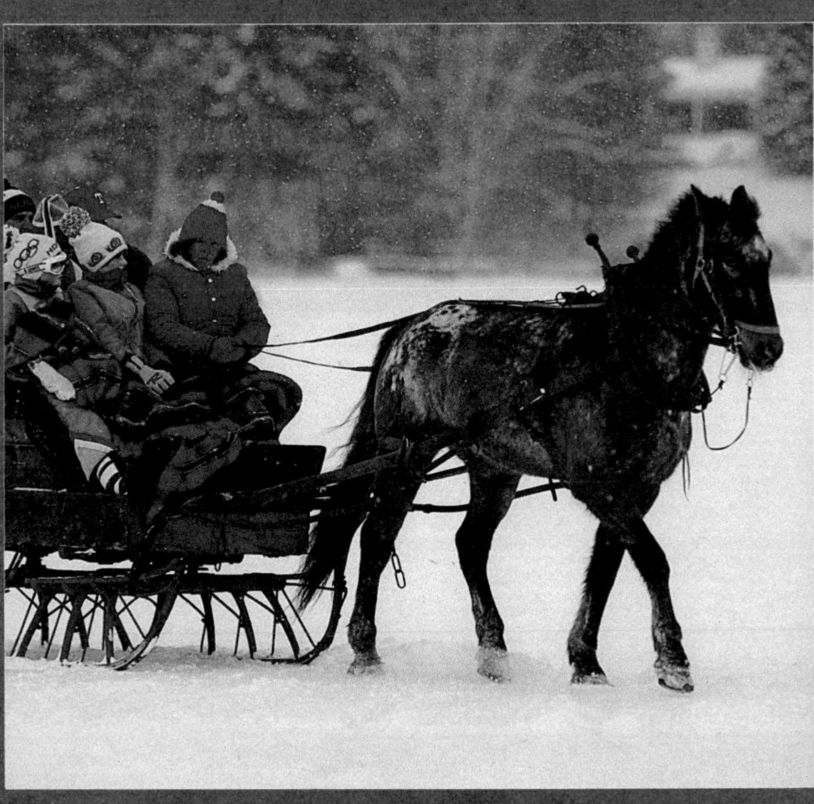

TOOLS FOR WRITING AND REVISING

pages 263–593

USING THE PICTURES

The pictures on this and the next page, along with those in the section "Picture the Possibilities" following page 226, provide students with sources of ideas for writing. The following suggestions will help you show students how to use the pictures, either singly or in combination, to generate ideas and gather information.

Sleigh

- Have students write a dialogue between two or more of the people in the sleigh. To help them create an interesting situation, work with them to develop questions such as these: *Who are the people? How well do they know each other? Do they live in the area, or are they visitors? What month, day, and time of day is it? Are the people going somewhere special, or are they just out for a ride?*
- Another possibility would be to have students imagine themselves as being one of the people in the sleigh and use questions such as these to gather concrete and sensory details: *What colors and textures do I see in my companions' clothing? In the horse's coat? In the landscape? What sound do the sleigh's runners make on the snow? What sound do the horse's hooves make? How does the wind feel on my face? What odors do I smell?* Students could then use the details to write a description or incorporate them into a

narrative along with the dialogue they develop for the preceding activity.

Old House/Horse

- Students could use the picture for descriptive writing by first asking themselves, *What main impression do I get from this picture?* They could then list concrete and sensory details, select the ones that help make their main impression clear, and arrange them in either spatial order or order of importance.
- Students who own horses or ride them regularly will enjoy writing stories or narrative paragraphs about their experiences. Other students might imagine that they have suddenly become the owner of a horse and write about the pleasures and problems such a situation would create in their family.
- Students might instead write paragraphs explaining a specialized term used by horse owners or a process involved in caring for or training a horse.
- Although the horse does not look underfed or mistreated, students could use the idea that no grass or other food is visible in the picture as the starting point for a persuasive paragraph. They might explain why they think the humane society should remove the horse from the property, for example, or, more generally, why a state or local agency should investigate people who buy horses.

Connecting the Pictures

Have students limit the subject "horses" on the basis of the ways in which they are used by human beings and write papers tracing the development of one use. They might instead write reports on books about horses.

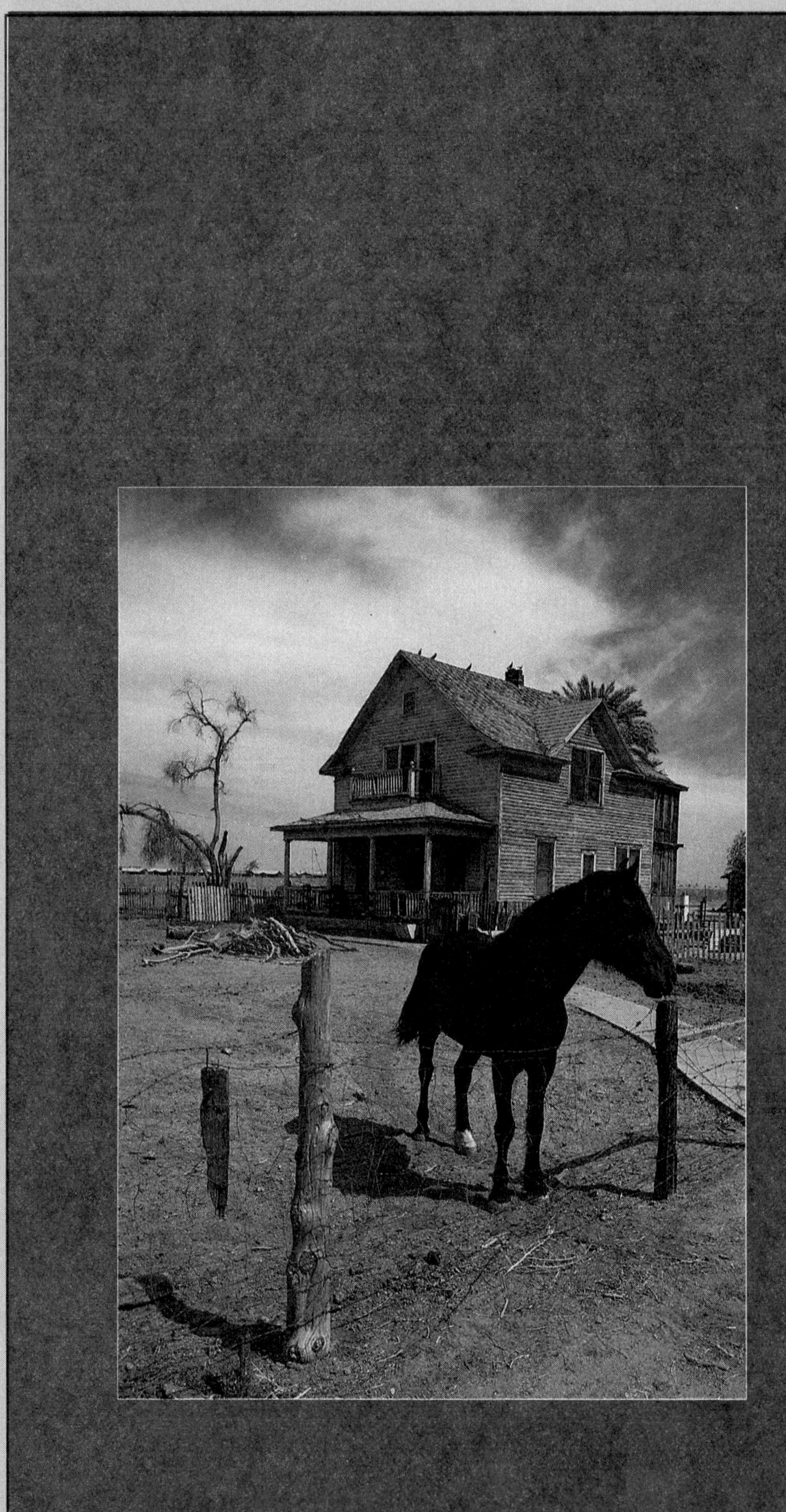

CHAPTER 10

The Sentence

SUBJECT AND PREDICATE, KINDS OF SENTENCES

Suppose that you began to read a story that opened as follows:

> Awakened in study hall John leaped from his seat into the balcony above him came the marching band led by the drum major playing "The Star Spangled Banner" on his hat a tall plume nodded to John it was a rude awakening.

This story is difficult to understand because it is not clear where one thought ends and a new one begins. When you communicate by speaking, you raise and lower your voice and you use pauses to help your listener understand your meaning. When you write, you have only words and punctuation as your means of communication. You need to use these in patterns that are familiar to your readers—in complete sentences that are set off clearly by punctuation.

DIAGNOSTIC TEST

A. Identifying Subjects and Predicates. Write each italicized group of words, and indicate whether it is the subject or the

GRAMMAR

Grammar (pages 265–416)

Chapter Overview

This chapter begins with the concept of the complete sentence and then takes up the two basic parts of a sentence, subject and predicate. After defining the simple subject and the verb, the chapter explains compound subjects and verbs, different kinds of sentences (declarative, interrogative, etc.), and elementary sentence diagraming.

Even with a class that has studied grammar in earlier grades, it is worthwhile to go over these basic ideas carefully. Take as much time as necessary to ensure that students understand "subject" and "verb." A grasp of these two fairly simple ideas is the key to much of the material in the book. Mastery of subject and verb will enable a student not only to understand related grammatical ideas but also to understand many problems in writing.

Chapter Objective

Students will identify subjects and predicates and complete sentences, and they will classify sentences according to purpose.

PRESENTING THE CHAPTER

LESS-ADVANCED STUDENTS These students should concentrate on learning to identify the essential parts of a sentence. You may wish to keep grammatical terminology to a minimum by teaching only these terms: *complete sentence, subject, predicate,* and *verb.* (You can refer to a *verb phrase* simply as "a verb that is made up of more than one word," to a *compound subject* as "two subjects connected by *and* or *or*," etc.) Less-advanced students should be required to write original sentences, but these sentences should be carefully checked and discussed. *(See listing of Alternative Worksheets on page 289.)*

ADVANCED STUDENTS If the class has studied grammar before, use the Diagnostic Test to determine which points, if any, need to be reviewed and retaught. With an advanced class, you can concentrate on exercises that assign original sentences. Spend more time on the writing applications, allowing these students to share their writing with the rest of the class.

WRITING APPLICATIONS

The writing applications in this chapter are designed to encourage students to use their knowledge of sentences in their own writing. Feel free to adapt these assignments to your students' writing needs, abilities, and interests.

DIAGNOSTIC TEST

This test will give you a clear picture of what your students already know about the parts and kinds of sentences. This test can be corrected immediately in class. You may want to instruct the students to use red pencils so that no answers will be changed. Going over the answers orally serves as a kind of review for some students. Remind your students that a *diagnostic* test does not count in their grade average.

GRAMMAR

predicate of the sentence. Underline the simple subject or the simple predicate (verb) in each.

EXAMPLES
1. *The mean dog next door* barks fiercely.
1. *The mean dog next door—subject*
2. The mean dog next door *barks fiercely.*
2. *barks fiercely—predicate*

1. Mr. Adams *gave me his old croquet set.* 1. pred.
2. Why did *that large new boat* sink on such a clear day? 2. subj.
3. *Trees and bushes all over the neighborhood* had been torn out by the storm. 3. subj.
4. On his way to school, Bill *was splashed by a passing car.* 4. pred.
5. *My old bicycle with the ape-hanger handlebars* is rusting away in the garage now. 5. subj. 6. subj.
6. *The creek behind my house* rises during the summer rains.
7. Sandy's little sister *bravely dived off the high board at the community pool.* 7. pred.
8. *Does* Max *want another serving of pie*? 8. pred.
9. My cousins and I *played basketball and walked over to the mall yesterday.* 9. pred.
10. *Fridays and other test days* always seem longer than regular school days. 10. subj.

B. Identifying Sentences by Purpose. Number your paper 11–20. After the proper number, identify each sentence as *declarative, interrogative, imperative,* or *exclamatory.*

EXAMPLE
1. What did you say?
1. *interrogative*

11. That may have been the longest string of train cars I have ever seen. 11. decl.
12. Follow these directions exactly. 12. imp.
13. No, I haven't seen Jenny all day. 13. decl.
14. Run for it—Tommy just knocked down a wasp's nest! 14. excl. *or* imp.
15. What's wrong with the television set? 15. int.
16. I don't care. 16. decl.
17. Take this book down to Mrs. Esteva's office. 17. imp.
18. Mai Lin and her family suffered many hardships at sea. 18. decl.

19. Ouch, that hurts! 19. excl.
20. May my dog have the rest of your sandwich? 20. int.

THE SENTENCE

10a. A *sentence* is a group of words expressing a complete thought.

A sentence begins with a capital letter and concludes with an end mark: a period or a question mark or an exclamation point. Sometimes a group of words looks like a sentence when it is not. You must examine the group of words closely to be sure that it expresses a complete thought. Reading it aloud will help you.

NOT A SENTENCE The music of Scott Joplin. [This is not a complete thought. What about the music of Scott Joplin?]

SENTENCE The music of Scott Joplin is popular again.

NOT A SENTENCE Upon hearing Jose Feliciano. [The thought is not complete. Who heard Feliciano? What was the response?]

SENTENCE Upon hearing Jose Feliciano, the audience applauded.

NOT A SENTENCE After she had worked a long time. [The thought is not complete. What happened after she had worked a long time?]

SENTENCE After she had worked a long time, Louise Nevelson completed the sculpture.

EXERCISE 1. Identifying and Writing Sentences. Capital letters and end marks have been omitted from the following groups of words. If a group of words is a sentence, write it after the proper number, using a capital letter and end punctuation. If the group of words is not a sentence, write *NS*. Then write the group of words, adding words to complete the thought and make it a sentence. Completed sentences will vary.

THE SENTENCE (rule 10a)

Review the examples in this section orally with your class. Have your students come up with a couple of their own examples of incomplete sentences. Then have them complete these sentences.

EXERCISE 1. The point of this exercise is not to teach students to correct sentence fragments (that is covered in Chapter 8) but to give them a clear sense of what "sentence" means before they begin to analyze the parts of a sentence. When you go over the answers in class, avoid being drawn into discussion of the various kinds of fragments—put the emphasis, instead, on completing the fragments. If students do well on this exercise, you might skip Exercises 2 and 3.

EXERCISE 2. You may also wish to have students rewrite the passage, correcting the fragments.

GRAMMAR

EXAMPLES 1. living alone in the mountains
1. *NS—Living alone in the mountains, the couple make their own furniture and clothes.*
2. classes in mountain climbing will begin soon.
2. *Classes in mountain climbing will begin soon.*

1. catching the baseball with both hands 1. NS
2. in the back of the room stands a tall pile of boxes.
3. a long narrow passage with a trapdoor at each end 3. NS
4. after waiting for six hours 4. NS
5. the gymnasium is open.
6. last night there were six television commercials every half-hour.
7. instead of calling the doctor about her sore throat 7. NS
8. beneath the tall ceiling of the church 8. NS
9. are you careless about shutting off unnecessary lights?
10. doing the multiplication tables 10. NS

EXERCISE 2. Identifying Sentences. Number your paper 1–20. After each number on your paper, write *S* if the group of words is a sentence and *NS* if it is not a sentence.
S—1, 3, 5, 8, 9, 10, 13, 15, 18, 19 NS—2, 4, 6, 7, 11, 12, 14, 16, 17, 20

1. One of the best-known women in our history is Sacajawea. **2.** A member of the Lemhi band of the Shoshoni Indians. **3.** She is famous for her role as interpreter for the Lewis and Clark expedition. **4.** Which was seeking the Northwest Passage.

5. In 1800 the Lemhis had encountered a war party of the Hidatsa. **6.** Who captured some of the Lemhis, including Sacajawea. **7.** Later, with Charbonneau, her French-Canadian husband, and their two-month old son. **8.** Sacajawea joined the Lewis and Clark expedition in what is now North Dakota. **9.** Her knowledge of Indian languages enabled the explorers to communicate with various tribes. **10.** Sacajawea also searched for eatable plants. **11.** And once saved valuable instruments during a storm. **12.** As they traveled further. **13.** The explorers came across the Lemhis. **14.** From whom Sacajawea had been separated years before. **15.** The Lemhis helped the explorers. **16.** By giving them guidance.

17. After they returned from the expedition. **18.** Clark tried to establish Sacajawea and Charbonneau in St. Louis. **19.** However, the couple moved back to Sacajawea's native land. **20.** Where this famous woman died in 1812.

EXERCISE 3. Writing Interesting Sentences. The following groups of words are not sentences. On your paper, add words to make interesting sentences. Answers will vary.

EXAMPLE 1. at the last minute
1. *At the last minute they remembered the secret message.*

1. on the last day of summer
2. found only in the country
3. a graceful ballerina
4. burning out of control
5. the old building by the lake

THE SUBJECT

You have learned that a sentence is a group of words expressing a complete thought. In order to express a complete thought, a sentence must have a subject and a predicate.

10b. The *subject* of a sentence is the part about which something is being said.

EXAMPLES A line of people (*subject*) | waited to see the movie.

Standing in line were | several sailors (*subject*).

Since the subject is that part of the sentence about which something is being said, you can usually locate it by asking yourself *Who?* or *What? Who* waited to see that movie? *Who* was standing in line? Notice that the subject comes at the beginning of the first example and at the end of the second.

EXERCISE 3. You may want to use this exercise as a class activity with less-advanced students.

THE SUBJECT (rules 10b and 10c)

For some students only a brief review of this material will be necessary. If your students have difficulty in identifying simple and complete subjects, write a short sentence on the board, such as *A girl is walking*. Have the class identify the simple and the complete subject. Then ask students to add words and phrases to the sentence. Finally, reverse the order of the subject and verb. For example:

A small girl is walking down the street.
A very small girl with a book satchel is walking down the street.
Walking down the street is a very small girl with a book satchel.

Explain that the simple subject remains the same in all the sentences and that the simple subject and related words constitute the complete subject.

EXERCISE 4. If students do well on this exercise, you can proceed to the next section. A class that does not do well should discuss the exercise thoroughly and then do Exercise 5 as homework.

GRAMMAR

In the subject part of each of these sentences, one word stands out as essential: in the first sentence, *line;* in the second sentence, *sailors.* These two words, which cannot be removed from the subject part of the sentences, are called *simple subjects.* The simple subject and the other words that belong with it, taken together, are called the *complete subject.*

10c. The *simple subject* is the main word in the complete subject.

The simple subjects in the following sentences are printed in boldface (heavy type).

complete subject
My **date** for the dance | arrived late.

complete subject
The long, hard **trip** across the desert | was finally over.

complete subject
Pacing back and forth in the cage was | a hungry **tiger.**

When the subject is only one word or one name, the complete subject and the simple subject are the same.

complete subject
EXAMPLES **Patsy Mink** | was elected to office in Hawaii.
She | was chosen congresswoman.

EXERCISE 4. Identifying Complete Subjects and Simple Subjects. Write the complete subject in each sentence. Then underline the simple subject.

EXAMPLE 1. The day of the performance arrived.
1. *The day of the performance*

1. A tense excitement filled the air.
2. Several students had been nervous all day.
3. The crew in charge of sets got ready for the first act.
4. The director of the play told everyone to "break a leg."
5. The curtain inched slowly upward.
6. Everyone in the audience stopped talking.

EXERCISE 5. Correct this exercise in class, calling on students to give answers.

7. The lights flooded the stage.
8. On the stage stood the actors.
9. They said their lines with confidence.
10. The first performance of the play was a great success.

From now on in this book, the word *subject* will refer to the simple subject.

EXERCISE 5. Identifying the Subject. Number your paper 1–20. After the proper number, write the subject (simple subject) of each sentence. Ask yourself what or whom the sentence says something about.

1. Mark Twain wrote many entertaining stories. **2.** Among them is "The Celebrated Jumping Frog of Calaveras County." **3.** One of the characters in this story will apparently believe anything. **4.** In a broken-down mining camp, this character meets Mr. Simon Wheeler. **5.** He asks the kindly old man a simple question. **6.** Instead of a simple answer, Mr. Wheeler gives a long, fantastic, and funny reply. **7.** This reply is in the form of a humorous tall tale. **8.** The tale features Jim Smiley, the owner of a very athletic frog. **9.** Mr. Smiley trained this frog for jumping contests. **10.** Confidently, Mr. Smiley bragged about his frog's leaping ability. **11.** Soon someone challenged Smiley's frog. **12.** The challenger, however, did not have a jumping frog for the contest. **13.** To Smiley, this was no problem. **14.** In a nearby swamp he found a frog for the challenger. **15.** Each creature was held on the starting line. **16.** Then, with a shout, each man released his frog. **17.** But Smiley's famous frog never jumped. **18.** The ordinary frog from the swamp easily won the contest. **19.** Smiley had been fooled by a trick. **20.** You will enjoy reading this story.

THE PREDICATE (rules 10d and 10e)

Students may have difficulty with sentences in which a subject appears in the middle of the predicate. If they do, go over the examples on page 273 carefully, and then ask students to give examples of their own. Write their examples on the board, underlining the predicates. As you teach this section on predicates, it may help to anticipate Chapter 12 by defining a verb as "a word that expresses action or helps to make a statement."

THE PREDICATE

The subject is one of the two essential parts of a sentence; the other essential part is the predicate.

GRAMMAR

GRAMMAR

10d. The *predicate* of a sentence is the part that says something about the subject.

EXAMPLES N. Scott Momaday | wrote several books. (*predicate*: wrote several books)

My whole family | heard Marian Anderson sing. (*predicate*: heard Marian Anderson sing)

On either side of me were | my two friends. (*predicate*: On either side of me were)

To find the predicate in a sentence, ask, *What is being said about the subject?* or *What happened?* In the normal order of an English sentence, the predicate follows the subject, but in some sentences the predicate comes before the subject. (See the sentence above.)

The Simple Predicate, or Verb

Just as the simple subject is the most important part of the complete subject, so the simple predicate is the most important part of the complete predicate. The simple predicate is usually called the *verb* of the sentence.

10e. The *simple predicate,* or *verb,* is the main word or group of words in the predicate.

In each of the following sentences the simple predicate, or verb, is in boldface.

The movie star | **signed** autographs for hours. (*complete subject*: The movie star; *complete predicate*: signed autographs for hours)

The trees | **sagged** beneath the weight of the ice. (*complete subject*: The trees; *complete predicate*: sagged beneath the weight of the ice)

The simple predicate may be a one-word verb, or it may be a verb of more than one word, such as *has signed* or *will be sagging*. A simple predicate of two or more words is called a *verb phrase*. Note the verb phrases in boldface in the following sentences:

The famous novel *Frankenstein* **was written** by Mary Wollstonecraft Shelley.
After the concert the guitarist **will sign** autographs.
Your vocabulary **can be increased** by the study of the origins of words.

The complete predicate, which consists of the verb or verb phrase and the other words that belong to it, usually comes after the subject, but it sometimes can appear at the beginning of a sentence, as in the following sentences.

complete predicate | *complete subject*
There on its back **was** | a large **tortoise.**

complete predicate | *complete subject*
At the top of the tree **sat** | a bird's **nest.**

The subject may come in the middle of the predicate so that part of the predicate is on one side of the subject and the rest is on the other side. In the following examples, the complete predicate is in boldface.

During the winter many birds **fly south.**
Do sparrows **fly south**?

The words *not* and *never,* which are frequently used with verbs, are not verbs. They may be part of the predicate, but they are never part of a verb or a verb phrase.

EXAMPLES She **did** not **believe** me.
We **had** never **met.**

From now on in this book, the simple predicate will be called the verb.

EXERCISE 6. Identifying Complete Predicates. Write the complete predicate from each of the following sentences. Then underline the verb or verb phrase twice.

GRAMMAR

EXERCISE 6. If students do well on this exercise, go on to Exercise 8 as a review of subjects and verbs. Otherwise, assign Exercise 7 as homework. Have the class pay special attention to sentence 5; point out that the opening prepositional phrase is related to the verb, not the subject, and so is part of the predicate.

EXERCISE 7. If students have difficulty finding the whole verb in a sentence, tell them to think about what action is being expressed. The action in sentence 1, for instance, is that of "writing," and the whole verb is not *had been* but *had been written.*

GRAMMAR

EXAMPLE 1. A ton and a half of groceries may seem like a big order for a family of five.
1. *may seem like a big order for a family of five*

1. Such a big order is possible in the village of Pang.
2. This small village is located near the Arctic Circle.
3. The people of Pang receive their groceries once a year.
4. A supply ship can visit Pang only during a short time each year.
5. In spring, families order their year's supply of groceries by mail.
6. The huge order is delivered to Pang a few months later.
7. The people store the groceries in their homes.
8. Frozen food is kept outdoors.
9. Too costly for most residents is the air-freight charge of two dollars a kilogram.
10. Villagers also fish in the icy water or hunt for wild game.

EXERCISE 7. Identifying Verbs and Verb Phrases. Number your paper 1–10. After the proper number, write the verb or verb phrase of the sentence.

1. For many years the diary had been written in a secret shorthand.
2. This secret shorthand was decoded after much hard work.
3. Samuel Pepys had kept this diary between 1660 and 1669.
4. A personal look at life in England during the seventeenth century is given in his diary.
5. Some of the entries tell about funny incidents of daily life.
6. Other entries are very serious.
7. In fact, in entries during 1666, Pepys described the great London fire.
8. What have accounts of the fire told us about this tragedy?
9. Pepys contributed his diaries and other works to Cambridge University.
10. These works are still read by people today.

WRITING APPLICATION A:
Expressing Your Ideas in Complete Sentences

Did anyone ever hold out two closed fists for you to choose the one that contained a surprise? When you communicate your thoughts to others, you offer them a surprise. You are sharing a thought that is unique and special. In conversations, you can tell by your listener's expression whether or not your message is clear. In writing, however, you cannot see your reader's expression. Therefore, when you communicate your thoughts in writing, you should use complete sentences to express your thoughts completely.

EXAMPLES *Groups of Words:* She'd been gone. Black-and-white. Missing for several days. Boy across the street. There on the side of the road. ASPCA

Sentences: Boots, our black-and-white cat, had been missing for days. Then, Monday morning, the boy who lived across the street knocked on our door. He said he had seen Boots. She had been found on the side of the road and taken to the ASPCA. We could claim her there.

GRAMMAR

Writing Assignment

Answers will vary.

You don't always know how you feel about something until you put your thoughts into words. Writing your ideas in complete sentences helps you organize your thinking. You may even discover thoughts you did not know you had. Discover what you think about the following subjects by making a complete sentence out of each group of words. Some groups are subjects and some are predicates.

1. the way to beat feeling lonely
2. always makes a class more interesting
3. dark, rainy days
4. really gets on my nerves
5. is a game that appeals to me

EXERCISE 8. This exercise serves as a review of subjects and verbs. If students have difficulty, it may help to tell them to find the verb first and then ask *Who?* or *What?* before the verb to find the subject. Use sentence 8 as an example.

EXERCISE 9. This is a creative exercise and will prove most useful with advanced students. If you think your less-advanced class would find the exercise too difficult, direct them instead to write five sentences, each containing a subject and a verb and expressing a complete thought. Have a number of students write their sentences on the board, and then ask the class: "Is the item a complete sentence? What is the subject? What is the verb? If it is not a complete sentence, what is missing?"

THE SENTENCE BASE

Ask a student to supply a word that can be used as a subject. Then ask a second student for a verb that can go with the subject. Ask other students to add words to the sentence. Point out that the two words the class began with are the essential parts of the sentence, the *sentence base.* Then write on the board a list of words and phrases such as these:

through the brush
fox
there
ran
red
quickly

Ask which of these words can serve as the essential parts of a sentence. Can any other words from the list be added to the

GRAMMAR

EXERCISE 8. Identifying Subjects and Verbs. Find the subject and the verb in each sentence and write them on your paper after the proper number.

1. Carla's mother drove us to the theater.
2. The bumblebee carries pollen from one plant to another.
3. A strong, gusty wind is blowing out to sea this morning.
4. My sister accidentally locked her keys inside the car.
5. From Maine to California the bicyclists made a cross-country journey.
6. The Medusa of Greek mythology was one of the three Gorgons, terrible in appearance.
7. For centuries she has been pictured with a head of snakes.
8. The picture of Medusa with her snaky hair appears in many books on mythology.
9. According to myth, a glance at the Medusa would turn a mortal to stone.
10. She was slain by Perseus with the aid of the goddess Athena.

EXERCISE 9. Writing Complete Sentences. Some of the following word groups are complete subjects and some are complete predicates. Write each group of words on your paper, adding whatever part is needed to make it a sentence. Then underline the subject once and the verb twice. Answers will vary.

EXAMPLE 1. marched for five hours
1. *The members of the band marched for five hours.*

1. should not be left alone
2. the vacant lot down the street
3. danced across the floor
4. looked mysteriously at us
5. their best player

THE SENTENCE BASE

You have been studying the two most important parts of the sentence: the subject and the verb. Because these two parts are essential to the sentence, they are called the *sentence base*. All other parts of the sentence are attached to the sentence base.

Sentence base: **Dogs play.**

Sentence base with other parts attached: Every day two frisky **dogs** named Bison and Stark **play** for hours on our lawn.

The parts that were added give additional information, but they would be meaningless without the sentence base.

EXERCISE 10. Using the Sentence Base. The following subjects and verbs are sentence bases that state complete thoughts. Add other parts to each of them to create more interesting sentences. Answers will vary.

EXAMPLE 1. Balloons floated.
1. *At dawn, fifty hot-air balloons floated over Nashville.*

1. Sparks flashed.
2. Car swerved.
3. Lion roars.
4. Band played.
5. Runner was sprinting.
6. Flower bloomed.
7. Girl laughed.
8. Child jumped.
9. Riders were sitting.
10. Years have passed.

COMPOUND SUBJECTS AND COMPOUND VERBS

Some sentences have more than one subject.

ONE SUBJECT **Alicia** carried her book.
THREE SUBJECTS **Alicia, Joy,** and **Carmen** carried their books.

ONE SUBJECT **New York City** is our destination.
TWO SUBJECTS Either **New York City** or **Niagara Falls** is our destination.

Notice that when two or more subjects have the same verb, a connecting word—usually *and* or *or*—is used between them. The connected subjects are referred to as a *compound subject.*

GRAMMAR

sentence? Why are these words not part of the sentence base? What other words might be added to the sentence?

EXERCISE 10. Less-advanced students may have trouble with this exercise and should probably be required to do only five of the sentences. Caution students not to attempt anything elaborate; generally the sentences should be no longer than ten or twelve words each.

COMPOUND SUBJECTS AND COMPOUND VERBS (rules 10f and 10g)

To introduce compound subjects and verbs, write on the board a sentence such as this: *The students played basketball.* Then ask your class to name the students and suggest other actions they performed. As the class supplies names and actions, write the resulting sentences on the board. Be sure your class sees the relationship between the original sentence and a sentence such as *Joe, Carol, and Larry played basketball and practiced jump shots,* where the subject *students* has become *Joe, Carol, and Larry.* Ask students to find the connecting words in the sentences.

Note: It is usually best to teach compound subjects and compound verbs in the same lesson, as suggested here. If compound subjects are taught alone, many students are likely to confuse compound with plural, and it may take some time to undo the confusion.

EXERCISES 11 and 12. You can use these exercises for practice in class and then assign Exercise 13 as homework.

GRAMMAR

10f. A *compound subject* consists of two or more connected subjects that have the same verb. The usual connecting words are *and* and *or*.

COMPOUND SUBJECT The **Senate** and the **House** are in session. [There are two subjects—*Senate* and *House*. They are joined by a connector word—*and*—and have the same verb —*are*.]

EXERCISE 11. Identifying Compound Subjects. Write the compound subject, including the connecting word, from each of the following sentences. Then write the verb or verb phrase.

EXAMPLE 1. Cicely Tyson and Paul Winfield starred in a film together.
1. *Cicely Tyson and Paul Winfield—starred*

1. Florida and California have world-famous amusement parks.
2. Records and tapes were sold at a discount.
3. The Aztecs, the Mayas, and the Incas developed impressive cultures in Central and South America.
4. Garlic or oregano may be used in the recipe.
5. Scarlett O'Hara and Melanie Wilkes are characters created by Margaret Mitchell.
6. The mayor and the governor were at the conference.
7. Suddenly, the sleet and the hail poured from the dark clouds.
8. Jim or Carol must take notes for me.
9. In the center ring were ten clowns, five acrobats, and three elephants.
10. Hawaii, Maui, and Oahu are three of the Hawaiian Islands.

Just as a sentence may have a compound subject, so it may have a compound verb.

10g. A *compound verb* consists of two or more connected verbs that have the same subject.

ONE VERB Surfing **has become** a very popular sport.

COMPOUND VERB The dog **barked** and **growled** at the thief. [There are two verbs—*barked* and *growled*—joined by *and*. Both verbs have the same subject—*dog*.]

COMPOUND VERB The man **was convicted** but later **was found** innocent of the crime. [There are two verb phrases—*was convicted* and *was found*—joined by *but*. Both verb phrases have the same subject—*man*.]

EXERCISE 12. Identifying Compound Verbs. Write the compound verb, together with the connecting word(s), from each of the following sentences. Then write the subject of the verb.

EXAMPLE 1. The hikers loaded their backpacks and studied the map of the mountain trails.
1. *loaded and studied—hikers*

1. Linda wrote her essay and practiced the piano last night.
2. Miami is the largest city in southern Florida and has been a popular resort area since the 1920's.
3. According to Greek mythology, Arachne angered Athena and was changed into a spider.
4. Martina Arroyo has sung in major American opera halls and has made appearances abroad.
5. Chip was bothered by the cold and was having a bad day.
6. During special sales, shoppers arrive early at the mall and search for bargains.
7. Maria Montessori studied medicine in Italy and developed new methods for teaching children.
8. Jim Rice autographed baseballs and made a short speech.
9. General Lee won many battles but lost the war.
10. In the summer many students go to music camps and improve their skills.

Sometimes you will see a sentence that has a compound subject and a compound verb. In such a sentence, both of the subjects go with both of the verbs.

EXERCISE 13. Have students write their homework answers on the board, and ask the class to decide whether each answer is right.

EXERCISE 14. A less-advanced class may omit this exercise.

GRAMMAR

EXAMPLE The **captain** (S) and the **crew** (S) **battled** (V) the storm and **prayed** (V) for better weather. [Both *captain* and *crew* performed both actions—*battled* and *prayed*.]

EXERCISE 13. Identifying Compound Subjects and Compound Verbs. Write the following sentences on your paper, underlining the subjects once and the verbs or verb phrases twice.

EXAMPLE 1. Several fine poems and novels were written by the Brontë sisters.
1. *Several fine poems and novels were written by the Brontë sisters.*

1. Charlotte and Emily are the most famous Brontë sisters.
2. Originally, they wrote and published under pen names.
3. *Jane Eyre* and *Wuthering Heights* are their well-known books.
4. In Charlotte Brontë's novel, Jane Eyre endured and overcame many hardships.
5. Emily Brontë's *Wuthering Heights* saddens me and makes me tearful.
6. Catherine Earnshaw and Heathcliff stand as unforgettable characters.
7. As children they wandered and explored the moor.
8. Catherine loved Heathcliff but married Edgar.
9. *Jane Eyre* and *Wuthering Heights* became movies.
10. I watched the movies and then read the books again.

EXERCISE 14. Writing Sentences with Compound Subjects and Compound Predicates. Using titles, words, and characters of songs, books, and poems, write ten sentences—five with compound subjects and five with compound predicates. Underline subjects once and verbs twice. Answers will vary.

EXAMPLE 1. *Tom Sawyer and Becky Thatcher were childhood sweethearts.*

WRITING APPLICATION B:
Adding Variety to Your Sentences by Placing the Subject in New Positions

Have you really looked at your room lately? You probably haven't unless something has been changed. When you see the same items in the same places over and over, you usually stop paying attention to them. This reaction holds true for writing: if you start every sentence with the subject, your reader may lose interest. In other words, you need to liven up your writing to hold your reader's interest. One way to do this is to place the subject of your sentence in a new place, perhaps in the middle or at the end of the sentence.

EXAMPLES In spite of everything, **I** still believe that people are really good at heart.—ANNE FRANK
Across the bottom of the television picture came the **words** *tornado watch.*

Writing Assignment

Answers will vary.

The lives of other people—even ordinary people—are often a source of entertainment and sometimes of inspiration, too. Write a mini-biography of a friend or relative. Add variety by occasionally placing the subject in the middle or at the end of your sentences.

CLASSIFYING SENTENCES BY PURPOSE

10h. Sentences may be classified according to purpose. There are four kinds of sentences.[1]

(1) A *declarative sentence* makes a statement. It is followed by a period.

EXAMPLES Miriam Colon founded the Puerto Rican Traveling Theater**.**

[1] The classification of sentences according to structure (simple, compound, complex, compound-complex) is taught in Chapter 16.

CLASSIFYING SENTENCES BY PURPOSE (rule 10h)

Advanced students should learn the terms *declarative, imperative, interrogative,* and *exclamatory,* because they will meet these words occasionally through the rest of their school careers—frequently in contexts where they are not explained. An average or below-average class, however, need not learn the terms unless you plan to use them repeatedly this year in talking about end punctuation or sentence structure. With less-advanced groups, many teachers use the easier names *statements, commands, questions,* and *exclamations.*

EXERCISE 15. Less-advanced students may have difficulty grasping the meaning of the quotations. Point out clues to sentence type in the structure of the sentence.

GRAMMAR

Curiosity is the beginning of knowledge.

(2) An *interrogative sentence* asks a question. It is followed by a question mark.

EXAMPLES What do you know about glaciers?
Why do we see only one side of the moon?
Was the game exciting?

(3) An *imperative sentence* gives a command or makes a request. It is followed by a period. Strong commands are followed by exclamation points.

EXAMPLES Do your homework each night.
Watch out!
Please close the door, John.

At first glance, none of these sentences seems to have any subject. Actually, the person or persons addressed in each case is the subject. The subject *you* is said to be "understood" in such sentences.

(You) Do your homework each night.
(You) Watch out!
John, (you) please close the door.

(4) An *exclamatory sentence* shows excitement or expresses strong feeling. It is followed by an exclamation point.

EXAMPLES What a sight the sunset is!
They're off!
Sarah won the videotape player!

Many students overuse the exclamatory sentence. Save your exclamation points for sentences that really do show strong emotion. If overused, the exclamatory sentence loses its impact.

EXERCISE 15. Classifying Sentences. Number your paper 1–10. Write the kind of sentence each quotation is and give the punctuation mark that should follow the sentence.

EXAMPLE 1. The only thing we have to fear is fear itself FRANKLIN D. ROOSEVELT

1. *declarative* **.**

1. Shall I compare thee to a summer's day 1. interrogative—? —WILLIAM SHAKESPEARE
2. Tact is after all a kind of mind-reading 2. declarative—. —SARAH ORNE JEWETT
3. Sail on, O Ship of State—HENRY WADSWORTH LONGFELLOW
4. The history of every country begins in the heart of a man or woman—WILLA CATHER 3. exclamatory—! 4. declarative—.
5. What happiness is there which is not purchased with more or less of pain—MARGARET OLIPHANT 5. interrogative—?
6. Bring me my bow of burning gold—WILLIAM BLAKE
7. No one can make you feel inferior without your consent 6. imperative—! (or.) 7. declarative—. —ELEANOR ROOSEVELT
8. Since when was genius found respectable 8. interrogative—? —ELIZABETH BARRETT BROWNING
9. 9. imperative—. (or !) Speak softly and carry a big stick—THEODORE ROOSEVELT
10. An expert is one who knows more and more about less and less—NICHOLAS MURRAY BUTLER 10. declarative—.

DIAGRAMING THE SUBJECT AND VERB

A diagram shows the structure of a sentence as a kind of picture. Making a diagram of the subject and the verb is a way of showing that you understand these two parts of the sentence.

PATTERN

subject	verb

EXAMPLES Lions roar.

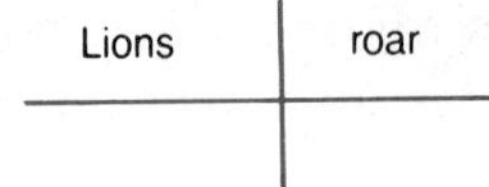

DIAGRAMING THE SUBJECT AND VERB

Almost all teachers make use of some kind of visual diagraming to explain sentence relationships. The formal diagram taught in the textbook is only one of several possible systems. Here are three different ways of diagraming the same sentence, according to the formal method, the arrow method, and the list method:

EXAMPLE The tall, bearded man walked slowly down the lane.

FORMAL METHOD

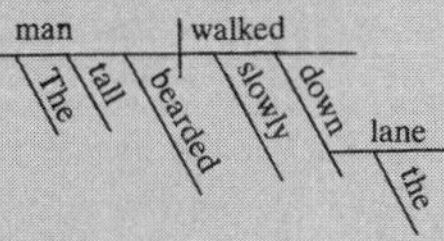

ARROW METHOD

LIST METHOD

man	walked
The	slowly
tall	down lane
bearded	the

You will frequently rely on some type of visual diagram in explaining grammatical structure. But whether you should teach your students to use one of the diagraming methods is another matter. Many teachers feel that practice in diagraming, if it is kept simple, does help students to develop a sense of sentence relationships. Others feel that diagraming is not effective. If you do teach diagraming, here are three points to remember:

1. *Sentences for diagraming should be short.* A diagram containing no more than ten or twelve

words makes sentence structure easier to see.

2. *Diagraming should be focused on one problem at a time.* For instance, if you want to use diagraming to help your students understand compound structures, avoid giving them sentences that raise irrelevant problems about the placement of adverbs or prepositional phrases.

3. *Diagraming is only a means to an end, never an end in itself.* If your students' diagrams show you that they understand the relationships between the parts of the sentence, that is what matters. For example, it does not matter if their lines are crooked.

EXERCISE 16. Do the first two sentences on the board as examples, asking the class to give you directions at each step. Then have students do the other sentences on their papers.

GRAMMAR

People speak.

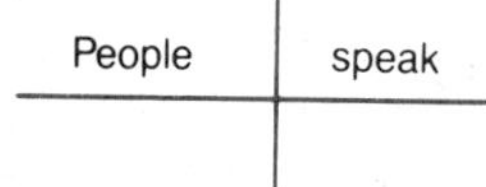

Notice that the parts of the sentence base—the subject and the verb—are placed on a horizontal line with a vertical line separating the subject from the verb. The capital marking the beginning of the sentence is used, but not the punctuation.

To diagram a sentence, you first pick out the subject and the verb and then write them on the horizontal line, separated by a crossing vertical line.

EXAMPLES The energetic reporter dashed to the fire.

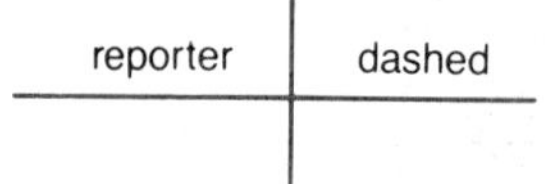

Have you been studying for the final test?

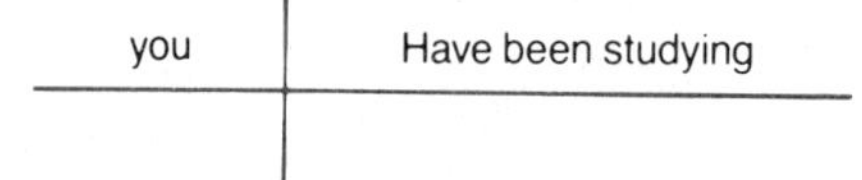

Listen to the beautiful music.

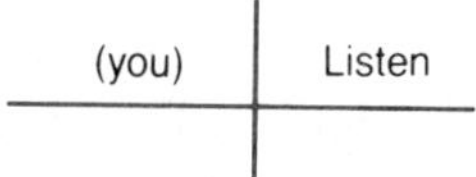

EXERCISE 16. Diagraming Simple Subjects and Verbs. Diagram only the simple subjects and verbs in the following sentences. Draw your diagrams with a ruler, leaving plenty of space between them. See Answer Key.

1. Midas is a character in Greek mythology.
2. He was the king of Phrygia.
3. One of the gods gave Midas a magic power.
4. With this power, Midas could turn anything into gold.
5. This could be done with a simple touch of Midas's hand.

EXERCISE 17. You may wish to diagram the first sentence on the board as an example and assign the rest of the exercise as homework.

GRAMMAR

6. For a while, this gift pleased Midas.
7. Soon it became a curse.
8. Do you know why?
9. Read the story of King Midas in a mythology book.
10. Today, people with "the Midas touch" can make money in any project at all.

The following example shows how to diagram a sentence with a compound subject. Notice the position of the connecting word *and*.

EXAMPLE Vines and weeds grew over the old well.

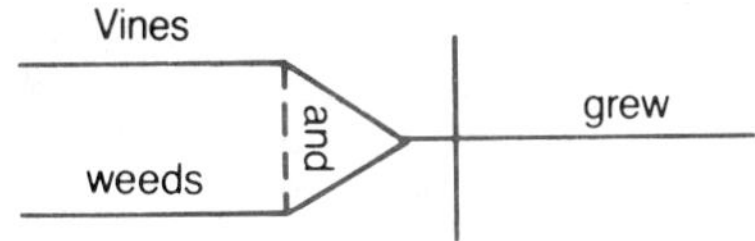

To diagram a sentence with a compound verb, you follow a similar pattern.

EXAMPLE The model walked across the platform and turned around.

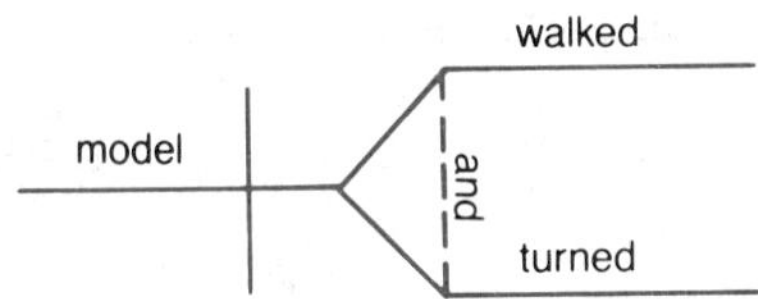

If the sentence has both a compound subject and a compound verb, it is diagramed this way:

EXAMPLE Ken and Marti dived into the water and swam across the pool.

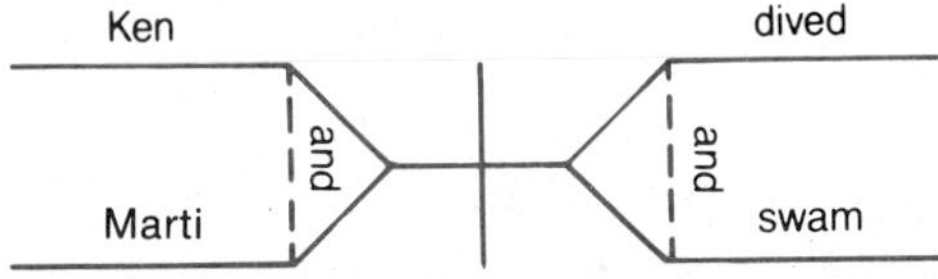

EXERCISE 17. Diagraming Subject and Verbs. Diagram the simple subjects and the verbs or verb phrases in the following sentences. See Answer Key.

REVIEW EXERCISE A. This exercise can also be used as a test. To find out how easily your class can do this work, you might assign a time limit of twenty minutes.

1. We ran to the railroad station and barely caught the train.
2. The students and the faculty combined their efforts and defeated the proposal.
3. The plane circled above the landing field but did not descend.
4. Pencil and paper are needed for tomorrow's assignment.
5. The actress and her costar prepared for the scene.

GRAMMAR

REVIEW EXERCISE A. Identifying Complete Subjects and Predicates. Write the following sentences on your paper. Separate the complete subject from the complete predicate with a vertical line. Then underline the simple subject once and the verb twice.

EXAMPLE 1. Legends and folk tales have been repeated and enjoyed throughout the Americas.

1. *Legends and folk tales have been repeated and enjoyed throughout the Americas.*

1. The Chorotega people| lived in Nicoya, Costa Rica, hundreds of years ago.
2. One Chorotega folk tale| tells the story of Nicoya's treasure and praises Princess Nosara for her protection of it from the enemy.
3. The warriors of the Chirenos| landed on the Nicoyan peninsula and attacked the Chorotegas.
4. The Indians of Nicoya| were surprised and could not react quickly.
5. Nosara| grabbed the treasure in her father's house.
6. Nosara and her suitor| took a bow and arrow and fled into the woods.
7. The two| ran from the enemy all night and at last reached a river.
8. The brave girl| dashed into the mountains, hid the treasure, and returned to the river.
9. The enemy| killed the princess and her friend.
10. The murderous tribe| never found the gold.

REVIEW EXERCISE B. Classifying Sentences. Write each sentence, adding the correct end punctuation. Then write what kind of sentence it is.

EXAMPLE 1. Turn left at the corner
1. *(you) Turn left at the corner.—imperative*

1. Several recent movies have shown the problems of life on a farm. 1. decl.
2. How many times have they tried to win the championship? 2. int.
3. Imagine a ride in the space shuttle! 3. (you) imp. (*or* excl.)
4. Because of its funny appearance, the frilled lizard looks like a comical monster. 4. decl.
5. Can you give me directions to the post office? 5. int.
6. How fresh the air feels after a storm! 6. excl.
7. Think about both sides of the problem. 7. (you) imp.
8. Many large museums in America have pottery from New Mexico by Maria Martinez. 8. decl.
9. What teams are playing in the World Series? 9. int.
10. What a fantastic world lies beneath the waves! 10. excl.

GRAMMAR

CHAPTER 10 REVIEW: POSTTEST 1

A. Identifying Subjects and Predicates. Write each italicized group of words and indicate whether it is the subject or the predicate of the sentence. Underline the simple subject or the verb in each word group you write.

EXAMPLES 1. *My aunt in Florida* took us to Sea World.
1. *My aunt in Florida—subject*
2. My aunt in Florida *took us to Sea World.*
2. *took us to Sea World—predicate*

Our whole family (1) *drove down to my aunt's house in Florida last summer.* (2) *The long drive and the steamy heat, especially in the southern states,* wore out all of us.

The first two days at my aunt's house, (3) *my mother and father and my brother and I* spent almost all of our time in my

REVIEW EXERCISE B. If you did not teach the section on classifying sentences by purpose, omit this exercise, or direct students instead to add the end punctuation and then underline the simple subject once and the verb twice.

CHAPTER 10 REVIEW: POSTTEST 1

Part A covers the identification of subjects and predicates, and Part B requires that your students classify sentences according to purpose.

CHAPTER 10 REVIEW: POSTTEST 2

You may wish to omit this test with your less-advanced students. An alternative would be to have them write sentences with just one directive, such as these:

1. Write an imperative sentence.
2. Write a sentence with a compound subject.

GRAMMAR

aunt's air-conditioned back room. Lounging on the couch, we (4) *could look out the picture windows at the lake and palm trees in the back yard*. My brother, (5) *naturally, was bored and pestered everyone*. (6) *Does* your little brother *always act that way, too?*

On the third day there, (7) *all of us* rode up to Sea World. (8) *The various exhibits and shows* featured all kinds of strange and wonderful animals. Many animals, particularly dolphins and killer whales, (9) *performed tricks and seemed very intelligent*.

In one huge tank swam (10) *scary-looking sharks*. A clear glass or plastic tunnel (11) *went right through the middle of the shark tank*. My mother and my brother (12) *did not like the tunnel*.

(13) *My brother's favorite part of Sea World* was the pirate ship. He (14) *ran and played all over the ship with a bunch of other children his age*. Even after a whole day there, (15) *none of us* wanted to leave.

B. Identifying Sentences by Purpose. Number your paper 16–20. After the proper number, identify each sentence as *declarative, interrogative, imperative,* or *exclamatory*.

EXAMPLE 1. Write your name at the top of your paper.
1. *imperative*

16. Maria plans to study architecture at the state university. 16. declarative
17. This isn't the right answer, is it? 17. interrogative
18. No, it definitely is not! 18. exclamatory
19. Clean up your room this instant, and don't make up any excuses or try to get out of it. 19. imperative
20. I can't right now, Mom; everybody's waiting for me down at Andy's house. 20. declarative

CHAPTER 10 REVIEW: POSTTEST 2

Writing a Variety of Sentences. Write ten sentences of your own according to the guidelines given. Make the subjects and predicates different for each sentence. Answers will vary.

1. A declarative sentence with a compound subject
2. An imperative sentence with a compound predicate
3. A declarative sentence with a single subject and a single predicate
4. An interrogative sentence with a compound subject
5. An interrogative sentence with a compound predicate
6. An exclamatory sentence with a single subject and a single predicate
7. An imperative sentence with a single subject and a single predicate
8. A declarative sentence with a compound predicate
9. An exclamatory sentence with a compound predicate
10. A declarative sentence with a compound subject and a compound predicate

Additional Practice

Teacher's Resource Book, Worksheet pages 97–109, Alternative Worksheet pages (for less-advanced students) 532–34

Testing

Teaching Tests booklet, pages 19–22, 23–24, 37–43
Teacher's Resource Book, Test pages 413–16, 417–18, 431–42

Chapter Overview

Students should become familiar with the terminology used in describing English sentences and the functions of the parts of speech. In teaching or reviewing parts of speech, remind the class that these are the building blocks out of which the complete subject and complete predicate of a sentence are made. Some students may fail to see any relationship between the material in Chapter 10 and the material in these chapters unless the connection is specifically pointed out.

Note: In class discussions of exercises, require students to explain their reasons for identifying words as particular parts of speech.

Chapter Objective

Students will identify common and proper nouns, pronouns, and adjectives and will use these parts of speech effectively in their own writing.

PRESENTING THE CHAPTER

LESS-ADVANCED STUDENTS These students should concentrate on the basic matter of identifying nouns, pronouns, and adjectives and should perhaps omit the study of compound nouns, proper nouns and adjectives, and words used as different parts of speech. *(See listing of Alternative Worksheets on page 308.)*

ADVANCED STUDENTS Advanced students who do well on the Diagnostic Test may review the chapter briefly, concentrating on the Writing Applications and other writing assignments.

CHAPTER 11

The Parts of Speech

NOUN, PRONOUN, ADJECTIVE

There are many thousands of different words in the English language, but there are only eight different *kinds* of words. These eight kinds, which are called "parts of speech," are the *noun,* the *pronoun,* the *adjective,* the *verb,* the *adverb,* the *preposition,* the *conjunction,* and the *interjection.* In this chapter you will study three of these eight parts of speech: the *noun,* the *pronoun,* and the *adjective.*

DIAGNOSTIC TEST

Identifying Nouns, Pronouns, and Adjectives. Number your paper 1–20. After the proper number, write each italicized word in the following sentences and indicate whether it is a noun (*n.*), a pronoun (*pron.*), or an adjective (*adj.*).

EXAMPLE 1. The biplane had four *wings* and a *wooden* propeller.
1. *wings—n., wooden—adj.*

1. Sometimes I don't feel well when *it* gets cloudy and the *dark* sky threatens rain. 1. pron., adj.

2. My little sister, *afraid* of thunder and *lightning,* hid under the bed. 2. adj., n.
3. Inger's mother gave *each* of us a tall glass of *cold* milk. 3. pron., adj.
4. One by one, *each* husky ventured out into the *cold.* 4. adj., n.
5. *Who* went to church *Sunday* morning? 5. pron., adj. 6. n., pron.
6. While the *Wilsons* were on vacation, Julio fed *their* dog.
7. The house across the street has been up for *sale* again since *Tuesday*. 7. n., n.
8. Under the *rotten* pine flooring my *brother-in-law* found a small tin canister. 8. adj., n.
9. *That* rifle doesn't belong to *anyone*. 9. adj., pron.
10. *That* is a *Persian* cat. 10. pron., adj.
11. Give me *some* iced *tea,* please. 11. adj., n.
12. *Somebody* said that there would be no more *discount* movie tickets. 12. pron., adj.
13. I got a *discount* on *our* tickets, though. 13. n., pron.
14. *Mr. Taylor* donated the *sports* equipment. 14. n., adj. 15. n., adj.
15. Barney is going to try out for *track* and several *other* sports.
16. *Everyone* liked one painting or the *other*. 16. pron., pron.
17. June went to the *mall* by *herself*. 17. n., pron.
18. Hobbies take up so *much* time that they often become *work*. 18. adj., n.
19. My father's *work* schedule often takes *him* out of town.
20. *This* parakeet screeches if you don't give him *enough* seed.

19. adj., pron. 20. adj., adj.

THE NOUN

If you were to travel to a foreign country where a language other than English is spoken, you would soon find yourself asking, "What's that called?" Knowing the names of things is basic to communication. A word that names something is called a *noun*.

11a. A *noun* is a word used to name a person, place, thing, or idea.

Persons Helen Hayes, Dr. Lacy, child, architect
Places Wyoming, Mexico, Europe, home, city

WRITING APPLICATIONS

The Writing Applications in this chapter are designed to encourage students to use their knowledge of pronouns and adjectives in their own writing. Feel free to adapt these assignments to your students' writing needs, abilities, and interests.

DIAGNOSTIC TEST

This test will give you a clear picture of what your students already know about nouns, pronouns, and adjectives. The results of the test will help you determine how much time you need to spend on the chapter.

THE NOUN (rule 11a)

To introduce the noun, write on the board sentences such as these:

The —— rode to the —— .
A —— ran up a —— .
The —— wagged its —— .
—— spoke to the —— at the —— .

Have the students suggest words to fill in the blanks. Ask what these words have in common; lead students to the answer that all the words name something. Providing further examples, point out that a noun can be singular or plural, capitalized or uncapitalized. Have students give additional examples for each point.

Students may offer a verb or an adjective as a "name." For instance, they may suggest that "*speak* is a name, since it names a thing you can do." Give the rule of thumb that *a word that names is ordinarily a word with which* a, an, *or* the *can be used.* (Exceptions would include proper nouns and abstract nouns.) Suggest that, although we don't speak of "a speak," we might speak of "a speech" or "a conversation."

Avoid a prolonged discussion of whether a particular noun names a person, thing, place, or idea. These categories obviously overlap.

EXERCISE 1. Ask ten students to write the nouns on the board (one student for each sentence). Then call on other students to tell whether each answer is correct.

COMPOUND NOUNS

Emphasize that a proper noun that is made up of several words counts as one noun, even if it contains words that are not in themselves nouns. *The Adventures of Huckleberry Finn* is one noun because it is the name of a particular book; but *the* and *of,* of course, are not themselves nouns.

GRAMMAR

Things money, shell, wind, worm, desk
Ideas courage, love, freedom, sorrow, luck

Some nouns name things that you can see, while others do not. The nouns that name unseen things, like ideas, can be more difficult to identify.

EXERCISE 1. Identifying Nouns. Number your paper 1–10. Pick out fifty nouns from the following sentences. (*Which, they,* and *all* arc not nouns.)

EXAMPLE 1. Both children and adults enjoyed the comedy.
1. *children, adults, comedy*

1. Rods, reels, and lines are called tackle.
2. Mines are important to the economy and industry of Utah.
3. Hobbies teach many people new skills and provide hours of entertainment.
4. During the war, women in our country worked in hospitals, factories, and offices.
5. The pollution of the air and water has been a serious problem for many years.
6. Computers have become a part of the daily lives of both children and adults.
7. Huge crowds of people attended the Olympics in summer.
8. All responsible citizens in a democracy should exercise the right to vote in elections.
9. Armadillos have an excellent sense of smell, which they use in their daily searches for food such as insects, lizards, and other small creatures.
10. A person never knows when courage will be needed in the face of danger or of a personal problem.

Compound Nouns

Sometimes a single noun is made up of two or more words. These words may be written as a single word (redwood), as two words (red pepper), or with a hyphen (self-esteem). Nouns that are names of particular people or things also often consist of more than one word: Rose Fitzgerald Kennedy, Buckingham Palace, *The Adventures of Huckleberry Finn* (the name of a book). Nouns such as these are called *compound nouns*. To be sure how a compound noun is written, look it up in your dictionary.

Proper Nouns and Common Nouns

There are two main classes of nouns: common nouns and proper nouns. While the *common noun* names a class or a group of persons, places, or things, the proper noun names a particular person, place, or thing. The *proper noun* begins with a capital letter. If it consists of more than one word, each important word is capitalized *(Declaration of Independence)*.

COMMON NOUNS	PROPER NOUNS
poem	"To a Skylark"
country	Kenya
man	Roberto Clemente
ship	*Mayflower*
newspaper	*New York Times*
ocean	Pacific Ocean
street	Market Street
date	November 6, 1987
city	Los Angeles

EXERCISE 2. Identifying Nouns. Number your paper 1–10. After each number, list the nouns you find in the corresponding sentence. (*Note: One* and *their* are not nouns.)

EXAMPLE 1. Forests come in many different shapes, kinds, and sizes.
1. *forests, shapes, kinds, sizes*

1. Trees in a tropical jungle have an ample supply of water.
2. Rain forests are usually located in tropical regions. 2. (or forests)
3. However, one rain forest is on a peninsula in the northwestern state of Washington. 3. (or forest)
4. Along the coast of California grow the famous redwoods, the tallest trees in the world.

GRAMMAR

PROPER NOUNS AND COMMON NOUNS

Write the words "girl" and "boy" in a column on the board. Then ask the class to supply specific girls' and boys' names. Write these in a second column. Ask someone to state the important difference between writing the words in the first column and writing the other words (capitalization).

EXERCISE 2. Compare common and proper nouns such as *state* and *Washington* (sentence 3) and *park* and *Sequoia National Park* (sentence 10). Ask why one kind of noun remains uncapitalized while the other kind should be capitalized. Also note that *rain forest* and *evergreens* are examples of compound nouns.

REVIEW EXERCISE A. A class unfamiliar with the rules of capitalizing proper nouns should probably omit this exercise. Such a class should study the material in Chapter 22, "Capital Letters."

THE PRONOUN (rule 11b)

Teach the use of pronouns by writing on the board sentences such as the following ones and having students give substitutes for the nouns in the sentences.

Joe has finished eating. (*He* has finished *that.*)
The skirt is much too big for Tina. (*It* is much too big for *her.*)

As students study the lists of words commonly used as pronouns (pages 295–96), call attention to the relatively small number of pronouns in the language by asking, "If words commonly used as nouns were listed in our textbook, how many nouns would there be?" Then point out that pronouns are easy to learn because there are so few of them.

You may wish to call attention to possessive pronouns such as *her, his,* and *my* and point out that they are pronouns because they take the place of nouns. Since possessive pronouns (like all possessives) also function as adjectives, some teachers prefer to call them *possessive adjectives.* See the paragraph near the bottom of text page 295. Decide now which term you will use, because you will have to refer to these words often during the year.

To teach interrogative and indefinite pronouns, write on the board the first sentence in each of the following pairs, and ask the class, "Does the speaker have a specific

GRAMMAR

5. The forests in Canada contain mostly evergreens, which adapt well to a cold climate.
6. Forests in the temperate zones have evergreens and also trees that shed leaves, such as oaks, beeches, and maples.
7. The giant Douglas fir, an evergreen tree, is a valuable source of lumber. 7. (or fir) 7. You may wish to refer students to dictionary for "Douglas fir."
8. Many other types of plants are dependent on trees for their life.
9. Forests swarm with insects, mammals, birds, and reptiles.
10. A national park such as Sequoia National Park protects large areas of forest.

REVIEW EXERCISE A. Classifying Nouns. Make two columns on your paper. Label one column *Proper Nouns* and the other column *Common Nouns.* Under the appropriate heading, list the nouns from the following paragraph. See Answer Key.

Each day several thousand people visit the Lincoln Memorial in Washington. The monument was designed by Henry Bacon and was dedicated on Memorial Day. Located in West Potomac Park, the Lincoln Memorial consists of a large marble hall that encloses a lifelike statue of Abraham Lincoln. The figure, which was made from blocks of white marble by Daniel Chester French, a distinguished sculptor, is sitting in a large armchair as if in deep meditation. On the north wall is found a famous passage from an inaugural address by Lincoln, and on the south wall is inscribed the Gettysburg Address.

THE PRONOUN

Once you can recognize nouns, you can learn to identify pronouns. A *pronoun* is a word that stands for a noun. Without pronouns we would be forced to repeat the same nouns again and again.

EXAMPLE When Kelly saw the signal, Kelly pointed the signal out to Teresa.
When Kelly saw the signal, **she** pointed **it** out to Teresa.

11b. A *pronoun* is a word used in place of one or of more than one noun.

Name the nouns that the pronouns in the following sentences stand for.

1. Gail read the book and returned **it** to the library.
2. The models bought **themselves** new dresses.
3. "Sam," the teacher said, "**you** will be the discussion leader tomorrow."
4. Sharon and Pat went fishing. **Both** caught six bass.

The noun that a pronoun stands for is called the *antecedent.* Sometimes the antecedent is not stated.

EXAMPLES **Catherine** (*antecedent*) told **her** (*pron.*) father **she** (*pron.*) would be late.

You (*pron.*) can't sleep now. [no antecedent stated]

There are several kinds of pronouns. The following pronouns are the *personal pronouns:*

I, me, mine, my, myself
you, your, yours, yourself, yourselves
he, him, his, himself
she, her, hers, herself
it, its, itself
we, us, our, ours, ourselves
they, them, their, theirs, themselves

In this book, pronouns that come directly before nouns and show possession (*my, his, her, its, your, their*) are called *possessive pronouns.* Your teacher may prefer that you call them *possessive adjectives.*

Make sure that you learn the differences between *its* and *it's* and between *their, they're,* and *there.* Avoid using *hisself* and *theirselves,* which are not standard English.[1]

Other common pronouns are

[1] *Standard* and *nonstandard* are the terms used in this book to describe kinds of usage. See pages 497–98 for a discussion of standard and nonstandard English.

GRAMMAR

person in mind when saying *who* or *everyone* or *nobody?*" Then write on the board the second sentence in each pair to demonstrate that pronouns, whether or not they take the place of a specific noun, do take the same positions as nouns in sentences.

Who knows the answer?
Sue knows the answer.

Bob likes *everyone.*
Bob likes *people.*

Nobody laughed.
Children laughed.

EXERCISE 3. You may want to do this exercise orally with your less-advanced students, especially if they have not studied pronouns before.

Answers: Exercise 3

1. its—cart, their—bags
2. their—passengers, they—passengers, their—passengers
3. me—salesperson, It—bag, my—salesperson, it—bag
4. you—unidentified, yours—unidentified, I—traveler, them—socks
5. Who—unidentified, This—shirt, ours—couple
6. many—people, several—people
7. themselves—travelers
8. I—person, my—person, Who—unidentified, it—comb

GRAMMAR

who, whom, whoever, whomever
everybody, everyone, someone, somebody
no one, nobody, none, others

The following words are pronouns when they are used in the place of nouns:

what, which, whatever, whichever, whose
this, that, these, those
one, each, some, any, other, another
many, more, much, most
both, several, few, all, either, neither

EXERCISE 3. Identifying Pronouns. List the pronouns in each of the following sentences after the proper number. After each pronoun, write the noun or nouns that the pronoun refers to.

EXAMPLE 1. Beth saw the kittens in the snow, and she decided to bring them inside.
1. *she—Beth*
them—kittens

1. When the luggage cart fell on its side, the bags and their contents scattered everywhere.
2. The passengers scrambled to find their luggage; they even got down on their hands and knees to pick up the belongings.
3. One salesperson shouted, "This bag belongs to me! It has my name on it."
4. "Are you sure these socks are yours?" asked another traveler. "I have a pair just like them."
5. One couple asked, "Who owns a pink-and-yellow shirt? This isn't ours."
6. As a crowd of people gathered, many just laughed, but several offered to help.
7. The travelers found themselves quibbling over toothbrushes, combs, and magazines.
8. "I lost my comb!" exclaimed one annoyed person. "Who has it?"

9. One worried traveler asked, "Where are the birthday presents for my cousin? He will be disappointed if I lose them."
10. Finally, the problem was resolved, and no one was unhappy.

WRITING APPLICATION A:
Using Pronouns to Avoid Unnecessary Repetition

Sometimes adults don't realize that they are telling you the same things over and over. At times they even repeat the exact words. How do you feel when this happens? You probably get irritated and impatient. In your writing, you can use pronouns to avoid irritating your reader with unnecessary repetition of nouns. You can see in the following example that the use of pronouns would make the information on Poe read much more smoothly.

> Edgar Allan Poe had a sad life. Edgar Allan Poe was the son of professional actors. Edgar Allan Poe was an orphan at age three. Edgar Allan Poe was raised and educated by a wealthy couple in Virginia. Edgar Allan Poe could not get along with Edgar Allan Poe's foster father. Edgar Allan Poe's young wife died of tuberculosis. Edgar Allan Poe did not take good care of Edgar Allan Poe, and Edgar Allan Poe survived Edgar Allan Poe's wife by only two years.

Writing Assignment

Answers will vary.

Select a well-known person from public life, the entertainment field, or sports. Describe this person without revealing his or her name until the end of your paragraph. Have the class guess who the person is.

EXERCISE 4. Writing Pronouns in Sentences. Rewrite the following paragraphs by filling in the blanks with appropriate pronouns. If necessary, refer to the lists of pronouns on pages 295–96. Answers will vary.

9. my—traveler, He—cousin, I—traveler, them—presents
10. no one—unidentified

EXERCISE 4. In a less-advanced class, you might want to put this exercise on the board and have the students suggest answers orally. Write in answers as they are supplied, and discuss each pronoun briefly. If your other classes write the answers individually, allow them to look back to the lists of pronouns on pages 295–96.

GRAMMAR

REVIEW EXERCISE B. A class that did well on Exercise 3 may omit this exercise.

GRAMMAR

Let —— tell —— about the experience that —— of my friends, Mary Tam, had on vacation. —— was taking a group tour through the dense Australian forests. After traveling for hours at night through wilderness, —— in the group wanted to make camp, but the guide insisted that —— continue. Finally, —— agreed to travel for just one more hour.

Soon —— were rewarded for the trip. At the edge of the forest, the guide pointed to the top of a large tree where several koalas were feeding. —— of the animals swung from one tree to —— .

The group watched —— from the ground. —— dared to speak a word. The koalas munched happily on the leaves of the trees. —— held onto branches with their sharp claws. —— of the animals carried a cub on her back. —— was feeding the cub while she also fed —— .

Although —— of the koalas have been hunted ruthlessly, a —— of the animals thrive within remote Australian forests. —— of the tour members marveled at the unique appearance of the koalas. —— look different from any other animal in the world.

REVIEW EXERCISE B. Identifying Pronouns. Number your paper 1–10. Write the pronouns from each sentence after the corresponding number. Circle all possessive pronouns.

1. All of us saw Rosemary Casals play in the tennis tournament.
2. Many of the spectators watching in the stands played tennis themselves.
3. Who would not like to be on the court playing during one of the sets?
4. Casals began to play, and the crowd was awed by the strength of her serve.
5. People were amazed that anyone could play with that much stamina.
6. Casals played such a strong game that she seemed to be rewarding us for our support.
7. Did you know that Rosemary Casals has played in many tennis tournaments?

8. I remembered that Casals had won my admiration by fighting for equal rights for women in professional tennis.
9. Several people in the audience showed by their enthusiasm that they had enjoyed watching the matches.
10. We met them for dinner after the tournament.

THE ADJECTIVE

Allen and Sonia have just finished the final exam for the history course they are taking. Neither of them will be satisfied with saying merely that it was a test. Rather, they will describe the test as being *long* or *difficult* or even *unfair.*

Not satisfied with just naming things, we often like to make a noun more definite by describing it in some way. The words that we use to make a noun more definite are called *adjectives.* When a noun is described by an adjective, it is said to be *modified.* Since a pronoun may be used in place of a noun, it too may be modified by an adjective.

11c. An *adjective* is a word used to modify a noun or a pronoun.

An adjective often answers one of these questions: *What kind? Which one? How much?* or *How many?*

WHAT KIND?	WHICH ONE?	HOW MUCH? or HOW MANY?
a *tall* woman	the *other* one	*five* times
a *steep* mountain	*this* year	*many* mistakes
a *long* hike	the *last* answer	*several* others
an *eager* clerk	*those* people	*no* supplies
a *tired* dog	*that* dress	*few* marbles

The most frequently used adjectives are *a, an,* and *the.* These adjectives are called *articles.*

EXERCISE 5. Writing Appropriate Adjectives. Rewrite the following sentences, replacing the italicized questions with adjectives that answer them. Answers will vary.

GRAMMAR

THE ADJECTIVE (rule 11c)

To introduce adjectives, write a noun on the board and ask students to "describe" this word by supplying one-word modifiers that tell *What Kind? Which one? How many?* List the modifiers before the noun. For example:

friendly
smart
fat dog
sick
healthy

Next, show how one of these simple phrases can be expanded by adding other adjectives: "a friendly dog," "an intelligent, friendly dog," "an intelligent, friendly, pug-nosed dog."

If your students want to know how an adjective can modify a pronoun, give them a sentence using a predicate adjective. For example, "They were noisy." Strictly speaking, this is one of the few ways an adjective can be used to modify a pronoun. (When an adjective precedes a word such as *one, somebody,* or *many,* the word is usually considered a noun. For instance, in the expression "the little one," *one* is considered a noun.)

EXERCISE 5. This exercise can be written in class immediately after the explanatory material is covered.

EXERCISE 6. Point out that sentence 10, in which two adjectives follow the noun they modify, illustrates the material immediately preceding the exercise.

EXAMPLE 1. They sold *how many?* tickets for the *which one?* show and *how many?* tickets for the *which one?* one.

1. *They sold fifty tickets for the first show and seventy-five tickets for the last one.*

GRAMMAR

1. Even though we had run *how many?* laps around the track, we still had to run *how many?* others.
2. *Which one?* weekend, *how many?* hikers went on a *what kind?* trip to the *what kind?* park.
3. We rode in a *what kind?* van that carried *how many?* people and went *how many?* miles to the basketball game.
4. There was *how much?* time left when I started to answer the *which one?* question on the test.
5. During the *what kind?* afternoon we washed more than *how many?* cars and earned *how many?* dollars.

An adjective sometimes follows the word it modifies. Note the position of the adjectives in the following sentences.

Each one of the students brought **used books** for the auction.

The **books,** although **old** and **worn,** were quickly bought.

EXERCISE 6. Identifying Adjectives and the Words They Modify. Write the following sentences, underlining the adjectives. Then draw an arrow from each adjective to the noun it modifies. Do not underline the articles *a, an,* and *the.*

EXAMPLE 1. It was a stormy night by the time the weary hikers reached the campground.

1. *It was a stormy night by the time the weary hikers reached the campground.*

1. Melville described whaling in his famous novel *Moby Dick.*
2. Whaling used to be considered a romantic adventure.
3. Whalers took long voyages on sailing ships with tall masts.
4. Modern whaling is a different kind of adventure. 3. *or* sailing
5. Today, ships that hunt for whales are huge floating factories.

6. Sharp harpoons are shot from guns and carry explosive tips.
7. In the nineteenth century, the products of whaling had great value, but today the products are not in much demand.
8. Some types of whales are becoming a rare sight.
9. Of the nine species of whales, six are now on the list of endangered species.
10. Citizens, both young and old, have been working for a long time to protect whales.

WRITING APPLICATION B:
Making Writing More Exact Through the Careful Use of Adjectives

Some words, especially adjectives, have been used so many times that they no longer carry much meaning. If you describe a friend with words like *nice,* or *great,* and other common adjectives, you are not saying much. Keep a notebook of new adjectives and use them in your writing and speaking. You will be able to communicate more information, and you will be more exact.

EXAMPLE The people of Florida raised money to restore the interior of the old capitol to the way it had been in 1845. Red, white, and blue were the original colors, but they had been natural colors and soft pastels. The ceiling over the entry hall has been painted in a *terra-cotta* red.

Do you know what *terra cotta* is? Other specific color adjectives include *azure, mauve, cerise, taupe* and *scarlet.*

Writing Assignment

Answers will vary.

Make up a new product that would be a magnificent discovery. Write a sales pitch or some other kind of advertisement for this product. Use at least three lively, exact adjectives describing your new product. Underline these adjectives.

EXERCISE 7. Have several students give answers orally for each sentence, and write the best answers on the board. Circle particularly interesting or vivid adjectives.

PROPER ADJECTIVES

If you omitted the section "Proper Nouns and Common Nouns," you should omit this section also. Proper adjectives cause little trouble except in connection with capitalization, and you may wish to postpone their study until you take up Chapter 22, "Capital Letters."

EXERCISE 8. You may prefer to instruct the class to copy the sentences and underline proper nouns once and proper adjectives, with the nouns they modify, twice.

GRAMMAR

EXERCISE 7. **Writing Sentences with Adjectives.** Except for *a, an,* and *the,* the following sentences contain no adjectives. Rewrite each sentence and, wherever possible, add interesting adjectives to modify the nouns and pronouns. Answers will vary.

EXAMPLE 1. The children took a nap.
1. *The five grumpy children took a long nap.*

1. Carolyn gave a cat to her aunt.
2. Luis donated books and jeans for the sale.
3. We watched the parade pass under our window.
4. The fielder caught the ball and made a throw to the catcher.
5. The dancer leaped across the stage.

Proper Adjectives

A *proper adjective* is formed from a proper noun, and like a proper noun, it begins with a capital letter.

PROPER NOUN	PROPER ADJECTIVE
Africa	**African** nations
China	**Chinese** calendar
Shakespeare	**Shakespearean** drama
Islam	**Islamic** law

EXERCISE 8. **Identifying Proper Nouns and Proper Adjectives.** Number your paper 1–10. Write each proper noun and proper adjective after its sentence number. Next to each proper adjective, write the noun it modifies.

EXAMPLE 1. In recent years many American tourists have visited the Great Wall in China.
1. *American—tourists, Great Wall, China*

1. The Colorado beetle has destroyed many potato crops in the United States.
2. The professor of African literature gave a lecture on the novels of Camara Laye, a writer who was born in Guinea.
3. Marian McPartland, a jazz pianist from New York City, played several songs that Scott Joplin wrote.

4. The program about the Egyptian ruins was narrated by an English scientist and a French anthropologist.
5. The exchange students from Europe were fascinated by the video games in America.
6. The society of Victorian England was the subject of many British novels in the late 1800's.
7. During the press conference the President commented on the Congressional vote.
8. My friend from Tokyo gave me a Japanese kimono.
9. We saw a display of Appalachian crafts in the public library.
10. Which Arthurian legend have you chosen for your report?

Changing Parts of Speech

Sometimes nouns are used as adjectives: *library* book, *airplane* ride, *school* mascot. *Library, airplane,* and *school* are nouns, but they act as adjectives when they are put in front of nouns. The way that a word is used in a sentence determines what part of speech it is.

Words such as *each, some,* and *whose* are sometimes pronouns and sometimes adjectives, depending on their use in a sentence. When they are used in place of nouns, they are pronouns; when they modify nouns, they are adjectives. When they are adjectives, they always precede a noun.

PRONOUN **Each** did the assignment.
ADJECTIVE **Each** person did the assignment.

PRONOUN **Some** have gone to their dressing rooms.
ADJECTIVE **Some** actors have gone to their dressing rooms.

PRONOUN **Whose** are these?
ADJECTIVE **Whose** gloves are these?

EXERCISE 9. Identifying Adjectives and Pronouns. Label the italicized word in each sentence as an adjective (*adj.*) or pronoun (*pron.*).

EXAMPLE 1. Say *whatever* you think.
1. *pron.*

GRAMMAR

CHANGING PARTS OF SPEECH

The fact that the same word can often be used as different parts of speech is difficult at first for students to grasp. Concentrate here on the words that can be used both as pronouns and as adjectives. Your class may profit from an oral exercise such as this one:

A. Each of these underlined adjectives will become a pronoun if you leave out the noun it modifies, because the underlined word will then stand for the whole idea.
   1. *All* people are mortal. (*All* are mortal.)
   2. Mom has *several* ideas. (Mom has *several.*)
   3. Although *one* guest did not eat the cake, *another* guest praised the cook. (Although *one* did not eat the cake, *another* praised the cook.)

B. If you add a noun after a pronoun, the underlined word will then be an adjective, modifying the noun.
   1. *Both* are intelligent. (*Both* girls. . . .)
   2. I don't like *that*. (. . . *that* idea.)
   3. *Either* would answer your question. (*Either* encyclopedia. . . .)

Note: The idea presented in this section may be confusing to a less-advanced class. You may wish to omit the section and take up the problem of different parts of speech later in connection with Chapter 26, "Using the Dictionary," or Chapter 28, "Vocabulary."

EXERCISE 9. Go over the answers orally in class. For sentences 2, 3, 5, 7, 8, and 10, ask students to identify the words modified by the italicized adjectives. For sentences 1, 4, 6, and 9, ask how adding a word would change the pronouns to adjectives.

REVIEW EXERCISE C. This exercise may be used as a test on adjectives.

GRAMMAR

1. *Both* passed the test. 1. pron.
2. At the tryouts *each* one of the students recited the lines from the first act. 2. adj.
3. *Many* high schools offer driver training. 3. adj.
4. It's hard to know what *one* should do in this situation. 4. pron.
5. *Some* twins do not look exactly alike. 5. adj.
6. After several days in Paris, *each* of the tourists flew to London. 6. pron.
7. They took *both* bicycles to be repaired. 7. adj.
8. Sally asked *another* friend to the party. 8. adj.
9. *Many* of us volunteered to help the teacher. 9. pron. 10. adj.
10. A unicycle has only *one* wheel, making it difficult to ride.

REVIEW EXERCISE C. Identifying Adjectives. There are twenty-five adjectives in the following paragraph. Make a list of them as they appear. Do not list articles.

1. The ancient Greeks and Romans worshiped twelve major gods. **2.** The one with the most power was Zeus, or Jupiter, who lived on a high mountain, Mount Olympus. **3.** From the cloudy peak he surveyed the various affairs of the world. **4.** He rode in a great chariot that was drawn by four white horses. **5.** Whenever he liked, he called for a great assembly of the gods. **6.** At the huge assembly would be Poseidon, or Neptune, the god of the sea; Hades, or Pluto, the god of the shadowy land of the dead; Hera, or Juno, the handsome but quarrelsome wife of his twin; Apollo, the shining god of the sun; Artemis, or Diana, the swift goddess of the hunt, who in time became known as the goddess of the moon; Hermes, or Mercury, the swift messenger of the gods; Hestia, or Vesta, the goddess of the hearth, who became a special protector of the home; Ares, or Mars, the dreadful god of war; Athena, or Minerva, the favorite daughter of Zeus, who was noted for her great wisdom; Hephaestus, or Vulcan, the ugly but useful god of fire and of the forge; and Aphrodite, or Venus, the lovely goddess of beauty.

DIAGRAMING NOUNS AND ADJECTIVES

Diagraming, as you recall from Chapter 10, is a way of seeing the relationships between words and groups of words. When you first studied the adjective, you drew an arrow from the adjective to the noun that it modified. This relationship can also be expressed in a diagram.

PATTERN

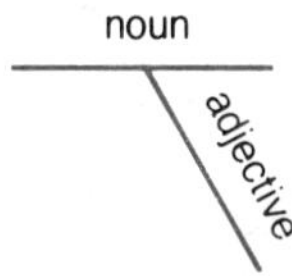

EXAMPLES bright star a special person

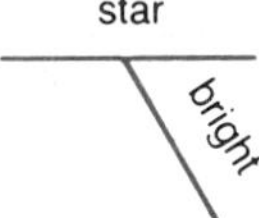

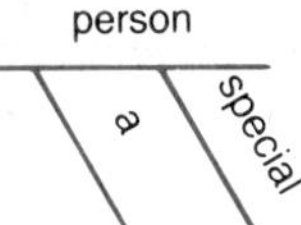

Two or more adjectives joined by a connecting word are diagramed this way.

PATTERN

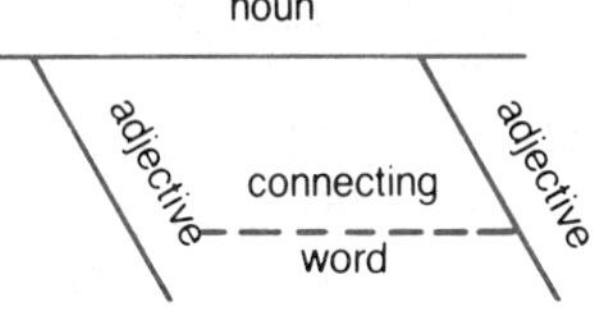

EXAMPLE a lovely and quiet place

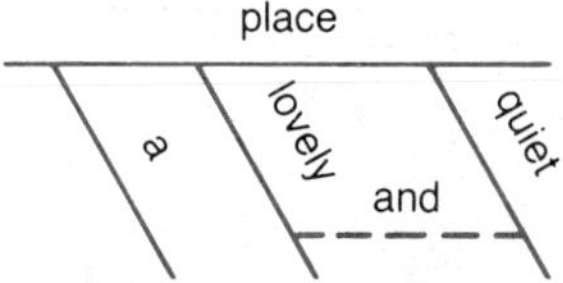

Possessive pronouns are diagramed in the same way adjectives are.

GRAMMAR

DIAGRAMING NOUNS AND ADJECTIVES

Emphasize that diagrams show relationships. Ask what relationship is shown by the position of an adjective on a diagram. If an adjective were placed elsewhere on the diagram, would the relationship be clear?

EXERCISES 10 and 11. Exercise 10 can be done in class immediately after the explanatory material is covered. To avoid spending too much time on the mechanics of diagraming, assign a time limit. Exercise 11 may be given as homework.

REVIEW EXERCISE D. Allow enough time for students to write the paragraph before identifying nouns, pronouns, and adjectives.

GRAMMAR

EXERCISE 10. Diagraming Nouns and Adjectives. Diagram the following items. Draw your diagrams with a ruler and allow plenty of space between diagrams. See Answer Key.

1. mighty warrior
2. big blue ox
3. a narrow path
4. long, exciting movie
5. his one purpose
6. the last one
7. short and funny story
8. many others
9. my final offer
10. the slow but persistent turtle

EXERCISE 11. Diagraming Sentences. Diagram the following sentences. See Answer Key.

EXAMPLE 1. A funny clown performed.

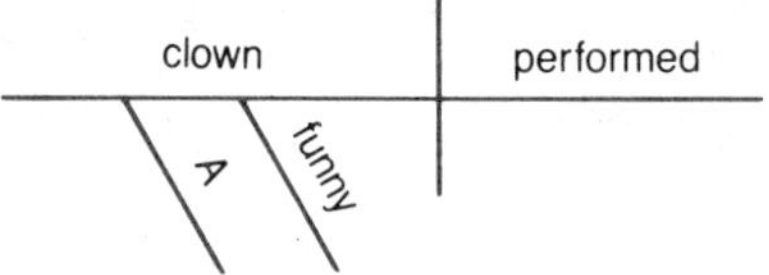

1. Our Swedish visitor arrived.
2. Several answers were given.
3. The small, shy boy won.
4. The poor but generous woman helped.
5. A house and a large barn have burned.

REVIEW EXERCISE D. Identifying Nouns, Pronouns, and Adjectives. Write the following paragraph on your paper, leaving an extra line of space between lines of writing. Over each noun, write *n.;* over each pronoun, write *pron.;* and over each adjective, write *adj.* Disregard the articles *a, an,* and *the.*

Charles Drew developed techniques that are used in the separation and preservation of blood. His research saved numerous lives during World War II. After he received his medical degrees, he taught at Howard University in Washington, D.C. He set up centers in which blood could be stored. The British government asked him to develop a storage system in England. During the war, Dr. Drew was director of an important effort for the American Red Cross that involved the donation of blood. Dr. Drew was also chief surgeon at Freedman's Hospital. We are indebted to this scientist for his great contributions. Many people who have needed blood owe their lives to his methods.

REVIEW EXERCISE E. Diagraming Sentences. Diagram the following sentences: See Answer Key.

1. Every minute counts.
2. Five days and five nights passed.
3. The powerful motor shook and roared.
4. The ventriloquist and the dummy talked and sang.
5. Black and gray ties have been sold.

CHAPTER 11 REVIEW: POSTTEST 1

Identifying Nouns, Pronouns, and Adjectives. Number your paper 1–25. After the proper number, write each italicized word in the following sentences, and indicate whether it is a noun, a pronoun, or an adjective. Use the abbreviations *n.* (noun), *pron.* (pronoun), and *adj.* (adjective).

1. Jenna prepared supper *herself* this *morning.* 1. pron., n. (adverbial noun)
2. *Everybody* says that *high school* will be more work, but more fun, too. 2. pron., n.
3. *This* is the biggest mistake *they* ever made. 3. pron., pron.
4. Jackie became a *high-school* senior *last* year. 4. adj., adj.
5. Does *anybody* know *whose* bicycle this is? 5. pron., pron. (*or* adj.)
6. *Mr. Lander* owns a grove of *citrus* trees. 6. n., adj.
7. That German shepherd *dog* is a *lively* animal. 7. n., adj.
8. The lady across the street owns a *Swiss* clock that has *ivory* numbers. 8. adj., adj.
9. Vincent lived in *Los Angeles* before *his* family moved here. 9. n., pron.
10. This is *their* fault because they ignored all the *danger* signals. 10. pron., adj.
11. I'm telling you, *you* are in *danger.* 11. pron., n.

GRAMMAR

REVIEW EXERCISE E. This exercise will indicate how well students have learned the diagraming taught up to this point. Assign a time limit of fifteen or twenty minutes.

CHAPTER 11 REVIEW: POSTTEST 1

This posttest contains twenty-five items. Students are asked to identify the italicized words as nouns, pronouns, or adjectives.

CHAPTER 11 REVIEW: POSTTEST 2

This test requires students to write a total of forty original sentences using prescribed words as nouns, pronouns, or adjectives. With less-advanced students, you may wish to omit the test, reduce the number of required sentences, or use a portion of the items as a class activity.

Additional Practice

Teacher's Resource Book, Worksheet pages 110–120, Alternative Worksheet pages (for less-advanced students) 535–37

Testing

Teaching Tests booklet, pages 19–22, 25–26, 37–43
Teacher's Resource Book, Test pages 413–16, 419–20, 431–42

GRAMMAR

12. *It* seemed that *whatever* happened always turned out all right. 12. pron., pron.
13. The answer, *plain* and simple, is that *somebody* needs to do more work. 13. adj., pron.
14. Give me *some* candy out of that *old* jar, will you? 14. adj., adj.
15. The *football* player had to retire after his third knee *injury*. 15. adj., n.
16. Are you going to *the* dance *Saturday* night? 16. adj., adj.
17. I told him to give you *something* for *your* stomachache. 17. pron., pron.
18. The dogcatcher picked up *my* dog last *Saturday*. 18. pron., n.
19. *Each* studcnt is rcquired to take *English*. 19. adj., n.
20. *Each* of them believed that the *best* response would be no response at all. 20. pron., adj.
21. *No one* gave Ms. Lucas *any* trouble. 21. pron., adj.
22. *That* drummer is the *best*. 22. adj., adj.
23. The *waiter* brought dessert even though Richard had said that he didn't want *any*. 23. n., pron.
24. *Mama* said to turn off the *television*, Billy. 24. n., n.
25. I learned a new *dance* step from that *television* show. 25. adj., adj.

CHAPTER 11 REVIEW: POSTTEST 2

Writing Sentences with Nouns, Pronouns, and Adjectives. Write two sentences with each of the following words. Use each one as two different parts of speech—noun and adjective or pronoun and adjective. Write the part of speech of the word after each sentence. Answers will vary.

EXAMPLE 1. this
1. *This bicycle is mine.* *adjective*
1. *This cannot be the right answer.* *pronoun*

just 1 sentence

1. game	6. that	11. Greek	16. one
✓ 2. their adj.	7. green	12. paper	17. many
3. American	8. school	13. lake	18. money
4. right	✓ 9. mine pro	14. square	19. date
5. whose	✓ 10. yours pro	15. bicycle	20. government

CHAPTER 12

The Parts of Speech

VERB, ADVERB, PREPOSITION, CONJUNCTION, INTERJECTION

In Chapter 11 you studied two of the workhorses of the sentence, the *noun* and the *pronoun;* and the part of speech that makes the noun or pronoun more definite, the *adjective.* In this chapter you will learn about the other workhorse of the sentence—the *verb*—and the remaining four parts of speech—*adverb, preposition, conjunction,* and *interjection.*

DIAGNOSTIC TEST

Identifying Verbs, Adverbs, Prepositions, Conjunctions, and Interjections. Number your paper 1–20. After the proper number, write the italicized word or word group in each of the following sentences and label it as an action verb (*a.v.*), a linking verb (*l.v.*), a helping verb (*h.v.*), an adverb (*adv.*), a preposition (*prep.*), a conjunction (*conj.*), or an interjection (*interj.*).

EXAMPLE 1. That girl has *traveled* widely with her family.
1. *traveled—a.v.*

1. Rosie *hit* a home run and tied up the score. 1. a.v.

GRAMMAR

Chapter Overview

Students should become familiar with the terminology used in describing English sentences and to learn the functions of the parts of speech. The writing applications encourage the students to demonstrate their facility with these abstract grammatical concepts and to produce lively, original writing.

Unless your students are unusually well prepared in grammar, introduce only one new part of speech each day. Encourage questions and discussion, and explain carefully any matters that confuse students. Use visual explanations, board diagrams, and plenty of example sentences.

Chapter Objective

Students will identify and use effectively in their own writing, verbs, adverbs, prepositions, conjunctions, and interjections.

PRESENTING THE CHAPTER

LESS-ADVANCED STUDENTS With a less-advanced class, stress examples rather than definitions or grammatical terminology. These students should learn the name and the most important function of each part of speech, but you need not insist that they master finer points such as the distinctions between action verbs and linking verbs or between coordinating and correlative conjunctions. *(See listing of Alternative Worksheets on page 335.)*

ADVANCED STUDENTS An advanced class that is already familiar with grammar should not need much review of the parts of speech. Work rapidly through the chapter, and give the students as many opportunities as possible to concentrate on original writing assignments.

WRITING APPLICATIONS

The writing applications in this chapter are designed to encourage students to use their knowledge of verbs and prepositions in their own writing. Feel free to adapt these assignments to your students' writing needs, abilities, and interests.

DIAGNOSTIC TEST

This test will give you a clear picture of what your students already know about verbs, adverbs, prepositions, conjunctions, and interjections. Use the results to guide you in planning how much time to spend on this chapter.

THE VERB (rule 12a)

Begin by reviewing the sentence base (Chapter 10). Elicit from the class the definition of a sentence and definitions of the two essential parts of a sentence (subject and predicate). Point out that the vital word in a predicate is the verb. Show that, although the other words in the predicate add something to the statement, they are not essential to it. Even if they are omitted, a statement remains. Now try omitting the verb from a sentence. The class will see that what is left is not a complete statement. Stress this primary function of the verb: It helps to make a statement; it says something about the subject. Stress also the grammatical importance of this function: It is impossible to make a complete statement without a verb.

GRAMMAR

2. *Wow,* that's the best meal I've eaten in a long time! 2. interj.
3. School can *be* fun sometimes. 3. l.v.
4. Neither Carlos nor Jan wanted to go *very* far out into the water. 4. adv.
5. That dog looks mean *in spite of* his wagging tail. 5. prep.
6. *Have* you ever seen any wild animals around here? 6. h.v.
7. If Ken will *not* help us, then he cannot share in the rewards. 7. adv.
8. My older sister was a cheerleader *during* her senior year. 8. prep.
9. The road that runs *close* to the railroad tracks is usually crowded. 9. adv.
10. Several of my friends *enjoy* working at the mall. 10. a.v.
11. No one could do much to help, *for* the damage had already been done. 11. conj.
12. *Where* have you been putting the corrected papers? 12. adv.
13. *Oh,* I didn't know he had already volunteered. 13. interj.
14. Jodie *was* taking in the wash for her mother. 14. h.v.
15. Surely Ms. Johnson doesn't *expect* us to finish by tomorrow.
16. May I have a glass of milk and a combination sandwich *without* onions? 15. a.v. 16. prep.
17. James *became* impatient, but he waited quietly. 17. l.v.
18. My uncle almost always brings us something *when* he visits during the holidays. 18. conj.
19. The car swerved suddenly, *yet* the driver remained in control. 19. conj.
20. The rose *smells* lovely. 20. l.v.

THE VERB

You know that the verb is one of the parts of the sentence base. It helps to make a statement about its subject. Some verbs do this by expressing the action of the subject: girl *ran;* monkeys *chatter;* sun *sets.* Other verbs help to make a statement without expressing action: I *am* an eighth-grader; this *is* good; they *seem* happy.

12a. A *verb* is a word that expresses action or otherwise helps to make a statement.

Action Verbs

The action expressed by a verb may be physical action or mental action.

PHYSICAL ACTION jump, shout, search, carry, run
MENTAL ACTION worry, think, believe, imagine

The action verbs in the following sentences are in boldfaced type.

Langston Hughes **wrote** volumes of poetry.
Julia Child **makes** gourmet cooking fun.
We **listened** to the *Jupiter* Symphony by Mozart.

EXERCISE 1. Identifying Action Verbs. Number your paper 1–11. After the proper number, write the verb or verbs in each sentence. There are twenty action verbs in the passage.

1. In the winter our house makes strange noises. **2.** Doors on old brass hinges creak as they open and close. **3.** Pipes in the basement shudder when the water heater starts up. **4.** Loose floorboards crack from the weight of footsteps. **5.** The window curtains rustle softly when the winds blow outside. **6.** The old china cabinet clatters each time a truck passes by. **7.** Beams and rafters in the attic strain and groan during the cold, windy nights.

8. Often members of my family sit silently and listen for these noises of the house. **9.** We disconnect the television and the appliances. **10.** We count the different kinds of noises. **11.** Sometimes we pretend that ghosts lurk upstairs and cause the eerie noises.

Linking Verbs

Many verbs do not express action. Instead, they help to make a statement by acting as links between a subject, which normally comes before the verb, and a word in the predicate, which usually follows the verb. Such verbs are called *linking verbs* because they link their subjects with nouns or adjectives in the predicate.

ACTION VERBS

Eighth-graders will probably find these easy to understand. Spend little time here.

EXERCISE 1. An advanced class may skip this easy drill.

LINKING VERBS

Emphasize that *linking* means *connecting* or *tying*—that a linking verb connects or ties the subject to a word or words in the predicate. Some teachers require students to memorize the forms of the most important linking verb, *be*, as well as the list of other common linking verbs (page 312). Explain, however, that these verbs are not *always* used as linking verbs. Put on the board a few sentences that show the same verb used in both ways. For example:

ACTION
She *appeared* on the stage.
He *looked* at the girl.
He *grew* tomatoes.

LINKING
She *appeared* happy.
He *looked* healthy.
He *grew* tall.

Your students may insist that some or all of these linking verbs seem to show action. Explain that they are used in the sense of *seem* or *become*. Do not be surprised if your students find this distinction difficult. Allow them to express their opinions. Agree with them that the difference is not always easy to see, and tell them that later, in their study of complements (Chapter 13), they will learn to apply some grammatical tests that are helpful on this point.

Introduce each of the other verbs in the list on page 312. Have your

EXAMPLES The star's name **is** Ruby Dee. [name = Ruby Dee]

Marie Curie **became** a famous scientist. [Marie Curie = scientist]

Wild animals **remain** free on the great animal reserves in Africa. [free animals]

The watermelon **looks** ripe. [ripe watermelon]

The verb most commonly used as a linking verb is the verb *be*. You should memorize its various forms.

***Forms of the Verb* Be**

am, is, are, was, were, be, being, been

Any verb ending in *be* or *been* is a form of *be: shall be, will be, can be, might be, has been, have been, had been, would have been, might have been,* etc.

In addition to *be,* there are several other verbs that are often used as linking verbs:

appear, look, seem	feel, smell, sound, taste
become, grow	remain, stay

EXERCISE 2. Writing Linking Verbs. Write the following sentences, inserting a different linking verb in each blank. Be prepared to tell which word each verb links to its subject.

Answers will vary.

EXAMPLE 1. Judith Jamison —— calm during the premiere of the dance.

1. *Judith Jamison remained calm during the premiere of the dance.* [*Remained* links *Jamison* and *calm.*]

1. The first day —— long.
2. Your suggestion —— good to me.
3. Our room —— festive after we decorated it for the party.
4. The orange —— a little too sweet.
5. In the novel the main character —— a doctor, and he returns home to set up a clinic.
6. Before a storm the air —— wet and heavy.
7. Did she —— happy living in Florida?
8. The diver —— more confident with each dive she made.

class try to give examples of each, both as linking verb and as action verb. Write these on the board. (The class may be unable to give an example of *become* as an action verb. Here is one: *That hat* **becomes** *you.*) For the verbs *taste, feel, look,* and *smell,* you can give amusing and convincing explanations of the difference between action verbs and linking verbs. Put on the board one or more pairs of sentences such as these:

He *smelled* the cake.
The cake *smelled* good.

Point out how ridiculous it would be to call *smelled* in the second sentence an action verb, since a cake has no nose.

Note: The verb be *is not always used as a linking verb (*We **were** there She **is** in the eighth grade*), but many teachers do not like to call* be *an action verb in such uses. If you wish, you may tell the class simply that* be *is a special verb and that it is usually, though not always, used as a linking verb.*

EXERCISE 2. All classes can do this exercise. An advanced class can do it orally and then write out Exercise 3.

9. They —— interested in the guest speaker.
10. The lilacs —— lovely.

Most linking verbs may also be used as action verbs. Whether a verb is used to express action or to link words depends on its meaning in a given sentence.

LINKING The tiger **looked** tame.
ACTION The tiger **looked** for something to eat.

LINKING The soup **tasted** good.
ACTION I **tasted** the soup.

LINKING She **grew** tired of playing.
ACTION She **grew** into a fine woman.

EXERCISE 3. Identifying Action Verbs and Linking Verbs. Number your paper 1–10. In the following sentences, when the verb is used as an action verb, write the verb and its subject beside the appropriate number. When the verb is used as a linking verb, write the verb, its subject, and the word or words that the verb links to its subject.

EXAMPLES
1. Ms. Brody appeared suddenly in the classroom.
1. *appeared, Ms. Brody*
2. Ms. Brody appeared quite cheerful.
2. *appeared, Ms. Brody—cheerful*

1. At Marla's request, we tasted the chili. 1. we
2. The chili tasted very spicy. 2. chili—spicy 3. cook—unhappy
3. The cook looked unhappy about our comments.
4. She looked at her sister Joan suspiciously. 4. She 5. chili—good
5. Yesterday the chili in the school cafeteria looked good.
6. Marla looked at Joan then, too. 6. Marla
7. Joan felt mischievous. 7. Joan—mischievous
8. She felt a laugh in the back of her throat. 8. She
9. The doorbell sounded down the hall. 9. doorbell
10. Marla's voice, usually pleasant, sounded angry. 10. voice—angry

EXERCISE 4. Identifying Verbs. Number your paper 1–14. After the proper number, list the verb or verbs that appear on

EXERCISE 3. If your students do poorly on this exercise, go over the answers in class, encouraging questions and discussion. If a less-advanced group still seems unable to grasp the distinction between action verbs and linking verbs, you may wish to take it up later in connection with Chapter 13, "Complements." A class that does well on this exercise may skip Exercise 4.

EXERCISE 4. This may be used as additional drill or as a test.

that line. If the verb is a linking verb, list also the subject and the word or words that the verb links to its subject.

1. Matt—musician

Matt is a young musician who loves all kinds of music. According to his parents, he practices the piano every day. No one knows how many hours he plays each week, although many people guess at least twenty. His parents worry about him. They think he remains indoors too much. Still, Matt seems happy. 5–6. Matt—happy

7. Matt—restless, notes—wrong

One day Matt becomes restless. The notes sound wrong, and everything appears impossible. However, Matt seems confident. He grabs some sheets of music paper and then writes down some notes. After some careful revisions Matt forms the notes into an original harmony.

That night he performs his song for his parents. They exclaim, "Matt, we are so proud of our son, the pianist and composer!" 8. everything—impossible, 8.–9. Matt—confident 13. we—proud

WRITING APPLICATION A:
Using Verbs That Make Your Writing Fresh and Lively

Verbs are vital to communication. To make your writing lively and original, try to use verbs that catch your reader's attention. Sportswriters often vary their verbs to give their reports more action and excitement.

EXAMPLE Celtics **rip** Lakers
Mississippi State **bashes** Michigan

Writing Assignment

Answers will vary.

When you use chronological order, you place events in the order in which they occurred. Write a summary of an incident from a book, a movie, or a television show that you consider to be exciting. Present the incident in chronological order, using verbs that are fresh and lively. Underline these verbs.

Helping Verbs

So far in this chapter you have been studying one-word verbs, sometimes called *main verbs*. Frequently, though, the main verb is accompanied by other verbs called *helping verbs*. The main verb and the helping verbs together make up a *verb phrase*. Notice in the following examples that the main verb may change its form when a helping verb is added.

MAIN VERB crawl
VERB PHRASE will crawl

MAIN VERB listen
VERB PHRASE have been listening

MAIN VERB find
VERB PHRASE would have been found

Here is a list of the most commonly used helping verbs.

Commonly Used Helping Verbs

be (am, is, are, etc.)	shall	should	must
has	will	would	do
have	can	may	did
had	could	might	does

The verb *be* in its various forms is the most frequently used helping verb. *Be* used as a helping verb is very easy to distinguish from *be* used as a linking verb. When *be* is used as a helping verb, there is always a main verb used with it; but when *be* is used as a linking verb, it is itself the main verb.

HELPING VERB These books **have been read** many times.
LINKING VERB The children **have been** good today.

The following sentences contain verb phrases. The verbs are in boldface, and the main verbs are also underlined.

Seiji Ozawa **has been praised** for his fine conducting.
His recordings **should be heard** by anyone interested in classical music.
He **will conduct** many outstanding orchestras.

GRAMMAR

HELPING VERBS

Point out that helping verbs are *not* a third kind of main verb, parallel to action verbs and linking verbs. In Chapter 10 your students learned that sometimes the verb in a sentence is made up of more than one word. Explain that helping verbs are simply the "extra" words that help the main verb make a statement. The *whole verb* consists of the *main verb* plus these *helpers,* and the whole verb is either an action or a linking verb, depending on how it is used.

Show how helping verbs are used with main verbs to make verb phrases. Selecting the complete verb phrase in a sentence may still be difficult for eighth-graders, especially when other words separate the parts of a verb phrase (page 316). Frequent drill in finding the *whole verb* is helpful. It is also useful for students to be able to identify helping verbs in a verb phrase. For this reason, some exercises in this chapter ask students to identify helping verbs. Review the basic ideas of subject and verb throughout the year by asking the class to pick out subjects and whole verbs in sentences they are discussing.

EXERCISE 5. You may want to use this exercise for drill in class, especially with less-advanced students.

REVIEW EXERCISE A. A less-advanced class may use this exercise for further practice in identifying verbs and verb phrases, without being required to distinguish between action verbs and linking verbs.

Answers: Review Exercise A

1. was used, a.v.
2. were, l.v.
3. were, l.v.
4. roamed, a.v.
5. considered, a.v.
6. invaded, a.v.
7. pillaged, a.v.
8. worshiped, a.v.
9. hoped, a.v.
10. would die, a.v.
11. believed, a.v.
12. died, a.v.
13. went, a.v.
14. could enjoy, a.v.
15. thought, a.v.
16. would go, a.v.
17. would receive, a.v.
18. would meet, a.v.
19. would heal, a.v.
20. could boast, a.v.

GRAMMAR

EXERCISE 5. Identifying Verb Phrases. Number your paper 1–10. Write the verb phrases in the order in which they appear in the following paragraph:

> Many people are earning their livings at unusual jobs. Even today people can find positions as shepherds, inventors, and candlestick makers. It may seem strange, but these people have decided that ordinary jobs can become too tedious for them. Some people have been working as messengers. You may have seen them when they were wearing costumes such as gorilla suits. Other people have been finding work as mimes. With a little imagination, anyone can find an unusual job.

Sometimes the verb phrase is interrupted by other parts of speech, as in the following examples:

> Because of the fog, we **could** not **see** the road.
> People **may** someday **communicate** with dolphins.
> How much **do** you **know** about Lucy Stone, the suffragist?

REVIEW EXERCISE A. Labeling Linking Verbs and Action Verbs. Number your paper 1–20. List the verbs and the verb phrases that appear in the following paragraph. After each action verb or verb phrase, write *a.v.;* after each linking verb or verb phrase, write *l.v.*

> The term *Viking* was used for all sailors of the North, whether they were Norwegians, Swedes, or Danes. The Vikings were a fierce people who roamed the seas for about three hundred years. For several centuries people considered the Vikings the scourge of Europe because they invaded and pillaged other countries. They worshiped such fierce gods as Thor and Odin, and they hoped that they would die in battle. The Vikings believed that when they died in battle, they went to Valhalla, where they could eternally enjoy battles and banquets. The Vikings thought that each day the warriors in Valhalla would go out to the battlefield and would receive wounds time and time again. Then, in spite of their injuries, at the end of each day they would all meet back at the banquet hall, where their wounds would promptly heal and they could boast about their great bravery in battle.

REVIEW EXERCISE B. Labeling Parts of Speech. Write the following sentences using every other line of your paper. Underline the italicized words, and over each of these, write an abbreviation to show its part of speech: *n.* for noun, *pron.* for pronoun, *adj.* for adjective, *a.v.* for action verb, and *l.v.* for linking verb. Treat proper names and verb phrases as single words.

EXAMPLE 1. *Mary McLeod Bethune* is a *major* figure in American history.

n. adj.
1. *Mary McLeod Bethune is a major figure in American history.*

1. *She* dedicated her *life* to helping young people. 1. pron., n.
2. In her *early* years she *began* a teaching career. 2. adj., a.v.
3. In 1904 she moved to Florida and *opened* a school of *her* own.
4. The school eventually *became* the Bethune-Cookman College, and Bethune served as its *president*. 3. a.v., pron. 4. l.v., n.
5. In 1930 Bethune *was invited* to a *Presidential* conference on child health and protection. 5. a.v., adj.
6. Then, during Roosevelt's administration, *she* helped in the establishment of the *National Youth Administration*. 6. pron., n.
7. Her outstanding efforts *impressed* Roosevelt, and *he* established an important office on minority affairs. 7. a.v., pron.
8. This office granted funds to *serious* students so that *they* could continue their education. 8. adj., pron.
9. In 1945 she *was* an observer at the conference that organized the *United Nations*. 9. l.v., n.
10. Bethune *remained* interested in education, and her *notable* efforts earned her national recognition. 10. l.v., adj.

THE ADVERB

12b. An *adverb* is a word used to modify a verb, an adjective, or another adverb.

REVIEW EXERCISE B. This exercise covers all the parts of speech that have been taught up to this point in the textbook.

THE ADVERB (rule 12b)

Students may have difficulty with adverbs modifying adjectives or other adverbs. Since these last two functions of the adverb do not cause glaring problems in usage, you may wish to skip them with a less-advanced class.

To introduce adverbs to an average or above-average class, write on the board sentences such as these, underlining the words that are here italicized.

1. We did the work *carefully*. (how?)
2. We do our homework *nightly*. (when?)
3. The balloon went *up*. (where?)
4. I am *too* hungry to think. (to what extent?)
5. The work was *very well* done. (to what extent? how?)

Draw from students the information that the underlined words give information about *how* the work was done, *when* the homework is done, etc. Some students will remember that these words are called adverbs. Ask the students *which* word each underlined adverb modifies. Help them discover that adverbs modify verbs, adjectives, or other adverbs. They should suggest original sentences that contain adverbs and should state which words the adverbs modify. Add their examples to those already on the board.

Point out that an adverb modifies a verb much more often than it modifies an adjective or adverb. Give them this helpful tip: Look at the verb first; if the adverb does not seem to "fit" the verb, then look for an adjective or an adverb.

Now have the class compose a rule about the adverb and its use in the sentence. Then have them open their textbooks and check their rule against the textbook definition (rule 12b, page 317).

List on the board information about adverbs that has resulted from class discussion. The list might look like this:

1. Adverbs often end in –ly—but not always.
2. Adverbs tell *how? when? where? to what extent?*
3. Adverbs usually modify verbs.
4. Sometimes an adverb modifies an adjective or an adverb rather than a verb.

You may then list common adverbs on the board as students suggest them. Ask each student who gives an example to prove that the word is an adverb by offering an example sentence.

EXERCISE 6. You can use this exercise as a class activity, or assign it as homework if you are sure that all the students have a fairly good grasp of adverbs.

GRAMMAR

An *adverb* usually answers one of these questions: *Where? When? How? To what extent (how much* or *how long)?*

WHERE?	WHEN?
The fire started **here.** The couple was married **nearby.**	The police arrived **promptly.** **Then** the suspects were questioned.
HOW?	TO WHAT EXTENT (HOW MUCH or HOW LONG)?
The accident occurred **suddenly.** The Prime Minister spoke **carefully.**	We should **never** deceive our friends. She has **scarcely** begun the lesson.

(1) An adverb modifies a verb more often than it modifies an adjective or an adverb.

Notice how an adverb makes the meaning of the verb more definite.

EXAMPLES The man crawled **down**. [The adverb tells *where* the man crawled.]
He halted **abruptly.** [The adverb tells *how* he halted.]
Now we are busy. [The adverb tells *when* we are busy.]
The speaker droned on **endlessly**. [The adverb tells *to what extent* the speaker droned.]

Adverbs are sometimes used to ask questions.

EXAMPLES **Where** are you going?
How did you do on the test?

EXERCISE 6. Identifying Adverbs That Modify Verbs. The following sentences contain twenty adverbs, all modifying verbs. Number your paper 1–9. After the proper number, write the adverbs in that sentence.

EXERCISE 7. Review predicate adjectives before assigning this exercise.

1. The snowstorm has completely blocked traffic and has temporarily grounded airplanes today.
2. How can you develop into a strong runner now?
3. Yesterday three police officers secretly followed the suspect.
4. The doctor came immediately, but the patient had already recovered.
5. Gymnastics has recently attracted many students, and the equipment is always in use.
6. The coach argued violently, but the umpire calmly ignored him.
7. February is never a warm month in Maine.
8. Her luncheon was well attended, and her speech was applauded loudly afterward.
9. Today astronomers can accurately chart the courses of planets, yet the motions of some celestial bodies are still a mystery.

GRAMMAR

(2) An adverb sometimes modifies an adjective.

An adverb is sometimes needed to make the meaning of an adjective more definite. An *extremely* good dancer is quite different from a *fairly* good dancer.

EXAMPLES An **unusually** fast starter, Karen easily won the hurdles event. [The adjective *fast* modifies the noun *starter*; the adverb tells *how fast* the starter was.]

Our committee is **especially** busy at this time of year. [The adjective *busy* modifies the noun *committee;* the adverb tells *how busy* the committee is.]

EXERCISE 7. Identifying Adverbs That Modify Adjectives. Number your paper 1–10. After the proper number, write the adverbs that modify adjectives in each sentence. After each adverb, write the adjective that it modifies.

EXAMPLE 1. Because so many bicycles have been stolen, the principal hired a guard.
1. *so, many*

EXERCISE 8. You will probably want to have your students do this exercise in class orally.

1. The team is extremely proud of its record.
2. All frogs may look quite harmless, but some are poisonous.
3. The class was unusually quiet today.
4. Newborn animals are very clumsy at first.
5. The coach said we were too careless when we made the routine plays.
6. The situation seemed utterly futile.
7. When kittens are with their mother, they look thoroughly contented.
8. Weekends are especially hectic for me when all of my teachers assign homework.
9. The lecture seemed much longer than one hour.
10. The new exchange student who comes from Norway is surprisingly fluent in English.

EXERCISE 8. Writing Adverbs to Modify Adjectives. The adverb *very* is used far too often to modify adjectives. Write an adverb to modify each adjective below. Do not use *very*.

Answers will vary.

EXAMPLE 1. strong
1. *incredibly strong*

1. cheerful	6. timid
2. sour	7. heavy
3. wide	8. long
4. messy	9. calm
5. honest	10. graceful

(3) An adverb occasionally modifies another adverb.

EXAMPLES Elena finished the problem **more** quickly than I did. [The adverb *quickly* modifies the verb *finished* and is, in turn, modified by the adverb *more,* which tells *how quickly* Elena finished the problem.]

Our guest left **quite** abruptly. [The adverb *abruptly* modifies the verb *left* and is modified by *quite,* which tells *how abruptly* our guest left.]

EXERCISE 9. Identifying Adverbs That Modify Other Adverbs. Number your paper 1–5. Beside the appropriate number, list each adverb that modifies another adverb. Then write the adverb that it modifies.

EXAMPLE 1. The new swimming pool is most certainly an improvement over the old one.
1. *most, certainly*

1. Condors are almost entirely extinct in the United States.
2. They are more frequently seen soaring over the Andes Mountains in South America.
3. Condors are the largest living birds, and some people think that they are most assuredly the ugliest.
4. Even though condors have not been welcomed too enthusiastically into the hearts of people, they still need protection.
5. The balance of nature quite definitely depends on all kinds of animals, even on the ones that are not cute and cuddly.

REVIEW EXERCISE C. Identifying Adverbs. Number your paper 1–10. Beside the appropriate number, list the adverbs in the order that they appear in each of the following sentences. After each adverb, write the word or expression that the adverb modifies. Some sentences have more than one adverb.

EXAMPLE 1. The movie ended too quickly.
1. *too—quickly; quickly—ended*

1. I have been a fan of mystery stories since I was very young.
2. My favorite stories are about detectives who cleverly match wits with equally clever villains.
3. Some stories are incredibly exciting from start to finish, but others slowly build suspense.
4. If I like a story, I can hardly put it down until I finish it.
5. I should never become involved in a story if I have tons of homework to do, because then I am too tempted to read.
6. If I am not able to guess the ending, I can scarcely prevent myself from peeking at the last chapter. 6. not may be taken to modify either am or able.

EXERCISE 9. A less-advanced class should probably omit this exercise.

REVIEW EXERCISE C. You can use this exercise as a test on adverbs. A less-advanced class should probably omit the exercise.

GRAMMAR

DIAGRAMING VERBS AND ADVERBS

Diagraming sentences that contain adverbs can be helpful to many students. If your less-advanced class has not studied adverbs that modify adjectives or other adverbs, however, you should naturally omit these points in diagraming activities.

GRAMMAR

7. well modifies restrain; unusually modifies well.

7. I restrain myself unusually well when I am tempted.
8. I wonder if I would have the nerve to creep around and look for clues in a terribly dark, spooky basement.
9. Clues are often found in carefully guarded places.
10. How do the mystery detectives find the answers to some of the most complicated cases?

8. around modifies to creep.

DIAGRAMING VERBS AND ADVERBS

The verb, like the noun and pronoun, always appears on a horizontal line. The adverb is diagramed on a slanting line under the word it modifies.

1. An adverb modifying a verb:

EXAMPLES studies hard does not exercise daily

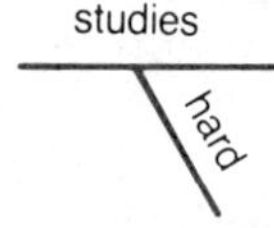

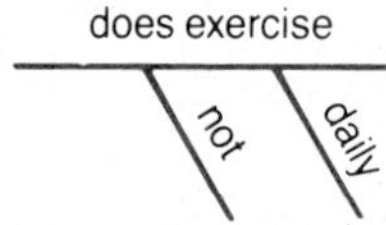

2. An adverb modifying an adjective:

EXAMPLES extremely strong wind much better swimmer

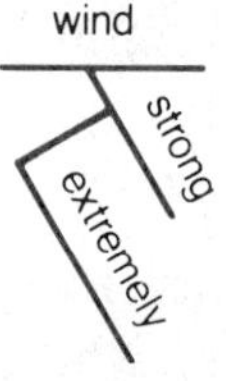

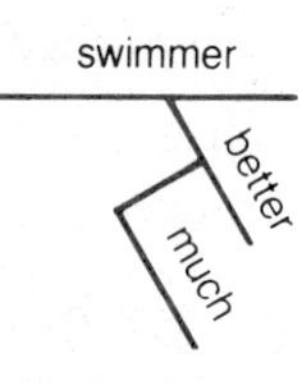

3. An adverb modifying another adverb:

EXAMPLES tried rather hard flew almost too high

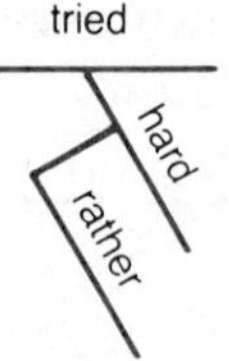

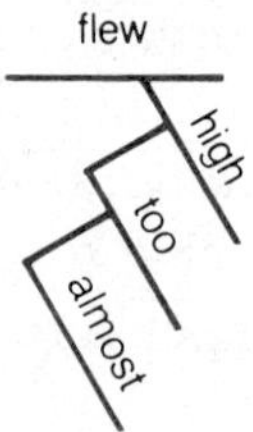

EXERCISE 10. Diagraming Verbs and Adverbs. Diagram the following groups of words. Use a ruler and leave plenty of space between diagrams. See Answer Key.

1. answered quickly
2. badly worn sail
3. listened quite intently
4. worked very late
5. dangerously sharp curve
6. never plans very carefully
7. walked proudly away
8. somewhat rickety bridge
9. may possibly happen
10. drove rather slowly

EXERCISE 11. Diagraming Sentences. Diagram the following sentences. Use a ruler and leave plenty of space between diagrams. See Answer Key.

1. The plane landed smoothly.
2. The shutters rattled quite noisily.
3. We are definitely leaving tomorrow.
4. The tired motorist drove much too far.
5. The unbelievably slow turtle got there first.
6. The guide limped noticeably.
7. The extremely nervous passenger collapsed.
8. Our turn finally came.
9. They tried very hard.
10. The new car had been slightly damaged.

THE PREPOSITION

12c. A *preposition* is a word used to show the relationship of a noun or a pronoun to some other word in the sentence.

Notice how a change in the preposition changes the relationship between *package* and *tree* in each of the following sentences.

The package **under** the tree is mine.
The package **in** the tree is mine.
The package **near** the tree is mine.
The package **behind** the tree is mine.
The package **beside** the tree is mine.

EXERCISES 10 and 11. These exercises contain many adverbs that modify adjectives or other adverbs. A class that has not studied these uses of the adverb should omit the exercises.

THE PREPOSITION (rule 12c)

The concept of *relationships* expressed by prepositions is often a stumbling block for students. Explain this point through a visual demonstration. Holding a book in one hand and a pencil in the other, keep the book in one spot and move the pencil *above, under, beside, inside, over, around, in, into, on* and *onto* the book. Each time, point out the position of the pencil in relation to the position of the book. Say, for instance, "The pencil is *above* the book. Now, the pencil is *under* the book." With a less-advanced class, you might write each preposition on the board after you demonstrate it. Such a demonstration can cover a surprisingly large number of the prepositions listed in the text (page 324). Then call attention to the fact that prepositions may show relationships not only in space but also in other dimensions, such as time (e.g., a meeting *before* noon, *at* dawn, *in* the morning, *after* five o'clock).

Urge your students to familiarize themselves thoroughly with the list of commonly used prepositions on text page 324. Go rapidly through the list, having students offer a brief sentence for each preposition. When the preposition is a word that may also be used as another part of speech, point out this characteristic and give an example.

Explain that compound prepositions, like verb phrases, may be considered as one word. An example will help: *She ran* **out of** *the room* is the equivalent of *She ran* **from** *the room.*

EXERCISE 12. Tell students to refer to the preceding lists of prepositions when doing this exercise.

Learn to recognize the following words, which are commonly used as prepositions.

Commonly Used Prepositions

aboard	behind	from	throughout
about	below	in	to
above	beneath	into	toward
across	beside	like	under
after	between	near	underneath
against	beyond	of	until
along	but (except)	off	unto
amid	by	on	up
among	down	over	upon
around	during	past	with
at	except	since	within
before	for	through	without

Occasionally you will find compound prepositions—prepositions of more than one word. A compound preposition may be considered as one word.

Compound Prepositions

because of	in spite of	instead of
on account of	according to	out of

EXERCISE 12. Identifying Prepositions. Number your paper 1–10. List the prepositions in order beside the appropriate number. Include all parts of any compound prepositions you find.

EXAMPLE 1. Many Roman myths were adaptations of Greek myths.
1. *of*

1. Mars, the god of war, is perhaps the most Roman god in Roman mythology.
2. Many Roman gods were borrowed from Greek mythology.
3. According to legend, Mars was the father of Romulus and Remus, twin brothers.
4. When the twins were babies, an evil ruler threw them into the Tiber River.

5. Romulus and Remus were rescued from the river, then were fed by a wolf, and were raised under the care of a shepherd.
6. These twins fought against each other in a deadly rivalry.
7. Instead of working with his brother, Romulus killed Remus.
8. It is said that Romulus founded the city of Rome around 753 B.C.
9. Throughout the centuries people have read about the legend of Romulus and Remus.
10. Out of hundreds of legends, this one has remained among the best known.

A preposition is always followed by a noun or a pronoun that the preposition relates to another word in the sentence. The noun or the pronoun following the preposition is called the *object* of the preposition. Words that modify the object may come between the preposition and the object. Taken together, the preposition, its object, and the modifiers of the object are called a *prepositional phrase*.

EXAMPLE **across** the dusty **prairie** [The entire prepositional phrase includes the preposition *across*, its object *prairie*, and two adjectives modifying the object—*the* and *dusty*.]

EXERCISE 13. Identifying Prepositional Phrases. Number your paper 1–10, and, after the proper number, write the prepositional phrase in each sentence. Underline each preposition.

EXAMPLE 1. Walt Whitman wrote a very moving poem, "O Captain! My Captain!", about Abraham Lincoln.
1. *about Abraham Lincoln*

1. In this poem the ship's captain represents Abraham Lincoln.
2. The ship has just completed a voyage through rough weather.
3. On the shore, people celebrate the ship's safe arrival.
4. One member of the ship's crew addresses his captain.
5. "For you they call, the swaying mass, their eager faces turning. . . ."

GRAMMAR

EXERCISE 13. Work on identifying prepositional phrases will be repeated in Chapter 14, "The Phrase." With less-advanced students, you may wish to save this exercise for use when you take up Chapter 14.

6. Everyone except the captain can hear the rejoicing.
7. He has died during the voyage.
8. The ship represents the ship of state.
9. The ship's voyage across rough seas symbolizes the Civil War.
10. Lincoln, the captain, directed his ship toward a safe harbor.

GRAMMAR

WRITING APPLICATION B: Using Prepositional Phrases To Create Vivid Similes

Color can add considerable appeal and interest to a picture. You know that you can use specific describing words to create the same kind of vivid impression in your writing. You can also try experimenting with *similes*. To form a simile, use *like* or *as* to show how one thing is similar to another thing, even though the two items are basically different. Notice how the following similes are expressed in prepositional phrases beginning with *like*.

EXAMPLES Her coat was red and silky, and there was a blaze of white down her chest and a circle of white around her throat. Her face was wrinkled and sad, **like a wise old man's.**

JAMES STREET

For nearly a year, I sopped around the house, the Store, the school and the church, **like an old biscuit.**

MAYA ANGELOU

Writing Assignment

Answers will vary.

A *tall tale* is a highly improbable humorous story that stretches the facts beyond any hope of belief. Tall tales include people as tall as mountains, woodsmen who use trees as toothpicks, and other impossible situations. Write a tall tale in which you use at least three similes that are expressed in prepositional phrases beginning with *like* or *as*. Underline these similes.

Sometimes the same word may be used either as a preposition or as an adverb. To tell an adverb from a preposition, remember that a preposition is always followed by a noun or pronoun object.

ADVERB The plane circled above.
PREPOSITION The plane circled above the field. [Note the object of the preposition—*field*.]

ADVERB We remained within.
PREPOSITION We remained within the shelter. [Note the object of the preposition—*shelter*.]

EXERCISE 14. Writing Sentences with Adverbs and Prepositions. Use each of the following words in two sentences, first as an adverb and then as a preposition. Underline the designated word. Answers will vary.

EXAMPLE 1. along
1. *"Why can't I go along?" asked the child.*
1. *Wildflowers were blooming along the riverbank.*

1. off 2. across 3. below 4. above 5. down

You must also be careful not to confuse a prepositional phrase beginning with *to* (*to town, to her club*) with a verb form beginning with *to* (*to run, to be seen*). Again, remember that a prepositional phrase always ends with a noun or pronoun.

THE CONJUNCTION

12d. A *conjunction* is a word that joins words or groups of words.

Conjunctions joining single words:

hot **or** cold
small **but** comfortable

Conjunctions joining groups of words:

through a forest **and** across a river
wanted to notify **but** not to alarm

GRAMMAR

EXERCISE 14. Less-advanced students may find this exercise too difficult.

THE CONJUNCTION (rule 12d)

Introduce conjunctions by writing on the board examples like those on pages 327–28. Most eighth-grade students already understand that the function of conjunctions is to connect words or groups of words. The names of the various *kinds* of conjunctions may be new to your class, however. The words *coordinating, correlative,* and *subordinating* may sound forbidding to less-advanced students; you may decide not to require them to learn these terms at this time. Explain to your other students the two main kinds of conjunctions—*coordinating* and *subordinating.* Then add that the correlative conjunction is merely a special kind of coordinating conjunction. Teach what is meant by *coordinating*—that a coordinating conjunction joins things that are equal or of the same value in a grammatical sense. Use examples to show that such conjunctions connect a word with a similar word (verb with verb, adjective with adjective, etc.), or phrase with phrase (prepositional phrase with prepositional phrase, etc.), or clause with clause. Contrast the *subordinating* conjunction, which joins groups of words that are not equal or of the same value in the grammatical sense. Point out the note about thse conjunctions immediately preceding Exercise 15. You may want your students to memorize the coordinating and correlative conjunctions.

EXERCISE 15. While the conjunctions covered in this exercise are not difficult, your students may overlook some of them. Going over the answers in class will usually clear up any difficulties.

GRAMMAR

Conjunctions joining groups of words that are sentences:

The stars seem motionless, **but** actually they are moving rapidly through space.
One leader was very powerful, **and** the other was very weak.

Conjunctions are of three kinds: *coordinating, correlative,* and *subordinating.*

The *coordinating conjunctions* are *and, but, or, nor, for, so,* and *yet.*

EXAMPLES The water was cold, **yet** refreshing.
You may take the test now, **or** you may wait until later.
I didn't like him, **nor** did he like me.

When *for* is used as a conjunction, it connects groups of words that are sentences. On all other occasions, *for* is used as a preposition.

CONJUNCTION We wrote to the tourist bureau, **for** we wanted information on places to visit.
PREPOSITION We waited patiently **for** a reply.

Correlative conjunctions are always found in pairs that have other words dividing them: *either . . . or, neither . . . nor, both . . . and, not only . . . but also.*

EXAMPLES Our class will furnish **either** the punch **or** the cookies for the party.
Both cats **and** dogs make good pets.
Clare Boothe Luce was **not only** a playwright **but also** an ambassador.

Subordinating conjunctions occur in complex sentences and are explained on pages 391–92.

EXERCISE 15. Identifying Coordinating and Correlative Conjunctions. Number your paper 1–20. After the proper number, write the coordinating or correlative conjunctions in each sentence. Be prepared to tell what words or groups of words each conjunction joins. Treat a pair of correlative conjunctions as one conjunction.

EXAMPLE 1. Our teacher bought either a jeep or a pickup truck.
1. *either—or*

1. The disc jockey played records and tapes for us.
2. We were afraid that neither the Ferris wheel nor the roller coaster was safe.
3. Some people like checkers, but others prefer chess.
4. We are working hard on the project, for the science fair starts tomorrow.
5. The players practiced hard and yet did not win the regional title.
6. Our club members will either make the decorations or bring refreshments.
7. Many players and coaches would like to change the rules of the game.
8. Ms. Whiting is both a teacher and a writer.
9. The girls' basketball team not only won the game but also scored the most points in our school's history.
10. If the girls rehearse, they will perform at the game and at the dance on Saturday.
11. Sarah speaks French or German.
12. I hope I improve my grades, for I have been studying hard this term.
13. They must practice fielding and batting.
14. We will be working on the balance beam or the trampoline this week in gym class.
15. I didn't receive a letter from my cousin today, nor did I really expect one.
16. The drivers braked and swerved to avoid the dog.
17. Either you or I should send the invitations.
18. The people waited patiently for the bus, but it never came.
19. The artist used neither oils nor acrylics to paint this picture.
20. The principal was excited, for the school board had approved his plan for a new cafeteria.

GRAMMAR

THE INTERJECTION (rule 12e)

Few students have trouble identifying interjections. They do not occur very often in student writing and cause no problems except in connection with punctuation.

DETERMINING PARTS OF SPEECH (rule 12f)

For average and above-average classes, this will perhaps be the most important section in the chapter. The fundamental principle underlying the study of the parts of speech is that **a word's use in a sentence determines its part of speech.** Give some examples of words that can be used as three, four, or even five parts of speech (e.g., *down*—sit *down, down* the hill, make the first *down,* to *down* your opponents, the *down* escalator). Toss out a few more words and see how many parts of speech the class can make of them (e.g., *cross, time, near*). Ask the class to give examples of other words used as more than one part of speech.

A less-advanced class, however, will usually have trouble grasping the idea that a word may be used as more than one part of speech. With these students, it may be best not to approach the idea directly. Do, however, require students to give reasons whenever they identify a word as being a particular part of speech in a given sentence.

REVIEW EXERCISES D and E. A less-advanced class may omit one or both of these exercises, which cover all eight parts of speech (Chapters 11 and 12). Note the "Summary of Parts of Speech" provided at the end of the chapter (pages 334–35).

GRAMMAR

THE INTERJECTION

12e. An *interjection* is a word that expresses emotion and that is not related grammatically to other words in the sentence.

EXAMPLES **Oh!** You surprised me.
Wow! Am I tired!
Well, I did my best.

DETERMINING PARTS OF SPEECH

You have now finished a study of the eight parts of speech. On page 334 is a chart that briefly summarizes what you have learned.

12f. A word's use determines its part of speech.

Although words are given as examples of particular parts of speech in the chart that follows, you cannot really tell what part of speech a word is until you know how the word is used in a sentence. For example, the same word can be used as a pronoun or an adjective or as an adverb or a preposition.

EXAMPLES **Each** did his part. [pronoun]
Each student baked a cake. [adjective]

The tired shoppers sat **down** for a while. [adverb]
The ball rolled **down** the hill. [preposition]

A member of the crew has spotted **land.** [noun]
The pilot can **land** here safely. [verb]

We didn't find her, **for** she had left. [conjunction]
Everybody searched **for** the lost child. [preposition]

Well, he seems to have recovered. [interjection]
He doesn't look **well** to me. [adjective]

REVIEW EXERCISE D. Identifying Parts of Speech. Number your paper 1–20. After each number, write the italicized word from the corresponding sentence. Then write the part of speech of the word. Be prepared to explain your answer.

EXAMPLES 1. The *ship* entered the harbor slowly.
1. *ship—noun*
2. Did they *ship* the package to Dee and Tom?
2. *ship—verb*

1. The English test was easy *for* him. 1. prep.
2. He didn't go to the movies, *for* he wanted to practice on the drums. 2. conj.
3. It was a steep *climb,* but we finally made it to the top of the hill. 3. n.
4. Instead of riding the elevator, June and I *climb* the stairs for exercise. 4. v.
5. *Some* volunteered to sell tickets. 5. pron.
6. We donated *some* clothes to the rummage sale. 6. adj.
7. Looking for shells, the girl strolled *along* the shore. 7. prep.
8. When we went sailing, Raul and Manuel came *along.* 8. adv.
9. I lost *my* book report! 9. pron.
10. *My!* This is not a good day! 10. interj.
11. No one *but* Jill saw it. 11. prep.
12. I play guitar, *but* Julianne sings. 12. conj.
13. Most club members voted in favor of the hayride, but *many* voted against it. 13. pron.
14. Christie has *many* lovely quilts in her room. 14. adj.
15. The *plan* for the trip has been confirmed. 15. n.
16. My parents *plan* to attend the school play. 16. v.
17. The hospital is located *nearby*. 17. adv.
18. After the movie we went to a *nearby* restaurant. 18. adj.
19. When the batter hit the ball, it popped *up*. 19. adv. 20. prep.
20. The neighbor's dog chased Fluffy *up* the crabapple tree.

REVIEW EXERCISE E. Identifying Different Parts of Speech. Number your paper 1–50. After the proper number, write each of the italicized words or groups of words in the following paragraphs. After each, write what part of speech it is, using these abbreviations: *n.* (noun), *pron.* (pronoun), *v.* (verb), *adj.* (adjective), *adv.* (adverb), *prep.* (preposition), *conj.* (conjunction), *interj.* (interjection).

CHAPTER 12 REVIEW: POSTTEST 1

This test requires students to identify verbs, adverbs, prepositions, conjunctions, and interjections. Verbs must be further identified as action, helping, or linking.

Before your students can identify the part of speech of *if* in item number 5, they will need to read the section on subordinating conjunctions on pages 391–92.

GRAMMAR

Dancing may be (1) *easy* for (2) *some,* but I have (3) *always* had (4) *two* left (5) *feet.* (6) *Yesterday* after (7) *school,* one of my friends (8) *tried* to teach (9) *me* the latest dance. (10) *Well!* I was (11) *so* embarrassed I could have hidden (12) *in* the (13) *closet.* My feet (14) *have* (15) *minds* of (16) *their* own, (17) *and* they do (18) *not* behave well. 1. adj. 2. pron. 3. adv. 4. adj. 5. n. 6. adv.

Today I (19) *thought* (20) *about* this (21) *problem* (22) *throughout* lunch. (23) *Later* I thought about it (24) *during* math class. I have considered every (25) *possible* solution. I have (26) *even* wanted to put (27) *down* cutouts of (28) *paper* feet (29) *with* numbers on them. 7. n. 8. v. 9. pron. 10. interj. 11. adv.

My (30) *mother* (31) *has shown* me (32) *some* dances that (33) *were* popular when (34) *she* was my age. I've tried (35) *hard* (36) *many* times to follow the (37) *steps,* (38) *but* all my efforts (39) *have seemed* (40) *useless.* 12. prep. 13. n. 14. v. 15. n. 16. pron.

"Either you are (41) *too* tense when you dance, (42) *or* you are trying too hard. (43) *You* should (44) *relax* more," people say to me. 17. conj. 18. adv. 19. v. 20. prep. 21. n. 22. prep. 23. adv.

(45) "*What!* (46) *How* can I relax?" I groan. (47) "*No one* can relax when the body goes (48) *left* and the feet go right!" At that point, I usually (49) *decide* to give up, but I always try (50) *again* the next day. 24. prep. 25. adj. 26. adv. 27. adv. 28. adj. 29. prep. 30. n. 31. v. 32. adj. 33. v. 34. pron. 35. adv. 36. adj. 37. n. 38. conj. 39. v. 40. adj. 41. adv. 42. conj. 43. pron. 44. v. 45. interj. 46. adv. 47. pron. 48. adv. 49. v. 50. adv.

CHAPTER 12 REVIEW: POSTTEST 1

Identifying Verbs, Adverbs, Prepositions, Conjunctions, and Interjections. Number your paper 1–25. After the proper number, write each italicized word or word group in the following sentences, and indicate whether it is a verb, an adverb, a preposition, a conjunction, or an interjection. Use the abbreviations *v.* (verb), *adv.* (adverb), *prep.* (preposition), *conj.* (conjunction), and *interj.* (interjection). For each verb, indicate whether it is an action verb, a helping verb, or a linking verb. (a.v., h.v., l.v.)

EXAMPLE 1. I *am reading* a book *about* dinosaurs.
1. *am reading—v. (action), about—prep.*

1. We *watched* the skywriter spell out the letters *carefully.* 1. a.v., adv.
2. *Both* the dog *and* the cat *are* dirty and need baths. 2. conj., l.v.
3. His cousins don't *know* much *about* sports. 3. a.v., prep.
4. When the horse reared *back,* the girl held *onto* its mane. 4. adv., prep.,
5. The teacher *would have been* late *if* the bell had rung on time. 5. l.v., conj.
6. Clever replies *never* occur to me until the situation is *long* past. 6. adv., adv.
7. If I *had known* how to identify verbs, I would have gotten a better grade *on* that test. 7. a.v., prep.
8. *When* do you usually feel your best and why *do* you *feel* that way then? 8. adv., a.v.
9. He won't go, *nor* will he *willingly* cooperate. 9. conj., adv.
10. Juan exercised *daily* for twenty minutes *before* breakfast. 10. adv., prep.
11. One of the runners *almost* tripped over the hurdle, *yet* he still placed third. 11. adv., conj.
12. There are times when Jill thinks that she *cares* almost *too* much about making the team. 12. a.v., adv. 13. interj., prep.
13. *Whoops*! I dropped my ring, and it rolled *under* the counter.
14. My scout leader said that she *had* never *tasted* stew like mine *before.* 14. a.v., adv.
15. Although *not* many people *like* the heat, the desert can be beautiful. 15. adv., a.v.
16. Be sure that you *sharpen* your pencil *now* because you won't be allowed to leave your seat after the test begins. 16. a.v., adv.
17. *Did* you *bring* a note *from* your parents? 17. a.v., prep.
18. The girl *tried* again *in spite of* her previous difficulty. 18. a.v., prep.
19. My mom took me *aboard* the ship where she once *worked.*
20. Nguyen *does* not *wish* to intrude, *nor* does he feel fully at ease in such situations. 19. prep., a.v. 20. a.v., conj.
21. Jill *cares* almost *too* much about making the team. 21. a.v., adv.
22. *Well,* I plan to help Andrea, for I believe in her cause. 22. interj.
23. The fish quickly darted *under* a rock. 23. prep.
24. Jeff loaned Anne a dollar and *then* found out that he didn't have *quite* enough money for his own lunch. 24. adv., adv.
25. I don't know *very* much *about* my great-grandparents. 25. adv., prep.

GRAMMAR

CHAPTER 12 REVIEW: POSTTEST 2

Less-advanced students may have difficulty writing sentences using specified words as assigned parts of speech.

GRAMMAR

CHAPTER 12 REVIEW: POSTTEST 2

Writing Sentences Using Different Parts of Speech. Write two sentences using each of the following words as the parts of speech given in parentheses. Underline the word in the sentence, and write its part of speech after the sentence. Answers will vary.

EXAMPLE 1. over (*adv.* and *prep.*)
1. *The skies began to clear when the storm was over. (adverb)*
2. *The horse jumped over the fence. (preposition)*

1. but (*conj.* and *prep.*)
2. like (*v.* and *prep.*)
3. run (*n.* and *v.*)
4. well (*adv.* and *interj.*)
5. that (*pron.* and *adj.*)
6. more (*adj.* and *adv.*)
7. last (*v.* and *adj.*)
8. one (*adj.* and *pron.*)
9. near (*v.* and *prep.*)
10. around (*prep.* and *adv.*)
11. all (*pron.* and *adj.*)
12. past (*n.* and *prep.*)
13. so (*interj.* and *adv.*)
14. for (*conj.* and *prep.*)
15. fight (*n.* and *v.*)
16. even (*v.* and *adv.*)
17. since (*prep.* and *adv.*)
18. taste (*n.* and *v.*)
19. boy (*n.* and *interj.*)
20. any (*pron.* and *adj.*)

SUMMARY OF PARTS OF SPEECH

Rule	*Part of Speech*	*Use*	*Examples*
11a	noun	names a person, a place, a thing, or an idea	Wilma, cave, Asia, freedom, honesty
11b	pronoun	takes the place of a noun	she, ourselves, who, anyone
11c	adjective	modifies a noun or pronoun	sick, tiny, purple, smooth
12a	verb	shows action or helps to make a statement	play, study, were, become
12b	adverb	modifies a verb, an adjective, or another adverb	very, too, usually, quickly, not

12c	preposition	relates a noun or a pronoun to another word; begins a prepositional phrase	beside [her], to [town], for [John], with [them]
12d	conjunction	joins words or groups of words	and, but, either . . . or
12e	interjection	shows strong feeling	Well! Wow! Oh!

GRAMMAR

Additional Practice

Teacher's Resource Book, Worksheet pages 121–36, Alternative Worksheet pages (for less-advanced students) 538–40

Testing

Teaching Tests booklet, pages 19–22, 27–28, 37–43
Teacher's Resource Boo, Test pages 413–16, 421–22, 431–42

Chapter Overview

An understanding of complements is basic to using complete sentences in writing and to mastering standard English usage.

Although the basic concepts in this chapter will be familiar to many eighth-graders, they may need a review of the terms and their meanings. Write on the board a few sentences illustrating a rule, and elicit explanations or definitions from the students. If they have done well on the Diagnostic Test and seem familiar with the rule in question, go on to the next point.

Chapter Objective

Students will identify the following grammatical concepts: direct object, indirect object, predicate nominative, and predicate adjective.

PRESENTING THE CHAPTER

LESS-ADVANCED STUDENTS For this class, you may want to use the term "completer" instead of "complement," and tell the class that the two kinds of completers are "object completers" and "subject completers." It is not important that these students learn to distinguish between direct and indirect objects or between predicate nominatives and predicate adjectives. *(See listing of Alternative Worksheets on page 351.)*

ADVANCED STUDENTS If these students do well on the Diagnostic Test, they can move through the chapter rapidly, perhaps doing only the review exercises. Emphasize the writing application, and have students write original sentences that illustrate the material in the chapter.

CHAPTER 13

Complements

DIRECT AND INDIRECT OBJECTS, SUBJECT COMPLEMENTS

Every sentence has a sentence base, which consists of, at the least, a verb and its subject.

S V
John shouted.

S V
The squirrels scampered across the campus.

The sentence base often has another part, in addition to the subject and verb, called a *complement.* The word *complement* means "completer." A complement completes the meaning begun by the subject and verb. The following word groups are not complete, even though they have subjects and verbs.

S V
Marlene brought [what?]

S V
I met [whom?]

S V
Her friend is [what?]

Here a complement completes the meaning of each.

S V C
Marlene brought a cake.

S V C
I met Carlos.

S V C
Her friend is a painter.

DIAGNOSTIC TEST

Identifying Direct Objects, Indirect Objects, and Subject Complements. Number your paper 1–20. After the proper number, write the italicized word or word group in the following sentences. Correctly identify each, using these abbreviations: *d.o.* (direct object), *i.o.* (indirect object), *p.n.* (predicate nominative), and *p.a.* (predicate adjective).

EXAMPLES
1. The rancher raised prize-winning *cattle.*
1. *cattle—d.o.*
2. The rancher became a rich *man.*
2. *man—p.n.*

1. Brenda caught the *ball* and threw it to first base. 1. d.o.
2. Your cousin seems *nice.* 2. p.a.
3. I'm not the *one* who did that. 3. p.n.
4. The sun grew *hotter* as the day went on. 4. p.a.
5. Mrs. Ford gave *me* a failing grade. 5. i.o.
6. That hamburger meat smells *bad* to me. 6. p.a.
7. Jane's father and mother are both *truck drivers.* 7. p.n.
8. Have you bought your *tickets* yet? 8. d.o.
9. My mother won't let me ride your *trail bike.* 9. d.o.
10. The irate customer sent the *store manager* a letter of complaint. 10. i.o.
11. The nurse gave *Virgil* a flu shot. 11. i.o.
12. Earl often looks *tired* on Monday mornings. 12. p.a.
13. With his calloused hands he cannot feel the *texture* of velvet. 13. d.o.
14. Her grades are always *higher* than mine. 14. p.a.
15. Heather, who is new at our school, is the nicest *girl* I know. 15. p.n.

GRAMMAR

WRITING APPLICATION

The writing application in this chapter is designed to encourage students to use their knowledge of predicate adjectives in their own writing. Feel free to adapt this assignment to your students' writing needs, abilities, and interests.

DIAGNOSTIC TEST

This test will give you a clear picture of what your students already know about complements. Use the results of this test to help you decide how much time to spend on the chapter.

The Sentence Base (rule 13a)

Introduce this chapter by asking your class to name the two essential parts of the sentence base (the subject and the verb). Stress the meaning of the word *base.* Point out that the sentence base is the foundation of the sentence. Put on the board a few short sentences having two-part (*subject-verb*) bases:

1. Harry ran.
2. I walked.
3. The little girl laughed loudly.

Then add a few sentences that have subjects and verbs but still do not express complete thoughts:

4. We like —— .
5. The man was —— .
6. The bus hit —— .
7. My work is —— .

By reading these aloud, make clear that each of them provokes in the hearer the question *What?* and that a word (or words) is necessary to complete each sentence. Then complete the sentences by adding nouns and adjectives. Ask someone to explain why these are called complements. Ask if anyone knows the difference between *complement* and *compliment.*

Explain that there are two kinds of complements: those that occur with action verbs and those that occur with linking verbs. Show that in two of the sentences on the board (4, 6) the complements are affected by the action expressed by the verb and that in two (5, 7) the complements are linked to (refer to) the subject.

Then erase the complements in the sentences and ask the class to suggest others. Stress these two points: (1) only nouns, pronouns, and adjectives can be complements; (2) a word in a prepositional phrase cannot be a complement. Now direct your students to rule 13a on page 338.

GRAMMAR

16. Overhead, the vultures circled the injured *gazelle*. 16. d.o.
17. Throw *Eric* a screen pass. 17. i.o.
18. When left to dry in the sun, plums become *prunes*. 18. p.n.
19. Why did Mr. Santos loan *Arnie* five dollars? 19. i.o.
20. Ms. Rossetti will be our Spanish *teacher* this fall. 20. p.n.

13a. A *complement* is a word or a group of words that completes the meaning begun by the subject and verb.

Jody redecorated her **room.** [*Room* completes the meaning by telling *what* Jody redecorated.]

My aunt sent **me** a **postcard** from Amsterdam. [*Me* and *postcard* complete the meaning by telling *what* was sent and *to whom* it was sent.]

The Ephron sisters are humorous **writers.** [*Writers* completes the meaning by telling something about the subject *sisters.*]

The *Mona Lisa* is very **famous.** [*Famous* completes the meaning by describing the subject *Mona Lisa.*]

In these four sentences, you see two kinds of complements. The first two sentences have complements that are affected by the action of the verb. The third and fourth have complements that refer to the subject. A noun, a pronoun, or an adjective can serve as a complement, but an adverb can never be a complement.

The bus is **here.** [*Here* is an adverb, not a complement.]

A complement, like a subject, is never in a prepositional phrase.

Sarah is reading the **dictionary**. [*Dictionary* is a complement; it completes the meaning begun by the subject and verb.]

Sarah is thumbing through the dictionary. [*Dictionary* is in the phrase *through the dictionary;* it is not a complement.]

Helen is an expert **skier** and **skater.** [*Skier* and *skater* are complements.]

Helen is in Colorado. [*Colorado* is in the phrase *in Colorado*; it is not a complement.]

EXERCISE 1. Identifying Subjects, Verbs, and Complements. Make three columns labeled *Subject, Verb,* and *Complement.* Enter the parts of the base of each of the following sentences in the appropriate columns. Remember that a complement is never in a prepositional phrase.

1. In Shakespeare's time, plays were very popular in England.
2. Many people watched plays at the Globe Theater in London.
3. William Shakespeare was one of the owners of the Globe.
4. The playhouse looked quite different from most of our modern theaters.
5. It was a building with eight sides.
6. The building contained an inner courtyard.
7. The stage was a platform at one end of the courtyard.
8. Many playgoers did not have seats during a performance.
9. The people without seats filled the courtyard in front of the stage.
10. Many of them watched the action of the play from a position next to the stage.

EXERCISE 2. Writing Sentences with Subjects, Verbs, and Complements. Write five sentences using the following sentence bases. Add enough words to make *interesting* sentences.
Answers will vary.

SUBJECT	VERB	COMPLEMENT
girl	delivered	telegram
days	are	long
Pam	won	contest
runner	appeared	tired
Venus	is	planet

DIRECT AND INDIRECT OBJECTS

There are two kinds of complements that are affected by the action of the verb: the *direct object* and the *indirect object.*

13b. The *direct object* receives the action expressed by the verb or names the result of the action.

GRAMMAR

EXERCISE 1. You may wish to do the first three or four sentences orally before assigning the rest as written work.

EXERCISE 2. The students may enjoy sharing their sentences with the rest of the class.

DIRECT AND INDIRECT OBJECTS (rules 13b and 13c)

Students usually find the direct object easy to understand; they sometimes find the indirect object more difficult. Teach the two kinds together. Put this series of questions on the board:

1. What is the verb and what is its subject?
2. Is it an action verb?
3. Is there a noun or pronoun that answers the questions *What?* or *Whom?* after the action verb?
4. Is there a noun or pronoun that is not in a prepositional phrase and that tells *to whom* or *to what* the action of the verb is done?

Have the class apply these questions to several example sentences. Emphasize that the indirect object cannot be in a prepositional phrase even though the meaning of the phrase is exactly the same as that expressed by the indirect object. (Compare "I gave *her* the book" with "I gave the book to *her.*")

Next you may point out these helpful facts: direct objects occur much more frequently than indirect objects; a direct object often occurs without an indirect object, but an indirect object almost never occurs without a direct object; the indirect object almost always precedes the direct object.

EXERCISE 3. The first few sentences may be done orally in class. If students have trouble with sentences 5, 7, and 10, remind them to turn the question into a statement before attempting to analyze it.

GRAMMAR

Dorothea Lange photographed **farmers** in the Midwest during the Depression. [*Farmers* is the direct object; it receives the action of the verb *photographed.*]

Lange built an impressive **collection.** [*Collection* is the direct object; it names the result of the action *built.*]

Direct objects follow action verbs only. They answer the question *What?* or *Whom?* after an action verb. Lange, in the first sentence, photographed *whom*? She photographed *farmers;* therefore, *farmers* is the direct object. In the second sentence, Lang built *what*? She built a *collection;* therefore, *collection* is the direct object.

EXERCISE 3. Identifying Direct Objects. Number your paper 1–10. Write the action verb and its object in each sentence. Say the verb to yourself and ask *What?* or *Whom?* Remember that objects are never in a prepositional phrase.

EXAMPLE 1. Volunteers distributed food to the flood victims.
1. *distributed—food*

1. On the plains the Cheyenne hunted buffalo for food and clothing.
2. We watched a performance of Lorraine Hansberry's *A Raisin in the Sun.*
3. During most of its history the United States has welcomed refugees from other countries.
4. The leading man wore a hat with a large plume.
5. Are you preserving the environment?
6. After the game the coach answered questions from the sports reporters.
7. Did you see her performance on television?
8. The researchers followed the birds' migration from Mexico to Canada.
9. Mayor Fiorello La Guardia governed New York City during the Depression.
10. Have the movie theaters announced the special discount for teen-agers yet?

13c. The *indirect object* of the verb precedes the direct object and tells *to whom* or *what* or *for whom* or *what* the action of the verb is done.

Sarita bought **us** a chess set. [*Us* is the indirect object because it tells *for whom* Sarita bought a chess set.]

Dad gave the **car** a coat of paint. [*Car* is the indirect object because it tells *to what* Dad gave a coat of paint.]

Notice that these two sentences contain direct objects as well as indirect objects. The indirect object is always used with a direct object and normally precedes the direct object.

The guide gave **me** clear **directions.** [*Me* is the indirect object; *directions* is the direct object.]

The indirect object, like the direct object, is never in a prepositional phrase.

She sent her **mother** some of her earnings. [*Mother* is an indirect object, telling *to whom* she sent some of her earnings.]

She sent some of her earnings to her mother. [*Mother* is not an indirect object; it is the object of the preposition *to*.]

EXERCISE 4. Identifying Direct Objects and Indirect Objects. Number your paper 1–10. Write the direct objects and the indirect objects from the following sentences and label each (*d.o.* or *i.o.*). Not every sentence has an indirect object.

EXAMPLE 1. They gave us their solemn promise.
1. *us, i.o.; promise, d.o.*

1. Sue's parents shipped her the books she had forgotten.
2. They sent me on a wild-goose chase.
3. Gloria mailed the company a check yesterday.
4. The speaker showed the audience the slides of Niagara Falls.
5. Juan would not deliberately tell you a lie.
6. Luckily, we had asked three of our friends to help.
7. I sent my cousins some embroidered pillows for their new apartment.

EXERCISE 4. You may decide to have your students copy the sentences, underlining the direct object once and the indirect object twice. Note that not every sentence has an indirect object.

REVIEW EXERCISE A. You may use this exercise as a test. You may want to do it orally with less-advanced students.

DIAGRAMING DIRECT AND INDIRECT OBJECTS

Diagraming is helpful in showing students the distinction between direct and indirect objects. Even if you do not teach diagraming, you may want to do a few explanatory diagrams on the board while teaching this chapter.

GRAMMAR

8. Several sports magazines have sent me subscription order blanks lately.
9. Carly and Doreen taught themselves the importance of hard work.
10. In European countries, Americans must carry their passports for identification.

REVIEW EXERCISE A. Identifying Direct and Indirect Objects. The following sentences contain ten direct objects and five indirect objects. Number your paper 1–10. After the proper number, write the object or objects in the sentence. Label direct objects *d.o.* and indirect objects *i.o.*

1. Mr. Luis told us many interesting stories about his childhood in Puerto Rico.
2. No one in the class finished yesterday's math assignment.
3. Allow yourselves more time for your homework assignments.
4. Television viewers in our country can watch events as they happen in any part of the world.
5. Who told you that ridiculous story about the gorilla in the gymnasium?
6. A permanent member of the United Nations Security Council can veto any resolution.
7. The Panama Canal greatly shortened the trip by boat between Europe and Japan.
8. Rudolf Diesel's first motor exploded during his experiments and nearly killed him.
9. The jeweler, Mrs. Adams, offered me a hundred dollars for my pearl necklace.
10. I brought her my antique silver bracelet, but she was not interested in it.

Diagraming Direct and Indirect Objects

All complements except the indirect object are diagramed on the main horizontal line, with the subject and the verb, as part of the sentence base. The direct object is diagramed on the horizontal line with a vertical line preceding it. The vertical line stops at the horizontal line to distinguish it from the line separating the subject and the verb.

PATTERNS

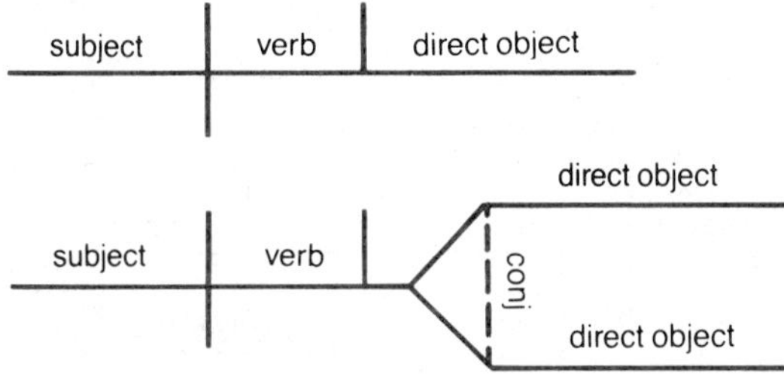

EXAMPLES The rain cleaned the street.

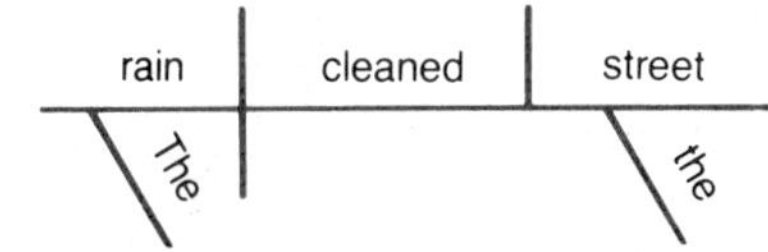

We sold lemonade and oranges.

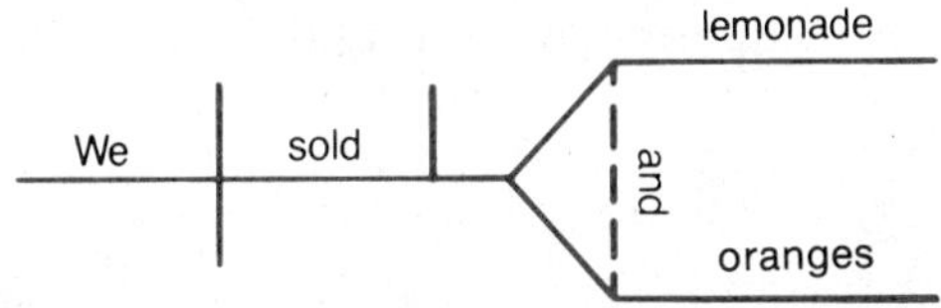

EXERCISE 5. Diagraming Sentences with Direct Objects. Diagram the following sentences, which contain direct objects. Use a ruler and leave plenty of space between diagrams.

See Answer Key.

1. The quarterback made the touchdown.
2. The distinguished conductor directed his own composition.
3. Our class collects leaves and rocks.
4. The audience saw a serious one-act play and two amusing skits.
5. We grow orchids and ferns.

EXERCISE 5. A less-advanced class should probably not be required to diagram these sentences. However, you can use these sentences for practice in identifying objects. Students can write the subject, the verb, and the object(s).

GRAMMAR

EXERCISE 6. See notes for Exercise 5.

To diagram an indirect object, write it on a short horizontal line below the verb. Connect it to the verb by a slanted line.

PATTERNS

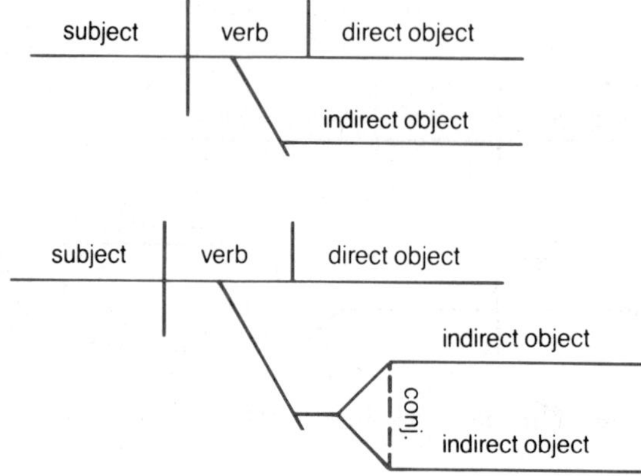

EXAMPLES The artist showed me his painting.

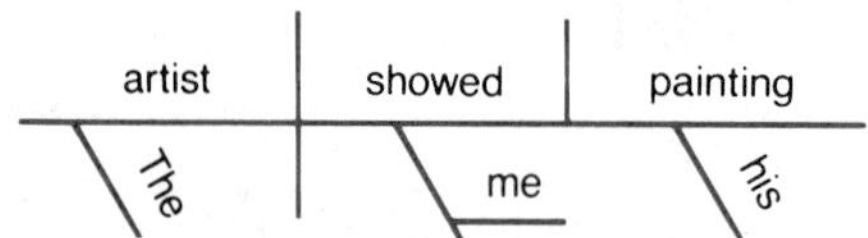

The company gave Jan and John summer jobs.

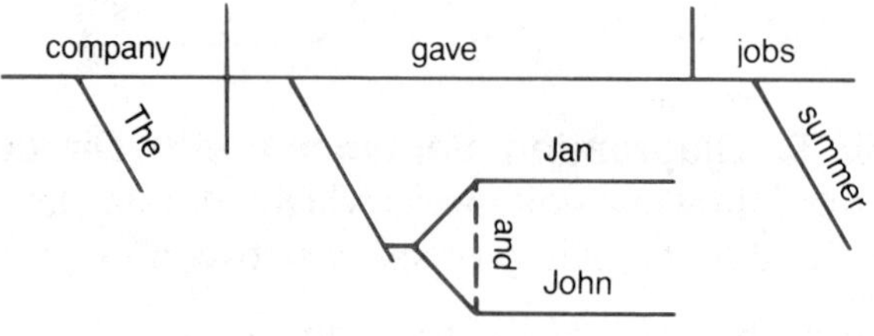

EXERCISE 6. Diagraming Sentences with Direct and Indirect Objects. Diagram the following sentences. See Answer Key.

1. The lifeguard gave us lessons.

2. Cara's sister taught her the rules.
3. The cashier handed the children balloons.
4. The judges awarded Jean and Rae the prizes.
5. Snow gives motorists and pedestrians trouble.

SUBJECT COMPLEMENTS

Sometimes a complement completes the meaning of a sentence by explaining or describing the subject. Such a complement is called a *subject complement.* While the direct and the indirect object follow action verbs only, the subject complement follows linking verbs only. (See page 312 for the list of linking verbs.)

13d. A *subject complement* is a word which follows a linking verb and refers to (explains or describes) the subject.

Alice Eng is a **teacher.** [*Teacher* follows the linking verb *is,* and explains something about *Alice Eng.*]

We are the **ones.** [*Ones* follows the linking verb *are* and refers to the subject *we.*]

A lemon tastes **sour.** [*Sour* follows the linking verb *tastes* and describes *lemon*—sour lemon.]

Nouns, pronouns, and adjectives can serve as subject complements.

Predicate Nominatives and Predicate Adjectives

There are two kinds of subject complements—*predicate nominatives* and *predicate adjectives.*

(1) If the subject complement is a noun or a pronoun, it is called a *predicate nominative.*

EXAMPLES Tuesday is my **birthday.** [*Birthday* is a predicate nominative. It is a noun referring to the subject *Tuesday.*]

He is **one** of the members. [*One* is a predicate nominative. It is a pronoun referring to the subject *he.*]

SUBJECT COMPLEMENTS (rule 13d)

Take time to review linking verbs (text pages 311–14). Put example sentences on the board, and point out that the subject complements answer the question *What?* or *Who?* after the verb. Use examples to show that a subject complement after a linking verb always refers to the subject of the sentence.

Students who recognize nouns, pronouns, and adjectives will have little difficulty distinguishing between predicate nominatives and predicate adjectives. However, they may confuse the *predicate adjective* that should follow a linking verb and the *adverb* that should follow an action verb. This material is included in Chapter 20, in connection with the difference between *good* and *well.* If you wish to explain the difference now, you can put on the board a few pairs of example sentences:

Bobby grew *rapidly.*
Bobby grew *tall.*
She looked *confidently* at her coach.
Her coach thought she looked *confident.*

By asking questions, get the class to tell you that *rapidly* in the first sentence describes the "growing" —it is an adverb modifying *grew;* and *tall,* in the next sentence, describes "Bobby"—it is an adjective. Repeat this procedure with further examples until students grasp the distinction.

EXERCISE 7. You may wish to do a few of the sentences orally before assigning the rest as written work.

Like subjects and objects, predicate nominatives never appear in prepositional phrases.

The result was a **declaration** of war.

The predicate nominative is *declaration,* not *war.* Not only is *war* part of a prepositional phrase, but the *result* was just a *declaration,* not the war itself.

GRAMMAR

(2) If the subject complement is an adjective, it is called a *predicate adjective.* A predicate adjective modifies the subject.

EXAMPLES An atomic reactor is very **powerful.** [*Powerful* is a predicate adjective modifying the subject *reactor.*]

This ground looks **swampy.** [*Swampy* is a predicate adjective modifying the subject *ground.*]

EXERCISE 7. Identifying Predicate Nominatives and Predicate Adjectives. Write the linking verb and the subject complement from each of the following sentences. Label each complement *p.n.* (predicate nominative) or *p.a.* (predicate adjective).

EXAMPLE 1. The raincoat looked too short for me.
1. *looked, short—p.a.*

1. My dog is playful. 1. p.a.
2. I am the one who called you yesterday. 2. p.n.
3. Many public buildings in the East are proof of I. M. Pei's architectural skill. 3. p.n.
4. The downtown mall appeared especially busy today. 4. p.a.
5. Sally Ride sounded confident during the television interview. 5. p.a.
6. The package felt too light to be a book. 6. p.a.
7. These questions seem easy to me. 7. p.a.
8. The singer's clothing became a symbol that her fans imitated. 8. p.n.
9. Some poems, such as "The Bells" and "The Raven," are delightfully rhythmical. 9. p.a.
10. While the mountain lion looked around for food, the fawn remained perfectly still. 10. p.a.

Some verbs, such as *look, grow,* and *feel,* may be used as either linking verbs or action verbs. They are followed by predicate nominatives or predicate adjectives only when the nouns or adjectives that follow them refer back to the subject. They are followed by objects when the nouns that follow them receive the action of the verb or name the result of the action.

LINKING VERB The sailor **felt happy.** [*Happy* is a predicate adjective after the linking verb *felt. Happy* refers back to sailor.]

ACTION VERB The sailor **felt** the **breeze.** [*Breeze* is a direct object after the action verb *felt*, and names what the sailor felt.]

WRITING APPLICATION:
Using Predicate Adjectives to Help Organize a Description

A good way to organize a paragraph is to start with a topic sentence that states three things about your topic. The pattern you would use would be subject—linking verb —predicate adjectives.

EXAMPLE A computer can be fascinating, challenging, and occasionally frustrating.

Using this pattern for the beginning sentence of your paragraph, you then could supply facts, reasons, or details that develop the adjectives into an organized description.

Writing Assignment

Answers will vary.

Describe a favorite spare-time activity in a paragraph that begins with a sentence containing a compound predicate adjective with three adjectives. Underline the predicate adjectives in your beginning sentence, and in your paragraph tell why or how each adjective describes the activity you are writing about.

REVIEW EXERCISE B. A class that did well on Exercise 7 may omit this exercise.

DIAGRAMING SUBJECT COMPLEMENTS

Diagram several sentences on the board as examples before assigning Exercise 8.

GRAMMAR

REVIEW EXERCISE B. Identifying Subject Complements. Number your paper 1–10. After the appropriate number, write the subject complement or complements in each of the following sentences, identifying each one as a predicate nominative (*p.n.*) or predicate adjective (*p.a.*).

EXAMPLE 1. The child was very restless.
1. *restless, p.a.*

1. Some varieties of apples taste tart. 1. p.a.
2. Some dishes are spicy, while others seem bland. 2. p.a., p.a.
3. Exotic orchids can be surprisingly easy to grow. 3. p.a.
4. Cheese is a valuable source of protein. 4. p.n.
5. After connecting the batteries to the engine, we will see whether our machine is a success. 5. p.n.
6. If the sky is clear and the water is warm enough, we will go. 6. p.a., p.a.
7. It could be worse. 7. p.a.
8. The saxophone is a popular instrument in the jazz band. 8. p.n.
9. Silver dollars have long been favorite collector's items. 9. p.n.
10. According to some, the new style looks ugly. 10. p.a.

Diagraming Subject Complements

A subject complement is diagramed somewhat like a direct object. But the short vertical line separating it from the verb is slanted toward the subject to show that the complement refers to the subject.

PATTERNS

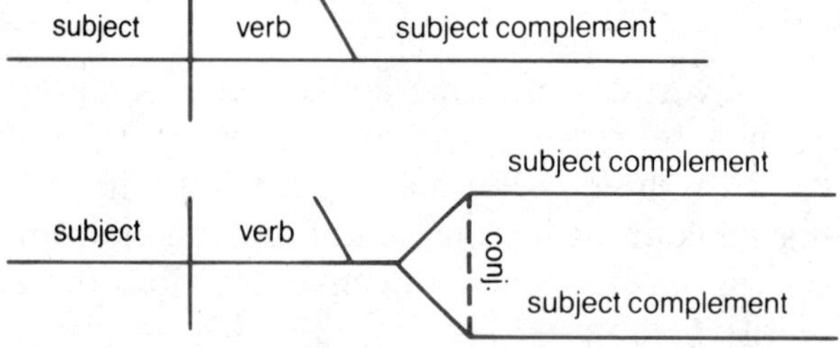

EXAMPLES The dancers are graceful.

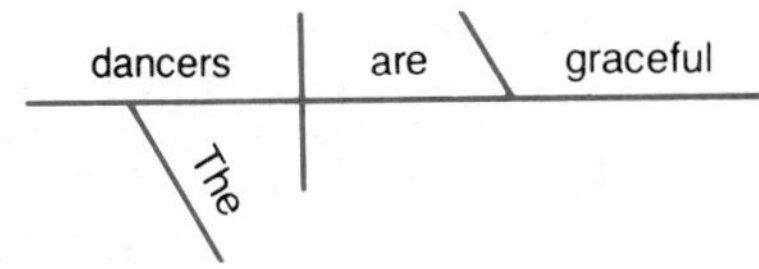

The contestants are Joan and Dean.

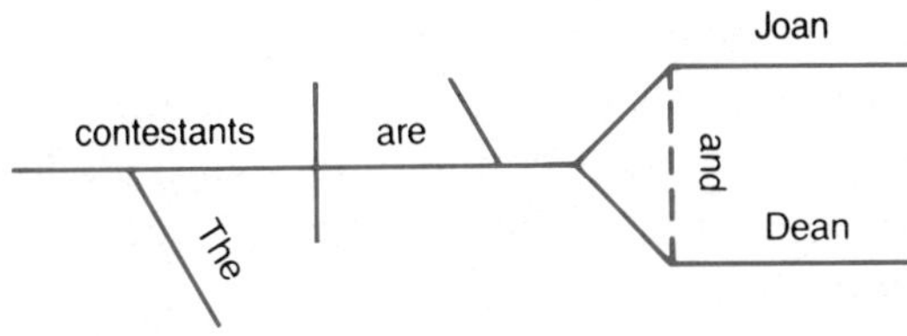

EXERCISE 8. Diagraming Subject Complements. Diagram the following sentences. See Answer Key.

1. Is Michael Jackson your favorite singer?
2. The cave was cold and damp.
3. One of the most daring explorers of the sixteenth century was Sir Francis Drake.
4. The chimpanzees seem happy in their new environment.
5. My shoes looked worn and dusty after the long walk.

REVIEW EXERCISE C. Identifying Verbs and Their Objects or Subject Complements. Number your paper 1–10. After the proper number, write the verb or verbs in the sentence. If a verb has one or more objects, write each object after it. If a verb is a linking verb, write the subject complement after it. Then identify each object or complement as direct object (*d.o.*), indirect object (*i.o.*), predicate adjective (*p.a.*), or predicate nominative (*p.n.*).

EXAMPLE 1. I have never seen a live manatee, but in pictures they look gentle.
1. *have seen, manatee—d.o.; look, gentle—p.a.*

1. The embarrassed guest accidentally broke the antique Chinese vase. 1. d.o.
2. The symphony conductor is the speaker for today. 2. p.n.

EXERCISE 8. A less-advanced class may use this exercise for further practice in identifying subject complements. If the class is not being taught to diagram, have them write the complements.

REVIEW EXERCISE C. A less-advanced class may omit this exercise. These sentences should not be assigned as diagraming practice because they would raise some problems for your eighth-graders.

REVIEW EXERCISE D. A less-advanced class should omit this exercise.

CHAPTER 13 REVIEW: POSTTEST 1
This test requires students to identify direct and indirect objects, predicate nominatives, and predicate adjectives. Since the complements appear in paragraphs, allow some time for students to check over their answers.

GRAMMAR

3. After thieves had stolen his money, the store owner installed a burglar alarm. 3. d.o., d.o., (or alarm)
4. Five of my relatives are politicians, but I would never cast my vote for any of them. 4. p.n., d.o.
5. The ladder by the doorway looks sturdier than the one in the corner. 5. p.a.
6. The book club sent me the wrong selection this month. 6. i.o., d.o.
7. These are only some of the popular songs from ten years ago. 7. p.n.
8. The performing seals gave us a good laugh. 8. i.o., d.o.
9. White gloves were once common in stylish circles. 9. p.a.
10. Whenever something is beautiful, some people will feel a need to destroy it. 10. p.a., d.o.

REVIEW EXERCISE D. Diagraming Complete Sentences. Diagram these sentences: See Answer Key.

1. Her mother was a leading ballerina with a famous ballet troupe.
2. Don and Maria acted the parts of Romeo and Juliet.
3. The origin of the Gypsies remains mysterious and fascinating.
4. The girls made themselves bracelets and necklaces.
5. Two world-famous canals are the Suez Canal and the Panama Canal.

CHAPTER 13 REVIEW: POSTTEST 1

Identifying Direct Objects, Indirect Objects, Predicate Nominatives, and Predicate Adjectives. Number your paper 1–20. After the proper number, write each italicized word and indicate whether it is a direct object (*d.o.*), an indirect object (*i.o.*), a predicate nominative (*p.n.*), or a predicate adjective (*p.a.*).

Girls aren't the only (1) *ones* who know how to cook. My mom got a (2) *job* last summer, so she gave (3) *me* cooking lessons before school began this year. At first, I felt (4) *reluctant* about learning what I considered a "girl's job." However, Dad

1. p.n. 2. d.o. 3. i.o. 4. p.a.

reminded me that he makes a (5) *number* of specialties, and he said that cooking lessons would be a good (6) *idea* for me. Boy, was he ever (7) *right!* 5. d.o. 6. p.n. 7. p.a.

When I began, I could hardly boil (8) *water* without fouling up, but my mom remained (9) *patient* and showed me the correct and easiest ways to do things. For example, did you know that water will boil faster if it has a little (10) *salt* in it or that cornstarch makes an excellent thickening (11) *agent* in everything from batter to gravy? 8. d.o. 9. p.a. 10. d.o. 11. p.n. (or) d.o.

My first attempts tasted (12) *awful,* but gradually I've become a fairly good (13) *cook.* Probably my best complete meal is beef (14) *stew.* Although stew doesn't require the highest (15) *grade* of beef, a good cut of chuck roast will give (16) *it* a much better taste. I am always very (17) *careful* about picking out the vegetables too. Our grocer probably thinks I am too (18) *picky* when I demand the best (19) *ingredients.* I don't care, though, because when I serve my (20) *family* my stew, they say it is their favorite dish.
12. p.a. 13. p.n. 14. p.n. 15. d.o. 16. i.o. 17. p.a. 18. p.a. 19. d.o. 20. i.o.

CHAPTER 13 REVIEW: POSTTEST 2

Writing Sentences with Direct Objects, Indirect Objects, and Subject Complements. Write sentences according to the following guidelines. Underline the direct object, the indirect object, or the subject complement in each sentence. Answers will vary.

1. a declarative sentence with a direct object
2. a declarative sentence with a predicate nominative
3. an interrogative sentence with a predicate adjective
4. an imperative sentence with an indirect object
5. an exclamatory sentence with a predicate adjective

GRAMMAR

CHAPTER 13 REVIEW: POSTTEST 2

This test may be difficult for less-advanced students. In addition to writing original sentences with specified complements, they must recall the kinds of sentences, classified according to purpose: declarative, interrogative, imperative, and exclamatory. You may wish to limit the instructions or use the test as a class activity.

Additional Practice

Teacher's Resource Book,
Worksheet pages 137–48,
Alternative Worksheet pages (for less-advanced students) 541–43

Testing

Teaching Tests booklet,
pages 19–22, 29–30, 37–43
Teacher's Resource Book,
Test pages 413–16, 423–24, 431–42

Chapter Overview

In both their speaking and their writing, students will benefit from instruction that increases their ability to use different kinds of phrases.

Beginning with a review of verb phrases and prepositional phrases, this chapter goes on to explain participles, infinitives, gerunds, and appositives. It discusses the functions of each as a phrase. Since many eighth-graders will find much new material in this chapter, you may need to go slowly.

Rule 14a, page 353, defines a *phrase* as "a group of related words that is used as a single part of speech and does not contain a verb and its subject." Accordingly, it treats as phrases all verbs and appositives that consist of two or more words. However, you may prefer to take up verbs and appositives as separate matters, and avoid using the term *phrase* in connection with them. *Verb phrase* and *verbal phrase* sound so much alike that less-advanced students, in particular, may confuse the two names. With such a class it may be better to use a term such as "the whole verb" instead of *verb phrase*. Since for practical purposes (such as the teaching of punctuation) there is little need to distinguish between a one-word appositive and an appositive phrase, some teachers simply use the term *appositive* to cover both situations.

Chapter Objective

Students will identify and use effectively in their own writing prepositional phrases, verbal phrases, and appositive phrases.

GRAMMAR

CHAPTER 14

The Phrase

PREPOSITIONAL, VERBAL, AND APPOSITIVE PHRASES

In Chapters 11 and 12, you studied single-word modifiers: the adjective and the adverb. Whole groups of words also may act as modifiers. Just as a verb phrase acts as a single verb, so an adjective or adverb phrase acts as a single adjective or adverb. An entire phrase may also serve as a noun. This chapter will focus on how to identify and use phrases in writing.

DIAGNOSTIC TEST

Classifying Phrases. Number your paper 1–20. After the proper number, write each italicized phrase and indicate what kind of phrase it is. Use the abbreviations *prep.* (prepositional phrase), *part.* (participial phrase), *inf.* (infinitive phrase), *ger.* (gerund phrase), and *app.* (appositive phrase). Do not separately identify a prepositional phrase that is part of a larger phrase.

EXAMPLE 1. He tried *to do his best.*
1. *to do his best—inf.*

1. *Fishing for bass* is my father's favorite pastime. 1. ger.
2. The seagulls *gliding through the air* looked like pieces of paper caught in the wind. 2. part.

3. The school bus was on time *in spite of the traffic jam.* 3. prep.
4. Ms. Hoban, *my science teacher,* got married last week. 4. app.
5. There is no time left *to answer your questions.* 5. inf.
6. *Under a white flag* of truce, the defeated soldiers glumly emerged from the fort. 6. prep.
7. My brother plans *to marry Maureen in June.* 7. inf.
8. Nobody seems to be interested in *going to the fireworks display.* 8. ger.
9. Have you seen my cat, *a striped Persian with yellow eyes?* 9. app.
10. Joel said that he can go *to the dance or the movies* on Friday. 10. prep.
11. *Hoping for a new bicycle and a toy robot,* my brother couldn't sleep at all on Christmas Eve. 11. part.
12. Tom Sawyer tricked his friends into *painting the fence for him.* 12. ger.
13. In America, citizens have the right *to speak their minds.* 13. inf.
14. My aunt's car, *an old crate with a beat-up interior and a rattly engine,* used to belong to my grandfather. 14. app.
15. Debbie's sister denied *taking the cookies.* 15. ger.
16. Last Sunday, we all piled in the car and went *to the beach, the bowling alley, and the mall.* 16. prep.
17. The shark *chasing the school of fish* looked like a hammerhead. 17. part.
18. Nobody wanted to read the book, *a thick hardback with a faded cover.* 18. app.
19. All of the invitations *sent to the club members* had the wrong date on them. 19. part.
20. Buddy's cousin ran off *to join the circus.* 20. inf.

14a. A *phrase* is a group of related words that is used as a single part of speech and does not contain a verb and its subject.

You have already studied the *verb phrase,* which is introduced by a helping verb (*have* bought). You have also been introduced to

PRESENTING THE CHAPTER

LESS-ADVANCED STUDENTS You may want to concentrate on the identification of prepositional phrases (without insisting that these students distinguish between adjective and adverb phrases) and on the identification of appositives. Verbals may be too difficult, although you may want to include infinitives without requiring that students learn how they are used. *(See listing of Alternative Worksheets on page 380.)*

ADVANCED STUDENTS These students may have no difficulty with prepositional phrases. Depending upon the results of the Diagnostic Test, you may want to go over verbals more carefully. Concentrate on original writing, starting with the writing applications. Encourage these students to use phrases to add variety to their own sentences.

WRITING APPLICATIONS

The writing applications in this chapter are designed to encourage students to use their knowledge of participial and gerund phrases in their own writing. Feel free to adapt them to your students' writing needs, abilities, and interests.

DIAGNOSTIC TEST

This test will give you a clear picture of what your eighth-graders already know about phrases. Since much of the material in this chapter will be new, assure your students that the results of this test will not affect their grades. You may prefer not to give the test if you know the material is new to your students.

THE PREPOSITIONAL PHRASE (rules 14b–14d)

Remind students who have difficulty identifying prepositional phrases that *a prepositional phrase begins with a preposition.* Then refer them to the list of prepositions on page 324. A less-advanced class need not be concerned about prepositions that consist of more than one word *(in front of, according to)*. Few of these prepositions appear in this chapter.

EXERCISE 1. This exercise provides practice in identifying prepositional phrases. If your students can already identify them easily, skip this exercise and proceed to adjective and adverb phrases.

GRAMMAR

the *prepositional phrase.* In this chapter you will learn more about the prepositional phrase, and you will meet several new kinds of phrases—the *participial phrase,* the *infinitive phrase,* the *gerund phrase,* and the *appositive phrase.*

THE PREPOSITIONAL PHRASE

14b. A *prepositional phrase* is a group of words that begins with a preposition and usually ends with a noun or pronoun.

In the following examples, the prepositional phrases are in boldface.

During the night the horse ran off.
Marian wore white pajamas **with red hearts.**

A single prepositional phrase may contain two or more objects.

The dish is filled **with crackers and rice cookies.**
The group traveled **through Spain and Italy.**

EXERCISE 1. Identifying Prepositional Phrases. Number your paper 1–10, using every other line. After the appropriate number, write the prepositional phrases in each sentence.

1. The daily schedule prepared by the camp directors was followed from dawn until late evening.
2. We were awakened at six by a bugle, played with cold fingers by a sleepy camper.
3. Standing attentively outside our cabins, we shivered in the early morning breeze coming across the lake.
4. After exercises, everyone swam in the icy water.
5. Fearing death from freezing, we raced back and dressed for breakfast.
6. Activity period included classes in painting, crafts, music, drama, and folklore.
7. The rest of the morning was devoted to sports.
8. After lunch, we spent an hour in our cabins.

9. Then we had two hours of water sports.
10. At night, talented campers and counselors entertained us.

The Adjective Phrase

14c. An *adjective phrase* is a prepositional phrase that modifies a noun or a pronoun.

Notice that the adjectives and the adjective phrases in boldface in the following sentences do the same work: they modify a noun.

ADJECTIVE The **lighthouse** beacon stayed on all night.

ADJECTIVE PHRASE The beacon **from the lighthouse** stayed on all night.

ADJECTIVE Their **varsity** players are bigger than our players.

ADJECTIVE PHRASE The players **on their varsity** are bigger than our players.

Like the adjective, an adjective phrase is usually located next to the word it modifies. But while the adjective generally precedes the word it modifies, the adjective phrase usually follows the word it modifies.

EXERCISE 2. Identifying Adjective Phrases. Number your paper 1–10. After the proper number, write the adjective phrase in each sentence and the noun or pronoun it modifies.

EXAMPLE 1. The dancers on the stage were thrilling.
1. *on the stage—dancers*

1. The strait between the Pacific Ocean and San Francisco Bay is called the Golden Gate.
2. The Golden Gate Bridge spans this narrow body of water.
3. San Francisco was once a small village on the bay but is now a busy metropolitan center.

GRAMMAR

THE ADJECTIVE PHRASE (rule 14c)

Write on the board pairs of sentences such as these:

He owns a *golden* lamp.
He owns a lamp *of gold*.

She owns some *rural* property.
She owns some property *in the country*.

Ask what part of speech *golden* is in the first sentence and what word it modifies. (Answer: Adjective; it modifies *lamp*.) Ask someone to identify the prepositional phrase in the paired sentence and to tell what word it modifies. Follow the same procedure with other paired sentences. The class will learn that these phrases are used, like single-word adjectives, to modify nouns.

Referring to the board, get the class to say that an adjective usually precedes the word it modifies, but an adjective phrase usually follows the word it modifies. Apply this idea to the improvement of writing by asking the class to rearrange some sentences with misplaced modifiers:

The girl was in the store in the navy blazer.
The purse belongs to the girl with the red initials.
The man was on the ladder with the broken arm.

EXERCISE 2. With advanced students you may decide to use only a few sentences from this exercise and the next one. With less-advanced students you might do this exercise in class and assign the next one as homework.

EXERCISE 3. If you assign this exercise as individual work, be sure to go over the answers in class.

THE ADVERB PHRASE (rule 14d)

Put on the board pairs of sentences such as these:

The job was done *carefully*.
The job was done *with care*.

We stayed *there* all afternoon.
We stayed *at home* all afternoon.

Follow the procedure suggested for adjective phrases to show that these phrases function like the single-word adverbs.

GRAMMAR

4. The California gold rush of 1849 swelled San Francisco's population. (or rush)
5. The 1906 earthquake destroyed the homes of many people.
6. Today sightseers from many different nations crowd San Francisco's streets.
7. Some of the streets are very steep.
8. Chinatown in San Francisco attracts many visitors.
9. This city beside the bay has many charms.
10. Do you know any songs about San Francisco?

Sometimes one adjective phrase follows another. The second phrase usually modifies the object in the first phrase.

EXAMPLE Sicily is an island **off the coast of Italy.**

EXERCISE 3. Identifying Adjective Phrases. Each of the following sentences contains two adjective phrases. Write each adjective phrase and the word it modifies after the appropriate number.

EXAMPLE 1. Sharon read a book on the origins of words.
1. *on the origins, book; of words, origins*

1. My sister Connie, a real terror with a whale of a temper, shouts "Beans!" when something goes wrong.
2. Some terms for the expression of anger were originally Latin or Greek words.
3. Many of us in English class wanted to discuss how people express their annoyance.
4. Imagine what would happen if everybody in every house in the city had a bad day.
5. We agreed that the best thing to do is to avoid people with chips on their shoulders.

The Adverb Phrase

When a prepositional phrase is used as an adverb to modify a verb, adjective, or adverb, it is called an *adverb phrase.* Like a single-word adverb, the adverb phrase answers the question *How? When? Where?* or *To what extent?*

14d. An *adverb phrase* is a prepositional phrase that modifies a verb, an adjective, or an adverb.

EXAMPLES The snow fell **like feathers.** [The adverb phrase modifies the verb *fell,* telling *how* the snow fell.]

Her dress is too long **in the back.** [The adverb phrase modifies the adjective *long,* telling *where* the dress is too long.]

We arrived early **in the morning.** [The adverb phrase modifies the adverb *early,* telling *when* we were early.]

EXERCISE 4. Identifying Adverb Phrases. Number your paper 1–10. After the appropriate number, write the adverb phrase from each sentence. Then write the verb, adjective, or adverb that the phrase modifies.

EXAMPLE 1. Our town was built over a river.

1. *over a river—was built*

1. The Cheery Oh Restaurant has opened across the road.
2. The food is fantastic beyond belief.
3. Almost everyone has gone to the new place.
4. At the Cheery Oh you can eat exotic food.
5. People sit late into the night drinking tropical fruit juices and chatting.
6. They enjoy themselves in the friendly atmosphere.
7. People appear happy with the service.
8. For three weeks the Cheery Oh has been crowded.
9. Some say in all seriousness that it resembles an English coffeehouse.
10. If the famous writers John Dryden and Joseph Addison were alive today, they could probably be found at this charming restaurant.

EXERCISE 4. A less-advanced class may have trouble identifying the word modified by an adverb phrase. You may ask these students simply to identify prepositional phrases.

EXERCISE 5. See notes for Exercise 4.

EXERCISE 6. You may want less-advanced students to write just five sentences and to skip the direction about labeling phrases as adjective or adverb.

GRAMMAR

Unlike an adjective phrase, an adverb phrase may be separated from the word it modifies by other words. Adverb phrases may be moved about in the sentence.

EXAMPLES **For many centuries** people searched **for a way** to make gold.

People searched **for many centuries for a way** to make gold.

EXERCISE 5. Identifying Adverb Phrases. Number your paper 1–5. After the proper number, write the adverb phrase or phrases in each sentence. After each adverb phrase, write the word or phrase it modifies.

EXAMPLE 1. I am going to camp during vacation.
1. *to camp—am going; during vacation—am going*

1. Mount Vernon is interesting for its history.
2. The house was named Mount Vernon by Lawrence Washington, who lived there for many years.
3. Somewhat later, George and Martha Washington moved to Mount Vernon.
4. After Washington's death the house was owned by a series of people.
5. In 1858, it was bought by the Mount Vernon Ladies' Association, which restored it.

EXERCISE 6. Writing Sentences with Prepositional Phrases. Write sentences of your own in which you use the following phrases as adjective or adverb phrases. In each sentence, underline the word or word group that the phrase modifies and label the phrase as *adj. phr.* (adjective phrase) or *adv. phr.* (adverb phrase). Answers will vary.

1. under the bridge
2. for our kitchen
3. outside the cabin
4. without any help
5. down the river
6. with bright lights
7. through the hallway
8. beside the path
9. in the laundry
10. through our efforts

Diagraming Adjective and Adverb Phrases

An adjective or adverb phrase is diagramed below the word it modifies. Write the preposition on a line slanting down from the modified word. Then write the object of the preposition (the noun or pronoun following the preposition) on a horizontal line extending from the slanting line.

PATTERNS

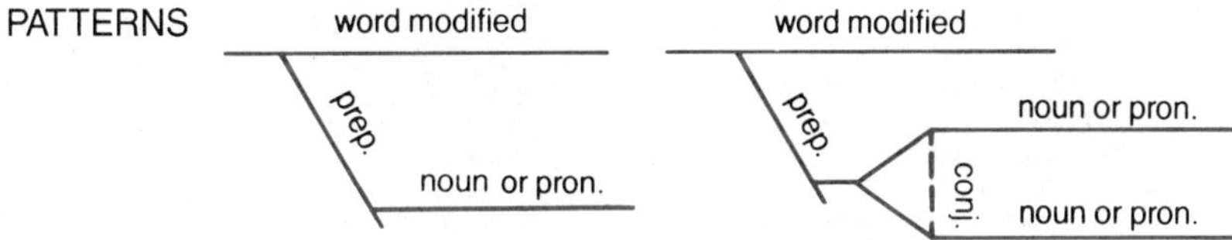

EXAMPLES walked along the road

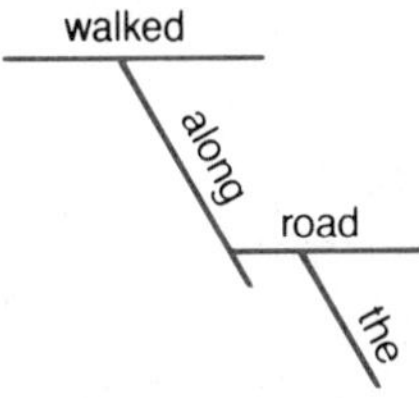

paintings by famous artists

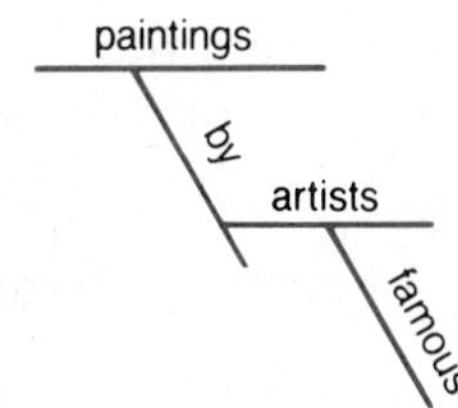

went with Hollis and Dave

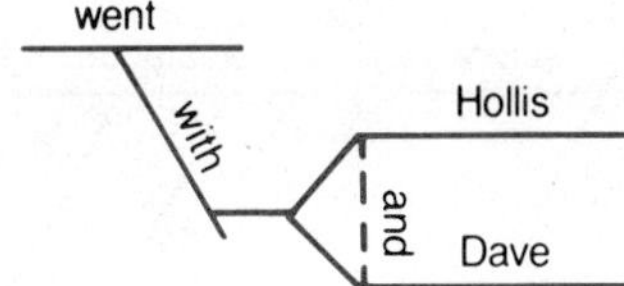

GRAMMAR

EXERCISES 7 and 8. The correct answers to these diagraming exercises should be written on the board.

If you have decided not to require a less-advanced class to identify the words modified by prepositional phrases, do not require them to diagram sentences containing prepositional phrases.

GRAMMAR

When a prepositional phrase modifies the object of another prepositional phrase, the diagram looks like this:

EXAMPLE camped on the side of a mountain

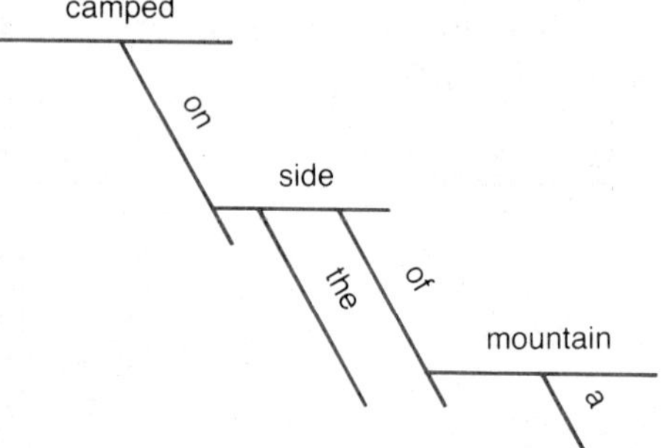

EXERCISE 7. Diagraming Prepositional Phrases. Diagram the following word groups, which contain prepositional phrases. Use a ruler, and leave plenty of space between diagrams.
See Answer Key.

1. invited to the celebrations
2. a glimpse of the famous ruler
3. one of the people in the room
4. read about King Midas and his golden touch
5. drove to a village near Paris

EXERCISE 8. Diagraming Sentences with Adjective Phrases and Adverb Phrases. Diagram the following sentences, each of which contains an adjective phrase or an adverb phrase or both. See Answer Key.

EXAMPLE The company of actors performed for an audience of children.

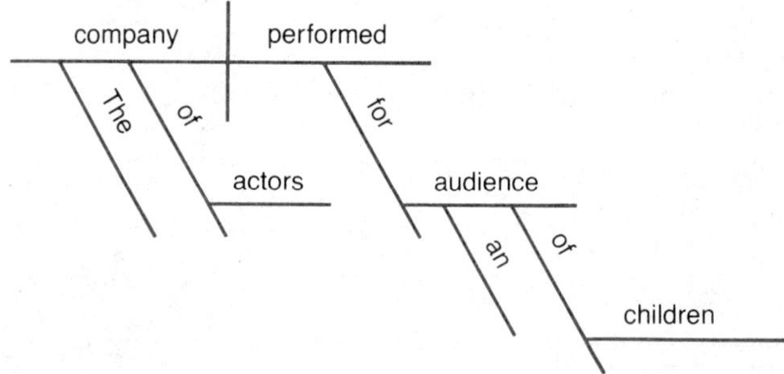

1. The number of whales is decreasing.
2. Some familiar animals can be found only in zoos.
3. Hundreds of species have vanished from the earth.
4. Citrus fruits are grown in California and Florida.
5. Many historic events have been decided by sudden changes in the weather.
6. The defeat of the Spanish Armada resulted from a violent ocean storm.

REVIEW EXERCISE A. Identifying Adjective Phrases and Adverb Phrases. After the proper number, list in order each adjective and adverb phrase in the following sentences. After each phrase, write the word or expression it modifies. Be ready to tell whether it is an adjective phrase or an adverb phrase.

EXAMPLE 1. Through old journals, our understanding of the pioneers has increased.
1. *Through old journals—has increased; of the pioneers—understanding*

1. Few of us appreciate the determination and courage of the pioneers who traveled west. 1. adj., adj.
2. The word *travel* comes from the French word *travailler,* which means "to work hard." 2. adv.
3. On the trip westward only small children rode in the wagons. 3. adv., adv.
4. Everyone else traveled on foot over the mountains. 4. adv., adv.
5. Sometimes a wagon train would stop in a valley and then spend the winter in houses that were built quickly. 5. adv., adv.
6. In one account of a harsh winter, a pioneer recorded* an incident of a roof collapsed under the weight of the snow.
7. Food was often scarce, and hundreds never recovered from the hardships. 7. adv.
8. A typical day's chores began long before dawn. 8. adv.
9. The pioneers who did survive by sheer determination often continued their journey. 9. adv.
10. At their western destination, many families often shared the same cabin. 10. adv.

6. adv., adj., adj., adv., adj., *(In one account modifies recorded; of a roof modifies incident; under the weight modifies collapsed.)

REVIEW EXERCISE A. You may use this exercise as a test. A less-advanced class should probably omit it. Note that these sentences are not suitable for diagraming, as they would present more advanced diagraming problems.

GRAMMAR

THE PARTICIPLE (rule 14e)

The concepts of the participle and of the participial phrase may be difficult even for eighth-graders who already have a good basic understanding of grammar. Review the forms of present and past participles. Students were probably introduced to these two forms in the seventh grade. For a review of participles, see text pages 443 and 446.

EXERCISE 9. Have your students do this exercise in class. If they have obvious difficulty distinguishing between a participle used as an adjective and a participle that is part of a verb phrase, they will need further help with this before they go on to the participial phrase.

GRAMMAR

VERBALS AND VERBAL PHRASES

A verbal is a word that is formed from a verb but is used in a sentence as a noun, an adjective, or an adverb. There are three kinds of verbals: the *participle,* the *gerund,* and the *infinitive.*

The Participle

14e. A *participle* is a verb form that can be used as an adjective.

There are two kinds of participles—present participles and past participles. Present participles end in *-ing.* Past participles often end in *-ed, -d,* or *-t.*

EXAMPLES The horses **trotting** past were not frightened by the crowd. [*Trotting* (a form of the verb *trot*) modifies the noun *horses—trotting horses.*]

Buried by pirates, the treasure lay undiscovered for centuries. [*Buried* (a form of the verb *bury*) modifies the noun *treasure—buried treasure.*]

Do not confuse participles used as in the examples above with participles used in a verb phrase.

PARTICIPLE **Broken,** the toy still ran.
VERB PHRASE The toy **was broken** by Tim, but it still ran.

PARTICIPLE **Planning** their trip, the class learned some geography.
VERB PHRASE While they **were planning** their trip, the class learned some geography.

The participle in a verb phrase is part of a verb and does not act as an adjective.

EXERCISE 9. Identifying Participles. Number your paper 1–10. After the proper number, write the participle from each sentence, then the noun or pronoun it modifies. Be prepared to identify the participle as a present participle or a past participle.

EXAMPLE 1. We heard the train whistling and chugging in the distance.
1. *whistling—train; chugging—train*

1. Records, cracked and warped, were in the old trunk in the attic.
2. Shouting loudly, Becky warned the pedestrian to look out for the car.
3. The sparkling water splashed in our faces.
4. The papers, aged and yellowed, are kept in the file.
5. For centuries the ruins remained there, still undiscovered.
6. Smiling politely, she gave directions to the post office.
7. The charging bull thundered across the field.
8. Cheering and clapping, the spectators greeted their team.
9. The children, fidgeting noisily, waited eagerly for recess.
10. Recently released, the movie has not yet come to our local theaters.

The Participial Phrase

When a participle introduces a group of related words that act together as an adjective, this word group is called a *participial phrase.*

14f. A *participial phrase* is a group of related words that contains a participle and that acts as an adjective.

A prepositional phrase often follows the participle. When it does, it is considered a part of the participial phrase. In the following examples, an arrow is drawn from each participial phrase (shown in boldface) to the word that it modifies.

Seeing itself in the mirror, the duck seemed bewildered.

It stood in front of the mirror, **watching its image closely.**

Then, **disgusted with the other duck,** it began to peck the mirror.

THE PARTICIPIAL PHRASE (rule 14f)

Write on the board a few sentences with short participial phrases.

1. **Laughing loudly,** the audience applauded the skit.
2. She saw the boys **waiting by the library**.
3. **Not seeing the woman and her dog**, I almost ran into them.
4. **Turning to her friend**, she whispered something.

Point out that each of these phrases is a participial phrase because the principal word in it is a participle. Have the class discover that the entire phrase (like a single-word participle) modifies the noun or pronoun—that, in other words, the phrase as a whole is used as an adjective. Emphasize that unlike a prepositional phrase, which can be used as either an adjective or an adverb, a participial phrase can be used *only* as an adjective.

Discuss each example on the board, asking the class what it contains. They should conclude that a participial phrase contains a participle and its modifiers and complements (if any).

Students sometimes mistakenly identify a word within the phrase as the word modified by the phrase. For example, a student might tell you that *seeing*, in example 3 above, modifies *woman*. If this should happen, point out that the word modified must be a word outside the phrase. The student can correct this error by asking "Who or what is *seeing*?"

EXERCISE 10. You may want to go over a few items with students before assigning the rest of the exercise for individual work.

EXERCISE 11. Caution students against using the participle as part of the main verb in a sentence ("We were *waiting for the bus in the rain*").

GRAMMAR

EXERCISE 10. Identifying Participial Phrases. Number your paper 1–10. After the appropriate number, write the participial phrase in each sentence. After the phrase, write the word or words that it modifies.

1. Noted for her beauty, Venus was sought by all the gods as a wife.
2. Bathed in radiant light, Venus brought love and joy wherever she went.
3. Jupiter, knowing her charms, nevertheless married her to Vulcan, the ugliest of the gods.
4. Mars, known to the Greeks as Ares, was the god of war.
5. Terrified by Ares' power, many Greeks did not like to worship him.
6. They saw both land and people destroyed by him.
7. Observing his path, they said that Ares left blood, devastation, and grief behind him.
8. The Romans, having great respect for Mars, made him one of their three chief deities.
9. They imagined him dressed in shining armor.
10. Mars, supposed to be the father of the founders of Rome, has a month named after him.

EXERCISE 11. Writing Sentences with Participial Phrases. Use the following participial phrases in sentences of your own. Place each phrase as close as possible to the noun or pronoun that it modifies. If you use a participial phrase to begin a sentence, put a comma after the phrase. Answers will vary.

EXAMPLE 1. standing in line
1. *Standing in line, we waited twenty minutes for the store to open.*

1. waiting for the bus in the rain
2. passing the store window
3. planning the escape
4. jumping from stone to stone
5. hearing the whistle blow and feeling the train lurch forward

WRITING APPLICATION A:
Using Participial Phrases to Combine Closely Related Sentences

When you were younger, you probably wrote mostly short, choppy sentences that contained simple ideas. As you have grown older, you have learned to combine ideas to pack more information into your sentences. One way you do this is by using participles.

EXAMPLE I sat down at the table. Mother was at the table. I took out my class schedule for next year. Mother and I discussed my classes. These classes were offered for ninth-graders. [The style of this example is short and choppy.]

Sitting down at the table, I took out my class schedule to show Mother. She and I discussed the classes **offered for ninth-graders next year.** [This is one way to improve the short, choppy sentences. Notice the participial phrases in boldface.]

Writing Assignment

Answers will vary.

Before people begin activities of various kinds, they often have warm-ups. This is true whether they are getting ready to swim in a race, play in a band concert, or perform in a dance recital. Describe either a person or a group of persons warming up. Use at least three participial phrases, and underline these phrases.

The Gerund

Besides acting as participial modifiers, verbs ending in *-ing* can also be another kind of verbal called a *gerund.* Gerunds function as nouns in sentences.

14g. A *gerund* is a verb form ending in *-ing* that is used as a noun.

THE GERUND and
THE GERUND PHRASE
(rules 14g and 14h)

Gerunds are used continually in everyday speaking and writing. However, since most of your students already use gerunds correctly, you may choose not to spend a great deal of class time on them. Students should be familiar, in any case, with the term.

Note: A few teachers use the term "participle used as a noun" instead of gerund, *and occasionally you may find that your students are familiar with gerunds under this name.*

The only usage problem directly related to the gerund is the use of the possessive case in sentences like these:

Did you hear about **Ms. Grant's** winning the election?
His parents did not approve of **his** going to the city alone.

In informal conversation many people would not use the possessive but would say *Ms. Grant* and *him* in these sentences. Show your class that the possessive is technically correct, however, by substituting ordinary nouns for the gerunds.

Did you hear about **Ms. Grant's** victory? (NOT "Ms. Grant victory")
His parents did not approve of **his** journey. (NOT "him journey")

To help your eighth-graders distinguish between verbs, participles, and gerunds, write the following sentences on the board:

VERB I *was studying*.
GERUND *Studying* is easy for him.
PARTICIPLE Anyone *studying* for an exam needs quiet.

Ask them to suggest their own sentences to illustrate these three terms.

EXERCISE 12. You may ask your more advanced students to write how each gerund is used.

GRAMMAR

EXAMPLES **Jogging** can be good exercise. [subject]
My favorite hobby is **fishing.** [predicate nominative]
Lock the door before **leaving.** [object of preposition]
Did they go **hiking?** [direct object]

Because the gerund acts as a noun, it can be modified by adjectives and adjective phrases.

EXAMPLE The **quiet** gurgling **of the water** was restful. [The adjective *quiet* and the adjective phrase *of the water* both modify the gerund *gurgling.*]

Because gerunds are also verb forms, they can be modified by adverbs and adverb phrases, too.

EXAMPLE We crossed the stream by stepping **carefully from stone to stone.** [The adverb *carefully* and the adverb phrase *from stone to stone* both modify the gerund *stepping.*]

Remember that gerunds are nouns. Do not confuse a gerund with a participle used as part of a verb or as an adjective.

EXAMPLE **Pausing,** (PART.) the deer **was sniffing** (V.) the wind before **stepping** (GER.) into the open meadow.

Pausing is a participle modifying *deer*, and *sniffing* is part of the verb phrase *was sniffing*. *Stepping* is a gerund, serving as the object of the preposition *before.*

EXERCISE 12. Identifying Gerunds. Number your paper 1–10. After the appropriate number, write the gerund in each sentence. If there is no gerund in the sentence, write *none.*

EXAMPLE 1. Typing is a useful skill.
1. *Typing*

1. Their singing caused the dogs to howl.
2. Jerry has been practicing pole vaulting every day after school. 2. (or vaulting)
3. My sister has always enjoyed horseback riding. 3. (or riding)

4. In the past, working took up most people's time six days a week.
5. I look forward to resting after this tiring job is done.
6. Uncle Eli's specialty is barbecuing on the outdoor grill.
7. Nobody could stand the child's unceasing whine. **7. none**
8. The colonel will be commending the scout for volunteering for the dangerous mission.
9. Studying usually pays off in higher scores.
10. Considering the other choices, Melinda decided on walking.

The Gerund Phrase

A gerund may be accompanied by modifiers and complements, which together with the gerund form a *gerund phrase.*

14h. A *gerund phrase* includes the gerund and all the words related to the gerund.

A gerund is formed from a verb. It may be modified by an adverb and may also have a complement, usually a direct object. Since a gerund functions as a noun, it may be modified by an adjective. A gerund phrase includes the gerund and all of its modifiers and complements.

EXAMPLE **Shouting at people** does not make them understand you better.

In the above example, *shouting* is a gerund, and *at people* is a prepositional phrase acting as an adverb that modifies *shouting.* Together, *shouting at people* is a gerund phrase that acts as the subject of the sentence.

EXAMPLE Most of the players obeyed **the stern warning from the coach.**

In the preceding example, the gerund *warning* is modified by the article *the,* the adjective *stern,* and the prepositional phrase *from the coach.* The word group *the stern warning from the coach* is a gerund phrase that serves as object of the verb *obeyed.*

EXERCISE 13. You may have your less-advanced students do this exercise orally with your help.

GRAMMAR

EXAMPLE The child spelled her name by **carefully printing each letter.**

Here the gerund *printing* is modified by the adverb *carefully* and takes a direct object, *each letter.* The phrase as a whole, *carefully printing each letter,* is the object of the preposition *by.*

NOTE Since a gerund acts as a noun, any noun or pronoun that comes immediately before it should be in the possessive case.

EXAMPLES **Michael's** cooking is the best I've ever tasted.
The vultures didn't let anything disturb **their** feeding.

EXERCISE 13. Identifying Gerund Phrases. After the appropriate number, write the gerund phrase in each of the following sentences.

EXAMPLE 1. The rain interrupted their building of the bonfire.
1. *their building of the bonfire*

1. Vincent's pleading did not influence his mother's decision.
2. The man was given a ticket for driving the wrong way on a one-way street.
3. We sat back and enjoyed the slow rocking of the boat.
4. The blue jay's screeching at the cat woke us up at dawn.
5. Give practicing the piano a chance.
6. When did that piercing clanging begin?
7. The frantic darting of the fish indicated that a shark was nearby.
8. She is considering running for class president.
9. Ants try to protect their colonies from storms by piling up sand against the wind.
10. The wading egret was intently searching for frogs and other small animals during its early-morning feeding.

EXERCISE 14. Writing Sentences with Gerund Phrases. Use each of the following gerund phrases in a sentence of your own. Underline the gerund phrase and identify it as subject, predicate nominative, direct object, indirect object, or the object of a preposition. Answers will vary.

EXAMPLE 1. Hiking up the hill
1. *Hiking up the hill took us all morning. subject*

1. getting up in the morning
2. arguing among themselves
3. refusing any help with the job
4. sharpening my pencil
5. peeling carrots carefully

WRITING APPLICATION B: Using Gerunds to Explain Activities Involving Action

The versatile paper clip can be used to fasten together pieces of paper, to hang up lightweight pictures, and to perform a number of other tasks. The gerund is the paper clip of the English language. It can be subject, direct object, predicate nominative, or anything else a noun can be. When you need a noun that expresses action, a gerund can be very helpful.

EXAMPLES **Learning to play a violin** is harder than I thought it would be. [gerund phrase used as subject.]
My brother dislikes **taking out the trash.** [gerund phrase used as object of the verb.]

Writing Assignment

Answers will vary.

If you could have any job you wanted, what would it be? Write a paragraph telling about this job and why you would choose it. Use three gerund phrases, and underline these phrases.

EXERCISE 14. Assign this exercise to all of your students. With your less-advanced students, omit the part of the assignment that tells them to identify how the phrase is used.

GRAMMAR

THE INFINITIVE and
THE INFINITIVE PHRASE
(rules 14i and 14j)

Infinitives, like gerunds, do not give rise to any critical usage problems. However, you may find it necessary to explain the infinitive with *to* to a class that confuses such structures with prepositional phrases. To remind students of the distinction between infinitives and prepositional phrases, write on the board the following phrases:

to town
to talk
to dance
to the dance
to the show
to show
to question
to a question
to have questioned

Have the class tell whether each is a prepositional or an infinitive phrase.

GRAMMAR

The Infinitive

Besides the participle and the gerund, there is a third kind of verbal called the *infinitive.* An infinitive can act as an adjective, a noun, or an adverb.

14i. An *infinitive* is a verb form that can be used as a noun, an adjective, or an adverb.

An infinitive has the word *to* directly before the plain form of the verb, as in *to win, to go,* and *to consider.*

To determine what part of speech an infinitive is, look at how the infinitive is used in the sentence.

Infinitives used as nouns: She expected **to finish** the race, but not **to win.** [*To finish* and *to win* are objects of the verb *expected.*

To forgive does not always mean **to forget.** [*To forgive* is the subject of the sentence; *to forget* is the predicate nominative.]

Infinitives used as adjectives: The best time **to visit** Florida is December through April. [*To visit* modifies *time.*]

If you want information about computers, that is the magazine **to read.** [*To read* modifies *magazine.*]

Infinitives used as adverbs: They were eager **to try.** [*To try* modifies the adjective *eager.*]

The caravan stopped at the oasis **to rest.** [*To rest* modifies the verb *stopped.*]

> ☞ **USAGE NOTE** *To* plus a noun or a pronoun (*to class, to them, to the dance*) is a prepositional phrase, not an infinitive. Be careful not to confuse infinitives with prepositional phrases beginning with *to.*

INFINITIVE	I want **to go.**
PREPOSITIONAL PHRASE	I want to go **to town.**

EXERCISE 15. This exercise should not be difficult. Go over the answers in class to make sure your students are not confusing infinitives with prepositions.

EXERCISE 15. Identifying Infinitives. Number your paper 1–10. After the appropriate number, write the infinitive in each sentence. If a sentence contains no infinitive, write *none.*

EXAMPLE 1. June doesn't know how to dance.
1. *to dance*

1. After school June and I like to walk home together.
2. Usually, we go to my house or her house to listen to tapes.
3. Sometimes I get up to move with the music, but June never does.
4. One day I asked her to join me.
5. She said that she had never been to dancing school or learned any steps. 5. none
6. "Do you want me to show you some?" I asked.
7. "I'm ready to try," she answered.
8. I didn't know which steps to start with.
9. After doing my best to teach her for three weeks, I gave up.
10. It's a good thing that June doesn't plan to become a dancer.

The Infinitive Phrase

An infinitive may be followed by a group of related words, which together with the infinitive form an *infinitive phrase.*

14j. An *infinitive phrase* consists of an infinitive together with its complements and modifiers.

An infinitive may be modified by an adjective or an adverb; it may also have a complement. Together, an infinitive and its modifiers and complements make up an infinitive phrase. The entire phrase may act as an adjective, an adverb, or a noun.

EXAMPLE **To lift those weights** takes a lot of strength.

The infinitive phrase *to lift those weights* is used as a noun that is the subject of the sentence. The infinitive *to lift* has an object, *weights,* which is modified by *those.*

EXAMPLE Peanuts and raisins are good snacks **to take on a camping trip.**

EXERCISE 16. Less-advanced students may have difficulty identifying whether the infinitive phrases are used as nouns, adjectives, or adverbs. You might omit this part of the exercise.

EXERCISE 17. Have all of your classes write the sentences. Omit the "identification" part of the assignment with your less-advanced students.

GRAMMAR

The infinitive phrase *to take on a camping trip* is used as an adjective modifying *snacks*. The infinitive *to take* is modified by the prepositional phrase *on a camping trip*.

EXAMPLE The crowd grew quiet **to hear the speaker.**

The infinitive phrase *to hear the speaker* is used as an adverb modifying the adjective *quiet*. The infinitive *to hear* has the complement *the speaker*.

EXERCISE 16. Identifying Infinitive Phrases. After the appropriate number, write the infinitive phrase in each sentence, and identify it as a noun, an adjective, or an adverb. If there is no infinitive phrase in the sentence, write *none*.

EXAMPLE 1. My uncle taught me to take care of my bicycle.
1. *to take care of my bicycle—noun*

1. Taking care of your bicycle will help to make it last longer. 1. n.
2. We used machine oil to lubricate the chain. 2. adv.
3. He said to place a drop of oil on each link. 3. n.
4. Then he showed me the valve to fill the inner tube. 4. adj.
5. Using a hand pump, we added air to the back tire. 5. none
6. We were careful not to put in too much air. 6. adv.
7. Next, we got out wrenches to tighten several bolts. 7. adv. or adj.
8. My uncle warned me not to pull on the wrench too hard. 8. n.
9. Overtightening can cause as much damage to a bolt as not tightening it enough can. 9. none
10. I thanked my uncle for taking the time to give me tips about taking care of my bicycle. 10. adj.

EXERCISE 17. Writing Sentences with Infinitives. Use each of the following infinitive phrases in a sentence of your own. Underline the infinitive phrase and identify it as a noun, an adjective, or an adverb. Answers will vary.

EXAMPLE 1. to leave school early on Tuesday
1. *The principal gave me permission to leave school early on Tuesday.—adj.*

1. to give the right answers
2. to go home after school
3. to run after the bus
4. to read the entire book
5. to spend the night

REVIEW EXERCISE B. Identifying and Classifying Verbals and Verbal Phrases. After the appropriate number, write the verbal or verbal phrase in each of the following sentences. Identify each verbal or verbal phrase as a *gerund, gerund phrase, infinitive, infinitive phrase, participle,* or *participial phrase.*

EXAMPLE 1. Raising his head, the steer eyed us lazily.
1. *Raising his head—participial phrase*

1. Even the people in charge didn't know what to do. 1. inf.
2. The "flying fox" is actually a bat. 2. part.
3. Bo was commended for organizing the clean-up campaign. 3. ger. phr.
4. What did you say to her to make her so mad? 4. inf. phr.
5. According to experts, swimming is the best form of exercise.
6. One of the women taking tickets at the door gave us directions to our seats. 6. part. phr.
7. The old hermit preferred living alone in the forest. 7. ger. phr.
8. The tourist looked exhausted, but he didn't stop for a rest.
9. One solution may be to offer them more money. 9. inf. phr.
10. His constant complaining grated on everyone's nerves.

5. ger. 8. part. 10. ger. phr.

Diagraming Verbals and Verbal Phrases

Participles alone are diagramed like any other adjective. Participial phrases are diagramed as follows:

EXAMPLE **Shaking her head,** my older sister winked at me.

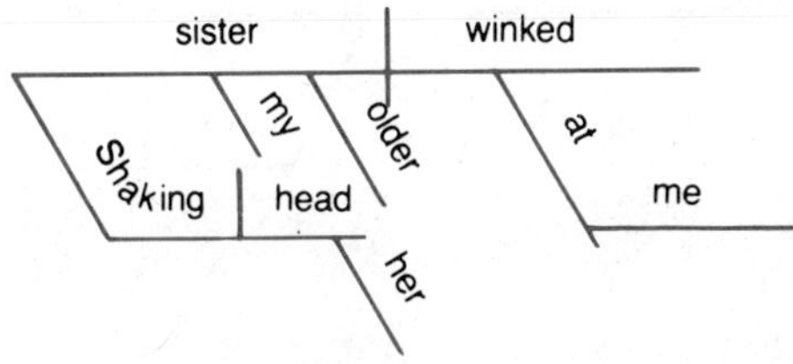

REVIEW EXERCISE B. You may decide to use this exercise as a test on verbals and verbal phrases.

DIAGRAMING VERBALS AND VERBAL PHRASES

Even if you do not plan to have your students diagram sentences, you may wish to put diagrams on the board to help explain the grammatical functions of verbal phrases. Diagraming clarifies the part that these phrases play in a sentence.

GRAMMAR

Gerunds and gerund phrases are diagramed as follows:

EXAMPLE **Being slightly ill** is no excuse for **missing two days of baseball practice.** [Gerund phrases used as subject and as object of preposition. The first gerund has a subject complement (*ill*); the second gerund has a direct object (*days*).]

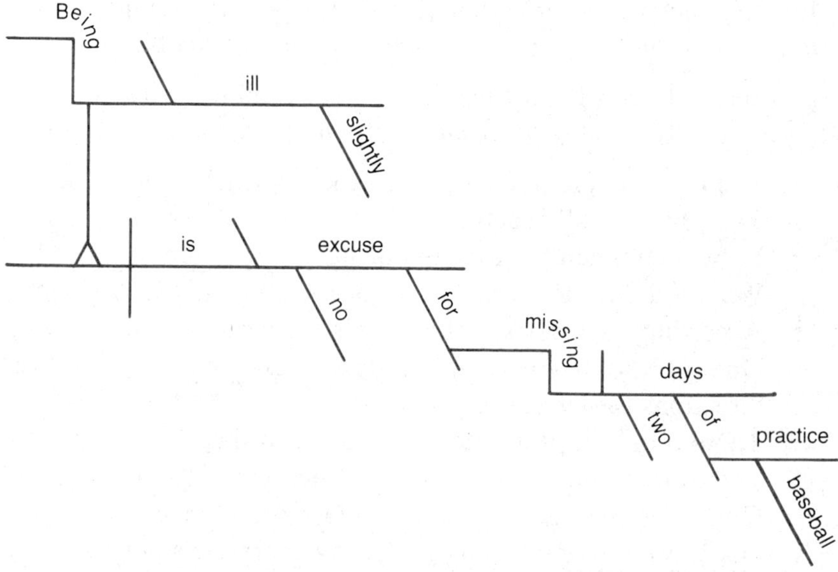

Infinitives and infinitive phrases used as modifiers are diagramed like prepositional phrases.

EXAMPLE He was the first one **to solve that tricky problem.**

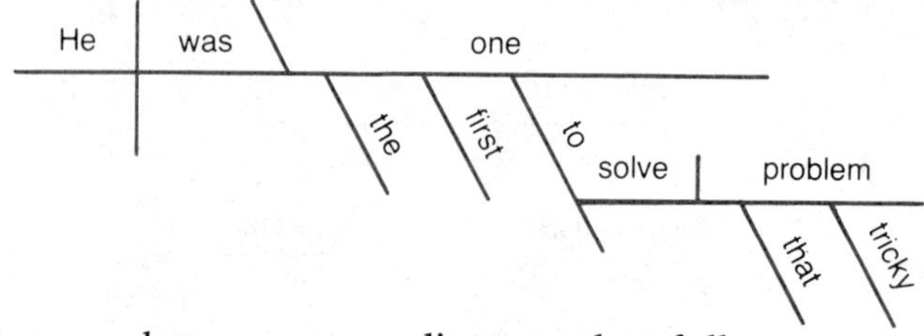

Infinitives used as nouns are diagramed as follows:

EXAMPLE Marge was hoping **to go with us.**

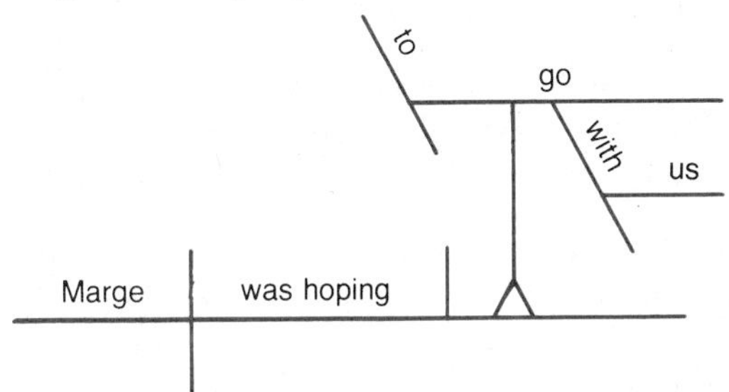

EXERCISE 18. Diagraming Sentences with Verbal Phrases. Diagram the following sentences: See Answer Key.

1. Taking that shortcut will cut several minutes off the trip.
2. I want to watch that program tonight.
3. That is my cat licking its paws.
4. Did they say what to do about this?
5. Checking the time, Wynetta rushed to the gym.

APPOSITIVES AND APPOSITIVE PHRASES

When you want to explain more exactly who or what you are talking about, you usually give additional information. You have already learned to add information by using complements. Another way is to use an *appositive* or an *appositive phrase.* Study these two ways to add information:

COMPLEMENT Mrs. Collins is **my English teacher.**
APPOSITIVE Mrs. Collins, **my English teacher,** went to school with my mother.

Notice that the sentence using the appositive gives more information about the subject than is possible with the complement alone.

14k. An *appositive* is a noun or a pronoun that explains the noun or pronoun it follows.

Appositives are often set off from the rest of the sentence by commas. However, when an appositive is necessary to the

EXERCISE 18. You might divide your class into five groups and assign one sentence to each group. Then have the groups select one person each to write the sentences on the board.

APPOSITIVES AND APPOSITIVE PHRASES (rules 14k and 14l)

Show your eighth-graders how the use of appositives and appositive phrases will help their writing sound more mature. Use examples such as the following ones:

I wrote to Ms. Simmons. She is the camp director. *(I wrote to Ms. Simmons, the camp director.)*

Johnny Tremain is Esther Forbes' best-known novel. It is about a boy who lived in Boston at the time of the American Revolution. (Johnny Tremain, *Esther Forbes' best-known novel, is about a boy who lived in Boston at the time of the American Revolution.)*

EXERCISE 19. Make sure your students realize that some sentences contain no appositives or appositive phrases. You might ask them to *add* appositives or appositive phrases to those sentences.

GRAMMAR

meaning of the sentence or is closely related to the word it follows, no commas are necessary.

EXAMPLES Troy, **a good friend of mine,** is camping with us.
The book ***Island of the Blue Dolphins*** is one of my favorites.

Sometimes you include modifiers in your appositive. When words are added to describe an appositive, an *appositive phrase* is created.

14l. An *appositive phrase* is made up of an appositive and its modifiers.

EXAMPLE The Newbery Medal, **an award for outstanding children's books,** was named for a man who sold children's books in the 1700's.

Diagraming Appositives and Appositive Phrases

To diagram an appositive, write it in parentheses after the word it explains. The modifiers in an appositive phrase are diagramed in the usual way beneath the appositive.

EXAMPLE Bill Cosby, **the popular TV star,** is now the author of a best-seller.

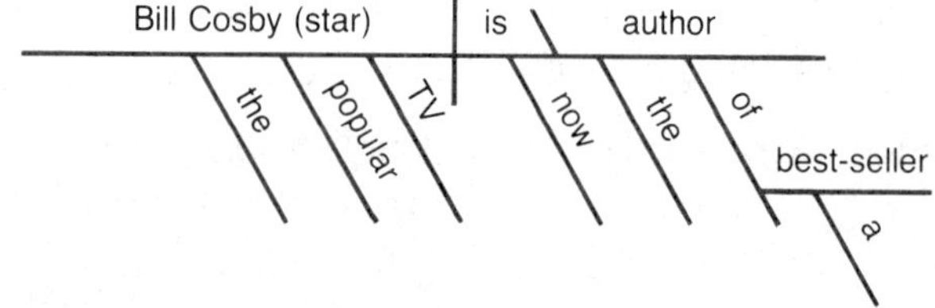

EXERCISE 19. Identifying Appositives and Appositive Phrases. After the appropriate number, write the appositive or appositive phrase in each of the following sentences. If a sentence has no appositive or appositive phrase, write *none.*

EXAMPLE 1. My dog, the mutt with floppy ears, can do tricks.
1. *the mutt with floppy ears*

REVIEW EXERCISE C. This exercise should help your students review for the posttests. Go over each answer carefully.

1. Don't lock that door, the exit out the back of the gym.
2. This color, midnight blue, is just what I've been looking for.
3. Two men, a truck driver and a fisherman, helped my father push the car off the road.
4. I'll have a sandwich, tuna salad on rye bread, please.
5. Ollie has the same class, American history, this afternoon.
6. My sister's friend forgot her sweater and her books. 6. none
7. Dee wondered where her friend Bonnie had gone.
8. Somebody reported the hazard, a pile of trash containing broken bottles, to the police.
9. Be sure to bring the exact change, fifty cents.
10. We sang the song "I've Been Working on the Railroad" over and over all the way down the path.

REVIEW EXERCISE C. Identifying Verbals and Appositives. Number your paper 1–10. After the appropriate number, write all verbals and appositives that appear in the following sentences. Write only the appositive or the verbal, not its modifiers or complements. In parentheses after each word, identify it as *appositive, infinitive, gerund,* or *participle.*

EXAMPLE 1. Skating on the sidewalk, my little brother Shawn tried to do some acrobatics, and that put an end to his playing for a while.
1. *Skating (participle), Shawn (appositive), to do (infinitive), playing (gerund)*

1. Instead of falling on the soft ground, Shawn managed to hit right on the concrete. 1. ger., inf.
2. The concrete, broken and crumbling, cut him in several places, mostly his knees and elbows. 2. part., part., app., app.
3. We heard his piercing wail all the way up at our house, and my mother and I rushed to see what had happened. 3. part., inf.
4. By the time we got to him, all the cuts had started bleeding, and he was struggling to get his skates off. 4. ger., inf.
5. Bending down, my mother pulled the skates off and dabbed at the seeping red cuts and scrapes. 5. part., part.

GRAMMAR

CHAPTER 14 REVIEW: POSTTEST 1

The students must identify the phrases as prepositional, participial, gerund, infinitive, or appositive. Allow enough time for your students to write the italicized phrases in each sentence.

GRAMMAR

6. Shawn, a brave little boy usually, could not control his crying. 6. app., ger.
7. Mom carried Shawn to the house, and I followed with the new skates, bent and ruined on the first day he used them. 7. part., part.
8. After cleaning Shawn's cuts, Mom decided to take him to the emergency clinic. 8. ger., inf.
9. The doctor, an Indian lady, said that she would have to close two of the cuts with stitches. 9. app., inf.
10. When we got home, Mom told Shawn that she wasn't going to get him another pair of skates until he was old enough to pay his own doctor bills. 10. inf., inf.

CHAPTER 14 REVIEW: POSTTEST 1

Identifying Prepositional, Verbal, and Appositive Phrases. After the proper number, write each italicized phrase in the following paragraphs, and indicate what kind of phrase it is. Use the abbreviations *prep.* (prepositional phrase), *part.* (participial phrase), *ger.* (gerund phrase), *inf.* (infinitive phrase), and *app.* (appositive phrase). Do not separately identify a prepositional phrase that is part of a larger phrase.

EXAMPLES After (1) *driving past the intersection,* my father had (2) *to drive over a mile farther before the next turn.*
1. *driving past the intersection—ger.*
2. *to drive over a mile before the next turn—inf.*

Jill, (1) *my best friend since elementary school,* and I decided (2) *to go to the mall after school yesterday.* Jill suggested (3) *taking the back way* so that we could jog, but I was wearing sandals (4) *instead of my track shoes,* so we just walked. Along the way we saw Cathy (5) *sitting on her front porch* and asked her if she wanted (6) *to join us.* She was earning a little spending money by (7) *baby-sitting her neighbor's children,* though, and couldn't leave. 1. app. 2. inf. 3. ger. 4. prep. 5. part. 6. inf. 7. ger.

(8) *Walking up to the wide glass doors at the mall,* Jill and I looked in our purses. We both had a few dollars and our student passes, so we stopped (9) *to get a glass of orange juice* while we checked what movies were playing. None of the four features looked (10) *interesting to us*. However, John Bowers, (11) *a friend from school and an usher at the theater,* said that there would be a sneak preview (12) *of a new adventure film* later, and we told him we'd be back then. 8. part. 9. inf. 10. part. 11. app. 12. prep.

Since most stores do not allow customers food or drinks inside, Jill and I gulped down our orange juice before (13) *going into our favorite dress shop*. We looked (14) *through the sale racks,* but none of the dresses, (15) *all of them formal or evening gowns,* appealed to us. A salesclerk asked if we were shopping (16) *for something special*. After (17) *checking with Jill,* I told the clerk we were just looking, and we left. 13. ger. 14. prep. 15. app. 16. prep.

We walked past a couple of shops— (18) *the health food store and a toy store*—and went into Record World. (19) *Seeing several cassettes of my favorite group,* I picked out one. By the time we walked out of Record World, I'd spent all my money, so we never did get (20) *to go to the movie that day*. 17. ger. 18. app. 19. part. 20. inf.

CHAPTER 14 REVIEW: POSTTEST 2

Writing Sentences with Prepositional, Verbal, and Appositive Phrases. Write ten sentences using the following phrases. Follow the directions in parentheses. Answers will vary.

1. after the game (*use as an adverb phrase*)
2. instead of your good shoes (*use as an adjective phrase*)
3. in one of Shakespeare's plays (*use as an adjective phrase*)
4. going to school every day (*use as a gerund phrase, as the subject of the sentence*)
5. living in a small town (*use as a gerund phrase, as the object of a preposition*)
6. walking through the empty lot (*use as a participial phrase*)

GRAMMAR

CHAPTER 14 REVIEW: POSTTEST 2

This test requires the students to use specified phrases in original sentences. In addition, the phrases must be used in certain ways: as prepositional, participial, gerund, infinitive, or appositive phrases. You probably will not want to assign this posttest to your less-advanced students.

Additional Practice

Teacher's Resource Book, Worksheet pages 149–71, Alternative Worksheet pages (for less-advanced students) 544–46

Testing

Teaching Tests booklet, pages 19–22, 31–32, 37–43
Teacher's Resource Book, Test pages 413–16, 425–26, 431–42

GRAMMAR

7. dressed in authentic costumes (*use as a participial phrase*)
8. to drive a car for the first time (*use as an infinitive phrase, as the direct object of the sentence*)
9. the best athlete in our school (*use as an appositive phrase*)
10. my favorite pastime (*use as an appositive phrase*)

CHAPTER 15

The Clause

INDEPENDENT AND SUBORDINATE CLAUSES

A phrase is a group of related words without a verb and its subject. In a sentence there may also be other groups of related words called *clauses,* which do contain both a verb and its subject.

PHRASES **on the tugboat** [no subject or verb]
have been laughing [no subject]

CLAUSES **as the tugboat crossed the river** [a verb—*crossed* —and its subject—*tugboat*]
who have been laughing [a verb—*have been laughing* —and its subject—*who*]

In this chapter you will learn about independent and subordinate clauses.

DIAGNOSTIC TEST

Identifying Independent and Subordinate Clauses; Classifying Subordinate Clauses. Number your paper 1–20. After the proper number, identify each of the italicized clauses in the following sentences as an independent clause or a subordinate clause. Classify each italicized subordinate clause as an *adj. cl.*

GRAMMAR

Chapter Overview

The material in this chapter will be new to some eighth-graders. They may know the term *clause,* but they may not know any kinds of clauses except the independent clauses in compound sentences. Go through the chapter one step at a time, making sure they recognize the *independent clause,* the *subordinate clause,* and the *adjective, adverb,* and *noun clauses,* as well as the terms *subordinating conjunction* and *relative pronoun.*

Working with subordinate clauses often encourages students to use this more mature sentence structure in their own writing. You may wish to tie this instruction to Chapter 9, "Writing Effective Sentences," which provides direct practice in using subordinate clauses to improve writing style.

Chapter Objective

Students will identify independent and subordinate clauses—adjective, adverb, and noun—and will use these clauses effectively in their own writing.

PRESENTING THE CHAPTER

LESS-ADVANCED STUDENTS You may wish to ask these students simply to identify subordinate clauses without requiring that they distinguish the various kinds. *(See listing of Alternative Worksheets on page 400.)*

ADVANCED STUDENTS Emphasize to these students that their knowledge of clauses will equip them with the technical terms useful for improving their writing. Give them considerable practice in original writing; use the writing assignments provided and other similar assignments.

WRITING APPLICATIONS

The writing applications in this chapter are designed to encourage students to use their knowledge of clauses—independent and subordinate—in their own writing. Feel free to adapt these assignments to your students' writing needs, abilities, and interests.

DIAGNOSTIC TEST

Give this test if you are unsure what your students already know about clauses.

GRAMMAR

(adjective clause), *adv. cl.* (adverb clause), or *n. cl.* (noun clause), to show how it functions in the sentence.

EXAMPLES
1. The customer thumbed through the book, but *it didn't seem to interest her.*
1. *independent clause*
2. Anyone *who gets a high score on this test* will not have to take the final exam.
2. *subordinate clause, adj. cl.*

1. *After it had been snowing for several hours,* we took our sleds out to Sentry Hill. 1. adv. cl.
2. The ring *that I lost at the beach last summer* had belonged to my great-grandmother. 2. adj. cl.
3. If he doesn't get here soon, *I'm leaving.*
4. *Who do you think* she is? 4. n. cl.
5. Nobody has seen Shawn *since the football game ended.* 5. adv. cl.
6. *In the morning they gathered their belongings and left* before the sun rose.
7. Nobody knew *that John had worked out the solution.* 7. n. cl.
8. *The dogs chased the deer onto the ice,* which was more than two feet thick.
9. My dad says not to trust strangers *who seem too friendly.* 9. adj. cl.
10. *That he had been right* became obvious as the problem grew worse. 10. n. cl.
11. Julio knew the right answer *because he looked it up in the dictionary.* 11. adv. cl.
12. Do you know *how a bill becomes a law?* 12. n. cl.
13. On our vacation we visited my dad's old neighborhood, *which is now an industrial park.* 13. adj. cl.
14. *It just doesn't seem right* that I have to do all this work without getting paid.
15. Did you get the message *that your mother called?* 15. adj. cl.
16. Andy raked up the leaves *while his father stuffed them into plastic bags.* 16. adv. cl.
17. Before the program began, *the band tuned their instruments,* and the audience got refreshments.

18. We will be over *as soon as Sandy finishes his lunch.* 18. adv. cl.
19. That is the man *whose dog rescued my sister.* 19. adj. cl.
20. Free samples were given to *whoever asked for them.* 20. n. cl.

15a. A *clause* is a group of words that contains a verb and its subject and is used as a part of a sentence.

Every clause, like every sentence, has a subject and a verb; however, not every clause expresses a complete thought, as all sentences do. Clauses that express a complete thought are called *independent clauses.* Clauses that do not express a complete thought by themselves are called *subordinate clauses.* Subordinate clauses, like phrases, can serve as nouns, adjectives, and adverbs.

THE INDEPENDENT CLAUSE

15b. An *independent* (or *main*) *clause* expresses a complete thought and can stand by itself as a sentence.

If you can recognize a sentence, you will be able to recognize independent clauses. Independent clauses can stand alone as sentences. They are usually called independent clauses only when they are part of a more complex sentence.

SENTENCE **I baked her a cake.**

INDEPENDENT CLAUSE Since it was my mother's birthday, **I baked her a cake.**

In the following sentences, the independent clauses are in boldface. Notice that the third sentence has more than one independent clause.

If you have worked with the soil, **you are familiar with *humus*.** ***Humus* comes from a Latin word** that means "earth." ***Humilis* means "on the ground,"** and **from this Latin word we derive the word "humility."**

GRAMMAR

Defining the Clause (rule 15a)

It will help the class if you make clear at the beginning the difference between a *phrase* and a *clause:* A phrase does not contain a verb and its subject; a clause does contain both these items. To point out the difference, use illustrations such as these:

The student *with the highest mark* wins a prize. (prepositional phrase)
The student *having the highest mark* wins a prize. (participial phrase)
The student *who earns the highest mark* wins a prize. (subordinate clause)

THE INDEPENDENT CLAUSE (rule 15b)

Emphasize that an independent clause is grammatically self-sufficient and can be used as a separate sentence. Write sentences like these on the board:

We expected you to be early.
You did not arrive until midnight.

Help the class see that these are sentences. Have someone identify the subject and verb in each. Now combine the sentences by placing *but* between them. Ask whether the result is one sentence or two. Tell the class that when a group of words that can be a sentence by itself becomes part of a longer sentence, it is called an *independent clause.* On the board now is one sentence with two independent, or main, clauses. Have your students suggest other examples.

THE SUBORDINATE CLAUSE (rule 15c)

Be sure your class understands the meaning of *subordinate* ("of lesser rank"). Stress the difference between an independent clause and a subordinate clause; the latter cannot stand alone as a separate sentence. Write on the board pairs of example sentences:

Jo had a slight fever, but she played for the first quarter.
Jo, who had a slight fever, played for the first quarter.

The class should see that in the first sentence the two clauses, *Jo had a slight fever* and *(but) she played for the first quarter* could each stand alone as a sentence. In the second example sentence, however, *who had a slight fever* cannot stand alone. (It could stand alone as a question, but the class will be able to see that it is not meant as a question in this context.) Encourage questions.

GRAMMAR

THE SUBORDINATE CLAUSE

Although an independent clause can stand alone as a complete thought, a subordinate clause cannot stand alone.

SENTENCE	Writers gathered at the home of Gertrude Stein when she lived in Paris.
INDEPENDENT CLAUSE	Writers gathered at the home of Gertrude Stein. [can stand alone]
SUBORDINATE CLAUSE	when she lived in Paris [cannot stand alone]

15c. A *subordinate* (or *dependent*) *clause* does not express a complete thought and cannot stand alone.

Subordinate means "lesser in rank or importance." Since a subordinate clause cannot stand by itself, it is considered "below the rank" of an independent clause.

Study the following sentences, which contain subordinate clauses set in boldface. Notice that the subordinate clauses all contain verbs and their subjects. Some subordinate clauses begin with words such as *since, when, if,* or *as.*

S V
As the monster appeared from beneath a huge rock, all of us in the movie theater held our breath.

S V
Since most plants die without light, we moved our house plants closer to the window.

Some subordinate clauses begin with words such as *who, which,* or *that.*

S V
The animals **that I saw in the game preserve** were protected from hunters.

S V
Michelle, **who was on the debating team last year,** won her argument with the teacher.

In the last example, notice that the word *who* is both the introductory word in the clause and the subject of the clause.

EXERCISE 1. Identifying Independent Clauses, Subordinate Clauses, and Phrases. Some of the following expressions are sentences, some are subordinate clauses, and some are phrases. Number your paper 1–10. If the expression is a sentence, write *S* after the proper number; if it is a subordinate clause, write *C;* if it is a phrase, write *P.*

EXAMPLE 1. as I answered the telephone
1. *C*

1. we memorized the lyrics 1. S
2. by the back porch 2. P
3. if no one is coming 3. C
4. who was born on Valentine's Day 4. C
5. which everyone enjoyed 5. C
6. after last year's flood 6. P
7. the singer wore a silk scarf 7. S
8. when the lights were flickering 8. C
9. since the first time we talked 9. C
10. beside the lion's cage 10. P

EXERCISE 2. Identifying Subordinate Clauses and Their Subjects and Verbs. After the proper number, write the subordinate clause from each of the following sentences. Underline the subject of the clause once and the verb twice.

EXAMPLE 1. In history class we learned about the plague that spread across Europe in the fourteenth century.
1. *that spread across Europe in the fourteenth century*

1. In 1347, trading ships arrived on the Mediterranean island of Sicily from Caffa (which was a port city on the Black Sea.)
2. (As they emerged from the boats,) many of the sailors carried a strange illness.
3. No medicine could save the sailors, (who died quickly and painfully.)

GRAMMAR

EXERCISE 1. You may want to work through the first five items orally before assigning the exercise as written work. As you do this, put the correct answers to items 1–5 on the board, and leave the answers there so that students can refer to them in doing the rest of the exercise. Then go over all the answers in class.

EXERCISE 2. By identifying the subject and verb in each subordinate clause, your students should have no difficulty distinguishing between subordinate and independent clauses. Go over their answers orally.

EXERCISE 3. This exercise requires that students write an independent clause for each subordinate clause. Point out to less-advanced students that they are merely writing groups of words similar to sentences to add to words that cannot stand alone as sentences.

THE ADJECTIVE CLAUSE (rule 15d)

To introduce adjective clauses, write on the board sentences illustrating adjectives, adjective phrases, and adjective clauses.

I have a new *cotton* blouse. (adjective)
I have a new blouse *of cotton.* (adjective prepositional phrase)
I have a new blouse *that is made of cotton.* (adjective clause)

Ask your students to suggest similar groups of sentences and write them on the board.

GRAMMAR

4. In the same year, many other people became sick and died (as the plague spread across Sicily and Europe.)
5. Even doctors caught the illness (when they hurried to the bedsides of sick patients.)
6. (If a person traveled to another city in Europe,) the disease probably traveled too.
7. The fast-spreading, deadly plague terrified the survivors, (who thought the world was coming to an end.)
8. (Since it originated in the Black Sea area,) the plague was called the Black Death.
9. No one is sure of the total number of people (who died.)
10. (Since medicine offers new ways for controlling plague,) the spread of this disease is unlikely today.

EXERCISE 3. Writing Sentences with Independent and Subordinate Clauses. Add an independent clause to each subordinate clause, and write the whole sentence. Draw one line under the subject and two lines under the verb of each clause.

Answers will vary.

EXAMPLE 1. who came late
1. *Susie is the volunteer who came late.*

1. when the ice melts
2. if my teacher approves
3. since you insist
4. when they act silly
5. who borrowed my notes
6. as she began to shout
7. when we danced on stage
8. who gave the report
9. since I sleep soundly
10. that I bought yesterday

THE ADJECTIVE CLAUSE

Like an adjective or an adjective phrase, a clause may modify a noun or a pronoun. In the following word groups, you see first an adjective phrase, then an adjective clause.

ADJECTIVE PHRASE the woman **in the car**
ADJECTIVE CLAUSE the woman **who is in the car**

ADJECTIVE PHRASE a tree **with red blossoms**
ADJECTIVE CLAUSE a tree **that has red blossoms**

15d. An *adjective clause* is a subordinate clause used as an adjective to modify a noun or a pronoun.

Observe how the adjective clauses in the following sentences modify nouns or pronouns. Notice that adjective clauses usually follow immediately after the words that they modify.

> Helen Keller was a remarkable woman **who overcame blindness and deafness.**
>
> Ms. Jackson showed slides **that she had taken in Egypt.**
>
> The ones **whose flight was delayed** spent the night in Detroit.

The Relative Pronoun

Adjective clauses are easy to identify because they are almost always introduced by a *relative pronoun. Who, whom, whose, which,* and *that* are called *relative* pronouns because they *relate* to another word or idea in the sentence.

EXAMPLES Leonardo da Vinci was the artist **who painted the Mona Lisa.** [The relative pronoun *who* begins the clause and relates to the noun *artist.*]

Everything **that could be done** was done. [The relative pronoun *that* begins the clause and relates to the pronoun *everything.*]

EXERCISE 4. Identifying Adjective Clauses. After the proper number, write each adjective clause, circling the relative pronoun. Then write the word that the pronoun refers to.

EXAMPLE 1. Our friends have a canary that is named Neptune.
1. *that is named Neptune—canary*

1. Proverbs are sayings that usually give advice.
2. Trivia questions have been organized into games that have become quite popular.
3. A black hole, which results after a star has collapsed, can trap energy and matter. 3. (or hole)

THE RELATIVE PRONOUN

Explain that an adjective clause is usually introduced by a special kind of pronoun called a *relative pronoun*. Write on the board common relative pronouns: *who, whom, whose, which, that*. Ask your students to suggest sentences using adjective clauses introduced by these relative pronouns. Then lead them to understand why they are called *relative*. (Because they relate to another word or idea in the sentence.) Have them point out in the sentences on the board which words the relative pronouns relate to. Make sure they understand that the relative pronoun is part of the adjective clause.

EXERCISE 4. You may want to use this exercise for practice in class.

4. A special award was given to the student whose work had improved most.
5. Frances Perkins, who served as Secretary of Labor, was the first woman to hold a Cabinet position.
6. The problem that worries us now is the pollution of underground sources of water.
7. We enjoyed the poems of Gwendolyn Brooks, who for years has been poet laureate of Illinois.
8. In *Walden,* Thoreau shared ideas that have influenced many.
9. Athena, who ranked as an important Greek goddess, protected the city of Athens.
10. A friend is a person whom you can trust.

GRAMMAR

WRITING APPLICATION A:
Using Adjective Clauses to Make Your Writing Specific

Improvements in technology have allowed us to store larger and larger amounts of information in smaller and smaller spaces. As you become more experienced in writing, you too learn how to pack more information into smaller spaces. Specific facts, for example, can sometimes be compressed into adjective clauses.

EXAMPLE The first library, *which contained a dining room, private studies, laboratories, and a walkway for strolling,* was located in Alexandria, Egypt.

Writing Assignment

Answers will vary.

In some cases people misunderstand each other because they do not have in mind the same meanings for words. For example, what *you* think is a "good" report card may not be the same as what your *parents* think is a "good" report card. Write a paragraph defining one of the following terms. Use at least two adjective clauses, and underline these clauses.

a clean room	a loyal friend	a fun weekend
a good teacher	an ideal pet	a good-looking outfit

Sometimes the relative pronoun is preceded by a preposition. Traditionally, this is the correct position when a relative pronoun is the object of a preposition; but nowadays you will often see the preposition at the end of the clause.

the day **which we looked forward to**
the day **to which we looked forward**
my friend, **whom I would do anything for**
my friend, **for whom I would do anything**

GRAMMAR

EXERCISE 5. Identifying Adjective Clauses. Write the adjective clause from each of the following sentences. Circle the relative pronoun. Remember that a relative pronoun may sometimes be preceded by a preposition.

1. Coco Chanel is the woman for whom the perfume is named.
2. Darth Vader, the enemy that Luke Skywalker fought, was an evil villain in *Star Wars*.
3. The cello, when played by Pablo Casals, is an instrument to which I could listen for hours.
4. Ella Fitzgerald, who started singing in New York City, is famous throughout the world.
5. Christopher Marlowe wrote of Helen of Troy, "Was this the face that launched a thousand ships?"
6. Anita was one of the sopranos who sang in the chorus.
7. In the play *My Fair Lady,* Eliza Doolittle, a poor flower merchant, becomes a woman whom everyone admires.
8. The Kinderhook was the creek in which we found the shells.
9. Janet Flanner, who wrote dispatches from Paris, used the pen name Genêt.
10. The astronauts, to whom travel in the space shuttle is routine, must always keep in shape.

EXERCISE 6. Writing Adjective Clauses in Sentences. Supply an adjective clause for each blank. Write the complete sentence on your paper. Circle each relative pronoun.
Answers will vary.

EXERCISE 5. If you used Exercise 4 as a class activity, assign this exercise as homework. Go over the answers in the following class session.

EXERCISE 6. You may want to help your less-advanced students by doing the exercise orally, writing the sentences on the board as they suggest the adjective clauses.

THE ADVERB CLAUSE
(rule 15e)

To illustrate how the adverb clause is different from an adverb and an adverb phrase, write on the board a set of example sentences:

We stayed *there*. (adverb)
We stayed *in the auditorium*. (adverb prepositional phrase)
We stayed *where we could hear the band*. (adverb clause)

Ask the class how the adverb phrase is different from the adverb clause. (The clause contains a subject and its verb.) Then help them see that both the phrase and the clause modify the verb *stayed*. Have your students suggest sentences that contain adverb clauses which tell *how, when, where, why, to what extent,* and *under what conditions*.

GRAMMAR

EXAMPLE 1. Pineapples —— thrive in Hawaii.
1. *Pineapples, (which) do not grow in many parts of the United States, thrive in Hawaii.*

1. Our club sponsored a dance —— .
2. The car —— is the sportiest one on the block.
3. The young paramedic quickly gave first aid to the motorist —— .
4. Suits of armor —— weigh hundreds of pounds.
5. Rita and Jon met the professional football player —— .

THE ADVERB CLAUSE

Like an adverb or an adverb phrase, a subordinate clause may modify a verb, an adjective, or an adverb. Such a clause is called an *adverb clause.*

ADVERB PHRASE **During the winter** many animals hibernate.
ADVERB CLAUSE **When winter sets in,** many animals hibernate.

15e. An *adverb clause* is a subordinate clause used as an adverb.

An adverb clause may modify a verb, an adjective, or an adverb by telling *how, when, where, why, to what extent* (*how much* or *how long*), or *under what conditions.*

There was a great sea wave **when the volcano erupted.** [The adverb clause tells *when* there *was* a great sea wave.]

Because the day was very hot, the cool water felt good. [The adverb clause tells *why* the water *felt* good.]

If it does not rain tomorrow, we will go to see Crater Lake. [The adverb clause tells *under what conditions* we *will go* to see Crater Lake.]

As these examples show, the adverb clause may be placed at various places in the sentence. When it begins the sentence, an adverb clause is usually followed by a comma.

WRITING APPLICATION B: Using Adverb Clauses to Explain a Process

It's fun to browse in bookstores. In the self-help section, you can find books on how to build things, how to cook, how to study, and even how to get over a broken heart! Adverb clauses are useful in explaining how to do something. They help a reader understand exactly how one thing is related to another in an explanation. Notice in the following example how the subordinating conjunction *if* helps relate the information in the adverb clause to information in the rest of the sentence.

EXAMPLE *If you want a tasty, nourishing dessert,* you should try combining an orange, an apple, and some pecans.

Writing Assignment

Answers will vary.

Write a paragraph explaining a process that you have used. List any equipment needed to complete the process, and include all of the steps. Use at least three adverb clauses. Underline these clauses, and circle the subordinating conjunctions that introduce them. Here are some ideas:

How to clean a trumpet
How to pack for a beach trip
How to study for a test

The Subordinating Conjunction

Chapter 12 discusses two kinds of conjunctions: coordinating conjunctions, such as *and* and *but;* and correlative conjunctions, such as *either . . . or* and *neither . . . nor.* A third kind, called a *subordinating conjunction,* introduces an adverb clause.

The following words are commonly used to begin adverb clauses. Remember that *after, before, since, until, as,* and many other subordinating conjunctions may also be used as prepositions or other parts of speech.

THE SUBORDINATING CONJUNCTION

In the sentences your students suggested, underline a conjunction (in one of them) that connects the clause to the rest of the sentence. Ask the students to point out the conjunctions in the other sentences that serve a similar function. Explain that these are *subordinating conjunctions*.

Call attention to the list of subordinating conjunctions on page 392, and encourage the class to refer to this list for help in identifying adverb clauses. Be sure students understand that unlike relative pronouns, subordinating conjunctions do not serve any grammatical function within the clauses that they introduce.

EXERCISE 7. This exercise may be somewhat difficult for less-advanced students. You might complete the whole exercise as a class activity, or you might do several sentences orally with the class before they begin to work individually.

Subordinating Conjunctions

after	as though	so that	whenever
although	because	than	where
as	before	though	wherever
as if	if	unless	while
long as	in order that	until	
as soon as	since	when	

EXERCISE 7. Identifying Adverb Clauses. There are ten adverb clauses in the following paragraph. Write the number of the line on which the clause begins. Then write the clause. In each clause, circle the subordinating conjunction, and underline the subject once and the verb twice.

EXAMPLE While we were listening to the radio, we heard the news bulletin.

1. *While we were listening to the radio*

What countries would you visit if you could travel anywhere in the world? After you had thought about all the possibilities for a few minutes, you would probably list some of the countries in Europe. Of course, England, France, Spain, Germany, or Italy would likely be on your list, since you have heard much about them. As you studied a map of Europe, you might also notice Liechtenstein and Andorra. Although you might need a magnifying glass to see them, these two European countries could go on your list. When you search for places to visit, you can often overlook some of the less famous areas. However, there are many charming spots in the world. Give some consideration to these whenever you make your travel plans. Because the world is so vast and full of interesting people and lands, it is worthwhile to search for different possibilities so that you can have a choice. When you are planning which places to visit, look beyond the obvious ones and consider some of the many small treats hidden away all over the world.

EXERCISE 8. Writing Adverb Clauses in Sentences. Add an adverb clause to each of the following sentences. Write the entire sentence; then circle the subordinating conjunctions, and underline the subject of each adverb clause once and the verb twice.

Answers will vary.

EXAMPLE 1. The movie finally ended.
1. *After we spent three hours in the theater, the movie finally ended.*

1. Members of the Drama Club auditioned.
2. Erica speaks three languages.
3. We prepared *moussaka,* a dish with lamb and eggplant, for our Cooking Club's international supper.
4. The Goldmans had flown to Acapulco many times.
5. Jill daydreams in class.

THE NOUN CLAUSE

In addition to acting as modifiers, subordinate clauses may also serve as nouns. A subordinate clause that acts as a subject, a predicate nominative, a direct object, an indirect object, or the object of a preposition in a sentence is called a *noun clause.*

15f. A *noun clause* is a subordinate clause used as a noun.

Like a noun, a noun clause can be used as a subject, a complement (predicate nominative, direct object, indirect object), or an object of a preposition.

NOUNS	NOUN CLAUSES
Subject Ann's **anger** was obvious.	**That Ann was angry** was obvious.
Predicate nominative Three dollars is their **offer.**	Three dollars is **what they offered.**
Direct object The judges determined the **winner.**	The judges determined **who won.**
Indirect object The sheriff gave each **volunteer** a flashlight.	The sheriff gave **whoever volunteered** a flashlight.

GRAMMAR

EXERCISE 8. Permit students who are having difficulty with adverb clauses to refer back to the list of subordinating conjunctions on page 392 as they write their sentences. Before assigning this exercise, remind your class that an introductory adverb clause is usually followed by a comma.

THE NOUN CLAUSE (rule 15f)

This use of the clause will probably be new to most eighth-graders. Review briefly the ways a noun functions in a sentence. Then write on the board a subordinate clause your students will enjoy working with as a noun clause. An example might be *what I'd like for my birthday*. Have them use this as a noun clause functioning as a subject, as a predicate nominative, and so forth.

SUBJECT *What I'd like for my birthday* is a ten-speed bicycle.

PREDICATE NOMINATIVE A ten-speed bicycle is *what I'd like for my birthday*.

DIRECT OBJECT Our conversation concerned *what I'd like for my birthday*.

OBJECT OF PREPOSITION We had a talk about *what I'd like for my birthday*.

You do not have to go over all the ways a noun clause functions in order to get the point across. Ask your students to suggest other noun clauses, which you can write on the board in a similar way.

The fact that adjective clauses and noun clauses can begin with the same introductory words (e.g., *who, whose, that*) may confuse students. Show that when one of the words begins an adjective clause, it is a relative pronoun that refers directly to an antecedent in the independent clause. If there is no antecedent word in the independent clause, the word must introduce a noun clause.

ADJECTIVE CLAUSE I have the book *that he wants.*
NOUN CLAUSE He told me *that he wanted it.*

EXERCISE 9. You may decide to have your students write the entire sentence. Then have them place parentheses around the noun clause, underlining the subject once and the verb twice.

GRAMMAR

NOUNS	NOUN CLAUSES
Object of preposition They agreed with his **statements.**	They agreed with **whatever he said.**

Most noun clauses are introduced by *that, what, whatever, who, whom, whoever,* and *whomever.* The introductory word sometimes has a function within the clause; at other times its only function is to introduce the clause.

EXAMPLES They told him **what he should do.** [The introductory word *what* is the direct object of the noun clause —*he should do what.* The entire noun clause *what he should do* is the direct object of the verb *told.*]

Give a free pass to **whoever asks for one.** [The introductory word *whoever* is the subject of the noun clause—*whoever asks for one.* The entire noun clause *whoever asks for one* is the object of the preposition *to.*]

Their complaint was **that the milk smelled sour.** [The introductory word *that* simply introduces the noun clause and has no other function in the clause. The noun clause *that the milk smelled sour* is the predicate nominative, referring to the subject of the sentence—*complaint.*]

EXERCISE 9. Identifying and Classifying Noun Clauses. After the proper number, write the noun clause in each of the following sentences. Then tell how the entire noun clause is used in the sentence: as *subject, predicate nominative, direct object, indirect object,* or *object of the preposition.*

EXAMPLE 1. We couldn't find what was making the noise in the car.
1. *what was making the noise in the car—direct object*

1. Whatever you decide will be fine with us. 1. subj.
2. Whoever takes us to the beach is my friend for life. 2. subj.
3. Do you know what happened to the rest of my tuna fish sandwich? 3. d.o.

4. Stu is looking for whoever owns that red bicycle. 4. obj. of prep.
5. Checking our supplies, we discovered that we had forgotten the flour. 5. d.o.
6. The worst flaw in the story is that it doesn't have a carefully developed plot. 6. p.n.
7. Unfortunately, these results are not what we had planned. 7. p.n.
8. The painter gave whatever spots had dried another coat of enamel. 8. i.o.
9. At lunch, my friends and I talked about what we should do as our service project. 9. obj. of prep.
10. That anyone could doubt their story seemed to amaze the children. 10. subj.

Diagraming Subordinate Clauses

Diagram an adjective clause by connecting it with a broken line to the word it modifies. Draw the broken line between the relative pronoun and the word that it relates to. The relative pronoun is either the subject or the object in the adjective clause.

EXAMPLE The grades that I got last term pleased my father.

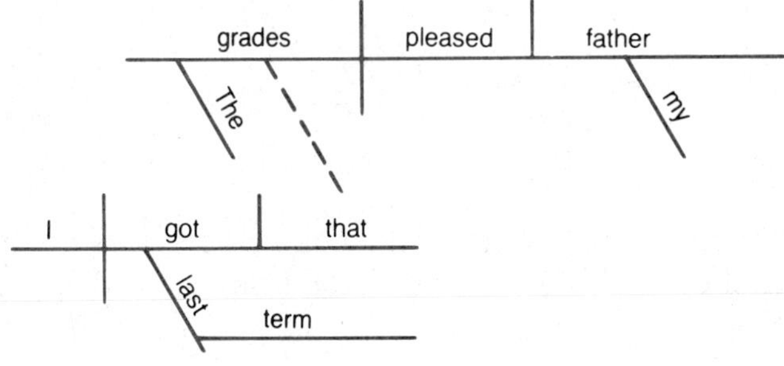

Diagram an adverb clause by using a broken line to connect the adverb clause to the word it modifies. Place the subordinating conjunction that introduces the adverb clause on the broken line.

DIAGRAMING SUBORDINATE CLAUSES

Consider giving students who understand diagraming an opportunity to help *teach* the class by presenting examples on the board.

GRAMMAR

EXAMPLE When I come home from school, I usually eat a sandwich.

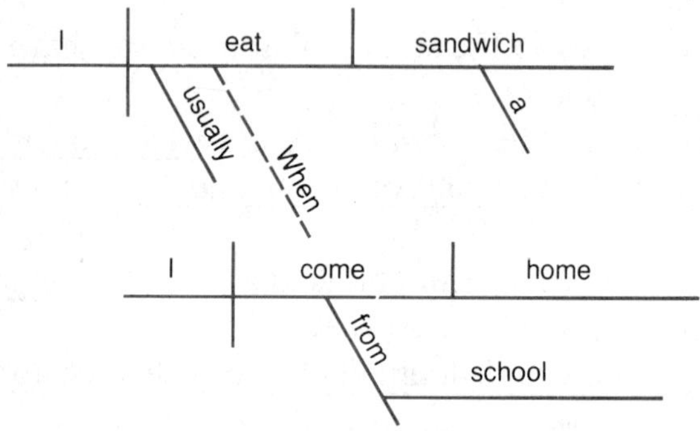

Diagram a noun clause according to how it is used in the sentence. Connect the noun clause to the independent clause with a solid line, as shown in the following two examples.

EXAMPLE Olive knew what she wanted. [The noun clause *what she wanted* is the direct object of the independent clause. The word *what* is the direct object in the noun clause.]

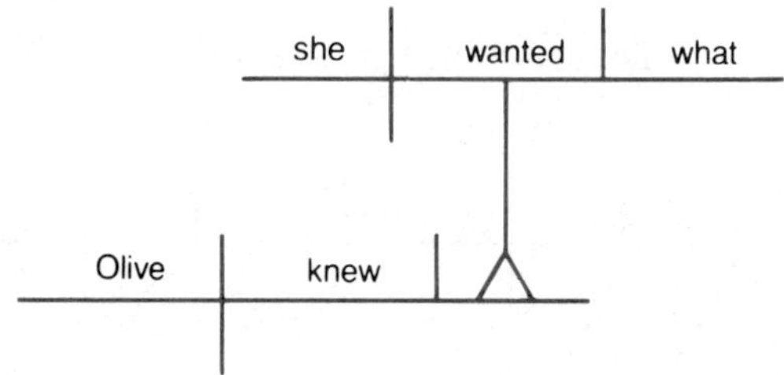

When the introductory word of the noun clause does not have a specific function in the noun clause, the sentence is diagramed in this way:

EXAMPLE The problem is that they lost the map. [The noun clause *that they lost the map* is the predicate nominative of the independent clause. The word *that* has no function in the noun clause except as an introductory word.]

GRAMMAR

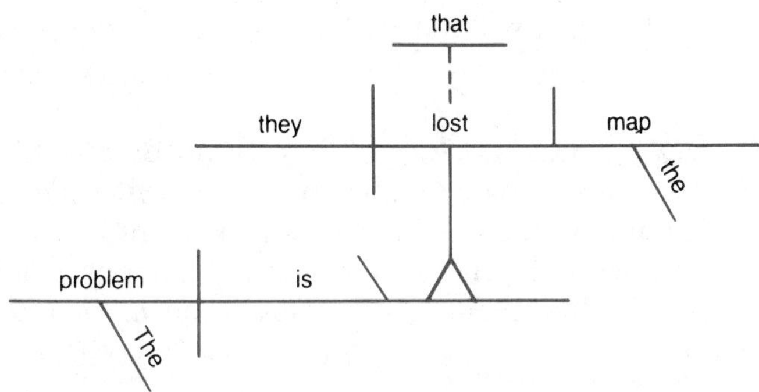

EXERCISE 10. Diagraming Sentences with Subordinate Clauses. Diagram the following sentences. See Answer Key.

1. The test that we took on Friday was hard.
2. If I had not studied Thursday night, I could not have answered half the questions.
3. Our teacher announced what would be on the test.
4. Several friends of mine were not paying attention when the teacher gave the assignment.
5. My friends who did not know what to study are worried now about their grades.

REVIEW EXERCISE A. Identifying Adjective, Adverb, and Noun Clauses. Each of the following quotations contains at least one adjective clause, adverb clause, or noun clause. Write the clause or clauses after the proper number. Write *adj. cl., adv. cl.,* or *n. cl.* where appropriate.

1. It's no use shutting the barn door after the horse is gone. 1. adv.cl.
—OLD PROVERB
2. They also serve who only stand and wait. 2. adj.cl. —JOHN MILTON
3. You gain strength, courage and confidence by every experience in which you really stop to look fear in the face. 3. adj.cl.
—ELEANOR ROOSEVELT
4. Let me not criticize any man until I have walked a mile in his moccasins.—OLD INDIAN PROVERB 4. adv.cl.

EXERCISE 10. If you do not teach diagraming, you can have your students write each subordinate clause and identify what kind it is.

REVIEW EXERCISE A. When your average or advanced students complete this exercise, they might select one of the quotations to define and illustrate with an anecdote in an original paragraph. Quotations 1, 3, and 4 are good possibilities for eighth-graders.

GRAMMAR

REVIEW EXERCISE B. This exercise may be too difficult for individual work by less-advanced students. Try assigning each paragraph to small groups. Have students write the paragraph, enclosing each subordinate clause in parentheses and writing the kind of clause over it.

CHAPTER 15 REVIEW: POSTTEST 1

This test requires students to label italicized clauses as independent or subordinate. Then they are to identify subordinate clauses as noun, adjective, or adverb.

GRAMMAR

5. n. cl.

5. I believe that man will not merely endure: he will prevail.

—WILLIAM FAULKNER

REVIEW EXERCISE B. Identifying Subordinate Clauses. There are ten subordinate clauses in the following paragraphs. Write the number of the line in which the first word of the clause appears. Then write the clause. Write *adj. cl.* after each adjective clause, *adv. cl.* after each adverb clause, and *n. cl.* after each noun clause.

1. adj. cl. 3. adj. cl. 5. n. cl. 6. adv. cl. 7. adj. cl. 8. n. cl. 9. adv. cl. 10. adj. cl. 11. n. cl.—adv. cl.

Robert Browning, who was a poet of the Victorian period, wrote a poem about Childe Roland, a daring knight who set out on a dangerous quest for the Dark Tower. Many brave knights had been killed searching for the tower, but Roland was determined that he would find it.

After Roland had searched for years, he came upon an old man who pointed the way to the tower. Following the old man's directions, Roland came to what he had been seeking. As he gazed upon the structure, he remembered the tales about all of the knights who had died in their searching. He knew that he must fulfill the quest for all of them. As he moved toward the tower, Roland raised his horn to his lips and blew: "*Childe Roland to the Dark Tower came.*"

CHAPTER 15 REVIEW: POSTTEST 1

Identifying Independent and Subordinate Clauses; Classifying Subordinate Clauses. After the proper number, identify each of the italicized clauses in the following paragraphs as an independent clause or a subordinate clause. Tell whether each italicized subordinate clause is a noun clause (*n. cl.*), adjective clause (*adj. cl.*), or an adverb clause (*adv. cl.*)

EXAMPLES When my father got a new job, (1) *we had to move to another town.*

1. *independent clause*

(2) *When my father got a new job,* we had to move to another town.
2. *subordinate clause-adv. cl.*

1. adv. cl. 2. adj. cl. 3. n. cl. 4. adv. cl.

Earlier this year I had to transfer to another school (1) *because my father got a new job*. This is the fourth time (2) *that I have had to change schools,* and every time I've wished (3) *that I could just stay at my old school.* (4) *As soon as I make friends in a new place,* I have to move again and leave them behind. Then at the new school (5) *I am a stranger all over again.*

We lived in our last house for three years, (6) *which is the longest time we've spent in any one place* (7) *since I was little.* Living there so long, (8) *I had a chance to meet several people* (9) *who became good friends of mine.* My two best friends, Chris and Marty, said (10) *that they would write to me,* and I promised to write to them, too. However, the friends (11) *that I had before* always promised to write, but (12) *after a letter or two we lost touch.* (13) *Why this happens* is a mystery to me, but it has happened every time. 6. adj. cl. 7. adv. cl. 9. adj. cl. 10. n. cl.

11. adj. cl. 13. n. cl.

I dreaded registering at my new school two months (14) *after the school year had begun.* By then, everyone else would already have made friends, and (15) *I would be an outsider,* (16) *as I knew from past experience.* There are always some students who bully and tease (17) *whoever is new at school* or anyone else (18) *who is different.* Back in elementary school I would get angry and upset (19) *when people would pick on me.* Since then, I've learned how to fit in and make friends (20) *in spite of whatever anyone does to hassle me or make me feel uncomfortable.* 14. adv. cl 16. adv. cl.

Everywhere (21) *that I've gone to school,* some students always are friendly and offer to show me around. (22) *I used to be shy,* and I wouldn't take them up on their invitations. Since they didn't know (23) *whether I was being shy or unfriendly,* they soon left me alone. Now (24) *whenever someone is friendly to me at a new school or in a new neighborhood,* I fight down my shyness and act friendly myself. It's still hard to get used to new people and places, but (25) *it's a lot easier with help from new friends.*

17. n.cl. 18. adj. cl. 19. adv. cl. 20. n. cl. 21. adj. cl. 23. n. cl. 24. adv. cl.

GRAMMAR

CHAPTER 15 REVIEW: POSTTEST 2

This test requires the students to write ten original sentences using specific guidelines. You will probably wish to omit this test in your less-advanced classes.

Additional Practice

Teacher's Resource Book, Worksheet pages 172–90, Alternative Worksheet pages (for less-advanced students) 547–49

Testing

Teaching Tests booklet, pages 19–22, 33, 37–43
Teacher's Resource Book, pages 413–16, 427–28, 431–42

GRAMMAR

CHAPTER 15 REVIEW: POSTTEST 2

Writing Sentences with Independent and Subordinate Clauses. Write your own sentences according to each of the following instructions. Underline the subordinate clauses.
Answers will vary.

EXAMPLE 1. A sentence with an independent clause and an adjective clause
1. I am going to the game with Jim, *who is my best friend.*

1. A sentence with an independent clause and no subordinate clauses
2. A sentence with an independent clause and one subordinate clause
3. A sentence with an adjective clause that begins with a relative pronoun
4. A sentence with an adjective clause in which a preposition precedes the relative pronoun
5. A sentence with an introductory adverb clause
6. A sentence with an adverb clause and an adjective clause
7. A sentence with a noun clause used as a direct object
8. A sentence with a noun clause used as a subject
9. A sentence with a noun clause used as the object of a preposition
10. A sentence with a noun clause and either an adjective clause or an adverb clause

CHAPTER 16

The Kinds of Sentence Structure

THE FOUR BASIC SENTENCE STRUCTURES

Chapter 10 explains how sentences may be classified according to their purpose: *declarative, interrogative, imperative,* and *exclamatory.* Another way to classify sentences is according to their construction—the kind and number of clauses they contain. In this chapter you will study the four kinds of sentence structure: *simple, compound, complex,* and *compound-complex.*

DIAGNOSTIC TEST

Identifying the Four Kinds of Sentence Structure. Number your paper 1–20. Identify each of the following sentences as simple, compound, complex, or compound-complex.

EXAMPLE 1. We bought a new computer program that helps with spelling and grammar.
1. *complex*

1. Nancy wanted to go to the dance, but she had to baby-sit. 1. cd.
2. When the rabbit saw us, it ran into the bushes. 2. cx.

GRAMMAR

Chapter Overview

No difficult new concepts are introduced here. Begin with a review showing clearly and simply the logical progression from a one-word part of speech through a phrase and a subordinate clause to an independent clause and a sentence. For example:

We went to a *country* school. *(one-word adjective)*
We went to a school *in the country. (adjective prepositional phrase)*
We went to a school *that was in the country. (adjective clause)*
We went to a school, *and it was in the country. (independent clause)*
We went to a school. *It was in the country. (sentence)*

After you write each sentence on the board, ask the class the characteristics of the underlined words (given above in parentheses). Emphasize the differences between the phrase and the subordinate clause and between the subordinate clause and the independent clause.

Chapter Objective

Students will identify simple, compound, complex, and compound-complex sentences. They will use these sentence structures to give variety to their own writing.

PRESENTING THE CHAPTER

LESS-ADVANCED STUDENTS A less-advanced class may have trouble with the terminology in this chapter. These students tend to identify any short, easy sentence as "simple" and any long or difficult sentence as "complex." Emphasize only the distinction between simple (one-clause) sentences and sentences that contain more than one clause, without requiring students to distinguish between compound and complex sentences. You should probably omit the compound-complex sentence entirely. *(See listing of Alternative Worksheets on page 416.)*

ADVANCED STUDENTS After advanced students have finished this chapter, you can have them apply what they have learned here to their written work: Require them, in their next composition assignment, to include at least one example of each kind of sentence. Have them underline and label these examples as they do for the writing assignment on page 413.

WRITING APPLICATION

The writing application in this chapter is designed to encourage students to use their knowledge of the kinds of sentence structure—simple, compound, complex, and compound-complex—in their own writing. Feel free to adapt this assignment to your students' writing needs, abilities, and interests.

DIAGNOSTIC TEST

This test will give you a clear picture of what your students already know about the kinds of sentence structure.

THE SIMPLE SENTENCE (rule 16a)

Your class should find simple sentences easy, except those that contain compound subjects or verbs. Review the meaning of *compound*. Give some examples of

3. Beyond that building and around the corner, the line stretched all the way down the block to the movie theater. 3. s.
4. You should either buy a new bicycle or fix your old one. 4. s.
5. Judy said that this was the shortest route, but I disagree. 5. cd.
6. There was no way to tell what had really happened. 6. cx.
7. Yes, that seems like the right answer to me. 7. s.
8. The steer broke out of its pen and trampled the roses. 8. s.
9. Do you know who wrote this? 9. cx.
10. I'm not sure what you said, but I think I agree. 10. cd.-cx.
11. Nobody is worried about that, for it will never happen. 11. cd.
12. Whatever you decide will be fine with me. 12. cx.
13. Is the movie that we wanted to see playing at the drive-in, or do we have to go to the theater in the mall? 13. cd.-cx.
14. Leroy knew the plan, and he assigned us each a part. 14. cd.
15. Amphibians and some insects can live both on the land and in the water. 15. s.
16. The detective searched for the man who had been wearing a beret, but there weren't many clues. 16. cd.-cx.
17. The tornado cut across the edge of the housing development, and seven homes were destroyed. 17. cd.
18. Until then, everyone had agreed with his main argument. 18. s.
19. Before the game started, all the football players ran out onto the field, and everyone cheered. 19. cd.-cx.
20. My father stopped to help the family whose car had broken down on the highway. 20. cx.

THE SIMPLE SENTENCE

Remember that a clause is a sentence part that contains a verb and its subject. An independent clause expresses a complete thought and may stand alone. A subordinate clause does not express a complete thought and cannot stand alone. When an independent clause stands alone with no other clauses attached to it, it is called a *simple sentence*.

16a. A *simple sentence* has one independent clause and no subordinate clauses.

In the following examples, the subjects and verbs are printed in boldface. Notice that a simple sentence may have a compound subject (second sentence), a compound verb (third sentence), or both (fourth sentence).

EXAMPLES The **hair stylist gave** John a new look.

Beth Heiden and **Sheila Young won** Olympic medals. [compound subject: *Beth Heiden* and *Sheila Young*]

Lawrence caught the ball but then **dropped** it. [compound verb: *caught* but *dropped*]

The **astronomer** and her **assistant studied** the heavens and **wrote** reports on their findings. [compound subject: *astronomer* and *assistant*; compound verb: *studied* and *wrote*]

EXERCISE 1. Identifying Subjects and Verbs in Simple Sentences. Number your paper 1–10. After the proper number, write the subjects and the verbs of the following sentences. Some sentences have compound subjects and verbs.

EXAMPLE 1. The first combustion engines were quite different from those of today.

1. *engines—were*

1. No kitten or puppy compares to my pet boa constrictor.
2. Officers in uniform boarded the ship in the harbor.
3. We gave apples to the trick-or-treaters.
4. Often juniors or seniors serve as tutors.
5. The amount of food will depend on the number of guests.
6. The first mayor of our town was elected in 1854 and won by a unanimous vote.
7. The accident occurred during the late-afternoon rush hour.
8. The Olympic Games inspired pride in our athletes and renewed interest in the support and training of amateur

sentences with simple subjects and verbs and some with compound subjects and verbs.

EXAMPLES

I left the party

Nelda and I left the party.

Nelda and I left the party and went home.

Ask the class to identify the subject and the verb in each example. Point out that *Nelda* and *I* in the last two sentences are parts of one subject, that *left* and *went* in the last sentence are parts of one predicate, and that the sentences are all simple sentences.

Ask someone to explain the function of the word *and* in these sentences. Then give examples of simple sentences with compound subjects and verbs connected by other coordinating conjunctions.

Neither he *nor* I was tired.

He weakened *but* continued in the game.

Mary *or* Jean should tell him the truth.

EXERCISE 1. You may have your class do the first few sentences orally before assigning the rest as written work.

THE COMPOUND SENTENCE (rule 16b)

Write examples such as the following sentences on the board.

He is a good friend, and she admires him.
Mary went home early, but I stayed later.
The house must have a big yard, or we will not buy it.
She did not laugh, nor did she even smile.
I gave her the money, for I knew she needed it.

Help the class discover that each of these sentences contains two independent clauses connected by a coordinating conjunction. Explain that a comma usually separates the two clauses.

EXERCISE 2. You may want to have your class do part of this exercise orally, then finish it in writing.

athletes in the United States.

9. Soldiers waiting for orders and volunteers waiting for supplies organized a system to help the flood victims.
10. After the dance the students, remembering their manners, thanked the chaperons.

GRAMMAR

THE COMPOUND SENTENCE

Sometimes two or more independent clauses appear in the same sentence without any subordinate clauses. Such a sentence is called a *compound sentence.*

16b. A *compound sentence* has two or more independent clauses but no subordinate clauses.

The independent clauses are usually joined by the coordinating conjunctions *yet, and, but, or, nor, for,* or *so.*

EXAMPLES **According to legend, Betsy Ross made our first flag,** but **there is little evidence.** [two independent clauses joined by the conjunction *but*]

The whistle blew, the drums rolled, and **the crowd cheered.** [three independent clauses, the last two joined by the conjunction *and*]

EXERCISE 2. Identifying Subjects, Verbs, and Conjunctions in Compound Sentences. For each sentence, write the subject and verb of the first independent clause, the coordinating conjunction that joins the independent clauses, and the subject and verb of the next clause. Insert a comma before the conjunction. Underline subjects once and verbs twice.

EXAMPLE 1. A director of a theater-in-the-round visited our class, and we listened to his humorous stories for almost an hour.

1. *director visited*, and *we listened*

1. Many strange things happen backstage during a performance, but the audience usually does not know about them.
2. Audiences at theaters-in-the-round add to the director's problems, for they sit very close to the stage.
3. Members of the audience sometimes use stage ashtrays, or they hang their coats on the actors' coat racks.
4. Sometimes these actions are overlooked by the stagehands, and the results can be very challenging for the actors.
5. The main clue in a certain mystery play depended on a scarf left lying on the stage floor, but the audience had gathered on the stage during intermission.
6. During the scene after the intermission, the detective in the play counted three scarves instead of one, but the actor showed no surprise.
7. Directors cannot always predict the reactions of the audience, nor can they always control the audience.
8. During the performance of another mystery drama, a spectator in the front row became too excited about the action of the play, for at one point, leaping up on the stage, the spectator tackled the killer.
9. The workers in charge of properties are usually alert and efficient, but they do sometimes make mistakes.
10. In one production of *Romeo and Juliet,* the character Juliet prepared to kill herself with a dagger, but unfortunately there was no dagger on the stage.

Sentences with Compound Parts

Although it consists of two or more subjects joined by a conjunction, a compound subject is still regarded as one subject. Similarly, a compound verb is still regarded as one verb. A simple sentence, which has only one subject and one verb, is still a simple sentence even when its subject or verb is compound. Do not confuse a simple sentence containing a compound subject or a compound verb with a compound sentence, which has a subject and a verb in each of its independent clauses.

EXERCISE 3. This exercise may prove difficult for many students. A less-advanced class should probably omit it.

GRAMMAR

SIMPLE SENTENCE Bill and Joe increased their speed and passed the other runners. [compound subject and compound verb]

COMPOUND SENTENCE Bill led half the way, and then Joe took the lead.

If a subject is repeated, then the sentence is considered compound.

SIMPLE SENTENCE I ran to the window and looked out at the snow.

COMPOUND SENTENCE I ran to the window, and I looked out at the snow.

EXERCISE 3. Distinguishing Between Compound Sentences and Compound Subjects and Verbs. After the proper number, write each subject and verb in the following sentences. Underline the subjects once and the verbs twice. Then write *S.* for each simple sentence and *Cd.* for each compound sentence.

EXAMPLES 1. David Attenborough has studied unusual creatures around the world and photographed their habitats and behavior.

1. *David Attenborough has studied, has photographed—S.*
2. He always manages to find unique animals, and he rarely misses a chance to observe them in their natural habitats.
2. *He manages, he misses—Cd.*

1. He has boundless curiosity about living creatures and treats them with respect. 1. s.
2. Many of his television programs focus on animal life, but several include information about plants and geology. 2. cd.
3. Some prefer the program *Life on Earth,* but I like *The Living Planet* better. 3. cd.
4. David Attenborough has also written books and has contributed many of the outstanding photos in them. 4. s.
5. Someday everyone might have the same enthusiasm for life on this planet, and then people will take care of the environment. 5. cd.

Diagraming Compound Sentences

The independent clauses in a compound sentence are diagramed like simple sentences. The second clause is diagramed below the first and is joined to it by a coordinating conjunction diagramed as shown.

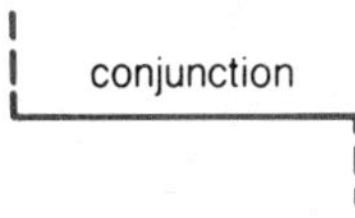

EXAMPLE The quarterback threw a good pass, but the end did not catch it.

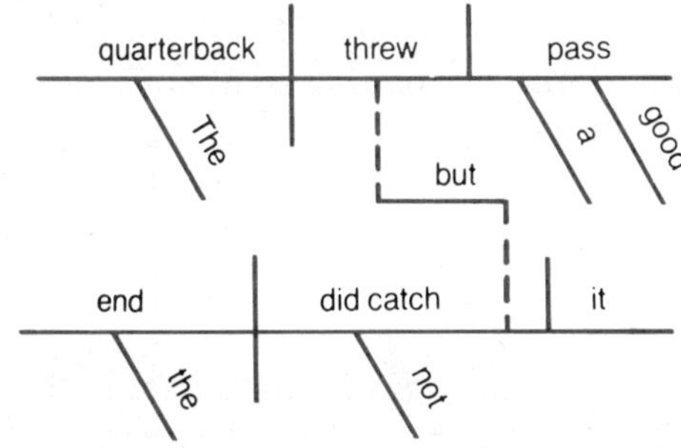

EXERCISE 4. Diagraming Compound Sentences. Diagram the following compound sentences. See Answer Key.

1. I want a motorboat, but Jan prefers a sailboat.
2. The bus stopped at the restaurant, and everyone got off.
3. Our club is very small, but it is growing.
4. Shall we meet you at the station, or will you take a taxi?
5. In Arizona the temperature is often high, but the humidity always remains low.

THE COMPLEX SENTENCE

Like a compound sentence, a complex sentence contains more than one clause. However, unlike the compound sentence, the complex sentence has at least one subordinate clause.

DIAGRAMING COMPOUND SENTENCES

Before assigning sentences to be diagramed, you will want to work out several examples on the board.

EXERCISE 4. If you are not teaching your class to diagram, you may want to use these sentences for easy practice in identifying independent clauses.

GRAMMAR

THE COMPLEX SENTENCE (rule 16c)

Review briefly what your students learned about subordinate clauses in Chapter 15. Ask someone to name the five relative pronouns (*who, whom, whose, which, that*). List them on the board and have the class give you a sentence using each. For example:

who The person who gambles often loses.
that The parrot that speaks Spanish is my pet.

Ask the class to name as many subordinating conjunctions from Chapter 15 as they can. List them on the board and have your students give you a sentence to write with each. For example:

after We left after the second act had started.
because She left because her mother called.

Have someone identify the independent clause and the subordinate clause in each sentence.

Point out that a complex sentence can have only one independent clause but can have several subordinate clauses. Challenge the class to produce a complex sentence with more than one subordinate clause. For example:

When the actor who had the principal part finally arrived, the rehearsal could begin.

EXERCISE 5. Go over the answers in class, and try to clear up difficulties that students may have. A less-advanced class should probably not attempt this exercise.

GRAMMAR

16c. A *complex sentence* has one independent clause and at least one subordinate clause.

A subordinate clause may be an adjective clause (pages 386–90), an adverb clause (pages 390–93), or a noun clause (pages 393–95).

Adjective clauses usually begin with a relative pronoun: *who, whom, whose, which,* or *that.* Adverb clauses usually begin with a subordinating conjunction such as *after, although, because, if, until, when,* or *where.* Noun clauses usually begin with *that, what, whatever, who, whoever, whom,* or *whoever.*

In the following examples, the subordinate clauses are printed in boldface.

EXAMPLE **When I watch Martha Graham's dances,** I feel like studying dance.

One independent clause I feel like studying dance
Subordinate clause When I watch Martha Graham's dances

EXAMPLE Some of the sailors **who took part in the mutiny on the British ship *Bounty*** settled Pitcairn Island.

One independent clause Some of the sailors settled Pitcairn Island
Subordinate clause who took part in the mutiny on the British ship *Bounty*

EXAMPLE In *Gone with the Wind,* **when she is faced with near-starvation,** Scarlett vows **that she will never be hungry again.**

One independent clause In *Gone with the Wind,* Scarlett vows
Two subordinate clauses when she is faced with near-starvation
that she will never be hungry again

EXERCISE 5. Identifying Independent and Subordinate Clauses in Complex Sentences. Write the following complex sentences. Draw one line under each independent clause and two lines under each subordinate clause. Circle subordinating conjunctions and relative pronouns. Be prepared to identify the subject and the verb in each clause. A sentence may have more than one subordinate clause.

EXAMPLES

1. China is a largely agricultural country that has a population of more than one billion people.
1. *China is a largely agricultural country that has a population of more than one billion people.*
2. Although my brother bought one of those coins for his collection, it was nearly worthless.
2. *Although my brother bought one of those coins for his collection, it was nearly worthless.*

1. The detective show appeared on television for several weeks before it became popular with viewers.
2. Most of the albums that we have from the 1960's are sitting in the corner of the basement behind the broken refrigerator.
3. Richard E. Byrd is but one of the explorers who made expeditions to Antarctica.
4. As studies continued, many important facts about nutrition were discovered.
5. A group of popular singers, who donated their time, recorded a song that made people aware of the problems in Ethiopia.
6. The players who were sent back to the minor leagues received a chance to improve their skills.
7. After we have written our report on the history of computers, we may be able to go to the picnic.
8. Although few students or teachers knew about it, a group of sociologists visited our school to study the relationship between the classroom environment and students' grades.
9. While the stage crew was constructing the sets, the performers continued their rehearsal, which went on into the night.
10. Because the park is maintained by the city, the citizens have complained to the mayor about vandalism.

DIAGRAMING COMPLEX SENTENCES

Diagram several sentences on the board. Use sentences that contain as *few words as possible.* Some teachers prefer to use "skeleton diagrams" instead of full diagrams for compound and complex sentences. A skeleton diagram includes only (1) the essential words in each clause—subject, verb, and complement (if any) and (2) the relative pronoun or the conjunction that connects the clauses.

EXAMPLE We had lunch in the student cafeteria when we visited the college.

We had lunch

we visited college

GRAMMAR

Diagraming Complex Sentences

Since a complex sentence has at least one subordinate clause, in order to diagram a complex sentence you need to know how to diagram subordinate clauses. The methods for diagraming subordinate clauses—adjective clauses, adverb clauses, and noun clauses—have been covered on pages 395–97.

Here is how to diagram each of the three kinds of subordinate clauses in a complex sentence:

EXAMPLES We had lunch in the student cafeteria when we visited the college. [complex sentence containing an adverb clause]

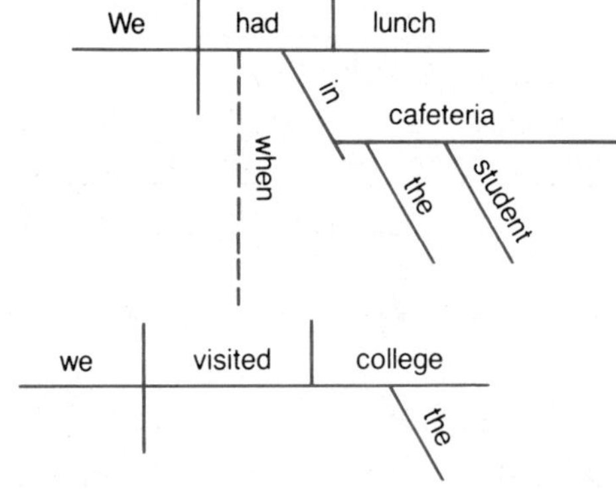

Blair has a ring that belonged to her great-grandmother. [complex sentence containing an adjective clause]

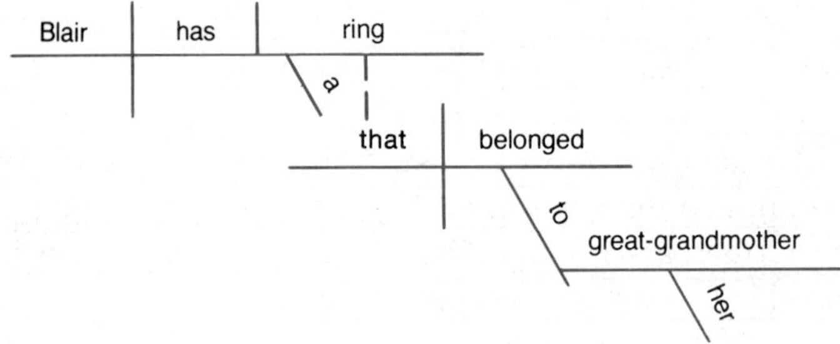

All of the children believed that they had actually seen Santa Claus. [complex sentence containing a noun clause]

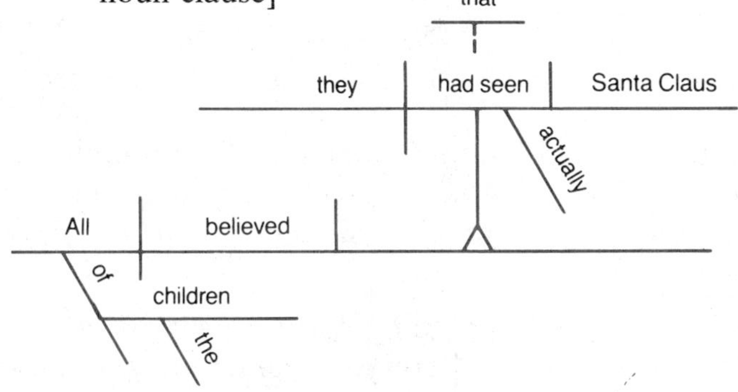

EXERCISE 6. Diagraming Complex Sentences. Diagram the following complex sentences. See Answer Key.

1. We felt sorry for the cub that had caught its leg in a trap.
2. Invite whomever you want.
3. The satellite will be launched if the weather remains good.
4. The knight in black armor fought whoever would challenge him.
5. Alexander the Great, who conquered most of the known world, died at the age of thirty-three.

THE COMPOUND-COMPLEX SENTENCE

A compound-complex sentence is a combination of the compound sentence and the complex sentence. Like a compound sentence, it has at least two independent clauses; like a complex sentence, it has at least one subordinate clause.

16d. A *compound-complex sentence* has two or more independent clauses and at least one subordinate clause.

EXAMPLE Isabel began painting only two years ago, but she has already been asked to hang one of her paintings at the art exhibit that is scheduled for next month.

GRAMMAR

EXERCISE 6. You may wish to have students do skeleton diagrams, rather than full diagrams, of these sentences. See the preceding example.

THE COMPOUND-COMPLEX SENTENCE (rule 16d)

If students have mastered the compound and the complex sentence, this section should not present any special difficulties. Have the class help you construct a table that summarizes the classification of sentences according to the kind and the number of clauses they contain. The table might include the following information:

	CLAUSES	
	INDEPENDENT	SUBORDINATE
Simple	One	None
Compound	Two or more	None
Complex	One	One or more
Compound-complex	Two or more	One or more

Students may copy this and refer to it when they do the review exercise.

EXERCISE 7. You may wish to have students write this exercise in class so that you can give help as it is needed.

Two independent clauses	Isabel began painting only two years ago
	she has already been asked to hang one of her paintings at the art exhibit
Subordinate clause	that is scheduled for next month

GRAMMAR

EXERCISE 7. Identifying Clauses in Compound-Complex Sentences. The following sentences are compound-complex. Write each clause separately, and identify it as *independent* or *subordinate.*

EXAMPLE 1. The little-theater group was happy with the performances, and everyone immediately set to work to find new plays so that next season would be successful, too.

1. *The little-theater group was happy with the performances—independent*
1. *everyone immediately set to work to find new plays—independent*
1. *so that next season would be successful, too —subordinate*

1. Before we conducted the experiment, we asked for permission to use the science lab, but the principal insisted on teacher supervision of our work.
2. Inside the old trunk up in the attic, which is filled with boxes and toys, we found some dusty photo albums, and one of them contained pictures from the early 1900's.
3. We told them that their plan wouldn't work, but they wouldn't listen to us.
4. Every expedition that had attempted to explore that region had vanished without a trace, yet the young adventurer was determined to map the uncharted jungle because he couldn't resist the challenge.
5. The smoke, which grew steadily thicker and darker, billowed through the dry forest, and the animals ran ahead of it as the fire spread quickly.

WRITING APPLICATION:
Using Different Kinds of Sentences to Achieve Variety

Wouldn't it be boring to wear the same clothes every day? Your writing can be just as boring if you always use the same kind of sentence. You can learn to include all four kinds of sentences in your writing, as in the following example.

EXAMPLE O. Henry had an unusual life. He grew up in North Carolina. He became a pharmacist's apprentice. He moved to Texas and became a rancher, a bank teller, and a newspaper writer. He was accused of embezzlement. He fled to Honduras. He returned to Texas. His wife was dying. He went to prison. He wrote short stories there. He wrote more than two hundred short stories. They became very popular. [The paragraph uses all simple sentences.]

O. Henry had an unusual life. [simple] He grew up in North Carolina, and he became a pharmacist's apprentice. [compound] After moving to Texas, he became a rancher, a bank teller, and a newspaper writer before he was accused of embezzlement. [complex] He fled to Honduras, but he returned to Texas because his wife was dying. [compound-complex] While he was in prison, he wrote short stories. [complex] His stories—more than two hundred—became very popular. [simple]

Writing Assignment

Answers will vary.

Write a summary of the life of an American author. Include all four kinds of sentences. At the end of each sentence, write in parentheses the kind of sentence it is. Here are some ideas for a subject:

John Steinbeck	Mark Twain	Robert Frost
Edgar Allan Poe	Emily Dickinson	Gwendolyn Brooks

GRAMMAR

REVIEW EXERCISE. Students will find this exercise fairly difficult. A less-advanced group should probably not attempt it.

CHAPTER 16 REVIEW: POSTTEST 1

This test requires students to identify the four kinds of sentence structure: simple, compound, complex, and compound-complex.

GRAMMAR

REVIEW EXERCISE. Identifying Simple, Compound, Complex, and Compound-Complex Sentences. Number your paper 1–10. Identify the kinds of sentences—simple (*S.*), compound (*Cd.*), complex (*Cx.*), or compound-complex (*Cd.—Cx.*) —in the following paragraphs.

1. People who are learning a new sport begin by mastering basic skills, and they usually are very enthusiastic. **2.** After people have been practicing the basic skills for several weeks or months, they usually progress to more difficult moves. **3.** At this point a beginner is likely to become discouraged, and the temptation to quit grows strong. 1. Cd.—Cx. 2. Cx. 3. Cd.

4. One of the most common problems that beginners face is coordination, and another is muscular aches and pains. **5.** If the student is not careful, the muscles can be injured, but the strenuous activity usually strengthens the muscle tissues. **6.** However, when enough oxygen reaches the warmed-up muscles, the danger of injury is lessened, and the muscles grow in size. **7.** At the same time, coordination grows, along with confidence.

8. The hours of practice that a beginner puts in often result in noticeable improvements. **9.** Obviously, learning something new takes time and work, or it would not be worthwhile. **10.** In sports, as in most activities, persistence and patience can earn rewards. 8. Cx. 9. Cd. 10. S.
4. Cd.—Cx. 5. Cd.—Cx. 6. Cd.—Cx. 7. S.

CHAPTER 16 REVIEW: POSTTEST 1

Identifying the Four Kinds of Sentence Structure. Number your paper 1–20. After the proper number, identify each of the following sentences as simple, compound, complex, or compound-complex.

EXAMPLE 1. When my grandmother came to visit at Christmas time, we decided to make our own ornaments for the Christmas tree.
1. *complex*

1. Last year my grandmother came to stay with us from the middle of December until my brother's birthday in January. **2.** While we were getting out the holiday decorations, Grandma told us all about how she and her family used to make their own decorations when my mother was a girl. **3.** Mom said that she remembered making splendid decorations and that it used to be fun, so we decided to try making some. 1. S. 2. Cx. 3. Cd.-Cx.

4. My dad, my brother, and I drove out to the woods to gather pine cones. **5.** We had forgotten to ask Grandma what size pine cones to get, and since Dad had never made decorations in his family, he didn't know. **6.** We decided to play it safe and get all different sizes, which was easy to do because there were pine cones everywhere. **7.** My brother picked up all the hard little ones, and my dad and I threw about a hundred medium and big ones into the trunk of the car. **8.** When Mom and Grandma saw how many we had, they laughed and said there were enough for decorating ten houses. 4. S. 5. Cd.-Cx. 6. Cx. 7. Cd. 8. Cx.

9. First we sorted the cones; the little hard ones went into one pile, and the bigger ones into another. **10.** Dad and I painted the little ones silver, and Mom and Grandma painted stripes, dots, and all sorts of designs on them. **11.** Then we tied strings to the tops of them, and later, when we put them up, they made great ornaments. 9. Cd. 10. Cd. 11. Cd.-Cx.

12. We painted the bigger pine cones all different colors and glued on cranberries and beads, which made each cone look like a miniature fir tree. **13.** We saved some of the smaller ones for the dining room table, and we put most of the others around on the windowsills and all over the house. **14.** My brother took some to school, too. 12. Cx. 13. Cd. 14. S.

15. Besides the pine-cone decorations, we made some strings to decorate the mantel. **16.** My mom got some needles and a spool of heavy thread out of her sewing basket, and we all strung the rest of the cranberries on six-foot lengths of the thread.

17. Mom and Grandma cut off more pieces of thread, and we made strings of popcorn, just like our strings of cranberries.
15. S. 16. Cd. 17. Cd.

GRAMMAR

CHAPTER 16 REVIEW: POSTTEST 2

This test requires the students to write original sentences according to specific directions. Your less-advanced students should probably omit sentences 5–10. You might assign them 1–4, asking them to write two sentences for each—for a total of eight.

Additional Practice

Teacher's Resource Book, Worksheet pages 191–201, Alternative Worksheet pages (for less-advanced students) 550–52

Testing

Teaching Tests booklet, pages 19–22, 35–36, 37–43
Teacher's Resource Book Test pages 413–16, 429–30, 431–42

GRAMMAR

18. We left some of the strings white and painted the others different colors. 18. S.

19. Decorating our tree was even more fun than usual, and I think that the tree looked prettier, too, with all our homemade ornaments. **20.** From now on, we're going to make decorations every year. 19. Cd.-Cx. 20. S.

CHAPTER 16 REVIEW: POSTTEST 2

Writing a Variety of Sentence Structures. Write your own sentences according to the following instructions: Answers will vary.

1. A simple sentence with a compound subject
2. A simple sentence with a compound predicate
3. A compound sentence with two independent clauses joined by *but*
4. A compound sentence with two independent clauses joined by *or*
5. A complex sentence with an adjective clause beginning with the relative pronoun *that*
6. A complex sentence with an adjective clause beginning with the relative pronoun *who*
7. A complex sentence with an adverb clause at the beginning of the sentence
8. A complex sentence with an adverb clause at the end of the sentence
9. A complex sentence with a noun clause
10. A compound-complex sentence

CHAPTER 17

Agreement

SUBJECT AND VERB, PRONOUN AND ANTECEDENT

Certain words in a sentence are closely related. The verb is closely related to its subject. A pronoun is closely related to the noun it stands for. Such closely related words have matching forms. When the related words are correctly matched, we say that they *agree.*

DIAGNOSTIC TEST

A. Identifying Verbs That Agree with Their Subjects. Number your paper 1–10. In each of the following sentences, if the italicized verb agrees with its subject, write *C* after the proper number. If the italicized verb does not agree with its subject, write the correct form of the verb.

EXAMPLES 1. Ms. Suarez, our gym teacher, *don't* know what happened.
1. *doesn't*
2. The answers to that question *don't* make sense.
2. *C*

USAGE

Usage (pages 417–510)

Chapter Overview

If students are not already familiar with the grammatical concepts of **number** and **agreement** and with the terms **singular** and **plural**, you should take them carefully through the first section of the chapter (pages 419–20) before beginning corrective work.

The second section of the chapter deals with specific errors in subject-verb agreement. Note that few students are likely to make all the errors covered here: For instance, a student who habitually uses a singular verb in sentences like "Ann and her sister *was* here" is not likely to make the opposite error and use a plural verb in sentences like "Either Ann or her sister *were* here." Concentrate on errors that your students actually make in their speaking and writing. The last part of the chapter covers agreement of pronoun and antecedent.

Chapter Objective

Students will practice two general usage rules for standard English: (1) a verb agrees with its subject in number and (2) a pronoun agrees with its antecedent in number and gender. Students will use verb forms and pronouns correctly to make their writing clear.

PRESENTING THE CHAPTER

LESS-ADVANCED STUDENTS A less-advanced class should usually concentrate on correcting major errors in usage. The class may omit study of less common problems. These students will probably learn more through oral drill than through studying rules. *(See listing of Alternative Worksheets on page 440.)*

ADVANCED STUDENTS In a community where standard English is rarely heard, even the students in an advanced class will have to study and practice correct verb forms. This will prepare them for special problems in agreement.

WRITING APPLICATIONS

The writing applications in this chapter are designed to encourage students to use correct agreement of subject and verb in their own writing. Feel free to adapt these assignments to your students' writing needs, abilities, and interests.

DIAGNOSTIC TEST

This test will give you a clear picture of what your students already know about agreement of subject and verb, pronoun and antecedent. Look at the results carefully to determine how much time you should spend on the material in the chapter.

1. Neither of the plants *need* water yet. 1. needs
2. Everyone who wears eyeglasses *is* having vision tests today. 2. c
3. Two minutes *are* long enough to boil an egg. 3. is
4. Mr. Adams said that it *don't* look like rain today. 4. doesn't
5. My baseball and my catcher's mitt *is* back in my room. 5. are
6. Neither Esteban nor Tina *have* tried out yet for the play. 6. has
7. All of the programs *have* been on television before. 7. c
8. *Don't* the team captain plan to put her into the game? 8. Doesn't
9. One of the men *have* decided to get his car washed. 9. has
10. The Bill of Rights *give* American citizens the right to worship where they please. 10. gives

B. Identifying Pronouns That Agree with Their Antecedents. Number your paper 11–20. In each of the following sentences, if an italicized pronoun agrees with its antecedent, write *C* after the proper number. If an italicized pronoun does not agree with its antecedent, write the correct pronoun.

EXAMPLES 1. Each of the boys brought *their* permission slips.
1. *his*
2. One of the does was accompanied by *her* fawn.
2. *C*

11. Have all the girls taken *their* projects home? 11. c
12. Paul, Mike, and Chip each sent in *their* application. 12. his
13. Many of the trees had lost *its* leaves. 13. their
14. Neither Sally nor Marilyn had worn *their* gym suit. 14. her
15. Every dog had a tag hanging from *their* collar. 15. its
16. Someone in the Boy Scout troop camped near poison ivy and has gotten it all over *themselves*. 16. himself
17. A few of the carpenters had brought tools with *them*. 17. c
18. My dog was one of the winners in the show who had *its* picture taken. 18. their
19. According to the teacher, both of those titles should have lines drawn underneath *it*. 19. them
20. No one was sure which of the streets had *its* names changed. 20. their

AGREEMENT OF SUBJECT AND VERB

Singular and Plural Number

17a. When a word refers to one person, place, thing, or idea, it is *singular* in number. When a word refers to more than one, it is *plural* in number.

SINGULAR book, woman, fox, one, I, he
PLURAL books, women, foxes, many, we, they

EXERCISE 1. Classifying Nouns and Pronouns According to Number. Number your paper 1–10. After each number, write *S* if the word is singular and *P* if it is plural.

EXAMPLE 1. cat
1. *S*

1. tomatoes 1. P
2. coach 2. S
3. they 3. P
4. I 4. S
5. many 5. P
6. basis 6. S
7. mice 7. P
8. we 8. P
9. parents 9. P
10. it 10. S

EXERCISE 2. *Oral Drill.* Classifying Nouns and Pronouns by Number. Read the following expressions aloud. Tell whether each is singular or plural.

1. The lion yawns. 1. S
2. The cubs play. 2. P
3. No one stays. 3. S
4. The refugees arrive. 4. P
5. She wins. 5. S
6. They have. 6. P
7. The actors rehearse. 7. P
8. The play opens. 8. S
9. Everyone goes. 9. S
10. All applaud. 10. P

17b. A verb agrees with its subject in number.

(1) Singular subjects take singular verbs.

SINGULAR AND PLURAL NUMBER
(rules 17a and 17b)

Adults tend to forget that the concept of *number* can be hard for students to grasp. In distinguishing between singular and plural, stress that the question is *How many?* If the answer is *one,* the word is singular; if *more than one,* it is plural. An average class that has studied grammar in earlier grades will probably be able to review this section quickly.

EXERCISE 1. You may wish to do this exercise orally.

EXERCISE 2. After your students have correctly identified the expressions as singular or plural, have them revise plural expressions, making them singular, and vice versa.

EXERCISE 3. Most students will have no trouble with this exercise. Students who speak nonstandard English, however, may need extensive drill with standard singular and plural verb forms. These students may not be ready to study the rest of the material in this chapter, which assumes that the class already knows standard singulars and plurals. (See the suggestions on Chapter 17 in Part Three of the front matter in this *Teacher's Edition* for teaching usage to a class that speaks nonstandard English.)

PREPOSITIONAL PHRASES BETWEEN SUBJECT AND VERB (rule 17c)

Ask students to suggest prepositional phrases like those below. (They may turn to the list of prepositions on page 324, if necessary.) Write the phrases on the board and enclose them in parentheses.

(at school)

(for the boys)

(near the carnival)

Ask the class to suggest a noun that could come before each phrase—e.g., *Teachers (at school)*—and write these words on the board. Finally, have the class turn each item into a complete sentence by adding a predicate.

Teachers (at school) work hard.
Uniforms (for the boys) have finally arrived.
Streets (near the carnival) were blocked by heavy traffic.

Ask for volunteers to identify the subject of each sentence and the verb that agrees with it.

EXAMPLES The **car comes** to a sudden stop.
On that route **the plane flies** at a low altitude.
[The singular subjects *car* and *plane* take the singular verbs *comes* and *flies*.]

(2) Plural subjects take plural verbs.

EXAMPLES The **prisoners walk** in the exercise yard.
Again and again the **dolphins leap** playfully.
[The plural subjects *prisoners* and *dolphins* take the plural verbs *walk* and *leap*.]

Generally, subjects ending in *s* are plural (*candles, prisoners, dolphins*), and verbs ending in *s* are singular (*burns, comes, flies*). The verb *be* is a special case.

SINGULAR	PLURAL	SINGULAR	PLURAL
I am	we are	I was	we were
you are	you are	you were	you were
he is	they are	she was	they were
Luis is	the boys are	Linda was	the girls were

EXERCISE 3. Identifying the Correct Number of Verbs. Number your paper 1–10. After the proper number, write the word in parentheses that agrees with the given subject.

EXAMPLE 1. it (is, are)
1. *is*

1. this (costs, cost)
2. plants (grows, grow)
3. the batter (swings, swing)
4. we (considers, consider)
5. the men (was, were)
6. she (asks, ask)
7. these (needs, need)
8. those colors (seems, seem)
9. that ink (lasts, last)
10. days (passes, pass)

Prepositional Phrases Between Subject and Verb

Errors in agreement often occur because words in prepositional phrases are mistaken for the subjects of verbs.

EXERCISE 4. With advanced students you may want to do this exercise orally.

NONSTANDARD[1] The many lights on the Christmas tree makes it look very festive. [*Lights,* not *tree,* is the subject.]

STANDARD The many **lights** on the Christmas tree *make* it look very festive.

17c. The number of a subject is not changed by a prepositional phrase following the subject.

Remember that a word in a prepositional phrase can never be the subject of a verb. If a sentence confuses you, imagine that the prepositional phrase is enclosed by parentheses, and go directly from the subject to the verb.

EXAMPLE The **silence** (in the halls) is unusual.

EXERCISE 4. Identifying Subjects and Verbs That Agree in Number in Sentences with Phrases Following the Subjects. Number your paper 1–10. After the proper number, write the subject and then the correct form of the verb. Remember that the subject is never part of a prepositional phrase.

EXAMPLE 1. The houses on my block (has, have) two stories.
1. *houses, have*

1. The launch of a space shuttle (attracts, attract) the interest of people throughout the world.
2. The thermos bottle in the picnic basket (is, are) filled with apple juice.
3. My favorite collection of poems (is, are) *Where the Sidewalk Ends.*
4. The chimes in the tower (plays, play) every hour.
5. The starving children of the world (needs, need) food and medicine.
6. The cucumbers in my garden (grows, grow) very quickly.
7. The koalas of Australia (eats, eat) eucalyptus leaves.

[1] For explanation of nonstandard and standard, see pages 497–98.

INDEFINITE PRONOUNS (rules 17d–17f)

Some teachers require their students to memorize the lists of singular and plural pronouns given in rules 17d and 17e. Some students may find it hard to accept *everybody* and *everyone* (rule 17d) as singular. Ask them whether one should say "Everybody *is* here" or "Everybody *are* here." In using *each, either,* and *neither* (also rule 17d), the students can avoid errors by mentally supplying the word *one*.

EXAMPLE Each (one) of the puppies chews on shoes.

Note: Some authorities regard usages such as the following ones acceptable in informal situations.

Everybody in Mr. Brown's freshman and sophomore English classes were invited to see the movie.
Neither of the buildings have elevators.
Either of the books answer that question adequately.

You may want to point out to students that these are cases where a usage that is often accepted in conversation may not be considered suitable in writing.

Ordinarily you need not spend much time on the rule about plural pronouns (17e). Few eighth-graders make mistakes in agreement with these words. If your class *does* need corrective work, you may require students to repeat orally pairs of sentences such as these:

Many players were hurt.
Many were hurt.
Several pages are missing.
Several are missing.

USAGE

8. The principal of each school (awards, award) certificates to honor students.
9. Ceramic tiles from Mexico (makes, make) a beautiful trivet for a Mother's Day gift.
10. The house beside the city park (is, are) where my grandfather was born.

Indefinite Pronouns

Certain pronouns do not refer to a definite person, place, thing, or idea and are therefore called *indefinite* pronouns.

You should learn the number of all the indefinite pronouns so that you will not make an error in agreement when an indefinite pronoun is the subject of the sentence.

17d. The following common pronouns are singular and take singular verbs: *each, either, neither, one, everyone, everybody, no one, nobody, anyone, anybody, someone, somebody.*

Pronouns like *each* and *one* are frequently followed by prepositional phrases. Remember that the verb agrees with the subject of the sentence, not with a word in a prepositional phrase.

EXAMPLES **One** of the chairs **looks** comfortable.
Either of the answers **is** correct.
Everyone with passports **was** accepted.
Someone in the stands **has been waving** at us.

17e. The following common pronouns are plural and take plural verbs: *both, few, several, many.*

EXAMPLES **Many** of the students **walk** to school.
Both of the apples **are** good.
Few of the guests **know** of the robbery.

17f. The words *some, any, none, all,* and *most* may be either singular or plural.

This rule is an exception to rule 17c because the number of the subjects *some, any, none, all,* and *most* is determined by a word in the prepositional phrase that follows the subject. If the word the subject refers to is singular, the subject is singular; if the word is plural, the subject is plural.

EXAMPLES **All** of the fans **rush** home. [*All* refers to plural *fans.*]

All of my work **is** finished. [*All* refers to singular *work.*]

Some of the birds **have** gone south.

Some of the glare **has** disappeared.

EXERCISE 5. Identifying Verbs That Agree with Indefinite Pronouns Used as Subjects. Number your paper 1–10. After the proper number, write the subject and then the correct one of the verbs in parentheses.

1. All of my friends (has, have) had the chicken pox.
2. Everyone at the party (likes, like) the cottage cheese and vegetable dip.
3. Both of Fred's brothers (celebrates, celebrate) their birthdays in July.
4. Some of my classmates (takes, take) tennis lessons after school.
5. None of the rosebushes in front of the house (blooms, bloom) in February. 5. (or blooms)
6. Several of those colors (appeals, appeal) to me.
7. Many of Mrs. Taniguchi's students (speaks, speak) fluent Japanese.
8. Nobody in the beginning painting class (displays, display) work in the annual art show.
9. Most of the appetizers on the restaurant menu (tastes, taste) delicious.
10. One of Georgia O'Keeffe's paintings (shows, show) an animal's skull.

USAGE

Concerning pronouns that may be either singular or plural (rule 17f), the only common error occurs with plural items: "Some of the apples was eaten." Native speakers of English rarely have trouble with the singular uses. Note that the pronouns *none* and *any* may be correctly construed as singular even when used with plural items: "None of the boys *was* hurt." Equally acceptable is "None of the boys *were* hurt."

EXERCISE 5. This exercise covers verb agreement with the three kinds of indefinite pronouns. If students complete the exercise as individual work, be sure to go over the answers orally.

REVIEW EXERCISE A. This exercise may not be suitable for a less-advanced class because these students might be confused by seeing incorrect usages in print.

WRITING APPLICATION A:
Using Indefinite Pronouns Correctly in Narration

Sometimes when you write, you may not want to use specific names because names are not important in what you are writing or because so many people are involved that using all their names would be confusing. In these cases, you probably will use indefinite pronouns, which do not refer to a particular person, place, thing, or idea. When you use these pronouns, be sure to proofread carefully to make certain that your pronouns match their verbs in number.

EXAMPLE Many of the students enjoys the water slide. [The indefinite pronoun *many* does not agree with the singular verb *enjoys.*]

Many of the students **enjoy** the water slide. [The plural pronoun *many* agrees with the plural verb *enjoy.*]

USAGE

Writing Assignment

Answers will vary.

Write a narrative in the present tense telling about a real or imaginary class or club trip. In your paragraph, use at least four indefinite pronouns, such as *many, few, several, either, all,* and *some.* Here is an idea about how you can begin your narrative:

Every year, at the end of May, my chorus class takes a trip to the beach. *Some* students bring fishing gear. *Many* bring inflatable rafts to float on. A *few* pack lotion to help prevent bad sunburns.

REVIEW EXERCISE A. Proofreading Sentences for Subject-Verb Agreement. Number your paper 1–10. Read each sentence aloud. If the verb agrees with the subject, write *C.* If the verb does not agree with the subject, write the correct form of the verb. Some sentences have more than one verb for you to consider.

17 g

EXAMPLES 1. One of the women practice medicine.
1. *practices*
2. Both of them work hard.
2. *C*

1. All of the concert chorus members harmonize very well with each other. 1. C
2. Several of the eighth-grade track stars also compete in the swimming meets. 2. C
3. Britain's prehistoric monument Stonehenge challenges tourists to uncover its mysteries. 3. C
4. Everybody want to know who erected the massive stones. 4. wants
5. Most of the visitors assumes that the ancient Druids built Stonehenge. 5. assume
6. Many of the archaeologists studying Stonehenge believe that it was built before the time of the Druids. 6. C
7. None of the tour guides at Stonehenge explain the secrets of the monument. 7. C or explains
8. All of the tourists wonders why the structure was built.
9. One of Justin's grandmothers visit Stonehenge once a year.
10. The stones in Stonehenge weighs as much as fifty tons.

8. wonder 9. visits 10. weigh

Compound Subjects

Most compound subjects that are joined by *and* name more than one person or thing; therefore, they are plural and require a plural verb.

17g. Subjects joined by *and* are plural and take a plural verb.

EXAMPLES **Antonia Brico** and **Sarah Caldwell are** famous conductors. [Two people are conductors.]

Last year a **library** and a **museum were** built in our town. [Two things were built.]

If the items in a compound subject actually refer to only one person or are thought of as one thing, the verb is singular.

USAGE

COMPOUND SUBJECTS (rules 17g–17i)

Few eighth-graders have any difficulty with subjects joined by *and* (rule 17g). Students who do have trouble with this agreement rule, however, should not be introduced to the "exceptions" covered in rules 17h and 17i until they have learned the basic usage habit.

When you discuss singular subjects joined by *or,* or *nor,* (rule 17h), use a visual demonstration to help put the point across. Take a red pencil and a yellow pencil (or any other two objects). Holding them up before the class, say, "I will use a red pencil AND a yellow pencil. How many pencils will I use?" (Two.) Then hold up the pencils one at a time and say, "I will use a red pencil—OR a yellow pencil. How many will I use?" (One.) Write on the board

Red pencil AND yellow pencil = two
Red pencil OR yellow pencil = one

Note: The rule that singular subjects joined by or *or* nor *take a singular verb is frequently not followed in informal conversation. It is, however, generally observed in written English. You may want to explain this difference in usage to your class.*

When discussing a singular subject and a plural subject joined by *or* or *nor* (rule 17i), stress that such constructions should be avoided, because any solution sounds awkward. Note that in conversation, a speaker usually uses the plural form of the verb, no matter which subject is nearer the verb.

EXERCISE 6. Warn students that in some of these sentences the subject comes after the verb.

EXERCISE 7. This exercise covers rules 17g and 17h.

EXAMPLES The **captain** and **quarterback** of the team is the speaker. [One person is both the captain and the quarterback.]

Chicken and dumplings is a favorite southern dish. [Chicken and dumplings is one dish.]

EXERCISE 6. Choosing Verbs That Agree in Number with Compound Subjects. Number your paper 1–10. Decide whether the compound subject of each sentence is singular or plural. Choose the correct verb form in parentheses, and write it after the proper number.

EXAMPLE 1. Cleon and Pam (is, are) here.
1. *are*

USAGE

1. March and April (is, are) windy months.
2. My mother and the mechanic (is, are) discussing the bill.
3. Virginia Wade and Tracy Austin (plays, play) today.
4. Steak and eggs (is, are) my favorite breakfast. *
5. (Does, Do) Carla and Jean take dancing lessons?
6. (Is, Are) the knives and forks in the drawer?
7. English and science (requires, require) hours of study.
8. (Here's, Here are) our star and winner of the meet.
9. Where (is, are) the bread and the honey?
10. (Does, Do) an Austrian and a German speak the same language?

*Steak and eggs can also be considered as two separate items, with a plural verb, *are*.

17h. Singular subjects joined by *or* or *nor* take a singular verb.

EXAMPLES A **pen or** a **pencil** is needed for this test. [Either one is needed.]

Neither Miami nor Jacksonville is the capital of Florida. [Neither one is the capital.]

EXERCISE 7. Choosing Verbs That Agree in Number with Compound Subjects. Number your paper 1–10. From each pair of verbs in parentheses, choose the one that agrees with the subject.

EXAMPLE 1. Either tea or coffee (is, are) fine with me.
1. *is*

1. Either Mrs. Gomez or Mr. Ming (delivers, deliver) the welcome speech on the first day of school.
2. Our guava tree and our fig tree (bears, bear) more fruit than our entire neighborhood can eat.
3. Tuskegee Institute or Harvard University (offers, offer) the best courses in Chester's field.
4. Armadillos and anteaters (has, have) tubular mouths and long sticky tongues for catching insects.
5. Either the president or the vice-president of the class (calls, call) roll every morning.
6. Georgia's frog and Sam's frog often (jumps, jump) out of the aquarium.
7. Red and royal blue (looks, look) nice in this bedroom.
8. Bridge or canasta (is, are) my favorite card game.
9. Neither my sister nor I (mows, mow) the lawn without protesting.
10. The tulips and the daffodils (blooms, bloom) every April.

17i. When a singular subject and a plural subject are joined by *or* or *nor*, the verb agrees with the nearer subject.

EXAMPLES Either Joan or her **friends are** mistaken. [The verb agrees with the nearer subject, *friends*.]

Neither the players nor the **director was** on time for rehearsal. [The verb agrees with the nearer subject, *director*.]

Whenever possible, avoid this kind of construction. The second sentence can be rewritten to read: *Both the players and the director were late for rehearsal.*

EXERCISE 8. Choosing Verbs That Agree with Singular and Plural Compound Subjects. Number your paper 1–5. From each pair of verbs in parentheses, choose the one that agrees with the subject, and write it after the proper number.

EXERCISE 8. This exercise covers rules 17g–17i. Students that did not study one or more of these three rules should skip the exercise.

USAGE

REVIEW EXERCISE B. This exercise covers all the rules of agreement presented in the chapter up to this point. It is best suited to an advanced class. Other groups should omit the exercise or do only selected sentences.

OTHER PROBLEMS IN AGREEMENT (rules 17j–17m)

You need not teach this section as a unit. Some teachers introduce the rules when the errors happen to appear in oral or written work.

When you present the rule about collective nouns (17j), note that students often waste their time worrying about when a collective noun "should" be regarded as singular or "should" be regarded as plural. Emphasize at the start that there is no "should" involved; either the singular or the plural is correct in almost any situation. The real point is that *speakers or writers should be consistent*—not switch from singular to plural, or vice versa, in mid-sentence. For example:

NONSTANDARD The class has finished the test and are working on a new project.
STANDARD The class have finished the test and are working on a new project.
STANDARD The class has finished the test and is working on a new project.

Rule 17k (page 429) focuses on a special problem that occurs only when a subject and a predicate nominative differ in number. You may wish to recommend that students avoid the problem by avoiding the structure; for instance, instead of using sentences like those in the examples on page 430, a

1. Either Sylvia or her brothers (washes, wash) the kitchen floor each Saturday morning.
2. This bread and this cereal (contains, contain) no preservatives or dyes.
3. Either the students or the teacher (reads, read) aloud during the last ten minutes of each class period.
4. The heavy rainclouds and the powerful winds (indicates, indicate) that a hurricane is approaching.
5. Neither the seal nor the clowns (catches, catch) the ball that the monkey throws into the circus ring.

REVIEW EXERCISE B. Choosing Verbs That Agree with Singular and Plural Subjects. Number your paper 1–10. Then choose from the words in parentheses the verb that agrees with the subject, and write it after the proper number.

1. Either the squirrels or the dog (digs, dig) a new hole in the yard at least once a day.
2. Jeffrey and his dad (builds, build) fireplaces for clients throughout the summer months.
3. Someone (places, place) the bricks around the inside of each of the fireplaces.
4. None of the bricks (cracks, crack) if they are installed very carefully.
5. Yellowstone National Park in Wyoming (fascinates, fascinate) many people.
6. The grizzly bears and coyotes (terrifies, terrify) would-be hikers.
7. A car or camper (provides, provide) protection from animals.
8. Some of the tourists foolishly (approaches, approach) the wild bears to give them food.
9. Unfortunately, several of these generous people (has, have) been killed or maimed by the bears.
10. Most of the park's visitors now (realizes, realize) that wild bears are truly wild.

Other Problems in Agreement

17j. Collective nouns may be either singular or plural.

A collective noun names a group of persons or things and is singular in form.

Common Collective Nouns

army	club	family	squadron
assembly	crowd	group	swarm
audience	fleet	herd	team
class	flock	public	troop

A collective noun takes a plural verb when the noun refers to the individual parts or members of the group. A collective noun takes a singular verb when the noun refers to the group as a unit.

EXAMPLES The **family were arguing** about where to spend the next vacation. [*Family* here refers to individuals acting separately.]

The **family was** calmed down by the grandparents. [*Family* here refers to a group considered as a unit.]

The **crowd are straining** to see the balloon. [The sentence leads you to picture the effort of individuals in the crowd.]

The **crowd is** gone. [The whole group is gone.]

EXERCISE 9. Writing Sentences with Collective Nouns. Select five collective nouns. Use each noun as the subject of two sentences. In the first, make the subject singular in meaning so that it calls for a singular verb. In the second, make the subject plural in meaning so that it takes a plural verb. Answers will vary.

17k. A verb agrees with its subject, not with its predicate nominative.

Sometimes the subject and the predicate nominative of a sentence are different in number. In this case the verb agrees with

writer could say, "The happiest time of my life was my childhood."

In a discussion of sentences beginning with *here* or *there* (rule 17l), note that current usage indicates this rule is often ignored. For example, a national leader recently said during a speech on television, "There's still sixty-two million people . . ." The choice of *is* before a singular part of a compound subject is also becoming common—as in, "Where's my book and pencil?" Eighth-graders should, however, follow the rule in their *written* work.

Teach the section on *don't* and *doesn't* (rule 17m) only if your students need corrective work. Many eighth-graders do not make the error of saying "he don't."

USAGE

EXERCISE 9. This exercise should be assigned only to average or above-average classes. Emphasize that the sentences should show clearly whether the subject is being considered singular or plural. Write on the board these two sentences, and insist that the class follow instructions by writing sentences like number 2.

1. The jury decided that the defendant was guilty. (No way to know whether *jury* is considered singular or plural.)
2. The jury has decided on a verdict. (*Has* shows clearly that *jury* is considered singular.)

EXERCISE 10. With advanced students you may decide to do this exercise orally.

the subject, not with the predicate nominative. The subject usually comes *before* the linking verb and the predicate nominative *after*.

EXAMPLES The happiest **time** of my life **was** my childhood days.
My childhood **days were** the happiest time of my life.

17l. When the subject follows the verb, as in sentences beginning with *there* and *here* and in questions, find the subject and make sure that the verb agrees with it.

EXAMPLES Here **is** my **seat.**
Here **are** our **seats.**
There **is** an exciting **ride** at the fair.
There **are** exciting **rides** at the fair.
Where **are** the programs?

USAGE

Be especially careful when you use the contractions *here's* and *there's*. These contain the verb *is* and should be used only with singular subjects.

NONSTANDARD There's the books.
STANDARD There **are** the **books.**

EXERCISE 10. Choosing Verbs That Agree in Number with Singular and Plural Subjects. Number your paper 1–10. Write the correct verb for each sentence.

1. The audience (loves, love) the mime performance.
2. (Here's, Here are) the answers to Chapter 8.
3. The club (sponsors, sponsor) a carwash each September.
4. Andy's gift to Jynelle (was, were) two roses.
5. (Here's, Here are) the letters I have been expecting.
6. The public (differs, differ) in their opinions on the referendum.
7. (There's, There are) only three people in the contest.
8. The tennis team (plays, play) every Saturday morning.
9. His legacy to us (was, were) words of wisdom.
10. (Where's, Where are) the bell peppers for the salad?

WRITING APPLICATION B:
Checking for Correct Agreement When the Subject Follows the Verb

One of the reasons that people from foreign countries sometimes have difficulty learning English is that the word order, or syntax, of English sentences can vary. The subject, the verb, and any modifiers may appear at the beginning, in the middle, or at the end of a sentence. For example, in sentences that begin with *here* or *there,* the subject usually follows the verb. In your writing, you need to proofread to make certain that each verb agrees with its subject in number, particularly when the verb comes *before* the subject.

INCORRECT There has been many exciting TV shows lately about historical figures. [The subject *shows* is plural; it does not agree in number with the singular verb *has been.*]

CORRECT There **have been** many exciting TV **shows** lately about historical figures. [The plural verb *have been* agrees with the plural subject *shows.*]

Writing Assignment

Answers will vary.

Pretend that you are welcoming a group of people to a new time or a new place. Explain to them the strange new things they will encounter. Start at least four sentences with *here* or *there.* Be sure to proofread carefully for agreement errors. Here are several ideas for new times and places for your explanation:

1. A new, previously unknown planet
2. A spaceship from another planet
3. Your home when you are twenty-five years old
4. The school your children attend in the year 2010

17m. *Don't* and *doesn't* must agree with their subjects.

EXERCISES 11 and 12. Students who say "he don't" will need much oral drill to form correct usage habits. You may also have to call attention to the spelling of *doesn't* (not "dosen't"), explaining that the word is made up of *does* plus *n't* for "not."

Use *don't* with plural subjects and with the pronouns *I* and *you*.

EXAMPLES These gloves **don't** fit.
You **don't** speak clearly.
I **don't** like that record.

Use *doesn't* with other subjects.

EXAMPLES The **music box doesn't** play.
She doesn't like cold weather.
It doesn't matter.

The most frequent errors in using *don't* and *doesn't* are made when *don't* is incorrectly used with *he, she,* or *it.* Remember always to use *doesn't* with these singular subjects: *he doesn't, she doesn't, it doesn't.*

USAGE

EXERCISE 11. *Oral Drill.* Using *Doesn't* with Singular Subjects. Read the following sentences aloud. By getting accustomed to hearing the correct use of *doesn't* and *don't,* you will get into the habit of using these two words correctly.

Oral drill.

1. It doesn't look like a serious wound.
2. She doesn't call meetings often.
3. One doesn't interrupt a speaker.
4. He doesn't play records loudly.
5. Doesn't the television set work?

EXERCISE 12. Writing *Doesn't* and *Don't* with Subjects. Number your paper 1–10. Write the subject of each sentence and then the correct verb, *doesn't* or *don't.*

EXAMPLE 1. —— they go to our school?
1. *they, Don't*

1. —— anyone in the class know about Susan B. Anthony? 1. Doesn't
2. My three-year-old sister —— use good table manners. 2. doesn't
3. They —— have enough people to form a softball team. 3. don't
4. Pearl and Marshall —— need to change their schedules. 4. don't
5. It —— hurt to practice the piano an hour a day. 5. doesn't

REVIEW EXERCISE C. A less-advanced class should probably omit this exercise or complete it as a class activity.

6. —— you think that the music is too loud? 6. Don't
7. Those snow peas —— look crisp. 7. (*or* peas) don't
8. Hector —— win every track meet, but he often places second. 8. doesn't
9. —— anyone know the time? 9. Doesn't
10. He —— know the shortest route from Dallas to Peoria. 10. doesn't

REVIEW EXERCISE C. Proofreading Sentences for Subject-Verb Agreement. Number your paper 1–20. If a sentence is correct, write *C* after the proper number. If a sentence contains an error in agreement, write the correct form of the ~~incorrect verb~~.

EXAMPLE 1. There is a man and a woman here to see you.
1. *are*

1. Walter or one of his assistants replaces the bald tires. 1. C
2. Leilani and Yoshi ~~doesn't~~ know how to swim. 2. don't
3. Either Maribeth or Wade ~~are~~ expected to win the speech contest. 3. is
4. The flock of geese flies over the lake at dawn. 4. C
5. The Seminole Indians of Florida ~~sews~~ beautifully designed quilts. 5. sew
6. ~~Here's~~ the sweaters I knitted for you. 6. Here are
7. Neither Frank nor his classmates ~~thinks~~ the test is fair. 7. think
8. The windmill generates power. 8. C
9. Each of the ten-speed bicycles ~~cost~~ over a hundred dollars. 9. costs
10. Few of the boxers leave the ring without some bruises. 10. C
11. Most of the puddle ~~disappear~~ after the sun comes out from behind the clouds. 11. disappears
12. Somebody in this room ~~know~~ where the car keys are hidden. 12. knows
13. The soccer team ~~celebrate~~ each victory with a pizza party.
14. The wheelchair division of the six-mile race was won by Randy Nowell. 13. celebrates 14. C
15. The caribou and the reindeer ~~is~~ closely related. 15. are
16. Don't you think three hours of homework is enough? 16. C
17. Both of the doctors ~~agrees~~ that she must have her tonsils removed. 17. agree

USAGE

AGREEMENT OF PRONOUN AND ANTECEDENT (rule 17n)

Most of the specific rules covering agreement in number of subjects and verbs apply also to agreement in number of pronouns and their antecedents. There is no need to repeat those rules in this section, but you may have to call attention to the fact that a subject that takes a singular (or plural) verb must be referred to by a singular (or plural) pronoun.

Since students ordinarily have no difficulty using pronouns that agree in gender with their antecedents, you may not wish to spend class time on the matter. A less-advanced class should probably not be required to master the concept of grammatical gender.

18. Any of those dresses look nice on you. 18. c
19. All of those books ~~smells~~ musty from being stored in the basement. 19. smell
20. Where's the bus schedule for downtown routes? 20. c

USAGE

AGREEMENT OF PRONOUN AND ANTECEDENT

Every pronoun refers to another word, called its *antecedent.* For example, in the phrase *the car with its windows open,* the pronoun *its* refers to the antecedent *car.* Whenever you use a pronoun, make sure that it agrees with its antecedent.

17n. A pronoun agrees with its antecedent in number and gender.

Some singular personal pronouns have forms that indicate gender. *He, him,* and *his* refer to masculine antecedents, while *she, her,* and *hers* refer to feminine antecedents. *It* and *its* refer to antecedents that are neither masculine nor feminine.

Here are several sentences containing pronouns that agree with their antecedents in both number and gender:

EXAMPLES **Bryan** lost **his** book.
Dawn loaned **her** book to Bryan.
The **book** had Dawn's name written inside **its** cover.

The antecedent of a personal pronoun can be another kind of pronoun, such as *each, either,* or *one.* To determine the gender of a personal pronoun that refers to one of these other pronouns, you may need to look in a phrase that follows the antecedent pronoun.

EXAMPLE **Each** of the men put on **his** hard hat.
Neither of those women got what **she** wanted.

Some antecedents may be either masculine or feminine, while others may be both. When referring to such antecedents, the masculine form of the personal pronoun may be used, or both the masculine and the feminine may be used.

EXAMPLES **No one** on the committee gave **his** approval.
or **No one** on the committee gave **his or her** approval.

Everyone in the class wanted to know **his grade.**
or **Everyone** in the class wanted to know **his or her** grade.

In conversation, you may be more accustomed to using a plural pronoun to stand for a singular antecedent that may be either masculine or feminine. Such usage is becoming more acceptable in writing, too, and may someday be considered acceptable in standard written English.

EXAMPLES **Everybody** rode **their** bicycle.
Each student paid for **their** ticket.

(1) Use a singular pronoun to refer to *each, either, neither, one, everyone, everybody, no one, nobody, anyone, anybody, someone,* or *somebody.*

EXAMPLES **Nobody** in the three classes would admit **his** (*or* **his or her**) guilt.

Each of the birds built **its** own nest.

A prepositional phrase does not affect the number of the antecedent. In both examples, the antecedent is singular and, therefore, takes a singular pronoun to agree with it.

(2) Two or more singular antecedents joined by *or* or *nor* should be referred to by a singular pronoun.

EXAMPLES **Julio or Van** will bring **his** football.
Neither **the mother nor the daughter** had forgotten **her** umbrella.

> **USAGE NOTE** Rules (1) and (2) are often disregarded in conversation; however, they should be followed in writing.

EXERCISE 13. Permit students to look back at the rules and examples when they write this exercise. Answer any questions to make certain they understand the concepts before going on to the next exercise.

(3) Two or more antecedents joined by *and* should be referred to by a plural pronoun.

EXAMPLES My **mother and father** send **their** regards.
My **dog and cat** never share **their** food.

EXERCISE 13. Proofreading Sentences for Pronoun-Antecedent Agreement. Number your paper 1–10. After the proper number, write *C* if the sentence is correct. If the sentence contains an ~~error in agreement~~, write the antecedent, then the correct form of the pronoun. Follow the rules for standard written English.

EXAMPLE 1. Everyone in my English class has to give their oral report on Friday.
1. *Everyone—his* (or *his or her*)

USAGE

1. Either Robert or Buddy will be the first to give ~~their~~ oral report. 1. his
2. Several others, including me, volunteered to give ~~mine~~ first. 2. theirs
3. Everybody else in class wanted to put off giving ~~their~~ report as long as possible. 3. his (*or* his or her)
4. Last year my best friend Sandy and I figured out that waiting to give our reports was worse than actually giving them. 4. C
5. I am surprised that more people didn't volunteer to give ~~his or her~~ reports first. 5. their
6. Someone else will be third to give ~~their~~ report; then I will give mine. 6. his (*or* his or her)
7. A few others in my class are going to try to get out of giving ~~his or her~~ reports at all. 7. their
8. However, my teacher, Mrs. Murray, said that anyone who does not give an oral report will get an "incomplete" as ~~their~~ course grade. 8. his (*or* his or her)
9. Most of us wish that ~~he or she~~ did not have to give an oral report at all. 9. we
10. Since no one can get out of giving ~~their~~ report, though, I'd rather get it over with as soon as possible. 10. his (*or* his or her)

EXERCISE 14. Identifying Antecedents and Writing Pronouns That Agree with Them. Number your paper 1–10. After the proper number, write a pronoun that will complete the meaning of the sentence. Then, write the antecedent for that pronoun. Follow the rules for standard written English.

EXAMPLE 1. Ann and Margaret wore —— cheerleader uniforms.
1. *their, Ann and Margaret*

1. The trees lost several of —— branches in the thunderstorm last night. 1. their
2. Each of these magazines has had the President's picture on —— cover. 2. its
3. Has anyone turned in —— paper yet? 3. his (*or* his or her)
4. The mob raised —— voices in protest. 4. their
5. The creek and the pond lost much of —— water during the drought. 5. their
6. One of my uncles always wears —— belt buckle off to one side. 6. his
7. No person should be made to feel that —— is worth less than someone else. 7. he (*or* he or she)
8. None of the dogs had eaten all of —— food. 8. its
9. A few of my neighbors have fenced —— backyards. 9. their
10. The fire engine and the police car went rushing by with —— lights flashing. 10. their

REVIEW EXERCISE D. Proofreading Sentences for Pronoun-Antecedent Agreement. Number your paper 1–10. After the proper number, write *C* if the sentence is correct. If the sentence contains an ~~error in agreement~~, write the antecedent, then the correct form of the pronoun. Follow the rules for standard written English.

1. Each member of the President's Cabinet gave ~~their~~ advice about what to do. 1. his (*or* his or her)
2. Nearly every one of the girls in our class had ~~their~~ hair cut short. 2. her

EXERCISE 14. Before assigning this exercise, explain that since in *conversational* situations we often use pronouns that do not agree with their antecedents, we cannot always depend upon what "sounds natural." Encourage the class to refer freely to the preceding rules and examples, which meet the demands of standard *written* English.

REVIEW EXERCISE D. This exercise gives your students additional drill in proofreading sentences for pronoun-antecedent agreement. If they are having difficulty, give additional instruction before you assign the posttest.

USAGE

CHAPTER 17 REVIEW: POSTTEST

In Part A of this test, the students are required to identify verbs that agree with their subjects. If there is an error, they must write the correct form. Part B includes similar directions concerning pronoun-antecedent agreement.

3. Was Mr. Avery or Mr. Jones going to show ~~their~~ classes that film today? 3. his
4. The guard said that anybody who didn't have ~~their~~ pass could not get in. 4. his (*or* his or her)
5. Some of the Boy Scouts had built an authentic Indian wigwam for their shelter. 5. C
6. Neither of those trees needs ~~their~~ limbs trimmed. 6. its
7. Every one of the soldiers carried extra rations in ~~their~~ pack. 7. his (*or* his or her)
8. Andrea, Tammy, and Laura trade outfits so that ~~she~~ can always have something different to wear. 8. they
9. All of the volunteers quickly went to work at ~~his or her~~ jobs. 9. their
10. A person should weigh ~~their~~ words carefully before criticizing someone else. 10. his (*or* his or her)

USAGE

CHAPTER 17 REVIEW: POSTTEST

A. Identifying Verbs That Agree with Their Subjects. Number your paper 1–15. If the italicized verb in a sentence agrees with its subject, write *C*. If an italicized verb does not agree with its subject, write the correct form of the verb.

EXAMPLES
1. The people on the bus have all been seated.
1. *C*
2. The fish, bass and perch mostly, *has* started feeding.
2. *have*

1. Pencil and paper *is* needed for this test. 1. are
2. Either Sol or Anthony *have* been assigned to give a report. 2. has
3. *Doesn't* any of the children ride the bus? 3. Don't
4. Mrs. Holmes and Mr. Davis *assigns* homework almost every night. 4. assign
5. Nearly every cat, no matter what breed, *go* crazy for catnip. 5. goes
6. James Fenimore Cooper's *Leatherstocking Tales is* a famous collection of stories about the early American wilderness. 6. C

7. None of the answers you gave *was* correct. 7. C *or* were
8. Up until recently hardly anyone *have* been able to own a personal computer. 8. has
9. The club often *argues* among themselves about finances and activities. 9. argue
10. Every player on the varsity teams *go* to daily exercise. 10. goes
11. Somebody said that he, of course, *don't* approve. 11. doesn't
12. There *is* probably a few children who don't like strawberries.
13. My spelling lessons and science homework sometimes *takes* me hours to finish. 12. are 13. take 14. C
14. The mice or the cat *has* eaten the cheese that was left out.
15. The swarm of bees *have* deserted its hive. 15. has

B. Identifying Pronouns That Agree with Their Antecedents. Number your paper 16–25. If the italicized pronoun in a sentence agrees with its antecedent, write *C*. If it does not agree with its antecedent, write the correct pronoun.

USAGE

EXAMPLES 1. Either of the men could have offered *their* help.
1. *his*
2. Both of the flowers had spread *their* petals.
2. *C*

16. Why doesn't somebody raise *their* hand and ask for directions? 16. his *or* her
17. In most cases, a dog or a cat that gets lost in the woods can take care of *themselves*. 17. itself
18. One of the birds had lost most of *their* tail feathers. 18. its
19. By the end of the day, all of the streets in our neighborhood had new yellow lines painted along *its* edges. 19. their
20. Everyone who will be going will need to bring a note from *their* mother. 20. his (*or* his or her)
21. I don't understand how chameleons sitting on a green leaf or a bush change *their* color. 21. C
22. Each of these tests has *their* own answer key. 22. its
23. Please ask some of these girls to pick up *her* own materials from the supply room. 23. their

Additional Practice

Teacher's Resource Book, Worksheet pages 202–219, Alternative Worksheet pages (for less-advanced students) 553–54

Testing

Teaching Tests booklet, pages 45–48, 49–50, 57–59, 61–63
Teacher's Resource Book, Test pages 443–46, 447–48, 457–68

24. The air conditioner and the refrigerator have switches that turn *it* off and on automatically. 24. them
25. The audience clapped *its* hands in approval. 25. their

USAGE

CHAPTER 18

Using Verbs Correctly

PRINCIPAL PARTS, REGULAR AND IRREGULAR VERBS

USAGE

Few errors in speaking or writing are more obvious than verb errors. Students who write *she done it, he begun, they drownded,* or *it bursted* immediately tag themselves as people who do not know the standard usages of their language.

DIAGNOSTIC TEST

A. Writing the Past and Past Participle Forms of Verbs. Number your paper 1–15. After the proper number, write the past or past participle of the verb given before the sentence.

EXAMPLES 1. *take* *We don't know why it —— them so long.*
1. *took*
2. *take* We don't know why it has —— them so long.
2. *taken*

1. *lie* The cat —— down in front of the warm fire. 1. lay
2. *raise* Since the storm began, the river has —— four feet. 2. risen
3. *go* Did you see which way they —— ? 3. went

Chapter Overview

If you have a class of students who still use expressions like "I knowed" and "I done" in their oral or written work, you may wish to concentrate on the irregular verb drills and ignore more advanced topics such as consistency of tense. On the other hand, a class that already uses the correct forms of verbs may need little or no review of regular and irregular verbs. If your students make relatively few errors in verb usage in their written work and do well on the Diagnostic Test, you will be able to go through the chapter rapidly.

Chapter Objective

Students will form the past and past participle forms of regular and irregular verbs and will be consistent in using verb tenses.

PRESENTING THE CHAPTER

LESS-ADVANCED STUDENTS Ordinarily, this class should concentrate on learning to use correctly the forms of irregular verbs. Avoid using grammatical terms such as *conjugation, infinitive,* and *consistency of tense. (See listing of Alternative Worksheets on page 463.)*

ADVANCED STUDENTS The results of the Diagnostic Test will help you determine which verb forms (if any) cause serious difficulty. Individual students who still have trouble with verbs that the rest of the class has mastered can be required to use each form correctly in original sentences. Do assign the writing applications to these students.

WRITING APPLICATIONS

The writing applications in this chapter are designed to encourage

441

students to use verbs correctly and consistently to make their writing clear. Feel free to adapt these assignments to your students' writing needs, abilities, and interests.

DIAGNOSTIC TEST

This test will give you a clear picture of what your students already know about using the past and past participle forms of irregular verbs and about using verb tense consistently.

4. *write* I should have —— you sooner. 4. written
5. *break* Two runners on our track team have —— the school record for the mile run. 5. broken
6. *burst* When the manager unlocked the door, a mob of shoppers —— into the store to take advantage of the sale. 6. burst
7. *shrink* Larry washed his wool sweater in hot water, and it —— . 7. shrank
8. *see* The witness said that she —— the blue car run through the red light. 8. saw
9. *rise* Look in the oven to see if the cake has —— yet. 9. risen
10. *ring* Everyone should be in class after the bell has —— .
11. *know* You have all —— for a week that we were going to have a test today. 11. known
12. *lay* Jeanette carefully —— her coat across the back of the chair. 12. laid
13. *freeze* Usually, by January the lake has —— hard enough to skate on. 13. frozen
14. *choose* No one could understand why Terry —— the striped one instead of the others. 14. chose
15. *swim* So far, Dena has —— fifteen laps around the pool.

10. rung 15. swum

USAGE

B. Correcting Verbs in the Wrong Tense. Number your paper 16–20. After the proper number, write the italicized verb in the correct tense.

EXAMPLE 1. He looked out the window and *sees* the storm approaching.
1. *saw*

16. Jan was late, so she *decides* to run the rest of the way. 16. decided
17. The man at the gate *takes* our tickets and said that we were just in time. 17. took
18. My uncle often travels in the Far East and *brought* me some fascinating souvenirs. 18. brings
19. When his mother told the little boy it was his bedtime, he *throws* a temper tantrum. 19. threw

20. The waitress brought my order and *asks* me if I wanted anything else. 20. asked

THE PRINCIPAL PARTS OF A VERB

Besides naming an action, a verb also shows its time. This expression of time by the verb is called *tense*. To express different times, a verb has different tenses. These tenses are formed from four *principal parts* of the verb.

18a. The principal parts of a verb are the *infinitive,* the *present participle,* the *past,* and the *past participle.*

From these four principal parts all the tenses of our language are formed. The four principal parts of *sing* are *sing* (infinitive), *singing* (present participle), *sang* (past), and *sung* (past participle). Notice in the following sentences how the four principal parts are used to express time.

I **sing** in the school glee club.
We **are singing** at the music festival tonight.
Mahalia Jackson **sang** gospels at Carnegie Hall.
We **have sung** all over the state.

Here are the principal parts of two familiar verbs:

INFINITIVE	PRESENT PARTICIPLE	PAST	PAST PARTICIPLE
work	working	worked	(have) worked
eat	eating	ate	(have) eaten

Notice that the present participle always ends in *-ing*. The past participle is the form used with *has, have,* or *had.*

THE SIX TENSES

By using the four principal parts of the verb, along with various helping verbs, you can form six tenses for every verb. When you give the forms for the six tenses of a verb, you are *conjugating* that verb.

USAGE

THE PRINCIPAL PARTS OF A VERB (rule 18a)

For less-advanced students, you may wish to simplify the presentation of principal parts. Since your goal is to help students use correct forms of the past tense and past participle, you can omit the present participle (which does not cause any special problems). Have students study verbs using this formula: "Today I *begin;* Yesterday I *began;* Often I have *begun.*" Some teachers use the names *first, second,* and *third* form in order to avoid terms such as *infinitive, participle,* and *tense.*

Show your students how to use the dictionary to find principal parts that have irregular formations or spellings (see text page 607).

THE SIX TENSES

If your students are taking foreign languages, ask the language teachers how they are presenting conjugations. If you can agree on form, it will be less confusing to students. Present material on conjugation before the foreign language teacher does so that the students learn it first in their native tongue. There is no point in asking students to *memorize* the conjugation of verbs in their own language. The sample conjugation in the textbook is given merely to show that all tenses are based on the four principal parts.

Note: Avoid a discussion of shall *and* will. *Today, respected speakers and writers rarely use* shall.

Conjugation of Write

Principal parts: write, writing, wrote, (have) written.

Present Tense

Singular	*Plural*
I write	we write
you write	you write
he, she, *or* it writes	they write

Past Tense

Singular	*Plural*
I wrote	we wrote
you wrote	you wrote
he, she, *or* it wrote	they wrote

Future Tense

Singular	*Plural*
I will (shall) write	we will (shall) write
you will write	you will write
he, she, *or* it will write	they will write

Present Perfect Tense

Singular	*Plural*
I have written	we have written
you have written	you have written
he, she, *or* it has written	they have written

Past Perfect Tense

Singular	*Plural*
I had written	we had written
you had written	you had written
he, she, *or* it had written	they had written

Future Perfect Tense

Singular	*Plural*
I will (shall) have written	we will (shall) have written
you will have written	you will have written
he, she, *or* it will have written	they will have written

REGULAR VERBS

18b. A regular verb forms its past and past participle by adding *-ed* or *-d* to the present form.

INFINITIVE	PRESENT PARTICIPLE	PAST	PAST PARTICIPLE
follow	following	followed	(have) followed
date	dating	dated	(have) dated
miss	missing	missed	(have) missed

Pay careful attention to pronunciation of the past and past participle. Avoid nonstandard pronunciation, which usually follows two patterns: (1) adding an extra syllable—*drownded* for *drowned, attackted* for *attacked;* (2) not pronouncing the *-ed* ending—*ask* for *asked, suppose* for *supposed.*

EXERCISE 1. *Oral Drill.* Forming the Past and Past Participle Forms of Regular Verbs. Use the following verbs in sentences. Put each verb in the past tense, or use the past participle and the helping verb *have* or *has.* Oral drill. Sentences will vary. Past tense is shown.

1. hope
2. talk
3. call
4. gallop
5. walk
6. own
7. decide
8. finish
9. support
10. love

1. hoped 2. talked 3. called 4. galloped 5. walked 6. owned 7. decided 8. finished 9. supported 10. loved

IRREGULAR VERBS

18c. An *irregular verb* forms its past and past participle in a different way than a regular verb does.

Irregular verbs form their past and past participle in several ways:

1. by a vowel change: *ring, rang,* (have) *rung*
2. by a consonant change: *make, made,* (have) *made*
3. by a vowel and consonant change: *bring, brought,* (have) *brought*
4. by no change: *burst, burst,* (have) *burst*

REGULAR VERBS (rule 18b)

Emphasize that *most* verbs are regular. Because students spend more time on irregular verbs, they sometimes think that these are more numerous.

Sometimes students fail to write the past tense suffix when it is not distinctly sounded in everyday speech. Write on the board the following words, asking the class to give attention to the endings.

voted
recited
protested
discussed
supposed, used
experienced
asked, risked
supposed to, used to
pleased the, pierced the

Although the endings may be hard to say and hard to hear, the *–d* or *–ed* is an important eye signal in writing, and its omission is a serious error.

EXERCISE 1. Emphasize that a person's speech can make an impression on others. Encourage your students to pronounce carefully the verb forms in their sentences.

IRREGULAR VERBS (rule 18c)

A class that has trouble with almost all the verbs on the list (text pages 446 and 447) should study a few verbs at a time instead of attacking the whole list at once. Divide the list into groups of four or five words each. Then spend a week on each group, giving five minutes each day to oral drill. Four of the verbs on the list (*lie, rise, set, sit*) receive special attention in the next section of this chapter.

If you do not know the principal parts of irregular verbs, you may make errors like this:

NONSTANDARD She has drank all her milk. [*Drunk,* not *drank,* is the past participle.]

To avoid errors, memorize the principal parts of irregular verbs. Include *have* with the past participle.

Irregular Verbs Frequently Misused

INFINITIVE	PRESENT PARTICIPLE	PAST	PAST PARTICIPLE
begin	beginning	began	(have) begun
blow	blowing	blew	(have) blown
break	breaking	broke	(have) broken
bring	bringing	brought	(have) brought
burst	bursting	burst	(have) burst
choose	choosing	chose	(have) chosen
come	coming	came	(have) come
do	doing	did	(have) done
drink	drinking	drank	(have) drunk
drive	driving	drove	(have) driven
eat	eating	ate	(have) eaten
fall	falling	fell	(have) fallen
freeze	freezing	froze	(have) frozen
give	giving	gave	(have) given
go	going	went	(have) gone
know	knowing	knew	(have) known
lie	lying	lay	(have) lain
ride	riding	rode	(have) ridden
ring	ringing	rang	(have) rung
rise	rising	rose	(have) risen
run	running	ran	(have) run
see	seeing	saw	(have) seen
set	setting	set	(have) set
shrink	shrinking	shrank	(have) shrunk
sing	singing	sang	(have) sung

sit	sitting	sat	(have) sat
speak	speaking	spoke	(have) spoken
steal	stealing	stole	(have) stolen
swim	swimming	swam	(have) swum
take	taking	took	(have) taken
throw	throwing	threw	(have) thrown
write	writing	wrote	(have) written

Caution: Be careful not to confuse irregular verbs with regular ones. Never say *knowed, throwed, shrinked,* or *bursted.*

EXERCISE 2. Writing the Past and Past Participle Forms of Irregular Verbs. As your teacher or a classmate reads aloud to you the infinitive forms of the thirty-two irregular verbs just listed, write the past and the past participle forms on your paper.
Written drill.

Merely knowing the principal parts of irregular verbs is not enough. You need to practice using them in sentence patterns. Use the following example to help you practice usage of irregular verbs.

Today I **bring** lunch.
Yesterday I **brought** lunch.
Often I **have brought** lunch.

EXERCISE 3. Identifying the Correct Forms of Irregular Verbs. Number your paper 1–10. Choose the correct one of the two verbs in parentheses, and write it after the proper number. After your paper has been corrected, read each sentence *aloud* several times.

EXAMPLE 1. The bread (rised, rose) as it cooked.
1. *rose*

1. Ray Charles, a blind musician, has (wrote, written) many beautiful songs.
2. Olympic champion Mary Lou Retton (began, begun) her gymnastics training when she was eight years old.
3. Leigh (did, done) everything the instructions said.
4. She (knew, knowed) we had planned a busy day.

USAGE

EXERCISE 2. With less-advanced students, use this exercise to go over short sections of the list rather than the whole list at one time.

EXERCISE 3. Be sure students do have an opportunity to read aloud the corrected sentences or to hear them read aloud.

EXERCISE 4 and REVIEW EXERCISE A. With a less-advanced class you may wish to rely chiefly on oral drill rather than on written work to teach correct usage.

5. Maria Tallchief (chose, choosed) a career as a dancer.
6. My woolen socks (shrinked, shrank) when I washed them in hot water.
7. He (eat, ate) chicken salad on whole-wheat bread for lunch.
8. The monkey had (stole, stolen) the food from its brother.
9. Henry and Tonya (sang, sung) a duet in the talent show.
10. The shy turtle (came, come) closer to me to reach the lettuce I was holding.

EXERCISE 4. Writing the Past and Past Participle Forms of Verbs. Number your paper 1–20. After the proper number, write the past or the past participle of the verb given before each sentence to complete the sentence correctly.

EXAMPLE 1. *do* Nobody knew why he —— that.
1. *did*

USAGE

1. *ring* The telephone —— while I was in the shower. 1. rang
2. *throw* The outfielder —— the ball to home plate. 2. threw
3. *swim* Diana Nyad —— sixty miles from the Bahama Islands to Florida. 3. swam
4. *choose* Did he say why he had —— that one? 4. chosen
5. *drive* We have —— all night to attend my sister's college graduation exercises. 5. driven
6. *write* I have —— a letter of complaint to the manufacturer. 6. written
7. *drown* He would have —— if the lifeguard hadn't noticed the splashing in the waves. 7. drowned
8. *give* Kay —— her dog a reward after each trick. 8. gave
9. *know* She —— that she could run the three-mile race. 9. knew
10. *run* On the day of the race, she —— the course in less than twenty minutes. 10. ran
11. *drink* After she finished the race, she —— three glasses of water. 11. drank
12. *break* He —— his arm when he fell on the pavement. 12. broke
13. *burst* The balloon —— when it strayed too near the flame. 13. burst

14. *freeze* The catfish —— in the pond last winter. 14. froze
15. *go* I have —— from one room to another looking for my lost shoe. 15. gone
16. *blow* The siren —— long and loud to warn the residents of danger. 16. blew
17. *ride* Uncle Olaf —— his snowmobile up to the remote mountain cabin. 17. rode
18. *sit* Peter —— quietly throughout the entire discussion. 18. sat
19. *see* Marianne —— that he disagreed with her. 19. saw
20. *steal* Our dog had —— a steak from the grill while we were inside. 20. stolen

REVIEW EXERCISE A. Proofreading Sentences for Correct Verb Forms. Number your paper 1–20. Write *C* after the number of each correct sentence. Write the correct form of the verb after the number of each incorrect sentence.

EXAMPLES 1. I broke a water glass.
1. *C*
2. We rung the door bell.
2. *rang*

1. Sally give me a menu from the new downtown restaurant. 1. gave
2. I had spoke to my parents last week about trying this restaurant. 2. spoken
3. We had never went there before. 3. gone
4. My big brother Mark drived us there in Mom's car. 4. drove
5. We had almost reached the restaurant when Mark hit a curb. 5. C
6. We falled off the curb with a big bounce. 6. fell
7. We all seen that he was very embarrassed. 7. saw
8. I shrinked down in the back seat so he wouldn't notice that I was laughing. 8. shrank
9. When we arrived at the restaurant, I runned ahead of everyone to tell the hostess we needed five seats. 9. ran
10. The waiter had brought our menus before we all sit down. 10. sat
11. We drunk water with lemon slices in the glasses. 11. drank
12. Have you ever ate spaghetti with clam sauce? 12. eaten

USAGE

13. Dad chose the ravioli. 13. C
14. My little sister Emily taked two helpings of salad. 14. took
15. The waiter bringed out our dinners on a huge platter as soon as we finished our salads. 15. brought
16. Mark give me a taste of his eggplant parmigiana. 16. gave
17. Emily stealed a bite of my lasagna. 17. stole
18. Mom breaked the last breadstick in half so that Emily and I could share it. 18. broke
19. Dad writed on the bill that the food was delicious and the service was excellent. 19. wrote
20. We had made a good decision to try that new restaurant. 20. C

SPECIAL PROBLEMS WITH VERBS

Sit and *Set*

Study the principal parts of the verbs *sit* and *set.* Notice that *sit* changes to form the past tense, but *set* remains the same in the past and the past participle.

INFINITIVE	PRESENT PARTICIPLE	PAST	PAST PARTICIPLE
sit (to rest)	sitting	sat	(have) sat
set (to place)	setting	set	(have) set

Sit and *set* are often confused. You will not make mistakes with these two verbs if you remember two facts about them:

(1) *Sit* means "to rest in an upright, seated position," while *set* means "to put or place (something)."

Let's **sit** under the tree.
Let's **set** the bookcase here.

The tourists **sat** on benches.
The children **set** the dishes on the table.

We **had sat** down to eat when the telephone rang.
We **have set** the reading lamp beside the couch.

USAGE

SPECIAL PROBLEMS WITH VERBS

For each of the troublesome pairs presented here, try this procedure: First make certain that your students understand the difference *in meaning;* then have them repeat the principal parts of each verb so often that the correct verb form automatically comes to mind. For example (present participle forms are omitted):

I *sit* down now.
I *sat* down yesterday.
I *have sat* down many times.

I *set* the chair there now.
I *set* it there yesterday.
I *have set* it there many times.

I *lie* on the floor now.
I *lay* there yesterday.
I *have lain* there many times.

I *lay* the book down now.
I *laid* it down yesterday.
I *have laid* it down many times.

I *rise* from my seat now.
I *rose* from it yesterday.
I *have risen* from it many times.

I *raise* the flag now.
I *raised* it yesterday.
I *have raised* it many times.

Give as much drill as you consider necessary, keeping in mind that classes vary widely in their need for it.

EXERCISES 5 and 6. When you find that students have serious difficulty distinguishing between the two verbs in a sound-alike pair, it is a good idea to drill them on each verb separately. In Exercise 5, for instance, select sentences requiring a form of the verb *sit* (sentences 1, 2, and 5, plus the last clause in sentence 8) and drill on these sentences first. Then use the other sentences for drill on the verb *set*. Do not introduce drills that mix the two verbs until students have learned each verb separately.

(2) *Sit* is almost never followed by an object, but *set* often does take an object.

My aunt **sits** in the large chair. [no object]
She **sets** the chair in the corner. [Sets what? *Chair* is the object.]

The audience **sat** near the stage. [no object]
The stagehand **set** a microphone near the Judds. [Set what? *Microphone* is the object.]

EXERCISE 5. *Oral Drill.* Using the Forms of *Sit* and *Set* Correctly. Read each sentence aloud, paying close attention to the meaning of *sit* and *set*. Pronounce each verb distinctly.
Oral drill.

1. Let's sit down here.
2. Look at the dog sitting on the porch.
3. Our teacher set a deadline for our term projects.
4. Have you set the clock?
5. I have always sat in the front row.
6. Please set the carton down inside the doorway.
7. She has set a high standard for her work.
8. After I set the mop in the closet, I sat down to rest.

USAGE

EXERCISE 6. Using the Correct Forms of *Sit* and *Set*. Number your paper 1–10. After the proper number, write the correct one of the two words in parentheses. If the verb you choose is a form of *set*, write its object after it.

EXAMPLE 1. Please (sit, set) the serving platter on the table.
1. *set, platter*

1. Will you (sit, set) down here?
2. It's Aaron's turn to (sit, set) the table for dinner.
3. Carolyn (sat, set) her notebook on the kitchen counter.
4. I have been (sitting, setting) here all day.
5. (Sit, Set) the fine crystal in the china cabinet.
6. The referee is (sitting, setting) the ball on the fifty-yard line.
7. The cat cautiously (sat, set) beside the Great Dane.

EXERCISES 7 and 8. See notes for Exercises 5 and 6.

8. Zachary (sits, sets) up in bed at night while he reads another chapter from his library book.
9. Let's (sit, set) that aside until later.
10. They have been (sitting, setting) there for fifteen minutes without saying a word to each other.

Lie and *Lay*

Study the principal parts of *lie* and *lay*.

INFINITIVE	PRESENT PARTICIPLE	PAST	PAST PARTICIPLE
lie (to recline)	lying	lay	(have) lain
lay (to put)	laying	laid	(have) laid

USAGE

Like *sit, lie*[1] has to do with resting, and it has no object. *Lay* is like *set* because it means "to put (something) down" and because it may have an object.

The cows **are lying** in the shade. [no object]
The workers **are laying** the foundation for the building. [*Are laying* what? *Foundation* is the object.]

The soldiers **lay** very still while the enemy passed by. [No object—*lay* here is the past tense of *lie.*]
The soldiers **laid** a trap for the enemy. [*Laid* what? *Trap* is the object.]

The injured man **had lain** in the cave for weeks. [no object]
The lawyer **had laid** the newspaper next to her briefcase. [*Had laid* what? *Newspaper* is the object.]

EXERCISE 7. *Oral Drill.* Using the Forms of *Lie* and *Lay* Correctly. Read each of the following sentences aloud several times. Be able to explain why the verb is correct. Oral drill.

1. The delegates laid the groundwork for future conferences.
2. Don't lie in the sun too long!
3. You shouldn't lay your papers on the couch.

[1] The verb *lie* meaning "to tell a falsehood" is a different word. Its past forms are regular: *lie, lying, lied, lied.*

4. The lion had been lying in wait for an hour.
5. The senator laid her notes aside after her speech.
6. He had lain still for a few minutes.
7. He has laid his books on his desk.
8. Our cat lies on the radiator.
9. She lays the sharp knives on the top shelf.
10. The exhausted swimmer lay helpless on the sand.

EXERCISE 8. Writing the Correct Forms of *Lie* and *Lay*. Number your paper 1–10. After the proper number, write the correct form of *lie* or *lay* for each of these sentences.

1. The television journalist —— aside her career while her children were young. 1. laid
2. My dad was —— down when I asked for my allowance. 2. lying
3. We need to —— down some club rules. 3. lay
4. Have you ever —— on a water bed? 4. lain
5. Andrew had —— his keys beside his wallet. 5. laid
6. My cat loves to —— in the tall grass behind our house. 6. lie
7. My brother left his clothes —— on the floor until they began to smell. 7. lying
8. Yesterday that alligator —— in the sun all day. 8. lay
9. The groundskeeper has —— new sod on the golf course.
10. The newspaper had —— in the yard until the sun faded it.

9. laid 10. lain

EXERCISE 9. Writing Sentences Using Forms of *Lie* and *Lay*. Use each of the following verbs or verb phrases correctly in a sentence of your own. Answers will vary.

1. lies	5. lays	9. will lie
2. laid	6. has been lying	10. are lying
3. was laying	7. lay (past tense of *lie*)	
4. has lain	8. have laid	

Rise and *Raise*

Study the principal parts of *rise* and *raise*.

EXERCISE 9. You may want less-advanced students to write only five sentences. Do some examples on the board before assigning the exercise, and share some of the students' correct sentences with the class.

USAGE

EXERCISES 10–12. See notes for Exercises 5 and 6.

INFINITIVE	PRESENT PARTICIPLE	PAST	PAST PARTICIPLE
rise (to go up)	rising	rose	(have) risen
raise (to lift up)	raising	raised	(have) raised

The verb *rise* means "to go up" or "to get up." Rise, like *lie,* never has an object. *Raise,* which means "to lift up" or "to cause to rise," usually, like *lay,* has an object.

My neighbors **rise** very early in the morning. [no object]
Every morning they **raise** their shades to let the sunlight in. [*Raise* what? *Shades* is the object.]

The moon **rose** slowly last night. [no object]
Last year Ana and Bill **raised** corn and tomatoes in their garden. [*Raised* what? *Corn* and *tomatoes* are the objects.]

The senators **have risen** from their seats to show respect for the Chief Justice. [no object]
The wind **has raised** a cloud of dust. [*Has raised* what? *Cloud* is the object.]

USAGE

EXERCISE 10. *Oral Drill.* Using the Correct Forms of *Rise* and *Raise*. Repeat each of the following correct sentences aloud several times, stressing the italicized verbs and thinking of the meanings of the verbs. Oral drill.

1. The reporters *rise* when the President enters the room.
2. The reporters *raise* their hands to be recognized.
3. The reporter who was recognized *rose* to her feet.
4. She *has raised* an interesting question.
5. Another reporter *was rising*.
6. Several reporters *rose* at the same time.
7. Who *had risen* first?
8. Will Congress *raise* taxes this year?

EXERCISE 11. Writing the Correct Forms of *Rise* and *Raise*. Number your paper 1–10. After the proper number, write the correct one of the two verbs in parentheses. If the verb you choose is a form of *raise*, write its object after it.

1. The steam was (rising, raising) from the pot of hot chicken soup on the stove.
2. That comment (rises, raises) a very good question.
3. The child's fever (rose, raised) during the night; she seems much better this morning.
4. The sun (rises, raises) later each morning.
5. The teacher will call only on students who (rise, raise) their hands.
6. We must (rise, raise) the flag in the courtyard each morning before school begins.
7. The student body's interest in this subject has (risen, raised) to new heights.
8. The kite has (risen, raised) above the power lines.
9. My father promised to (rise, raise) my allowance if I pull the weeds.
10. The department store (rose, raised) the price on that clock radio last week.

USAGE

EXERCISE 12. Writing the Correct Forms of *Rise* and *Raise*. Number your paper 1–10. After the proper number, write the correct form of *rise* or *raise* in each blank in the following paragraphs.

We girls —1— early to start our hike to Lookout Mountain. From our position at the foot of the mountain, it looked as though it —2— straight up to the heavens. 1. rose 2. rose 3. risen

But we had not —3— at daybreak just to look at the high peak. We —4— our supply packs to our backs and started the long climb up the mountain. With every step we took, the mountain seemed to —5— that much higher. Finally, after several hours, we reached the summit and —6— a special flag that we had brought for the occasion. When our friends at the foot of the mountain saw the flag —7— , they knew that we had reached the top safely. They —8— their arms and shouted. 4. raised 5. rise

Our friends' shouts were like an applause that seemed to —9— from the valley below. Then we felt glad that we had —10— early enough to climb to the top of Lookout Mountain.
6. raised 7. rise (*or* raised) 8. raised 9. rise 10. risen

REVIEW EXERCISE B. You may use this exercise as a test on the three troublesome verb pairs.

WRITING APPLICATION A: Using Irregular Verbs Correctly When Writing About Experiences in the Past

When you talk with other people and when you write, you often deal with past personal experiences. One of the most common errors in English usage is misuse of the past and past participle forms of irregular verbs. Since these verbs do not add a simple *-ed* for the past tense, you have to memorize their correct forms.

EXAMPLE Drivers in England *have* always *drove* on the left side of the street. [The past participle *driven* should be used with the helping verb *have.*]

Drivers in England *have* always *driven* on the left side of the street. [The error in agreement is corrected.]

USAGE

Writing Assignment

Answers will vary.

Select several of the irregular verbs discussed in this chapter. Using their correct forms, write a paragraph about a personal experience. Following are some ideas.

Learning to Swim	A Horseback Ride
Making Ice Cream	The Time I Ate Too Much

REVIEW EXERCISE B. Using the Correct Forms of *Sit* and *Set*, *Lie* and *Lay*, and *Rise* and *Raise*. Number your paper 1–25. Choose the correct verb from the two in parentheses, and write it after the proper number. If a sentence has two verbs, write both of them on the same line in the order in which they occur. Be prepared to explain your choices in class.

1. The sun has (risen, raised), and you are still (lying, laying) in bed.
2. While their grandmother (sat, set) in the shade, Marilyn and Ed (sat, set) the table for the picnic.

3. The water level has not (risen, raised) since last summer.
4. Cooks often (lie, lay) their spoons in special spoon rests.
5. Key West (lies, lays) off the southwestern coast of Florida.
6. To study how solar energy works, our class (sit, set) a solar panel outside the window of our classroom.
7. The golfer carefully (sits, sets) the ball on the tee.
8. Since I have gotten taller, I have (rose, raised) the seat on my bicycle.
9. We all (sit, set) in alphabetical order in algebra class.
10. (Lie, Lay) the grass mats on the sand so that we can (lie, lay) on them.
11. (Sit, Set) the groceries on the table while I start dinner.
12. The squirrels (rose, raised) their heads when they heard me tapping on the window.
13. (Rise, Raise) the car higher so that we can change the tire.
14. When the sun (rises, raises), I sometimes have difficulty (sitting, setting) aside my covers and getting up.
15. When the sun had (sit, set), I wearily (lay, laid) on the hard earth in my tent.
16. I (lay, laid) my flashlight beside my sleeping bag.
17. My dog Beau (lay, laid) just outside the tent.
18. We (sat, set) under a beach umbrella.
19. Mr. DeLemos (lay, laid) the foundation for our new patio.
20. Your grades must (rise, raise), or you will not make the honor roll this term.
21. Would you please (sit, set) the sofa down here?
22. The people in front of me (raised, rose) up in their seats.
23. You'd better (sit, set) down while I tell you this.
24. He left his books (lying, laying) on the table.
25. The crane (rose, raised) the steel beam into place.

CONSISTENCY OF TENSE

You should never shift tenses needlessly. When you are writing about events in the past tense, you should use the past tense

USAGE

CONSISTENCY OF TENSE (rule 18d)

Shifting tenses needlessly is an error many eighth-grade students make. The class may comprehend the concept behind the rule and do correctly all the drills, but you may still find inconsistent use of tenses in their written work. The only way to correct the error is by checking written work and continuing to provide constant drill.

An excellent source for extra drill in tense shift is the composition work the students submit. Copy sentences that contain errors involving tense sequence and give each student a sheet of errors to correct. You could also use an overhead projector, letting the class correct the errors.

EXERCISE 13. You may wish to have students write this exercise. If so, do the first two sentences as examples, making it clear that the past tense is required.

consistently unless there is a reason to change tenses. You should not shift without reason to the present tense.

18d. Do not change needlessly from one tense to another.

NONSTANDARD After we were comfortable, we begin to do our homework. [*Were* is past tense and *begin* is present.]

STANDARD After we **were** comfortable, we **began** to do our homework. [Both *were* and *began* are in the past tense.]

NONSTANDARD Suddenly the great door opened, and an uninvited guest comes into the dining hall. [*Opened* is past tense and *comes* is present.]

STANDARD Suddenly the great door **opens,** and an uninvited guest **comes** into the dining hall. [Both *opens* and *comes* are in the present tense.]

STANDARD Suddenly the great door **opened,** and an uninvited guest **came** into the dining hall. [Both *opened* and *came* are in the past tense.]

USAGE

EXERCISE 13. Proofreading a Paragraph to Make the Tenses of the Verbs Consistent. Read the following paragraph, and decide what tense you should use to tell about the events. Prepare to read the paragraph aloud, making the verb tense consistent throughout. See Answer Key.

At my grandparents' house that morning, I wake up before anyone else and quietly grabbed the fishing pole and head for the pond. Across the water, I saw ripples. "I have to catch the fish," I say to myself. I threw my lure near where I see the ripples and reeled in the line. The fish don't seem interested. I saw more ripples and throw the line in the water again. "I've got a strike!" I shout to the trees around me. As I reeled in the line, a beautiful trout jumps out of the water and spit out the hook. Discouraged, I go back to the house. Grandpa was sitting at the table with a bowl of hot oatmeal for me. I say, "Maybe tomorrow we'll have trout for breakfast."

REVIEW EXERCISE C. This exercise provides further practice with irregular verb forms. You may wish to use it as a test.

WRITING APPLICATION B: Being Consistent in Using Verb Tenses

Every day you encounter many things that indicate the time, such as sunrise, bells, and alarm clocks. The way you signal the time to your readers is through the use of *tense.* Avoid shifting tenses unless you have a good reason. An important rule to remember is *be consistent.*

EXAMPLE In *The Secret Life of Walter Mitty,* by James Thurber, the main character *was henpecked* by his wife. [past tense] When she *fusses* at him, [present tense] he *will dream* about being some famous person. [future tense]

In this example, the tenses are not consistent. They switch from past to present to future. The example could be corrected by writing all three verbs in either the present or the past tense to make them consistent.

Writing Assignment

Answers will vary.

Select a story or book that you have read recently. Write a paragraph summarizing the plot. Proofread your paragraph to make sure that you have used verb tense consistently.

USAGE

REVIEW EXERCISE C. Using the Correct Verb and the Correct Verb Form. Number your paper 1–20. Write the correct one of the verb forms in parentheses from each sentence. Some sentences have more than one verb.

1. He (knew, knowed) he would not get his wish even though he (blew, blowed) out all his birthday candles.
2. Buffy Sainte-Marie has (sang, sung) professionally for more than twenty years.
3. Have you (began, begun) your homework yet?
4. Cindy Nicholas was the first woman who (swam, swum) the English Channel both ways.

REVIEW EXERCISE D. This exercise provides more practice with irregular verb forms. It can be used as a test.

5. I'm glad you (come, came) with us to the lake.
6. When the baby sitter (rose, raised) her voice, the children (knew, knowed) it was time to behave.
7. After we had (saw, seen) all the exhibits at the county fair, we (ate, eat) a snack and then (went, go) home.
8. The egg (burst, bursted) in the microwave oven.
9. I was very nervous when I (go, went) on the ski lift for the first time.
10. He (lay, laid) his lunch money on his desk.
11. When he tried to claim the money later, he found that it had been (stole, stolen).
12. The loud noise (breaked, broke) my concentration.
13. Grandma (give, gave) me a belt for my birthday.
14. For the creative writing assignment, I had (wrote, written) a story about my deep-sea fishing trip.
15. Robbie had (chose, chosen) to take band this year.
16. The thirsty plants (drank, drunk) all the rainwater.
17. The truck has (rode, ridden) over the rough country road with ease.
18. We had (rode, ridden) halfway across the desert when I began to wish I had (brought, brung) more water.
19. The oranges and grapefruit had (froze, frozen) on the trees last winter.
20. We liked that movie so much that we (sat, set) through it three times on Saturday.

USAGE

REVIEW EXERCISE D. Using the Correct Verb and the Correct Verb Form. Number your paper 1–10. After the proper number, write the form of the verb at the left that correctly fills the blank in each sentence.

1. *sing* Stevie Wonder —— at the concert hall here last week. 1. sang
2. *run* Have you ever —— in a race with Alberto Salazar? 2. run
3. *break* Pearl Moore —— a record in basketball by scoring 4,061 points during her college career. 3. broke

4. *fall* The newly hatched sparrow —— from its nest. 4. fell
5. *steal* The bandits —— over seven million dollars in cash. 5. stole
6. *shrink* The meat patties —— while they were being cooked. 6. shrank
7. *ring* The child cried each time a Halloween goblin —— the doorbell. 7. rang
8. *speak* Have you —— to the counselor about your schedule for next year? 8. spoken
9. *take* Who —— a bite from my blueberry muffin? 9. took
10. *do* He —— the best he could on the paper but received only a B for his efforts. 10. did

CHAPTER 18 REVIEW: POSTTEST

A. Writing the Past and Past Participle Forms of Verbs. Number your paper 1–15. After the proper number, write the past or past participle of the verb given before the sentence.

EXAMPLES 1. *run* The deer —— across the road in front of our car.
1. *ran*
2. *run* Her dog has —— away from home.
2. *run*

1. *shrink* The older girl —— from the responsibility of caring for her younger brothers and sister. 1. shrank
2. *write* Have you —— your history report yet? 2. written
3. *eat* I don't think I should have —— that last handful of sunflower seeds. 3. eaten
4. *sit* The blue jay that —— on the telephone wire called to its mate. 4. sat
5. *know* She is the nicest person I have ever —— . 5. known
6. *break* When the medicine finally began to work, his fever —— . 6. broke
7. *ring* That phone has —— every five minutes since I got home. 7. rung

USAGE

CHAPTER 18 REVIEW: POSTTEST

This test is divided into three parts: writing the past and past participle forms of verbs; determining the correct forms of *lie–lay, sit–set,* and *rise–raise;* and correcting verbs in the wrong tense.

8. *come* Earl thought and thought, but the answer never —— to him. 8. came
9. *freeze* If that had happened to me, I would have —— with fear. 9. frozen
10. *sing* Through the murky depths the whales —— to one another. 10. sang
11. *give* The coach —— us all a pep talk before the game. 11. gave
12. *begin* We knew that it would rain soon because the crickets had —— chirping. 12. begun
13. *take* That job shouldn't have —— you all day. 13. taken
14. *bring* Everyone else had —— along a warm sweater. 14. brought
15. *fall* Though he had —— from the top of the tree, the baby squirrel was all right. 15. fallen

USAGE

B. Writing the Correct Forms of *Lie—Lay, Sit—Set,* and *Rise—Raise* in Sentences. Number your paper 16–20. Choose the correct verb from the two verbs given in parentheses, and write it after the proper number on your paper.

EXAMPLE 1. My cat (lies, lays) around the house all day.
1. *lies*

16. We had to wait for the drawbridge to (rise, raise) before we could sail out to the bay.
17. (Sit, Set) that down in the chair, will you?
18. The treasure had (lay, lain) at the bottom of the ocean for more than four hundred years.
19. My grandfather and grandmother like to (sit, set) on the porch and talk.
20. Look on the other side of any logs (lying, laying) in the path to avoid stepping on a snake.

C. Correcting Verbs in the Wrong Tense. Number your paper 21–25. In each of the following sentences, the italicized verb is in the wrong tense. After the proper number, write the italicized verb in the correct tense.

EXAMPLE 1. My father looked at his watch and *decides* that it was time to leave.
1. *decided*

21. Marjorie's sister refused to give us a ride in her car, and then she *asks* us to loan her some money for gas. 21. asked
22. He says he's sorry, but he *didn't* mean it. 22. doesn't
23. The trees grow close together and *had* straight trunks. 23. have
24. When the show ended, we *get* up to leave, but a crowd had already gathered. 24. got
25. Several mechanics worked on my aunt's car before one of them finally *finds* the problem. 25. found

USAGE

Additional Practice

Teacher's Resource Book, Worksheet pages 202–33, Alternative Worksheet pages (for less-advanced students) 555–56

Testing

Teaching Tests booklet, pages 45–48, 51–52, 57–59, 61–63
Teacher's Resource Book, Test pages 443–46, 449–50, 457–68

Chapter Overview

Some of the errors covered in the chapter are careless mistakes—such as "him and me went" and "between you and I." If your students still make errors of this kind, concentrate on these first.

Some of the other errors explained here are usages often accepted in conversational English but out of place in most written English—such as "it was him." A class that already has a good command of standard conversational usage will usually be ready to master more formal usage. To find out where your own class stands, you can use the Diagnostic Test.

Note: The distinction between who *and* whom *is not covered in the eighth-grade textbook.*

Chapter Objective

Students will use the nominative and objective forms of personal pronouns correctly in both speaking and writing.

PRESENTING THE CHAPTER

LESS ADVANCED STUDENTS If these students still have difficulty using correct pronouns in compound subjects and objects (*he and I, him and me*), concentrate on this point. Give them the simple rule "Use the form you would use if the pronoun occurred alone." This class might skip rule 19b. *(See listing of Alternative Worksheets on page 475.)*

ADVANCED STUDENTS If these students make few errors in pronoun usage and do well on the Diagnostic Test, assign original writing similar to the writing application on

USAGE

CHAPTER 19

Using Pronouns Correctly

NOMINATIVE AND OBJECTIVE CASE FORMS

The case of a noun or a pronoun depends on how the noun or pronoun is used in the sentence. A word used as a subject is in the *nominative* case; a word used as an object is in the *objective* case; and a word used to show ownership or relationship is in the *possessive* case.

The case of nouns presents no problem because a noun has the same form in the nominative and objective cases.

The **woman** [nominative] said she saw another **woman** [objective] in the park.

The possessive case of a noun usually requires only the addition of an apostrophe and an *s*.

The **woman's** friend has arrived.

Personal pronouns, however, change form in the different cases.

DIAGNOSTIC TEST

Using Pronouns Correctly in Sentences. Number your paper 1–20. Write the correct one of the two pronouns in parentheses.

EXAMPLE 1. Just between you and (I, me), I think he's wrong.
1. *me*

1. When I got home, a package was waiting for (I, me).
2. Everyone thought that (she, her) was very intelligent.
3. We saw (they, them) riding their bikes to school.
4. The winners in the contest turned out to be Jill and (I, me).
5. The wasp flew in the window and bit (he, him) on the arm.
6. Elton and (she, her) will give reports this morning.
7. The two scouts who have earned the most merit badges are Angelo and (he, him).
8. Several people in my neighborhood helped (we, us) boys clear the empty lot and measure out a baseball diamond.
9. Nina has promised to give Ralph and (I, me) some help with our music lessons.
10. My father and (he, him) are planning to go into business together.
11. We thought that we'd be facing (they, them) in the finals.
12. May I sit next to Marvin and (he, him)?
13. After class the teacher asked Kim and (she, her) to help erase the chalkboard.
14. My little sister always gives (me, I) a lot of trouble.
15. Did you know that it was (I, me) who called?
16. Corey's mother and my father said that (we, us) could go on the field trip.
17. The bears wanted (we, us) to feed them our sandwiches.
18. Invite (she, her) and the new girl in class to the party.
19. We hoped that the job would fall to Leon and Greg instead of (we, us).
20. The best soloists in the band are (they, them), apparently.

THE CASE FORMS OF PERSONAL PRONOUNS

Study the following list of pronouns to see how their forms differ in the three cases.

page 471 to reinforce the concepts in this chapter.

WRITING APPLICATION

The writing application in this chapter is designed to encourage students to use pronouns correctly in their own writing. Feel free to adapt this assignment to your students' writing needs, abilities, and interests.

DIAGNOSTIC TEST

This test will give you a clear picture of what your students already know about identifying the correct forms of pronouns.

THE CASE FORMS OF PERSONAL PRONOUNS

A less-advanced class should study only the simplified list given in the middle of page 466. Some teachers of less-advanced students use the terms *subject form* and *object form* instead of *nominative case* and *objective case.*

An eighth-grade class that already has a firm understanding of the nominative and objective forms of pronouns should not be required to memorize and recite the list.

THE NOMINATIVE CASE (rules 19a and 19b)

Note that these two rules for the use of the nominative case cover several different levels of usage, ranging from the clearly nonstandard "him and me went" to the generally accepted "it's me." If your students still say "him and me went," concentrate on this error in teaching the section.

You probably already recognize that expressions like "we boys" sound prissy to many students. Eighth-graders may prefer to avoid such expressions in their written work, changing a sentence like "Us boys went downtown" simply to "*We* went downtown."

USAGE

Personal Pronouns

NOMINATIVE CASE	OBJECTIVE CASE	POSSESSIVE CASE
	Singular	
I	me	my, mine
you	you	your, yours
he, she, it	him, her, it	his, her, hers, its
	Plural	
we	us	our, ours
you	you	your, yours
they	them	their, theirs

The pronouns *you* and *it* cause few usage problems because their forms remain unchanged in the nominative and objective cases. The possessive case forms, which show ownership or relationship, need care in spelling. (See pages 562–63.) Omitting *you* and *it* and the possessive pronouns from the above list leaves the following pronouns, which have different forms in the nominative and objective cases. Memorize the list for each case.

NOMINATIVE CASE	OBJECTIVE CASE
I	me
he	him
she	her
we	us
they	them

THE NOMINATIVE CASE

19a. The subject of a verb is in the nominative case.

EXAMPLES **I** like music. [*I* is the subject of the verb *like.*]

He and **she** sold tickets. [*He* and *she* are the subjects of the verb *sold.*]

They called while **we** were away. [*They* is the subject of *called; we* is the subject of *were.*]

EXERCISES 1 and 2. A class that does not make errors with these usages may omit the exercises.

Pronoun usage errors occur most frequently when the subject is compound. It is easy to say, "Lois and me study together" when you should say, "Lois and I study together." "Lois and I" is a compound subject. If you test the pronoun by itself with the verb, you can tell which form is correct.

EXAMPLE Lois and me study together. [me study—nonstandard]
Lois and **I** study together. [I study—standard]

Use the same test in sentences such as "We girls work together" and "Us girls work together." Use the pronouns alone before the verb. "Us work together" is incorrect. "We work together" is correct; consequently, "We girls work together" is correct.

EXERCISE 1. *Oral Drill.* Practicing Correct Pronoun Usage. Read the following sentences aloud, stressing the italicized pronouns. Oral drill.

1. *He* and *she* collect seashells.
2. My grandmother and *I* are painting the boat.
3. Both *they* and *we* were frightened.
4. Did Sally or *she* answer the phone?
5. *We* girls are giving a fashion show.
6. *You* and *I* will stay behind.
7. Where are *he* and *she*?
8. My parents and *they* are good friends.

EXERCISE 2. Writing Pronouns in Sentences. Number your paper 1–10. Beside the proper number, write a pronoun that will correctly fill each blank. Use a variety of pronouns. Don't use *you* or *it*. Answers will vary.

EXAMPLE 1. —— and —— will have a debate.
1. *We, they*

1. Yesterday she and —— went shopping.
2. Our cousins and —— are ready for the race.
3. Neither —— nor Kathy was nominated.
4. —— and Margie have copies of the book.
5. When are —— and —— coming?

Predicate Nominative (rule 19b)

The rule about predicate nominatives is often ignored in informal spoken English. An advanced class may be taught that the rule *does* apply to standard written English, including t heir own composition work. (The one exception might be written dialogue, which is supposed to reflect realistic spoken usage.)

EXERCISE 3. Have the answers to this exercise read aloud. It is important that students hear the formally correct forms often enough to become accustomed to the way they sound.

6. Everyone remembers when —— won the big game.
7. Someone said that —— and —— are finalists.
8. Did you or —— ride in the hot-air balloon?
9. Both —— and —— gave excellent speeches.
10. Has —— or Eduardo seen that movie?

19b. A predicate nominative is in the nominative case.

A *predicate nominative* is a noun or a pronoun that completes the meaning of a linking verb. A pronoun used as a predicate nominative usually follows a form of the verb *be* (*am, is, are, was, were*) or a verb phrase ending in *be* or *been,* such as *will be* or *has been.*

Read these examples aloud; stress the boldfaced words.

The speakers are **she** and **I.** [*She* and *I* are predicate nominatives following the linking verb *are.*]

Do you think it was **they**? [*They* is a predicate nominative following the linking verb *was.*]

EXERCISE 3. Identifying Correct Pronoun Usage for Predicate Nominatives. Number your paper 1–10. Write the linking verb in each sentence; then write the correct pronoun.

EXAMPLE 1. It was (I, me) at the door.
1. *was, I*

1. We hoped it was (her, she).
2. That stranger thinks I am (she, her).
3. Luckily, it was not (them, they) in the accident.
4. It could have been (she, her) that he called.
5. Everyone believed it was (we, us) students.
6. It might have been (him, he), but I'm not sure.
7. Our opponents could have been (them, they).
8. I thought it was (they, them) to whom he spoke.
9. If the singer had been (her, she), I would have listened.
10. Was that Claudia or (she, her)?

> ☞ **USAGE NOTE** You should understand two facts about English usage. First, some usages are acceptable in conversational English, but not in written English. Second, from time to time usage changes, so that expressions that were once considered nonstandard may become standard. The application of rule 19b provides examples of both these facts. The expressions *It's me, That's her, It was them,* etc., although they violate the rule, have now become acceptable spoken English. In writing, however, standard usage still follows the rule.

SPOKEN No one would believe it was her. (him, etc.)
WRITTEN No one would believe it was she. (he, etc.)

Of course, it would be correct to use *she* in speaking, even though *her* is acceptable.

In doing the exercises in this book, base your answers on the usage of written English.

THE OBJECTIVE CASE

19c. Direct and indirect objects of a verb are in the objective case.

EXAMPLES You surprised **us.** [*Us* is the object of the verb *surprised.*]

Our neighbor gave **her** and **me** a job. [*Her* and *me* are indirect objects; they tell *to whom* our neighbor gave a job.]

The ranger guided **us** boys to the camp. [*Us* is the object of the verb *guided.* Using the pronoun alone after the verb shows that the ranger guided *us* (not *we*) to the camp.]

Most errors in the use of the objective case occur when the object is compound. You can often avoid making an error with a compound object by trying each pronoun separately with the verb, as in the following example.

USAGE

THE OBJECTIVE CASE (rules 19c and 19d)

You may wish to begin with a review of objects of the verb, which were studied in Chapter 13. Explain that a pronoun following a verb is usually in the objective case. Predicate nominatives are comparatively rare. Normal word order for a huge percentage of English sentences follows these patterns:

SUBJECT	VERB
Kathryn	met

DIRECT OBJECT
Marvin and him.

SUBJECT	VERB
Kathryn	gave

INDIRECT OBJECT	DIRECT OBJECT
Marvin and him	the assignment.

Ask your students to write original sentences with compound objects containing pronouns, following the patterns above.

The mistaken use of nominative forms where objective forms are needed ("Clyde thanked she and I") is usually a result of overcorrection. Many students get the idea that nominative forms like "she and I" or "we boys" are always more acceptable than "her and me" or "us boys." Remind students to use the form they would use if the pronoun occurred alone—"thanked *her,*" "thanked *me,*" "thanked *her and me.*"

EXERCISE 4. By stressing the italicized pronouns, your students will become accustomed to correct usage of object pronouns.

EXERCISE 5. If your students seem to have mastered the use of pronouns as objects of verbs, you might omit this exercise.

The representative met (she, her) and (he, him).

NONSTANDARD The representative met she.
The representative met he.

STANDARD The representative met **her.**
The representative met **him.**
The representative met **her** and **him.**

EXERCISE 4. *Oral Drill.* Practicing Correct Pronoun Usage for Objects. Read the following sentences aloud at least twice, stressing the italicized pronouns. Oral drill.

1. The hot soup burned Gail and *me.*
2. Karen showed *her* and Allen her houseplants.
3. The dog followed *her* and *him* to school.
4. Did you expect *us* or *them*?
5. The doctor gave *her* and *me* flu shots.
6. Let's help Sarah and *him* with their chores.
7. Have you seen the Romanos or *them*?

USAGE

EXERCISE 5. Writing Pronouns as Direct and Indirect Objects. Number your paper 1–10. Write a correct pronoun for each blank. Use a variety of pronouns, but do not use *you* and *it.* When your answers have been checked, read aloud at least three times the corrected form of each sentence you missed.
Answers will vary.

EXAMPLE 1. The teacher asked —— some hard questions.
1. *us*

1. The judges picked —— and —— as the winners.
2. They asked —— and Ms. Shore for permission.
3. Rita can usually find Alberto and —— at our house.
4. Did you know Jarvis and —— ?
5. My grandmother helped —— girls make homemade bread.
6. Aunt Aggie took —— and —— to the zoo.
7. The driver left my sister and —— at the corner.
8. Should we call Mark and —— ?
9. Do you remember —— and —— ?
10. The dog chased Adam and —— .

WRITING APPLICATION: Using Pronouns Correctly in Compound Subjects and Objects

Have you ever seen someone whose socks didn't match? When you are in a hurry, sometimes it's easy to make a mistake. Pronoun usage errors often occur when writers are in too much of a hurry. These mistakes are particularly easy to make when a subject or an object is compound.

EXAMPLE Me and Jana waited for a tennis court so that we could play. [The pronoun *me* should not be used as the subject of a verb.]

Jana and I waited for a tennis court so that we could play. [The nominative case pronoun *I* is correct as the subject of the verb *waited.*]

Writing Assignment

Answers will vary.

Write a paragraph about an incident that involved you and a friend. Supply details that make this incident memorable. Include two compound subjects and two compound objects. Underline these constructions. Be sure to use nominative case pronouns for subjects and objective case pronouns for objects.

19d. The object of a preposition is in the objective case.

A prepositional phrase begins with a preposition and ends with an object, which is always a noun or a pronoun. When the object is a pronoun, you must be careful to use the objective case. Note the case of the objects in the following prepositional phrases.

with **me**	near **her**	except **them**
to **him**	by **us**	for **us**

Most errors in usage occur when the object of the preposition is compound. Notice that in the prepositional phrases in the following exercise all pronouns are in the objective case.

Objects of Prepositions (rule 19d)

Since these pronouns raise the same kind of problem as pronouns that are objects of verbs (rule 19c), you can probably teach the two rules together. Note that pronouns after *between* sometimes confuse students. Remind the class that *between* is a preposition. You may wish to give them the following rhyme as a memory aid:

Just between me
And the deep blue sea.

EXERCISE 6. Many students who recognize the correct use of written object pronouns still have difficulty with correct use in speech. This oral exercise will give additional drill.

EXERCISE 7. When your students finish this exercise, go over the sentences aloud so that they will hear the correct forms.

REVIEW EXERCISE A. Have the answers read aloud in class, so that all students can hear the correct forms again.

EXERCISE 6. *Oral Drill.* Practicing Correct Pronoun Usage. Read each of the following sentences several times, stressing the correct, italicized pronouns. Oral drill.

1. The safari continued without *her* and *me.*
2. Everyone except *us* counselors had left the camp.
3. We stood beside their families and *them* during the ceremony.
4. Do you have any suggestions for Jane or *me*?
5. The clowns talked to Claire and *him.*
6. Give this to either your father or *her.*
7. With the help of Juan and *her,* we built a fire.
8. There was a spelling bee between *us* and *them.*

USAGE

EXERCISE 7. Writing Pronouns as Objects of Prepositions in Sentences. Write the prepositional phrase in each sentence, adding a pronoun that will complete the phrase correctly. Use a variety of pronouns, but do not use *you* or *it.* Answers will vary.

EXAMPLE 1. We could not find all of —— .
1. *of them*

1. You always give advice to Bob and —— .
2. I made an appointment for —— and you.
3. There are some seats behind Jenny and —— .
4. No one except —— and Beth was studying.
5. I couldn't have done it without you and —— .
6. Why didn't you speak to —— and Christie?
7. Our team has played soccer against the Jets and —— .
8. I was near you and —— during the parade.
9. Just between you and ——, I think our chances are good.
10. About your cousin and ——, there is no doubt.

REVIEW EXERCISE A. Identifying Correct Pronoun Usage in Sentences. Number your paper 1–20. After the proper number, write the correct pronoun of the two in parentheses. After each answer, write an abbreviation showing how the pronoun is used: *subj., p.n., d.o., i.o., obj. prep.*

REVIEW EXERCISE B. You may use this exercise to determine whether your students are ready for the Chapter Review Posttest.

EXAMPLE 1. Say hello to (she, her) and Ann.
1. *her, obj. prep.*

1. The mayor congratulated (we, us) volunteers for our effort. 1. d.o.
2. The election resulted in a tie between Diane and (he, him). 2. obj. prep.
3. Last year's winner was (she, her). 3. p.n.
4. Where should you and (I, me) meet after school? 4. subj.
5. The audience clapped for (he, him) and Ned. 5. obj. prep.
6. (We, Us) sisters should help Dad with the lawn. 6. subj.
7. The best singer in the choir is (she, her). 7. p.n.
8. We beat Betty and (they, them) at tennis. 8. d.o. 9. obj. prep.
9. The poet dedicated the book to Greg and (she, her).
10. The film editor showed the visitors and (we, us) students around the television station. 10. d.o.
11. Deborah and (he, him) will recite next. 11. subj.
12. Have you given Arlene and (they, them) directions? 12. i.o.
13. Please invite your cousin and (they, them) to the horse show this Saturday. 13. d.o.
14. She sewed Aunt Elsie and (I, me) matching vests. 14. i.o.
15. The one by the yellow car is (he, him). 15. p.n.
16. The officer gave (we, us) girls a ride to the gas station.
17. The oldest members are Jerry and (she, her). 17. p.n. 16. i.o.
18. Tomorrow you and (they, them) can distribute posters.
19. I was standing by Consuelo and (she, her). 19. obj. prep. 18. subj.
20. I wrote a story about my great-grandmother and (he, him).

20. obj. prep.

REVIEW EXERCISE B. Identifying Correct Pronoun Usage. Number your paper 1–10. After the proper number, write the correct one of the two pronouns in parentheses.

EXAMPLE 1. It was news to (I, me).
1. *me*

1. Craig and (he, him) are washing the car.
2. Honorable mention was given to Mary and (I, me).
3. The first speakers will be you and (she, her).
4. Members of the decorating committee for the dance include four juniors and (we, us).

USAGE

CHAPTER 19 REVIEW: POSTTEST

In this test, which contains twenty items, students must determine if a pronoun is used incorrectly in a sentence; if it *is* used incorrectly, they must write the correct form.

5. Everyone except Steve and (I, me) will be at the game.
6. Did you get these books from Cindy or (she, her)?
7. She will tell (we, us) runners when to line up.
8. It was (they, them) who rescued you.
9. That could have been (they, them) at the store.
10. The Jensens and (we, us) watched the fireworks display.

CHAPTER 19 REVIEW: POSTTEST

Determining the Proper Case of Pronouns in Sentences. Number your paper 1–20. After the proper number, write any incorrect pronoun and then its correct form. If the sentence is correct, write *C.*

USAGE

EXAMPLE 1. The teacher told Jim and I to stop talking.
1. *I—me*

1. Several people have asked if you and me are related. 1. I
2. The winning science project was entered by Carol and he.
3. That announcer always irritates my father and I. 2. him 3. me
4. Did you give she the answer? 4. her
5. The last person I would have suspected was him. 5. he
6. Let's ask Neil and him for help. 6. C
7. The coach taught we linemen not to budge an inch. 7. us
8. We split the pie between him and I. 8. me
9. Shirley and him generously donated their time to the fund drive. 9. he
10. The ones who deserve a reward are the Thompsons and them. 10. they
11. After reading the inscription, they awarded she the plaque. 11. her
12. Us teammates have to stick together, right? 12. We
13. When my mother finally found me sitting on the curb, she was mad at me. 13. C
14. Would they suggest what Irene and me should make for dinner? 14. I

15. The shop teacher said he was pleased with Ling and I. 15. me
16. Why don't they give we girls a chance? 16. us
17. At the movies we met Julia and she while buying popcorn. 17. her
18. The strongest discus thrower we have is him. 18. he
19. Was that Hank or him? 19. he
20. My mother never tires of telling Mary Anne and I what it was like when she was our age. 20. me

Additional Practice

Teacher's Resource Book, Worksheet pages 234–41, Alternative Worksheet pages (for less-advanced students) 557–58

Testing

Teaching Tests booklet, pages 45–48, 53–54, 57–59, 61–63
Teacher's Resource Book, Test pages 443–46, 451–52, 457–68

Chapter Overview

The first part of this chapter covers the correct use of adjectives and adverbs: the distinction between *good* and *well*, the use of comparatives and superlatives, and the avoidance of double negatives. The second part deals with the correct placement of modifying phrases and clauses in a sentence.

Your students have almost certainly studied most of the material in the first part of the chapter in earlier grades. However, the material in the second part (misplaced or dangling modifiers) will be new to most eighth-graders. With an average or advanced class you will probably want to concentrate your teaching on this part of the chapter.

Chapter Objectives

Students will use comparatives and superlatives of adjectives and adverbs correctly. Students will correct dangling and misplaced modifiers and will use modifiers correctly in their own writing.

PRESENTING THE CHAPTER

LESS-ADVANCED STUDENTS These students should concentrate on the material in the first part of the chapter if they still make those kinds of errors. The material on placement of modifiers may be difficult but you may decide to introduce certain examples and exercises you think will be helpful to them. *(See listing of Alternative Worksheets on page 494.)*

ADVANCED STUDENTS Give the Diagnostic Test to see which rules in the first part of the chapter need

USAGE

CHAPTER 20

Using Modifiers Correctly

COMPARISON AND PLACEMENT

A modifier describes or makes more definite the meaning of another word. Adjectives modify nouns or pronouns, and adverbs modify verbs, adjectives, or other adverbs. Phrases and clauses may also be used as modifiers. This chapter will help you learn to use modifiers correctly and more effectively.

DIAGNOSTIC TEST

A. Using the Correct Comparative, Superlative, and Negative Forms. The following sentences contain errors in the use of comparison modifiers and negatives. After the proper number, write the incorrect words from each sentence. Then write the correct form, adding or omitting words if necessary. In some cases you may need to write the entire sentence.

EXAMPLES
1. Sara is more neater than her sister is.
1. *more neater—neater*
2. I never get to have no fun.
2. *never, no—I never get to have fun.*

1. Of all the rides, the roller coaster was the most funnest.
2. Alan thinks that this pie tastes gooder than the others.

1. most fun 2. better

3. I couldn't hardly believe she said that. 3. couldn't (*or* could hardly)
4. Yoshi is the tallest of the twins. 4. taller 5. more curious
5. The detective kept getting curiouser about the suspect's alibi.
6. The movie doesn't cost much, but I don't have no money.
7. They offer so many combinations that I don't know which one I like more. 6. have no (*or* don't have any) 7. most
8. The house on Drury Avenue is the one we like the bestest.
9. There's nothing I like more better than barbecued ribs.
10. Why doesn't the teacher give us questions that are more easier? 8. best 9. more (*or* better) 10. easier

B. Revising Sentences by Correcting Misplaced and Dangling Modifiers. Each of the following sentences contains a dangling or misplaced modifier in italics. After the proper number, revise each sentence by placing the italicized modifier where it will make the meaning of the sentence logical and clear. In some cases you will need to add or omit words. See Answer Key.

EXAMPLE 1. *Waiting at the curb for the bus,* a car splashed water on me.
1. *Waiting at the curb for the bus, I had water splashed on me by a car.*

or

1. *A car splashed water on me while I was waiting at the curb for a bus.*

11. *Under the doormat,* I looked for the key.
12. The library has several books about dinosaurs *in our school.*
13. *Sleeping soundly,* Howard woke his father when supper was ready.
14. The book is not in the library *that I wanted to read.*
15. Aunt Joan sent away a coupon for a free recipe book *in a magazine.*
16. The band is my favorite *that will perform next week.*
17. *Left alone for the first time in his life,* strange sounds in the night scared my little brother.
18. *After eating all their food,* we put the cats outside.

USAGE

to be taught or reviewed. An advanced class may be able to proceed directly to the section on "Placement of Modifiers" (pages 487–93). Do assign the writing applications to encourage original writing.

WRITING APPLICATIONS

The writing applications in this chapter are designed to encourage students to use comparative and superlative forms correctly to make their writing clear. Feel free to adapt these assignments to your students' writing needs, abilities, and interests.

DIAGNOSTIC TEST

This test will give you a clear picture of what your students already know about the correct use of modifiers. Have the class exchange papers, and go over the sentences one at a time. Ask for both corrections and reasons for corrections. Note which items seem to give your students the most difficulty.

GOOD AND WELL (rule 20a)

The common error here is the use of *good* as an adverb—"Dina swims good." If your students do not make this error, skip this section. If they do need practice on this point, use the drill approach, giving only sentences using *well* as an adverb; it would probably be confusing to introduce sentences using *good* and *well* as adjectives.

EXERCISES 1 and 2. It is important that a student's ear be trained. Exercise 2 (after correction) may be used for additional oral drill.

19. *Often slaughtered only for their tusks,* many African nations prohibit the hunting of elephants.
20. *Sitting in the bleachers,* the outfielder caught the ball right in front of us.

USAGE

GOOD AND *WELL*

20a. Distinguish between *good* and *well* as modifiers.

Use *good* to modify a noun or a pronoun, never use *good* to modify a verb. Use *well* to modify a verb.

NONSTANDARD Doris bowls good.
STANDARD Doris bowls **well.**

NONSTANDARD The orchestra played very good.
STANDARD The orchestra played very **well.**

In the following examples, *good* is correct because it is a predicate adjective modifying the subject. Like all predicate adjectives, it follows a linking verb.

STANDARD The pie tastes especially **good.** [good pie]
STANDARD Over the microphone her voice sounds **good.** [good voice]

Well can also be used as an adjective when it refers to a person's health or appearance.

EXAMPLES Doug feels **well** today. [*Well* is a predicate adjective modifying the subject *Doug.*]
You look **well** in red. [*Well* is a predicate adjective modifying the subject *you.*]

EXERCISE 1. *Oral Drill.* Practicing the Correct Use of the Modifier *Well.* Read aloud each of the following sentences, stressing the italicized words. Oral drill.

1. Everyone did *well* on the test.
2. We work *well* together.

3. Do you sing as *well* as your sister does?
4. I can't water-ski very *well.*
5. How *well* can you write?
6. All went *well* until the actor forgot his lines.
7. Our class pictures turned out *well.*
8. The freshman quarterback can pass as *well* as the senior.

EXERCISE 2. Identifying the Correct Use of *Good* and *Well.* Number your paper 1–10. If *good* or *well* is correctly used in a sentence, write *C* after the corresponding number. If *good* or *well* is not correctly used, write the correct word.

EXAMPLE 1. We danced good at the recital.
1. *well*

1. Peg did not run as good during the second race. 1. well
2. The casserole tasted good to us. 2. C
3. How good does she play the part? 3. well
4. I didn't answer the questions very well. 4. C
5. He certainly looks well in spite of his illness. 5. C
6. I gave them directions as well as I could. 6. C
7. The children behaved very good. 7. well
8. Spinach salad always tastes good to them. 8. C
9. The debate did not go as good as we had hoped. 9. well
10. How good the pool looks on such a hot day! 10. C

COMPARISON OF MODIFIERS

Adjectives and adverbs may be used in comparing two or more things. When adjectives and adverbs are used to make comparisons, they express degrees of comparison. *Degrees of comparison* show the degree to which one word states a quality, as compared with another word that states the same quality.

This building is **tall.**
This building is **taller** than that one.
This building is the **tallest** one in the world.

COMPARISON OF MODIFIERS (rules 20b–20d)

To explain the degrees of comparison, hold up three books of different sizes. Of the first, say, "This book is *large*." Of the second, "This book is *larger* than the first." Of the third, "This book is the *largest* of the three." Then put the following chart on the board:

POSITIVE	COMPARATIVE
large	larger

SUPERLATIVE
largest

Ask the class to give you a few adjectives and adverbs. Write these in the POSITIVE column. Then have students use the adjectives and adverbs in sentences expressing comparisons. Write in the proper columns the comparative and superlative forms used in these sentences. If a student makes an error, have someone else in the class supply the correct form.

I ski **frequently.**
I ski **more frequently** than she does.
Of the three of us, I ski **most frequently.**

20b. There are three degrees of comparison of modifiers: ***positive, comparative,*** **and** ***superlative.***

POSITIVE	COMPARATIVE	SUPERLATIVE
weak	weaker	weakest
ancient	morc ancicnt	most ancient
loud	louder	loudest
loudly	more loudly	most loudly
good	better	best
bad	worse	worst

There are two regular ways to compare modifiers. To form the comparative degree, the letters *-er* may be added to the end of a word, or the word *more* may precede it. To form the superlative, the letters *-est* may be added to the end of a word, or the word *most* may precede it.

(1) Most one-syllable modifiers form their comparative and superlative degrees by adding ***-er*** **and** ***-est.***

POSITIVE	COMPARATIVE	SUPERLATIVE
near	nearer	nearest
meek	meeker	meekest

(2) Some two-syllable modifiers form their comparative and superlative degrees by adding ***-er*** **and** ***-est,*** **but most two-syllable modifiers form their comparative and superlative degrees by means of** ***more*** **and** ***most.***

POSITIVE	COMPARATIVE	SUPERLATIVE
simple	simpler	simplest
drowsy	drowsier	drowsiest
modern	more modern	most modern
pleasant	more pleasant	most pleasant

When you are in doubt about which way a modifier forms its degrees of comparison, consult a dictionary.

(3) Modifiers having three or more syllables form their comparative and superlative degrees by means of *more* and *most*.

POSITIVE	COMPARATIVE	SUPERLATIVE
ignorant	more ignorant	most ignorant
happily	more happily	most happily

EXERCISE 3. Forming the Degrees of Comparison of Modifiers. Write the forms for the comparative and superlative degrees of the following modifiers:

EXAMPLE 1. long
1. *longer, longest*

1. slowest, slowest 2. more cautious, most cautious 3. more agilely, most agilely 4. more thankful, most thankful 5. more possible, most possible

1. slow
2. cautious
3. agilely
4. thankful
5. possible
6. short 6. shorter, shortest
7. easy 7. easier, easiest
8. confident 8. more confident, most confident
9. forcefully 9. more forcefully, most forcefully
10. plain 10. more plain, most plain *or* plainer, plainest

(4) Comparisons to indicate *less* and *least* of a quality are accomplished by using the words *less* and *least* before the modifier.

POSITIVE	COMPARATIVE	SUPERLATIVE
skillful	less skillful	least skillful
delicate	less delicate	least delicate

Irregular Comparison

When adjectives and adverbs do not follow the regular methods of forming their comparative and superlative degrees, they are said to be compared irregularly. You should learn the comparative and superlative degrees of these five modifiers:

POSITIVE	COMPARATIVE	SUPERLATIVE
bad	worse	worst
good	better	best
well	better	best
many	more	most
much	more	most

USAGE

EXERCISE 3. The chief purpose of this exercise is to help students relate the terms *comparative* and *superlative* to modifiers they use in speaking and writing.

IRREGULAR COMPARISON

If your students have trouble with any of the words on the list, you might require them to memorize and recite the three forms of the word.

REVIEW EXERCISE A. Writing the Comparative and Superlative Degrees of Modifiers. Write the comparative and superlative degrees of the following modifiers. When in doubt about words of two syllables, consult a dictionary.

EXAMPLE 1. wasteful
1. *more wasteful, most wasteful*

1. sheepish	6. quick	11. furious	16. hot
2. simply	7. weary	12. enthusiastic	17. good
3. much	8. suddenly	13. easily	18. well
4. surely	9. many	14. tasty	19. near
5. gracious	10. frequently	15. generous	20. old

Use of Comparative and Superlative Forms

20c. Use the *comparative* degree when comparing two things; use the *superlative* when comparing three or more.

Comparing two things:

The second problem is **harder** than the first.
This blouse is **larger** than the other one.
She is **more studious** than her sister.
This book is **more carefully** written than that one.

Comparing three or more things:

This road is the **narrowest** of the three we've traveled.
Of all the performers, she was the **best.**
This is the **simplest** recipe for bread that I've seen.
Monday is the **worst** day of the week.

Most mistakes in the use of modifiers are made when two things are being compared. Remember that the comparative degree should be used when two things are compared.

NONSTANDARD Of the two soups, this is the best one.
STANDARD Of the two soups, this is the **better** one.

NONSTANDARD Marie is the youngest of the two girls.
STANDARD Marie is the **younger** of the two girls.

USAGE

REVIEW EXERCISE A. An advanced class can skip this exercise. Note that many modifiers normally formed with *-er* and *-est* will, under certain circumstances, be used instead with *more* or *most*. Tell students to give the more usual forms in their answers, but do not tell them that the other forms are always wrong.

Answers: Review Exercise A

(Note: Some modifiers can be compared in more than one way. The following list gives the more usual forms.)

1. more sheepish, most sheepish
2. more simply, most simply
3. more, most
4. more surely, most surely
5. more gracious, most gracious
6. quicker, quickest
7. wearier, weariest
8. more suddenly, most suddenly
9. more, most
10. more frequently, most frequently
11. more furious, most furious
12. more enthusiastic, most enthusiastic
13. more easily, most easily
14. tastier, tastiest
15. more generous, most generous
16. hotter, hottest
17. better, best
18. better, best
19. nearer, nearest
20. older, oldest

USE OF COMPARATIVE AND SUPERLATIVE FORMS (rules 20c and 20d)

At the bottom of page 482 are usages that are generally avoided in written English but are not necessarily out of place in everyday speech. A class that is still struggling to master basic concepts

When comparing one thing with a group to which it belongs, do not omit the word *other*.

NONSTANDARD She is taller than any girl on her team. [She is a member of her team, and she obviously cannot be taller than herself.]

STANDARD She is taller than any **other** girl on her team.

WRITING APPLICATION A:
Using Modifiers Correctly When Comparing Two Things

It's fun to have a pet. If you could have any pet you wished, what kind would you choose? Would you like an unusual pet such as a seal or a chimpanzee, or would you prefer a more common pet such as a cat or dog? You would probably narrow your decision down to two kinds of pets before selecting one. When you make comparisons between two things, you use the comparative degree of a modifier. To form the comparative degree, you add *-er* to the end of the word or use the word *more* before it.

EXAMPLES A snake would be *more amusing* than a tropical fish.
An elephant would be *harder* to feed than a parrot.

Writing Assignment

Answers will vary.

Select two books, two movies, or two TV shows that interest you. Write a comparison of the two. Use comparative forms to give specific reasons why you prefer one to the other. Proofread for inaccuracies in the use of modifiers.

20d. Avoid the double comparison.

A *double comparison* occurs when *-er* or *-est* is added to a modifier and, at the same time, the modifier is preceded by *more* or *most.* Words should be compared in only one of these two ways; you should never use both ways at the same time.

should probably skip these technical points. If you do teach your class to use the comparative in expressions like *the taller of the two boys*, warn them against overcorrections. Some students may begin to use the comparative in all expressions of this kind—"the taller of the three boys," "the taller of the four boys," and so on. Do not spend class time on the rule about double comparisons (20d) unless your students actually use double comparisons in their speech or writing.

EXERCISE 4. Have your class read the corrected sentences aloud.

THE DOUBLE NEGATIVE (rule 20e)

Almost all eighth-graders have been warned previously against expressions like "I didn't say nothing." Many of them, however, may not realize that expressions like *hardly, barely,* and *scarcely* are incorrect when coupled with *not*. Point out that sentences such as "We *couldn't hardly* lift it" and "We *could hardly* lift it" are intended to express the same meaning; therefore, there is an *unnecessary element* in the first sentence. Another approach is to ask the class, "*Could* we lift it, or *couldn't* we?" (The meaning of the sentence is that we *could*, although just barely.)

NONSTANDARD Our dog is more smaller than yours.
STANDARD Our dog is **smaller** than yours.

NONSTANDARD It was the most beautifulest waterfall I had ever seen.
STANDARD It was the **most beautiful** waterfall I had ever seen.

EXERCISE 4. Identifying Correct Usage of Degrees of Comparison. Write *C* after the number of each correct sentence. After the number of each ~~incorrect~~ sentence, revise the sentence, using the correct form of comparison.

EXAMPLE 1. It's the most homeliest dog in the world.
1. *It's the homeliest dog in the world.*

1. The rehearsals are getting ~~more longer~~ every day. 1. longer
2. Judith, the pitcher, is worse at bat than ~~any member~~ of the team. 2. any other member
3. That modern sculpture is the ~~most strangest~~ I've ever seen. 3. strangest
4. After watching the two kittens for a few minutes, Rudy chose the ~~most playful~~ one. 4. more playful
5. This morning was ~~more sunnier~~ than this afternoon. 5. sunnier *or* more sunny
6. Your cough sounds ~~worser~~ today. 6. worse
7. The music on this album is better for dancing than the music on that one. 7. C
8. New York City has a larger population than ~~any city~~ in the United States. 8. any other city
9. I can see ~~more better~~ with my new glasses. 9. better
10. She was the most talented singer in the show. 10. C

THE DOUBLE NEGATIVE

Words like the following ones are called negatives: *no, not, none, never, no one, nothing, hardly, scarcely.* (Notice that many negatives begin with the letter *n*.) When such a word is used in a sentence, it makes an important change in the meaning.

EXERCISE 5. A class that does not make errors involving double negatives should skip this exercise.

I have found the wallet that I lost.
I have **never** found the wallet that I lost.

20e. Avoid the use of double negatives.

We often make negative statements such as "I never ran in a marathon." Negative statements in standard English require only one negative word. Use of more than one negative word is called a *double negative*. For example, the sentence "I never ran in no marathon" contains a double negative. Double negatives are considered nonstandard English.

NONSTANDARD We don't have no extra chairs.
STANDARD We have **no** extra chairs.
STANDARD We do**n't** have any extra chairs.

NONSTANDARD He couldn't hardly talk.
STANDARD He **could hardly** talk.

EXERCISE 5. Correcting Sentences with Double Negatives.

Revise the following sentences, eliminating the double negatives.
See Answer Key.

EXAMPLE 1. We don't hardly have time to relax.
1. *We hardly have time to relax.*
or *We don't have time to relax.*

1. Josie hasn't never been to Tennessee.
2. Because of the heavy rain, we couldn't scarcely find our way home.
3. He never had no problem with public speaking.
4. The athletes don't hardly have a break between events.
5. Don't use no forks to get toast out of the toaster.
6. By the time I had made sandwiches for everyone else, I didn't have nothing left for me.
7. I never hardly listen to gossip.
8. Your answer doesn't make no difference to me.
9. Don't never say *not* and *scarcely* together.
10. The goalie doesn't have no excuse.

REVIEW EXERCISE B. This exercise may be used as a mastery test on the chapter up to this point.

WRITING APPLICATION B: Using Modifiers Correctly When Comparing More Than Two Things

All through your life you are faced with decisions. Some are just small decisions, such as whether to order chicken, beef, or fish. Other decisions, however, such as whether to go to college, get a job, or volunteer for military service, are much more serious. You must makc many comparisons in order to come to a decision. When you are describing a decision involving more than two options, use the superlative degree of modifiers instead of the comparative degree.

EXAMPLE I plan to work with children. Of the three activities, teacher helper, candy striper, and camp assistant, I think being a teacher helper will best prepare me for my career. [The use of the superlative modifier *best* is correct because more than two things are being compared.]

Writing Assignment

Even though graduation is a long way off, you may have given some thought to what you would like to do after you graduate. Sometimes your goal can affect what subjects you take in high school. Select three possible career choices. Write a paragraph comparing these three. Based on this comparison, indicate which job you think would suit you best. Remember to use the superlative degree for your modifiers.

REVIEW EXERCISE B. Correcting Improperly Used Modifiers. Revise each incorrect sentence, eliminating ~~errors in the use of modifiers.~~ If a sentence is correct, write *C* after its number.

EXAMPLE 1. We don't never stay after school.
1. *We never stay after school.*

1. Which did you like ~~best~~—the book or the movie? 1. better
2. Gina has more ideas for the festival than ~~anyone~~. 2. anyone else
3. Since the defeat, we have worked ~~more harder~~. 3. harder
4. I ~~can't hardly~~ reason with her. 4. can hardly
5. Jean and Frank work ~~good~~ as a team. 5. well
6. Lana's bruise looks worse today than it did yesterday. 6. c
7. They ~~haven't said nothing~~ to us about it. 7. have said nothing (*or* haven't said anything)
8. Of the two singers, Rose has the ~~best~~ voice. 8. better
9. Which has better sound, your stereo or mine? 9. c
10. The cast performed extremely well. 10. c

PLACEMENT OF MODIFIERS

Notice how the meaning of the following sentence changes when the phrase *from Canada* is moved about in the sentence.

> The professor **from Canada** gave a televised lecture on famous writers.
>
> The professor gave a televised lecture on famous writers **from Canada.**
>
> The professor gave a televised lecture **from Canada** on famous writers.

The first of the three sentences above says that the *professor* was from Canada; the second sentence, that the *famous writers* were from Canada; the third, that the *televised lecture* came from Canada. As you can see, shifting the position of the modifying phrase has resulted in important changes in meaning.

20f. Place modifying phrases and clauses so that they clearly and sensibly modify a word in the sentence.

Prepositional Phrases

You know that prepositional phrases are used as adjectives and adverbs. To make a sentence clear and sensible, you should place a prepositional phrase near the word it modifies.

PLACEMENT OF MODIFIERS (rule 20f)

Many students find sentences containing misplaced modifiers comical. Less-advanced students may also appreciate the humor once the teacher has pointed it out, but they are often not ready to apply the principles covered here. A less-advanced class will ordinarily skip this section.

The presentation is divided according to grammatical classifications covering the several kinds of incorrectly used modifiers. In each case the *right* way to use the modifier is the same—it should always be placed near the word it modifies. *Your teaching should concentrate on the correct use of modifiers, not on the identification of misplaced modifiers as prepositional phrases, participial phrases, or clauses.*

Since dangling or misplaced modifiers are usually considered faults only in writing (and in formal speeches), all the exercises in this part of the chapter should be written out. Everyday conversation is full of modifiers that are thrown in as a person thinks of them. But written English, which cannot rely on tone of voice to express meaning, has to be more precise.

EXERCISE 6. This exercise covers misplaced prepositional phrases. If you use it with less-advanced students, you might have them work in small groups to revise the sentences. With all students, go over their written answers in class.

☞ **NOTE** As was said on page 358, adverb phrases are more flexible than adjective phrases and do not have to come immediately after the modified word. However, to avoid confusion, an adverb phrase should be placed near the modified word. Often, as in the standard sentence in the following example, it precedes the modified word.

NONSTANDARD I read about the lost puppy that was found in today's newspaper. [The puppy was not found in the newspaper.]

STANDARD **In today's newspaper** I read about the lost puppy that was found.

USAGE

Be careful to avoid having a prepositional phrase come between two words that it might modify. Instead, place it next to the *one* word that you intend it to modify.

UNCLEAR She said in the morning she was going to Chicago.

CLEAR She said she was going to Chicago **in the morning.**

CLEAR **In the morning** she said she was going to Chicago.

EXERCISE 6. Identifying the Appropriate Placement of Modifiers. The meaning of each of the following sentences is not clear and sensible, because the modifying phrase is in the wrong place. Decide where the phrase belongs; then revise the sentence. See Answer Key.

EXAMPLE 1. I read about the satellite that was launched in the news today.

1. *I read in the news today about the satellite that was launched.*

1. The nature photographer told us about filming a herd of water buffalo in class today.
2. Inside the ring we watched the antics of a dancing bear.
3. The mannequins drew a huge crowd in the window display.
4. Hundreds of people were watching the show in their cars.

5. The assignment required three articles from magazines on the Statue of Liberty.
6. My aunt promised me on Saturday she would take me to the symphony.
7. There is one gymnast who can tumble as well as vault on the gymnastics team.
8. The marathon runner twisted his ankle with the blue T-shirt.
9. The model posed gracefully in front of the statue in the designer gown.
10. We saw the trapeze artist swinging dangerously through our field binoculars.

Participial Phrases

A participial phrase modifies a noun or pronoun. When a participial phrase begins the sentence, it modifies the noun or pronoun immediately following it. Notice that the participial phrases below are separated from the other parts of the sentences by commas. (For a review of participles, see page 362.)

EXAMPLES **Screaming wildly,** the bandits chased the stagecoach.

Arriving after the others, we waited until intermission to be seated.

When you begin a sentence with a participial phrase, you should be sure that it modifies the noun or pronoun that immediately follows it; otherwise, your sentence will have a *dangling participle.* A dangling participle is a participle that is not closely connected to the noun or pronoun it modifies. The following examples show the methods of correcting dangling participles.

DANGLING Coming in for a landing, the tower radioed the plane. [The participial phrase dangles because the *tower* was not coming in for a landing.]

CORRECTED **Coming in for a landing,** the plane was radioed by the tower.

CORRECTED The tower radioed the plane **coming in for a landing.**

USAGE

EXERCISE 7. Note that students may suggest an acceptable correction that does not retain the modifier as a phrase, as in, "I had to repair my bicycle tire, *which was punctured* by a nail." (See Sentence 4.)

Answers: Exercise 7
(Answers will vary somewhat.)

1. Standing on the dock, we saw a boat almost sink right in front of us.
2. C
3. Having bolted the cabin door, we were never really frightened by the hungry bear.
4. My bicycle tire, punctured by a nail, had to be repaired.
5. The governor, surrounded by reporters, was asked many questions.
6. Suffering from blisters, last year's winner lost the race.
7. While I was reading a book, my cat crawled into my lap.
8. C
9. C
10. Exhausted after our exercises, we craved a tall, cool glass of water.

DANGLING Broken in many pieces, I saw my watch lying on the floor. [The participial phrase dangles because *I* was not broken in many pieces.]

CORRECTED **Broken in many pieces,** my watch was lying on the floor.

DANGLING Jogging down the sidewalk, my dog followed me. [The dog was not jogging.]

CORRECTED My dog followed me **as I jogged down the sidewalk.**

EXERCISE 7. Identifying the Correct Placement of Participial Phrases in Sentences. Some of the following sentences are nonsensical or awkward because they contain dangling participial phrases. If a sentence is correct, write *C* after its number. Revise all incorrect sentences. (You may have to supply some words.) Set off a participial phrase beginning a sentence with a comma.

EXAMPLE 1. Dressed in our costumes, the police officer waved to us clowns.
1. *The police officer waved to us clowns dressed in our costumes.*

1. Standing on the dock, a boat almost sank right in front of us.
2. Exploring the old house, Janet and Patty found a secret passageway.
3. Having bolted the cabin door, the hungry bear never really frightened us.
4. Punctured by a nail, I had to repair my bicycle tire.
5. Surrounded by reporters, many questions were asked of the governor.
6. Suffering from blisters, the race was lost by last year's winner.
7. Reading a book, my cat crawled into my lap.
8. The old suit hanging in the closet would make the perfect costume for the play.
9. Balancing precariously on the wire, the tightrope walker performed amazing tricks.
10. Exhausted after our exercises, a tall, cool glass of water was what we craved.

USAGE

EXERCISE 8. Writing Sentences with Introductory Participial Phrases. Use correctly the following introductory participial phrases in sentences of your own. Answers will vary.

EXAMPLE 1. Sitting near the stage,
1. *Sitting near the stage, I was able to see the dancers clearly.*

1. Locked in the old trunk,
2. Hanging from the ceiling,
3. Expecting a phone call from her boyfriend,
4. Almost lost in the confusion,
5. Looking toward the sunset,

Clauses

Like modifying phrases, adjective clauses should be placed as close as possible to the words they modify. Notice in the following examples how the confusion resulting from misplaced clauses is cleared up when the clauses are placed near the words they modify.

MISPLACED My parents traded an old television for a new tape recorder that they no longer wanted. [The parents no longer wanted the new tape recorder?]

CORRECTED My parents traded an old television **that they no longer wanted** for a new tape recorder.

MISPLACED The book was about insects that we read. [Did you read the insects?]

CORRECTED The book **that we read** was about insects.

EXERCISE 9. Correcting the Placement of Clauses in Sentences. Decide which word each misplaced clause should modify. Write the sentence, placing the clause near the right word. See Answer Key.

EXAMPLE 1. I retyped the first draft on clean paper which I had corrected.
1. *I retyped the first draft, which I had corrected, on clean paper.*

USAGE

EXERCISE 8. Go over your students' written answers and select those sentences containing errors. Write them on the board or use an overhead projector. Without identifying the authors, present them to the class. Encourage your students to discover what the errors are and how they can be corrected.

EXERCISE 9. Assign this exercise as written work. You might ask students to circle the word that is modified and place the clause near it.

REVIEW EXERCISE C. This exercise is most suitable for advanced students. Less-advanced students should omit it or do only selected items.

1. The soldiers were far from their base camp who had volunteered for the mission.
2. We tiptoed over the ice in our heavy boots, which had begun to crack.
3. The spaniel belongs to Bernie that won the dog show.
4. Several gospel songs were presented at yesterday's assembly that were often sung by Mary Lou Williams.
5. The telethon had achieved its goal that ran for thirty-six hours.
6. The game was canceled by the two schools that was scheduled for tomorrow.
7. The strange messenger gave Mr. Johnson a dozen balloons who was dressed as a chicken.
8. The sweater belongs to my best friend that I have lost.
9. My married sister Becky came for the weekend to see me who lives in Michigan.
10. The documentary was filmed at several locations which will be broadcast in the fall.

USAGE

REVIEW EXERCISE C. Identifying the Correct Use of Modifiers in Sentences. In each of the following sentences, a modifier is used incorrectly. The mistake may result from (1) a confusion of *good* and *well,* (2) incorrect comparison, (3) the use of a double negative, or (4) a dangling or misplaced modifier. Revise the sentences, correcting the mistakes. See Answer Key.

EXAMPLE 1. This is the most interesting of the two articles.
1. *This is the more interesting of the two articles.*

1. During last night's concert, the singing group was protected from being swarmed by guards.
2. Attempting to raise money for the homeless, many sad songs were sung by the group.
3. Years ago the singers wore strange costumes and makeup so that fans couldn't hardly tell what their faces looked like.
4. When the fans began to tire of these gimmicks, the singers tried out a new look who were also tired of gimmickry.

5. They finally chose the most simply tailored look of the two they had considered.
6. Warned about the fickleness of fans, a different style of singing was also practiced by the group.
7. Few fans could tell the first time they appeared in public after changing their style how nervous the singers were.
8. "That was the most scariest performance of my career," one singer remarked.
9. Cheering heartily, the singers' fears were relieved.
10. Both the concert and the fund raising ended exceptionally good.

CHAPTER 20 REVIEW: POSTTEST

A. Using the Correct Comparative and Superlative Forms. Number your paper 1–15. The sentences in the following paragraphs contain double negatives and errors in the use of comparative and superlative modifiers. After the proper number, write the incorrect word or words. Then write the correct form, adding or omitting words if necessary.

EXAMPLES
1. We don't want none of that food.
1. *don't, none—We don't want any of that food.*
2. Gail was even more later than I was.
2. *more later—later*

1. most wonderful 2. an 3. other 4. better

(1) The ~~wonderfullest~~ place in the whole world is my grandmother's house. (2) We used to live there when we didn't have ~~no~~ apartment of our own. (3) Since her house is bigger than any ^ house in the neighborhood, we all had plenty of room. (4) My grandmother was glad to have us stay because my dad can fix things so that they're ~~gooder~~ than new. (5) He plastered and painted the walls in one bedroom so that I wouldn't have to share a room ~~no~~ more with my sister. (6) I don't know which was ~~best~~—having so much space of my own or having privacy from my sister. 5. any 6. better

USAGE

CHAPTER 20 REVIEW: POSTTEST

This test is divided into two sections: comparative and superlative forms (fifteen items) and misplaced and dangling modifiers (ten items). Give your students enough time to complete the test. After identifying errors, the students must make corrections and in some cases revise the entire sentence.

Additional Practice

Teacher's Resource Book, Worksheet pages 242–51, Alternative Worksheet pages (for less-advanced students) 559–60

Testing

Teaching Tests booklet, pages 45–48, 55–56, 57–59, 61–63
Teacher's Resource Book, Test pages 443–46, 453–54, 457–68

(7) My grandmother can sew better than anybody^can. (8) She taught my sister and me how to make the ~~beautifullest~~ clothes. (9) She has three sewing machines and my mother has one, but I like Grandma's older one ~~better~~. (10) We started with the ~~more~~ simpler kinds of stitches. (11) After my sister and I could do those, Grandma showed us ~~elaborater~~ stitches and sewing tricks. (12) For instance, she taught us to wrap thread behind buttons we sew on so that they will be ~~more~~ easier to button. (13) We learned how to make dresses, skirts, blouses, and all sorts of things, until now there ~~isn't~~ hardly ~~nothing~~ we can't make.

(14) I was sad when we left Grandma's house, but I like our new apartment ~~more~~ better than I thought I would. (15) Luckily, we moved to a place near my grandmother's, and after school I can go over there or go home—whichever I want to do ~~most~~.
7. else 8. most beautiful 9. best 10. simpler (*or* more simple) 11. more elaborate 12. easier 13. is hardly anything 14. better 15. more

USAGE

B. Revising Sentences by Correcting Misplaced and Dangling Modifiers. After the proper number, revise each sentence by correcting the misplaced or dangling modifier. In some cases you will need to add or omit words. See Answer Key.

EXAMPLE 1. Tearing away his umbrella, Mr. Perez became drenched in the storm.
1. *Tearing away his umbrella, the storm drenched Mr. Perez.*

16. Our teacher told us that she had been a nurse in class today.
17. The woman helped us who runs the store.
18. Destroyed by the fire, the man looked sadly at the charred house.
19. After missing the bus, my mother gave me a ride in the car.
20. The fox escaped from the hounds pursuing it with a crafty maneuver.
21. Walking through the park, the squirrels chattered at me.
22. My uncle lives in Germany who is in the Army.
23. The squid fascinated the students preserved in formaldehyde.
24. Keeping track of the race with binoculars, the blue car with a yellow roof pulled into the lead.
25. We watched the snow pile up in drifts inside our warm house.

CHAPTER 21

Glossary of Usage

COMMON USAGE PROBLEMS

This chapter contains a short glossary of English usage for you to use as a reference when you are uncertain about a question of usage.

Several kinds of usage problems are treated in this glossary. Some require the writer or speaker to choose between two words, according to the meaning intended. Others involve a choice between two words in which one word is less acceptable than the other. A few of the words and expressions discussed here should be avoided altogether. (Spelling problems arising from the confusion of similar words are treated in Chapter 25.)

DIAGNOSTIC TEST

Revising Sentences by Correcting Errors in Usage. One sentence in each of the following sets contains an error in usage. After the proper number, write the letter of the sentence that contains an error, and revise the sentence to agree with standard formal usage.

EXAMPLE 1. (a) I rode a unicycle. (b) Everyone came except Michael. (c) The side affects of the medicine are well known.

1. *(c) The side effects of the medicine are well known.*

USAGE

Chapter Overview

The words and expressions listed in this chapter often appear in eighth-grade work. Students should recognize these words and expressions and use them appropriately (some are to be avoided altogether).

After you cover the introductory material on standard and nonstandard English, you may decide to go ahead and teach the chapter as a unit. However, some teachers use the chapter for reference, teaching the items throughout the year as the need arises or referring individual students to explanations of troublesome items whenever necessary. If you plan to approach the chapter as a unit, use the results of the Diagnostic Test to determine which items to emphasize.

Chapter Objective

Students will use correctly words that are often confused and will identify and correct nonstandard usages and informal usages that are usually avoided in written English.

PRESENTING THE CHAPTER

LESS-ADVANCED STUDENTS These students should not try to cover all the items in the chapter, but should concentrate instead on the serious errors they most frequently make.

ADVANCED STUDENTS Unless these students have unusual difficulty mastering standard usage, they can use this chapter primarily for reference. However, these students should investigate some of the finer points of usage. As a project for an oral or written report, they can research usage patterns. Do assign the writing application.

WRITING APPLICATION

The writing application in this chapter asks students to illustrate the standard formal usage of "kind of." Feel free to adapt this assignment to your students' needs, interests, and abilities.

DIAGNOSTIC TEST

Use this test to determine which of the items in this chapter your class needs to study.

USAGE

1. (a) They bought themselves new pens. (b) The balloon busted. (c) Use less flour. 1. burst
2. (a) She did not feel well. (b) Jack ought to help us. (c) John hisself bought that. 2. himself
3. (a) Tom could of come. (b) This book has fewer pages. (c) He sang well. 3. have
4. (a) We had already been there. (b) She feels alright now. (c) We looked everywhere for him. 4. all right
5. (a) He behaved badly. (b) She felt badly about being late. (c) There is no talking between classes. 5. bad
6. (a) We saved ten dollars between the four of us. (b) Bring a salad when you come. (c) The chair broke. 6. among
7. (a) She set down. (b) This news may affect his decision. (c) They left less milk for me. 7. sat
8. (a) I cannot go unless I finish my work first. (b) Your my friend. (c) She laid the packages on the table. 8. You're
9. (a) My father use to play the piano. (b) We have a long way to go. (c) Yesterday I read in the newspaper that the governor is in town. 9. used
10. (a) I know how come she left. (b) It's windy. (c) He likes this kind of movie. 10. why
11. (a) I am somewhat hungry. (b) Will you learn me how to ski? (c) Do as the leader does. 11. teach
12. (a) She looks as though she is exhausted. (b) Meet me outside of the building. (c) He wrote the letter and mailed it. 12. outside
13. (a) The reason why he works is that he wants to save money for a trip. (b) Your backhand has improved somewhat. (c) Their are not enough chairs. 13. The reason he works . . .
14. (a) I just bought those shoes. (b) This here ride is broken. (c) Try to relax. 14. This
15. (a) I am real happy. (b) Study now. Then go outside. (c) They're new in school. 15. really *or* very
16. (a) Take the report when you go. (b) She might have gone. (c) Mr. Bennigan he is my English teacher. 16. Mr. Bennigan is

17. (a) We worked for a hour. (b) She accepted your invitation. (c) They can hardly see the sign. 17. an
18. (a) Where do you study? (b) Divide the tasks among the two of us. (c) If he had been there, I would have seen him.
19. (a) You should have come. (b) Less sugar is needed. (c) It's pedal is stuck. 18. between 19. its
20. (a) He likes these kinds of ties. (b) It looks like a rabbit. (c) She raised up on her tiptoes. 20. rose on

LEVELS OF USAGE

To use the glossary properly, you will need to be familiar with the terms *standard English, formal English, informal English,* and *nonstandard English.* To identify special uses of English, you need to know the terms *slang, colloquialisms,* and *jargon.*

Standard English

Standard English is the form of English most widely accepted by educated people. It conforms to the rules and conventions given throughout this textbook, such as those concerning subject-verb agreement, pronoun-antecedent agreement, and pronoun usage.

Formal English is the standard English used most often in formal writing or speaking situations, such as in formal reports that have footnotes and bibliographies, formal essays, and speeches given on serious occasions. Formal English avoids contractions and slang. Presidential State of the Union speeches are examples of formal English.

Informal English is the standard English that most of us use every day in our conversation and in much of our personal writing. It is used in many newspapers, magazines, and books; on radio and television; by professional and business people; and by students. Informal English is not appropriate for formal occasions.

USAGE

LEVELS OF USAGE

Ask your students if they know what the word *standard* means. You may find that they have a difficult time trying to define it. They might come up with a definition like "how things should be." Before you assign the textbook reading, write these terms on the board:

STANDARD ENGLISH
1. *Formal English*
2. *Informal English*
NONSTANDARD ENGLISH

Give the students some examples for each category. After they read the material in the textbook, ask them for additional examples.

By writing more examples on the board, help your students understand the special characteristics of *slang, colloquialisms,* and *jargon.* They will probably be able to suggest examples of each. Write them on the board. As you discuss these terms, show your appreciation for the flexibility of the English language. Eighth-graders can learn to distinguish between informal and formal, standard and nonstandard English. They probably can also already switch levels in their own communication—both spoken and written.

USAGE GLOSSARY

Students who make many errors on the list should probably concentrate this year on overcoming clearly nonstandard usages like "them pencils" and "this here dress." Provide such a class with much more oral and written drill on standard forms. Do not confuse these students by asking them to master all the items in the chapter; omit the less common errors and the finer points. If your students already speak and write standard English, omit the nonstandard items such as "them pencils" and "this here dress."

Note: See Part Three in the front of this Teacher's Edition *for a list of words in the glossary. The list groups the items by type and may be helpful as you decide which ones to teach.*

USAGE

Nonstandard English

Nonstandard English is the form of language that does not conform to the rules and conventions discussed in this textbook.

EXAMPLE My hands are more smaller than his. [nonstandard]
My hands are **smaller** than his. [standard]

Special Uses of English

Slang and colloquialisms are most often found in informal spoken English. **Jargon** may be found in formal or informal English.

Slang consists of new words, or old words in new uses, that are adopted because they seem colorful and clever and they show that the user is up to date. Slang is often found in the speech of young people and those who belong to groups set apart from the community.

EXAMPLE My older brother always **hassles** me.

Colloquialisms are words or phrases usually found in the speech, but not in the writing, of educated speakers. Colloquialisms are more widespread than slang.

EXAMPLE Let's **put our heads together** to solve this problem.

Jargon consists of words and phrases used in a particular activity, such as a sport, hobby, or field of study, or by people engaged in a particular occupation. Often jargon assigns a specified meaning to a word already in common use.

EXAMPLE The base runner tried to **steal** second base.

In most of the writing that you do for school, you should use standard formal English. Sometimes a writing assignment may use informal English. When choosing your words, always keep your purpose and audience in mind.

USAGE GLOSSARY

a, an Use *a* before words beginning with consonant sounds; use *an* before words beginning with vowel sounds.

EXAMPLES Mike will stay at **a** hotel.
I live on **a** one-way street.
Susan is **an** honest person.
My older sister gave me **an** orange sweater.

accept, except *Accept* is a verb; it means "to receive." *Except* may be either a verb or a preposition. As a verb, it means "to leave out" or "to omit"; as a preposition, it means "excluding."

EXAMPLES I **accept** your apology.
Some students will be **excepted** from this assignment.
Mark has written all his friends **except** John.

affect, effect *Affect* is a verb meaning "to influence." *Effect* used as a verb means "to accomplish." Used as a noun, *effect* means "the result of some action."

EXAMPLES His score on this test will **affect** his final grade.
Bo and Alice's hard work **effected** a solution to the problem.
The **effects** of the medicine were immediate.

ain't Avoid this word in speaking or writing; it is nonstandard English.

all ready, already *All ready* means "completely prepared" or "in readiness." *Already* means "previously."

EXAMPLES We had **already** seen that film.
The soup is **all ready** to be served.

all right Used as an adjective, *all right* means "satisfactory" or "unhurt." Used as an adverb *all right* means "satisfactory." *All right* is always two words. *Alright* is not an acceptable spelling.

EXAMPLES Your work is **all right.** [adjective]
Maria fell, but she is **all right.** [adjective]
You did **all right** at the track meet. [adverb]

anywheres, everywheres, nowheres, somewheres Use these words without the final *s.*

EXAMPLE I didn't go **anywhere** [not *anywheres*] yesterday.

as See **like, as.**

as if See **like, as if.**

at Do not use *at* after *where.*

NONSTANDARD Where will you be at?
STANDARD Where will you be?

bad, badly *Bad* is an adjective; in most uses, *badly* is an adverb. The distinction between the two forms should be observed in standard formal usage.

EXAMPLES The fish tastes **bad.** [The adjective *bad* modifies *fish.*]
The boy's wrist was sprained **badly**. [The adverb *badly* modifies *was sprained.*]

In informal usage, however, the expression "feel badly" has become acceptable, though ungrammatical, English.

INFORMAL Marcia felt badly about her low grade.
FORMAL Marcia felt **bad** about her low grade.

because See **reason . . . because.**

between, among Use *between* when you are thinking of two things at a time, even though they may be part of a group consisting of more than two.

EXAMPLES In English, Marc sits **between** Bob and me.

Some players practice **between** innings. [Although there are more than two innings, the practice occurs only *between* any two of them.]

Next year we will study the War **Between** the States. [Although thirty-five states were involved, the war was *between* two sides.]

USAGE

Use *among* when you are thinking of a group rather than of separate individuals.

EXAMPLES There was disagreement **among** the players about the coach's decision. [The players are thought of as a group.]

We saved twenty dollars **among** the three of us. [Three people together saved twenty dollars.]

bring, take *Bring* means "to come carrying something." *Take* means "to go carrying something." Think of *bring* as related to *come* and of *take* as related to *go.*

EXAMPLES Please **bring** my book when you come.
Take this dish when you go.

bust, busted Avoid using these words as verbs. Use a form of either *burst* or *break.*

EXAMPLES The balloon **burst** [not *busted*] when June sat on it.
The dish **broke** [not *busted*] when I dropped it.

can't hardly, can't scarcely The negative words *hardly* and *scarcely* should never be used with another negative word.

EXAMPLES I **can** [not *can't*] **hardly** read Jack's handwriting.
We **had** [not *hadn't*] **scarcely** enough food for everyone.

could of *Could have* sometimes sounds like *could of* when spoken. Do not write *of* with the helping verb *could.* Write *could have.* Also avoid *ought to of, should of, would of, might of,* and *must of.*

EXAMPLE Sally **could have** [not *of*] played the piano for the reception.

effect See **affect, effect.**

everywheres See **anywheres,** etc.

USAGE

fewer, less *Fewer* is used with plural words, *less* with singular words; *fewer* tells "how many," *less* "how much."

EXAMPLES We have **fewer** balloons than we need.
This recipe calls for **less** flour.

good, well *Good* is always an adjective. Never use *good* to modify a verb; use *well,* which is an adverb.

NONSTANDARD Nancy sang *good* at the audition.
STANDARD Nancy sang **well** at the audition.

Although it is usually an adverb, *well* is used as an adjective to mean "healthy."

USAGE

☞ **USAGE NOTE** *Feel good* and *feel well* mean different things. *Feel good* means "to feel happy or pleased." *Feel well* means "to feel healthy."

EXAMPLES He did not feel **well** yesterday. [predicate adjective meaning "healthy"]
I felt **good** when I received an A in English.

had of See **of.**

had ought, hadn't ought Unlike other verbs, *ought* is not used with *had.*

NONSTANDARD Gary had ought to help us; he hadn't ought to have missed our meeting yesterday.
STANDARD Gary **ought to** help us; he **oughtn't to have** missed our meeting yesterday.
or
Gary **should** help us; he **shouldn't have** missed our meeting yesterday.

he, she, they In writing, do not use an unnecessary pronoun after a noun. This error is called the *double subject.*

NONSTANDARD Mrs. Pine she is my mother's friend.
STANDARD Mrs. Pine is my mother's friend.

hisself *Hisself* is nonstandard English. Use *himself.*

EXAMPLE Ira bought **himself** [not *hisself*] a yellow tie.

how come In informal English, *how come* is often used instead of *why;* but in formal English, *why* is always preferable.

INFORMAL I don't know how come she's not here.
FORMAL I don't know **why** she is not here.

its, it's *Its* is a personal pronoun in the possessive form. *It's* is a contraction of *it is* or *it has.*

EXAMPLES **Its** window is broken. [*Its* is a possessive pronoun.]
It's a hot day. [*It's* means "it is."]
It's been a good trip. [*It's* means "it has."]

USAGE

kind, sort, type In writing, the demonstrative words *this, that, these,* and *those* must agree in number with the words *kind, sort,* and *type.*

EXAMPLE Maria likes **this kind** of book better than any of **those** other **kinds.**

kind of, sort of In informal English, *kind of* and *sort of* are used to mean "somewhat" or "rather"; but in formal situations, *somewhat* or *rather* is always preferable.

INFORMAL It was kind of embarrassing.
FORMAL It was **somewhat** embarrassing.

learn, teach *Learn* means "to acquire knowledge." *Teach* means "to instruct" or "to show how."

EXAMPLES I am **learning** how to use this computer.
My father is **teaching** me how.

less See **fewer, less.**

WRITING APPLICATION:
Using *Kind of* Correctly in Writing Definitions

If you are not a basketball fan, you might not know what a *slam-dunk* is. If you are not a climber, you have probably never heard of *chimneying:* Sometimes words are familiar only to people who have a special interest in a particular subject. Your reader might be eager to learn about a new subject that you know much about. To explain a particular subject, you would give a definition of it. Definitions often include the phrase *kind of,* which should not be followed by *a.*

EXAMPLE A piranha is a **kind of** tropical fish with very sharp teeth that attacks and destroys its prey. [Notice that *kind of* is not followed by *a.*]

Writing Assignment

Answers will vary.

Write a paragraph in which you define a term that is familiar to you but may not be well known to other people. Here are some ideas:

woofer *or* tweeter   Siamese cat   word processor   ceramics

Use the phrase *kind of* at least twice, and underline it each time you use it.

USAGE

lie, lay See pages 452–53.

like, as *Like* is a preposition, introducing a prepositional phrase. In informal English, *like* is often used as a conjunction meaning "as"; but in formal English, *as* is always preferable.

EXAMPLES This tastes **like** pineapple juice. [Like is a preposition introducing the phrase *like pineapple juice.*]

Please do **as** he suggests. [*He suggests* is a clause

and needs the conjunction *as* (not the preposition *like*) to introduce it.]

like, as if In formal English, *like* should not be used for the compound conjunctions *as if* or *as though.*

EXAMPLE You looked **as though** [not *like*] you knew the answer.

might of, must of See **could of.**

nowheres See **anywheres,** etc.

of Do not use *of* with prepositions such as *inside, off,* and *outside.*

EXAMPLE He quickly walked **off** [not *off of*] the stage and left the theater.
She waited **outside** [not *outside of*] the school.
What is **inside** [not *inside of*] this large box?

Of is also unnecessary with *had.*

EXAMPLE If I **had** [not *had of*] seen her, I would have said hello.

ought to of See **could of.**

real In informal English, *real* is often used as an adverb meaning "very" or "extremely"; but in formal English, *very* or *extremely* is preferable.

INFORMAL I am real tired.
FORMAL I am **very** tired.

reason . . . because In informal English, *reason . . . because* is often used instead of *reason . . . that.* In formal English, use *reason . . . that,* or revise your sentence.

INFORMAL The reason I did well on the test was because I had studied hard.

FORMAL The **reason** I did well on the test was **that** I had studied hard.

or

I did well on the test **because** I had studied hard.

rise, raise See pages 453–54.

shall, will Some people prefer to use *shall* with first person pronouns and *will* with second and third person in the future and future perfect tenses. Nowadays, most Americans do not make this distinction. *Will* is acceptable in the first person as well as in the other two.

sit, set See pages 450–51.

so Because this word is usually overworked, avoid it in your writing whenever you can.

INFORMAL I want to get a good grade, so I will study tonight.
FORMAL Because I want to get a good grade, I will study tonight.

or

I want to get a good grade; therefore, I will study tonight.

some, somewhat In writing, do not use *some* for *somewhat* as an adverb.

NONSTANDARD My math has improved some.
STANDARD My math has improved **somewhat.**

than, then Do not confuse these words. *Than* is a conjunction; *then* is an adverb.

EXAMPLES Margo is a faster runner **than** I am.
First we went to the department store; **then** we went to the library.

their, there, they're *Their* is the possessive form of *they. There* is used to mean "at that place" or to begin a sentence. *They're* is a contraction of *they are.*

USAGE

EXAMPLES **Their** team won the game.
We will go **there** in the spring.
There were twenty people at the party.
They're the best players on the team.

theirself, theirselves *Theirself* and *theirselves* are nonstandard English. Use *themselves.*

EXAMPLE They bought **themselves** [not *theirself* or *theirselves*] new basketballs.

them *Them* should not be used as an adjective. Use *these* or *those.*

EXAMPLE I gave you **those** [not *them*] records yesterday.

this here, that there The *here* and the *there* are unnecessary.

EXAMPLE Do you like **this** [not *this here*] shirt or **that** [not *that there*] one?

this kind, sort, type See **kind,** etc.

try and In informal English *try and* is often used for *try to;* but in formal English *try to* is always preferable.

INFORMAL Try and be early.
FORMAL **Try to** be early.

use to, used to Be sure to add the *d* to *use. Used to* is the past form.

EXAMPLE We **used to** [not *use to*] own a dog.

very Avoid overusing this word. Try to use more precise words in its place.

EXAMPLES I was **trembling** [instead of *very* afraid].
He was **delighted** [instead of *very* happy] with his gift.

way, ways Use *way,* not *ways,* in referring to a distance.

USAGE

EXAMPLE They still had a long **way** [not *ways*] to go before reaching the town.
We took the short **way** [not *ways*] home.

when, where Do not use *when* or *where* incorrectly in writing a definition.

NONSTANDARD Listening is when a person pays close attention to what the other person is saying.
STANDARD Listening is paying close attention to what the other person is saying.

where Do not use *where* for *that.*

EXAMPLE I read in our newspaper **that** [not *where*] John will be the new sportswriter.

USAGE

which, that, who Remember that the relative pronoun *who* refers to people only; *which* refers to things only; *that* refers to either people or things.

EXAMPLES She is the student **who** had the lead in the school play. [person]
I rode my bike, **which** is blue and has ten speeds. [thing]
This is the pen **that** I want to buy. [thing]
He is the person **that** can help you. [person]

without, unless Do not use the preposition *without* in place of the conjunction *unless*.

EXAMPLE I will not be able to go to the party **unless** [not without] I finish my homework first.

would of See **could of.**

your, you're *Your* is the possessive form of *you. You're* is the contraction of *you are.*

EXAMPLES **Your** dinner is on the table.
You're one of my closest friends.

CHAPTER 21 REVIEW: POSTTEST

Revising Sentences by Correcting Errors in Usage. After the proper number, write the letter of the sentence in each set that contains an error in usage. Then revise the sentence, following standard formal usage.

EXAMPLE 1. (a) The chicken tastes bad. (b) Where is the book at? (c) There was agreement among the five dancers.
1. *(b) Where is the book?*

1. (a) Bring your notes when you come. (b) The dish busted. (c) He could have danced. 1. broke
2. (a) I drew an apple. (b) The cold affects the plant. (c) We are already to go. 2. all ready
3. (a) Mike feels alright today. (b) She went everywhere. (c) We have fewer chairs than we need. 3. all right
4. (a) They danced good at the party. (b) If I had sung, you would have laughed. (c) You ought to help. 4. well
5. (a) It's cold. (b) He made it hisself. (c) Its knob is broken. 5. himself
6. (a) Teach me the song. (b) That story is kind of funny. (c) The dog lay down. 6. rather *or* somewhat
7. (a) Mr. Barnes is here. (b) I know why he left. (c) This kinds of bikes are expensive. 7. These
8. (a) These taste like oranges. (b) Sing as she does. (c) She might of moved. 8. have
9. (a) Please come inside the house. (b) I am real happy. (c) The reason she laughed was that your dog looked funny. 9. very *or* really
10. (a) I wanted the book but someone had lost such. (b) Your forehand has improved somewhat. (c) He sings better than I do. 10. it.
11. (a) Your coat is beautiful. (b) You're a fast runner. (c) I cannot leave without I wash the dishes first. 11. unless
12. (a) She is the student which plays the violin. (b) We only

CHAPTER 21 REVIEW: POSTTEST

This test requires that students select the one sentence out of three that contains an error in usage. They must identify the sentence and then revise it. Be sure to allow enough time for the sentence revisions.

USAGE

Additional Practice

Teacher's Resource Book, Worksheet pages 252–53

Testing

Teacher's Resource Book, Test pages 443–46, 455–56, 457–68

have a short way to go. (c) We read in our newspaper that a new store is opening in town. 12. who

13. (a) I use to read mysteries. (b) Set that crate down here. (c) This hat is old. 13. used
14. (a) I gave you them books. (b) They bought themselves new shirts. (c) There is the cat. 14. those
15. (a) Sit down. (b) They're smiling. (c) There team is good. 15. Their
16. (a) Gail did not feel well. (b) Have a orange. (c) You invited everyone except Sue. 16. an
17. (a) I raised at 8:00 this morning. (b) Have you read about the effects of the sun's rays? (c) We already read the book in class. 17. rose
18. (a) You did all right. (b) They went nowheres. (c) He looks as if he is sad. 18. nowhere
19. (a) Nancy's ankle was hurt bad. (b) We listened to the discussion among the three governors. (c) The pipe burst. 19. badly
20. (a) I cannot hardly dance. (b) Warm days make me feel good. (c) It's pretty. 20. can
21. (a) He must be somewhere. (b) I can scarcely ride this bike. (c) The reason why I like him is because he is kind. 21. The reason I like him is that . . .
22. (a) We have fewer shelves than we need. (b) Those kinds of shirts are warm. (c) This morning I laid in bed too long.
23. (a) Pat always lays her books on the couch. (b) Learn how to play this game. (c) Do like he does. 22. lay 23. as
24. (a) They are inside of the house. (b) I will have a sandwich. (c) He set the chair down. 24. inside
25. (a) Their my cats. (b) Do you need those books? (c) This house has fourteen rooms. 25. They are *or* They're

USAGE

CHAPTER 22

Capital Letters

RULES FOR CAPITALIZATION

Capital letters indicate important words—the beginnings of sentences and quotations, titles, and other words that deserve special attention. You have probably already mastered most of the rules for capitalization. Perhaps there are some that you still find troublesome. In this chapter you will review the rules for using capital letters correctly.

DIAGNOSTIC TEST

Correcting Sentences by Using Capitalization Correctly. Number your paper 1–20. Each of the following sentences contains incorrect capitalization. After the proper number, write the word or words correctly, supplying capitals where they are necessary and omitting capitals where they are unnecessary.

EXAMPLE 1. The Maxwells enjoyed visiting the southwest, particularly the Alamo in San Antonio.
1. *Southwest*

1. Dr. Powell's office is at Twenty-first street and Oak Drive.
2. On labor day we always go to Three Trees State Park.
3. We invited aunt Mae and her two children to go with us.
4. Our junior high school had a much more successful carnival than Lakeside junior high school did.

MECHANICS

Mechanics (pages 511–93)

Chapter Overview

The great majority of eighth-graders already observe the basic rules of capitalization. The chapter concentrates, therefore, on other rules of capitalization: It gives lists of the various kinds of proper nouns and proper adjectives that are regularly capitalized; it explains the capitalization of titles; and it takes up instances where capital letters are often *incorrectly* used.

Most of the new material will be in the form of notes and of exceptions that are given after the rules. Go over all the explanatory matter accompanying the rules before you assign exercises. Pay particular attention to the examples, and then have the class suggest their own. Write these on the board.

In planning how you will approach this chapter, do not forget the *Summary Style Sheet* on page 527. As you teach each rule, you may wish to have your students write the related example from this style sheet in their notebooks. You might have them formulate their own style sheets with new examples. The *Summary Style Sheet* can also serve as a dictation exercise, a quick review, or a reference tool.

Chapter Objective

Students will recognize correct capitalization and will apply seven rules of capitalization to their own writing.

PRESENTING THE CHAPTER

LESS-ADVANCED STUDENTS These students will profit more from seeing examples than from studying rules. Correct capitalization of geographical names (pages 514–15) may be the most important point. Make sure that students learn how to capitalize other names that they use frequently in their writing. You can make a list of such frequently used names and add them to the class spelling list. *(See listing of Alternative Worksheets on page 527.)*

ADVANCED STUDENTS An advanced class will usually have mastered many capitalization rules in earlier grades. With these students, you may want to concentrate on the exceptions and finer points presented throughout the chapter as "Notes."

WRITING APPLICATION

The writing application in this chapter is designed to encourage students to use the rules for correct capitalization in their own writing. Feel free to adapt this assignment to your students' writing needs, abilities, and interests.

DIAGNOSTIC TEST

This test will give you a clear picture of what your students already know about capitalization. The test is structured as a proofreading exercise consisting of twenty sentences that contain errors in capitalization. If you discover that your students do extremely well, you may decide to have them use this chapter as a reference tool.

The First Word in a Sentence, The Pronoun *I*, and The Interjection *O* (rules 22a–22c)

5. When our class read *a Tale of two Cities,* we also studied the French Revolution.
6. My cousin joined the Peace corps and lived in a small village on the west coast of Africa for a year.
7. No fish live in the Great salt lake in Utah.
8. One famous hero of World War I is sergeant Alvin York.
9. We have studied Japanese culture and the shinto religion.
10. This year I have English, American History, Spanish, and shop in the afternoon.
11. On sunday my mother and I are going to an antique car show.
12. The Robinsons live near route 41 just off the Memorial Parkway on the south side of town.
13. At our Wednesday night meeting, the reverend Terry Witt gave a short talk on the beliefs of Lutherans.
14. We salute you, o Caesar!
15. Thursday was named after the Norse God Thor.
16. An icy gust of Winter air chilled the scouts to the bone.
17. Dale Evans and Roy Rogers always sang "Happy trails to you" at the end of their television programs.
18. Ms. Morelli's class has studied the Supreme court.
19. My uncle served in the U.S. Army during the War in Vietnam.
20. The American revolution took place toward the end of the Age of Enlightenment in the eighteenth century.

MECHANICS

22a. Capitalize the first word in every sentence.

To capitalize the first word in a sentence, you must be able to identify the beginning of a sentence. The section on run-on sentences (pages 236–37) will help you.

INCORRECT More and more people are discovering the benefits of exercise daily workouts at the gymnasium or on the running track strengthen the heart.

CORRECT More and more people are discovering the benefits

of exercise. **D**aily workouts at the gymnasium or on the running track strengthen the heart.

The first word of a sentence that is a direct quotation is capitalized even if the quotation begins within a sentence.

EXAMPLE *Elinor shouted, "**W**e did it!"*

For a fuller explanation of this rule, see the section on writing quotations, pages 555–61.

> NOTE Traditionally, the first word in a line of poetry is capitalized, whether or not the word begins a sentence:
>
> *W*hen I am dead, my dearest,
> *S*ing no sad songs for me

Some modern poets do not follow this style. When copying a poem, be sure to follow the capitalization the poet used.

22b. Capitalize the pronoun *I*.

EXAMPLE Recently **I** have begun to enjoy classical music.

22c. Capitalize the interjection *O*.

The interjection *O* is most often used on solemn or formal occasions. Notice that it is most often used with a word in direct address and that no mark of punctuation follows it.

EXAMPLES Hear our prayer, **O** Lord.
Protect us in the battle, **O** great Athena!

The interjection *oh* requires a capital letter only at the beginning of a sentence. It is usually followed by a comma.

EXAMPLES **Oh,** wait till you see tomorrow's assignment.
We haven't seen her for some time—**oh,** perhaps two or three months.

22d. Capitalize proper nouns.

MECHANICS

Rules 22a (Capitalize the first word in every sentence) and 22b (Capitalize the pronoun *I*) can be omitted for most eighth-graders. If you are in doubt after the Diagnostic Test, ask your students to write an original paragraph about a personal experience. Youngsters this age rarely use the interjection *O* (rule 22c). These rules are included primarily for reference.

Proper Nouns (rule 22d)

It may be confusing to introduce all this material at once. Pick out the two or three problems that your class most needs to work on, and concentrate on these. You can deal with other problems as they come up in students' written work.

The proper noun, which you studied on page 293, names a particular person, place, or thing. It is always capitalized. The common noun is capitalized only when it begins a sentence or is part of a title.

PROPER NOUNS	COMMON NOUNS
Cicely Tyson	actress
February	month
Tennessee	state

(1) Capitalize the names of persons.

EXAMPLES **J**ames **B**aldwin is my favorite writer.
Is **A**lice coming, too?
According to **M**rs. **S**andoz, **A**nnie **S**ullivan is a good subject for a biography.

(2) Capitalize geographical names.

Cities, Towns: **J**amestown, **S**an **D**iego, **A**kron
States: **G**eorgia, **I**daho, **H**awaii
Countries: **G**hana, **N**icaragua, **T**hailand
Sections of the Country: the **M**idwest, the **N**orth

> ☞ **NOTE** Do *not* capitalize *east, west, north, south,* or any combination like *southwest* when these words indicate direction; do capitalize them when they name a region: *If you fly west across the Pacific Ocean, you will arrive in the Far East.*

Islands: **I**sle of **W**ight, **M**olokai, **W**ake **I**sland, **A**ttu
Bodies of Water: **D**anville **R**eservoir, **T**ennessee **R**iver, **L**ake **E**rie, **N**iagara **F**alls, **T**ampa **B**ay, **I**ndian **O**cean, **P**uget **S**ound, **B**ering **S**ea, **S**traits of **G**ibraltar
Streets, Highways: **C**herry **L**ane, **T**aconic **A**venue, **C**rescent **C**ircle, **W**est **N**inety-fourth **S**treet, **R**oute 44, **S**kyline **D**rive

NOTE In a hyphenated street number, the second word begins with a small letter: *East Seventy-eighth Street, South Forty-third Place.*

Parks: **E**stes **P**ark, **W**hite **M**ountain **N**ational **F**orest
Mountains: **B**ig **H**orn **M**ountains, **M**ount **W**ashington, **S**awtooth **R**ange, **P**ikes **P**eak
Continents: **N**orth **A**merica, **E**urope, **A**frica, **A**sia

(3) Capitalize names of organizations, business firms, institutions, and government bodies.

Organizations: **D**ebating **C**lub, **F**uture **F**armers of **A**merica
Business Firms: **G**arcia's **H**ardware **S**tore, **U**nited **T**ool and **D**ie **C**orporation
Institutions: **C**ary **M**emorial **H**ospital, **H**illcrest **S**chool, **A**ntioch **C**ollege
Government Bodies: **A**ir **N**ational **G**uard, **D**epartment of **A**griculture, **G**overnor's **C**ouncil on **I**ndian **A**ffairs

NOTE Do *not* capitalize words like *school, circus, restaurant, club* unless they are part of a proper name: *an elementary school—Irving Elementary School; a circus —Ringling Brothers' Circus.*

MECHANICS

(4) Capitalize special events and calendar items.

EXAMPLES		
	World **S**eries	**F**ourth of **J**uly
	National **C**hess **T**ournament	**F**riday
	Rockland **L**obster **F**estival	**O**ctober

NOTE Do *not* capitalize the names of seasons: *We go on fishing trips in the spring and the fall.*

EXERCISE 1. Before assigning this exercise, you may wish to present the following activity as a kind of warm-up exercise. Write on the board a number of small letters and capital letters, and then require students to supply common or proper nouns using the letters correctly.

EXAMPLES

a (ccident) *A* (merica)
b (alloon) *B* (arbara)
c (alendar) *C* (alifornia)

(5) Capitalize the names of historical events and periods.

EXAMPLES Ice Age, Revolutionary War, Battle of Bunker Hill, Middle Ages, Renaissance, Crusades

(6) Capitalize the names of nationalities, races, and religions.

EXAMPLES Spanish, Egyptian, Caucasian, Eskimo, Lutheran

(7) Capitalize the brand names of business products.

EXAMPLES Cannon towels, Buick sedan, Ivory soap [Notice that only the brand name is capitalized; the common noun following it begins with a small letter.]

(8) Capitalize the names of ships, planets, monuments, awards, and any other particular places, things, or events.

Monuments, Memorials: Washington Monument, Vietnam Veterans Memorial
Awards: Pulitzer Prize, Newbery Medal
Ships, Trains: U.S.S. *Maine, Queen Elizabeth, Silver Rocket*
Planets, Stars: Venus, Saturn, the Milky Way, the Big Dipper

☞ **NOTE** Planets, constellations, stars, and groups of stars are capitalized; *sun, moon,* and *earth* are not capitalized unless they are listed with other heavenly bodies.

MECHANICS

EXERCISE 1. Writing Common Nouns and Proper Nouns. Number your paper 1–10. For each proper noun, write a corresponding common noun. For each common noun, write a proper noun. Answers will vary. Some possible answers are given.

EXAMPLES 1. Chien Shiung Wu
1. *physicist*
2. city
2. *San Francisco*

1. Rockies 2. politician 3. Civil War
4. Tiber River 5. state 6. country 7. monument, building
8. "To a Skylark" 9. Wheaties 10. government agency

1. mountain range
2. Geraldine Ferraro
3. historical event
4. river
5. North Dakota
6. Ethiopia
7. Washington Monument
8. poem
9. cereal
10. Environmental Protection Agency

EXERCISE 2. Using Capital Letters Correctly. After the proper number, rewrite each of the following expressions, using capital letters where they are needed.

EXAMPLE 1. a member of the peace corps
1. *a member of the Peace Corps*

1. veterans day ceremony
2. decisions of the united states supreme court
3. eastern half of iowa
4. eleanor roosevelt park
5. cree indians of north america
6. boulder dam
7. graduate of bryn mawr college
8. the statue of liberty
9. enid bagnold
10. saint patrick's day parade
11. general foods corporation
12. one street east of north fairview drive
13. 512 west twenty-fourth street
14. pictures of saturn sent by *voyager II*
15. the hawaiian island called maui
16. the great lakes
17. a catholic
18. sealtest cottage cheese
19. monday, april 29
20. the stone age

EXERCISE 3. Correcting Sentences by Capitalizing Words. Number your paper 1–10. After the proper number, rewrite all words that need capital letters in the sentence. Treat a compound word as one word.

EXERCISES 2 and 3. In class, be sure to have students give reasons for their choices. A less-advanced class should probably work on small groups of selected items rather than an entire exercise at once.

MECHANICS

Proper Adjectives (rule 22e)

The material on proper adjectives in Chapter 11 (pages 302–303) supplements this section. You can teach or review that part of Chapter 11 now if your students seem to have difficulty understanding proper adjectives.

EXERCISE 4. A good way to supplement this exercise is to use similar items taken from the compositions of your students. You may also want to refer to pages 302–303 in Chapter 11.

EXAMPLE 1. our class visited abraham lincoln's home in springfield, illinois.
1. *Our, Abraham Lincoln's, Springfield, Illinois*

1. according to the federal aviation administration, united states airlines are the safest in the world.
2. ethel waters lived in chester, pennsylvania as a child.
3. the sacred muslim city of mecca is in saudi arabia.
4. in chicago, the sears tower and the museum of science and industry attract many tourists.
5. the detroit tigers won the world series in 1984.
6. the valentine's day dance is always the highlight of the winter.
7. several of my friends bought new adidas shoes at the big sporting goods sale in the mall.
8. the city-wide food pantry is sponsored and operated by protestants, catholics, and jews.
9. the second-place winners will receive polaroid cameras.
10. jane bryant quinn writes a magazine column on money management.

22e. Capitalize proper adjectives.

A proper adjective, which is formed from a proper noun, is always capitalized.

PROPER NOUN	PROPER ADJECTIVE
China	Chinese doctor
Egypt	Egyptian cotton
Ireland	Irish wolfhound
Middle East	Middle Eastern tour

MECHANICS

EXERCISE 4. Correcting Sentences by Capitalizing Proper Nouns and Proper Adjectives. Number your paper 1–10. After the appropriate number, write and capitalize all proper nouns and proper adjectives in the sentence.

EXAMPLE 1. A finnish architect, eliel saarinen, designed a number of buildings in the detroit area.
1. *Finnish, Eliel Saarinen, Detroit*

1. Have you seen the exhibit of african art at the library?
2. The egyptian and israeli leaders met in jerusalem.
3. The european cities I plan to visit are paris and vienna.
4. Our english literature book includes hopi poems and cheyenne legends.
5. The south american rain forests contain many different kinds of plants and animals.
6. Maria has watched two shakespearean plays on television.
7. The alaskan wilderness is noted for its majestic beauty.
8. Our program will feature irish and scottish folk songs.
9. The language most widely spoken in brazil is portuguese.
10. The baptist leader heard the ruling of the supreme court.

22f. Do *not* capitalize the names of school subjects, except languages and course names followed by a number.

EXAMPLES I have tests in **E**nglish, **L**atin, and **m**ath.
You must pass **H**istory II before taking **H**istory III.

EXERCISE 5. Correcting Phrases by Capitalizing Words. Number your paper 1–5. After the proper number, write each phrase, inserting capitals where they are needed.

1. a lesson in spanish
2. report for english II
3. a program on chinese customs
4. problems in geometry
5. studying latin, history, chemistry, and government II

22g. Capitalize titles.

(1) Capitalize the title of a person when it comes before a name.

EXAMPLES There will be a short address by **G**overnor Halsey.
Report to **L**ieutenant Engstrom, please.
Dr. Politi has a new associate, a **M**s. Tam.
Is **M**s. Tam the new associate of **D**r. Politi?

MECHANICS

Names of School Subjects (rule 22f)

This rule, which is clearly important for student writing, is one that often cannot be found in a dictionary or in a general reference book on spelling and capitalization. Go over the explanation carefully in class. You might have students write five sentences of their own using names of school subjects and school classes. Note that some schools do not use names such as *History II* and *Science I* for eighth-grade courses. However, students should still learn to capitalize them correctly. The point may appear on standardized tests.

EXERCISE 5. Have students write the correct answers on the board.

Titles (rule 22g)

Although some of this material is challenging even for advanced students, the rules can be mastered by most eighth-graders if each subrule is taught separately. Do not try to cover all the subrules in one lesson.

Students often have difficulty learning when to capitalize words such as *aunt, cousin, mother, dad, grandfather.* Ask the class to give you sentences that include these words. As you write the sentences on the board, ask whether the words showing family relationships should be capitalized and why.

When you teach subrule (4), which concerns the capitalization of titles of books, poems, stories, etc., discuss how your students' knowledge of grammar (the parts of speech—articles, prepositions, and conjunctions) will help them. *Articles* are found in Chapter 11 and *prepositions* and *conjunctions* in Chapter 12 of their text if they need to refer to them.

This is the church in which the **R**everend Henry Ward Beecher preached.
How many terms did **P**resident Cleveland serve?

(2) Capitalize a title used alone or following a person's name only if it refers to a high official or to someone to whom you wish to show special respect.

EXAMPLES The **S**ecretary of **L**abor will hold a news conference this afternoon. [*Secretary of Labor* is a high office.]

The White House is the official residence of the **P**resident. [The word *President* is usually capitalized when it refers to the President of the United States.]

The **t**reasurer of our scout troop has the measles. [The title is not that of a high office.]

Ellen Rafferty, **c**hairperson of the program committee, reported on plans for the Winter Carnival. [The office is not a high one.]

> ☞ **NOTE** When a title is used instead of a name in direct address, it is usually capitalized: *Could you tell me how my sister is feeling, Nurse?*

(3) Capitalize words showing family relationships when used with a person's name but *not* when preceded by a possessive.

EXAMPLES **A**unt Christine, **G**randfather Smith
Maria's **m**other, our **b**rother, her **a**unt

Exception: When family-relationship words are *usually* used before a name, so that they are considered part of the name, they are capitalized even when preceded by a possessive.

EXAMPLE Kim's **A**unt **B**etty

When family-relationship words are used in place of a person's name, they may or may not be capitalized.

EXAMPLE Ask **M**other, *or* Ask **m**other. [Either is correct.]

(4) Capitalize the first word and all important words in titles of books, magazines, newspapers, poems, stories, movies, paintings, and other works of art.

Unimportant words in a title are *a, an, the,* and prepositions and conjunctions of fewer than five letters. Such words should be capitalized only if they come first or last in the title.

EXAMPLES My sister asked me to read Denise Levertov's poem, "**W**ith **E**yes **a**t **t**he **B**ack **o**f **O**ur **H**eads."

Katharine Hepburn and Humphrey Bogart starred in *The African Queen.*

Curtain Going Up! is a biography of Katharine Cornell.

Exception: When you write the names of newspapers and magazines within a sentence, do not capitalize the word *the* before the name.

EXAMPLES Is that the late edition of **t**he *New York Times*?

(5) Capitalize words referring to the Deity.

EXAMPLES **L**ord, **J**ehovah, the **C**reator, **S**on of **G**od, **A**llah

> ☞ **NOTE** The word *god* is not capitalized when referring to the gods in mythology: *The Roman god of war was Mars.*

MECHANICS

EXERCISE 6. Correcting Sentences by Capitalizing Words. Number your paper 1–10. After the proper number, write and capitalize the words requiring capitals. If a sentence is correct, write *C.*

1. During Woodrow Wilson's term as president of the united states, sheep grazed on the front lawn of the White House.
2. When aunt Jo visits, she shows slides of her most recent trip.

EXERCISE 6. Do not permit students to look back at the rules as they complete this exercise, but go over the answers when they are done.

REVIEW EXERCISE A. Students who turn in perfect papers for this exercise might be excused from doing Review Exercise B. Announcing such an exemption in advance may encourage them to be careful.

3. All of these pronunciations are taken from *the american heritage dictionary*.
4. Some of the gods in greek mythology were also worshiped in ancient asian and egyptian cultures.
5. Did you hear commissioner of education smathers' speech recommending a longer school day?
6. Was Carrie Fisher in *return of the jedi*?
7. After the secretary read the minutes, the treasurer reported on the club's budget. 7. C
8. Lillian Hellman wrote *watch on the rhine*.
9. My older brother subscribes to *field and stream*.
10. The first politician to make a shuttle flight was senator Jake Garn of Utah.

REVIEW EXERCISE A. Correcting Sentences by Capitalizing Words. Number your paper 1–10. After the proper number, write and capitalize the words requiring capitals.

1. The browns hosted an exchange student from argentina.
2. The king ranch in texas is as large as rhode island.
3. Ms. epstein is taking courses in computer programming I, french, and english at rand community college.
4. The sixth day of the week, friday, is named for the norse goddess of love, freya.
5. Both the christian holiday of christmas and the jewish holiday of chanukah are celebrated in december.
6. My uncle ron was stationed in the south pacific. 6. (*or* uncle Ron)
7. The liberty bell, on display in independence hall in philadelphia, was rung to proclaim the boston tea party and to announce the reading of the declaration of independence.
8. Is your mother still teaching an art appreciation class at the swen parson gallery?
9. Emily dickinson and robert frost, both new england poets, are among the best-loved american poets.
10. I walk to the eagle supermarket each sunday for the *miami herald* and a quart of tropicana orange juice.

MECHANICS

WRITING APPLICATION: Using Capital Letters Correctly

Using capital letters correctly helps you make your writing clear. A capital letter signals your readers that you mean a specific person, place, or thing. Compare the following pairs of sentences:

EXAMPLES Exit at the third street ramp.
Exit at the Third Street ramp.

This new Mexican bracelet was a gift.
This New Mexican bracelet was a gift.

She perched on the back of the mustang to have her picture taken.
She perched on the back of the Mustang to have her picture taken.

To make your meaning clear, always proofread your writing carefully to make sure that you have used capital letters correctly.

Writing Assignment

Answers will vary.

Write ten sentences, using one of the items in the following list in each sentence. Proofread carefully to make sure that you have used capital letters correctly to make your meaning clear.

1. The name of a magazine
2. A business
3. A mountain range
4. The title of a person
5. The title of a book
6. A geographical section of the country
7. The name of a street
8. A language and two other school subjects
9. A historical event
10. A continent

MECHANICS

REVIEW EXERCISE B. Students correcting their errors should look up the correct rule or subrule and write its letter and number after the error.

REVIEW EXERCISE B. Correcting Sentences by Correcting Capitalization Errors. Number your paper 1–20. For each sentence, write in order the words that should be capitalized and capitalize them. Also write the words that are incorrectly capitalized, omitting the capitals.

1. The president's saturday talks from the white house were broadcast on the radio.
2. In History class, we learned about women suffragettes elizabeth cady stanton, susan b. anthony, and lucretia c. mott.
3. A great many words came into the english language from greek and latin.
4. At elgin larkin high school, students must complete three years of Math, three of Science, and four of English.
5. Each summer a group from the methodist youth fellowship travels to appalachia to help poor people in the area.
6. The empire state building is taller than the eiffel tower.
7. In April, the cherry blossom festival will be celebrated by a Parade in the heart of the City.
8. The 1984 summer olympics were held in los angeles.
9. The rio grande flows along the Southern border of Texas; it is one of the most famous rivers in north america.
10. jane addams, an American Social Reformer who founded hull-house in chicago, was awarded the 1931 nobel peace prize.
11. Many of the countries of europe are smaller than some states in our country.
12. The President of the local volunteer society received the outstanding volunteer award two years in a row.
13. My parents subscribe to *national geographic* and *time*.
14. William Least Heat Moon began his journey around America in the southeast.
15. Seeing the Redwood forests was a highlight of our trip to California.
16. Bonds were sold to raise money for the construction of a new

MECHANICS

Junior High School in Sycamore.

17. Can we have a surprise Birthday party for grandpa, mom?
18. The University was the site of a convention of african and south american scientists.
19. The panama canal connects the atlantic ocean and the pacific ocean; the new york state barge canal connects the hudson river and lake erie.
20. Edna Ferber's *so big, cimarron,* and *giant* give a colorful picture of american life during times of rapid growth.

CHAPTER 22 REVIEW: POSTTEST

Correcting Sentences by Using Capitalization Correctly. Number your paper 1–25. Each of the following sentences contains an error in capitalization. After the proper number, write the word or words correctly, supplying capitals where they are necessary and omitting capitals where they are unnecessary.

EXAMPLE 1. The shubert Theater is located at 225 West Forty-fourth Street in New York.
1. *Shubert*

1. Several planets in our solar system were named for Roman Gods.
2. In history class we memorized the Capitals of all the states.
3. Uncle Ron owns one of the first honda motorcycles that were sold in America.
4. My cousin gave me a terrific book, *Rules of the game,* which illustrates the rules of all sorts of games.
5. My grandmother makes delicious boston brown bread.
6. Rajiv Gandhi, the prime minister of India, visited Washington, D.C., in June of 1985.
7. The Indus river flows from the Himalaya Mountains to the Arabian Sea.

MECHANICS

CHAPTER 22 REVIEW: POSTTEST

This test requires students to identify words which are capitalized incorrectly or which *should* be capitalized but are not. You may wish to have your students copy the sentences, correcting errors in capitalization as they write. Then have them underline any words they changed.

8. Appearing on television and writing popular books, dr. Carl Sagan has done much to increase public interest in science.
9. In the afternoons i used to help Mrs. Parkhurst deliver the *Evening Independent,* a local Newspaper.
10. Stavros and his friend belong to the Civil air Patrol.
11. As economic conditions changed, people began leaving Northern states and moving to the South and West. *
12. Ernest Hemingway and Robert Service are famous writers who served in the red cross during the Spanish Civil War.
13. My brother owns an olivetti typewriter. *or Northern
14. Next year my sister will graduate from mayfair high school and go to the university in the state capital, where she intends to study mathematics and english.
15. When we found the injured german shepherd, we took it to our veterinarian, dr. Rita Molina.
16. Could you please tell me how to get to the chrysler Factory on highway 21 and riverside road?
17. The woman in the bait shop said to steer the boat North across the lake to the mouth of Fish-eating creek.
18. For father's day, we bought Dad a new power saw.
19. The Ohio department of education provided buses to help evacuate the victims of the tornado in June.
20. Anwar Sadat was one of the most famous egyptian leaders in Modern Times.
21. In the south, the civil war is sometimes called the war between the States.
22. When We read "fire and ice" by Robert Frost, I understood what the Poem meant.
23. At the beginning of their long journey, the Pioneer families knelt beside their wagons and prayed to god for guidance.
24. When I ate Supper at Cam's house, I tried *nuoc mam,* a vietnamese fish sauce.
25. To get to woodside mall, turn left at the deep pit barbecue palace; then turn right at park street, and you'll see the Mall on the Left.

MECHANICS

SUMMARY STYLE SHEET

This list gives examples of the rules of capitalization in this chapter. Use it as a review by studying each item and explaining the use of each capital or small letter. The list will also be convenient for quick reference.

Johnson **C**ity	a **c**ity in Tennessee
Aztec **M**otel	a **m**otel in Miami
Second **S**treet	a **s**treet in Pasadena
Milton **P**ond	a **p**ond in Milton
the **N**ortheast	a **n**ortheasterly gale
North Dakota	**n**orth of South Dakota
the Music **C**lub	a **c**lub for musicians
Slater **W**oolen **C**ompany	a **w**oolen **c**ompany
Topeka **H**igh **S**chool	a **h**igh **s**chool in Topeka
the Korean **W**ar	a **w**ar in Korea
the John Hancock **B**uilding	an insurance **b**uilding
Washington's **B**irthday	Christine's **b**irthday
the Industrial **R**evolution	a **r**evolution in manufacturing
God, our **F**ather	the **g**ods of Greek mythology
the **W**inter **P**rom	a **p**rom in the **w**inter
the **S**ophomore **C**lass	a **c**lass of **s**ophomores
French, **E**nglish, **R**ussian	**m**athematics, **m**usic, **g**eography
Science II	a lesson in **s**cience
Principal Harris	Ms. Harris, the **p**rincipal
the **P**resident of the United States	the **p**resident of the company
Will you call **M**other (*or* **m**other)?	My **m**other is here.
Aunt Marie	her **a**unt
the ***A**merican **G**irl*	a monthly **m**agazine
the ***D**allas **T**imes **H**erald*	a **n**ewspaper
***T**he **W**ar **o**f **t**he **W**orlds*	an exciting **b**ook
customs of the **J**apanese	**n**ational customs
an **E**piscopalian	a sermon in **c**hurch
Ford truck	a **p**ickup truck

MECHANICS

SUMMARY STYLE SHEET

As you teach each rule, you may wish to have students write the related example from this sheet in their notebooks. They might add another example of their own. The sheet can also serve as a dictation exercise, a quick review, or a reference tool.

Additional Practice

Teacher's Resource Book, Worksheet pages 254–63, Alternative Worksheet pages (for less-advanced students) 561–62

Testing

Teaching Tests booklet, pages 65–68, 69–70, 77–83
Teacher's Resource Book, Test pages 469–72, 473–74, 481–92

Chapter Overview

Chapters 23 and 24 present a short but comprehensive guide to punctuation. The uses of the period, question mark, and exclamation point, as well as some of the uses of the comma and colon, are already familiar to eighth-graders. But other colon uses and the semicolon uses in this chapter may be new to many classes.

For ease in reference, all the material on punctuation is grouped in one place in the textbook. Many teachers, however, give punctuation work as it is needed instead of trying to teach everything in these chapters as one unit. For example, the natural time to take up the punctuation of friendly letters is when the class is studying letter writing (Chapter 7), and the natural time to teach the use of quotation marks is when they are writing compositions containing dialogue (Chapter 4).

Chapter Objective

Students will use end marks, commas, colons, and semicolons correctly in their own writing.

PRESENTING THE CHAPTER

LESS-ADVANCED STUDENTS Give these students careful directions for writing sentences of their own to illustrate punctuation rules. An assignment such as the following one might serve as a chapter review.

MECHANICS

CHAPTER 23

Punctuation

END MARKS, COMMAS, SEMICOLONS, COLONS

In spoken language the voice indicates pauses and full stops, but in written language punctuation does this work. Although it might seem as if writing would be easier without using periods or commas or other marks of punctuation, the result would be very difficult to read. In this chapter and the next one, you will learn to master punctuation so that your writing will be clear.

DIAGNOSTIC TEST

Correcting Sentences by Adding End Marks, Commas, Semicolons, and Colons. Write the following sentences, inserting end marks, commas, semicolons, and colons where they are needed. Circled commas are optional.

EXAMPLE 1. Have you seen our teacher Ms. O'Donnell today
1. *Have you seen our teacher, Ms. O'Donnell, today?*

1. My neighbor,the lady with red hair,used to be my baby sitter when I was younger,and I still visit her sometimes.
2. We made a salad with the following vegetables from our garden:lettuce,cucumbers,carrots,and cherry tomatoes.
3. Running after the bus,Melody tripped and fell in a puddle.

4. My first pet, which I got when I was six, was a beagle; I named it Bagel.
5. Sit in the back row, Randy, and don't disturb the class. (or !)
6. The award was given for the best-written, most interesting report about air pollution.
7. My mother said that we could go to the lake; however, it looks as if it's going to rain.
8. Does anyone know where the crank that we use to open the top windows is?
9. The chickens clucked, the dogs barked, and the ducks squawked.
10. Over the weekend I saw Charlie's twin brother, who used to work at the grocery store, at the motocross bike course.
11. Wow! That's the longest homer I've ever hit!
12. After the rain stopped falling, the blue jays hopped around the lawn in search of worms.
13. Wasn't President John F. Kennedy assassinated on November 22, 1963?
14. Why wasn't Sid's last letter, which was mailed May 5, delivered until June 5?
15. Everybody had told her, of course, that it was useless to try.
16. Preparing for takeoff, the jetliner rolled slowly toward the runway.
17. Hand in your test, your answer sheet, and your scratch paper.
18. What shall we do after 3:00, when school lets out, Yolanda?
19. Her address is 142 Oak Hollow Court, Mendota, CA 93640.
20. My cousins will stay here tonight, or they will drive on to Aunt Cindy's house.

END MARKS

23a. A statement is followed by a period.

EXAMPLES The lens is the most important part of a camera.
One of the figure skaters was Sonja Henie.

1. Write a complete sentence with a series of nouns. Tell about three or four things you recently bought.
2. Write a compound sentence telling about your lunch period yesterday. Use the conjunction *but* to connect the two complete thoughts.
3. Answer the following questions in *one* complete sentence: (1) Where were you born? (2) When were you born?

(See listing of Alternative Worksheets on page 551.)

ADVANCED STUDENTS These students should proofread their written work carefully before handing it in.

WRITING APPLICATIONS

The writing applications in this chapter are designed to encourage students to use the rules for correct punctuation in their own writing. Feel free to adapt these assignments to your students' writing needs, abilities, and interests.

DIAGNOSTIC TEST

This test will give you a clear picture of what your students already know about end marks, commas, colons, and semicolons.

END MARKS (rules 23a–23e)

Students usually find end marks easy. If they are unable to tell where a sentence ends, refer to Chapter 8.

Note: Rule 23e (concerning abbreviations) is included primarily for reference.

EXERCISE 1. Review here the kinds of sentences—declarative, imperative, interrogative, and exclamatory (see pages 281–83 of the textbook).

23b. A question is followed by a question mark.

EXAMPLES Have you watched Barbara Walters?
Is photography a science or an art?

23c. An exclamation is followed by an exclamation point.

EXAMPLES What a good time we had!
Wow! What a view!

23d. An imperative sentence is followed by either a period or an exclamation point.

EXAMPLES Please give me the scissors. [making a request]
Give me the scissors! [showing strong feeling]

EXERCISE 1. Correcting Paragraphs by Adding End Marks. Number your paper 1–10. In the following paragraphs, sentences have been run together without end marks. Write the last word of every sentence and the first word of the next sentence, inserting the proper end mark. There are ten end marks to supply. Use one line of your paper for each end mark.

In New Salem Park, Illinois, you will find a reproduction of the little village of New Salem, just as it was when Abraham Lincoln lived there.If you visit this village, you will find that life in Lincoln's time was much harder than it is today.

The cabin of the Onstats is not a reproduction but the original cabin where Lincoln spent many hours.In that living room, on that very floor, young Abe Lincoln studied with Isaac Onstat.It was the cabin's only room.

Across the way hangs a big kettle once used by Mr. Waddell for boiling wool.Mr. Waddell, the hatter of the village, made hats of wool and fur.

Do any of you feel you would like to go back to those days? What endurance those people must have had! Could we manage to live as they did?

23e. An abbreviation is followed by a period.

MECHANICS

EXAMPLES	min.	minute	Dr.	Doctor	Mr.	Mister
	St.	Street	Aug.	August	Co.	Company
	in.	inch	Neb.	Nebraska		

COMMAS

A *comma* does not indicate a full stop, as a period does. Instead, it divides a sentence into readable parts by indicating pauses. If you master the use of the comma, your written work will improve in clarity. One word of warning: Have a reason for every comma you put into a sentence.

Items in a Series

23f. Use commas to separate items in a series.

Words, phrases, and clauses in a series should be separated by commas so that the reader can tell where one item in the series ends and the next item begins.

(1) Use commas to separate words in a series.

EXAMPLES We have read poems by Longfellow, Teasdale, and Dickinson this week.

Tobacco, *hammock*, *canoe*, and *moccasin* are three of the words that English-speaking people owe to American Indians.

In the early morning, the lake looked cold, gray, and uninviting.

Get into the habit of using a comma before the *and* joining the last two items in a series. Although many writers omit this comma, it is sometimes necessary to make your meaning clear.

UNCLEAR Susie, Zack and I are going riding.
CLEAR Susie, Zack, and I are going riding.

The first sentence is perfectly clear if you are addressing Susie and informing her that Zack and you are going riding; but not if

COMMAS (rules 23f–23m)

Many of these rules for comma use have been taught in earlier grades. Use the Diagnostic Test to find out which rules you need to emphasize.

Do not try to teach more than one or two comma rules a day, or your students may become bored and confused. Simply memorizing rules is not recommended. Instead, when they have completed the assigned exercises, encourage them to apply the rules to their own writing.

After you have reviewed comma usage, have the class copy the following principles:

FOUR IMPORTANT COMMA RULES

Use commas to *separate*

1. Items in a series
2. Independent clauses joined by *and, but, or, nor, for, yet*

Use commas to *set off* expressions that

3. Interrupt the sentence
4. Introduce the sentence

ITEMS IN A SERIES (rule 23f)

Students will be familiar with the use of the comma to separate single-word items in series, but they may not be familiar with its use to separate phrases and clauses in series. Review briefly the definitions of phrases and clauses and give examples of them in series:

She played the piano *in the orchestra, in the band,* and *for the chorus.*

The chickens cackled, the pigs squealed, and *the poor farmer had to yell to make himself heard.*

Current usage seems to favor the comma before the *and;* as page 531 states, it often helps to clarify meaning.

EXERCISE 2. After students complete the exercise, go over the answers in class.

you mean to tell some other person that all three of you—Susie, Zack, and you—are going riding.

(2) Use commas to separate phrases in a series.

EXAMPLES We found seaweed in the water, on the sand, under the rocks, and even in our shoes.

It makes no difference whether that hamster is in a cage, on a string, or under a net—it always escapes.

(3) Use commas to separate subordinate clauses and short independent clauses in a series.

EXAMPLES Everyone wondered when he had been in the house, what he had wanted, and where he had gone.

We worked, we played, and we rested.

(4) If all items in a series are joined by *and* or *or,* do not use commas to separate them.

EXAMPLE Have you read *Huckleberry Finn* or *Tom Sawyer* or *A Connecticut Yankee in King Arthur's Court*?

EXERCISE 2. Correcting Sentences by Adding Commas. Number your paper 1–10. After the proper number, show where commas are needed in each sentence by writing the word before a necessary comma and adding the comma. Optional commas are circled.

EXAMPLE 1. I read that each American eats an average of 117 pounds of potatoes 116 pounds of beef and 100 pounds of fresh vegetables each year.

1. *potatoes, beef,*

1. Carlos and Anna and Francie ran across the park, climbed over the fence, and hurried to the bus stop.
2. The three states that have produced the most U.S. Presidents are Virginia, Ohio, and New York.
3. The school band includes clarinets, saxophones, trumpets, trombones, tubas, flutes, piccolos, and drums.

MECHANICS

4. Most flutes used by professional musicians are made of sterling silver, 14-carat gold, or platinum.
5. We discussed what we would write about, where we would find sources, and how we would organize our reports.
6. No one knew what had started the argument, when the two had begun to fight, or why they were now both laughing.
7. Financial writer Sylvia Porter has written a book explaining how to earn money and how to spend it, borrow it, and save it.
8. Last summer I read *The Red Badge of Courage*, *The Wizard of Earthsea*, *The Virginian*, and *A Wrinkle in Time*.
9. The San Joaquin kit fox, the ocelot, the Florida panther, and the red wolf are all endangered mammals in North America.
10. I would like to visit Thailand, Nepal, China, and Japan, the Land of the Rising Sun.

23g. Use a comma to separate two or more adjectives preceding a noun.

EXAMPLES An Arabian horse is a fast**,** beautiful animal.
The rancher of old often depended on the small**,** tough**,** sure-footed mustang.

When the final adjective is so closely connected to the noun that the words seem to form one expression, do not use a comma before the final adjective.

EXAMPLE Training a frisky colt to become a gentle, dependable riding horse takes great patience.

In the above example, no comma is used between *dependable* and *riding* because the words *riding horse* are closely connected in meaning and may be taken as one term.

A comma should never be used between an adjective and the noun immediately following it.

INCORRECT Mary O'Hara wrote a tender, suspenseful, story about a young boy and his colt.
CORRECT Mary O'Hara wrote a tender, suspenseful story about a young boy and his colt.

Adjectives in a Series (rule 23g)

Most students find it hard to decide when to omit the comma before the final adjective. It will help them to try the word *and* between the adjectives—if *and* makes sense, they should use a comma. For example:

I have a new, expensive watch.
I have four white shirts.

"New *and* expensive watch" makes sense; hence a comma is used. "Four *and* white shirts" does not make sense; hence no comma is used.

EXERCISE 3. Some of these series of adjectives could be correctly punctuated in more than one way. Be prepared to explain that there is room for a difference of opinion.

COMPOUND SENTENCES (rule 23h)

Here you have an opportunity to review compound subjects and verbs as well as compound sentences.

EXERCISE 3. Correcting Sentences by Adding Commas. Write the following sentences, inserting commas where needed.

EXAMPLE 1. A squat dark cooking stove stood in one corner.
1. *A squat, dark cooking stove stood in one corner.*

1. They made a clubhouse in the empty,unused storage shed.
2. This book describes the harsh,isolated lives of pioneer women in Kansas.
3. What a lovely,haunting melody that tune has!
4. A group of proud,smiling parents watched the nervous young musicians take their places on the stage.
5. The delicate,colorful wings of the hummingbird vibrate up to two hundred times each second.

Compound Sentences

23h. Use a comma before *and, but, or, nor, for,* and *yet* when they join independent clauses.

EXAMPLES The musical comedy originated in America**,** and it has retained a distinctly American flavor.

Grand opera is a popular form of entertainment in Europe**,** but few Americans take the opportunity to see live productions of operas.

If the clauses in a compound sentence are very short, the comma before the conjunction may be omitted.

EXAMPLE Hart wrote the words and Rodgers wrote the music.

To follow rule 23h, you must be able to tell a compound sentence from a simple sentence that has a compound verb.

COMPOUND SENTENCE Margo likes golf**,** but she doesn't enjoy archery. [comma between independent clauses joined by a conjunction]

SIMPLE SENTENCE WITH COMPOUND VERB Margo likes golf but doesn't enjoy archery. [no comma between parts of compound verb joined by a conjunction]

MECHANICS

EXERCISE 4. Correcting Compound Sentences by Adding Commas. After the proper number, write the words in the sentence that should be followed by commas according to rule 23h. Add the commas.

EXAMPLE 1. Have you read this article in *Nature* or do you want me to tell you about it?
1. *Nature,*

1. Human beings must study to become architects,yet some animals build amazing structures by instinct.
2. One kind of male gardener bird builds a complex structure, and he decorates it carefully to attract a mate.
3. This bird constructs a dome-shaped garden in a small tree, and underneath the tree he lays a carpet of moss covered with brilliant tropical flowers.
4. As a finishing touch, the bird gathers twigs,and he arranges them in a three-foot-wide circle around the display.
5. Prairie dogs might be called the city planners of the plains,for they create huge networks of underground burrows.
6. These burrows may stretch hundreds of miles,and they may house millions of prairie dogs.
7. The prairie dogs do not often leave their own small territories within the complex,but they can somehow tell their neighbors from strangers.
8. The female European water spider builds a waterproof nest underwater,and she stocks the nest with air bubbles.
9. This air supply is very important,for it allows the spider to hunt underwater.
10. The water spider also lays its eggs in the waterproof nest,and they hatch there.

Phrases and Clauses

Participial phrases, as you learned on page 363, act as adjectives to modify nouns or pronouns. Subordinate clauses may also act as adjectives (see pages 386–87).

MECHANICS

EXERCISE 4. Have your students identify the independent clauses and their subjects and predicates.

PHRASES AND CLAUSES (rules 23i and 23j)

The rule about nonessential phrases and clauses (23i) may be new for some students. They may find it difficult at first. In fact, you may want less-advanced students to skip this part of the section. If you do present it, review the participial phrase and the adjective clause, including the relative pronoun. Then go over the explanatory material in the text. Emphasize that participial phrases and adjective clauses that follow proper nouns ordinarily require commas. Have the class discuss the differences in meaning of example sentences such as these:

A student who is not making passing grades is not eligible for a class office. (The adjective clause is essential, because it tells *what kind of* student is not eligible. If the clause were omitted, the sentence would not be true.)

Terry, who is not making passing grades, is not eligible for class office. (The adjective clause gives additional information, but it is not essential. If the clause were omitted, the meaning of the sentence would not change.)

The rule about introductory phrases and clauses (23j) may also be new for your students, but they should not find it difficult. Review the adverb clause, including subordinating conjunctions. Once they can identify the introductory phrase or clause, insertion of the comma follows automatically. A funny example may help the class to see a reason for the rule:

After eating my father usually takes a nap.

In some sentences, the participial phrase or adjective clause is essential to the thought. It cannot be removed without destroying the meaning of the sentence.

EXAMPLE All farmers **growing hybrid corn** owe a debt to an Austrian monk named Gregor Mendel.

In the preceding example, the participial phrase in boldfaced type tells *which* farmers. It is essential to the meaning of the sentence.

EXAMPLE Mendel made the discoveries **that have become the basis of modern genetics.**

The adjective clause in the example above modifies *discoveries.* It cannot be removed without destroying the meaning of the sentence.

In other sentences, the participial phrase or adjective clause is *not* essential to the thought. Such a phrase or clause can be removed without changing the basic meaning.

EXAMPLE Sometimes seeds and nuts**, forgotten by the squirrels that hid them,** germinate far away from their parent plants.

Here the participial phrase can be removed without changing the basic meaning of the sentence: *Sometimes seeds and nuts germinate far away from their parent plants.*

EXAMPLE Migrating birds**, which often fly hundreds or thousands of miles,** are one of the main carriers of seeds.

Here the adjective clause can be removed without changing the basic meaning of the sentence: *Migrating birds are one of the main carriers of seeds.*

MECHANICS

23i. Use commas to set off participial phrases and adjective clauses that are not essential to the basic meaning of the sentence. Do not use commas with phrases or clauses that are essential to the meaning.

EXAMPLES A new spider web**, shining in the morning light,** is an impressive example of engineering. [nonessential participial phrase; commas needed]

Anyone **who finishes early** may start on tomorrow's assignment. [essential adjective clause; no commas needed]

To set off with commas means to separate from the rest of the sentence. If the nonessential phrase or clause comes in the middle of the sentence, a comma is needed before and after it. If the phrase or clause comes at the end, a comma is needed before it; if the phrase or clause comes at the beginning of the sentence, a comma is needed after it.

EXERCISE 5. Using Commas Correctly in Sentences with Participial Phrases and Adjective Clauses. Number your paper 1–10. Write the words that should be followed by commas and add the commas.

1. Ynes Mexia,hoping to find new kinds of plants,explored the dense jungles of Brazil.
2. The plants that she gathered,carefully dried and preserved, became the basis for a collection.
3. Traveling and working alone for many months,she found a tremendous variety of new and unusual plants.
4. Mrs. Nina Floy,who was an assistant to Ynes Mexia,kept detailed records of Mexia's jungle discoveries.
5. Ynes Mexia,who spent a year in search of unknown plants on the South American continent,collected nearly one thousand new varieties of plants on her expedition.
6. President Carter, whose full name is James Earl Carter, prefers to be known as Jimmy.
7. Jimmy Carter was born in Plains,which is a small town in Georgia.
8. Carter,who graduated from the U.S. Naval Academy,studied nuclear physics.
9. After his Navy service,he returned to Georgia,serving first as a state senator and later as Governor.
10. Winning the Democratic Party's nomination for the Presidency,Carter defeated President Ford in the 1976 election.

MECHANICS

EXERCISE 5. Have students write out the answers; then go over each answer in class, encouraging questions and discussion. A less-advanced class should probably omit this exercise.

EXERCISE 6. Your students should write this exercise and go over the answers in class.

23j. Use a comma after a participial phrase or an adverb clause that begins a sentence.

EXAMPLES **Forced onto the sidelines by a torn ligament,** Harris was restless and unhappy. [introductory participial phrase]

When March came, the huge ice pack began to melt and break up. [introductory adverb clause]

An adverb clause that comes at the end of a sentence does not usually need a comma.

EXAMPLE The huge ice pack began to melt and break up **when March came.**

EXERCISE 6. Using Commas Correctly in Sentences with Participial Phrases and Introductory Clauses. Number your paper 1–10. After the proper number, if a comma is needed in a sentence, write the word before it and add the comma. If no comma is needed, write *C* after the number.

EXAMPLE 1. Stopping at the post office I mailed the letters.
1. *office,*

1. Although mail delivery is as old as recorded history, the first postage stamps were not used until the nineteenth century.
2. The idea of using prepaid postage stamps was adopted after it had been suggested by a British educator. 2. C
3. Originally picturing government officials or national symbols, stamps soon began to feature a wide variety of other items.
4. Stamp collecting became a popular hobby when stamps became more varied. 4. C
5. Because stamps provide a colorful record of many areas of life, they are fascinating.
6. Although most stamps are issued to pay for the delivery of mail, special issues are produced for sale to collectors.
7. Enjoyed by more than twenty million people in the United States alone, stamp collecting is a favorite pastime of both young and old.

MECHANICS

8. Collectors can always look forward to adding new stamps because new designs are issued often. 8. C
9. Since a collection of every type of stamp ever issued would be too bulky,many collectors concentrate on a single topic.
10. Filling albums with their treasures,collectors enjoy examining their first stamps as well as their latest ones.

Interrupters

When an expression such as *of course* or *well* or a person's name interrupts a sentence, commas are needed to set off the interrupter. If the interrupting expression comes first or last in the sentence, only one comma is needed. If it comes in the middle of the sentence, two commas are needed—one before the interrupter, and one after.

23k. Use a comma after a word such as *well, yes, no, why* when it begins a sentence.

EXAMPLES Why, you really should know that!
Well, I don't.

> NOTE Words such as *well, yes, no* and *why* are not followed by a comma if they do not interrupt the sentence; that is, if no pause follows them: *Why is Rebecca early?*

23l. Use commas to set off an expression that interrupts a sentence.

(1) Appositives and appositive phrases are usually set off by commas.

An appositive is a word that means the same thing as the noun it follows; usually it explains or identifies the noun. It is set off by commas to show that it is not essential to the meaning of the sentence.

INTERRUPTERS
(rules 23k and 23l)

Caution your students against omitting the comma that should follow the interrupting expression. You may have to go over this point several times throughout the year. Use examples taken from recent student papers whenever possible. This will supplement the exercises in the text.

Take up the four kinds of interrupters separately. Your students are probably already familiar with words used in direct address, parenthetical expressions, and words such as *well* and *yes* at the beginning of a sentence. Appositives may be new to some of them.

To teach appositives, put on the board sentences such as these:

Mumbo and Jumbo two performing elephants were the stars of the show.

Gwendolyn Brooks the author of *Maud Martha* grew up in Chicago.

Many climbers have tried to climb the Matterhorn one of the most dangerous peaks in the Alps.

Ask the class to punctuate the sentences. Then ask if anyone sees any similarity between the three phrases that have been set off by commas. Draw out two facts: (1) Each phrase names the same thing as the word (or words) it follows, and (2) each phrase interrupts the flow of the sentence. Read the sentences aloud without these phrases to show that they are not part of the body of the sentence in question. Then ask the class to give you other sentences containing appositives and to tell how they should be punctuated.

EXERCISES 7 and 8. Have students read the answers aloud and give a reason for using or not using commas in each sentence.

EXAMPLES My best friend**, Nancy,** is studying ballet. [*Nancy* is an appositive with exactly the same meaning as *My best friend.*]

We're out of our most popular flavor**, vanilla.**

Often an appositive is modified by other words, taking the form of an appositive phrase. The entire phrase is set off by commas.

EXAMPLES Nancy**, my best friend,** has won a dance scholarship. [In this sequence, *my best friend* is the appositive phrase.]

The Rio Grande**, one of the major rivers of North America,** forms part of the border between Texas and Mexico.

When the appositive is short, closely related to the noun it follows, and essential to the meaning of the sentence, no comma should be used.

EXAMPLES My ancestor **Alberto Pazienza** emigrated to America on the ship *Marianna.*

White House spokesman **Larry Speakes** issued a statement.

EXERCISE 7. Using Commas Correctly in Sentences with Introductory Words and Appositives. After the proper number, write the sentences that require commas. Insert the commas. If a sentence is correct, write *C.*

MECHANICS

EXAMPLE 1. The dog a boxer is named Brindle.
1. *The dog, a boxer, is named Brindle.*

1. The composer Mozart wrote five short piano pieces when he was only six years old. 1. C
2. Katy Jurado, the actress, has appeared in many fine films.
3. Harper Lee, author of *To Kill a Mockingbird*, is from Alabama.
4. Did you know that the card game canasta is descended from mah-jongg, an ancient Chinese game?
5. Jupiter, the fifth planet from the sun, is so large that all the other planets in our solar system would fit inside it.

6. No, I do not enjoy murder mysteries.
7. The writing of Elizabeth Bowen, an Irish novelist, shows her keen, witty observations of life.
8. Charlemagne, the king of the Franks in the eighth and ninth centuries, became Emperor of the Holy Roman Empire.
9. Why, those soldiers are only children!
10. Sarah Winnemucca, a Paiute Indian, opened a school in Nevada.

(2) Words used in direct address are set off by commas.

When someone speaks directly to another person, using that person's name, commas precede and follow the name.[1]

EXAMPLES **Mrs. Clarkson,** I just want to get to the beach.
Can you tell me**, Hazel,** when the next bus is due?

EXERCISE 8. Correcting Sentences by Adding Commas to Set Off Words in Direct Address. Number your paper 1–5. After the proper number, write the words in the sentence that should be followed by a comma, and add the comma.

EXAMPLE 1. Are you hungry Jan or have you had lunch?
1. *hungry, Jan,*

1. Ms. Wu, will you schedule me for the computer lab tomorrow?
2. Have you signed up for a baseball team yet, Aaron?
3. Your time was good in the hurdles, Juanita, but I know you can do better.
4. Wear sturdy shoes, girls; those hills are hard on the feet!
5. Run, Susan; the bus is pulling out!

MECHANICS

(3) Parenthetical expressions are set off by commas.

Occasionally a sentence is interrupted by an expression such as *to tell the truth, in my opinion, in fact.* Such expressions are called *parenthetical* because, like words enclosed in parentheses, they

[1] For rules governing the use of commas in dialogue, see page 558.

EXERCISE 9. Go over the answers in class.

are not grammatically related to the rest of the sentence. These expressions are set off by commas.

EXAMPLES The President said**, off the record,** that he was deeply disappointed.

To be honest, I thought the movie was fairly good.
It wasn't very good**, in my opinion.**

The following expressions are often used parenthetically.

in fact	however	as I was saying
for example	mind you	to tell the truth
of course	nevertheless	on the contrary
I suppose	I know	I believe
I hope	in my opinion	if you ask me

Such expressions are not always parenthetical. Be careful to use commas only if they are needed.

EXAMPLES What**, in her opinion,** is the best closing hour? [a parenthetical expression set off by commas]

I have no faith **in her opinion.** [not a parenthetical expression; no commas needed]

Traveling by boat may take longer**, however.** [a parenthetical expression, preceded by a comma]

However you go, it will be a delightful trip. [*However* not used parenthetically; no commas needed]

MECHANICS

EXERCISE 9. Correcting Sentences by Adding Commas to Set Off Parenthetical Expressions. Number your paper 1–5. After the proper number, write the words in the sentence that should be followed by commas, and add the commas.

EXAMPLE 1. Mathematics I'm afraid is my hardest subject.
1. *Mathematics, afraid,*

1. The situation is,if you ask me,very unfortunate.
2. Your subject,I think,should be limited further.
3. I'm not saying,mind you,that I agree with their methods.

4. Flying,however,will be more expensive.
5. Nevertheless,his honesty pleased his parents.

23m. Use a comma in certain conventional situations.

English usage requires that commas be used in dates, in addresses, and after the salutations and closings of letters.

(1) Use a comma to separate items in dates and addresses.

EXAMPLES The delegates to the Constitutional Convention signed the Constitution on September 17, 1787, in Philadelphia, Pennsylvania.

Passover begins on Wednesday, April 14, this year.

My friend has just moved to 6448 Higgins Road, Chicago, Illinois.

In an address, you should leave some space between the ZIP code and the state (unless you are writing it in a sentence). No comma should come before it.

EXAMPLE Jackson Heights, New York 11372

> ☞ **NOTE** If a preposition is used between items of an address, a comma is not necessary: *He lives at 144 Smith Street in Moline, Illinois.*

(2) Use a comma after the salutation of a friendly letter and after the closing of any letter.

EXAMPLES Dear Aunt Margaret,
Sincerely yours,
Yours truly,

EXERCISE 10. Correcting Dates, Addresses, and Letter Parts by Adding Commas. After the proper number, write the following items on your paper, inserting necessary commas.

MECHANICS

Conventional Situations (rule 23m)

Eighth-graders probably know that they should insert a comma between the day and the year in a date and between the city and the state in an address, but they may not know that such dates and addresses in the middle of a sentence should be followed by commas. Subrule (2) is included for reference in presenting letter writing.

EXERCISE 10. For additional practice, you may wish to have your students write complete sentences using some of these items.

REVIEW EXERCISE A. This exercise may be used as an additional drill, as remedial work for individual students, or as a test.

1. 11687 Montana Avenue, Los Angeles, CA 90049
2. 1615 West Touhy Avenue, Chicago, IL 60626
3. Monday, December 2, 1985
4. after January 1, 1986
5. Dresser Road at North First Street in Lynchburg, Virginia
6. Memorial Day, 1985
7. from December 1, 1985 to March 15, 1986
8. either Thursday, April 18, or Monday, April 22
9. Dear Joanne,
10. Sincerely yours,

WRITING APPLICATION A: Using Commas to Separate Items

Using commas between words, phrases, and short independent clauses tells your reader that each item is a separate one. Compare the following examples:

EXAMPLES We invited Mary Beth Hardy and Bill.
We invited Mary Beth, Hardy, and Bill.
We invited Mary, Beth, Hardy, and Bill.

The first sentence indicates that two persons were invited. The second sentence shows that three were invited, while the third sentence increases the guest list to four. As you can see, using commas to separate items can make a big difference in the meaning of a sentence.

Writing Assignment

Answers will vary.

Write a paragraph describing a busy scene, using words that appeal to the senses—sight, sound, touch, taste, and smell. After you revise your paragraph, proofread it carefully to be sure that you have used commas correctly to make your meaning clear. Then prepare a clean copy of your paragraph.

MECHANICS

REVIEW EXERCISE A. Correcting Sentences by Adding Commas and End Marks. Number your paper 1–20. After the proper number, supply commas and end marks in the following sentences by writing the word before a mark of punctuation and adding the comma or end mark. Circled commas are optional.

1. If we include New York City in our vacation plans, we will certainly go to the Statue of Liberty.
2. The famous statue was dedicated on October 18, 1886.
3. Few people know its full name, *Liberty Enlightening the World.*
4. The statue, which was given to the United States by France, has become a symbol of freedom.
5. Have you ever made the long, tiring trip up the stairs to the head of the statue, Alan?
6. When you travel in Canada, Joe, you will know you are no longer in the United States.
7. Notice, for example, the signs that allow speeds up to 100 kilometers per hour.
8. How fast is that in miles per hour?
9. Well, it converts to about 62 miles per hour, I think.
10. Brenda and Beverly, the twins next door, have given their old bikes to Goodwill.
11. If a piece of a supernova the size of a baseball were brought to earth, it would weigh more than the Empire State Building.
12. The blue whale weighs as much as thirty elephants, grows as long as three buses, and has an upper jawbone three feet long.
13. Turtles, crocodiles, alligators, frogs, and dolphins must breathe air in order to survive.
14. Lanolin, a smelly fatty substance taken from the wool of sheep, is used in many cosmetics.
15. Although they were much bigger than other animals, dinosaurs had very small brains.
16. On May 29, 1953, Sir Edmund Hillary, a New Zealand explorer, became the first person to climb Mount Everest, the highest point on the earth's surface.
17. Junko Tabei, one of a team of Japanese women, reached the summit in 1975.

MECHANICS

SEMICOLONS (rules 23n–23p)

Most of your students should be able to understand the three rules presented here. Review briefly the independent clause as you teach rule 23n. Call attention to the boxed note on page 546 concerning short independent clauses. Rule 23o can be taught along with transitional expressions. You should point out that a semicolon is not mandatory before these expressions, but it is correct if the writer chooses to use it.

When you put examples on the board to illustrate these rules, it is often a good idea to use down-to-earth sentences about familiar matters such as current school activities. This kind of sentence makes a punctuation usage seem more realistic to your students.

EXAMPLES

We will be in the cafeteria for the English test; consequently, the English classrooms will be vacant.

The next drama rehearsal will be held on Tuesday, not Monday; however, student actors will be expected to know the whole act, not just the first scene.

18. Many people who love climbing have been inspired by these feats.
19. Will the first day of the twenty-first century begin officially on January 1,2000,or on January 1,2001,Sarah**?**
20. What a great fireworks display that was!

SEMICOLONS

The *semicolon* signals a pause stronger than a comma but not as strong as a period.

23n. Use a semicolon between independent clauses in a sentence if they are not joined by *and, but, or, nor, for, yet.*

EXAMPLES On our first trip to Houston I wanted to see the Astrodome**;** my little brother wanted to visit the Johnson Space Center.

Our parents settled the argument for us**;** they took us to see a rodeo in a nearby town.

A period (and capital) between the independent clauses would change each of these examples into two sentences. Creating two sentences would be correct, but it would not show how closely related the ideas are.

☞ **NOTE** Very short independent clauses without conjunctions may be separated by commas: *The leaves whispered, the brook gurgled, the sun beamed benignly.*

MECHANICS

23o. Use a semicolon between independent clauses joined by such words as *for example, for instance, that is, besides, accordingly, moreover, nevertheless, furthermore, otherwise, therefore, however, consequently, instead, hence.*

EXAMPLES Mary Ishikawa decided not to stay at home**;** instead, she went to the game.

EXERCISE 11. Be sure to go over the answers in class after students complete the exercise.

The popular names of certain animals are misleading**;** for example, the koala bear is not a bear.

English was Louise's most difficult subject**;** accordingly, she gave it more time than any other subject.

23p. A semicolon (rather than a comma) may be needed to separate the independent clauses of a compound sentence if there are commas within the clauses.

Ordinarily, a comma is used to separate independent clauses that are joined by *and, but, or, nor, for,* or *yet.* However, if there are already commas *within* the independent clauses, an additional comma *between* the clauses might be confusing. In such a case, a stronger mark of punctuation—the semicolon—is needed.

EXAMPLE A tall, slender woman entered the large, drafty room**;** and a short, slight, blond woman followed her.

EXERCISE 11. Correcting Sentences by Using Semicolons Between Independent Clauses. Number your paper 1–10. If a sentence requires a semicolon, write the words before and after the semicolon and insert the mark of punctuation. If the sentence does not require a semicolon, write *C.*

EXAMPLE 1. The gym is on the ground floor the classrooms are above it.
1. *floor***;** *the*

1. Map-makers have explored almost all areas of the earth, they are now exploring the floors of the oceans. 1. earth; they
2. Some scientists predict the development of undersea cities, but this prediction seems at least questionable. 2. c
3. In the future, perhaps, people will choose to live in a city in space, or they may prefer to live in an undersea city. 3. c
4. Roger Maris hit his sixty-first home run during the last game of the 1961 baseball season, until then Babe Ruth had held the record for the most home runs in a season. 4. season; until
5. Some reptiles like a dry climate, but others prefer a wet climate. 5. c

COLONS (rules 23q and 23r)

The use of the colon after the salutation of a business letter and in certain conventional situations should be easy for your students. When you present the use of a colon before a list of items, make it clear that a colon is *not* used between a verb and a series of items:

I have the following teachers: Ms. Hawkins, Mr. Stein, and Ms. Kelso.
My teachers are as follows: Ms. Hawkins, Mr. Stein, and Ms. Kelso.
BUT My teachers are Ms. Hawkins, Mr. Stein, and Ms. Kelso.

Adult writers employ introductory colons in other ways which are not covered here. But learning when—and when not—to place a colon before a list is usually the first problem for a younger writer.

6. Many of today's office buildings look like glass boxes, they appear to be made entirely of windows. 6. boxes; they
7. In April 1912, a new "unsinkable" ocean liner, the *Titanic,* struck an iceberg in the North Atlantic, as a result, 1,493 persons lost their lives. 7. Atlantic; as
8. The *Titanic* carried nearly 2,200 passengers and crew, however, it had only enough lifeboats to accommodate 950. 8. crew; however
9. The tragedy brought stricter safety regulations for ships, for example, the new laws required more lifeboats. 9. ships; for
10. Today's shipwrecks can produce a different kind of tragedy, for instance, if a large oil tanker is wrecked, the spilled oil damages beaches and kills wildlife. 10. tragedy; for

COLONS

The colon says, in effect, "Note what follows."

23q. Use a colon before a list of items, especially after expressions like *as follows* or *the following.*

EXAMPLES Minimum equipment for camping is as follows**:** bedroll, utensils for cooking and eating, warm clothing, sturdy shoes, jackknife, rope, and flashlight.

This is what I have to do**:** clean my room, shop for a birthday present, baby-sit for Mrs. Magill for two hours, and do my Spanish homework.

MECHANICS

23r. Use a colon in certain conventional situations.

(1) Use a colon between the hour and the minute when you write the time.

EXAMPLES 11**:**30 P.M. 4**:**08 A.M.

(2) Use a colon after the salutation of a business letter.

EXAMPLES Gentlemen**:**
Dear Ms. Gonzalez**:**
Dear Sir**:**

REVIEW EXERCISE B. You may prefer to require that the sentences be written out in full. A less-advanced class should probably omit this exercise.

REVIEW EXERCISE B. Correcting Sentences by Adding Colons and Commas. Number your paper 1–5. Supply necessary colons and commas by writing the word before a mark of punctuation and adding the punctuation. Optional commas are circled.

1. During the field trip our teacher pointed out the following trees: sugarberry, pawpaw, silverbell, and mountain laurel.
2. The first lunch period begins at 11:00 A.M.
3. This is my motto: laugh and the world laughs with you.
4. These languages are offered: Spanish, French, Russian and German.
5. The artist showed me how to obtain a flesh color simply mix white, yellow, and a little red.

WRITING APPLICATION B:
Using Semicolons to Join Closely Related Ideas

Using semicolons between independent clauses signals your reader that the ideas in the clauses are closely related. However, few ideas are so closely related that they are equal in importance. Thus, you will probably not use the semicolon often. Compare the following examples:

EXAMPLES The rain began before dawn; I went shopping.
The rain began before dawn; it lasted all day.

The connection between the two ideas in the first example is not at all clear to the reader. The second sentence correctly combines two closely related ideas with a semicolon. When you use a semicolon, always check to make sure that the ideas it combines are closely related.

Writing Assignment

Answers will vary.

Write a paragraph explaining how something you said or did brought about an unexpected event. As you revise your paragraph, make sure that you have used semicolons to connect only closely related ideas. Then make a clean copy of your paragraph.

CHAPTER 23 REVIEW: POSTTEST

This posttest requires that the students rewrite paragraphs adding end marks, commas, semicolons, and colons. Your less-advanced students should probably not attempt this test.

CHAPTER 23 REVIEW: POSTTEST

Correcting Sentences by Adding End Marks, Commas, Semicolons, and Colons. Rewrite the following paragraphs, inserting punctuation as needed. Optional commas are circled.

EXAMPLE 1. Did I ever tell you how our washing machine which usually behaves itself once turned into a foaming monster

1. *Did I ever tell you how our washing machine, which usually behaves itself, once turned into a foaming monster?*

(1) "Oh, no! The basement is full of soapsuds!" my younger sister Sheila yelled. (2) When I heard her, I could tell how upset she was. (3) Her voice had that tense, strained tone that I know so well. (4) Running downstairs to the basement, I immediately saw why she was excited. (5) Imagine the following scene: the washing machine was completely hidden in a thick, foamy flow of bubbles. (6) I ran across the slippery floor, fought my way through the foam, and turned off the machine.

(7) This, of course, only stopped the flow. (8) Sheila and I now had to clean up the mess, for we didn't want Mom and Dad to see it when they got home. (9) We mopped up soapsuds, we sponged water off the floor, and we dried the outside of the washing machine. (10) After nearly an hour of exhausting effort, we were satisfied with our work and decided to try the washer.

(11) Everything would have been fine if the machine had still worked; however, it would not even start. (12) Can you imagine how upset we both were then? (13) Thinking things over, we decided to call a repair shop.

(14) We frantically telephoned Mr. Hodges, who runs the appliance-repair business nearest to our town. (15) We told him the problem; then we asked him to come to 21 Crestview Drive, Ellenville, as soon as possible.

(16) When he arrived, Mr. Hodges inspected the machine, asked us a few questions, and said that we had no real problem. (17) The

MECHANICS

wires had become damp,and we were to let the machine sit for a day before we tried to use it again.

(18) Surprised and relieved ,we thanked Mr .Hodges and started toward the stairs to show him the way out.(19) He stopped us,however,and asked if we knew what had caused the problem with the suds.(20) We didn't want to admit our ignorance,but our hesitation gave us away.(21) Well,Mr.Hodges suggested that from now on we should measure the soap instead of just pouring it into the machine.

(22) Looking at the empty box of laundry powder,I realized what had happened.(23) It was,I believe,the first time Sheila had used the washing machine by herself,and no one had told her to read the instructions on the box.

(24) This incident occurred on November 10,1983,and we have never forgotten it.(25) Whenever we do the laundry now,we remember the lesson we learned the day the washer overflowed.

MECHANICS

Additional Practice

Teacher's Resource Book, Worksheet pages 264–82, Alternative Worksheet pages (for less-advanced students) 563–64

Testing

Teaching Tests booklet, pages 65–68, 71–72, 77–83
Teacher's Resource Book, Test pages 469–72, 475–76, 481–92

Chapter Overview

Eighth-graders should begin to use marks of punctuation correctly and confidently in their own writing. The exercises and writing applications in this chapter give them a chance to practice these marks.

All students should work toward mastering the use of the apostrophe in possessives and contractions. This work has already been taught in the earlier grades, and for many students an occasional reminder may be sufficient. The two uses of the hyphen and thc usc of quotation marks and italics with titles are also fairly simple.

Chapter Objective

Students will use italics, quotation marks, apostrophes, and hyphens to make their writing clear.

PRESENTING THE CHAPTER

LESS ADVANCED STUDENTS These students may have difficulty remembering many of the rules in the chapter. They should form the habit of referring to this and the preceding chapter whenever they are in doubt about punctuation. Encourage this habit by writing marginal notes in their compositions telling them to look up specific rules whenever they make errors in punctuation. Some teachers omit teaching the punctuation of written dialogue to a less-advanced class. Note that some students have greater difficulty mastering the use of the apostrophe in the possessive plural form. Give these students plenty of drill. *(See listing of Alternative Worksheets on page 571.)*

MECHANICS

CHAPTER 24

Punctuation

ITALICS, QUOTATION MARKS, APOSTROPHES, HYPHENS

Just as you use different facial expressions, gestures, and intonations to convey meaning when you speak, you need a variety of different marks of punctuation to make the meaning of your writing clear. In this chapter you will study the use of four more marks of punctuation.

DIAGNOSTIC TEST

A. Proofreading Sentences for the Correct Use of Apostrophes and Hyphens. Number your paper 1–10. Each of the following sentences contains one or two errors in the use of apostrophes or hyphens. After the proper number, write each sentence correctly.

EXAMPLE 1. Rays mother said that hed have to mow the lawn before he could play soccer.
1. *Ray's mother said that he'd have to mow the lawn before he could play soccer.*

1. Marsha is this years captain of the girls basketball team.
   1. year's, girls'
2. The plants leaves had wilted and its stem had shriveled.
   2. plant's

3. At one time or another, Ive tried to play the piano, the guitar, and the clarinet. 3. I've
4. We couldnt have done the job without you're help. 4. couldn't, your
5. Shes strict about being on time. 5. She's
6. On my older brothers last birthday, he turned twenty one. 6. brother's, twenty-one
7. Wed have forgotten to turn off the computer if Maggie hadnt reminded us. 7. We'd, hadn't
8. The recipe said to add two eggs, a teaspoon of salt, and a three quarter cup of milk. 8. three-quarter
9. My fathers office is on the twenty second floor. 9. father's, twenty-second
10. The soldiers supplies had run out, and its doubtful whether they could have survived without reinforcements. 10. soldiers', it's

B. Proofreading Sentences for the Correct Use of Quotation Marks and Underlining (Italics). Number your paper 11–20. Each of the following sentences contains one or two errors in the use of quotation marks or underlining (italics). After the proper number, rewrite each sentence correctly. See Answer Key.

EXAMPLE 1. Mary asked, "Did you read Robert Frost's poem Nothing Gold Can Stay out loud in class?"
1. *Mary asked, "Did you read Robert Frost's poem 'Nothing Gold Can Stay' out loud in class?"*

11. Uncle Ned reads the Wall Street Journal every day.
12. Fill in all the information on both sides of the form, the secretary said.
13. How many times have you seen the movie of Margaret Mitchell's novel Gone with the Wind?
14. Many of the students enjoyed the humor and irony in O. Henry's short story The Ransom of Red Chief.
15. My little sister asked, Why can't I have a hamster?
16. Please don't sing I've Been Working on the Railroad.
17. Over the summer my older sister played in a band on a Caribbean cruise ship named Bright Coastal Star.
18. "Read E. B. White's essay The Decline of Sport, and answer the study questions," the teacher announced.

MECHANICS

ADVANCED STUDENTS Encourage these students to apply the rules in this chapter to their own writing. For example, they should be able to include dialogue, correctly punctuated, in their narratives.

WRITING APPLICATIONS

The writing applications in this chapter are designed to encourage students to use the rules for correct punctuation in their own writing. Feel free to adapt these assignments to your students' writing needs, abilities, and interests.

DIAGNOSTIC TEST

This test will give you a clear picture of what your students already know about these punctuation marks. Use the results of the test to help you plan your teaching. Allow enough time for your students to write the sentences.

19. Dudley Randall's poem Ancestors questions why people always seem to believe that their ancestors were aristocrats.
20. "Wait here," the clerk said, while I go to check the price.

UNDERLINING (ITALICS)
(rule 24a)

Make sure students understand that underlining is equivalent to italics. Rule 24a (on page 554) and rule 24k (on page 560) should usually be taught at the same time, so that you can make it clear which kinds of titles require underlining and which kinds require quotation marks.

UNDERLINING (ITALICS)

Italics are printed letters that lean to the right, *like this.* In handwritten or typewritten work, italics are indicated by underlining. If your composition were to be printed in a book or some other publication, the typesetter would use italics for underlined words. For example, if you wrote

Born Free is the story of a lioness that became a pet.

the printed version would look like this:

Born Free is the story of a lioness that became a pet.

24a. Use underlining (italics) for titles of books, periodicals, works of art, plays, films, television programs, ships, and so on.

EXAMPLES *Big Red* is a book about an Irish setter.
Van Gogh's *Sunflowers* is a well-known painting.
The *Philadelphia Inquirer* has won many of the nation's top journalism awards.
Jacques-Yves Cousteau has outfitted the *Calypso* as a seagoing research lab.
Star Wars was one of the most popular movies ever made.

MECHANICS

> ☞ **NOTE** When writing the title of a newspaper or a magazine within a sentence, underline the title. Do not underline or capitalize the word *the* with the name of a newspaper or magazine within a sentence. The name of a city in a newspaper title is usually underlined.

EXAMPLE My parents subscribe to two newspapers published in other cities: the *St. Louis Post-Dispatch* and the *San Francisco Chronicle.*

EXERCISE 1. Using Underlining to Indicate Titles. Number your paper 1–10. After the proper number, write and underline the words in the sentence that should be italics.

EXAMPLE 1. Have you read The Call of the Wild?
1. *The Call of the Wild*

1. Popular Mechanics, Sports Illustrated, and Seventeen are all popular magazines in our library.
2. In Wednesday's edition of the Globe-Democrat, there is a section on baking bread.
3. The final number will be a medley of excerpts from George Gershwin's opera Porgy and Bess.
4. Elizabeth Speare won the Newbery Medal twice, for her books The Witch of Blackbird Pond and The Bronze Bow.
5. Picasso's painting Guernica is named for a Spanish town that was destroyed during the Spanish Civil War.
6. Katharine Graham, the publisher of the Washington Post, is one of this year's commencement speakers.
7. The first battle between ironclad ships took place between the Monitor and the Merrimac in 1862.
8. Have you seen both versions of the movie Close Encounters of the Third Kind?
9. Betty Comden and Adolph Green have written such Broadway shows as Bells Are Ringing and Fade Out, Fade In.
10. The magazine rack held issues of National Wildlife, Time, Popular Photography, Ladies Home Journal, and The Runner.

WRITING QUOTATIONS

Quotations are words spoken or written by someone and reported directly. In your writing you will often find it necessary to tell

MECHANICS

EXERCISE 1. If you wish to give additional drill, ask your students to write original sentences illustrating rule 24a.

WRITING QUOTATIONS (rules 24b–24k)

The rule for the use of quotation marks with titles appears, with examples, on page 560 of the text, at the end of this section. The first several pages of the section concern the punctuation of written dialogue.

Learning to punctuate dialogue correctly may seem difficult because it involves—in addition to the distinction between indirect and direct quotations—the use of commas, capital letters, and properly placed end marks. However, students do not seem to have any more trouble learning to punctuate dialogue than they do learning to punctuate other constructions. Perhaps the very complexity of the skill poses a challenge that students enjoy.

Write several examples of correctly punctuated dialogue on the board. Then ask students to suggest rules for the use of the comma, capitals, and other punctuation with quotation marks. Write their suggestions on the board. Dictate other examples for students to write at their desks (you may take these from exercises in the text), while they can refer to the rules on the board. Have the students write the answers on the board.

Finally, have the class open their books and check the rules on the board against those in the text.

EXAMPLES FOR BOARD WORK

"Where have you been?" Mother asked. "Your father

wants you. He says that he wants you to wash the car."

"Oh, no!" I exclaimed. "I'm supposed to meet Pam in ten minutes. Where is Dad?"

"Well," Mother said, "he's probably in the garage. You had better go and talk to him."

what someone has said, whether you are describing a true happening or an imaginary one. This section explains how to write quotations in a standard form that can be easily read by others.

24b. Use quotation marks to enclose a direct quotation—a person's exact words.

Quotation marks before and after a person's words show exactly what was said.

EXAMPLES **"**Has anyone in the class swum in the Great Salt Lake?**"** asked Ms. Estrada. [Ms. Estrada's exact words]

"I swam there last summer,**"** said June. [June's exact words]

Do not confuse a person's exact words with a rewording of the person's speech. If you tell what someone said without repeating the exact words, you are using an *indirect* quotation. No quotation marks are needed for an indirect quotation.

INDIRECT Pauline asked for **my interpretation of the poem.** [not Pauline's exact words; no quotation marks needed]

DIRECT Pauline asked, **"What is your interpretation of the poem?"** [Pauline's exact words; quotation marks needed]

INDIRECT I told her that **I thought the poet was expressing awe at the power of nature.**

DIRECT **"I think the poet is expressing awe at the power of nature,"** I said.

MECHANICS

24c. A direct quotation begins with a capital letter.

EXAMPLES Jimmy shouted, "**A** parade will be held tomorrow!"

"Is it true?" asked Sandra.

24d. When a quotation is divided into two parts by an interrupting expression such as *he said* or *Mother asked,* the second part begins with a small letter.

EXAMPLES "What are some of the things," asked Mrs. Perkins, "**t**hat the astronauts discovered on the moon?"

"One thing they discovered," answered Gwen, "**w**as that the moon is covered by a layer of dust."

"Gee," George added, "**m**y room at home is a lot like the moon, I guess."

If the second part of an interrupted quotation starts a new sentence, it should start with a capital letter.

EXAMPLE "Any new means of travel is exciting," she remarked. "**S**pace travel is no exception." [The second part begins with a capital because it is a new sentence.]

EXERCISE 2. Correcting Sentences by Adding Capital Letters and Punctuation. Write the following sentences, supplying whatever capitals and marks of punctuation are needed. For the two sentences that require no changes, write *C*.

EXAMPLE 1. Now, said the teacher, you may go to the library.
1. *"Now," said the teacher, "you may go to the library."*

1. I hope, said Elizabeth, that we will reach Atlanta soon.
2. if the traffic does not get worse, the driver predicted, we should be there in half an hour.
3. Mrs. Yamasaki, our physical education teacher, told us we would begin the volleyball unit Monday.
4. We took the injured young owl into the house, said Dick, and we made a nest for it in a basket.
5. Mr. Howard said that we might have trouble persuading the owlet to eat.

24e. A direct quotation is set off from the rest of the sentence by commas or by a question mark or exclamation point.

EXAMPLES "I've just finished reading a book about Narcissa Whitman**,**" Ellen said.

"Was she one of the early settlers in the Northwest**?**" asked Janet.

EXERCISE 2. Have volunteers write the corrected sentences on the board.

Answers: Exercise 2

1. "I hope," said Elizabeth, "that we will reach Atlanta soon."
2. "If the traffic does not get worse," the driver predicted, "we should be there in half an hour."
3. C
4. "We took the injured young owl into the house," said Dick, "and we made a nest for it in a basket."
5. C

EXERCISES 3 and 4. After students complete the assignments individually, have the sentences written on the board so that the entire class can see the correct punctuation.

Answers: Exercise 3

1. "Mother, will you take us to the soccer field?" asked Libby.
2. "Please hold my viola case for a minute, Dave," Josh said. "I need to tie my shoelace."
3. Cary asked, "What is pita bread?"

"What an adventure**!**" exclaimed Carol.
Tom said**,** "I wish I had been there."

24f. A period or a comma following a quotation should be placed inside the closing quotation marks. A period is only used if the quotation comes at the end of the sentence that includes it.

EXAMPLES Ramon said, "Hank Aaron was better than Babe Ruth because he hit more home runs in his career**.**"

"But Hank Aaron never hit sixty in one year**,**" countered Paula.

24g. A question mark or an exclamation point should be placed inside the closing quotation marks if the quotation is a question or an exclamation. Otherwise, it should be placed outside.

EXAMPLES "What is the time difference between Los Angeles and Chicago**?**" asked Ken. [The quotation is a question.]

Linda exclaimed, "I thought everyone knew that**!**" [The quotation is an exclamation.]

Is the right answer "two hours"**?** [The quotation is not a question, but the sentence as a whole is.]

If the sentence and the quotation are both questions, you still use only one question mark.

EXAMPLE Who said, "What's in a name?"

MECHANICS

EXERCISE 3. Correcting Sentences by Adding Capital Letters and Punctuation. Revise the following sentences, supplying capitals and marks of punctuation as needed. See Answer Key.

EXAMPLE 1. Why she asked can't we leave now
1. *"Why," she asked, "can't we leave now?"*

1. Mother, will you take us to the soccer field asked Libby
2. Please hold my viola case for a minute, Dave Josh said I need to tie my shoelace
3. Cary asked What is pita bread

4. Did Therese answer It's a round, flat Middle Eastern bread
5. Run Run cried the boys a tornado is headed this way

4. Did Therese answer, "It's a round, flat Middle Eastern bread"?
5. "Run! Run!" cried the boys. "A tornado is headed this way!"

24h. When you write dialogue (conversation), begin a new paragraph each time you change speakers.

EXAMPLE "What did you think of that movie about Japan?" Sara asked Ron as they left the school building.

"I was surprised at the scenes in Tokyo. I didn't know it was so much like Chicago or New York."

"I guess a lot of the young people don't wear traditional Japanese clothes nowadays," Sara said.

24i. When a quotation consists of several sentences, put quotation marks only at the beginning and at the end of the whole quotation, not around each sentence in the quotation.

INCORRECT "Memorize all your lines for Monday." "Have someone at home give you your cues." "Enjoy your weekend!" said Ms. Goodwin.

CORRECT **"**Memorize all your lines for Monday. Have someone at home give you your cues. Enjoy your weekend!**"** said Ms. Goodwin.

EXERCISE 4. Punctuating and Paragraphing Dialogue. Revise the following dialogue, punctuating and paragraphing it correctly. See Answer Key.

Lynette, did you enjoy reading *The Yearling* Miss Bishop asked I think it's the best book I have ever read, Miss Bishop Can you tell us why you liked it The characters seemed so real Lynette replied and their struggles made me like them even more What were some of the struggles Jody and his family faced They struggled to raise crops and to gather food to get through the winter Jody was lonely until he found Flag What conflicts did keeping the deer as a pet cause Flag ate some of the crops, and Jody pleaded with his father to keep the deer Jody loved his pet and had trouble admitting it couldn't live with the family Good, Lynette

EXERCISE 5. For additional drill, you can ask students to write sentences of their own about books, periodicals, articles, short stories, and poems.

Answers: Exercise 5

1. "Has anyone read the story 'To Build a Fire'?" asked the teacher.
2. "I have," said Eileen. "It was written by Jack London."
3. Do you know the poem "To Make a Prairie"?
4. *New Yorker*
5. "Did you read," asked Ms. Carlson, "the article 'Animal Architects' in the *St. Louis Post-Dispatch*?"

24j. Use single quotation marks to enclose a quotation within a quotation.

EXAMPLES "I said, 'The quiz will cover Unit 2 and your special reports,'" repeated Mr. Allyn.

"What poem begins with the line, 'I'm going out to clean the pasture spring'?" Carol asked.

24k. Use quotation marks to enclose titles of short works such as poems, short stories, articles, songs and individual episodes of television programs; and of chapters and other parts of books.[1]

EXAMPLES Irwin Shaw's "Strawberry Ice-Cream Soda" is a story of an older and a younger brother.

Our assignment for tomorrow is the first part of Chapter 11, "Americans Create New States out of the Wilderness."

The poetry of Elizabeth Madox Roberts is the subject of an article called "A Tent of Green" in the *Horn Book Magazine.*

EXERCISE 5. Using Punctuation Marks, Quotation Marks, and Underlining (Italics). Write the following sentences, inserting punctuation marks and quotation marks where needed. Underline words that should be in italics.

MECHANICS

EXAMPLE 1. We sang Greensleeves for the assembly.
1. *We sang "Greensleeves" for the assembly.*

1. Has anyone read the story To Build a Fire asked the teacher.
2. I have said Eileen. It was written by Jack London.
3. Do you know the poem To Make a Prairie?
4. The New Yorker magazine features excellent short stories.
5. Did you read asked Ms. Carlson the article Animal Architects in the St. Louis Post-Dispatch?

[1] For the use of italics for titles, see rule 24a on page 554.

REVIEW EXERCISE A. Correcting Sentences by Adding Punctuation and Capital Letters. If a sentence is correct, write *C* after its number on your paper. Revise the incorrect sentences, making all necessary corrections.

1. "Won't you stay," pleaded Wynnie, "there will be refreshments and music later."
2. "Why, Jason," said Irv, "you play the drums like an expert!"
3. The girls asked if we needed help finding our campsite.
4. "Elise, do you know who said a chicken in every pot" asked the teacher.
5. "What a wonderful day for a picnic!" exclaimed Susan.
6. Dear me whispered Connie doesn't this speaker know when to say In conclusion. . .
7. When President Lincoln heard of the South's defeat, he requested that the band play Dixie.
8. The latest issue of National Geographic has an article on rain forests.
9. What can have happened to Linda this time, Tina Didn't she say I'll be home long before you are ready to leave?
10. Langston Hughes's Dream Deferred is a moving poem.

WRITING APPLICATION A:
Using Dialogue in Narration

Using dialogue helps make your readers feel as though they are hearing an actual conversation. When you write narration, using dialogue that is natural and realistic can help show the personalities of your characters.

Writing Assignment

Answers will vary.

Write a one-page narrative using dialogue between two characters that reveals their personalities. After you revise what you have written, proofread it carefully: Make sure that you have used quotation marks and paragraphing correctly so that your readers will know which character is speaking. Then make a clean copy of your paper.

REVIEW EXERCISE A. This exercise is most suitable for an average or advanced class. Less-advanced students may need your help; you might use the exercise as a class activity.

Answers: Review Exercise A

1. "Won't you stay?" pleaded Wynnie. "There will be refreshments and music later."
2. C
3. C
4. "Elise, do you know who said, 'A chicken in every pot'?" asked the teacher.
5. C
6. "Dear me," whispered Connie, "doesn't this speaker know when to say, 'In conclusion . . .'?"
7. "Dixie."
8. *National Geographic*
9. What can have happened to Linda this time, Tina? Didn't she say, "I'll be home long before you are ready to leave"?
10. "Dream Deferred"

APOSTROPHES
(rules 24l–24o)

Although your eighth-graders are familiar with apostrophes used in possessives and contractions, they probably still make errors. The use of apostrophes with possessives is especially troublesome for many students.

THE POSSESSIVE CASE
(rules 24l and 24m)

Put on the board this summary of the rules and ask your class to memorize it:

1. To form the possessive of a singular noun, add an apostrophe and an *s*.
   EXAMPLES mouse—*mouse's* tail
   cat—*cat's* tail
2. To form the possessive of a plural noun—
   Add only an apostrophe if the plural noun ends in *s*.
   EXAMPLE cats—*cats'* tails
   Add an apostrophe and an *s* if the plural noun does not end in *s*.
   EXAMPLE mice—*mice's* tails

The class may need to study or review the plurals of nouns (text pages 577–79) in connection with this work.

Give your students the following reminders about when *not* to use an apostrophe.

1. Do *not* use an apostrophe with a possessive pronoun: *his, hers, its, ours, yours, theirs*.
2. Do *not* use an apostrophe with plurals which are not possessives.
   EXAMPLE *Cats* have tails.

MECHANICS

APOSTROPHES

The *apostrophe* has two uses: to show ownership or relationship, and to show where letters have been omitted in a contraction.

The Possessive Case

The possessive case of a noun or pronoun shows ownership or relationship.

OWNERSHIP	RELATIONSHIP
Sandra's boat	an hour's time
Mother's job	Julio's father
a book's title	person's responsibility

☞ **NOTE** Personal pronouns in the possessive case require no apostrophe: Is this bat *ours, yours,* or *theirs*?

24l. To form the possessive case of a singular noun, add an apostrophe and an *s*.

EXAMPLES a dog's collar
a moment's thought
one cent's worth
Charles's typewriter

Exception: A proper name ending in *s* may take only an apostrophe to form the possessive case under these conditions:

1. The name consists of two or more syllables.
2. Adding *'s* would make the name awkward to pronounce.

EXAMPLES Mr. and Mrs. Rogers' house
Marjorie Kinnan Rawlings' novels
Hercules' feats

EXERCISE 6. Supplying Apostrophes for Possessive Nouns. Number your paper 1–5. After the proper number, write the noun or nouns that are in the possessive case and supply the necessary apostrophes.

Note: *If your students are having trouble mastering the basic uses of the apostrophe, avoid teaching the exception given below rule 24l on page 562. Relatively few nouns fall under this exception, and even for those few, the use of 's (instead of just the apostrophe) is allowable.*

EXERCISES 6 and 7. Most students will profit from doing both of these exercises.

EXAMPLE 1. The dogs leash is too short.
1. *dog's*

1. That trucks taillights are broken. 1. truck's
2. The judges were impressed with Veronicas project. 2. Veronica's
3. Last weeks meals were meatless ones. 3. week's
4. Matthias dream is to have a horse like his sisters palomino. 4. Matthias', sister's
5. Please pack your mothers books and Joans toys. 5. mother's, Joan's

24m. To form the possessive case of a plural noun ending in *s*, add only the apostrophe.

EXAMPLES friends' invitations doctors' opinions
citizens' committee pupils' records

The few plural nouns that do not end in *s* form the possessive just as singular nouns do, by adding an apostrophe and an *s*.

EXAMPLES men's suits geese's noise
mice's tracks children's voices

> ☞ **NOTE** Do not use an apostrophe to form the *plural* of a noun. The apostrophe shows ownership or relationship, not number.

INCORRECT The new car's are sporty this year.
CORRECT The new cars are sporty this year. [plural]
CORRECT The new car's styling is sporty. [possessive]

A noun in the possessive case (shown by an apostrophe) is usually followed by a noun.

EXAMPLES car's styling women's group
book's cover Jean's friends

EXERCISE 7. Forming Plural Possessives. Number your paper 1–10. After the proper number, write the possessive for each of the following plural expressions.

EXERCISE 8. This exercise continues the drill on possessives. Assign it even if you assigned both of the two preceding exercises.

CONTRACTIONS (rule 24n)

Take the class over the examples and the lists of common contractions on pages 564–65. (You may wish to point out that *she'd* and *you'd* can also stand for *she had* and *you had*.) Most students have little trouble with contractions except for confusion between the sound-alike pairs *its–it's*, *whose–who's* and *your–you're*. Teachers often find that they have to review the differences between these words frequently during the course of the year. It is sometimes effective to give students the following rule for the three pairs: *If you can turn the word into two separate words (it is, who is, you are), it is a contraction and needs an apostrophe; if you cannot separate it into two words, it does not need an apostrophe.*

EXAMPLE 1. artists paintings
1. *artists' paintings*

1. boys' 2. women's 5. girls' 6. Joneses' 9. cities' 10. oxen's

1. boys boots
2. women careers
3. friends comments
4. three days work
5. girls parents
6. Joneses cabin
7. men shoes
8. children games
9. cities mayors
10. oxen yokes

3. friends' 4. days' work 7. men's 8. children's

EXERCISE 8. Writing Singular Possessives, Plurals, and Plural Possessives. Number your paper 1–10. Divide your paper into three columns. Label the columns *Singular Possessive, Plural,* and *Plural Possessive.* In each column, write the form of the following nouns that the column label calls for. See Answer Key.

1. stove
2. puppy
3. donkey
4. mouse
5. calf
6. potato
7. elephant
8. tooth
9. school
10. valley

MECHANICS

Contractions

24n. Use an apostrophe to show where letters have been omitted in a contraction.

A *contraction* is a word made by combining two (or more) words to make one shorter word. An apostrophe takes the place of the letters that are omitted.

EXAMPLES **Where is** the exit?
Where's the exit?

We will have gone by then.
We'll have gone by then.

The word *not* is contracted *n't,* and is often added to a verb to form a contraction. Usually the spelling of the verb is unchanged.

is not	isn't	has not	hasn't
are not	aren't	have not	haven't
does not	doesn't	had not	hadn't
do not	don't	should not	shouldn't
was not	wasn't	would not	wouldn't
were not	weren't	could not	couldn't

However, in some cases the spelling does change, as in the following contraction: *won't* for *will not.*

Contractions may also be formed with nouns or pronouns and verbs:

I am	I'm	you will	you'll
you are	you're	they are	they're
she would	she'd	Ann is	Ann's

Its and *It's*

The word *its* is a pronoun in the possessive case. It does not have an apostrophe.

The word *it's* is a contraction of *it is* or *it has* and requires an apostrophe.

EXAMPLES **Its** front tire is flat. [*Its* is a possessive pronoun.]
It's wet paint. [*It's* means *it is.*]
It's been a long time. [*It's* means *it has.*]

Whose and *Who's*

The word *whose* is a pronoun in the possessive case. It does not have an apostrophe.

The word *who's* means *who is* or *who has.* Since it is a contraction, it requires an apostrophe.

EXAMPLES **Whose** idea was it? [*Whose* is possessive.]
Who's next in line? [*Who's* means *who is.*]
Who's been in my room? [*Who's* means *who has.*]

Your and *You're*

The word *your* is a possessive pronoun. It does not have an apostrophe.

You're is a contraction of *you are.* It requires an apostrophe to show where the letter *a* is omitted.

EXAMPLES **Your** paper shows great improvement, Leon. [*Your* is a pronoun in the possessive case.]
You're going to get a better mark this term. [*You're* means *you are.*]

PLURALS (rule 24o)

If your students still have trouble distinguishing between plurals and possessives, do not teach this rule. It will come up rarely, if at all, in your eighth-graders' writing.

WRITING APPLICATION B:
Using Underlining, Quotation Marks, and Apostrophes to Make Your Writing Clear

Using underlining, quotation marks, and apostrophes correctly helps make your writing clear. Compare the following sets of sentences.

EXAMPLES Have you seen the sun today?
Have you seen the *Sun* today?
He said he cannot go with us.
He said, "He cannot go with us."
Well, take care of it right away.
We'll take care of it right away.

As you can see, the punctuation makes a great deal of difference. Always proofread your writing carefully to make sure that you have used punctuation marks correctly to make your meaning clear.

Writing Assignment

Answers will vary.

Write six sentences, using one of the following words in each sentence: *its, it's, whose, who's, your, you're.* Proofread your sentences to make sure that you have used the words correctly.

MECHANICS

Plurals

24o. Use an apostrophe and *s* to form the plurals of letters, numbers, and signs, and of words referred to as words.

EXAMPLES Doesn't he know the *ABC*'s?
Your *2*'s look like *5*'s.
Don't use *&*'s in place of *and*'s.
I hope to make all A's.

EXERCISE 9. Correcting Sentences by Adding Apostrophes. Number your paper 1–10. Rewrite the items that require apostrophes in the following sentences, and insert the apostrophes where they belong.

EXAMPLE 1. Do you know what youre doing?
1. *you're*

1. The girls didnt say when theyd be back. 1. didn't, they'd
2. Lets find out when the next game is. 2. Let's
3. Dorothy usually gets all *A*s and *B*s on her report card. 3. *A*'s, *B*'s
4. It isnt correct to use *&*s in your compositions. 4. isn't, *&*'s
5. Many of the scores were in the 80s and 90s. 5. 80's, 90's
6. They cant come with us; theyre studying. 6. can't, they're
7. Theyll meet us later, if its all right to tell them where were going. 7. they'll, it's, we're
8. Whos signed up for the talent show? 8. Who's
9. Dont those *2*s look like *z*s to you? 9. Don't, *2*'s, *z*'s
10. Your capital *L*s and *F*s are hard to tell apart. 10. *L*'s, *F*s

HYPHENS

24p. Use a hyphen to divide a word at the end of a line.

Sometimes you will find that there is not enough space for a whole word at the end of the line. When this happens, you may divide the word, using a *hyphen* to indicate the division.

EXAMPLES How long has the building been under construction?
If you want to know, look it up in the almanac.

Be careful to divide words only between syllables. For the rules on dividing words, see page 42.

24q. Use a hyphen with compound numbers from twenty-one to ninety-nine and with fractions used as adjectives.

EXERCISE 9. You may want to have your students write out the sentences in full.

HYPHENS (rules 24p and 24q)

If your students do not know how to use the dictionary to find syllables of a word, give them practice on this point. Most eighth-graders know that compound numbers and fractions are hyphenated. With an advanced class, you may wish to explain the additional point that fractions used as nouns are *not* hyphenated.

EXERCISE 10. Permit your students to refer to the examples when they write this exercise.

REVIEW EXERCISE B. This exercise provides an easy review of contractions.

REVIEW EXERCISE C. Go over students' answers in class, referring to the rules in the chapter whenever a question arises.

EXAMPLES There were twenty-one ducks in that flock.

A two-thirds majority will decide the issue, and the other one third will have to abide by the decision.

In the first use, *two-thirds* is a compound adjective modifying *majority;* in the second use, *third* is a noun modified by the single adjective *one.*

EXERCISE 10. Hyphenating Numbers and Fractions. Number your paper 1–5. After the proper number, write the words from the following expressions that require hyphens. Supply hyphens. If an expression is correct, write *C.*

1. a three-fourths majority
2. one half of the money 2. c
3. one hundred twenty-five contestants
4. Twenty-third Street
5. forty-eight decorated eggs

REVIEW EXERCISE B. Forming Contractions. Number your paper 1–20. Form contractions from the following groups of words.

1. won't 2. there's 3. who'll 4. they're 5. who's 6. aren't 7. it's 8. shouldn't 9. let's 10. can't 11. you're 12. doesn't 13. he'd 14. hasn't 15. we're 16. I'm 17. hadn't

1. will not	6. are not	11. you are	16. I am
2. there is	7. it is	12. does not	17. had not
3. who will	8. should not	13. he would	18. she is
4. they are	9. let us	14. has not	19. you will
5. who is	10. can not	15. we are	20. could not

18. she's 19. you'll 20. couldn't

MECHANICS

REVIEW EXERCISE C. Inserting Apostrophes and Hyphens. Number your paper 1–10. After the proper number, write the words in the following sentences that require apostrophes or hyphens. Supply the apostrophes and hyphens.

1. Theres where they live. 1. There's
2. Wholl volunteer to participate in next weeks campaign? 2. Who'll, week's
3. The Lockwood sisters golden retriever is named Storm. 3. sisters'
4. One third of Hollys allowance goes into the bank. 4. Holly's

5. From Fifty-third Street down to Forty-fifth, there are ninety-seven businesses.
6. Twenty- six student council members voted to change the school song that theyd selected. 6. they'd
7. Shelly signed up for the writing class because shed heard how helpful it was. 7. she'd
8. If two thirds of the class has a score below seventy-five, well all have to retake the test. 8. we'll
9. Lets see whats happening at the park today. 9. Let's, what's
10. Ninety-seven years ago my great-grandparents left Scotland for the United States.

REVIEW EXERCISE D. Correcting Sentences by Adding Punctuation. Rewrite the following sentences, supplying the needed punctuation marks, including quotation marks.

See Answer Key.

1. Ill see you at the sale tomorrow at Sport World said Vera Its on the corner of Thirty ninth and Vine.
2. Today's Geneva Gazeteer has a story about the fire at the Pattersons home; its roof was destroyed.
3. Belinda, Bill, Don, and Vickie have each read at least twenty one books since last years book fair.
4. I cant imagine remarked Judy a more terrifying short story than The Most Dangerous Game.
5. Seventy three percent of the legislators voted to extend the school day.
6. Lisa reported that one third of the students interviewed said they usually had no homework, while a two thirds majority said that they had too much.
7. Although I offered to help with the cleanup, Renee explained, Brian said that he could manage alone.
8. Augusta Savages Lift Every Voice and Sing is the sculpture Id most like to see for myself.
9. Larues eyes twinkled as he replied Why, Ive no idea what youre talking about nobodys planning a party.
10. Shelly ride to todays meeting with us.

REVIEW EXERCISE D. A less-advanced class should probably omit this exercise, or you may want to use it as a class activity with these students.

MECHANICS

CHAPTER 24 REVIEW: POSTTEST

This test, which contains twenty items, requires students to write the sentences, so allow enough time for the test. Punctuating these sentences correctly will test students' knowledge of underlining, quotation marks, apostrophes, and hyphens.

CHAPTER 24 REVIEW: POSTTEST

A. Proofreading Sentences for the Correct Use of Apostrophes and Hyphens. Number your paper 1–10. Each of the following sentences contains one or two errors in the use of apostrophes or hyphens. After the proper number, write each sentence correctly. Some words will require respelling.

EXAMPLE 1. Our ad appeared in todays paper, but our phone number wasnt included.
1. *Our ad appeared in today's paper, but our phone number wasn't included.*

1. The dog's havent been fed yet. 1. dogs haven't
2. Its a two-thirds mixture. 2. It's
3. The decoration committees purchases included crepe paper, confetti, and seventy-two balloons. 3. committee's
4. The car wouldn't start; its battery was dead. 4. C
5. Alinas sister looked at all the greeting cards and finally took the one shed selected to the cashier. 5. Alina's, she'd
6. You're tour of Chicago should include a drive along Lake Michigan to see the citys skyline. 6. Your, city's
7. This work cant wait any longer; well have to do it now. 7. can't, we'll
8. There was a big party at the Rogers house when Mr. Rogers was forty-seven years old. 8. Rogers'
9. My great-grandfather often tells us to mind our *p*s and *q*s. 9. *p*'s, *q*'s
10. My aunt, who's job takes her all over the world, sends me postcards from the places she visits. 10. whose

MECHANICS

B. Proofreading Sentences for the Correct Use of Quotation Marks and Underlining (Italics). Number your paper 11–20. Each of the following sentences requires underlining (italics), quotation marks, or both. After the proper number, write each sentence correctly. See Answer Key.

EXAMPLE 1. Ted, can you answer the first question? Ms. Simmons asked.
1. *"Ted, can you answer the first question?" Ms. Simmons asked.*

11. The best chapter in our vocabulary book is the last one, More Word Games.
12. "I answered all the questions, Todd said, but I think that some of my answers were wrong."
13. There is a legend that the band on the Titanic played the hymn Nearer My God to Thee as the ship sank into the icy sea.
14. Mr. Washington asked Connie, "Which flag included the slogan Don't Tread on Me?"
15. Star Wars was more exciting on the big movie screen than it was on our small television set.
16. Play the Gene Autry tape again, Mom, Jonathan said, grinning at his mother.
17. Wendy wrote an article called Students, Where Are You? for our local newspaper, the Morning Beacon.
18. In the short story The Tell-Tale Heart, Edgar Allan Poe explores the theme of guilt.
19. "Can I read Treasure Island for my book report? Carmine asked.
20. Every Christmas Eve my uncle recites The Night Before Christmas for the children in the hospital.

Additional Practice

Teacher's Resource Book, Worksheet pages 283–97, Alternative Worksheet pages (for less-advanced students) 565–66

Testing

Teaching Tests booklet, pages 65–68, 73–74, 77–83
Teacher's Resource Book, Test pages 469–72, 477–78, 481–92

Chapter Overview

In most eighth-grade English classes, spelling will be a regular part of the classwork throughout the year. Although you may want to set aside a week or two at some point for special attention to spelling (perhaps for a systematic review of the rules on text pages 573–79), this chapter is intended not to be taught as a single unit but to provide material for the year's program.

The chapter begins by suggesting five methods students can use to improve their spelling. It then presents a list of basic rules for spelling and a discussion of seventy-four "sound-alike" words which are often confused. It concludes with two spelling lists, "50 Spelling Demons" and "250 Spelling Words."

Spelling *is* difficult for many students, but there is no eighth-grader who cannot, with effort, meet a certain minimum standard: the correct spelling of the easy, familiar words that are used constantly by students in this age group and that have been taught again and again. Misspelling of the long, unusual words is relatively unimportant (although even this should be checked, if for no other reason than to teach students not to guess, but to use the dictionary).

There is no single best way to teach spelling. For a discussion of some suggested teaching procedures, see Section III, pages T78–79, in the front of this *Annotated Teacher's Edition*.

Chapter Objective

Students will demonstrate good spelling habits, observe spelling

MECHANICS

CHAPTER 25

Spelling

IMPROVING YOUR SPELLING

English is a language that is not consistent in its representation of sounds. For this reason, learning to spell in English is a challenging task. You have learned to spell many thousands of words, but there are probably others that give you trouble. You can improve your ability to spell provided you approach the task slowly and easily—and provided you have the will and patience to learn.

GOOD SPELLING HABITS

1. *Keep a list of your own errors.* As your ability to spell improves, you will notice that some words seem to be especially difficult for you. But don't be discouraged; make your own spelling book. The best way to master words that you find troublesome is to list them and review them frequently.

2. *Use the dictionary as a spelling aid.* Develop the habit of consulting a dictionary whenever you have a spelling problem.

3. *Spell by syllables.* If you have trouble spelling long words, break them up into syllables. A syllable is a part of a word that can be pronounced by itself. The word *remember* has three syllables: *re·mem·ber.* A long word then becomes a group of short parts, and you can learn it syllable by syllable.

4. *Avoid mispronunciations that lead to spelling errors.* If you listen and speak carefully, you will be less likely to misspell words because you are not pronouncing them correctly. Be sure that you are saying *chimney*, not *chimbly; library*, not *liberry; modern*, not *modren.*

5. *Proofread your papers to avoid careless spelling errors.* Half the trouble in spelling comes from careless haste. Whenever you do any writing, proofread your paper for errors in the spelling not only of difficult words but also of the ordinary, easy words that you may have misspelled through carelessness.

SPELLING RULES

The following rules are helpful, even though there are exceptions to them. If you learn them thoroughly, you will find it easier to spell correctly.

ie and *ei*

25a. Except after *c*, write *ie* when the sound is long *e*.

EXAMPLES bel**ie**ve, rel**ie**f, f**ie**ld, dec**ei**ve, c**ei**ling
EXCEPTIONS n**ei**ther, l**ei**sure, s**ei**ze, w**ei**rd

Write *ei* when the sound is not long *e,* especially when the sound is long *a.*

EXAMPLES r**ei**gn, w**ei**ght, **ei**ght, fr**ei**ght, h**ei**ght, sl**ei**ght
EXCEPTIONS fr**ie**nd, misch**ie**f

EXERCISE 1. Writing Words with *ie* and *ei*. Write the following words, supplying the missing letters (*e* and *i*) in the correct order. Be able to explain how the rules apply to each word.

1. fr...nd [ie]	4. w...ght [ei]	7. br...f [ie]	9. n...ghbor [ei]
2. p...ce [ie]	5. bel...ve [ie]	8. h...ght [ei]	10. fr...ght [ei]
3. rec...ve [ei]	6. c...ling [ei]		

rules, and correctly spell words that are often confused or commonly misspelled.

PRESENTING THE CHAPTER

LESS-ADVANCED STUDENTS Some of the spelling rules may serve only to confuse this class. Skip those rules which you think will not prove helpful, and instead drill students on the spelling of other words they are most likely to use. The study of the spelling demons on page 590 is especially important to these students. Also give a good deal of class time to explaining the distinctions between words frequently confused, pages 580–89.

ADVANCED STUDENTS These students often feel that a grade of 85 or 90 on a test means excellent work. Point out to them, however, that where spelling is concerned, no grade short of 100 shows good command of the subject. After a list of spelling words has been taught and drilled, you may want to mark any test score below 100 as "unsatisfactory."

The poor spellers in an advanced class can be required to memorize the rules in the chapter and to memorize the correct spelling of words which cause them difficulty. Students who have a slight case of "spelling blindness" but who are otherwise advanced can usually learn to spell well by this approach. However, they may not make the effort unless you firmly insist on it.

GOOD SPELLING HABITS

Introduce students to this list early in the school year. Remind them of this reference whenever they are working on spelling.

SPELLING RULES
(rules 25a–25i)

You will want to have your class study spelling rules one by one—not in large blocks. You may want to spread the teaching of the rules over the entire year.

IE AND EI **and**
–CEDE, –CEED, –SEDE
(rules 25a and 25b)

If your students do not already know the rhyme about *ie* and *ei*, teach it to them now:

I before *e,* except after *c*
Or when sounded like *a,*
As in *neighbor* and *weigh.*

While this rule holds true ninety percent of the time, students should note carefully the exceptions listed in the text.

Learning the simple rule about *–cede, –ceed,* and *–sede* can help students overcome a spelling problem. Less-advanced students, however, may not be ready for the rule if they are not yet familiar with the meanings of the words.

EXERCISE 1. As a homework assignment, you can have your students write sentences using these words.

EXERCISE 2. Have students write sentences with these words to make sure they understand the meanings.

ADDING PREFIXES and ADDING SUFFIXES
(rules 25c–25i)

Learning to spell words with prefixes and suffixes will be more meaningful if the student learns at the same time how these prefixes

MECHANICS

-cede, -ceed, -sede

25b. Only one word in English ends in *-sede—supersede;* only three words end in *-ceed—exceed, proceed,* and *succeed;* all other words of similar sound end in *-cede.*

EXAMPLES con**cede,** re**cede,** pre**cede**

EXERCISE 2. Writing Words with *-ceed, -cede,* and *-sede.* Write the following words, supplying *-ceed, -cede,* or *-sede.*

1. pre... cede
2. pro... ceed
3. con... cede
4. super... sede
5. ex... ceed

Adding Prefixes

A prefix is one or more letters added to the beginning of a word to change its meaning.

EXAMPLES un + able = **un**able
pre + arrange = **pre**arrange

25c. When a prefix is added to a word, the spelling of the word itself remains the same.

EXAMPLES il + logical = **il**logical
in + elegant = **in**elegant
un + selfish = **un**selfish
mis + apply = **mis**apply
over + see = **over**see

EXERCISE 3. Writing Words with Prefixes. Number your paper 1–10. Write correctly the words formed.

1. immigrant 2. misinform 3. reenter 4. overrule 5. unnatural 6. dissimilar 7. illegible 8. semiannual 9. innumerable 10. unnecessary

1. im + migrant
2. mis + inform
3. re + enter
4. over + rule
5. un + natural
6. dis + similar
7. il + legible
8. semi + annual
9. in + numerable
10. un + necessary

Adding Suffixes

A suffix is one or more letters added to the end of a word to change its meaning.

EXAMPLES care + less = care**less**
walk + ed = walk**ed**
comfort + able = comfort**able**

25d. When the suffixes *-ness* and *-ly* are added to a word, the spelling of the word itself is not changed.

EXAMPLES mean + ness = mean**ness**
casual + ly = casual**ly**

EXCEPTIONS Words ending in *y* usually change the *y* to *i* before *-ness* and *-ly:* misty—mist**iness;** happy—happ**ily.** One-syllable adjectives ending in *y* generally follow rule 25d: shy—shy**ly.**

25e. Drop the final *e* before a suffix beginning with a vowel.

EXAMPLES line + ing = lin**ing**
approve + al = approv**al**
desire + able = desir**able**

EXCEPTIONS In some words, the final *e* must be kept to retain the soft sound of a *c* or *g:* notice + able = notic**eable;** courage + ous = courag**eous.**

25f. Keep the final *e* before a suffix beginning with a consonant.

EXAMPLES hope + less = hope**less**
care + ful = care**ful**

EXCEPTIONS true + ly = tru**ly**
argue + ment = argu**ment**
judge + ment = judg**ment**

EXERCISE 4. Writing Words with Suffixes. Number your paper 1–10. Write correctly the words formed.

MECHANICS

and suffixes affect the meaning of a word. You may want to teach the material on text pages 631–35 in connection with this section of the spelling chapter. In addition, you may want your students to keep a list of common prefixes and suffixes, with examples of words in which they occur.

EXERCISES 3 and 4. Students should find these exercises easy to do. Caution them, however, not to race ahead and complete an assignment in a few minutes. Tell them to work carefully and check their answers. You might ask students to write sentences in which the words are used correctly.

1. finally 2. lovable 3. truly 5. outrageous 6. prettily 9. pleasing

1. final + ly
2. love + able
3. true + ly
4. one + ness

4. oneness

5. outrage + ous
6. pretty + ly
7. advantage + ous 7. advantageous
8. change + able 8. changeable

9. please + ing
10. hope + ful 10. hopeful

25g. With words ending in *y* preceded by a consonant, change the *y* to *i* before any suffix not beginning with *i*.

EXAMPLES cry + ed = cr**ied**
lovely + ness = love**liness**
but cry + ing = cr**ying**

Note that words ending in *y* preceded by a vowel generally do not change their spelling when a suffix is added.

EXAMPLES pray + ing = pray**ing**
pay + ment = pay**ment**
boy + hood = boy**hood**

25h. With words of one syllable ending in a single consonant preceded by a single vowel, double the consonant before adding *-ing, -ed,* or *-er*.

EXAMPLES sit + ing = si**tt**ing
swim + ing = swi**mm**ing
drop + ed = dro**pp**ed

MECHANICS

25i. With words of more than one syllable ending in a single consonant preceded by a single vowel, double the consonant before adding *-ing, -ed,* or *-er* if the word is accented on the last syllable.

EXAMPLES occur′+ ed = occu**rr**ed
begin′+ er = begi**nn**er
permit′+ ing = permi**tt**ing

If the word is *not* accented on the last syllable, the final consonant is not doubled before a suffix.

EXAMPLES trav′el + er = trave**l**er
can′cel + ed = cance**l**ed

EXERCISE 5. Writing Words with Suffixes. Number your paper 1–10. Write correctly the words formed. 1. studied 2. hurrying 3. quizzing 4. fitted 5. cried

1. study + ed
2. hurry + ing
3. quiz + ing
4. fit + ed
5. cry + ed
6. deploy + ing
7. prefer + ed
8. plan + ed
9. admit + ing
10. run + er

6. deploying 7. preferred 8. planned 9. admitting 10. runner

THE PLURAL OF NOUNS

Plurals are formed in several ways, most of them covered by rules. To learn irregular plurals, you should enter them in your private spelling list and memorize them.

25j. Observe the rules for spelling the plural of nouns.

(1) The regular way to form the plural of a noun is to add an *-s*.

EXAMPLES desk, desks
idea, ideas

(2) The plural of some nouns ending in *s, x, z, ch,* or *sh* is formed by adding *-es*.

EXAMPLES pass, passes
fox, foxes
buzz, buzzes
clutch, clutches
dish, dishes

EXERCISE 6. Writing the Plurals of Nouns. Number your paper 1–10. Write the plurals of the following words:

1. wish
2. pilot
3. machine
4. match
5. automobile
6. porch
7. dance
8. mechanic
9. reflex
10. box

1. wishes
2. pilots
3. machines
4. matches
5. automobiles
6. porches
7. dances
8. mechanics
9. reflexes
10. boxes

(3) The plural of nouns ending in *y* preceded by a consonant is formed by changing the *y* to *i* and adding *-es*.

MECHANICS

EXERCISE 5. See notes for Exercises 3 and 4.

THE PLURAL OF NOUNS (rule 25j)

Probably the best way for students to learn the spellings of plurals is by a combination of (1) memorizing the rules and (2) drilling repeatedly on the spellings of individual plural words. Since many eighth-graders confuse plurals ending in *–s* with possessives and write *boy's* or *boys'* instead of *boys,* you may wish to review the spelling of possessives, text pages 562–64, in connection with the spelling of plurals.

EXERCISE 6. For additional drill, have students write five of the plurals in sentences.

EXERCISES 7 and 8. You might require your students to say both singulars and plurals aloud and to write the plurals in sentences.

EXAMPLES	army, arm**ies**	city, cit**ies**
	country, countr**ies**	pony, pon**ies**

(4) The plural of nouns ending in *y* preceded by a vowel is formed by adding *-s*.

EXAMPLES	journey, journey**s**
	key, key**s**

(5) The plural of most nouns ending in *f* is formed by adding *-s*. Some nouns ending in *f* or *fe,* however, form plurals by changing the *f* to *v* and adding *-s* or *-es*.

EXAMPLES	grief, grief**s**	shelf, shel**ves**
	belief, belief**s**	knife, kni**ves**

(6) The plural of nouns ending in *o* preceded by a vowel is formed by adding *-s;* the plural of nouns ending in *o* preceded by a consonant is formed by adding *-es*.

EXAMPLES *o* following a vowel:

radio, radio**s** patio, patio**s**

o following a consonant:

tomato, tomato**es** echo, echo**es**

EXCEPTIONS Eskimos, silos, pianos, sopranos, altos

Note that many nouns ending in *o* that pertain to music are exceptions to this rule.

MECHANICS

(7) The plural of a few nouns is formed in irregular ways.

EXAMPLES	child, child**ren**	goose, g**ee**se
	ox, ox**en**	foot, f**ee**t
	woman, wom**e**n	mouse, m**ice**
	tooth, t**ee**th	

EXERCISE 7. Writing the Plurals of Nouns. Number your paper 1–10. Write the plurals of the following nouns:

1. chimney s	6. roof s	2. companies
2. company	7. volcano s (*or* oes)	4. libraries
3. valley s	8. child	5. leaves
4. library	9. tooth	8. children
5. leaf	10. woman	9. teeth
		10. women

(8) The plural of compound nouns consisting of a noun plus a modifier is formed by making the noun plural.

EXAMPLES passer-by, passers-by
maid of honor, maids of honor
brother-in-law, brothers-in-law
editor in chief, editors in chief

(9) The plural of a few compound nouns is formed in irregular ways.

EXAMPLES drive-in, drive-ins
fourteen-year-old, fourteen-year-olds

(10) Some nouns are the same in the singular and plural.

EXAMPLES trout, salmon, sheep, Sioux, deer, moose

(11) The plural of numbers, letters, signs, and words considered as words is formed by adding an apostrophe and *s*.

EXAMPLES 1900 1900**'s** + +**'s**
ABC ABC**'s** *and* *and***'s**

MECHANICS

EXERCISE 8. Writing the Plurals of Nouns. Number your paper 1–10. Write the plurals of the following nouns:

1. sheep 1. sheep
2. weekend 2. weekends
3. trout 3. trout*
4. daughter-in-law
5. *a* 5. *a*'s
6. teen-ager 6. teen-agers
7. guard of honor 7. guards of honor
8. deer 8. deer
9. cupful 9. cupfuls
10. 1800 10. 1800's

**sometimes* trouts
4. daughters-in-law

WORDS OFTEN CONFUSED

Concentrate on the items in this list that actually cause difficulty for your students. To find out which are the most troublesome items, you can either keep a list of words misspelled in student themes or use diagnostic testing. (The example sentences on these pages can be dictated, in groups of six or eight, as diagnostic tests.) Your eighth-graders have probably met most of these spelling words in earlier grades, and the class as a whole need not spend time on those words that the great majority of them have already mastered. Individual students who need extra work can use this section for reference.

Less-advanced students may misspell some words on a diagnostic test simply because the words are not part of their vocabulary and they have never written them before. These students should learn to spell correctly the words they *do* use, rather than be drilled on pairs such as *formerly* and *formally,* which may never appear in their written work.

Less-advanced students will often enjoy exercises with sound-alikes, but these students may take longer to learn than other students. You may wish to devote part of each day's work (say the first five minutes) over a long period of time to teaching these sets of words. Review the words frequently and give many short quizzes based on them.

Memory tricks such as the following ones are helpful for some students:

all right If it's not *all right*, it's *all wrong*.
dessert When this is served, we often want *two*.

MECHANICS

WORDS OFTEN CONFUSED

The words grouped together in the following lists are frequently confused with each other. Some of the words are homonyms—that is, their pronunciation is the same but their meanings and spellings are different. Others have the same or similar spellings. Study them carefully, and learn to distinguish both their meanings and their spellings.

---

accept *to receive with consent; to give approval to*
Many of his contemporaries did not *accept* Copernicus' theory that the earth moves around the sun.

except *[verb] leave out from a number; [prep.] with the exclusion of; but*
We were *excepted* from the assignment.
Everyone will be there *except* Mark.

---

advice *a recommendation about a course of action*
Good *advice* may be easy to give but hard to follow.

advise *to recommend a course of action; to give advice*
I *advise* you to continue your music lessons if you possibly can.

---

affect *to influence; to produce an effect upon*
The explosion of Krakatoa *affected* the sunsets all over the world.

effect *the result of an action; consequence*
It has long been observed that the phases of the moon have an *effect* on the tides of the oceans.

---

all right *everything is right* or *satisfactory* [This must be written as two words. The spelling *alright* is never correct.]
Maria did *all right* in the track meet.
Was my answer *all right?*

all ready *all prepared* or *in readiness*
The players are *all ready* for the big game.

already *previously*
Our class has *already* taken two field trips.

EXERCISE 9. Selecting Spelling Words to Complete Sentences. Number your paper 1–10. After the proper number, write the word given in the parentheses that makes the sentence correct.

1. Everyone likes to give (advice, advise).
2. The (affect, effect) of the victory was startling.
3. Why did you (accept, except) Carla from the class rule?
4. The scientists were (all ready, already) to watch the launching of the rocket.
5. The coach (advices, advises) us to stick to the training rules.
6. Her weeks of practice finally (affected, effected) her game.
7. Most of the rebels were offered a pardon and (accepted, excepted) it, but the leaders were (accepted, excepted) from the offer.
8. Juan has (all ready, already) learned how to water-ski.
9. Do you think my work is (all right, alright)?
10. Whose (advice, advise) are you going to take?

altar *a table for a religious ceremony*
The *altar* was banked with lilies.

alter *to change*
The outcome of the election *altered* the mayor's plan.

all together *everyone in the same place*
The director called us *all together* for rehearsal.

altogether *entirely*
Your story is *altogether* too late for this issue.

MECHANICS

hear We do this with our *ears*.
piece A *pie* contains this.
stationery We write letters on this.
stomach His stomach *aches*.

You might want to try the game "Spelling Algebra" in review work as a welcome departure from routine drill. Students are individually assigned a pair of sound-alike words. They write one or two sentences, using both sound-alikes. Then they read to the class what they have written, substituting the algebraic terms "x" and "y" for the sound-alikes, and the class must figure out what the words are. For example:

All the members were able to *x* the invitation to the party, *y* the girl whose parents were away. (Answer: *accept* and *except*)
My dog did not *x* me when I said, "Come *y*." (Answer: *hear* and *here*.)

EXERCISE 9. It is important to back up this kind of drill with further drill, frequent review, and reminders whenever students misspell any of the words in their written work. Use this exercise and the following ones selectively, according to your students' needs.

EXERCISE 10. Advanced students might write new sentences using the "incorrect" words.

brake — *a device to stop a machine*
Can you fix the *brake* on my bicycle?

break — *to fracture, to shatter*
The winner will be the one who *breaks* the tape.

---

capital — *a city; the seat of a government*
Olympia is the *capital* of Washington.

capitol — *building; statehouse*
Where is the capitol in Albany?

---

choose — [present tense, rhymes with *lose*] *to select*
Will you *choose* speech or civics as your elective next year?

chose — [past tense, rhymes with *grows*] *selected*
Janet *chose* to play in the band rather than in the orchestra.

EXERCISE 10. Selecting Spelling Words to Complete Sentences. Number your paper 1–10. After the proper number, write the word given in parentheses that makes the sentence correct.

1. The building with the dome is the (capital, capitol).
2. By working (all together, altogether) we can do the job easily.
3. Because she loved dramatics, Alice (choose, chose) a difficult part in the school play.
4. Be careful not to (brake, break) those dishes.
5. That book is (all together, altogether) too complicated for you to enjoy.
6. The candles on the (altar, alter) glowed beautifully.
7. We don't know whether to (choose, chose) band or chorus.
8. A car without a good emergency (brake, break) is a menace.
9. Will Joan's accident (altar, alter) her plans?
10. Tallahassee is the (capital, capitol) of Florida.

clothes *wearing apparel*
One can learn a lot about a historical period by studying its fashions in *clothes.*

cloths *pieces of fabric*
You'll find some cleaning *cloths* in the bottom desk drawer.

coarse *rough, crude*
The beach is covered with *coarse* brown sand.

course *path of action; planned program or route* [also used in the expression *of course*]
The wind blew the ship slightly off its *course.*

consul *a representative of a government in a foreign country*
Who is the American *consul* in Nigeria?

council *a group of people who meet together*

councilor *a member of a council*
The king called a meeting of the *council* and informed the *councilors* that the royal treasury was nearly empty.

counsel *advice; to give words of advice*

counselor *one who advises*
When choosing a career, seek *counsel* from your teacher.
Who is your guidance *counselor*?

desert [des′ ert] *a dry, sandy region*
The Sahara is the largest *desert* in Africa.

desert [de sert′] *to abandon; to leave*
Most dogs will not *desert* a friend in trouble.

dessert [des sert′] *the final course of a meal*
Fruit salad is my favorite *dessert.*

EXERCISES 11 and 12. You might have students work in small groups to complete this exercise and write new sentences with the "incorrect" words.

EXERCISE 11. Selecting Spelling Words to Complete Sentences. Number your paper 1–10. After the proper number, write the word or words given in the parentheses that will make the sentence correct.

1. Each class has four representatives on the student (council, counsel).
2. The guide threatened to (desert, dessert) us as we crossed the (desert, dessert).
3. Most young people are interested in (clothes, cloths).
4. Your guidance (councilor, counselor) can help you.
5. The (coarse, course) for the cross-country race is rugged.
6. The cleaning (clothes, cloths) must be washed often.
7. Do we have a Canadian (consul, council) in this city?
8. (Coarse, Course) gravel lines the driveway of our house.
9. The meal didn't seem complete without (desert, dessert).
10. The members of the losing team looked to their coach for (council, counsel).

---

formally *with dignity; following strict rules or procedures*
The Governor delivered the speech *formally.*

formerly *previously; in the past*
Formerly, I knew the Zubalsky family very well.

---

hear *to perceive sounds by ear*
Dogs can *hear* some sounds that are inaudible to people.

here *in this place*
The campsite is right *here.*

---

its possessive [of the pronoun *it*]
Mount Fuji is noted for *its* beauty.

it's [a contraction of *it is* or *it has*]
It's an extinct volcano.
It's been a long time.

MECHANICS

lead [lēd] — [present tense] *to go first, to be a leader*
A small town in New Hampshire often *leads* the nation in filing its election returns.

lead [lĕd] — *a heavy metal*
A *lead* pencil actually has no *lead* in it.

led — [past tense] *went first*
The Governor *led* the slate with an impressive majority.

---

loose — [rhymes with *noose*] *not securely attached; not fitting tightly*
If a tourniquet is too *loose,* it will not serve its purpose.

lose — [pronounced looz] *to suffer loss*
Vegetables *lose* some of their vitamins when they are cooked.

EXERCISE 12. Selecting Spelling Words to Complete Sentences. Number your paper 1–10. After the proper number, write the word or words given in parentheses that will make the sentence correct.

1. (Its, It's) a long way from (hear, here) to the park.
2. The plumber is removing the (lead, led) pipes and putting in brass ones.
3. We don't want to (loose, lose) you in the crowd.
4. Before the club takes up new business, the secretary (formally, formerly) reads the minutes of the previous meeting.
5. (Its, It's) too bad that the tree has lost (its, it's) leaves.
6. Do you (hear, here) me, Ann? Come (hear, here) now!
7. The Yankees were ten runs behind, and it seemed certain that they were going to (loose, lose).
8. The marshal (lead, led) the class into the chapel.
9. Had Pepita ever done any running (formally, formerly)?
10. That (loose, lose) bolt can cause trouble.

---

passed [past tense of *pass*] *went by*
Our airplane *passed* over the Grand Canyon.

past *that which has gone by; beyond*
Some people live in the *past.*
They moved *past* the dozing sentry.

---

peace *security and quiet order*
We are striving for *peace* and prosperity.

piece *a part of something*
Some people can catch fish with a pole, a *piece* of string, and a bent pin.

---

plain *simple, common, unadorned; a flat area of land*
A *plain* jackknife is often as useful as one with several blades.
What is the difference between a prairie and a *plain*?

plane *a tool; an airplane; a flat surface*
The *plane* is useful in the carpenter's trade.
Four single-engine *planes* are in the hangar.
Rhoda says she likes *plane* geometry.

---

principal *the head of a school; main or most important*
The *principal* is the chief officer of a school.
What are the *principal* exports of Brazil?

principle *a rule of conduct; a main fact or law*
She listed some of the *principles* of economics.

---

quiet *still and peaceful; without noise*
A *quiet* room is needed for concentrated study and reflection.

quite *wholly or entirely; to a great extent*
Winters in New England can be *quite* severe.

EXERCISE 13. See notes for Exercise 9.

EXERCISE 13. Selecting Spelling Words to Complete Sentences. Number your paper 1–10. After the proper number, write the word or words given in parentheses that make the sentence correct.

1. A bright smile often makes a (plain, plane) face attractive.
2. The summer was (quiet, quite) over before the beginning of school brought a (quiet, quite) household once more.
3. This is an important (principal, principle) in mathematics.
4. On July 20, 1963, the moon (passed, past) between the earth and the sun, causing a total eclipse.
5. A (plain, plane) is a useful tool.
6. Save me a (peace, piece) of that blueberry pie.
7. Our (principal, principle) is leaving the school this year.
8. We should try to learn from (passed, past) experience.
9. The nation was working hard to attain (peace, piece).
10. Cattle were grazing over the (plain, plane).

---

shone [past tense of *shine*] gleamed, glowed
They polished the silver until it *shone.*

shown [past participle of *show*] *revealed*
The statue will be *shown* to the public.

---

stationary *in a fixed position*
Most of the furnishings of a space capsule must be *stationary.*

stationery *writing paper*
I need a new box of *stationery.*

---

than [a conjunction used for comparisons]
The Amazon River is longer *than* the Mississippi River.

then *at that time*
If the baby is awake by four o'clock, we will leave *then.*

MECHANICS

EXERCISE 14. For additional practice, students might write brief paragraphs in which they try to use all of these words correctly.

there *a place [also used to begin a sentence]*
Go *there* in the fall when the leaves are turning.
There were no objections.

their [a possessive pronoun]
Their team seems very skillful.

they're *they are*
They're taller than most of our players.

threw [past tense of *throw*] *hurled*
Our pitcher *threw* four balls in succession.

through [a preposition]
Have you ever seen a ship go *through* the locks of a canal?

EXERCISE 14. Selecting Spelling Words to Complete Sentences. Number your paper 1–10. After the proper number, write the word or words given in parentheses that make the sentence correct.

1. We go (there, their, they're) often, for the children can get (there, their, they're) instruction in swimming, and we can see how (their, there, they're) progressing.
2. She has more (stationary, stationery) than she'll ever use.
3. The stars (shown, shone) brilliantly.
4. The city was so much larger (then, than) I expected.
5. The desks in our art room are not (stationary, stationery).
6. We often hear the planes break (threw, through) the sound barrier.
7. Sue will have the first ride; (than, then) it will be your turn.
8. The goal posts on the football field have been made (stationary, stationery).
9. We were (shone, shown) all the points of interest in the downtown area.
10. The pitcher (threw, through) a wild ball that hit the batter.

MECHANICS

to — [a preposition, also used with the infinitive of a verb]
A visit *to* Chinatown is an exciting treat.
Many small nations throughout the world are eager *to* be independent.

too — *also; more than enough*
We have lived in Iowa and in Alaska, *too*.
It is *too* cold for rain today.

two — *one plus one*
Americans can visit *two* foreign countries without leaving the continent.

---

weak — *not strong; feeble*
My mother likes to drink *weak* tea.

week — *seven days*
Your pictures will be ready in about a *week*.

---

weather — *condition of the air or atmosphere*
Weather prediction is an important branch of meteorology.

whether — [a conjunction] *if*
Jane Gordon is wondering *whether* the bond issue for the new school will be approved.

---

whose — [a possessive]
Whose report are we hearing today?

who's — *who is* or *who has*
Who's read today's newspaper?
Who's representing the yearbook staff?

---

your — [a possessive]
Your work in math is improving.

you're — *you are*
You're right on time!

MECHANICS

EXERCISE 15. See notes for Exercise 9.

50 Spelling Demons

Try to make sure that no student finishes the year without having mastered these words. If your students object to studying the spelling of these words, complaining that they are too easy, have them close their books and take a quiz on fifteen or twenty of the words to see how many they can spell correctly. Point out that making even one or two mistakes means that they should go over this list attentively.

250 Spelling Words

Do not assign more than twenty spelling words at a time. It is probably best to assign words in groups of ten. The list is arranged with a space break after every tenth word, to make such grouping easy.

The spelling list has been composed in accordance with the needs and abilities of average eighth-graders. Together with the lists in the other six books of the *English Composition and Grammar* series, it is part of a long-range spelling program that extends from the sixth grade to the senior year in high school. Both average and advanced students will find much to challenge them in the eighth-grade list. You may want to simplify the list, however, for less-advanced students.

EXERCISE 15. Selecting Spelling Words to Complete Sentences. Number your paper 1–10. After the proper number, write the word or words given in parentheses that make the sentence correct.

1. Lack of exercise made the runner's legs (weak, week).
2. (Weather, Whether) we'll go or not depends on the (weather, whether).
3. (Whose, Who's) books are you carrying?
4. Find out (whose, who's) going if you can.
5. Allen thought algebra was (to, too, two) difficult for him (to, too, two) master.
6. (Your, You're) a long distance off your course, captain.
7. We took (to, too, two) (weaks, weeks) for our trip.
8. The (weather, whether) was cloudy in Orlando, Florida.
9. Would you enjoy a trip (to, too, two) Mars, Flo?
10. Aren't you using (your, you're) compass?

50 Spelling Demons

ache	doctor	laid	tear
again	does	meant	
always	don't	minute	though
answer	early	often	through
blue	easy		tired
built	every	once	tonight
busy	friend	ready	trouble
buy		said	wear
can't	guess	says	where
color	half	shoes	which
	hour	since	whole
cough	instead	straight	women
could	knew	sugar	
country	know	sure	

250 Spelling Words

In studying the following list, pay particular attention to the letters in italics.

abandon
absolutely
acceptance
accidentally
accommodate
accompany
accomplish
achieve
acquaintance
acquire

actually
advertisement
against
aisle
amount
analysis
anticipate
anxiety
apology
apparent

appearance
application
appreciation
approach
arguing
argument
article
assistance
authority
basis

beginning
believe
benefit
boundary
bouquet

bulletin
business
canceled
capacity
careless

carrier
ceiling
challenge
choice
choir
chorus
circuit
colonel
column
coming

commercial
committees
competition
completely
conceive
condemn
congratulations
conscience
conscious
control

convenience
courteous
criticism
cylinder
dealt
deceit
decision
definite
definition
describe

description
desirable
despair
develop
difficulties
disappointment
discipline
discussion
diseased
distinction

distribution
doctrine
duplicate
economic
eligible
embarrass
engineering
enthusiasm
equipped
eventually

exactly
exaggerate
excellent
existence
experience
experiment
explanation
fascinating
favorite
February

finally
flu
forty
fourth
friendliness

MECHANICS

gener*al*ly
govern*o*r
gramm*a*r
gra*ti*tude
gu*a*r*a*nt*ee*

g*u*ardi*a*n
g*y*mnasium
hatr*e*d
h*eigh*t
heroin*e*
hes*i*tate
hum*o*r*ous*
h*y*pocrit*e*
ignor*a*nce
i*m*ag*i*nation

i*mm*edi*a*t*e*ly
incident*al*ly
ind*i*vi*du*al
inf*e*rior
ini*ti*al
insp*i*ration
intell*i*gence
interf*ere*
inte*rr*upt
*i*nvolve

judg*m*ent
knowle*dge*
lab*o*ratory
l*ei*sure
l*e*ngthen
l*ieu*tenant
lon*e*l*i*ness
lunch*e*on
major*i*ty
manufac*t*ure

marr*i*age
me*ch*an*i*cal
med*ie*val
mil*i*tary
m*ou*rn
mult*i*pl*i*cation
muscul*ar*
m*y*st*e*ry
natur*al*ly
ne*c*e*ss*ary

nick*el*
nonsen*se*
n*ui*s*ance
numer*ou*s
o*b*vious
occa*s*ion*ally*
occu*rre*nce
*o*pinion
opp*o*rtunity
or*ch*estra

origin*al*ly
pa*id*
pa*r*a*ll*el
parl*ia*ment
pa*tie*nce
p*er*formance
person*al*
personal*i*ty
pers*ua*de
philoso*ph*er

picnic*k*ing
pla*nn*ed
ple*a*s*a*nt
po*ssess*
prec*ede*

prefe*rr*ed
prej*u*d*ice*
priv*i*l*ege*
prob*a*bly
proc*e*dure

pro*f*ess*o*r
p*u*rs*ui*t
qual*i*fied
re*a*lize
rece*ipt*
recognize
re*c*o*mm*end
re*f*e*rr*ing
reg*u*l*a*rly
rel*ie*ve

rep*e*tition
res*ea*rch
respon*s*e
r*hy*thm
sat*i*sfied
s*au*cer
s*ch*edule
s*c*i*ss*ors
sen*s*e
sent*i*ment

sep*arate*
ser*gea*nt
shep*he*rd
sim*i*l*a*r
sim*ply*
sole*mn*
so*u*rce
spon*sor*
stra*igh*ten
subscrip*t*ion

MECHANICS

succeed
success
sufficient
suggest
suppress
surprise
surround
suspense
suspicion
tailor

temperament
tendency
theory
therefore

thorough
tobacco
tonsils
tradition
tragedy
transferred

tries
truly
unanimous
unnecessary
unsatisfactory
until
useful
using

utilized
vacuum

variety
various
vein
view
villain
violence
warrant
weird
wholly
writing

Additional Practice

Teacher's Resource Book, Worksheet pages 298–309

Testing

Teaching Tests booklet, pages 65–68, 75–76, 77–83
Teacher's Resource Book, Test pages 469–72, 479–80, 481–92

PART FOUR

RESOURCES FOR WRITING AND STUDYING

RESOURCES FOR WRITING AND STUDYING

pages 595–668

USING THE PICTURES

The pictures on this and the next page, along with those in the section "Picture the Possibilities" following page 226, provide students with sources of ideas for writing. The following suggestions will help you show students how to use the pictures, either singly or in combination, to generate ideas and gather information.

Mauna Loa Volcano, Hawaii

- To find topics for library reports, students could analyze the subject "volcanoes" on the basis of examples, features, time periods, places, or causes. They could then select one topic and use the *5 W-How?* questions to gather information.
- Students could use the scene as the setting for a story in which the eruption of the volcano is the problem facing the main character.
- Advanced students might enjoy reporting on the myth of the Roman god Vulcan. One good source is Edith Hamilton's *Mythology: Timeless Tales of Gods and Heroes* (New York: New American Library, 1969).
- Have students write process paragraphs explaining how rubber is vulcanized. They might instead compare the properties of natural rubber and vulcanized rubber.
- Another possibility would be to have students report on the life of Charles Goodyear, who invented the vulcanization process, or on

how natural rubber is obtained from plants.

Clouds

- One way to use this picture would be to have students imagine themselves in the scene and use questions such as these to gather concrete and sensory details for a description: *What colors, shapes, and patterns do I see in the clouds? In the light from the sun? In the mountains? What is the temperature? What texture is the surface on which I am standing? What sounds do I hear? How does the wind feel on my skin?*
- Have students write reports on the main types of clouds. They might instead write paragraphs on only one of the types.
- You might be able to arrange to have a meteorologist from the local U. S. Weather Bureau office (or from a television station) visit your class, giving students the opportunity to interview him or her. You will want to work with the class in advance of such a visit to help them develop appropriate topics and generate questions that will elicit relevant details. Possible topics for such an interview might include "how to become a meteorologist," "the duties of a meteorologist," "precautions to take when a tornado (hurricane, blizzard, etc.) threatens the area," or "how radar is used in weather forecasting."
- Have students write papers explaining the difference between *weather* and *climate*.

Connecting the Pictures

Have students write paragraphs comparing a cloud of steam with a cloud in the sky.

CHAPTER 26

Using the Dictionary

ARRANGEMENT OF A DICTIONARY, INFORMATION IN A DICTIONARY

Early Phoenician (late 2nd millenium B.C.)	Early Etruscan (8th century B.C.)
Phoenician (8th century B.C.)	Monumental Latin (4th century B.C.)
Early Greek (9th–7th centuries B.C.)	Classical Latin
Western Greek (6th century B.C.)	Uncial
Classical Greek (403 B.C.onward)	Half Uncial
	Caroline miniscule

A good dictionary tells you what meanings a word has, how it is usually spelled and pronounced, what its history is, and, often, the kind of situations in which it is appropriate or inappropriate. Since dictionaries differ from one another in their methods of presenting information, the best guide to the use of your dictionary is the introductory section that explains the arrangement of entries, the system of showing pronunciations, and special features of that particular book. This chapter will show you how to use the general features that you will find in all dictionaries.

Chapter Overview

Since the dictionary is probably the reference book most frequently used by students, it is important that they learn to use it intelligently and efficiently. Most eighth-grade classes have already had several years of basic dictionary instruction, but very few eighth-graders make as full use of the dictionary as they should.

To help students acquire the "dictionary habit," you can (1) make sure that each student has a dictionary (even a paperback dictionary will serve the purpose); (2) make sure there is a dictionary, either unabridged or "college size," in the English classroom at all times; and (3) *make sure these dictionaries are used almost daily in English class and in doing homework assignments.*

Note: You will find that your work in the dictionary unit will be made much easier if all students are using the same dictionary. Some schools provide class sets of dictionaries for this purpose. In other schools, all students are urged to buy the same dictionary.

Chapter Objective

Students will use the various features of the dictionary effectively.

PRESENTING THE CHAPTER

LESS-ADVANCED STUDENTS It is almost essential in this class that all students use the same dictionary. Less-advanced students will need help from the teacher at every step; and if they use different dictionaries, you will find yourself having to give individual instruction to each pupil in the class. The points to emphasize in such a class are probably (1) how to locate a word in the dictionary, (2) how to find correct spellings (teach students to keep trying until they find the word), and (3) how to find the right definition for a particular use of a word.

ADVANCED STUDENTS With this class, you can use the Review Exercise on page 612 as a diagnostic test to see how well students know their way around the dictionary. If possible, give the test in class and set a ten-minute limit for its completion. An advanced class can usually work through this chapter fairly quickly and then continue to use their dictionaries for the work in Chapter 28, "Vocabulary."

ARRANGEMENT (rule 26a)

This material will be review work for most classes. An advanced class may be able to skip the section. To find out how familiar your students are with the alphabetical arrangement of the dictionary, give them a short list of words to look up. When they have found a word, they should write the number of the page on which it occurs. Set a time limit on the exercise. If students frequently take more than one minute to find a word, you should plan to give some drill in this area.

EXERCISES 1 and 2. These exercises provide drill in the skills needed to locate words in the dictionary. A class that did well on a diagnostic test of the kind described above may omit the exercises.

ARRANGEMENT

26a. Learn how to find a word in the dictionary.

The words in a dictionary are listed in alphabetical order. This does not mean simply that all words beginning with a particular letter are found in one section. It means that words having *a* as a second letter come before those that have *b* as a second letter, and so on through all the other letters in the word.

Two special problems should be kept in mind: abbreviations and entries of more than one word.

Some dictionaries explain abbreviations in a special section, but most dictionaries define them in the main part of the book. In such dictionaries, abbreviations are entered according to the letters in them, *not* according to the complete words that they stand for. The abbreviation *pt.* (meaning *pint* or *part*) comes after *psychology,* even though both words that the abbreviation can stand for would come before *psychology.* In a dictionary, the abbreviation *St.* (for *saint*) comes after *squirt* and before *stab.* A name like *St. Denis,* however, would appear under the full spelling—*saint.*

Two or more words used together as a single word (*open season, prime minister*) are treated as though they were a single word. Thus *open shop* appears after *openly.*

EXERCISE 1. Arranging Words, Phrases, and Abbreviations in Alphabetical Order. Arrange the following words, phrases, and abbreviations in alphabetical order.

18. watermelon	7. dept.	8. Mrs.	13. munificence
4. department	15. st.	5. departmental	14. munificent
2. curtain	3. curvature	1. curtail	19. water moccasin
16. stateside	17. static	11. mudguard	20. water wheel
12. municipal	10. muddy	9. mt.	6. department store

Guide Words

Guide words are printed in boldfaced type at the top of each dictionary page. The one on the left is the same as the first word defined on that page; the one on the right is the same as the last word on that page. Words that fall between guide words in the alphabet will appear on that page.

EXERCISE 2. Using Guide Words. Number your paper 1–10. Suppose that the guide words *needy* and *neither* appear on a particular dictionary page. After the proper number, make a plus sign if the corresponding word would appear on that page. Write *before* if it would appear on an earlier page and *after* if it would appear on a later page.

EXAMPLES 1. nefarious
1. +
2. navy
2. *before*

1. negative 1. +
2. needle 2. before
3. neophyte 3. after
4. ne'er-do-well 4. +
5. newcomer 5. after
6. necktie 6. before
7. negligent 7. +
8. Neanderthal 8. before
9. New Zealander 9. after
10. negotiate 10. +

FINDING THE RIGHT MEANING

26b. Learn to find the meaning you want.

Most English words have a number of different meanings. When you go to the dictionary, you are usually interested in a particular meaning of a word—one that will fit into the particular sentence or situation in which you heard or read the word. Nevertheless, it is a good idea to scan all of the meanings given. By doing so you will form a general impression of the range of meanings that word may have.

Each separate meaning of a word is explained in a numbered definition. Some dictionaries use letters within numbered definitions to distinguish between closely related meanings. To see how this works, examine the following dictionary entry for the word *offensive:*

FINDING THE RIGHT MEANING
(rule 26b)

Experienced teachers know that the ability to find the correct definition of a word cannot be taken for granted in an eighth-grade class. Even advanced students will often accept the first definition given in the dictionary, whether it makes sense in context or not. Throughout the year, you can occasionally send a student to the classroom dictionary to look up a word that has come up in class reading or discussion. Insist that the student read through all the definitions and select the definition that best fits the context the word was used in.

EXERCISE 3. Go over students' answers in class. Have the students explain in each case why they chose a particular definition.

[1]**of•fen•sive** \ə-'fen-siv\ *adj* **1 a** : of, relating to, or designed for attack ⟨*offensive* weapons⟩ **b** : being on the offense ⟨the *offensive* team⟩ **2** : giving unpleasant sensations ⟨*offensive* smells⟩ **3** : causing displeasure or resentment : INSULTING ⟨an *offensive* remark⟩ — **of•fen•sive•ly** *adv* — **of•fen•sive•ness** *n*

[2]**offensive** *n* **1** : the act of an attacking party ⟨on the *offensive*⟩ **2** : ATTACK ⟨launch an *offensive*⟩

Suppose you want to find the meaning of *offensive* in the sentence "The child was scolded for making such an offensive remark." By recognizing that the word is used as an adjective in this sentence, you can concentrate your search on the entry that gives definitions for the adjective (*adj.*) *offensive.* Definitions 1 and 2 do not fit the context, but definition 3 does. What is more, the illustrative example for 3 provides a context very similar to the one you have in mind.

Now look back at the sample entry and notice that *offensive* is listed again, this time as a noun (*n.*). This particular dictionary gives separate entries for each part of speech. The small numeral 2 before the entry word shows that it is the second entry for the same word. Other dictionaries may not list parts of speech in this way. They may have all the definitions of a word in one entry, with each part of speech in its own subgroup. The following definition, taken from a different dictionary, illustrates the latter method. Notice that the definitions for the noun subgroup, marked by —*n* for *noun*, begin with the numeral 1.

of•fen•sive |ə fĕn′sĭv| *adj.* **1.** Offending the senses; unpleasant: *an offensive smell.* **2.** Causing anger, displeasure, resentment, etc.: *offensive language.* **3.** |ô′fĕn′sĭv| *or* |ŏf′ĕn′-|. Of an attack; aggressive; attacking: *an offensive play in football.* —*n.* **1.** An aggressive action; an attack: *their third major offensive of the war.* **2.** An attitude of attack: *take the offensive.* —**of•fen′sive•ly** *adv.* —**of•fen′sive•ness** *n.*

EXERCISE 3. Finding the Correct Meaning in the Dictionary. Below are two groups of sentences, each group followed by a dictionary definition. Number your paper 1–5. After the appropriate number, write the number (3) or the number and letter

(2b) of the definition that gives the correct meaning of the word as it is used in the sentence.

1. This morning we had a *rough* exam in science. 1. 2b
2. Mrs. Logan made a *rough* sketch of the model. 2. 4
3. Joan's coat is made of *rough* material. 3. 1a

[1]**rough** \'rəf\ *adj* **1 a** : having an uneven surface : not smooth **b** : covered with or made up of coarse and often shaggy hair or bristles ⟨a *rough*-coated terrier⟩ **c** : difficult to travel over or penetrate : WILD ⟨*rough* country⟩ **2 a** : characterized by harshness, violence, or force **b** : DIFFICULT, TRYING ⟨a *rough* day at the office⟩ **3** : coarse or rugged in character or appearance: as **a** : harsh to the ear **b** : crude in style or expression **c** : marked by a lack of refinement or grace : UNCOUTH **4** : marked by incompleteness or inexactness ⟨a *rough* draft⟩ ⟨*rough* estimates⟩ [Old English *rūh*] — **rough·ly** *adv* — **rough·ness** *n*

4. Astronomers will *train* their telescopes on Halley's comet. 4. 4
5. Ms. McConnell *trains* every morning for the marathon race. 5. 3

[2]**train** *vb* **1** : to direct the growth of (a plant) usually by bending, pruning, and tying **2 a** : to teach something (as a skill, profession, or trade) to ⟨was *trained* in the law⟩ **b** : to teach (an animal) to obey **3** : to make ready (as by exercise) for a test of skill **4** : to aim (as a gun) at a target **5** : to undergo instruction, discipline, or drill [Middle French *trainer* "to draw, drag"] **syn** see TEACH — **train·able** \'trā-nə-bəl\ *adj* — **train·ee** \trā-'nē\ *n*

CONTENT

26c. Learn what different kinds of information a dictionary gives you about words.

The typical dictionary definition contains a large amount of information. To take advantage of this information, you need to become familiar with the labels used in the dictionary. Examine the sample dictionary column on page 602. The explanations that follow correspond to the labels on this column. Consult the column as you study the notes.

CONTENT (rule 26c)

As an introduction to this part of the chapter, spend a few minutes questioning the class on what they already know about the kinds of information given in dictionaries. List on the board the various features and uses of a dictionary.

You will probably find, if your students are using different dictionaries, that their dictionaries do not always agree even about simple matters such as spelling, capitalization, and syllable division, and that different dictionaries are even more likely to give different answers regarding exact meanings and current levels of usage. As a general rule, any spelling, pronunciation, or definition given as a standard form by a reputable dictionary can be regarded as being in good standing. By the same token, the fact that one particular dictionary does not list a certain form or meaning does not necessarily indicate that the form or meaning is incorrect.

You can take this opportunity to point out to the class that when there are several right ways to spell or pronounce a word, a person should choose one way and stick to it. It is not correct, for instance, for a writer to use the spelling *moustache* in one sentence and the spelling *mustache* a few sentences later, even though both ways of spelling the word are considered correct by most dictionaries.

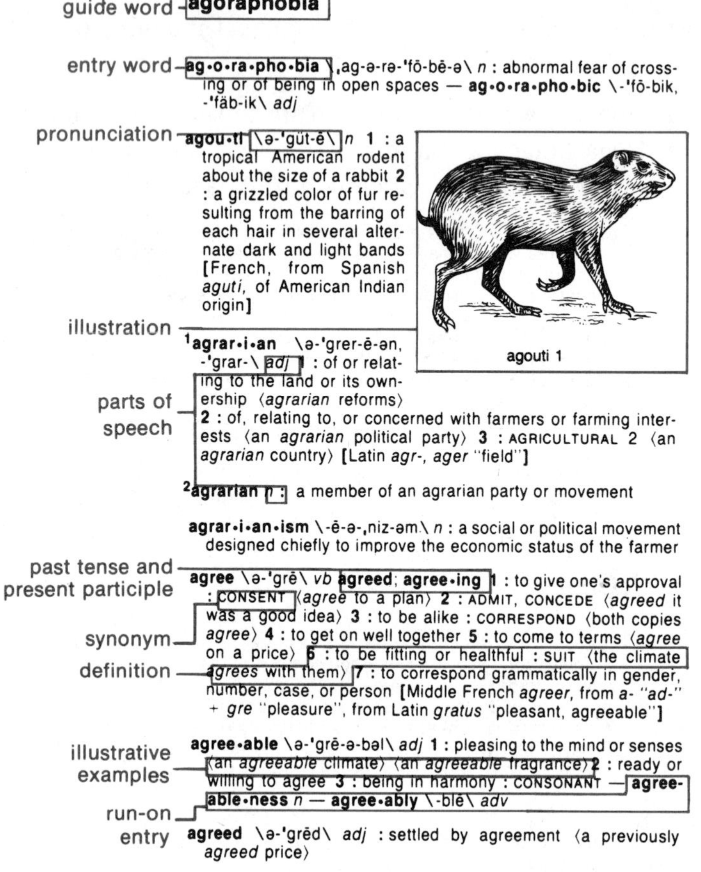

agoraphobia

ag•o•ra•pho•bia \ˌag-ə-rə-ˈfō-bē-ə\ *n* : abnormal fear of crossing or of being in open spaces — **ag•o•ra•pho•bic** \-ˈfō-bik, -ˈfäb-ik\ *adj*

agou•ti \ə-ˈgüt-ē\ *n* **1** : a tropical American rodent about the size of a rabbit **2** : a grizzled color of fur resulting from the barring of each hair in several alternate dark and light bands [French, from Spanish *aguti*, of American Indian origin]

agouti 1

[1]**agrar•i•an** \ə-ˈgrer-ē-ən, -ˈgrar-\ *adj* **1** : of or relating to the land or its ownership ⟨*agrarian* reforms⟩ **2** : of, relating to, or concerned with farmers or farming interests ⟨an *agrarian* political party⟩ **3** : AGRICULTURAL 2 ⟨an *agrarian* country⟩ [Latin *agr-*, *ager* "field"]

[2]**agrarian** *n* : a member of an agrarian party or movement

agrar•i•an•ism \-ē-ə-ˌniz-əm\ *n* : a social or political movement designed chiefly to improve the economic status of the farmer

agree \ə-ˈgrē\ *vb* **agreed**; **agree•ing** **1** : to give one's approval : CONSENT ⟨*agree* to a plan⟩ **2** : ADMIT, CONCEDE ⟨*agreed* it was a good idea⟩ **3** : to be alike : CORRESPOND ⟨both copies *agree*⟩ **4** : to get on well together **5** : to come to terms ⟨*agree* on a price⟩ **6** : to be fitting or healthful : SUIT ⟨the climate *agrees* with them⟩ **7** : to correspond grammatically in gender, number, case, or person [Middle French *agreer*, from *a-* "ad-" + *gre* "pleasure", from Latin *gratus* "pleasant, agreeable"]

agree•able \ə-ˈgrē-ə-bəl\ *adj* **1** : pleasing to the mind or senses ⟨an *agreeable* climate⟩ ⟨an *agreeable* fragrance⟩ **2** : ready or willing to agree **3** : being in harmony : CONSONANT — **agree•able•ness** *n* — **agree•ably** \-blē\ *adv*

agreed \ə-ˈgrēd\ *adj* : settled by agreement ⟨a previously *agreed* price⟩

1. *Entry word*. The word to be defined is called the *entry word*. It appears in boldfaced type. You use the entry word to locate a definition, to get the correct spelling of a word, and to find out how it is divided into syllables, if it has more than one syllable. Most dictionaries also indicate words that are capitalized by beginning the entry word with a capital letter. However, capitalization may be indicated in other ways, especially in dictionaries not specially designed for high-school students. If there is more than one acceptable spelling of a word, the alternative is usually listed immediately after the entry word:

EXAMPLE **moustache** or **mustache**

In most cases the first spelling listed is the one that most people prefer to use.

2. *Illustration*. Sometimes the best way to indicate the meaning of a word is through an illustration. *Agouti* on page 602 is such a word.

3. *Pronunciation*. The pronunciation of a word is usually indicated immediately after the entry word by means of a special respelling, which is explained in detail on pages 610–11. The sounds represented by the symbols in the pronunciation respelling are explained in a key that usually appears inside the front cover of the dictionary. A shorter key may appear at the bottom of each page or of every other page. (For more about pronunciation, see pages 609–11.)

4. *Definition*. The definition gives the meaning or meanings of a word. When a word has more than one meaning, each meaning is defined separately in a numbered definition. (Some dictionaries use letters to distinguish between meanings so closely related that they are defined in a single numbered definition.)

5. *Illustrative example*. For many words, and for different meanings of the same word, sample contexts are provided to show how the word is used. Illustrative examples often provide the clues that will prevent you from making mistakes in usage.

6. *Synonyms*. Synonyms are words that have similar meanings. In the sample column on page 602, for example, *consent* is given as the synonym for *agree*. (The word *consent* is printed in block letters to indicate that it is a synonym.) Words that are synonyms can be used alike in some contexts but not in others. For example, the words *deep* and *profound* are synonyms when the subject is mystery.

7. *Run-on entry*. Many English words have companion forms that are closely related to them in meaning. Dictionaries include these words at the end of an entry as *run-on entries*. At the end of the adjective *bad,* for instance, you may find the notation "**—bad′ly** *adv.* **—bad′ness** *n.*" Although often no definitions are

given in a run-on entry, a part-of-speech label is provided for each companion form. Some dictionaries also give the pronunciation for the companion form. (For more about companion forms, see page 633.)

8. *Part of speech.* The part of speech is indicated by an italicized abbreviation:

n.	noun	*adv.*	adverb
pron.	pronoun	*prep.*	preposition
v. or *vb.*	verb[1]	*conj.*	conjunction
adj.	adjective	*interj.*	interjection

Many English words can be used as more than one part of speech. For such words, a dictionary will indicate how the definitions are related to the part-of-speech labels. In some dictionaries, all the definitions for one part of speech are grouped together after the label, as on page 602. Other dictionaries provide consecutively numbered definitions, with the part-of-speech label after each numeral. The most frequent usages are given first.

A dictionary also provides the following information:

Usage label. Not all words entered in a dictionary are equally acceptable in all situations. A usage label is a mild warning that people use a word (or use a particular meaning of a word) only in certain situations. For example, the label *slang* indicates a word that may be used in certain informal situations but is likely to call attention to itself when used in other situations. Another label, *archaic,* indicates that a word was once common but is now rarely used. A third label, *dialect,* indicates that a word is used in only one part of the country. The introduction to your dictionary explains the meaning of all the usage labels employed by your dictionary.

[1] Unabridged dictionaries and those designed for older students distinguish between verbs like *wonder* in the sentence "I wonder" and verbs that require another word to show who or what is receiving the action; for example, *hit* in "The batter hit a home run." Such dictionaries label verbs like *wonder,* in the first example, *v.i.,* and verbs like *hit,* in the second, *v.t.* The abbreviation *v.i.* stands for *intransitive verb; v.t.* stands for *transitive verb.* Transitive verbs always have to have an object—a word showing who or what was affected by the action expressed by the verb.

Origin. For some words, school dictionaries provide information about the history of a word, usually by indicating the language from which it was borrowed. Such information may appear near the beginning of the definition or at the end, as in the following example:

> **dex·ter·ous** [dek′strəs *or* dek′stər·əs] *adj.* **1** Skillful in using the hands or body; adroit: a *dexterous* billiard player. **2** Mentally quick; keen. — **dex′ter·ous·ly** *adv.* ◆ *Dexterous* comes from a Latin word meaning *skillful,* which in turn comes from a Latin root meaning *on the right* or *right-handed.*

Encyclopedia information. A small number of dictionary entries deal with people and places. There are better places, including encyclopedias, to find out about important people and places than in a dictionary—these are described in Chapter 27. However, if all you need is a general identification or location, the dictionary will usually provide it, as in the following entry:

> **Pierce** (pirs), **Franklin** 1804–69; 14th president of the U.S. (1853–57)

EXERCISE 4. Writing Synonyms of Words. Number your paper 1–5. Write a synonym for each of the following words. If necessary, use the dictionary.

1. coax
2. distinct
3. diversity
4. find
5. plain

1. persuade 2. separate 3. variety 4. discover 5. ordinary

EXERCISE 5. Understanding Usage Labels. Copy from your dictionary the usage labels for five of these words. Be prepared to explain what the labels tell you and how they would affect your use of the words.

1. afeared
2. corny
3. davenport
4. gabby
5. loco
6. lorry
7. ope
8. petrol
9. pone
10. raspberry

EXERCISES 4 and 5. If possible, insist that all students in the class use the same dictionary for these exercises. If this is not feasible, tell students to write at the top of their paper the exact name of the dictionary they use for an exercise. Although in this latter case you probably cannot check each student's answers against the dictionary that was used, you can at least compare the answers with those given by other students who also used that dictionary.

Answers: Exercise 5

(Answers will vary, according to which dictionary students use. Some dictionaries will not give usage labels for all of these words. These answers are based on the Thorndike-Barnhart Advanced Junior Dictionary.*)*

1. *Archaic; Dialect*
2. *Slang*
3. *U.S.*
4. *Informal*
5. *U.S., Slang*
6. *Brit.*
7. *Poetic*
8. *Brit.*
9. *Southern U.S.*
10. *Slang (in one use)*

EXERCISES 6–8. See notes for Exercises 4 and 5.

Answers: Exercise 8
(Answers will vary in wording.)

1. A Moabite widow deeply devoted to her mother-in-law, Naomi
2. The beautiful wife of Menelaus, king of Sparta
3. Seaport in northeast Egypt
4. River in Venezuela
5. American Indian who recorded the Cherokee language

SPELLING, CAPITALIZATION, and **SYLLABLE DIVISION**
(pages 606–609, rule 26d)

All students should get into the habit of looking up a word in the dictionary when they are not sure of the spelling. Show them examples of the information they can get about the spelling of plurals, past tenses, participles, and various other forms by looking in a dictionary.

EXERCISE 6. Finding Run-on Entries for Specific Words. Copy from your dictionary a run-on entry for each of the following words.
Answers will vary. Some dictionaries may not give run-on entries for all these words.

1. celebrate
2. reform
3. fair
4. foolish
5. liquidate

1. celebration
2. reformer
3. fairness
4. foolishly
5. liquidation

EXERCISE 7. Writing Definitions According to Parts of Speech. Copy from your dictionary two definitions for each of the following words, each definition for a different part of speech. Following the definitions, indicate the parts of speech by using part-of-speech labels. Answers will vary.

EXAMPLE 1. flower
1. *a. The part of a plant that normally bears the seed, n.*
   b. To blossom; to bloom, v.

1. back
2. Chinese
3. maneuver
4. net
5. tag

EXERCISE 8. Finding Information About Persons and Places in the Dictionary. Look up the following persons and places in your dictionary. Be able to tell what information the dictionary provides about them.

1. Ruth
2. Helen of Troy
3. Port Said
4. Orinoco
5. Sequoya

SPELLING

26d. Learn to use your dictionary for spelling and capitalization.

The dictionary is the authority on correct spelling. In English, the spelling of the initial sound of a word is much more regular than the spelling of sounds in the middle or at the end of words. To find how most words are spelled, simply follow the principles of alphabetical order and let the guide words help you.

Variant Spellings

A dictionary occasionally gives two spellings for a word: *abridgment* and *abridgement, coconut* and *cocoanut.* Both spellings are correct, but usually a dictionary indicates which spelling is preferred by listing it first.

EXERCISE 9. Finding Variant Spellings of Specific Words. Copy from your dictionary a variant spelling for the following words. Be able to tell whether one spelling is preferred.

1. demon
2. judgment
3. likeable
4. savior
5. sulfur

1. daemon
2. judgement
3. likable
4. saviour
5. sulphur

Unusual Plurals

If the plural of a noun is formed in an unusual way, a dictionary will give the plural form with the abbreviation *pl.* preceding it. For example, the plural of *datum* is given as *data.* Some dictionaries list plurals that are formed in the regular way if there is a chance that the plural will be misspelled. The plural of *valley* might be given (*valleys*) so that no one will make the mistake of ending the plural in *-ies.*

Unusual Verb Forms

If a verb forms its past tense, its past participle, or its present participle in an unusual way, a dictionary will list these irregular forms.

Comparatives and Superlatives

If the comparative and superlative forms of an adjective are spelled in an unusual way, a dictionary provides these forms either near the beginning or the end of an entry. Sometimes the abbreviations *compar.* and *superl.* are used.

EXERCISE 9. Different dictionaries may give slightly varying answers for some items in this exercise and the next one. See the notes for Exercises 4 and 5. You might point out here that in compositions, students should choose one correct spelling and use it consistently.

EXERCISE 10. Make sure students understand what kind of forms they are finding—noun, adjective, and verb forms.

EXERCISE 11. You might first dictate these words as a capitalization test, using them in sentences of your own, and then have students look up the words in a dictionary. Then point out that all the mistakes in capitalization that were made could be avoided in the future by using the dictionary. Doing the exercise in this fashion may impress students with the dictionary's usefulness.

love·ly [luv′lē] *adj.* **love·li·er, love·li·est** **1** Having qualities that make people love one: a *lovely* child. **2** Beautiful: a *lovely* rose. **3** *informal* Enjoyable; pleasant: to have a *lovely* time at a party. —**love′li·ness** *n.*

EXERCISE 10. **Finding Unusual Spelling Forms for Specific Words.** Copy from your dictionary the unusual spelling forms (if any) for the following words. After the forms, write (*1*) if they are unusual plurals, (*2*) if they are unusual verb forms, or (*3*) if they are unusual comparatives and superlatives.

EXAMPLE 1. swim
1. *swam, swum, swimming (2)*

1. choose
2. index
3. mad
4. needy
5. rise

1. chose, chosen (2)
2. indexes *or* indices (1)
3. madder, maddest (3)
4. needier, neediest (3)
5. rose, risen (2)

CAPITALIZATION

If you are not sure about capitalizing a certain word, the dictionary will help you. Sometimes a word should be capitalized in one sense but not capitalized in another. In such a case, the dictionary indicates which meaning requires a capital. For example, some dictionaries print *Mass,* meaning "a religious ceremony," with a capital; but *mass,* meaning "a large amount or number," appears uncapitalized.

EXERCISE 11. **Using the Dictionary for Capitalization.** Look up the following words in a dictionary to see when they are capitalized. Be able to explain why they are or are not capitalized in each usage. Your dictionary may not give capitalized uses for all the words. See Answer Key.

1. cupid
2. democrat
3. nativity
4. senate
5. west

SYLLABLE DIVISION

A dictionary divides all words into syllables. If your dictionary uses small dots or dashes between the syllables of a word, be careful not to confuse these marks with a hyphen. Look up a hyphenated word like *flip-flop* or *open-minded* to be sure you can tell the difference.

EXERCISE 12. Dividing Words into Syllables. Copy the following words, dividing them into syllables. Use the same method to indicate syllable division that your dictionary uses.

1. endurance
2. flexible
3. junior
4. socialize
5. underdog

PRONUNCIATION

26e. Learn to use your dictionary for pronunciation.

One of the most important pieces of information given in a dictionary is the pronunciation of a word. This information usually comes immediately after the entry word and is enclosed within slant bars or within parentheses.

The Accent Mark

In words of two or more syllables, one syllable is always pronounced with greater force than the others. A dictionary indicates which syllable needs emphasis by using an *accent mark*. Most dictionaries use one of two kinds of accent marks: either the mark (ˈ) appearing before the syllable or the mark (′) placed after the syllable.

In a word of three or more syllables, a dictionary usually indicates two accent marks, one primary, the other secondary. The word *elevator* has a primary accent on the syllable *el* and a weaker accent on *vat*. Dictionaries generally show the secondary accent in one of three ways. When the mark (′) is used to indicate primary accent, the secondary accent is indicated by a weaker mark (') or by two marks (″). When the primary accent (ˈ) is used, the secondary accent is a similar mark placed at the bottom of a syllable (ˌ).

EXERCISE 12. Less-advanced students especially should learn to use the dictionary when they want to divide a word at the end of a line. Tell all students that if they have difficulty in remembering the rules for syllabication, they should rely on the dictionary as a guide. Then assign the exercise.

Answers: Exercise 12

(Answers will vary, according to which dictionary students use. The following answers are based on the Thorndike-Barnhart Advanced Junior Dictionary.*)*

1. en dur ance
2. flex i ble
3. jun ior
4. so cial ize
5. un der dog

PRONUNCIATION (rule 26e)

It would not be worthwhile to ask students to memorize the pronunciation symbols used by a dictionary, since these symbols are not standardized and vary from one dictionary to the next. It is, however, worthwhile to go over in class the pronunciation key in the dictionary that students are using and to give students practice with the pronunciations. You might put on the board some frequently mispronounced words and have students look up the words in their own dictionaries to find the correct pronunciations.

EXERCISES 13 and 14. Advise students to read the words aloud after they have written them to check whether their customary pronunciation of a word agrees with that given in the dictionary. In reviewing the answers in class, have students pronounce the words again.

Answers: Exercise 13

(Answers will vary, according to which dictionary students use. The following answers are based on the Thorndike-Barnhart Advanced Junior Dictionary.*)*

1. det′ri men′tal
2. dis′tri bu′tion
3. fru′gal
4. mas′quer ade′
5. O lym′ pi an

EXERCISE 13. Dividing Words into Syllables and Indicating Accented Syllables. Copy the following words, dividing them into syllables, and indicate the accented syllables. Use the kinds of accent marks that are used in your dictionary.

1. detrimental
2. distribution
3. frugal
4. masquerade
5. Olympian

Pronunciation Symbols

A dictionary uses pronunciation symbols to indicate the pronunciation of a word. Most symbols are regular letters of the alphabet, but they are used more strictly than in ordinary writing. For example, the letter *c* can have several different pronunciations, as in the words *city, control,* and *cello.* A dictionary would indicate the beginning sounds of these words as *s, k,* and *ch.* To show the pronunciation of vowels, which is harder to indicate than the pronunciation of consonants, a dictionary uses *diacritical* marks—special symbols placed above the letters.

Dictionaries vary in their use of symbols. A key to these symbols usually appears inside the front cover and sometimes on each page as well.

In this chapter you will study several diacritical marks that are used by most dictionaries.

Long Vowels

To indicate a long vowel, a dictionary generally uses a diacritical mark called a *macron*—a long straight mark over the vowel. When a macron is used, the long vowel is said to have the sound of its own name.

EXAMPLES	main	/mān/
	mean	/mēn/
	mine	/mīn/
	moan	/mōn/
	immune	/imūn/

Short Vowels

The vowels in the words *mat, head, bid, dot,* and *cut* are called short vowels. Dictionaries differ in their methods of showing the sound of short vowels.

One method uses a symbol called a *breve* (pronounced *brĕv* or *brēv*) over the vowel. Another method is to leave short vowels unmarked.

EXAMPLES	mat	(măt)	or	/mat/
	head	(hĕd)	or	/hed/
	bid	(bĭd)	or	/bid/

Sometimes, when all that we pronounce in an unaccented syllable is the sound of the consonant, the pronunciation indication in certain dictionaries may omit the short vowel altogether.

The Schwa

Most recent dictionaries use an upside-down *e*, called a *schwa,* to represent the neutral vowel sound "uh." This sound occurs in the phrase *the pen* (thə pen) and in the following words:

minute (min′ ət), permit (pər mit′), police (pə lēs′).

Most dictionaries use the schwa for the "uh" sound only when it occurs in unaccented syllables, but several dictionaries also use this symbol when the sound occurs in accented syllables and in one-syllable words.

EXERCISE 14. Finding the Pronunciations of Specific Words. Copy from your dictionary the pronunciation of each of the following words. Follow the practice of your dictionary in using parentheses or slant lines to enclose the pronunciation. Be able to explain all the diacritical marks used.

1. diet	6. poverty
2. erase	7. puny
3. bumblebee	8. revolve
4. matriarchy	9. seldom
5. nation	10. sidesaddle

Answers: Exercise 14

(Answers will vary, according to which dictionary students use. The following answers are based on the Thorndike-Barnhart Advanced Junior Dictionary.*)*

1. (dī′ət)
2. (i rās′)
3. (bum′b′l bē′)
4. (mā′tri ar′ki)
5. (nā′sh n)
6. (pov′ər ti)
7. (pū′ni)
8. (ri volv′)
9. (sel′dəm)
10. (sīd′sad′əl)

REVIEW EXERCISE. If not already used as a diagnostic test, this exercise can serve as a chapter review.

Additional Practice

Teacher's Resource Book, Worksheet pages 312–14

Testing

Teaching Tests booklet, pages 85–86, 89–91
Teacher's Resource Book, Test pages 493–94, 497–99

REVIEW EXERCISE. Understanding the Arrangement and Content of Dictionaries. Use complete sentences in writing the answers to the following questions. If necessary, look the information up in the chapter. See Answer Key.

1. Define
   a. synonym c. guide word
   b. macron d. schwa
2. Name three kinds of information about spelling that a dictionary provides.
3. After which of the following words would *mother-in-law* occur in a dictionary?
   a. motherly c. motherhood
   b. mother d. motherland
4. What kind of information is given by the following terms: *slang, informal, archaic*?
5. List the types of information—other than spelling and pronunciation—that a dictionary entry gives about a word.

CHAPTER 27

Using the Library

ARRANGEMENT OF A LIBRARY, REFERENCE MATERIALS

The best place to look for information is a library or media center. To use a library efficiently, you must understand its system of arranging the books, magazines, pamphlets, and other materials it contains so that you can find what you want easily and quickly.

THE ARRANGEMENT OF A LIBRARY

Fiction

27a. Learn to locate books of fiction.

In most libraries all books of fiction are located in one section. The books are arranged in alphabetical order according to authors' last names. If you were looking for *The Good Earth* by Pearl S. Buck, you would go to the fiction section and find the books by authors whose last names begin with *B*. There you would find several books by Buck. Books by the same author are arranged in alphabetical order according to the first word in the title, unless that word is *a, an,* or *the.* In that case, the second word of the title is used. *The Good Earth* would then come in the *G* position.

Chapter Overview

Most eighth-graders are already familiar with the arrangement of the school library and with the use of the card catalog. Review work on these matters can usually be covered in one or two periods, and the rest of the time spent on this chapter can be devoted to the different kinds of reference books and to assignments that require students to find information in the library. In fact, you might teach the section on reports in Chapter 6 in connection with this work, since the reports will provide opportunities for library research. For students' use, a Summary List of Library Reference Tools appears at the end of the chapter (page 625).

Whenever possible, library instruction should take place in the library itself. If you do not have a library in your school, however, the material may be reviewed with aids such as wall charts of the Dewey decimal system, sample cards like those in the card catalog, and so forth. Either require students to take notes or else hand out duplicated sheets that summarize the information. Make arrangements to take the class on a field trip to a nearby library. Have some drills prepared that the class will do when they visit the library—for instance, titles of books that they are to look up in the card catalog and locate on the shelves.

Chapter Objective

Students will use the library and its reference materials.

PRESENTING THE CHAPTER

LESS-ADVANCED STUDENTS For these students, the fiction shelf and

613

the magazine collection will usually be the most attractive parts of the library. It is worthwhile to teach this class to use the card catalog to find books by their favorite authors or about their favorite subjects. If the card catalog in your library has subject listings for certain types of fiction—such as "Mystery stories," "Sports stories," "Adventure"—be sure to point this out to the class and give them practice looking up books under these subject heads.

The encyclopedia, the atlas, and the almanac (plus the dictionary, which was covered in the last chapter) will probably be the most important reference materials for such students, both while they are in school and in later life. Instead of introducing more specialized reference books, therefore, it may be wise to give a less-advanced class further training in using these basic tools.

ADVANCED STUDENTS An advanced class, if they have already mastered the shelving system and the use of the card catalog, can concentrate on learning to use some of the specialized reference materials. If your students are not yet familiar with the *Readers' Guide,* you might want to concentrate this year on that important but rather difficult tool.

Do not expect any class, no matter how advanced, to be able to study thoroughly all the reference books mentioned in the chapter in a single year. You can pick out four or five books for class work and recommend some of the other books to students who may need special resources for their individual reports.

☞ **NOTE** Books by authors whose names begin with *Mc* are arranged as though the name were spelled *Mac; St.* is arranged as though it were spelled out, *Saint.*

EXERCISE 1. Arranging Books of Fiction. Write the authors and titles of the following fiction books in the order in which the books would be arranged in the library.

1. *The Light in the Forest* by Conrad Richter 8
2. *Curtain* by Agatha Christie 6
3. *Jane Eyre* by Charlotte Brontë 2
4. *Dirt Track Summer* by William Campbell Gault 7
5. *Crooked House* by Agatha Christie 5
6. *The Incredible Journey* by Sheila Burnford 4
7. *The Friendly Persuasion* by Jessamyn West 10
8. *Wuthering Heights* by Emily Brontë 3
9. *The Tamarack Tree* by Betty Underwood 9
10. *The Martian Chronicles* by Ray Bradbury 1

Nonfiction

27b. Learn the Dewey decimal system of arranging nonfiction.

The Dewey decimal system is named for Melvil Dewey, the American librarian who developed it. Under this system, books are classified under ten headings, and each heading has a number. The numbers and headings are as follows:

000–099 General Works (encyclopedias, reference materials)
100–199 Philosophy
200–299 Religion
300–399 Social Sciences (economics, government, etc.)
400–499 Language
500–599 Science
600–699 Technology (engineering, aviation, inventions, etc.)
700–799 The Arts (architecture, music, sports, etc.)

800–899 Literature
900–999 History (including geography, travel, and biography)

The number given to a book is known as the book's call number. To see how the Dewey system works, take as an example Arthur Zaidenberg's *How to Draw Cartoons*. Since the book is about art, its number will be in the 700's. Within this broad category, the numbers 740–749 are used for books on drawing and decorative arts. Books on freehand drawing are given the number 741. By means of a decimal, the classification is narrowed further. The number 741.5 is given to books about drawing cartoons, and 741.5-Z is the call number for the book *How to Draw Cartoons*.

Biographies are arranged in alphabetical order according to the names of the persons written about, not according to the names of the persons who wrote the biographies. For example, *The Helen Keller Story* by Catherine Owens Peare will appear among the K's. The call number may consist of **B** (for biography) with **K** (for Keller) under it: **B**/**K**. Or it may consist of 92 with **K** under it: 92/**K**. Some librarians use the **B;** others use the 92, which is a short form of the Dewey number (920) for biography. Still others use 921.

EXERCISE 2. Classifying Nonfiction According to the Dewey Decimal System. Within which number range in the Dewey decimal system would you find each of the following?

EXAMPLE 1. A book on modeling in clay
1. *700-799*

1. A book about travels in Africa
2. A book about the Presidency
3. A book about baseball
4. A book about poetry
5. A collection of biographies of pioneer men and women

1. 900–999 4. 700–799
2. 300–399 5. 900–999
3. 700–799

THE CARD CATALOG

You can find out the call number of any book in the library by looking the book up in the card catalog.

THE ARRANGEMENT OF A LIBRARY (rules 27a and 27b)

If this is the first time that you have taught a unit on the school library, be sure to visit the library yourself and find out exactly how it is arranged before you present this section to your class. You may want to take the textbook with you and check each piece of information against the system actually used in your library.

EXERCISE 1. A less-advanced class should probably write out this exercise. In an average class, you can have students list the books orally, while you write their answers on the board.

EXERCISE 2. Students should refer to the preceding list as they complete this exercise. There is no point in students' memorizing the list, because they would still need to look up a book in the card catalog and find its exact Dewey decimal number in order to locate it quickly on the shelves.

THE CARD CATALOG (rule 27c)

Work on the card catalog should include a visit to the school library so that students can look through an actual card catalog. If you maintain a classroom library, you may want to have each student make a title, author, and subject card for one of the books in this collection.

27c. Learn to use the card catalog.

The card catalog is a cabinet with small drawers that contain file cards arranged in alphabetical order for all the books in the library. For each book of fiction there are at least two cards, an *author card* and a *title card.* For each book of nonfiction, there are usually three cards, an *author card,* a *title card,* and a *subject card.* If the book is by two or more authors, there is an author card for each name.

Each card provides a different means of finding a book. If you are looking for a book by a particular author, you would look for the *author card.* If you know the title of the book but not the name of the author, you would look for the *title card.* If you need information about a particular subject (rockets and rocketry, for instance), look for a *subject card* with the word *ROCKETS* at the top.

Study the following sample cards and explanations:

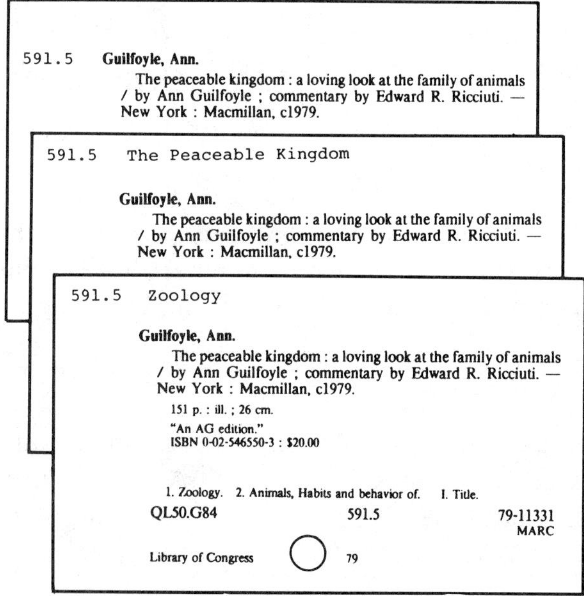

591.5 **Guilfoyle, Ann.**
The peaceable kingdom : a loving look at the family of animals / by Ann Guilfoyle ; commentary by Edward R. Ricciuti. — New York : Macmillan, c1979.

591.5 The Peaceable Kingdom

Guilfoyle, Ann.
The peaceable kingdom : a loving look at the family of animals / by Ann Guilfoyle ; commentary by Edward R. Ricciuti. — New York : Macmillan, c1979.

591.5 Zoology

Guilfoyle, Ann.
The peaceable kingdom : a loving look at the family of animals / by Ann Guilfoyle ; commentary by Edward R. Ricciuti. — New York : Macmillan, c1979.
151 p. : ill. ; 26 cm.
"An AG edition."
ISBN 0-02-546550-3 : $20.00

1. Zoology. 2. Animals, Habits and behavior of. I. Title.
QL50.G84 591.5 79-11331
MARC
Library of Congress 79

Principal Items of Information on a Card

1. *Name of author.* This information appears first on author

cards, which are filed alphabetically under the author's last name. All books by one author are then arranged in alphabetical order by titles.

2. *Call number.* This Dewey decimal number tells you where to find the book in the nonfiction section of the library.

3. *Title of book.* On title cards this information appears first. Title cards are filed alphabetically in the card catalog according to the first word of the title, not counting the words *a, an,* or *the.*

4. *Subject.* The subject of a book appears first on subject cards. Like author cards and title cards, they are arranged alphabetically in the card catalog.

5. *Publisher and date of publication.* The date of publication is an important guide if you want recent information on a subject. Always check each source's date of publication to make sure that you are using the most current edition. The place of publication is often given before the publisher's name.

6. *Number of pages.* Occasionally this fact will be useful. Obviously, a book about the history of the Supreme Court that is only seventy pages long cannot give much detailed information on the subject.

7. *"See" and "see also" references.* Sometimes a subject card has a "see" reference or a "see also" reference sending you to another card in the catalog. For example, if you looked up *Revolutionary War,* you might find a card saying, "See United States—History—Revolutionary War." If you looked up *Diving,* you might find, "See also Skin Diving."

EXERCISE 3. Using the Card Catalog. Using the card catalog, list the call number, title, author, and date of publication of one book on each of five of the following topics. Answers will vary.

1. French Impressionist painters
2. Lasers
3. Birds of Europe
4. Baseball
5. Florence Nightingale
6. South America
7. American poets and poetry
8. Computer games
9. Japanese Americans
10. Scientists

EXERCISE 3. You might check these items with the card catalog in your library before you assign the exercise to the class. If some of the items are not listed in your library's catalog, you may want to use substitute items.

REFERENCE BOOKS
(rules 27d and 27e)

Before teaching this section, check to see which of the reference materials dealt with in the textbook are actually available in your library. Few school libraries, for instance, will have all three of the junior encyclopedias listed in the textbook. Find out which encyclopedias your library does have and concentrate on these.

REFERENCE BOOKS

27d. Learn to use the reference books available in the library.

The section devoted to reference books is one of the most important parts of a library. These books contain information on a great many subjects or tell where such information can be found. Once you become familiar with the reference books in your library, they will prove a valuable aid to your studies.

Encyclopedias

An encyclopedia contains articles by experts on a wide range of subjects. Many articles contain pictures, charts, maps, lists of facts, and tables of figures. An encyclopedia article will give you a good overall view of the subject and may also suggest more detailed sources of information.

You will likely find the following three encyclopedias handy for most reports:

Compton's Encyclopedia
World Book Encyclopedia
Collier's Encyclopedia

All these encyclopedias consist of many volumes and arrange their articles alphabetically by subject. The guide letter or letters on the spine of each volume will help you to find information about a particular subject. Guide words at the top of each page will help you to find a specific article. Use them as you would use guide words in a dictionary. (See page 598.) If you cannot find an article under a particular subject, look for a larger subject that includes yours. For example, information on *supersonic flight* can probably be found in an article on *aviation.*

You can also find information in an encyclopedia by using the index. Most encyclopedias have indexes, but the indexes are not always located in the same place. For example, the index of *Collier's Encyclopedia* is the last volume, while the index in *Compton's Encyclopedia* is at the end of each volume. You can use the index to locate maps, charts, tables, and illustrations, as well as articles about a particular subject. Usually there is a guide to using the index at the beginning of the index itself.

The index in the last volume of the *World Book Encyclopedia* is in somewhat different form. It is a "Reading and Study Guide," which is arranged by subjects. Each subject is divided into a series of smaller subjects for which a list of articles available in the encyclopedia is given.

EXERCISE 4. Using an Encyclopedia. Look up two of the topics below in an encyclopedia and take half a page of notes on each of them. Below each group of notes, write the title of the article, the name of the encyclopedia, the volume number, and the number of the page on which you found the information.
Answers will vary.

EXAMPLE 1. The tourist industry in Hawaii

1. *Each year, several million tourists enjoy vacations in Hawaii. They spend about 3 billion dollars. The busiest months are July, August, and December. In 1903, business people on the islands established an agency that later became the Hawaii Visitors Bureau. The bureau, with state assistance, conducts advertising campaigns to attract tourists.*
"Hawaii," World Book Encyclopedia, *volume 9, page 102*

1. Soft-coal mining in the United States
2. The paintings of Mary Cassatt
3. Famous volcanoes
4. Dinosaurs
5. The Battle of Hastings
6. The origin of bowling
7. Penguins
8. The native tribes of Australia
9. The rules and strategy of backgammon
10. The invention of the Diesel engine

Atlases

Atlases are reference books made up mainly of maps. Often they contain much other information, such as the population figures

EXERCISE 4. If students have chosen topics for research reports (Chapter 6) and are beginning to gather information for the reports, you may wish to have them use their report topics for this assignment.

EXERCISES 5 and 6. Note that students are asked to write answers to only *two* questions in each of these exercises. Assigning all the questions would merely provide busywork. If you wish to give further practice in using atlases and almanacs, however, you might get together with the social studies teacher and make a list of questions that are directly related to the class's work in history or geography and which can be answered by using atlases or almanacs.

Answers: Exercise 5

1. *Answers may include* Kings Canyon National Park, Lassen Volcanic National Park, Sequoia National Park, Yosemite National Park.
2. a. France, Germany, Liechtenstein, Austria, Italy
   b. Colombia, Brazil, Guyana
   c. Greece, Bulgaria, U.S.S.R., Iran, Iraq, Syria
3. Answers will vary.
4. a. Soviet Union c. East Germany
   b. Saudi Arabia d. Japan
5. Illinois, Florida, Virginia, Maine

for cities, states, and countries; principal crops; natural resources; and major industries.

Some atlases contain maps for all the countries of the world. Others contain maps for a particular country only. Historical atlases show how countries have changed through the years, while economic atlases show such things as trade routes and natural resources. Some of the common atlases are

The Encyclopaedia Britannica Atlas
Hammond Contemporary World Atlas
National Geographic World Atlas
Rand McNally Popular World Atlas

Atlases will prove valuable in your history and geography courses. You should learn about the different kinds of information that atlases provide and become thoroughly familiar with at least one atlas.

EXERCISE 5. Using a World Atlas. Consult a world atlas and write answers to two of the following questions.

1. Name three national parks in California.
2. List the countries that border on each of the following:
   a. Switzerland b. Venezuela c. Turkey
3. List four major products of each of the following:
   a. Bolivia b. Ethiopia c. Pakistan d. Iraq
4. In which country is each of the following cities situated?
   a. Volgograd b. Riyadh c. Jena d. Sapporo
5. List the following states in order of population, beginning with the most populous:
   a. Illinois b. Virginia c. Maine d. Florida

Almanacs

An almanac contains lists of miscellaneous information, including sports statistics, names of government officials, population figures, and birth and death rates. In addition, an almanac is a good source of recent information since almanacs are published annually. For instance, if you want a review of the important events of last year, you should consult this year's almanac.

Three useful almanacs are *The World Almanac and Book of Facts, Information Please Almanac,* and *The CBS News Almanac.* The various kinds of information in an almanac are not always organized alphabetically or even systematically. The best way to find information in an almanac is to use the index.

EXERCISE 6. Using an Almanac. Consult one of the almanacs mentioned above and answer two of the following questions:
See Answer Key.

1. Give the birth dates and birthplaces of the following persons (look up "Personalities, noted" or "Celebrated persons"):
   a. Eudora Welty
   b. Stephen Spielberg
   c. Chris Evert Lloyd
   d. Robert Redford
   e. Jesse Jackson
2. Give the names of the Secretaries of State during the administration of the following Presidents:
   a. John Quincy Adams
   b. William Harrison
   c. Abraham Lincoln
   d. William Taft
   e. Warren Harding
3. Who won the Nobel Prize for physics in 1923? 1938? 1946? 1970? 1976?
4. Give the name of the author and title of the novel that won the Pulitzer Prize for fiction in each of the following years: 1926, 1928, 1947, 1955, 1959, 1980.

Biographical Reference Books

A biographical reference book contains short biographies of famous persons. The following are among the most useful:

Who's Who and *Who's Who in America*—useful for principal biographical facts about living persons only.

Webster's Biographical Dictionary—very short biographies of famous persons, modern and historical.

Contemporary Authors and *Contemporary Authors: First Revision*—interesting profiles of modern writers.

Current Biography—lives of persons currently prominent in the news. Published monthly.

THE *READERS' GUIDE*
(rule 27e)

If students did not have a thorough introduction to the *Readers' Guide* in an earlier grade, you may wish to order for the class copies of the H. W. Wilson Company's "How to Use the *Readers' Guide to Periodical Literature*" and then spend two or three days of class time going over the explanations, examples, and exercises in the booklet. The booklets are free to classroom teachers.

In order to retain what they have learned about using the *Readers' Guide,* students should be given several assignments during the rest of the year that will require searching for information with the help of the *Readers' Guide*. If you do not plan to give writing assignments that will require finding background information in magazine articles, however, you might well consider omitting this section when you teach the library chapter. A less-advanced class, in particular, may not be ready to handle assignments that would involve the use of the *Readers' Guide*.

The *Readers' Guide*

27e. To find a magazine article, use the *Readers' Guide.*

To find a magazine article on any subject, you use a reference book called the *Readers' Guide to Periodical Literature.* Published eighteen times a year, the *Readers' Guide* indexes articles in more than one hundred magazines. Every year the issues are collected and published in a large volume. You can look up an article by its subject or by its author. To save space, the listings use the abbreviations listed in the keys in the front of the *Readers' Guide.*

Suppose you are writing an article about ancient Egypt and wish to include some information about King Tut's tomb. You could begin by looking up the subject *Tutenkhamun.* Scanning the listings under *Tutenkhamun,* you would come to the subdivision *Tomb.*

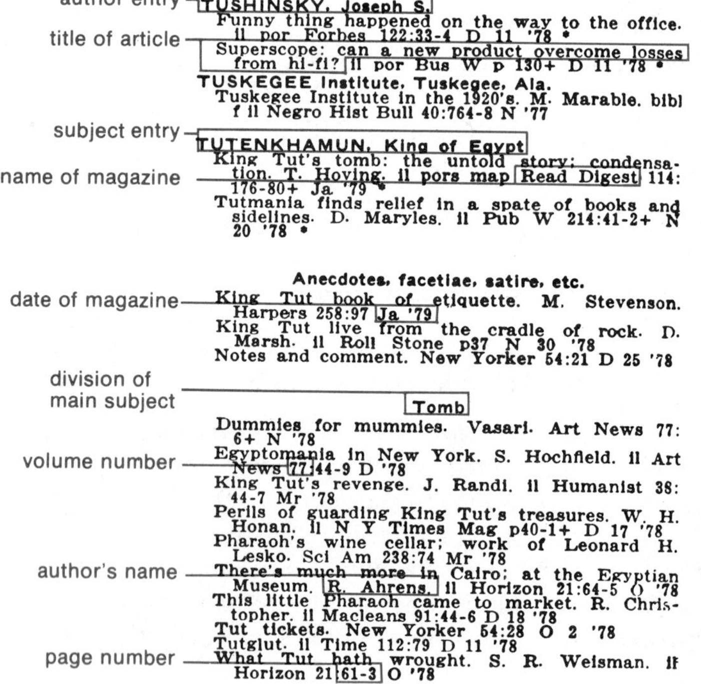

TUSHINSKY, Joseph S.
Funny thing happened on the way to the office. il por Forbes 122:33-4 D 11 '78 •
Superscope: can a new product overcome losses from hi-fi? il por Bus W p 130+ D 11 '78 •
TUSKEGEE Institute, Tuskegee, Ala.
Tuskegee Institute in the 1920's. M. Marable. bibl f il Negro Hist Bull 40:764-8 N '77
TUTENKHAMUN, King of Egypt
King Tut's tomb: the untold story: condensation. T. Hoving. il pors map Read Digest 114:176-80+ Ja '79 •
Tutmania finds relief in a spate of books and sidelines. D. Marlyes. il Pub W 214:41-2+ N 20 '78 •

Anecdotes, facetiae, satire, etc.
King Tut book of etiquette. M. Stevenson. Harpers 258:97 Ja '79
King Tut live from the cradle of rock. D. Marsh. il Roll Stone p37 N 30 '78
Notes and comment. New Yorker 54:21 D 25 '78

Tomb
Dummies for mummies. Vasari. Art News 77:6+ N '78
Egyptomania in New York. S. Hochfield. il Art News 77:44-9 D '78
King Tut's revenge. J. Randi. il Humanist 38:44-7 Mr '78
Perils of guarding King Tut's treasures. W. H. Honan. il N Y Times Mag p40-1+ D 17 '78
Pharaoh's wine cellar; work of Leonard H. Lesko. Sci Am 238:74 Mr '78
There's much more in Cairo; at the Egyptian Museum. R. Ahrens. il Horizon 21:64-5 O '78
This little Pharaoh came to market. R. Christopher. il Macleans 91:44-6 D 18 '78
Tut tickets. New Yorker 54:28 O 2 '78
Tutglut. il Time 112:79 D 11 '78
What Tut hath wrought. S. R. Weisman. il Horizon 21:61-3 O '78

An article about King Tut's tomb titled "Perils of Guarding King Tut's Treasures" by W. H. Honan can be found in the *New York Times Magazine*. The article, which is illustrated (il), begins on page 40 and is continued on later pages (p40–1+) of the December 17, 1978, issue (D 17 '78).

EXERCISE 7. Using the *Readers' Guide.* In the *Readers' Guide,* find an article listed under any four of the following subjects. Copy the entry for the article. Be ready to explain the information for the entry. Answers will vary.

1. Scandinavia
2. Lakes
3. Colleges and universities
4. Space probes
5. Elephants
6. Submarines, atomic-powered

THE VERTICAL FILE

27f. To find a pamphlet, use the vertical file.

In addition to books and magazines, pamphlets can be a valuable resource when you are studying a topic. The U.S. Government publishes hundreds of pamphlets each year. In addition, state and local governments, businesses, colleges and universities, and health and other organizations publish pamphlets regularly. These pamphlets are found in a special filing cabinet called a vertical file. Sometimes newspaper clippings of special interest will also be included. Each pamphlet or clipping is placed in a folder and filed in alphabetical order by subject. For current information, you will find the vertical file very helpful.

MICROFILM AND MICROFICHE

27g. Use microfilm and microfiche to find information.

To save space, many libraries store some magazines, newspapers, and documents on microfilm or microfiche. *Microfilm* is a roll or

EXERCISE 7. If students are working on report topics on which they will be able to find information through the *Readers' Guide,* have them look up their own topics at this time. Remind them that each hardcover volume of the *Readers' Guide* covers only one year and that they may have to go through several back volumes, plus the current issues, in order to find appropriate articles.

THE VERTICAL FILE (rule 27f)

It is a good idea to consult the librarian to find out how extensive the library's vertical file is and what subjects it covers before teaching this section. Some libraries may not keep such material on file or may keep only very specialized material. The vertical file can be an excellent source of information on many current topics that are of interest to your students.

MICROFILM AND MICROFICHE (rule 27g)

If your students will be writing reports this year, knowledge about the materials stored on microfilm or microfiche and about how to use microfilm and microfiche projectors will be useful to them. Consult with the librarian to find out if the library's resources include microfilm and microfiche.

COMPUTERS (rule 27h)

Though your students probably will not use computers to find the names and locations of books in their libraries, it is a good idea to explain to them that some libraries have computerized their catalogs.

REVIEW EXERCISE. This exercise may be used as an open-book test on the chapter. If students have difficulty with any of the questions, it is a sign that they need more practical work in that area. Give them projects that they can carry out at the school library.

Note: A combined test on this chapter and the dictionary chapter appears in Teaching Tests, Second Course.

reel of film containing photographically reduced pages. *Microfiche* is a small sheet of film containing photographically reduced pages. Both microfiche and microfilm can contain hundreds of pages. To use the microfilm and microfiche, you use special projectors which enlarge the microscopic images to a readable size. Your librarian can help you to use microfilm and microfiche.

COMPUTERS

27h. Use computers to find information.

Some libraries have computerized their book lists, periodical lists, and catalogs. In using a computerized system, type the information you need into the computer—for example, "subject: plant collecting." The computer will search for the titles and locations of books and periodicals on your subject and will print the information onto its screen. The computer might even be able to give a printed list. Your librarian can help you to use the computers.

REVIEW EXERCISE. Using Library Reference Tools. Number your paper 1–10. Write the reference tool from the list on page 625 to which you would turn first to get information on the corresponding subject in the list below.

1. Latest developments in cancer research *1. Reader's Guide*
2. History of the Nobel Prize 2. Encyclopedia
3. Antarctica—climate, terrain, etc. 3. Atlas (*or* encyclopedia)
4. Title and author of a library book on outer space 4. the card catalog
5. Origins of jazz music 5. Encyclopedia 6. *Reader's Guide*
6. A list of magazine articles on a recent international crisis
7. Winners of the World Series since 1977 7. Almanac
8. Height of Mount Everest 8. Atlas (*or* almanac *or* encyclopedia)
9. Facts about Ralph Ellison, the American author
10. The biography of a person who has only recently become prominent in the news *10. Current Biography*

9. *Contemporary Authors* or *Contemporary Authors: First Revision*

SUMMARY LIST OF LIBRARY REFERENCE TOOLS

The card catalog
Computers
Microfilm or microfiche
Reference books
- Encyclopedias
- Atlases
- Almanacs
- Biographical reference books
  - *Who's Who*
  - *Who's Who in America*
  - *Webster's Biographical Dictionary*
  - *Contemporary Authors*
  - *Contemporary Authors: First Revision*
  - *Current Biography*
- *Readers' Guide to Periodical Literature*
- The vertical file

SUMMARY LIST OF LIBRARY REFERENCE TOOLS

This list provides students with a handy reminder of the various library resources available to them. They can refer to it any time they are planning a search for information.

Additional Practice

Teacher's Resource Book, Worksheet pages 315–18

Testing

Teaching Tests booklet, pages 85–86, 89–91
Teacher's Resource Book, Test pages 493–94, 497–99

Chapter Overview

The vocabulary words presented in this chapter are not fancy or unusual—they are words that eighth-graders encounter in their reading and listening. None of the words treated in this chapter are beyond the grasp of average eighth-grade students, and almost all of them are words that the students have already met, not just once or twice, but dozens of times in their own reading.

The list of vocabulary words on text pages 644–46 should be the basis for regular weekly work on vocabulary. The list can be covered at the rate of ten words a week. Have students copy the words in their notebooks. Dictate a synonym or a brief definition for each word and a brief sentence illustrating use of the word. Designate the part of speech of the word. *Note: After you dictate the meanings of the words to the class, it is not always practical to require students also to look up these words in the dictionary. Students may tend to select rare or technical meanings instead of the common definitions.*

Mastery of these words does not mean, for eighth-graders, putting the words to immediate use in their own writing or conversation, but only the ability to recognize the meaning of the words when they come across them in their reading. In time, most words will become a part of their spoken vocabulary.

When you are teaching a vocabulary list, concentrate on practical application of the vocabulary words. Be sure to call attention to vocabulary words the class has studied recently when they come up in literature selections, in class discussions, in assembly speeches,

CHAPTER 28

Vocabulary

LEARNING AND USING NEW WORDS

Although there is no simple way to acquire a large vocabulary, there are ways in which you can learn and remember more of the words you encounter every day. This chapter will give you practice in using these methods. It will also introduce you to a number of words that are widely used in the books you will be reading this year and in the future.

An effective way to develop a wide vocabulary is to set aside a section of your notebook in which to enter the new words you learn. Along with this list of words, write a definition and a sentence or phrase illustrating how each word is used. You can begin your vocabulary notebook with any unfamiliar words that you encounter in the following diagnostic test.

DIAGNOSTIC TEST

A. Number your paper 1–10. After the proper number, write the letter of the word or phrase that is closest in meaning to the numbered word.

EXAMPLE 1. hamper a. build c. hinder
b. revise d. search

1. *c*

1. abashed	a. beaten	c. lowered
	b. ashamed	d. fallen
2. belligerent	a. dull	c. swift
	b. warlike	d. gentle
3. dexterity	a. sugar	c. handiness
	b. duplicate	d. kindness
4. fatigue	a. war	c. fatalist
	b. weariness	d. explosion
5. haughty	a. moderate	c. proud
	b. smiling	d. slow
6. humdrum	a. melodious	c. aggressive
	b. loud	d. dull
7. menace	a. army	c. song
	b. threat	d. rival
8. primitive	a. undeveloped	c. violent
	b. prominent	d. religious
9. remorse	a. repetition	c. justice
	b. guilt	d. reason
10. revile	a. abuse	c. rebuild
	b. correct	d. bury

B. Number your paper 11–20. After each number, write the letter of the word or phrase that best defines the italicized word in each sentence. Look for clues in the context to help you find the best meaning. You will not need to use all the definitions on the list.

a. pale	g. lack of seriousness
b. friendship	h. torn down
c. face	i. flooded; overwhelmed
d. lukewarm	j. religious
e. skillful	k. energetic or of great intensity
f. buried	l. a hearty burst of laughter

11. Julio should get a good grade in art because he's very *adept* at drawing. 11. e
12. The United States and Canada, its northern neighbor, have shared years of *amity*. 12. b

or in newspaper articles. Throughout the year, take time to review words the class has studied earlier, and ask students to use the words in sentences of their own.

Chapter Objective

Students will increase their vocabularies.

PRESENTING THE CHAPTER

LESS-ADVANCED STUDENTS With these students you may wish to use a vocabulary list intended for a lower grade instead of the one presented at the end of this chapter. Such students often have difficulty learning words out of context, and you will probably want to dictate their vocabulary words to them in short illustrative sentences rather than as a word list.

It is especially effective with a less-advanced class to do day-to-day teaching of vocabulary, stopping frequently to discuss the meanings of words that come up in class reading or discussion and asking students to paraphrase the expressions or sentences that contain the words. Asking for paraphrases of short sentences is also often a more accurate way of testing students' knowledge of word meanings than asking them to give synonyms or definitions for out-of-context words. Many standard types of vocabulary tests (e.g., tests where the blanks in sentences are to be filled in from an accompanying list of words) involve skills not directly related to a student's understanding of the meaning of a word, and a less-advanced student's score on such a test may not be an accurate measure of the student's vocabulary.

13. The radio station was *deluged* with telephone calls from people who wanted to win the car. 13. i
14. His loud *guffaw* during the play embarrassed the entire class. 14. l
15. The night before a test is not the time for *levity*. 15. g
16. Her *pallid* complexion warned us that she was still ill. 16. a
17. The historic hotel had to be *razed* for the new expressway. 17. h
18. Bathing in *tepid* water, not hot water, is now recommended by doctors. 18. d
19. We thought that Robert was the culprit until we heard his *vehement* denial. 19. k
20. The snow-covered *visage* at the window frightened us. 20. c

LEARNING NEW WORDS

Occasionally we see or hear a word used alone, but most of the time we encounter words used in combination with other words. If the word is unfamiliar, these surrounding words often supply valuable clues to meaning.

28a. Learn new words from context.

The *context* of a word means the words that surround it in a sentence and the whole situation in which the word is used. The context of the word supplies the main clue to the meaning of *inedible* in this sentence:

> The cook was told not to use toadstools in the stew because they are inedible.

Since the cook was warned against using the toadstools in a stew, it stands to reason that something *inedible* is something "not fit to eat." If you know that much about toadstools already, you can be even surer about your guess.

Many common English words have several meanings. The context often provides clues to their meanings. For example, *pound* means one thing in a grocery store, another in a story about a dogcatcher, and still another in a British movie. Context

ADVANCED STUDENTS These students are usually enthusiastic about vocabulary study and enjoy keeping vocabulary notebooks. You may have to curb their enthusiasm for collecting rare and unusual words, however, if their performance on some of the tests and exercises in this chapter shows that they have not thoroughly mastered more ordinary words.

DIAGNOSTIC TEST

An average eighth-grade class should score about 65–70 percent on this test (about 16–18 right, out of 25). If your own students score notably higher or notably lower than this average, you may want to modify your approach to the rest of the material in the chapter.

LEARNING NEW WORDS (rules 28a and 28b)

While it is true that the great majority of the words we know are words whose meanings we have learned from context, this method is no longer very reliable by the time students have reached the eighth grade. They will continue to learn some new words from context, but most often these will be rather specialized or technical words (the set of terms used to refer to the equipment in a science classroom, for instance) rather than general vocabulary words of the kind that are emphasized in this chapter.

In teaching this section, therefore, emphasize the dictionary work. Each student should, if possible, own a dictionary and be required to bring it to class while studying vocabulary. Throughout the school year, keep a classroom clues will aid you in understanding these words when you encounter them in your reading.

EXERCISE 1. Using Context Clues to Define Words. Number your paper 1–10. For each italicized word in the sentences that follow, write the letter of the definition that is closest in meaning. You will not need all the definitions in the list. Check your answers in the dictionary.

a. calm	e. pronounced	i. fearful
b. peak	f. honesty	j. avoid
c. guidance	g. delight	k. ambition
d. respect	h. swung to hit	l. without success

1. Mrs. Tompkins has been the treasurer for twenty-seven years, and no one doubts her *integrity*. 1. f
2. At thirty, Lisa Chin is at the *summit* of her tennis career. 2. b
3. He is so *timorous* that he cannot sleep in the dark. 3. i
4. Unhappy, the baby *flailed* angrily at the bars of her playpen. 4. h
5. The doctor spoke comforting words to *allay* the patient's fears. 5. a
6. The speaker *articulated* her words with care. 6. e
7. The soldiers bowed to the emperor as a sign of *deference*. 7. d
8. With a roar, the crowd expressed its *jubilation* at the victory. 8. g
9. People should not attempt to *evade* their duties as citizens. 9. j
10. Jose's *aspiration* is to win the lead in the school play. 10. k

Using the Dictionary

28b. Learn to find the meaning you want in your dictionary.

If you cannot guess the meaning of a word from context, you should go to your dictionary. Context is still important, however. Most words have a number of different meanings, and the best way of finding the one you want is to look for the definition that fits the context in which you originally encountered the word. Consider the following sentence.

dictionary available and make it a practice to have students use this dictionary to settle questions that arise about the meanings of words. Instilling the dictionary habit is one of the best ways of developing students' vocabularies.

Learning Words from Context (rule 28a)

This section is particularly appropriate for use with a less-advanced class. These students sometimes skip over words that are unfamiliar without trying to puzzle out their meanings, even when the meaning is clearly spelled out in the context. Teaching them to look for context clues is really a part of teaching them how to read more efficiently, and it is a technique that should be used throughout the year in connection with all their reading assignments.

EXERCISE 1. Go over the answers in class. Have students point out the context clues that helped them decide on an answer.

USING THE DICTIONARY (rule 28b)

Emphasize the point that the dictionary often lists several different meanings of a word, and that a student should be able to tell *from the context* which meaning is appropriate. Even a less-advanced student will grasp this point if the teacher takes the class through several dictionary exercises: Have the class open their dictionaries to the appropriate page and read the definitions aloud one at a time, asking after each definition, "Is this the meaning we are looking for?" You may wish to teach or review pages 599–601 of the dictionary chapter in connection with this work.

EXERCISE 2. Have students enter in their vocabulary notebooks (or on a special sheet in their regular notebooks) any unfamiliar words in this exercise.

Your jokes are in poor taste, Harold, and we can dispense with any more of them.

Dispense has the following meanings: (1) to give; (2) to distribute; (3) to get rid of; (4) to get along without. By trying each of these meanings in place of the word *dispense* in the example, you can easily eliminate all of the choices except the last one—the meaning you want.

Which of these numbered meanings for *dispense* fits the following sentence?

The Red Cross dispensed clothing to the flood victims.

Dictionaries often supply sample contexts to help you distinguish between the various meanings of a word (see pages 599–600). Such phrases can be very helpful in showing you how to use the new word in your own speech and writing.

EXERCISE 2. Finding the Correct Meaning of a Word. The italicized words in the following sentences have a number of different meanings. Using your dictionary, select the meaning that best fits each sentence, and write it after the proper number.
Answers will vary in wording.

EXAMPLE 1. A candidate for the presidency is likely to be an *eminent* political figure.
1. *prominent*

1. The doctor said that there was nothing to be feared from the *benign* swelling. 1. harmless
2. The old man gave us a *benign* smile. 2. kindly
3. The professor's lecture *illuminated* the subject for us. 3. made clear
4. With the flick of a switch, he can *illuminate* the garden. 4. light up
5. As we drove into the valley, a beautiful *pastoral* scene unrolled before us. 5. rural
6. The minister attended to his *pastoral* duties. 6. of a pastor
7. Your argument seems *valid* and has convinced us all. 7. sound
8. Since this is a *valid* contract, you will have to live up to it.
9. The manager's *bland* words calmed the angry customer.
10. I don't like this cereal because it is too *bland*.

8. legally binding 9. agreeable 10. lacking in flavor

PREFIXES, ROOTS, AND SUFFIXES

Some words can be divided into parts, and some cannot. Those that can be divided, like *workbook* and *unhappy*, often consist of parts that mean something separately. By learning how to divide words into their parts, you can sometimes discover additional clues to meaning.

The basic part of a word is called a *root.* A part added before the root is called a *prefix;* a part added after the root is called a *suffix.* Becoming familiar with the common prefixes and suffixes discussed here will provide you with helpful leads to finding the meaning of a large number of new words.

Prefixes

28c. Learn how common prefixes change the meaning of words.

The following common prefixes occur in thousands of English words.

PREFIX	MEANING	EXAMPLE
auto-	self	automobile
bi-	two	bimonthly
circum-	around	circumference
con-	together	concord
de-	down or from	degrade
dis-	away or apart	disagree
ex-	out	expel
im-	not	impractical
mis-	wrong	misjudge
multi-	many	multiply
pre-	before	preview
semi-	half or partly	semiprecious

EXERCISE 3. Using Prefixes to Define Words. Number your paper 1–10. After the proper number, give the meaning of the italicized word in each of the sentences. Be prepared to tell how the prefix of the word helps determine its meaning. Use the dictionary if necessary. Answers will vary in wording.

PREFIXES, ROOTS, AND SUFFIXES (rules 28c and 28d)

Some classes may find the terms *root, prefix,* and *suffix* difficult to learn. You might speak instead of "the main part of the word" and "added syllables." You will probably wish to present the material on prefixes and suffixes (pages 574–77) in Chapter 25, "Spelling," in connection with the material in this section.

EXERCISE 3. A less-advanced class should probably not be asked to discuss the ways in which the prefixes contribute to the meanings of the italicized words, since these students will not be familiar with the meanings of most of the root words.

EXERCISE 4. You might use the words in this exercise as the basis for additional dictionary practice for less-advanced students.

1. The assistant principal *convened* the student council to draft a new student code of conduct. 1. called together
2. An artillery shell completely *demolished* the hut. 2. destroyed
3. Our newspaper is published *biweekly*. 3. every two weeks
4. Some of the czars of Russia were cruel *autocrats* who were feared by the people. 4. rulers with absolute power
5. To call Alvin a worker is a *misnomer* because he is always asleep with a broom in his hands. 5. wrong designation
6. Ferdinand Magellan, the Portuguese sailor and explorer, *circumnavigated* the globe. 6. sailed around 7. many-colored
7. The girl held a large, *multicolored* ball in her hands.
8. The mechanic had to *dismantle* the motor to find the faulty part. 8. take apart
9. The theft of the jewels showed careful planning and must have been a *premeditated* crime. 9. previously planned
10. We finally *dissuaded* Tom from writing a letter to the author. 10. persuaded not to

EXERCISE 4. Using Prefixes to Define Words. Follow the directions for Exercise 6. Answers will vary in wording.

1. Frank has become so efficient at packaging toys that he moves like an *automaton*. 1. robot
2. The people, angry over years of misrule, *deposed* the unjust king. 2. removed from the throne
3. Remember Shakespeare's *immortal* words: "This above all, to thine own self be true." 3. undying, imperishable
4. The Smiths own *extensive* lands in this valley. 4. of great extent, broad, large
5. Mrs. Slocum showed how to *bisect* an angle. 5. divide into two equal parts
6. Is the prisoner truly sorry for his *misdeeds,* or is he only sorry he was caught? 6. wrong acts 7. not completely private
7. Ms. Feinstein stayed in a *semiprivate* hospital room.
8. The prisoner was allowed to move freely within a *circumscribed* area. 8. restricted, limited
9. Next year our city will hold its *bicentennial* celebration.
10. Melba MacHenry Gardner, who donated the money for our new Civic Center, is a *multimillionaire*. 10. person having many millions

9. two-hundredth anniversary

Suffixes

28d. Learn to recognize common suffixes when they occur in *companion forms.*

There are many English words to which suffixes can be added. The new words formed by adding suffixes are *companion forms* of the basic word. Adding suffixes to the root *free* results in the companion forms *freedom* and *freely.* If you are on the alert for companion forms and learn some common suffixes, you will often be able to guess the correct meanings of new words. One fact to keep in mind is that the spelling of the root may change when a suffix is added. For example, when *-ly* is added to *day,* the resulting word is not *dayly* but *daily.* When *-ition* is added to *repeat,* the resulting word is spelled *repetition.*

Sometimes adding a suffix will result in a word that is a different part of speech from the original word. For example, the suffix *-ly* added to the adjective *free* results in *freely,* an adverb. The suffix *-ly* occurs at the end of an adjective or an adverb but never at the end of a noun. Therefore, words ending in this suffix are never nouns. (When the letters *-ly* occur at the end of a noun such as *lily,* they are not a suffix but part of the basic word.)

Learn the following suffixes that occur in nouns.

SUFFIX	MEANING	EXAMPLE
-hood	condition	childhood
-ness	quality	goodness
-ance, -ence	state, act, fact	independence
-ation, -ition, -tion	action or state	celebration
-ity, -ty	quality	ability
-ment	result or action	employment

EXERCISE 5. Using Noun-forming Suffixes. Number your paper 1–10. Form nouns from the following words by using the suffixes just listed; then give the meanings of the new words. In some cases it will be necessary to change the spelling of the root. Check your answers in the dictionary.

EXERCISE 5. Students of all levels of ability should be able to do this exercise and the next two. Tell the class to use their dictionaries if they have trouble thinking of the companion forms.

Answers: Exercise 5
(Answers will vary somewhat.)

1. replacement—that which replaces
2. likelihood—possibility
3. articulation—expression, wording
4. acceptance—approval; act of accepting
5. intensity—strength
6. manhood—state of being a man
7. fragility—delicacy
8. aspiration—desire
9. improvisation—art of composing, making up
10. friendliness—kindliness

EXERCISES 6 and 7. See notes for Exercise 5.

Answers: Exercise 6
(Answers will vary somewhat.)

1. lonesome—alone
2. picturesque—colorful
3. harmonious—tuneful
4. devilish—mischievous
5. gracious—courteous
6. babyish—childish
7. luxurious—costly
8. dependable—reliable
9. meddlesome—interfering
10. riotous—noisy

EXAMPLES
1. kind
1. *kindness—the quality of being kind*
2. create
2. *creation—the act of creating*

1. replace	4. accept	7. fragile	9. improvise
2. likely	5. intense	8. aspire	10. friendly
3. articulate	6. man		

The following suffixes occur in adjectives.

SUFFIX	MEANING	EXAMPLE
-ish	like or suggesting	foolish
-able, -ible	able	tolerable
-ous	having the quality of	religious
-esque	like	statuesque
-some	like or tending to	tiresome

EXERCISE 6. Using Adjective-forming Suffixes. Number your paper 1–10. Form adjectives from the following words by using the suffixes just listed; then give the meanings of the new words. Check your answers in the dictionary.

1. lone	4. devil	7. luxury	9. meddle
2. picture	5. grace	8. depend	10. riot
3. harmony	6. baby		

The following suffixes occur in verbs.

SUFFIX	MEANING	EXAMPLE
-ate	cause to become	animate
-en	make or become	deepen
-fy	make or cause	fortify
-ize	cause to be	motorize

EXERCISE 7. Using Verb-forming Suffixes. Number your paper 1–10. Form verbs from the following words by using the suffixes just listed; then give the meanings of the new words. Check your answers in the dictionary.

1. captive
2. system
3. strength
4. nausea
5. glory
6. active
7. civil
8. sweet
9. illumine
10. beauty

USING EXACT WORDS

28e. Use the exact word in your speaking and writing.

In English, many thousands of words are available to help you express exactly what you mean. If you use the same few words to describe many different people or things or actions or situations, you are not taking advantage of the variety of your language. Avoid overworked words that are used in so many different contexts that they lose precise meaning. *Good* is one such word. If you were to refer to someone as "a good person," would you mean that he is capable, kind, or dependable? If you were to say, "I had a good day," would you mean an enjoyable, a productive, or a tranquil day? *Good* might be the first word that occurs to you to describe a person or a day, but a moment's thought will usually supply a better word to express your meaning.

Using Precise Adjectives to Describe

The English language is rich in adjectives. You should learn to use adjectives to express your meaning exactly. In talking about a book you enjoyed, for example, you might say it was *interesting,* but you would be more expressive if you called it *exciting* or *engrossing* or *stimulating*. Build your vocabulary by taking time to find the exact adjective to express your thought.

EXERCISE 8. Selecting Precise Adjectives. Each of the following sentences contains a vague or overworked adjective, in italics, which should be replaced by a more precise word. Number your paper 1–10. After the proper number, write the more precise adjective from the list preceding the sentences. You will not need all the words in the list. Use the dictionary, if necessary, to check your answers and make corrections.

Answers: Exercise 7
(Answers will vary somewhat.)

1. captivate—charm
2. systematize—organize
3. strengthen—make stronger
4. nauseate—sicken
5. glorify—make glorious
6. activate—make active
7. civilize—tame
8. sweeten—make sweet
9. illuminate—light up
10. beautify—make beautiful

USING EXACT WORDS (rule 28e)

Since it will take time for students to learn the meanings of these vocabulary words, it is best to go through this section slowly. You may want to teach some of this material at the time the class is studying narration and description.

EXERCISE 8. Have students enter in their vocabulary notebooks any unfamiliar words in this exercise. You may also want to have students enter the pronunciation of the word and one or two original sentences in which the word is correctly used.

EXERCISES 9 and 10. See notes for Exercise 8.

eccentric	decrepit	devout	tangible
casual	customary	insipid	eligible
titanic	burly	appalling	boisterous
fragrant	sallow	fluent	

1. That rice pudding had a rather *flat* taste. 1. insipid
2. The *old* car drove slowly down the road. 2. decrepit
3. The damage done by the hurricane was *shocking*. 3. appalling
4. The *muscular* sailor pushed against the door. 4. burly
5. Paul is regarded as *odd* because he puts mustard on ice cream. 5. eccentric
6. When we began to sing and shout, our counselor warned us that we were being too *lively*. 6. boisterous
7. With a *great* effort, Samson tore down the pillars of the Philistine temple. 7. titanic
8. The foreman of the jury said that no *real* evidence of guilt had been produced. 8. tangible
9. No student who is failing one or more subjects is *qualified* for a student council position. 9. eligible
10. The roses were *sweet-smelling*. 10. fragrant

Using Interesting Verbs to Express Action

Your ability to express yourself is directly dependent on your verb vocabulary. Verbs give action and color to your sentences. The following exercise includes a number of verbs that will add variety to your speaking and writing.

EXERCISE 9. Selecting Verbs to Complete Sentences. Number your paper 1–10. After the proper number, copy the verb whose meaning best completes the sentence. Change the tense if necessary to fit the sentence, and use your dictionary. You will not need all the verbs in the list.

soar	restrain	capitulate	browbeat
saturate	liberate	stray	wheedle
diverge	carouse	restore	elapse
confiscate	pollute	obliterate	

1. Because they could not pay their taxes, the government —— their property. 1. confiscated
2. The fighter was badly beaten but refused to —— to his opponent. 2. capitulate
3. Realizing that the bird would die in captivity, the girl took it to the woods and —— it. 3. liberated
4. As the plane —— above the clouds, the earth disappeared from view. 4. soared
5. Several hours —— before the weary hikers returned home. 5. elapsed
6. She is extremely timid and allows people to —— her. 6. browbeat
7. Skillful detective work —— the stolen painting to its rightful owners. 7. restored
8. The two hunters parted company when their paths ——. 8. diverged
9. Two centuries of wind and weather have almost —— the words carved on the stone. 9. obliterated
10. Although we may be tempted to overeat, we should —— ourselves. 10. restrain

Using Vivid Adverbs to Modify Verbs

Because adverbs answer such questions as *How? When?* and *Where?* in connection with verbs, they are a very important part of your vocabulary. The exactness and vividness of your writing and speaking depend a great deal on your using adverbs well. In the exercise that follows, there are a number of adverbs for you to learn. Many of these adverbs are formed from words in the list beginning on page 644.

EXERCISE 10. Using Vivid Adverbs to Modify Verbs. Number your paper 1–10. After the proper number, write an adverb from the list that answers the question. You will not need all the adverbs in the list. Use the dictionary, if necessary.

immensely	resonantly	superficially
covertly	scrupulously	rigidly
abruptly	urgently	cautiously
excessively	anonymously	ostentatiously

1. How did the conscientious bookkeeper keep the company's records? 1. scrupulously
2. How did the woman who found there were burglars in her house call for the police? 2. urgently
3. How did the opera star sing the low notes in his aria? 3. resonantly
4. How did the audience like the actor's superb performance?
5. How did the newly engaged girl display her engagement ring?
6. How did the tired student check her homework? 6. superficially
7. How did the little boy try to get a cookie from the cookie jar when his mother was in the next room? 7. covertly
8. How would a person stand if imitating a statue? 8. rigidly
9. How does a doctor leave a dinner party upon receiving an emergency call? 9. abruptly
10. How does a person cross a busy city street during rush hour?

4. immensely 5. ostentatiously 10. cautiously

Synonyms and Antonyms

A *synonym* is a word that means nearly the same thing as another word. Although words that are synonyms are close in meaning, they rarely have *exactly* the same meaning. At times you will be able to use one of several words in a sentence, but at other times only the exact word will do.

Pleasure, delight, and *joy* all have roughly the same meaning, yet each expresses a different shade of meaning. *Pleasure* is the most general of the three words; it covers a variety of situations, none of them very specifically. *Delight* indicates a sharp feeling of pleasure that lasts only a short time. *Joy* may indicate a deep and long-lasting happiness. In the following sentence, which of the three words fits most exactly?

I receive great —— from my study of mathematics.

Pleasure fits, of course, but is not very specific. *Delight* does not fit very well because the feeling indicated in this sentence would seem to last for some time. The synonym that most exactly expresses the desired meaning is *joy*.

When you look up a word in a dictionary, you will often find several synonyms listed. To help you to distinguish between synonyms, some dictionaries give *synonym articles*—brief explanations of a word's synonyms and how they differ in meaning. The more often you encounter a word in different contexts, the better you will be able to determine its meaning.

EXERCISE 11. Selecting Synonyms to Complete Sentences. Number your paper 1–10. After the proper number, write the synonym you have selected that best fits the sentence. Use the dictionary to learn the exact meaning of each synonym.

1. My jacket is made of a new (fabricated, imitation, synthetic) material.
2. Our (invincible, victorious, triumphant) army never has been and never should be defeated in battle.
3. The monks in several medieval monasteries kept (histories, annals, records) summarizing the important events of each year.
4. Medieval artists had a special (fashion, technique, system) for making stained-glass windows.
5. The young couple fondly (fed, nourished, sustained) their baby daughter.
6. You can imagine how (ridiculous, shaming, humiliating) it was to be spanked in front of all my relatives.
7. Her (guess, conjecture, estimate) that there would be a test the next day was based on the fact that Mrs. Brown had assigned no homework that night.
8. Although the lawyer stayed within the law, he relied on (guile, cunning, fraud) to win his case.
9. Under the new government, many citizens were (dispossessed, deprived, divested) of their rights.
10. After studying the problem I formed a working (theory, hypothesis, supposition), which I tested by experiment.

The antonym of a word is a word with the opposite meaning. *Bad* is the antonym of *good,* and *happy* is the antonym of *sad.* Sometimes an antonym of a word is formed by adding a prefix meaning *not:* an antonym of *wise* is *unwise.* Knowing the antonym of a word will often help you to understand the word's exact

EXERCISE 11. With less-advanced students, you may want to use this exercise as a class activity and do only five of the items.

EXERCISE 12. Allow time for students to use their dictionaries. Be sure to discuss the answers with the class and clarify misconstrued meanings.

SPECIAL VOCABULARIES (rule 28f)

Students should keep a vocabulary section in each of their subject notebooks. Point out that the boldface words or italicized words in their textbooks belong in this section.

meaning (or at least one exact meaning). For example, knowing that *dexterity* is the antonym of *clumsiness* will lead you to a correct meaning for this word. A dictionary sometimes lists antonyms at the end of an entry for a word.

EXERCISE 12. Selecting Antonyms for Specific Words. Antonyms for words in the first column may be found in the second column. Number your paper 1–10. After the proper number, write the letter of the correct antonym. You will not need all the words in the second column. Use the dictionary, if necessary.

1. frustrate	a. tiny	1. e
2. contemptible	b. dawn	2. k
3. colossal	c. ornamental	3. a
4. impertinent	d. spiteful	4. i
5. upbraid	e. satisfy	5. m
6. twilight	f. wordiness	6. b
7. brevity	g. biased	7. f
8. neutral	h. probity	8. g
9. functional	i. courteous	9. c
10. random	j. eventual	10. l
	k. admirable	
	l. orderly	
	m. praise	

SPECIAL VOCABULARIES

Each of your school subjects has special words that you must learn if you are to understand the concepts. Some of the words are new, while others, which are used in everyday speech, have special meanings in a particular subject.

A textbook often calls attention to these new words by printing them in italics or in boldfaced type. Printing a word in a special way shows that it is important. Often a definition immediately follows the word. If not, turn to the back of the book to see if there is a glossary—a short dictionary of special words. There, you will usually find a definition for the word. Always use a glossary when a textbook provides one. It is one of the most valuable features of a book.

EXERCISE 13. Defining Mathematics Words. The words in this exercise are used in mathematics books designed for students in your grade. Write each word on your paper, and follow it by a short definition. Then write a sentence using each word correctly. Use a dictionary or the glossary in your mathematics book.

See Answer Key.

acute	diameter	intersection	obtuse	radical
bisect	exponent	numeral	quotient	radius

EXERCISE 14. Defining Social Studies Words. The following words are likely to appear in your social studies assignments. Follow the directions for Exercise 13. See Answer Key.

History: blockade, capitalism, depression, filibuster, gerrymander, initiative, recall, referendum, totalitarian, vassal

Geography: arid, fiord, fissure, meridian, monsoon, plateau, peninsula, precipitation, topography, tributary

EXERCISE 15. Defining Science Words. The following words are likely to appear in your science assignments. Follow the directions for Exercise 13. See Answer Key.

antibody	electron	friction	nebula	satellite
condensation	embryo	fulcrum	radiation	spectrum

28f. Use the words from specialized vocabularies in your everyday speaking and writing.

Many words in a special field are often used outside the field. *Condensation* and *inertia* are often found in nonscientific books, while *exponent* and *radical* can be used by a political speaker as well as a mathematician. Learn the meanings of these words as used outside their fields. Use them in your own speaking and writing when they help to express your ideas exactly.

EXERCISE 16. Using Special Words in Everyday Writing. The following words used in mathematics, science, and social

EXERCISES 13–15. Some eighth-graders, especially in a less-advanced class, may not have encountered all these terms in their studies. You can check with the teachers of other subjects to find out which of the words should be familiar to your students and which ones may be too advanced.

EXERCISE 16. A less-advanced class may omit this exercise. Although a number of the expressions are probably familiar to these students, such students are often confused by having to select the right word out of a long list. Unless a student is able to fill in all, or almost all, the blanks correctly, the teaching point of the exercise will not come across.

REVIEW EXERCISE. If you have omitted some of the earlier exercises in the chapter because you felt they might be too difficult for your class, you should also omit the corresponding words in this exercise. For most classes of average or above-average ability, however, this exercise can be used as a mastery test on the work in the vocabulary chapter. (The exercise does not, of course, cover all the words in the following word list, which is meant to provide a full year's vocabulary studies.)

Note: It may be a good idea to spot-check students' textbooks to make sure that answers for this exercise have not been written in by previous users of the books. You may wish to have the exercise duplicated or written on the board to prevent students from using written-in answers.

studies have meanings outside these fields. Use these words appropriately in the blanks in the sentences. You will not use all the words.

blockade	embryo	initiative	radical
condensation	fulcrum	intersection	spectrum
depression	inertia	obtuse	vassal

1. Harriet displayed great —— in forming a drama club and recruiting members for it. 1. initiative
2. When you have trouble getting started on your work, you are suffering from —— . 2. inertia
3. The newspapers have called Mayor Tompkins "a —— of special-interest groups." 3. vassal
4. George is so —— that he didn't get the joke even after she explained it. 4. obtuse 5. radical
5. The department store has been completely reorganized; you will discover some pretty —— changes when you go there.
6. To save space, the magazine published a —— of Madeleine L'Engle's new book. 6. condensation
7. The fugitive ran up the stairs to the attic and —— d the entry by pushing a heavy table against the wooden door. 7. blockade
8. Ann met us at the —— of Vernon Street and Third Avenue.
9. The student council was responsible for the entire —— of homecoming activities. 8. intersection 9. spectrum
10. After receiving his test grade, Juan couldn't shake his mood of —— . 10. depression

REVIEW EXERCISE. Defining Words. The words in this exercise have been chosen from all those you have studied in this chapter. Number your paper 1–20. After the proper number, write the letter of the word or phrase that is closest in meaning to the numbered word.

1. appalling	a. revealing	c. shocking
	b. annoying	d. rewarding
2. boisterous	a. lively	c. treacherous
	b. supporting	d. weak

3. concord — a. sympathy; b. conformity; c. agreement; d. boredom
4. covertly — a. swiftly; b. gaily; c. badly; d. secretly
5. decrepit — a. decoyed; b. feeble; c. wise; d. proud
6. deference — a. pressure; b. deceit; c. respect; d. loyalty
7. divest — a. clothe; b. deprive; c. retreat; d. amble
8. flail — a. shrink; b. beat; c. reveal; d. forget
9. jubilation — a. anniversary; b. ceremony; c. terror; d. rejoicing
10. nourish — a. hate; b. regret; c. love; d. feed
11. premeditated — a. deliberate; b. fiendish; c. foolish; d. great
12. random — a. close; b. emotional; c. aimless; d. knowing
13. restrain — a. hold back; b. teach; c. dress up; d. remember
14. rigidly — a. stiffly; b. stubbornly; c. cleverly; d. rudely
15. saturate — a. wring out; b. imitate; c. treat badly; d. fill completely
16. stray — a. wander; b. direct; c. lonely; d. puzzled
17. synthetic — a. tiring; b. expensive; c. careless; d. artificial
18. technique — a. detail; b. method; c. instruction; d. reason
19. titanic — a. metallic; b. huge; c. backward; d. alive
20. wheedle — a. grow; b. correct; c. coax; d. crawl

Word List

You will find it worthwhile to distribute study of the words in this list over the entire year instead of encouraging students to "cram" vocabulary study into a period of two or three weeks. Introduce the words at the rate of about ten a week, starting at the beginning of the year. Having distributed the work load, you will find that your students are far better prepared for a special unit on vocabulary in the second semester than they would be without this regular work.

Word List

The following list of 300 words should form the basis of your vocabulary study for the year. You have already encountered some of them (or related forms) in this chapter. When you encounter a new word, add it to your vocabulary notebook. Write a definition of the word, and use the word in a sentence.

abuse
acceptance
access
accessory
accommodations
activate
adapt
adept
adequate
adjacent

advantageous
advent
aeronautics
affliction
aggressive
alliance
anonymous
antibiotics
anxiety
appalling

aristocrat
aroma
articulate
aspiration
assumption
attain
automaton
badger
baffle
bankrupt

barbarism
basis
baste
bewilder
blockade
boisterous
boycott
burly
calamity
calculation

capital
casual
catastrophe
category
censorship
charitable
chronic
circulate
circumnavigate
clarify

climax
colossal
commute
complement
condemn
confederation
confide
confiscate
conjecture
consecutive

considerate
contagious
contemporary
controversy
convert
creative
customary
decade
deceased
deceive

dedicate
deduction
defy
delegate
demolish
denial
depose
derive
descend
despise

detach
dictate
dilapidated
dilute
diminish
dingy
diplomat
disagreeable
discord
disintegrate

dismantle
dispatch
dispense
dissect
distraction
durable
eccentric
ecology
elegant
eligible

embarrass
emigrate
eminent
emphasize
endorse
enhance
epidemic
erosion
essay
evacuate

exaggeration
exertion
extensive
falter
famine
famished
feasible
felony
ferocious
fictitious

folklore
foresight
foreword
fortnight
fragile

fragment
fraudulent
frequency
gallery
generate

glorify
gnarled
gracious
grieve
hamper
harmonious
haughty
haven
hilarious
homicide

hospitable
humidity
humiliate
hydraulic
hypothesis
illuminate
immense
immigrate
immune
imperative

imply
impose
improvise
impulsive
inanimate
inclination
incomparable
inconsiderate
indelible
inevitable

inflexible
ingenious
inherit
inquisitive
insoluble
integrity
intelligible
intensity
intentional
intercept

intervene
intrigue
invariable
isolation
jeopardize
jubilation
knoll
latent
liable
liberate

literal
malfunction
malnutrition
manageable
maroon
massage
meddlesome
memento
menace
menagerie

miscellaneous
misdeed
modify
monopoly
morale

Additional Practice

Teacher's Resource Book, Worksheet pages 319–37

Testing

Teaching Tests booklet, pages 87–88, 89–91
Teacher's Resource Book, Test pages 495–96, 497–99

multicolored
multitude
mutual
myriad
nationality

negligent
neutral
notify
nourish
novelty
obituary
obscure
occupant
occurrence
omission

optimism
pacify
pamphlet
parasitic
persistent
petition
petty
pewter
phenomenon
photogenic

picturesque
pious
planetarium
pleasantry
pollute
populate
posterity
potential
prearrange
predicament

premier
premiere
presume
primitive
privilege
probable
probation
propaganda
proposal
provision

pulverize
pun
punctual
quaint
quench
rebate
recuperate
refuge
regime
remorse

remote
resolute
respiration
restore
restrain
revelation
rigid
riotous
romantic
ruthless

sable
salutation
sanctuary
sarcasm
satire

saturate
secluded
sedate
sincerity
sinew

spacious
sphere
sterile
strategy
successor
summit
superficial
sustain
synthetic
tangible

tariff
tarnish
technology
temperament
testify
therapy
thrifty
thrive
titanic
transit

tumult
unique
upbraid
urban
urgent
valid
valor
verify
vitality
warranty

CHAPTER 29

Studying and Test Taking

SKILLS AND STRATEGIES

In many of your classes, you are expected to study textbook materials, complete oral and written assignments, and take tests. This chapter provides strategies for making your studying more effective and your test taking more successful than before.

STUDY SKILLS

You study to gain information about a topic and to understand and evaluate knowledge that you have acquired. The following strategies and skills can help you improve your study skills.

Following the SQ3R Study Method

29a. Use the SQ3R Study Method.

The *SQ3R Method* was developed by Francis Robinson, an educational psychologist. The method consists of five steps.

1. *Survey.* Survey your selection by glancing quickly at the title, the subheadings, important terms in **boldface** and *italics,* and all charts, diagrams, illustrations, summaries, and questions.

Chapter Overview

Although eighth-graders have been studying and taking tests throughout their schooling, many are not very good at doing so. Sometimes the reason is a lack of study skills and test-taking "savvy." Academic skills that are second nature to successful students may be totally unknown to those who perform unsuccessfully. Consequently, this chapter has been devoted to spelling out study and test-taking strategies that may appear to less-advanced students as "insiders'" knowledge about how to succeed in school. Capable students who perform well in class can also benefit from this chapter, as they may learn a new skill or strategy.

Since the information in this chapter can prove immediately useful to students and can facilitate their grasping the material covered in other chapters, you may wish to cover this section during the first two weeks of the term.

Chapter Objective

Students will use a variety of study and test-taking skills and strategies that can apply to a wide range of assignments in school.

PRESENTING THE CHAPTER

LESS-ADVANCED STUDENTS These students stand to gain a great deal from direct instruction in how to succeed in school. You may wish to generate class discussion of specific problems faced by students and then apply solutions from this chapter, from your own experience, or from students' suggestions. Additional review of these solutions may prove useful when you are discussing graded tests and assignments.

ADVANCED STUDENTS Though these students will know many of the skills and strategies discussed in this chapter, they will probably learn some new ones.

STUDY SKILLS
(rules 29a–29h)

Students can use the studying strategies in this chapter to help them complete class and homework assignments and prepare for tests. Impress upon your students that learning these skills will be helpful only if they are actually applied to schoolwork and other learning assignments—they must be used to be useful.

FOLLOWING THE SQ3R STUDY METHOD (rule 29a)

Be sure students understand the task or tasks involved in each step of the method.

EXERCISE 1. You may need to point out to students that the homework they select should be a reading assignment, not an exercise assignment.

In addition, read the introduction and the summary paragraph quickly to find the main ideas.

2. ***Question.*** Make a list of questions that you want to answer after you have read the selection. One way to do this is to use the subheadings. For example, if a subheading is *The Industrial Revolution,* you might write *What was the Industrial Revolution?* Sometimes such questions are included in the text. At other times, your teacher may provide them.

3. ***Read.*** Read your selection *carefully* to find answers to your questions. Look for main ideas and supporting details. Look up any unfamiliar words. Take notes as you read.

4. ***Recite.*** Read the questions that you have written down. Think carefully about the answers, and recite them in your own words. (Refer to your notes to make sure your answers are correct.) Write down the answers to the questions.

5. ***Review.*** Review the selection by asking yourself the questions and answering them without looking at your notes. Check your answers by consulting the selection and your notes. Then immediately review the selection to reinforce your knowledge.

EXERCISE 1. Applying the SQ3R Method to a Homework Assignment. Select a homework assignment in your science or social studies textbook. Follow the steps of the SQ3R Method to complete the assignment. Answer each question as you work.

Answers will vary.

1. *Survey.* What is the title? What are the subheadings? What are the new terms in boldface or italics? What charts, illustrations, diagrams, or summaries are there? What do the introductory and summary paragraphs say?
2. *Question.* Make a list of questions to be answered after you have read the selection. (If your teacher has assigned specific questions, use those instead.)
3. *Read.* Take notes on the main ideas and important details.
4. *Recite.* Recite the answers in your own words. Then write the answers to your questions.
5. *Review.* Use your questions to review the selection.

Adjusting Your Reading Rate to Your Purpose

29b. Adjust your reading rate according to your purpose.

Depending on what you are reading, you may need to read quickly, at a moderate rate, or very slowly. You should learn to adjust your reading rate to your reading purpose.

(1) Scan to find information quickly.

Scanning means to read quickly to find *specific* information, such as facts, dates, or names. For example, you scan a dictionary to find a particular word by moving your eyes quickly down the page until you find the word you seek. Materials that you scan include telephone directories, indexes, and tables of contents.

(2) Skim to get a general idea of what the selection covers.

Skimming means to read at a fast rate to get the *general* idea of a selection. In the Survey step of the SQ3R Method, you skim when you quickly read the title, subheadings, charts, diagrams, key terms, introductory and summary paragraphs, and questions.

(3) Read closely to understand the main ideas and details.

Reading closely means to read slowly and thoughtfully. You read closely to identify not only the main ideas but also the supporting details. You read closely to find answers to study questions. In the Read step of the SQ3R Method, you read closely.

(4) Read recreational materials lightly.

Reading lightly means to read at a fast rate. Light novels and some magazines are examples of materials that you read lightly.

EXERCISE 2. Determining Reading Approaches for Particular Situations. Determine the appropriate reading approach (scanning, skimming, reading closely, or reading lightly) for each situation. Be prepared to explain your answers.

ADJUSTING YOUR READING RATE TO YOUR PURPOSE (rule 29b)

After students have read through this section, explain to them that adjusting their reading rate will help them complete assignments more easily. For example, if they need to find a word in the dictionary, scanning will help them complete that task more quickly than skimming would.

EXERCISE 2. You might want to discuss with your students other reading situations that call for scanning, skimming, reading closely, or reading lightly.

RECOGNIZING MAIN IDEAS (rule 29c)

This section may be especially important for less-advanced and average students. Both stated and implied main ideas are discussed.

EXAMPLE 1. You need to find the term *comma* in an index.
1. *scanning*

1. You need to find rule 29c in this chapter. 1. scanning
2. You want to get a general idea of what the next chapter in this textbook will cover. 2. skimming
3. You completed the Survey and Question parts of the SQ3R Method for your social studies assignment. Now you need to read the selection. 3. reading closely
4. You want to read a novel for entertainment. 4. reading lightly

Recognizing Main Ideas

29c. Find the main ideas of the material being studied.

The main idea of a piece of writing is the most important point that the author wants to make. Sometimes the main idea is stated. Sometimes it is implied, or suggested.

(1) Main ideas may be stated.

The main idea of a piece of writing is usually stated as a complete sentence. For example, the main idea of a paragraph about cats may be *Cats are easier to care for than dogs.*

The following paragraph is from "Bears," by Ben East. The topic is "a bear track." The main idea is *A bear track is calculated to send shivers up the human spine.*

> A bear track is calculated to send shivers up the human spine. You stare at the footprints, printed big and deep in the sand of a woods road or the mud along a stream bank, and you say to yourself, "A bear walked here, in the black of night, cloaked in darkness, furtive and silent. On what bloody errand was he bent? What prey did he finally find? Did he surprise and brain a young deer? Sniff out a wild turkey on her nest? Raid a pigpen on some settler's brush-bordered farm? Or did he only tear a log apart for ants? What would have happened if I had met him face to face?"
>
> BEN EAST

EXERCISE 3. This exercise gives students practice in identifying main ideas (stated and implied) in passages. You may wish to provide additional practice with paragraphs from a literature text.

Note that the main idea in this paragraph is stated in the first sentence. The main idea may also be stated in the middle or at the end of a paragraph.

(2) Main ideas may be implied.

When a main idea is implied, you will need to read closely, examine details, and state the main idea in your own words. As you read the following paragraph from "Nature's Medicines: Spearmint," think about the main idea that the writer implies.

> Ancient Greeks used to perfume their arms with spearmint so they could smell its refreshing scent wherever they went. Romans placed fresh sprigs of spearmint on their dining tables and in their sleeping chambers. Today many gardeners simply go out to their spearmint patches and breathe deeply. The smell is said to help them if they are nervous or have a headache.
>
> LOIS WICKSTROM

The subject of this paragraph is "spearmint." What does this paragraph tell us about spearmint? It tells us that ancient Greeks used spearmint as a perfume, that Romans used spearmint to scent their homes, and that today many gardeners grow spearmint and use its scent to relieve nervousness or headaches. These details support the main idea of the paragraph: For thousands of years people have valued the spearmint plant for its fragrant odor and beneficial effects.

EXERCISE 3. Finding the Main Idea. Write the stated or implied main idea for each of the following paragraphs.

Answers may vary in wording.

1

> The January wind has a hundred voices. It can scream, it can bellow, it can whisper, and it can sing a lullaby. It can roar through the leafless oaks and shout down the hillside, and it can murmur in the white pines rooted among the granite ledges where lichen makes strange hieroglyphics. It can whistle down a chimney and set the hearth-flames to dancing. On a sunny day it can pause in a sheltered spot and breathe a

FINDING DETAILS THAT SUPPORT MAIN IDEAS
(rule 29d)

You may also wish to emphasize this section with less-advanced and average students. Point out to your students that they are often asked to recall specific details (dates, facts, figures, or names) for tests. Explain that finding and memorizing these details while reading will help them complete tests more easily.

promise of spring and violets. In the cold of a lonely night it can rattle the sash and stay there muttering of ice and snowbanks and deep-frozen ponds.

HAL BORLAND

2

Imagine waiting all your life for a dream to come true! Some people achieve greatness during their lifetime. Others are recognized only after their deaths. John James Audubon was labeled a failure for most of his life. He knew a small measure of success before he died. Years later, organizations were named for him, and his monumental work was finally recognized for the magnificent achievement that it is.

ELEANOR P. ANDERSON

2. The work of John James Audubon, largely unrecognized during his lifetime, has brought him great fame and honor posthumously.

Finding Details That Support Main Ideas

29d. Find details that support main ideas.

In addition to identifying main ideas, you will need to identify their supporting details. Such details may include reasons, examples, or descriptions.

In the following paragraph, the main idea is expressed in the topic sentence (the first sentence). The other sentences contain details that explain the main idea.

Are you prepared to give your pet lifetime care? Even a fully grown pet is totally dependent on you for all of its needs. Every day, you must provide it with food and water, change its litter box or walk it and make sure that it gets sufficient exercise. You're also responsible for keeping it clean, watching over its health and taking it to the vet if necessary. What's more, you'll have to train and discipline your pet so that it doesn't become a nuisance, and give it attention and affection so that it remains loving and companionable. When your pet becomes a senior citizen, he will probably need even more affection and care.

ALICE HERRINGTON

EXERCISE 4. Encourage students to write the answers in their own words.

The main idea of the paragraph above is *You must be prepared to care for a pet throughout its life.* To support this main idea, the writer uses the following details: (1) You must feed the pet, care for its needs, and make sure that it gets exercise. (2) You must keep it clean and healthy. (3) You need to train your pet and give it attention and affection. (4) When your pet ages, you will have to give it additional love and care.

EXERCISE 4. Using Supporting Details to Answer Questions. Read the following paragraphs, noting the main ideas and the supporting details. Then complete each activity.

See Answer Key.

1

That first winter in St. Catharines was a terrible one. Canada was a strange, frozen land, snow everywhere, ice everywhere, and a bone-biting cold the like of which none of them had ever experienced before. Harriet rented a small frame house in the town and set to work to make a home. The fugitives boarded with her. They worked in the forests, felling trees, and so did she. Sometimes she took other jobs, cooking or cleaning house for people in the town. She cheered on these newly arrived fugitives, working herself, finding work for them, finding food for them, praying for them, sometimes begging for them.

ANN PETRY

1. The details in the paragraph above explain why the first winter in St. Catharines was hard for Harriet Tubman. List at least four of these details.

2

In ancient times an elephant was as powerful and feared a weapon as a missile with a nuclear warhead is today. Generals depended on these animals, and it isn't hard to understand why. A group of elephants could trample an army or batter down the walls of a city. When sent into battle carrying a tower full of armed men, an elephant was the equivalent of a modern armed tank. Warrior elephants could inflict tremendous physical damage on the enemy, but that wasn't the most important reason for using them. When soldiers saw elephants

DISTINGUISHING BETWEEN FACT AND OPINION (rule 29e)

This section might be difficult for your less-advanced students, so review it carefully with them.

for the first time, they were often so frightened that they forgot to fight; they simply dropped their weapons and ran. Horses panicked and refused to charge, and the elephants won easy victories. In the ancient world, elephants were such valuable weapons that every king wanted to have some, and a few rulers, like Queen Semiramis of Assyria, went to incredible lengths just to get hold of a few of these remarkable animals.

SUZANNE JURMAIN

2. Write four sentences explaining why the elephant, in ancient times, was powerful and feared. Use your own words.

Distinguishing Between Fact and Opinion

29e. **Distinguish between fact and opinion.**

Most of what you read and hear contains both facts and opinions. It is important to be able to distinguish between these two types of information.

(1) A statement of fact contains information that can be proved true.

A statement of fact contains information about things that have happened in the past or are happening in the present. For example, here are three statements of fact.

Amelia Earhart was born in 1898.
Oranges are a source of vitamin C.
Edgar Allan Poe wrote "The Raven."

(2) A statement of opinion contains information that cannot be proved.

A statement of opinion expresses a personal belief or attitude. The following examples state two different opinions.

Birthday parties are fun.
Soccer is a more exciting game than baseball.

Sometimes a statement of opinion contains expressions such as "Everyone knows that. . . " or "The truth is that. . . " or "It's a fact that. . . ." Do not let these expressions mislead you into thinking that a statement of opinion is a statement of fact.

Remember also that not everything presented as a fact is true or accurate. Be prepared to use a reliable source to prove that a given statement is true. Among the sources you might use are direct experience, an expert, an encyclopedia, a dictionary, an almanac, or any other authoritative reference.

EXERCISE 5. Distinguishing Between Facts and Opinions. Number your paper 1–5. After the proper number, write whether each of the following items is a fact or an opinion. If it is a fact, write some kind of evidence or a source (such as direct experience, an encyclopedia, a textbook, or an almanac) that you could use to determine that it is truly a fact.

EXAMPLES
1. The Bill of Rights was ratified in 1791.
1. *fact—social studies textbook*
2. Oranges are more delicious than apples.
2. *opinion*

1. Twenty-six times two equals fifty-two. 1. fact-math textbook
2. The United Nation's Children's Fund (UNICEF) aids children and teen-agers in developing countries. 2. fact-encyclopedia
3. Blue jeans are the most comfortable of all clothing. 3. opinion
4. Denver is the capital of Colorado. 4. fact-encyclopedia
5. Everyone knows that Denver is the best place for skiing. 5. opinion

Taking Effective Study Notes

29f. Take effective study notes.

Notes that you take while reading your textbooks will help you remember what you have read.[1] Your notes should be brief, but you need to be able to understand them. The following strategies will help you take effective study notes.

[1] See pages 691–96 for strategies in taking notes from class lessons.

EXERCISE 5. In addition to this exercise, you might want to have students write down statements of fact and opinion that they hear on television or radio or read in the newspaper. Go over as many statements as possible, checking that the students have correctly identified facts and opinions.

TAKING EFFECTIVE STUDY NOTES (rule 29f)

Emphasize that the exact form of study notes will vary from person to person.

1. Make sure that you have read your selection once closely.
2. Take notes on paper instead of on note cards.
3. Use the section title and subheadings in your textbook as the subject and topics in your notes. Leave room for main ideas and details under the topics.
4. As you read, look for statements that introduce main ideas. Be aware of transitional words or phrases, such as *first, next, therefore, however, more importantly,* and *on the other hand,* which often introduce main ideas.
5. Write the main ideas and details under the topics.
6. Use your own words.
7. Use words, phrases, or short sentences.
8. Use abbreviations when possible. Omit articles (*a, an, the*).
9. Review your notes soon after you have taken them.

Now read the following passage about how to make an artificial ant colony. Then read the sample study notes for the passage.

> The simplest way to have an artificial ant colony to study in your home is to take a large jar and fill it with soft black earth. Then find a colony of small black or brown ants. You must dig this colony out with a *trowel,*[1] keeping a sharp eye out for the queen, who is much larger and fatter than the small workers. When you find her, put her into the jar along with a couple of hundred workers. They will quickly get busy making passageways down into the earth, and if you feed them a little sugar, honey, meat, and bread crumbs each day, they will make their ant town right in your jar. To see their passageways under the earth, cover the jar up to the level of the dirt with black cloth or paper, and take this off only at rare intervals. When you do take it off, you will see passageways running next to the glass and will be able to watch the ants going about their work underground.
>
> VINSON BROWN

Study Notes: How to Make an Artificial Ant Colony
—Fill large jar with soft black dirt.
—Find colony of small black or brown ants.

[1] *trowel:* a tool with a scoop, used for digging up plants in gardens.

—Look for queen—fatter, larger.
—Put her and about two hundred others into jar with dirt.
—Feed each day—sugar, honey, meat, bread crumbs.
—Cover jar up to level of earth with black paper.
—Seldom take paper off.
—Will be passageways running down sides of jar.
—Can watch ants working.

EXERCISE 6. Taking Study Notes. Select a homework assignment in your science, social studies, or English textbook. Take study notes, using the strategies on pages 655–57. Be prepared to share your notes. Answers will vary.

Writing a Summary of Study Material

29g. Write a summary to help you understand your study material.

A *summary* is a brief composition that covers the main ideas and important supporting details of a piece of writing. It should be approximately one-third the length of the original writing and should be written in your own words. Study the following steps for writing a summary.

1. Skim the selection.
2. Read the selection closely, looking for the author's main ideas.
3. Read the selection again to identify not only the main ideas but also the supporting details. Look up any unfamiliar words. Take notes as you read.
4. Identify the author's main ideas and important supporting details. (You might put a check mark [✔] next to those ideas in your notes.)
5. Write a summary in your own words. Include only the author's main ideas and *important* supporting details.
6. Revise your summary to make sure that you have covered the main ideas and important supporting details.
7. Revise your summary until it is approximately one-third the length of the original piece of writing.

EXERCISE 6. You may want to allow some class time for one or two volunteers to share the study notes they wrote and explain the strategies they used for the assignment.

WRITING A SUMMARY OF STUDY MATERIAL (rule 29g)

This section is probably better suited to your average and advanced students. Emphasize that only the main ideas and *important* supporting details are included in a summary. You might want to provide students with some practice in selecting important details: Have them read a passage and then arrange the topic, main idea, and supporting details in *descending* order of importance.

EXERCISE 7. This exercise provides students with an opportunity to write a summary of a passage found in one of their textbooks. Review their work to the extent that time permits.

WRITING IN OTHER COURSES (rule 29h)

Emphasize to students that they can more easily succeed in their other courses if they apply to those subjects the writing, thinking, and studying skills they learn in the English classroom.

Now read the passage on page 656 again. Then read the following example summary for that passage. Note that it is about one-third the length of the original.

Summary

> To make an artificial ant colony, fill a jar with earth. Then find an ant colony and put the queen (the largest ant) and about two hundred other ants into the jar. Feed them every day. Cover the jar to the top of the earth with black paper. Remove the paper when you want to see the ants working.

EXERCISE 7. Writing a Summary. Select a homework assignment in your science or social studies textbook. Write a summary of one passage, using the strategies on pages 655–57.
Answers will vary.

Writing in Other Courses

29h. Use writing to learn about ideas in social studies or history.

You can better understand a content-area subject, such as social studies or history, if you write about its important ideas. Most often you will write factual reports in these subjects (see pages 178–94). You can also explore ideas in social studies or history with other forms of writing.

One way to use writing in history or social studies is to write dialogues and narratives about historical figures. For example, you might write an imaginary dialogue between Thomas Jefferson and Meriwether Lewis, the explorer, about the Lewis and Clark expedition. Or, you might write an interview (using dialogue form) between Susan B. Anthony, the suffragette, and a television reporter. You might even want to be the reporter or a participant in the situation. (For more on writing dialogue, see pages 79–83.)

You might also write a narrative in which you are a person telling about an important historical event. For example, you might be Charles Lindbergh describing his historic flight across the Atlantic Ocean in 1927. Or, you might be Amelia Earhart describing her attempt to fly around the world in 1937. No matter which person you write about, use the same process you follow to write any other personal experience narrative (see pages 79–83).

For each of these activities, you will use your knowledge of writing and your understanding of history. You will have to write from the point of view of the historical figure. (See page 81 on point of view.) You will also have to use what you know about that time in history. This kind of writing might help you to see history from a new angle.

Another way to use writing in social studies or history is to keep a journal. In this journal, you can write about the ideas and people you are studying. In this way, your journal is like the writer's notebook you might keep in English class (see page 14).

You can use your journal in two ways. First, you can record what you think about the events, ideas, and people you are studying. This will help you understand the course material from your own point of view. Second, you can use your journal to answer specific questions or discussion items your teacher gives you. For example, your history or social studies teacher might ask you to write about one of the following items:

1. Summarize the main ideas in the Bill of Rights.
2. Discuss how a country's geography and agriculture are related.
3. What were some of the major changes in the United States in the years between the Civil War and 1900?
4. Describe three of George Washington Carver's most important discoveries.

Items like these will also help you to understand the ideas, people, and events you are studying. When you write in your journal, be sure to apply your knowledge of writing sentences and paragraphs.

You can also use writing in social studies or history by writing book reports. You may already write book reports in your English class (see pages 195–200). In history or social studies class, your book report should be on a book that discusses an

EXERCISE 8. Less-advanced students might best complete activity 1. With all students, you may want to review briefly the stages of the writing process and refer students to Chapter 1.

historical person or event, such as *The Battle of the Alamo,* by Keith Murphy. This also includes biographies and autobiographies, such as *Osceola: Seminole Warrior* by Joanne Oppenheim, or *The Story of My Life,* by Helen Keller.

In your book report, you should summarize the book's main events, without including every detail. You should also explain why you did or did not like the book. This means that you should include reasons for your opinion. These reasons should be specific details from the book. You might also want to read an encyclopedia article about the book's subject. This will help you to understand more about the subject.

Prepare for your book report by carefully reading the book. Jot down notes about important ideas or details as you read. Then, write your book report. Explain what the book is about and give your opinion of the book. You might also want to answer one of the following questions in your book report: How does this book help you to understand history or social studies? Does the book present the person or the event accurately? How do you know it does (or does not)? After you write a first draft of your book report, evaluate, revise, and proofread it—just as you would do for any other piece of writing.

No matter what kind of writing you do in history or social studies, or in your other classes, apply what you know about narration, description, and exposition (Chapters 4 and 5) and about writing paragraphs and compositions (Chapters 2, 3, and 5). Also remember to use what you know about the writing process (Chapter 1) to improve all the writing you do in school.

EXERCISE 8. Writing in Social Studies or History. Use the writing process to complete one of the following activities.
Answers will vary.

1. Write a dialogue, an interview, or a narrative about a person you are studying now.
2. Write a journal entry about an idea, person, or event you are studying now. Use the discussion items on page 659, or use questions your teacher gives you.
3. Write a book report on a book that discusses an important person or event in history. In your report, answer one of the questions above.

PREPARING FOR AND TAKING TESTS

Tests are designed to measure different things. Some tests measure how well you remember specific information; others determine how well you understand ideas. Some questions call for brief answers; others ask you to write a paragraph or more. The following skills and strategies will prepare you for different kinds of tests.

Preparing for Objective Tests

Objective tests measure how well you remember specific information, such as dates, names, terms, and definitions. Objective tests include multiple-choice, true-or-false, and fill-in-the blank questions as well as short-answer identifications and matching questions.

29i. Prepare for objective tests by studying the specific information that will be included on the test.

Follow these steps to prepare for objective tests.

1. Know what will be included on the test.
2. Gather the materials you will need, such as your textbook, study notes, and homework assignments.
3. Review your notes and assignments. Pay attention to names, dates, terms, and definitions. If your notes are not clear, reread the appropriate section in your textbook.
4. Make up questions that might be on the test. Then answer these questions. (Use your notes to check your answers.)

Taking Objective Tests

Follow these steps to take objective tests.

1. Read the directions closely. Note *exactly* what the directions ask you to do; for example, "Answer *three* of the following five questions."
2. Skim the rest of the test. Note how many questions there are, which ones are difficult, and which ones are easy. Complete

PREPARING FOR AND TAKING TESTS (rules 29i–29k)

This section includes strategies for taking both objective and essay tests.

PREPARING FOR OBJECTIVE TESTS AND TAKING OBJECTIVE TESTS (rule 29i)

Be sure students understand that objective tests ask them to recall specific information, such as facts, dates, figures, and descriptive details. Encourage students to discuss the problems they encounter in taking each kind of objective test. Have them apply these strategies to the tests they take in this and other classes.

the easy ones first; then work through the more difficult ones.

3. Note how much time you have for the test and figure out how much time you can spend on each question. (Plan less time for easy questions and more time for difficult ones.)

4. If you do not understand something on the test, ask your teacher for help.

In addition, keep in mind these points about the specific kinds of objective tests.

Multiple-choice Questions

Multiple-choice questions ask you to choose the correct answer from three or more options. Follow these steps.

1. Read the question carefully.
2. Read *all* of the choices *before* you answer the question.
3. Eliminate choices that you know are incorrect. (Usually there will be one or two.)
4. Think carefully about the remaining choices. Based on what you know, determine which choice makes the most sense.

Now read the following multiple-choice question and its solution.

EXAMPLE A single entry word in the dictionary appears divided into two parts to show (a) that it is sometimes written as two words (b) the origin of the word (c) that the word consists of two syllables. [Having studied the dictionary, you would be able to eliminate choice *b*—information about origin follows the entry word. Of the two remaining choices, choice *c* makes more sense—the single word is divided into two syllables, not spelled as two words. The correct choice is *c*.]

True-or-false Questions

True-or-false questions ask you to determine whether a given statement is true or false. Follow these steps.

1. Read the entire statement carefully.
2. Look to see if *any* part of the statement is false. If this is the case, mark the statement false.

3. If all the parts of the statement are true, mark the statement true.

Now read the following true-or-false questions and solutions.

EXAMPLES
1. In 1875 Edison invented the phonograph. [This statement is false. Though Edison invented the phonograph, he invented it in 1877, not in 1875.]
2. The sun is the center of the solar system. [All parts of this statement are true; therefore, the statement is true.]

Fill-in-the-blank questions

Fill-in-the-blank questions ask you to fill in the missing word or words that correctly complete the sentence. Follow these steps.

1. Read the question carefully.
2. Write a specific answer, using the terminology found in your notes or textbook.
3. Try to fill in all the blanks.

Now read the following fill-in-the-blank questions and solutions.

EXAMPLES
1. A —— gives inventors exclusive rights to make and sell their inventions. [patent]
2. Jimmy Carter was elected President in —— . [1976]
3. Sandra Day O'Connor was the first woman ever appointed to —— . [the United States Supreme Court]

Note that the first item asks you to fill in a term, the second asks you to fill in a figure, and the third asks you to fill in a name. Note also that all answers are appropriate to the subject.

Short-answer Identifications

Short-answer identifications usually ask you to answer a question with a word or a phrase or with one or two sentences. Follow these steps.

1. Read the question carefully.

2. Write a specific answer, using the terminology found in your notes or textbook.
3. Try to answer all questions.

Now read the following short-answer identifications and solutions.

EXAMPLES
1. In American politics, what does ERA stand for? [the Equal Rights Amendment]
2. Who was Nelson A. Rockefeller? [a former New York State governor who was chosen by President Ford as Vice-President.]

Notice that each of the answers is specific and that the terminology is appropriate to the subject matter.

Matching Questions

Matching questions ask you to match the items in one list with the items in another list. Follow these steps.

1. Read the directions carefully. Some directions may explain that you do not have to use all the items. Other directions will inform you that you may use some items twice.
2. Read both lists and note how they are related. For example, one list may contain the names of famous people, and the other may include their accomplishments.
3. Skim through the items. Identify the easy ones and the difficult ones. Do the easy ones first.
4. Complete the rest of the test by making informed guesses, that is, by using clues to help you.

Now read the following matching questions and solutions for a test on the Constitution of the United States.

EXAMPLE

1. To accuse an official in the executive branch or a judge in a federal court of wrong doing	a. impeach
2. Proposal for a law	b. bill
3. Set number of members required to conduct the business of Congress	c. amendment
	d. quorum
	e. elastic clause

4. A change or an addition to a constitution
5. Provision that allows Congress to stretch its powers to meet new situations

Note that the list on the left contains definitions and the list on the right contains the corresponding terms. First, you might identify items 1, 2, and 4 as easy items and match item 1 with *a*, item 2 with *b*, and item 4 with *c*. Then, of the two remaining choices, you could examine the words in item 5 and determine that the word *stretch* is a clue: something that can be stretched is said to be elastic. Thus you would match item 5 with choice *e*. Last, you would correctly match item 3 with choice *d*.

EXERCISE 9. Applying Test-Taking Skills. Write the answers to the following questions: See Answer Key.

1. Identify ten key terms that might appear in an objective test on this chapter.
2. Using the terms you chose, prepare for a test on this chapter by writing sample questions. Include at least two of each of the following types of test questions:
   a. multiple-choice
   b. true-or-false
   c. fill-in-the-blank
   d. short-answer identifications

Preparing for Essay Tests

Essay tests are intended to measure your understanding of what you have learned. You express your understanding by writing an essay of one paragraph or more.

To prepare for essay tests, reread the appropriate parts of your textbook and your notes to identify main ideas and important supporting details. Study this information until you understand it. Try answering any questions in your textbook that ask you to write a paragraph or more. Then try making up your own essay questions.

EXERCISE 9. Many students will enjoy this exercise—making up their own test questions. Provide help as needed.

PREPARING FOR ESSAY TESTS and **TAKING ESSAY TESTS (rule 29j)**

These sections include steps students can follow to prepare for essay tests and strategies they can use to write better essay-type answers. After reviewing with students the steps on pages 666 and 667, ask them to discuss the problems they encounter when taking essay tests.

Although there is no *right* answer on an essay test, your teacher will expect specific details in your essay answer. Therefore, be prepared to use your main ideas and important details to write complete, well-supported answers.

Taking Essay Tests

29j. Plan your time and your answer for an essay question.

Follow these steps when taking an essay test.

1. Read the directions closely. Note whether you have a choice of questions to answer.
2. Skim the rest of the test. Note how many questions there are, which ones are easy, and which ones are difficult.
3. If you have a choice of essay questions, decide which one(s) you will answer.
4. Figure out how much time you can spend on each question. (Be sure to leave enough time to plan and write your essay.)
5. Begin by reading the directions carefully. Note *what* task you are being asked to do, for example, to *compare* (point out likenesses *or* differences between) two characters or to *explain* (give reasons for) the causes of a war. In addition, note *how many* tasks are involved. For example, the following directions ask you to do two tasks: *Briefly describe the character traits and activities of Paul Bunyan and Pecos Bill. Then contrast (discuss the differences between) these two legendary folk heroes.*
6. Work through the stages of the writing process.
   a. *Prewriting.* Gather ideas for your answer. Write a sentence that expresses your main point. Be sure your sentence uses the key words of the question.
   b. *Writing.* Use your prewriting notes to help you write your answer. Begin by writing either the topic sentence of a paragraph or the thesis statement of a composition. Be sure that your supporting sentences develop this main idea.
   c. *Revising.* In most cases you will not have much time for revising. Reread the question and your answer to make sure that you have answered the question.

d. *Proofreading.* Proofread your paragraph for errors in grammar, usage, spelling, and mechanics.

Answering the Different Kinds of Essay Questions

29k. Know the different kinds of essay questions and what is expected in the answer for each type.

Essay questions generally ask you to complete one of several tasks. Each of these tasks is expressed by a verb. The following list shows some key verbs and the tasks each verb signals.

Essay Test Questions

KEY VERB(S)	TASK
analyze	Take something apart to show how each part works.
compare	Point out likenesses *or* differences.
contrast	Point out differences.
compare and contrast	Point out similarities *and* differences.
describe	Give a picture in words or an account of.
list, outline, trace	List events, show development.
discuss	Examine in detail.
explain	Give reasons for something's being the way it is.
demonstrate, illustrate, show	Provide examples to support a point.
interpret	Give the meaning or significance of something.

Now read the following example of an essay question:

EXAMPLE Contrast the Pilgrims' reasons for coming to North America with those of the Jamestown settlers.

ANSWERING THE DIFFERENT KINDS OF ESSAY QUESTIONS
(rule 29k)

This section includes a list of *key* verbs that are often used in essay questions. Each verb signals a specific task that the student is supposed to do. You might want to have your students memorize the list of key verbs and the task each suggests, and then test them on the verbs.

EXERCISE 10. This exercise tests the students' recognition of key words in sample essay questions and of the task each key word suggests.

Answers: Exercise 10

1. Compare—point out likenesses (or differences) between the Versailles Treaty and President Wilson's Fourteen Points
2. Interpret—explain the significance of the poem; give reasons—back up explanation with quotes from poem and discussion of poetic devices
3. Explain—give reasons for the struggle between Antigone and Creon
4. Describe—give an account of the geography and climate of Costa Rica
5. Show—provide examples, giving ways the selections illustrate American beliefs; identify—make note of or list

Additional Practice

Teacher's Resource Book, Worksheet pages 338–39

This essay question asks you to point out the differences between the Pilgrims' reasons for coming to North America and those of the Jamestown settlers. The sentence that expresses your main idea might be *The Pilgrims' reasons for coming to North America were different from those of the Jamestown settlers.* Your details would include the Pilgrims' main reason for coming to North America (religious persecution in England) and the Jamestown settlers' reasons (lack of jobs in England, conflict with the government). You would provide details to support these reasons. You might arrange your essay test answer by first expressing your main idea, next discussing the Pilgrims' reasons, and then discussing the Jamestown settlers' reasons.

EXERCISE 10. Analyzing Essay Questions. For each of the following sample essay questions, identify the key word or words that state the specific task in the question. State briefly what task you must do to answer the question.

EXAMPLE 1. Explain why the United States replaced the spoils system with the merit system for hiring federal employees during the late 1800's.

1. *Explain—give reasons for the replacement of the spoils system with the merit system.*

1. Compare the Treaty of Versailles with President Wilson's Fourteen Points.
2. Interpret Robert Frost's poem "The Road Not Taken." Be sure to give reasons to support your point of view.
3. The conflict of the myth of Antigone involves two strong wills. In a single paragraph, explain the struggle between Antigone and Creon.
4. Describe the geography and climate of Costa Rica.
5. Several selections presented in this unit focus on beliefs that are part of America's heritage, particularly belief in independence, tolerance, and personal freedom. Choose two selections you have read, and in a brief essay show how they demonstrate characteristic American beliefs. Identify the selections by title and author.

PART FIVE

SPEAKING AND LISTENING

PART FIVE

SPEAKING AND LISTENING

pages 669–96

USING THE PICTURES

The pictures on this and the next page, along with those in the section "Picture the Possibilities" following page 226, provide students with sources of ideas for writing. The following suggestions will help you show students how to use the pictures, either singly or in combination, to generate ideas and gather information.

Moon over Mountains

- Have students limit the subject "moon" on the basis of events or time periods and use the *5 W-How?* questions to gather information for a report or a speech. For the topic "the first human landing on the moon," for example, they might ask, *Who* made the landing? *How* did they reach the moon? *When* and *where* did the landing take place? *How long* did the human beings remain on the moon? *What* did they do while they were there? *How* did the people on Earth learn about the landing? *Why* was the landing made?
- Another possibility would be to have students report on the composition of the lunar rocks brought back to Earth by the various Apollo missions.
- Students might enjoy finding out about the beliefs earlier people had about the moon and either reporting on their findings or adapting them for use in imaginative stories. They might, for example, read about Greek or Roman gods or

goddesses associated with the moon or about traditional American Indian legends involving the moon.

Backpackers in Mountains

• One way to use this picture would be to have students write a dialogue between two or more of the people in the group. To help them create an interesting situation, have them consider questions such as these: *Who are the people? How well do they know each other? Where are they? Are they visiting the area, or do they live nearby? What month, day, and time of day is it?*

• For a process paragraph, students could explain how to pack a backpack (for a one-day hike, for an overnight trip, etc.); how to select good hiking shoes; or how to reach a scenic area in or near your community.

• The subject "camping" suggests many possibilities for oral or written reports, such as "good places to camp in our county," "planning a camping trip," "easy-to-fix meals for camping trips," "freeze-dried foods," and "preparing a first-aid kit."

• Students who have been camping (or have gone to summer camp) could write stories about their experiences. Other students might write stories about an overnight stay at a friend's or relative's home.

Connecting the Pictures

The fact that both pictures show mountains might give students the idea of writing a report on or a description of a particular mountain or mountain range. They might instead write paragraphs giving information about the points of highest and lowest elevation in your state.

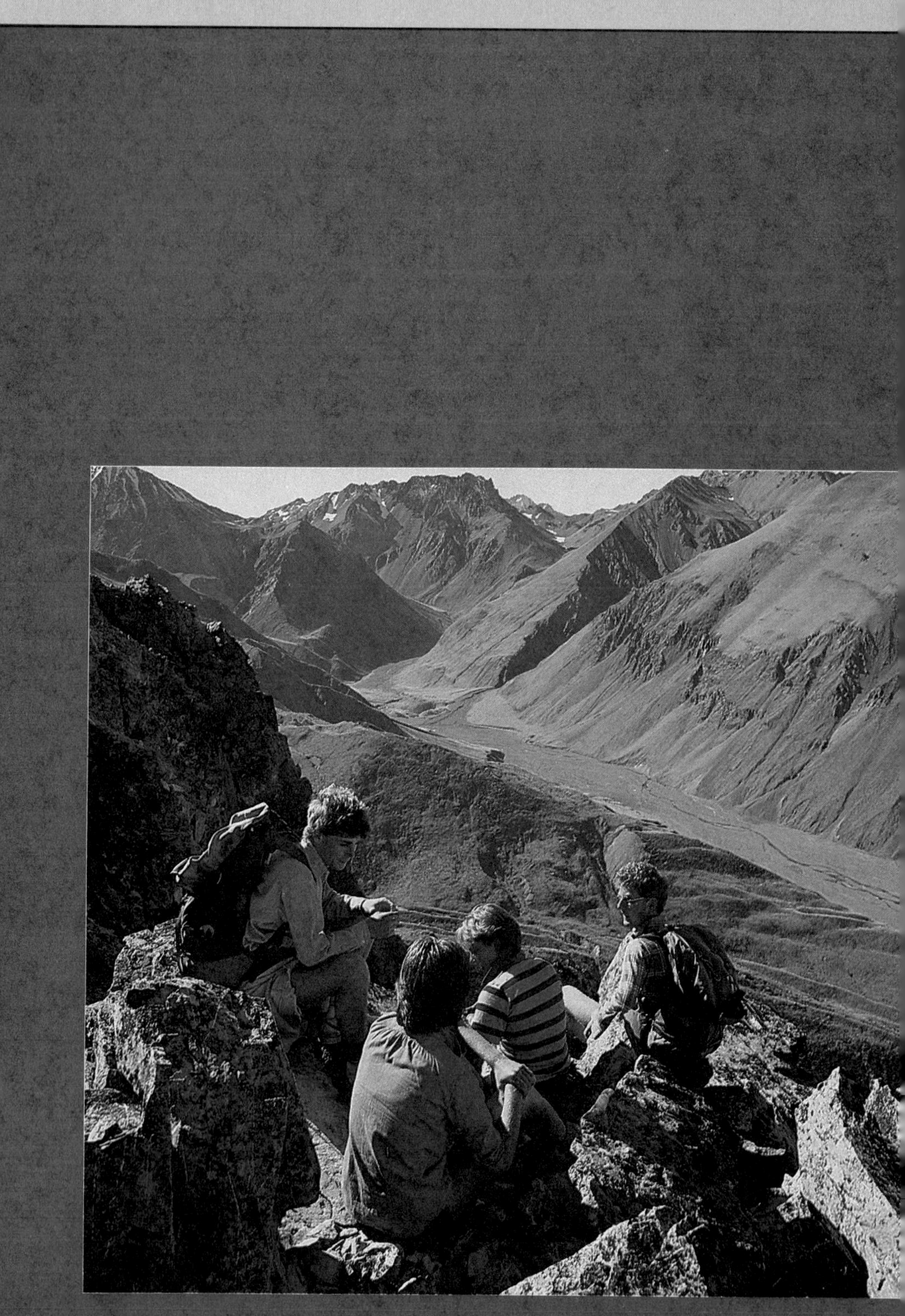

CHAPTER 30

Speaking

FORMAL AND INFORMAL SPEAKING SITUATIONS

Learning how to speak well and comfortably before groups or in unfamiliar situations is an important part of everyone's education. This chapter will help you to improve your speaking skills.

MAKING ANNOUNCEMENTS

To announce information about an event to other students, you do not need to make elaborate notes. Nevertheless, you should write down the information you are to give and check it over to be sure it includes all the essential facts. You have already used the *5 W-How?* questions to gather information for your writing. These same questions can help you organize information for your announcement.

30a. In making an announcement, be sure to include all the necessary facts.

Most announcements should include the following information: (1) the kind of event, (2) the time, (3) the place, (4) the admission fee, if any, and (5) special features. The following example includes four of these items, omitting only the admission fee.

Chapter Overview

Many eighth-graders are apprehensive about speaking before a group. Your first task is to help them overcome their fears. This chapter gives instructions for preparing and delivering announcements and oral reports. The chapter also includes work on evaluating speeches and participating in group discussions.

Chapter Objective

Students will compose and deliver oral presentations, evaluate speeches, and participate in group discussions.

PRESENTING THE CHAPTER

LESS-ADVANCED STUDENTS Some students find oral work less difficult than written work. However, they will need careful training in learning to plan and organize talks. It is often a good idea to begin this training by having students give "how-to" demonstrations—for instance, how to mend a torn page in a book, how to tie a square knot, or how to wrap a present. Students might stand in front of the class and give their demonstrations, explaining each step orally. Then each student might be assigned to give another "how-to" speech on the same subject, this time without an accompanying demonstration. The rest of the class should listen closely to make sure that the speaker's explanation includes each necessary step and presents the steps in logical order.

ADVANCED STUDENTS After their initial experience in public speaking, advanced students should speak on topics that challenge their ability to think and that require some research. If you set your sights high, you will be surprised at the high quality of content and thinking that can characterize their talks.

MAKING ANNOUNCEMENTS (rule 30a)

You may want to teach your students the essential requirements of an announcement by having them memorize the first stanza of Kipling's "The Elephant Child":

I keep six honest serving-men
(They taught me all I know);
Their names are What and Why and When
and How and Where and Who.

You might write the stanza on the board and have the class copy it.

EXERCISES 1 and 2. You can follow up the training provided here by having students make real announcements throughout the remainder of the year. Some teachers make it a practice to have all class events and extracurricular activities announced by members of the class. Additional examples of announcements can be found in *Your Speech* by Griffith, Nelson, and Stasheff (Harcourt Brace Jovanovich, 1979, pp. 245–46).

PREPARING AN ORAL REPORT (rule 30b)

The class will need at least as much help in choosing and developing topics for oral reports as they need in choosing and developing topics for written compositions. You may wish to review Chapters 1 and 5 with the class before they begin to prepare their speeches.

EXAMPLE The Microcomputer Club will meet Tuesday, January 15, at 3:05 P.M. in Room 27. All members and any other interested students are invited for a program called "Using Computers to Create Sound Effects."

Go over the facts of an announcement several times in your mind before you speak. If you are not sure that you will remember them all while you are speaking, carry a note card with the information on it. You can glance at this card as you speak.

Use a normal rate of speaking, and make sure that you give your audience time to take in what you are saying. Speak loudly enough so that everyone will hear.

EXERCISE 1. Correcting Announcements. The following announcements omit essential items of information. What are these items? Rewrite each announcement so that it includes all the necessary information.

Answers will vary. Omitted information is listed.

1. Students in Ms. Robertson's class who are going to the art museum tomorrow should be ready to leave at 11:15. The only expense will be for lunch in the museum cafeteria.
2. The Junior Philharmonic needs more members. Even if you are not sure of your musical talent, why not come to a rehearsal and join the preparation for the next concert?

1. place of departure; special features 2. time; place

EXERCISE 2. Preparing and Delivering Announcements. Prepare and deliver an announcement for one of the following events or for an actual event at your school. Give all the necessary information, using the *5 W-How?* questions as a guide.

Answers will vary.

1. A five-mile bicycle race to benefit handicapped children
2. The annual Spring Talent Show
3. The eighth-grade class trip to Washington, D.C.
4. Teacher Recognition Day
5. A science fair

PREPARING AN ORAL REPORT

30b. Learn how to prepare an oral report.

Some students will tend to write out their reports and try to memorize them word for word, unless you caution against this practice. If you encourage students to speak at first on subjects from their personal experience (such as "How I Raised My Kitten"), they will probably not feel a need to memorize. Later, when they give talks that include items such as quotations or statistical figures, they may use note cards as memory aids.

There are several similarities between planning an oral report and planning a piece of writing. In fact, you use the same skills to organize each form of communication: choosing a suitable subject, limiting the subject to a topic, and gathering and arranging information. These skills are the same as the prewriting steps in the writing process. For a review of these prewriting steps, refer to pages 6–28 in Chapter 1.

Oral reports and written reports, which are discussed in Chapter 6, are planned in much the same way. Also, both oral and written reports have the same purpose: to present information, to explain something about a subject, or to express and support an opinion. Still, there is one important difference: Oral reports are not written out word for word. Instead, you make some notes to help you remember your material as you speak. Be sure to use the following steps to prepare oral reports for any of your school subjects.

(1) Choose a suitable subject for your oral report.

If you are given a subject to report on, you have no problem of selection. If you are asked to choose your own subject, however, you can find subjects to talk about just as you find subjects to write about. You can use the methods discussed in Chapters 1 and 5 to find subjects for your talk: observation, brainstorming, clustering, and a writer's journal.

Choose a suitable subject, that is, one that is right for your report. Two ideas can guide your choice. First, focus on your interests and experiences. By discussing a subject you know about or are interested in, you will be able to speak confidently and enthusiastically. Your confidence and enthusiasm should also make your report more interesting to your audience.

Second, select a subject that will interest your audience. A report on how to identify types of clouds might bore some people, and a report on how to hang up your clothes would bore everybody. But a report on ways to earn money after school or on a new probe of a distant planet would be likely to interest many of your listeners.

EXERCISE 3. This exercise provides practice in selecting suitable subjects for oral reports. You may want to refer students to text pages 11–17, where techniques for finding subjects are discussed.

EXERCISE 4. This exercise provides students with practice in limiting subjects to topics for an explanatory or informative talk. You may want to refer students to pages 17–20 for help on limiting subjects.

EXERCISE 3. Choosing Suitable Subjects. Suppose that you must give an oral report that explains a subject to your classmates or supports an opinion. Using your interests and experiences and your audience's interests as guides, list at least five subjects that would be suitable for your report. Answers will vary.

(2) Limit your subject to a narrow topic.

Once you have chosen a subject, you should limit it. That is, you should narrow your subject to a topic that can be covered reasonably well in the time you have for your report. Remember that the purpose of an oral report is to give information or an opinion about or to explain a particular subject to an audience. If the subject is too large, you will not be able to achieve this purpose.

To limit a subject to a narrow topic, divide it into smaller parts. Suppose you chose the subject "dinosaurs" for an oral report in science class. This subject is very broad—there is a great deal of information about dinosaurs that you could discuss.

To limit this broad subject, divide it into smaller parts: "how scientists identify dinosaur bones," "the climate when dinosaurs roamed the earth," and "places to see dinosaur exhibits in the United States." Notice how each topic focuses on a small part of the broad subject "dinosaurs." You could easily develop an oral report on any one of these limited topics. Depending on the time you have to present your report, sometimes you may need to continue narrowing your subject to even more limited topics. For more help on limiting subjects, see pages 17–19 in Chapter 1.

EXERCISE 4. Limiting Subjects. Each of the following subjects is too broad for an oral report. Limit each one to at least two narrow topics by dividing it into smaller parts. If your teacher prefers, you may instead limit the broad subjects you selected in Exercise 3. Keep the report's explanatory, informative, or persuasive purpose in mind. Answers will vary.

1. Modern transportation
2. Great cities
3. Clothing
4. Community recreation
5. Women writers and artists

(3) Gather information for your report.

Your next step is to gather information for your report. There are at least three sources of information: (1) your own ideas and experiences, (2) other people who know something about your topic, and (3) books and periodicals. Consult all of these sources, and get as much information as you can.

The methods you use to gather information for your writing can also be used to gather information for your oral report. These methods include using a writer's journal, brainstorming, clustering, changing your point of view, and asking the *5 W-How?* questions. Refer to the information-gathering sections of Chapters 1 and 5 for more help. Be sure to write notes or brief summaries of the information you are gathering. You will use these notes to prepare your oral report.

EXERCISE 5. Gathering Information. Gather information for an oral report. Use any one of the narrow topics you developed in Exercise 4 on page 672, or use another narrow topic of your own. Be sure to write notes or brief summaries of the information you gather. Answers will vary.

(4) Prepare an outline of your oral report.

From your notes, prepare an outline for your oral report. (Look at pages 151–53 in Chapter 5 to refresh your memory on how to prepare an outline.)

Suppose that you have decided to give a report in your science class on shooting stars. Having discovered that shooting stars are meteors, go to the library (see pages 613–25) and read articles on meteors in various reference works. Take notes and study them until the material is familiar to you. Prepare an outline from the notes. The outline might have four main headings:

I. Time: when meteors are seen
II. Nature: what the characteristics of meteors are
III. Place: where and why meteors are seen
IV. Fate: how speed, size, and course determine the final end of meteors

EXERCISE 5. This exercise provides students with practice in gathering information. Emphasize that they must make notes or summaries of the information they find. You may want to refer students to pages 20–25, where information-gathering techniques are discussed.

EXERCISE 6. In this exercise, students prepare outlines for their reports. Refer to the model of a topic outline on pages 151 and 152.

Under each heading, arrange your material in logical order. For some topics, you will give the major ideas first, with the details following them. For other topics—such as how to conduct an experiment—you will arrange ideas in chronological, or time, order. The logical order you use depends on your topic.

EXERCISE 6. Preparing an Outline. Using the information you have gathered on your topic, prepare an outline of your oral report. Answers will vary.

(5) Write note cards to use as reminders when delivering your report.

It is not necessary to write out a speech word for word and memorize it. Instead, read and reread your material and your outline until they are so familiar that you need only an occasional reminder to help you talk freely about your topic.

Write these reminders on 3- × 5-inch note cards. Arrange the cards to correspond to the order of your outline. These cards make up the body of your oral report.

Reminder cards do not have to contain complete sentences; key words or phrases will do. Include the subheadings under the main idea on the card. Remember: These cards are not to be read aloud. They are meant to aid your memory.

A reminder card for a talk on shooting stars might look like this:

I. Time
A. More after midnight than before
B. More in the fall than in any other season
C. Five per hour - 500 per minute

When giving your speech, you would start with this card. The items on the card are reminders. The main point tells what this part of the speech is about; the subheadings identify details to discuss. You might start your speech by saying:

> We are all familiar with shooting stars, or meteors. Often, on summer evenings, we have seen them streak across the dark sky. Most of us, however, are unaware that we can see more shooting stars after midnight than before and that we can see more in the fall of the year than in other seasons. Usually, about five shooting stars per hour can be sighted. However, when meteor showers occur, sometimes as many as five hundred meteors fall each minute. . . .

In some cases write full and exact details on a note card. If, for example, you want to give the ingredients of a recipe or the measurements of material needed to make a greenhouse, write out the full details on a note card.

You may want to use direct quotations from people whom you've interviewed. (Direct quotations will make your talk livelier and give it the weight of authority.) Write out quotations exactly, to avoid misquoting the person you interviewed.

If you are explaining a process to your audience, you may use charts and pictures. You may also want to use the chalkboard to write figures and dates or draw illustrations. A reminder card can tell you when to use these visual aids.

You may need only a few reminder cards if you know the material well—perhaps one for each main heading, plus one or two additional cards with details. Prepare as many cards as you think necessary.

As you speak, hold the cards in your hand. Glance at the top card, and talk about the subject on it. Then move this top card to the bottom, uncovering the next topic of your speech. Continue until you have spoken on every topic listed on your cards.

As you practice your speech, practice using your note cards also. You should be able to use them smoothly so that they do not distract your audience.

(6) Plan an interest-arousing introduction and a strong conclusion.

EXERCISE 7. Explain to the students that they should use their notes and outlines to write out their note cards. Emphasize that they should use words and not sentences.

REVIEW EXERCISE A. Before students tackle this exercise, they should practice delivering brief informal speeches to the class. Some teachers use students' writing assignments as the basis for informal speeches. For example, on the day that book reports are due, the teacher will call on five or six students to stand up and tell about the books on which they have written their reports. Or, when students have just finished making outlines for longer compositions, several members of the class will be asked to speak briefly on topics they are going to write about.

Write out an exciting first sentence, one that will arouse your audience's interest. Memorize this sentence so that you can look at your audience and speak the sentence naturally.

Similarly, work out a strong ending statement for your talk—a sentence or paragraph that ties your main ideas together. You may write this statement on a card. However, try not to spoil the effect of a good speech by reading the last part of it. (For more help in writing introductions and conclusions, see pages 155 and 157 in Chapter 5.)

EXERCISE 7. Completing an Oral Report. Prepare note cards and plan an introduction and a conclusion for a topic of your own. You may use the topic and information you have developed in previous exercises. Answers will vary.

REVIEW EXERCISE A. Planning an Oral Report. Plan a short oral report on one of the following topics or on a topic of your own. Follow each of the steps explained in this chapter. Answers will vary.

1. UFO's: reality or illusion?
2. Progress made to save the whales
3. What makes an airplane fly?
4. The monster called Sasquatch
5. Why —— is the best career
6. Family birthday customs in China
7. Can cars run on solar energy?
8. My choice for a personal hero
9. Programs I'd like to see on television
10. A hobby that earns money

DELIVERING AN ORAL REPORT

By planning your oral report, you have focused on the content of your speech: *what* you will explain to your audience about your topic. It is also important for you to consider *how* you will communicate this content to your audience. As you deliver your report, you need to think about nonverbal communication, pronunciation and enunciation, and expression.

Nonverbal Communication

People often communicate with unspoken, or nonverbal, signals. For example, someone who cannot talk may use sign language to converse. An umpire at a baseball game raises one thumb in the air to say, "You're out!"

Nonverbal communication—also called body language—is an important part of giving a speech. An audience will read, or interpret, a speaker's gestures and body movements in the same way that they will listen to words. Nonverbal signals should communicate exactly what a speaker wants to say.

30c. Learn how to use nonverbal signals as you speak.

You can improve your speech by using good posture and natural gestures.

Stand straight. Keep your weight on both feet. If you are sitting, place both feet squarely on the floor, and keep your back straight in the chair. Good posture communicates confidence.

Look at your audience as you speak. Glance around the room, and focus on the faces of your listeners. Eye contact is an effective way to hold the audience's attention. If you are using note cards, glance—but do not stare—at them as you speak. While speaking, try to smile occasionally. Smiling usually helps to relax the audience.

Keep gestures under control. Although it is natural to feel nervous about giving a talk, avoid nervous, random gestures, such as fidgeting with your hair or your note cards.

Think about what gestures may mean. Choose gestures that help rather than hinder your spoken words. Keeping your hands in your pockets, for example, suggests you are not well prepared to give the speech. Scratching your head suggests that you are not sure of what to say next. Avoid any gestures that detract from your message.

Pause for transition. A short pause between parts of your speech can be a nonverbal signal to your audience that you are about to introduce another topic. A pause can also give you a chance to take a deep breath and relax.

DELIVERING AN ORAL REPORT (rules 30c–30e) and **NONVERBAL COMMUNICATION** (rule 30c)

You might introduce this section with a discussion of how many meanings a wave of the hand can have—to say hello or to say good-bye, either politely or enthusiastically; to say "I don't believe that"; to shoo or to warn someone away; and so on.

EXERCISE 8. Doing this exercise orally may provide an opportunity for some of the shyer students to speak before the group.

PRONUNCIATION AND ENUNCIATION (rule 30d)

Make it clear to the class that this part of the chapter deals with the kind of clear, distinct speech that is necessary in *speaking to an audience.* In relaxed conversation, of course, a certain amount of slurring is natural and normal. Point out that you are not asking students to reform their private conversational habits, but only to learn a special set of habits that they will need for speaking in public.

Note: Individual speech defects such as lisping or stammering cannot usually be overcome by classroom drill. Students with speech defects need help from specialists. Many school systems have remedial speech teachers to whom such students can be referred; other school systems may refer students instead to private specialists or to a local speech clinic.

EXERCISE 8. Thinking About Nonverbal Communication. Write down at least five different forms of nonverbal communication that you notice at school, at home, and on television. Next to each form, write what you think it means. Prepare to discuss your list with your classmates. Answers will vary.

Pronunciation and Enunciation

30d. Pronounce words correctly, and enunciate carefully.

Your audience must hear your speech plainly. An audience that must strain to hear becomes restless, and a talk that is not heard is wasted.

Take care to speak correctly and distinctly. In many cases the meaning of a word varies with the way it is pronounced. Remember that if your words are mispronounced or if you mumble or run words together, your audience will have difficulty in following you.

Vowel Sounds

Each vowel in our language may be pronounced in different ways. In some words vowels or combinations of vowels have sounds that you might not expect from the spelling. Make sure you use standard pronunciation for the following words:

despite	fertile	opaque	thorough
despot	genuine	suite	through
drought	mischievous	superfluous	vitamins

Consonant Sounds

Enunciation, the careful sounding of every syllable, is as important as pronunciation. Be especially careful with words that end in *-ing* and words that contain similar consonants—*p* and *b, m* and *n, t* and *th.*

For practice, say the following groups of words aloud, taking care to make the consonant sounds clearly distinguishable so that no one in the room mistakes the word you used.

EXERCISES 9 and 10. Some of the errors attacked in these exercises are mispronunciations (such as "fillum" for *film*), but many of them (for instance, "lib'ary" for *library*) represent slurred pronunciations that are common in conversational speech and are to be avoided in more formal speaking situations.

d—t		*t—th*	
dent	tent	tank	thank
dare	tear	taught	thought
send	sent	tinker	thinker
bed	bet	ten	then
madder	matter	wetter	weather

b—p		*v—f*	
blank	plank	vendor	fender
bin	pin	veil	fail
bowl	pool	viewer	fewer
robe	rope	vault	fault
bunk	punk	veal	feel

EXERCISE 9. Practicing Vowel and Consonant Sounds. Practice reading aloud the following tongue twisters. Oral reading.

1. She said severely. "Son, shun the hot sun."
2. The tinker muttered thanks in a thin, throttled tone.
3. Jane's chuckles and antics jarred her ailing aunt and uncle.
4. The tank of thin tin was dank and dented.
5. His mother muttered that wetter weather would wash his wrath away.

Omitting Sounds

Take care not to omit sounds that belong in words. Here is a list of words frequently subject to nonstandard pronunciation.

arctic (not "artic")
asked (not "ask" or "ast")
exactly (not "zactly" or "exackly")
finally (not "finelly")
library (not "liberary" or "liberry")
mystery (not "mystry")
probably (not "probly" or "proely")

EXERCISE 10. Including Frequently Omitted Sounds. Use five of the words in the preceding list in sentences to be spoken aloud in class. Include all the sounds in each word. Sentences will vary.

EXERCISE 11–13 and REVIEW EXERCISE B. Students are likely to understand the mispronunciation errors immediately, but you will have to explain carefully that commonly slurred pronunciations may be "errors" only in relatively formal speaking situations.

You might use the expressions listed in Exercise 13 to put this point across; ask students where they have seen such spellings. (They are occasionally used in written dialogue—for instance, in comic-strip balloons and in some contemporary novels and short stories.) Point out that these spellings therefore seem to represent very informal conversational usage. Then ask whether it would sound right if a speaker addressing a public gathering said something like "Wyncha gi't trial?" for "Why don't you give it a trial?" Would most of the audience grasp the meaning? Would they feel that this was the right way to deliver a public speech?

Adding Sounds

Take care not to add sounds to a word—either inside a word or at the end. Do you add sounds to any of these words?

arithmetic (not "arith*uh*metic")
athlete (not "ath*uh*lete")
barbarous (not "barbar*i*ous")
chimney (not "chim*bl*ey" or "chim*uh*ney")
column (not "col*y*um")
corps (the *p* and *s* are silent)
height (ends in *t*, not *th*)
subtle (the *b* is silent)
umbrella (not "umbrell*er*" or "umb*e*rella")
vehicle (the *h* is silent)

EXERCISE 11. Practicing Frequently Mispronounced Words. Practice each of the preceding frequently mispronounced words. Choose a partner and take turns pronouncing each word twice. Do not add sounds to the words. Oral reading.

Changing Position of Sounds

Be careful not to change the position of a sound within a word. Sometimes such nonstandard pronunciation is based on the similarity of a word to another word that is almost like it in spelling. *Perspire* and *prescribe*, for example, have first syllables that are almost alike. *Perspire* is often mispronounced *prespire*, and *prescribe* is often mispronounced *perscribe*.

Here are some words whose sounds are often transposed.

apron (not "apern")
cavalry (not "calvary")
children (not "childern")
contradict (not "conterdict")
modern (not "modren")

EXERCISE 12. Pronouncing Words Correctly. Review all of the preceding lists. Be prepared to write words on the board and to pronounce them. Pronunciation review.

REVIEW EXERCISE B. Practicing Mispronounced Words. Here is a list of frequently mispronounced words. Be prepared to read them aloud to the class. Use the dictionary if you are not sure of the correct pronunciation. Oral reading.

admirable	hearth	partner
architect	hurtle	remembrance
champion	incomparable	scythe
favorite	infamous	superfluous
film	jubilant	theater
finale	mischievous	toward
gesture	museum	tremendous
handkerchief	ogre	yacht

Running Words Together

Another form of mispronouncing words is running them together when speaking. Telescoping words makes a wreckage of sense. Too often, for example, we run together the words of such a sentence as *I'm glad to meet you* into *Gladdameecha.*

EXERCISE 13. Pronouncing Words Distinctly. Translate the following mangled words into understandable language.

didja	gonna	woncha
thankslot	whereya	didjaseer
gimeyahan	lemmetry	wassamaddawichoo
wachasay	begyaparn	wyncha

Expression

30e. Learn to speak with expression and meaning.

We give meaning to language not only by our choice of words but also by the *feelings* we put into them—the tone of voice, the grouping of words, the emphasis, and the variety of tone. The tone and emphasis we use can greatly influence the meaning our words convey. Differing emphases on certain words or syllables can convey different meanings and emotions.

You can increase the effectiveness of your speech by giving attention to your tone of voice and to the amount and kind of expression you use.

Answers: Exercise 13

did you
Thanks a lot.
Give me a hand.
What did you say?

going to
Where are you?
Let me try.
Beg your pardon?

won't you
Did you see her?
What's the matter with you?
why didn't you

EXPRESSION (rule 30e)

Ask students if anyone has ever said to them, "I don't think I like your tone of voice." Emphasize that learning to control expression, which can be practiced by giving talks, will help students become more effective communicators in all speaking situations. The discussions here should also help students see how expression is handled in written communication, with word choice and punctuation.

EXERCISES 14 and 15. You may wish to call attention to the specific ways in which pauses and changes in pitch affect the meanings of these expressions and to ask the class whether they could convey the same shades of meaning if they wrote the expressions out on paper. Less-advanced students in particular may profit from being shown the connection between spoken patterns and conventional punctuation symbols such as question marks, exclamation points, commas, and periods.

EVALUATING A SPEECH (rule 30f)

Because most teachers call for brief oral or written evaluations after student speeches, it is wise to set up guidelines for these evaluations with the class. Tact and courtesy may be the points to stress most strongly. You may wish to have your class work out an evaluation sheet of their own instead of using the sheet suggested on text page 686. There is also a Peer Evaluation Form on page 522 of the *Teacher's Resource Book.*

EXERCISE 14. Speaking with Expression. Study these sentences before reading them aloud. The class will discuss how well each person expresses the different feelings. Oral reading.

1. You are taking care of a six-year-old. Tell her, "Susan, put that puppy down!"
   a. Say it as if the mother dog, growling furiously, is getting out of her box to leap at Susan.
   b. Say it as if you know Susan is going to plead with you to buy the puppy and you don't have the money.
2. Someone has just walked through your room with muddy feet, leaving tracks on the rug. You ask, "Kyle, did you just walk through my room?"
   a. Say it as if you have told him before to stay out of your room.
   b. Say it as if you have just cleaned your room.
3. You have started on a long walk when you discover that your small brother is walking behind you. You tell him, "Andy, go home and go to bed."
   a. Say it as if he is feverish with a bad cold, and you are very worried about him.
   b. Say it as if you've told him before that he could not come along.

EXERCISE 15. Changing Tone and Emphasis. See how many meanings you can put into the following remarks by varying your tone and the words you emphasize. Oral reading.

1. I'll go now, if you don't mind.
2. Bring all your money tomorrow.
3. I told you not to play with him.
4. You earned all that money yourself?
5. Did you say yes?

EVALUATING A SPEECH

30f. Learn to evaluate another person's report politely and constructively.

Often, after a student has given a report, the class is asked to evaluate the talk. The purpose of such an evaluation is to help the speaker improve by getting reactions. Another purpose is for the group to give recognition to the fine qualities as well as the weak points of the talk.

Be clear and definite. Always give reasons for your evaluation. Be generous with praise. If you find serious faults in a talk, begin by discussing strong points; then show how the talk might have been even stronger if certain faults had been corrected.

WEAK "I thought it was very interesting."
BETTER "His description of Mount Rainier was very interesting because his details were so sharp that I could almost see the mountain trail."

WEAK "I just couldn't follow the talk."
BETTER "Her explanation was clear and easy to follow except in a couple places. I wonder if she left out some steps."

Do your part in helping the class to establish an atmosphere of kind and constructive evaluation. When you evaluate a classmate's oral report, use the following guidelines.

1. Give praise when it is merited.
2. Avoid discussing points of little importance.
3. Point out strengths as well as weaknesses.
4. Be definite and constructive.

Your class may decide to use an evaluation sheet like the one on page 686 for evaluating speakers. After a talk each listener rates the speech, and the sheets are given to the speaker.

Knowing how to accept an evaluation is as important as knowing how to evaluate a speech. When your classmates evaluate your speech, keep the following points in mind:

1. Do not take the remarks personally. They are made to help you improve.
2. Study your weaknesses and take steps to improve them. Think about ways to make your strengths even stronger!
3. If evaluations are given orally, thank your classmates for their help.

EXERCISE 16. If you wish, encourage applause after each talk. Class comments should be brief and commendatory. After several talks have been heard, ask the class to suggest ways in which the talks could be improved. You might focus attention on the suggestions offered in the text: an interesting introduction, a strong conclusion, appropriate nonverbal communication, the use of charts and pictures, etc. For your convenience, a speech evaluation form is provided on page 520 of the *Teacher's Resource Book.*

EXERCISE 17. This exercise provides students not only with practice in evaluating a peer's oral report but also with practice in writing a paragraph expressing an opinion.

PARTICIPATING IN GROUP DISCUSSIONS (rule 30g)

Encourage students to refer to the eight subrules presented here any time they will be participating in a class meeting, club meeting, or other group discussion.

EXERCISE 16. Delivering an Oral Report. Deliver the talk that you prepared in Exercise 7 or in Review Exercise A. Remember the importance of nonverbal communication, pronunciation and enunciation, and expression. Oral report.

EXERCISE 17. Evaluating an Oral Report. Write a paragraph evaluating a talk someone has given in class. Use the following evaluation sheet as a basis for your evaluation, but also give your opinion of the talk as a whole. Answers will vary.

EVALUATION SHEET

Speaker ______________________

Topic ______________________

Critic ______________________

	Very good	Good	Fair	Weak
Introduction				
Organization				
Conclusion				
Use of notes				
Posture				
Gestures				
Voice				
Pronunciation				

Other comments

PARTICIPATING IN GROUP DISCUSSIONS

Another situation in which you can use your speaking skills is the group discussion. Throughout your schooling and later in adult life, you might often join with other people to discuss important issues or to explore solutions to problems. To discuss an issue or problem intelligently and fairly, you need to learn how to participate in a group discussion.

You already have some experience with participating in group discussions. You often converse with friends, teachers, and family members. These conversations are an informal, or unplanned, form of group discussion.

You may have already participated in group discussions that are more focused or planned than informal conversations. In school your teachers may have asked you to meet with classmates to discuss school-related topics, for example, ways to involve parents in tutoring or reasons for allowing students to help plan lunch menus.

Think about the group discussions you have participated in. Some may have had a discussion leader and an audience, but others may not. Some discussions may have gone very smoothly: the group discussed an issue or problem and came up with creative or useful ideas. In other cases, the group may have argued constantly and accomplished very little, so that the time spent together was wasted. To make a group discussion worthwhile and satisfying, you should learn several simple rules based on courtesy and common sense. By following these rules, you and your fellow group members should be able to express your ideas in an atmosphere of consideration and respect.

30g. Learn to participate in a group discussion.

(1) Be sure the discussion topic is manageable.

A discussion topic should be narrow, or limited, enough for the time you have available. Suppose your group wants to discuss ways to expand your school's extracurricular activities. If you only have thirty minutes for your discussion, you should divide this broad subject into smaller parts and discuss each one separately at a different time. For example, your group could instead discuss ways to expand after-school musical activities. This topic is more manageable for the time you have.

(2) Learn the duties of each participant in a group discussion.

A group discussion can have three different participants: a discussion leader, speakers or discussion members, and an audience. The *discussion leader* organizes and guides the discussion. He or she introduces the topic and the speakers, asks questions, keeps the speakers on the topic, and summarizes the discussion's main points. The *speakers* actively participate in the discussion. They should listen carefully and courteously to the other speakers, speak clearly, and stay on the topic. The *audience* should also listen quietly and carefully, and audience members can ask questions when the discussion leader invites them to do so.

(3) Prepare thoroughly for a discussion.

Whenever possible, prepare for the discussion beforehand. Gather information about the discussion topic by reading magazines, books, and encyclopedias and by discussing the topic with people who know about it. If each group member has spent some time studying and thinking about the topic, the discussion should proceed smoothly and intelligently.

(4) Be sure all group members have a chance to participate in the discussion.

Because some people feel more comfortable expressing their ideas in a group, it is always possible that one or two group members will dominate, or take over, the discussion. A group discussion should have *all* group members participating equally. Be sure that all members have a chance to express their ideas on the topic. Listening respectfully to each other should make group members feel comfortable sharing their ideas.

(5) Listen with an open mind.

Members of a group discussion who have different interests and experiences often express ideas and opinions that may be very different from your own. As you hear these different ideas, listen with an open mind. Remember that a group discussion should be a learning experience that allows an exchange of ideas.

(6) Focus on the discussion topic only.

With several people meeting together, it is easy to get off the subject and discuss ideas that are not related to the topic. Remember that your group is talking together for a specific purpose. Stay on the topic yourself, and politely remind your fellow group members to stay on the topic if the discussion begins to wander.

(7) Listen attentively to every speaker in the group.

Every speaker in your discussion group should have your full attention. Listen carefully to others as they express their ideas about the discussion topic, and do not chat with other members of the group while a speaker is talking. Rules of courtesy that apply to informal conversations apply to group discussions as well. Allow one speaker to talk at a time, and avoid shouting when group members disagree. Instead, calmly discuss your different ideas, and allow each person to contribute his or her views on the point of disagreement.

(8) Continue to improve your participation in group discussions.

It is likely that you will participate in group discussions throughout your schooling and your adult life. Learning to be a better participant in a group discussion is an important skill to work on. One way to improve is to focus on the preceding seven rules of courtesy and common sense for a group discussion.

Another way to improve is to ask yourself several questions after a group discussion. These questions will focus your attention on how well the discussion went and whether the group accomplished its purpose:

a. Did group members prepare beforehand? Did they study and think about the topic before the group met?
b. Did all group members contribute in some way to the discussion?
c. Did all group members understand and fulfill their role in the discussion?
d. Did the group stay on the discussion topic?

EXERCISE 18. Students will need some time to gather information about their topics. Provide help with the discussion as needed.

EXERCISES 19 and 20. These exercises provide students with opportunities to evaluate discussion groups. Encourage further class discussion of the evaluation results.

e. Did group members show respect and courtesy toward one another?

You and the group members should ask these questions after your discussion. Try to answer *yes* to each one, and improve how you participate in group discussions in the future.

EXERCISE 18. Participating in a Group Discussion. Join a discussion group assigned by your teacher, or form a discussion group with three or four classmates. Select one of the following topics or a topic of your own, and discuss it in the time period your teacher assigns. Remember that your group has a specific purpose to accomplish during this time. Your teacher may ask you to select a discussion leader. Class discussion.

1. Three reasons for allowing students to help establish school rules
2. Our class's most memorable contributions to school life
3. How to raise money for school projects without having bake sales or carwashes
4. A famous man and a famous woman that young people can respect
5. Three things you can do to contribute to a happy family life

EXERCISE 19. Evaluating a Group Discussion. After your group completes its discussion in Exercise 18, evaluate your group's work. Use the five questions on page 689 to evaluate your discussion, and be prepared to discuss your evaluation in class. Answers will vary.

EXERCISE 20. Evaluating a Group Discussion You Observe. Observe a group discussion—one your classmates are having or one on a television news program. Use the five questions on page 689 to evaluate what you observe. Be prepared to explain whether the group accomplished its purpose and to discuss how the group could have improved its work together. Answers will vary.

CHAPTER 31

Listening

IMPROVING YOUR LISTENING

Listening well is important. In school, at home, and among friends, you can learn more by listening well to others.

LISTENING TO MEDIA

You may spend many hours each week watching television, going to the movies, and listening to the radio. It is good to enjoy such entertainment, but you owe it to yourself to develop a critical appreciation of what you see and hear.

31a. Choose radio programs, television programs, and movies intelligently.

You can learn a great deal from radio, television, and movies if you plan ahead and decide what you want to see and hear. Newspaper reviews, suggestions from friends, and your own interests should guide your choice of these media.

EXERCISE 1. Identifying Preferences for Particular Movies and Radio and Television Programs. Look at the television, radio, and movie schedules for the next week. Make a list of the

Chapter Overview

Your first step should be to show students their need for instruction in listening. One way of doing this is by inviting someone to speak to your class for about ten minutes on a topic that is of interest to students and is suited to their level of maturity. Either record the speech on a tape recorder or else have the speaker give you a written copy of the talk. When the speaker has finished, ask students to write a prècis of what was said. (Do not tell them beforehand that they will be asked to do this.)

Then have several volunteers read their summaries aloud, and ask the class to judge whether these summaries are full and correct statements of the speaker's main points. Usually, members of the class will not agree about what the main points were—or even about whether the speaker made or did not make certain statements. When it has become clear that there are a number of items about which the students do not agree, play back the recorded speech or read aloud the written copy. All students will probably discover that the speech contained points that they remembered wrongly or missed entirely. This procedure will prove to them, rather dramatically, that they need to develop their listening skills.

Chapter Objective

Students will improve their listening skills.

PRESENTING THE CHAPTER

LESS-ADVANCED STUDENTS These students may become distracted easily because their span of attention tends to be short. Abbreviate the length of lessons, provide frequent reviews and drills, make use of visual aids, and summarize often. Stress courtesy and attentiveness in listening.

ADVANCED STUDENTS An advanced class should apply what they learn to school-assembly talks by invited speakers and to speeches, political or otherwise, on television. Ask students to consider questions such as these: What idea was important? Which ideas were of less importance? What facts did the speaker present? What was the speaker's interpretation of these facts?

LISTENING TO MEDIA
(rule 31a)

In order to best appreciate radio and television programs and movies, students should be encouraged to plan what they see and hear in advance. They should develop their own standards of viewing and listening and should select their programs wisely.

EXERCISE 1. You can encourage your students to judge radio and television programs—and movies and plays—in much the same way that they judge the books they read for book reports. You may want to have students write several reports on television programs during the course of the year and compare them with those of their classmates.

shows you want to see or hear. Next to each show, give the reason for your interest. In class, compare your list with others. Did you list the same shows? Do you have the same reasons?
Class discussion. Answers will follow.

LISTENING TO INSTRUCTIONS

A large part of what we listen to is informative. As students, much of your listening is done for the purpose of gaining information.

31b. Listen alertly to directions and class assignments.

You can save time and avoid errors by listening carefully to directions. If the directions are lengthy, jot down each step on a piece of paper. Do not interrupt with questions while the directions are being given. Wait, and ask your questions when the speaker has finished. Be sure that you have noted *all* the instructions and have understood them.

EXERCISE 2. **Following Oral Directions.** Someone in the class will read the following directions aloud. See if you can follow the directions after hearing them. Listening for directions.

> Take out a piece of paper and write your name in the upper left-hand corner. Beneath your name write the day you were born.
>
> Draw a line down the middle of the page. Mark the left column with the letter *A* and the right column with the letter *B*. In column A, write the months of the year that begin with the letter *J*. In column B, write the days of the week that begin with the letter *T*. Compare the lists. If column B has more words, fold your paper in half.

LISTENING TO OTHERS

31c. Listen to talks and oral reports with an open mind.

The basis of good listening is *interest* and *purpose*. You listen very attentively to something that interests you. You also listen attentively to, and remember vividly, information that will serve a purpose that you consider important.

When listening to a talk, ask, *How can this information be of real help to me?* If you determine ways in which the content is important to you, listening and remembering will be easier.

Suppose you are listening to a talk on how a particular club serves the community. You may not be very interested. The club has staged a benefit dance to buy a record player and records for a local hospital. To you, this is of no immediate concern. If you pay attention, however, you may discover that the club sponsors trips for students or that it compiles job opportunities for summer employment.

Sometimes you know what you are listening for—as when you listen to directions or assignments. At other times you should keep an alert, open mind—you may learn something unexpectedly useful.

EXERCISE 3. Determining Purposes for Listening. Suppose the following people spoke in assembly programs at your school. What would be your purpose in listening to each? Answers will vary.

1. The manager of a local department store talks on "How to Tell a Bargain from a Rip-off."
2. A graduate of your school gives a talk on two years spent with the Peace Corps in South America.
3. A professional guitarist speaks on "What to Listen for in Music," illustrating points on the guitar.
4. The head of a research laboratory gives a talk on new ways of using solar energy.

31d. Listen actively.

If you intend to use the information you are hearing, you must be alert to select the ideas that you can use and retain them so clearly that you will remember them later when you need them.

(1) Listen for the speaker's purpose.

LISTENING TO INSTRUCTIONS and **LISTENING TO OTHERS (rules 31b–31e)**

Acquiring good listening habits takes a good deal of practice. You can use classroom situations to provide some of it. The daily homework assignment offers a particularly good opportunity for training in listening. Go over each assignment, explaining difficult points and inviting questions. Require students to jot down notes about it. After this kind of preparation, decline to accept "I didn't know what I was supposed to do" as an excuse.

EXERCISE 2. If you introduced this chapter by having the class write brief summaries of a speech, as suggested earlier, emphasize to students that their performance on this exercise should show definite improvement over those first efforts.

EXERCISE 3. This exercise can provide the basis for classroom discussion of purposeful listening.

EXERCISES 4 and 5. As noted for Exercise 2, student performance on these exercises should show marked improvement over earlier attempts.

Sometimes, while listening to a talk, you want to know the speaker's intention. Is the speaker trying to persuade you to do something? Are you expected to agree or disagree with the speaker? In such situations, concentrate on grasping the speaker's point of view. Ask yourself why the speaker wants you to do something or why the speaker holds certain opinions.

(2) Listen for a few main ideas.

Listen to understand the *main points* of the speech: the reasons the speaker gives for taking action or the ideas with which the speaker supports one side of an issue. Try to understand and remember each main idea presented.

When you are listening for the main ideas of a speech, pay special attention to the start and finish of the talk. A speaker's introduction often presents the main points that will be developed, and the conclusion often sums them up. An able speaker emphasizes important ideas so that you can easily recognize them.

EXERCISE 4. Listening for Main Ideas. Select six short news stories in a newspaper. Read each story aloud. Listeners will write down, in their own words, the main idea of each story. Compare the answers. Answers will vary. Class discussion.

(3) Listen for specific details.

On some occasions your purpose in listening to a talk will be to get specific details. Suppose, for example, that you are listening to a talk on how to start a model airplane engine or how to tell edible mushrooms from poisonous ones. A general idea of the method will not be sufficient; you will want exact details.

EXERCISE 5. Listening for Specific Details. Your teacher will read aloud a set of instructions or directions. When the teacher has finished, write the details of the instructions or directions from memory. Then the teacher will reread the instructions and ask you to check the accuracy of what you remembered. Listening for instructions.

EXERCISE 6. Take this opportunity to encourage less-open students to describe nonverbal communication before the class.

(4) Evaluate nonverbal signals such as gestures.

A speaker may use gestures for emphasis. Some of these gestures may be appropriate; for example, a comedian will often rely on gestures to draw laughs. Other gestures may be inappropriate; for example, nervous speakers will often wave one or both hands in the air as they speak. The best gestures add to a speech and communicate nonverbally what the speaker is trying to say.

EXERCISE 6. Evaluating Nonverbal Signals. Watch a popular comedian or other personality speaking. Notice how gestures are used. Describe these gestures to your classmates and indicate what they mean to you. Class discussion.

31e. Listen critically. Distinguish fact from opinion. Judge whether statements are backed up by evidence from dependable sources.

When you listen to a speaker, you do not wish to be fooled by trickery or unreliable sources of information. Ask yourself questions as you listen: Is this statement a fact or an opinion? If the speaker is presenting it as a fact, is it backed up with proof from a dependable source or a trustworthy expert? Is the speaker talking from experience?

Know the difference between fact and opinion. A fact is a statement that can be proved true or false, such as, "Winter temperatures averaged 12° Celsius this year." An opinion is a statement that cannot be proved true or false, such as, "It feels colder this winter than last."

Study the following examples. Can you see why two are opinions and two are facts?

OPINION The library facilities in this school are inadequate.
FACT There are 10 library books available for the assignment, but 50 students must do the assignment at once.

OPINION The referee is being unfair to our players!
FACT The referee has given our players three penalties in the last five minutes.

EXERCISE 7. Only three items (2, 4, and 10) are facts. Students may disagree about whether some of the other items represent facts or opinions. Lead them to see that some of the statements (3, 5, and 6) may sound as if they are supposed to be facts, but they are actually sweeping generalizations that could not be literally true in all cases. A person making one of these statements would merely be stating a private prejudice—an opinion. The remaining statements (1, 7, 8, and 9) all contain signals of opinion ("ought to," "too much," "best," and "greatly"). Stress the idea that an opinion may be considered right or wrong but that a speaker or writer should give facts in order to support it.

EXERCISE 7. Distinquishing Between Fact and Opinion. If you heard the following statements, would you accept them as fact or interpret them as opinion? After each number on your paper, write *fact* if you think the statement would be a fact or *opinion* if you think it would be an opinion. Be prepared to explain each choice.

1. We ought to irrigate our desert lands with fresh water made from sea water. 1. opinion
2. A tornado in Kansas today wrecked fifty homes. 2. fact
3. Sunbathing is harmful. 3. opinion
4. Stanford beat Oregon at football today, 28 to 14. 4. fact
5. There's no place like home. 5. opinion
6. TV comedies are all alike. 6. opinion
7. Mrs. Currier gives too much homework. 7. opinion
8. American cars give the best value among low-priced compacts. 8. opinion
9. The orchestra has improved greatly this year. 9. opinion
10. Mrs. Townsend has never been introduced to my family. 10. fact

INDEX

Index

INDEX

699

B

INDEX

INDEX

INDEX

E

INDEX

F

G

H

I

N

P

INDEX

INDEX

INDEX

INDEX

T

INDEX

U

INDEX

Y

Z

INDEX